"If you are looking for a job ... before you go to the newspapers and the help-wanted ads, listen to Bob Adams, editor of *The Metropolitan New York JobBank*."
-Tom Brokaw, NBC News

"*The Chicago JobBank* has proven to be an extremely useful resource for finding a job in the Chicagoland area."
-George Pinder, Sr., *John Crane, Inc.*

"For those graduates whose parents are pacing the floor, conspicuously placing circled want ads around the house and typing up resumes, *[The Carolina JobBank]* answers job search questions."
-*Greensboro News and Record*

"This well-researched, well-edited job hunter's aid includes most major businesses and institutional entities in the New York metropolitan area ... Highly recommended."
-Cheryl Gregory-Pindell, *Library Journal*

"*The Houston JobBank* is a good reference tool for the job hunter. It's $15.95 and worth it."
-L.M. Sixel, *Houston Chronicle*

"One of the best sources for finding a job in Atlanta!"
-Luann Miller
Human Resources Manager
Prudential Insurance

"*The San Francisco Bay Area JobBank* ... is a highly useful guide, with plenty of how-to's ranging from resume tips to interview dress codes and research shortcuts. "
-A.S. Ross, *San Francisco Examiner*

"No longer can jobseekers feel secure about finding employment just through want ads. With the tough competition in the job market, particularly in the Boston area, they need much more help. For this reason, *The Boston JobBank* will have a wide and appreciative audience of new graduates, job changers, and people relocating to Boston. It provides a good place to start a search for entry-level professional positions."
-*The Journal of College Placement*

"A timely book for Chicago job hunters follows books from the same publisher that were well received in New York and Boston ... A fine tool for job hunters ..."

-Clarence Peterson, *The Chicago Tribune*

"Job hunting is never fun, but this book can ease the ordeal ... *[The Los Angeles JobBank]* will help allay fears, build confidence, and avoid wheel-spinning."

-Robert W. Ross, *The Los Angeles Times*

"Job hunters can't afford to waste time. *The Minneapolis-St. Paul JobBank* contains information that used to require hours of research in the library."

-Carmella Zagone
Minneapolis Human Resources Administrator

"Because our listing is seen by people across the nation it generates lots of resumes for us. We encourage unsolicited resumes. We'll always be listed *[in The Chicago JobBank]* as long as I'm in this career."

-Tom Fitzpatrick
Director of Human Resources
Merchandise Mart Properties, Inc.

"Through *The Dallas-Ft. Worth JobBank,* we've been able to attract high-quality candidates for several positions."

-Rob Bertino
Southern States Sales Manager
Compuserve

"I read through the "Basics of Job Winning" and "Resumes" sections *[in The Dallas-Ft. Worth JobBank]* and found them to be very informative, with some positive tips for the job searcher. I believe the strategies outlined will bring success to any determined candidate."

-Carmilla Norder
Professional Recruiter
Presbyterian Hospital of Dallas

"The Seattle JobBank is an essential resource for job hunters."

-Gil Lopez
Staffing Team Manager
Battelle Pacific Northwest Laboratories

"*The Boston JobBank* provides a handy map of employment possibilities in Greater Boston. This book can help in the initial steps of a job search by locating major employers, describing their business activities, and for most firms, by naming the contact person and listing typical professional positions. For recent college graduates, as well as experienced professionals, *The Boston JobBank* is an excellent place to begin a job search."

-Juliet F. Brudney
Career Columnist
Boston Globe

What makes the JobBank Series the nation's premier line of employment guides?

With vital employment information on thousands of employers across the nation, the JobBank Series is the most comprehensive and authoritative set of career directories available today.

Each book in the series provides information on **dozens of different industries** in a given city or area, with the primary employer listings providing contact information, telephone numbers, addresses, a thumbnail sketch of the firm's business, and in many cases descriptions of the firm's typical professional job categories, the principal educational backgrounds sought, and the fringe benefits offered.

In addition to the **detailed primary employer listings,** the new 1994 JobBank books give telephone numbers and addresses for hundreds of other large employers as well as for **thousands of smaller and medium-sized employers.**

All of the reference information in the JobBank Series is as up-to-date and accurate as possible. Every year, the entire database is thoroughly researched and verified, first by mail and then by telephone. Bob Adams Inc. publishes **more local JobBank books more often** than any other publisher of career directories.

In addition, the JobBank Series features important information about the local job scene--**forecasts on which industries are the hottest, overviews of local economic trends,** and even **lists of regional professional associations,** so you can get your job hunt started off right.

Hundreds of discussions with job hunters show that they prefer information organized geographically, because most people look for jobs in specific areas. The JobBank Series offers **twenty regional titles,** from Minneapolis to Houston, and from Washington, DC, to San Francisco. The future employee moving to a particular area can review the local employment data not only for information on the type of industry most common to that region, but also for names of specific employers.

A condensed, but thorough, review of the entire job search process is presented in the chapter **"The Basics of Job Winning",** a feature which has received many compliments from career counselors. In addition, each JobBank directory is completed by a section on **resumes and cover letters** *The New York Times* has acclaimed as "excellent."

The JobBank Series gives job hunters the most comprehensive, most timely, and most accurate career information, organized and indexed to facilitate the job search. An entire career reference library, JobBank books are the consummate employment guides.

Published by Bob Adams, Inc.
260 Center Street, Holbrook, MA 02343

Manufactured in the United States of America.

While the publisher has made every reasonable effort to obtain accurate information and verify same, occasional errors are inevitable due to the magnitude of the data base. Should you discover an error, or if a company is missing, please write the editors at the above address so that we may update future editions.

"This publication is designed to provide accurate and authoritative information with regard to the subject matter covered. It is sold with the understanding that the publisher is not engaged in rendering legal, accounting, or other professional advice. If legal advice or other expert assistance is required, the services of a competent professional person should be sought."
--From a *Declaration of Principles* jointly adopted by a Committee of the American Bar Association and a Committee of Publishers and Associations

The appearance of a listing in the book does not constitute an endorsement from the publisher.

Cover design by Peter Gouck and Chris Ciaschini.

ISBN: 1-55850-458-3

This book is available at quantity discounts for bulk purchases.
For information, call 1-800-872-5627.

The Greater
Philadelphia
JobBank
1995

Managing Editor
Carter Smith

Series Editor
Steven Graber

Editorial Assistants
Kenny Brooks
Peter Hale
Jennifer Greene
Emily Merowitz
Erin O'Neill
Chris Baker

BOB ADAMS, INC.
Holbrook, Massachusetts

Top career publications from Bob Adams, Inc.

The Atlanta JobBank, 1995 ($15.95)
The Boston JobBank, 1995 ($15.95)
The Carolina JobBank, 2nd Edition
($15.95)
The Chicago JobBank, 1995 ($15.95)
The Dallas-Ft. Worth JobBank, 1995
($15.95)
The Denver JobBank, 6th Edition ($15.95)
The Detroit JobBank, 5th Edition ($15.95)
The Florida JobBank, 1995 ($15.95)
The Houston JobBank, 1995 ($15.95)
The Los Angeles JobBank, 1995 ($15.95)
The Minneapolis-St. Paul JobBank, 1995
($15.95)
The New York JobBank, 1995 ($15.95)
The Ohio JobBank, 1995 ($15.95)
The Philadelphia JobBank, 1995 ($15.95)
The Phoenix JobBank, 4th Edition
($15.95)
The San Francisco Bay Area JobBank,
1995 ($15.95)
The Seattle JobBank, 1995 ($15.95)
The St. Louis JobBank, 5th Edition
($15.95)
The Tennessee JobBank, 1st Edition
($15.95)
The Washington DC JobBank, 1995
($15.95)

The National JobBank, 1995
(Covers 50 states: $250.00)

The JobBank Guide to Employment
Services, 1994-1995
(Covers 50 states: $150.00)

OTHER CAREER TITLES:

The Adams Jobs Almanac, 1995 ($10.95)
The Adams Resume Almanac ($10.95)
America's Fastest Growing Employers,
2nd Edition ($16.00)
Career Shifting ($9.95)

Careers and the College Grad ($9.95)
Careers and the Engineer ($9.95)
Careers and the MBA ($9.95)
Cold Calling Techniques that Really
Work, 3rd Edition ($7.95)
Cover Letters that Knock 'em Dead, 2nd
Edition ($7.95)
The Elements of Job Hunting ($4.95)
Every Woman's Essential Job Hunting &
Resume Book ($10.95)
Harvard Guide to Careers in the Mass
Media ($7.95)
High Impact Telephone Networking for
Job Hunters ($6.95)
How to Become Successfully Self
Employed ($9.95)
The Job Hunter's Checklist ($5.95)
The Job Search Handbook ($6.95)
Job Search Networking ($9.95)
Knock 'em Dead--The Ultimate
Jobseeker's Handbook, 1995 ($9.95)
The Minority Career Book ($9.95)
The National Job Line Directory ($7.95)
Outplace Yourself ($25.00)
Over 40 and Looking for Work ($7.95)
The Resume Handbook, 2nd Edition
($5.95)
Resumes that Knock 'em Dead, 2nd
Edition ($7.95)
300 New Ways to Get A Better Job
($7.95)

To order these books or additional copies
of this book, send check or money order
(including $4.50 for postage) to:

Bob Adams, Inc.
260 Center Street
Holbrook MA 02343

Ordering by credit card?
Just call 1-800-USA-JOBS
(In Massachusetts, call 617-767-8100)

TABLE OF CONTENTS

SECTION FOUR: EMPLOYMENT SERVICES OF GREATER PHILADELPHIA/357

Employment Agencies and Temporary Services/358

Includes the address, phone number, description of each company's services, contact name, and a list of positions commonly filled.

Executive Search Firms/376

Includes the address, phone number, description of each company's services, contact name, and a list of positions commonly filled.

Section Five: Index/389

An alphabetical index of Greater Philadelphia's primary employer listings only. Due to space constraints, employers that fall under the headings "Large Employers", or "Small to Medium Sized Employers" are not indexed here.

INTRODUCTION

How to Use This Book

Right now, you hold in your hands one of the most effective job hunting tools available anywhere. In *The Greater Philadelphia JobBank*, you will find a wide array of valuable information to help you to either launch or continue a rewarding career. But before you open to the book's employer listings and start calling about current job openings, take a few minutes to learn how best to put the resources presented in *The Greater Philadelphia JobBank* to work for you.

The Greater Philadelphia JobBank* will help you to stand out from other jobseekers. While many people looking for a new job rely solely on newspaper help-wanted ads, this book offers you a much more effective job-search method -- direct contact. The direct contact method has been proven to be twice as effective as scanning the help-wanted ads. Instead of waiting for employers to come looking for you, you'll be far more effective going to them. While many of your competitors will use trial and error methods in trying to set up interviews, you'll learn not only how to get interviews, but what to expect once you've got them.

In the next few pages, we'll take you through each section of the book so you'll be prepared to get a jump-start on your competition:

The Philadelphia Job Market: An Overview

To get a feel for the state of the Philadelphia job scene, read the introductory section called *The Greater Philadelphia Job Market*. In it, we'll recap the economy's recent performance, and the steps that local governments and business leaders are taking to bring new jobs to the area.

Even more importantly, you'll learn where things are headed. What are the prospects for the industries that form the core of the region's economy? Which new industries are growing fastest and which older ones are laying off? Are there any companies that are especially hot, and why?

To answer these questions for you, we've pored over local business journals and newspapers, and interviewed local business leaders and labor analysts. Whether you are new to the Philadelphia area and need a source of regional information, or are a life-long Philadelphian just looking for a fresh start in a new job, you'll find this section to be a concise thumbnail sketch of where Philadelphia's jobs are.

This type of information is potent ammunition to bring into an interview. Showing that you're well versed in current industry trends helps give you an edge over job applicants who haven't done their homework.

Basics of Job Winning

Preparation. Strategy. Time-Management. These are three of the most important elements of a successful job search. *The Basics of Job Winning* helps you address these and all the other elements needed to find the right job.

One of your first priorities should be to define your personal career objectives. What qualities make a job desirable to you? Creativity? High pay? Prestige? Use *Basics of Job Winning* to weigh these questions. Then use the rest of the chapter to design a strategy to find a job that matches your criteria.

In *Basics of Job Winning,* you'll learn which job hunting techniques work, and which don't. We've reviewed the pros and cons of mass mailings, help-wanted ads and direct contact. We'll show you how to develop and approach contacts in your field; how to research a prospective employer; and how to use that information to get an interview and the job.

Also included in *Basics*: interview dress code and etiquette, the "do's and don'ts" of interviewing, and sample interview questions. The often forgotten art of what to do after the interview is also discussed.

Resumes and Cover Letters

The approach you take to writing your resume and cover letter can often mean the difference between getting an interview and never being noticed. In this section, we discuss different formats, as well as what to put on (and what to leave off) your resume. It also reviews the benefits and drawbacks of professional resume writers, and the importance of a follow-up letter. Also included in this section are sample resumes and cover letters which you can use as models.

The Employer Listings

Employers are listed alphabetically by industry, and within industry, by company names. When a company does business under a person's name, like "John Smith & Co.", the company is usually listed by the surname's spelling (in this case 'S'). Exceptions occur when a company's name is widely recognized, like 'JCPenney' or 'Howard Johnson Motor Lodge'. In those cases, the company's first name is the key ('J' and 'H' respectively).

The Greater Philadelphia JobBank covers thirty-six industries. Each company profile is assigned to one of the following:

Accounting/Management Consulting
*Advertising/Marketing and Public
    Relations*
Aerospace
Apparel and Textiles
*Architecture, Construction and
    Engineering*
Arts and Entertainment/Recreation

Automotive
Banking/Savings and Loans
*Biotechnology/Pharmaceuticals/
    Scientific R&D*
*Business Services and Non-Scientific
    Research*
*Charities/Social Services/Membership
    Organizations*

Chemicals/Rubber and Plastics
Communications: Telecommunications/
    Broadcasting
Computer Hardware, Software and
    Services
Educational Services
Electronic/Industrial Electrical
    Equipment
Environmental Services
Fabricated/Primary Metals and
    Products
Financial Services
Food and Beverage/Agriculture
Government
Health Care: Service, Equipment and
    Products
Hotels and Restaurants

Insurance
Legal Services
Manufacturing and Wholesaling: Misc.
    Consumer
Manufacturing and Wholesaling: Misc.
    Industrial
Mining/Gas/Petroleum/Energy Related
Paper and Wood Products
Personal Services
Printing and Publishing
Real Estate
Retail
Stone, Clay, Glass and Concrete
    Products
Transportation
Utilities: Electric/Gas/Sanitation

While most of these industry headings are self-explanatory, a few may need clarification. *Business Services and Non-Scientific Research* contains companies that 1) provide services to other companies; and 2) aren't classified elsewhere (under advertising, or computer or financial services, for example). Examples include companies which do laundry for hotels, conduct personnel checks of job applicants, or provide security guards for warehouses. *Personal Services* addresses the services provided to individuals, such as hair stylists, house painters, or funeral homes.

Many of the company listings offer detailed company profiles. In addition to company names, addresses, and phone numbers, these listings also include contact names or hiring departments, and descriptions of each company's products and/or services. Many of these listings also include a variety of additional information including:

Common positions - A list of job titles that the company commonly fills when it is hiring. Note: keep in mind that *The Greater Philadelphia JobBank* is a directory of major employers in area, not a directory of openings currently available. Many of the companies listed will be hiring, others will not. However, since most professional job openings are filled without the placement of help-wanted ads, contacting the employers in this book directly is still a more effective method that browsing the Sunday papers.

Common positions are listed under many of the entries in alphabetical order, and range from Accountant to Wholesale Buyer.

Educational backgrounds sought - A list of educational backgrounds that companies seek when hiring.

Benefits - What kind of benefits packages are available from these employers? Here you'll find a broad range of benefits, from the relatively common (medical insurance) to those that are much more rare (health club membership; child daycare assistance).

Special programs - Does the company offer training programs, internships or apprenticeships? These programs can be important to first time job seekers and college students looking for practical work experience. Many employer profiles will include information on these programs.

Parent company - If an employer is a subsidiary of a larger company, the name of that parent company will often be listed here. Use this information to supplement your company research before contacting the employer.

Hires/layoffs in 1993 - This offers a quick glimpse at the company's recent employment trends. Some companies have given both local and national figures.

Number of employees: The number of workers a company employs.

Projected number of hires/layoffs - An estimate of hiring for the next year. Again, some firms have provided both national and local figures.

Companies may also include information on other U.S. locations, annual revenues, and any stock exchange the firm may be listed on.

Because so many job openings are with small and mid-sized employers, we've also included the addresses and phone numbers of additional Philadelphia area employers. While none of these listings include any additional hiring information, many of them also offer rewarding career opportunities. These listings are also organized under each industry heading. Within each industry, they are organized by the type of product or service offered.

A note on all employer listings that appear in *The Greater Philadelphia JobBank*. This book is intended as a starting point. It is not intended to replace any effort that you the jobseeker should devote to your jobhunt. Keep in mind that while a great deal of effort has put into collecting and verifying company information that is provided in this book, addresses and contact names change regularly. Inevitably, some contact names listed herein have changed even before you read this. We recommend you contact a company before mailing your resume to insure nothing has changed.

At the end of each industry section, we have included a directory of other industry-specific resources to help you in your job search. These include:

employment advice and job search help; magazines that cover the industry; and additional directories that may supplement the employer listings in this book.

Employment Services and Executive Search Firms

Immediately following the employer listings section of this book are listings of Philadelphia area employment services and executive search firms. Many jobseekers supplement their own efforts by contracting "temp" services, head hunters, and other employment search firms to generate potential job opportunities.

This section is a comprehensive listing of such firms, arranged alphabetically under the headings Employment Agencies/Temporary Services, and Executive Search Firms. Each listing includes the firm's name, address, telephone number and contact person. Each listing may also include the firm's founding date, the areas it specializes in, whether an appointment is necessary, if unsolicited resumes are accepted, the type of positions the company commonly fills, how many jobs are filled annually, and who pays the finder's fee.

Index

The Greater Philadelphia JobBank index is a straight alphabetical listing.

The Greater Philadelphia Job Market:
An Overview

The Delaware Valley region of eastern Pennsylvania, southern New Jersey, and Delaware is rich with employment opportunities. In the fourth quarter of 1993, the combined job growth for the three states was the strongest it had been in five years. Services, especially business services, are amongst the fastest growing sectors in the area. There was a marked increase in the number of jobs in manufacturing as well. The region continues to advance steadily as the Delaware Valley's job market improves.

The Philadelphia job market represents a diverse range of industries. The area is stocked with high-tech and health care companies. In metropolitan Philadelphia, as with the rest of the nation, business services are growing rapidly. Financial services also plays a significant role in the regional economy. Manufacturing is not the dominant employer of the Philadelphia region that it formerly was, and jobs in this industry are expected to continue to decline in the coming years. Despite these losses, some segments of manufacturing are expected to expand in the region. Manufacturing jobs in pharmaceuticals and printing are among those expected to grow over the course of the decade.

There are currently twenty-two *Fortune 500* companies in the metro Philadelphia area. Many of these companies have been actively seeking new employees. **Harsco**, a manufacturer of valve and pipe fittings, increased its number of employees by 48% nationwide to reach 14,200 in 1993. **Vishay Intertechnology**, an electronics manufacturer, increased its staff by 27% for a total of 14,208 employees. **VF**, a clothing manufacturer, increased its staff by 9% to 62,000. **AMP**, another electronics company, increased its number of employees by 7% bringing its grand total to 26,900. Finally, in 1993, **Teleflex**, a manufacturer of industrial farm equipment, hired 3,700 employees nationwide.

Economic Overview

Unfortunately, not all employers in metro Philadelphia will be hiring. Recent economic trends in the Philadelphia metro area indicate that many companies will continue to downsize and restructure in order to adapt to increasingly competitive economic conditions.

According to the first quarter 1994 report of the **Federal Reserve Bank of Philadelphia**, combined job growth for the metro Philadelphia area has been its strongest in five years. The three state area's unemployment rate dropped almost a full percentage point between the first quarters of 1993 and 1994, from 7.4% to 6.5%.

Business Services

According to the Federal Reserve, the business services sector is one of the healthiest sectors in metro Philadelphia. According to the *Philadelphia Business Journal*, earnings between 1992 and 1994 have increased by a total of 132% in the business services sector. *Among the fastest growing industries:* Employment Services. Right Management Consultants Inc., a human resources consulting and out-placement counseling firm, for example, experienced a 432% increase in quarterly earnings from 1992-94. CDI Corp., a temporary personnel service in Philadelphia, increased its quarterly profits by 127%, from 1.3 million to 2.9 million.

Manufacturing

Although the Pennsylvania Bureau of Labor Statistics projects a state-wide decline of 39,000 manufacturing jobs over the course of this decade, there are signs that the industrial sector in metro Philadelphia is at least stabilizing. Data from the first quarter of 1994 indicated an increase of almost 5,000 manufacturing jobs in the Philadelphia region -- the first quarterly increase in five years. **Crown Cork and Seal**, a *Fortune 500* company located in Philadelphia, produces metal and plastic containers; crowns and closures; and packaging machinery. In 1993, Crown Cork and Seal increased its number of employees by 4% to 21,254.

Health Care and Biotechnology

Graced by 85 hospitals and 186 nursing homes, the health care industry is an integral part of the Philadelphia region's economy. A study compiled by the Pennsylvania Economy League determined that hospitals are the largest employers by payroll in Montgomery, Philadelphia, Delaware, and Bucks counties. Indeed, this sector accounts for 15% of the Philadelphia area's jobs. The PEL study also revealed that Delaware Valley hospitals pay out more than $5.5 billion in wages.

Jobseekers should note however that many hospitals are consolidating in response to skyrocketing health care costs. Such measures have recently resulted in the elimination of nearly 1,000 jobs in Delaware Valley hospitals. Moreover, health care reform, if and when it happens, will likely bring new changes to the health care industry. Despite the decrease of available jobs in local hospitals, opportunities in outpatient care and group-managed care are expected to expand as the nation's health care needs continue to change with the aging population.

Jobseekers will find many more opportunities in Philadelphia's biotech industry. The "Medical Mile", a stretch of U.S. Route 202 just west of the city, hosts a number of biotech companies. These include upstarts **Magainin Pharmaceuticals Inc.** and **Cephalon**. Major labs from **Merck**, **SmithKline Beecham** and **Rhone-Poulenc Rorer** also reside within the Philadelphia metro area. Overall, the pharmaceutical and biotech companies on the Medical Mile employ more than 50,000 people, and include thirty research and development labs for many pharmaceutical companies, both large and small.

High-tech and Education

Route 202 is also home to a large number of high-tech companies. Eighty-nine colleges and universities in the region graduate 50,000 students annually, and these colleges and universities provide the high-tech industry with a skilled work force. Moreover, there exists both public and private initiatives to promote the development of the high-tech industry. For example, the **University of Pennsylvania, Drexel University**, and **Thomas Jefferson University** have been actively involved in filing for patents and commercializing laboratory developments.

The Ben Franklin Partnership, a government funded agency which promotes economic development by encouraging relationships between different industries, assists the development of this industry by promoting the transfer of technological innovation to commercial use. *The Philadelphia Business Journal* reports that 36% of local high-tech companies expect staff increases of at least 10% through 1997. With over 250 firms engaged in the computer industry, computer programmers and computer systems analysts continue to be in demand throughout the Delaware Valley. Many Philadelphia businesses are recruiting data processing and software professionals from outside the region. In fact, the Pennsylvania Department of Labor and Industry anticipates that almost 1,000 of these positions will be available annually throughout the '90s.

Finance and Insurance

Philadelphia's reputation as a financial center is driven by the fact that it is home to the **Philadelphia Stock Exchange** and the Federal Reserve Bank, as well as a variety of large commercial banks, insurance companies, and national accounting firms. During the last half of the 1980's, however, bad loans to the third world, the 1987 stock market crash, and the savings and loan crisis hampered growth in the local financial sector. Insurance agency employment, despite an annual growth rate of 3% in the past few years, is not expected to have any significant increases in local employment.

Falling rates of unemployment, a government continuation of initiatives intended to strengthen and diversify the local economy, a possible tax cut to lure businesses to the area, and the improving national economy promise a continued recovery for the Philadelphia region in 1995.

Conclusion

In the past few years the tri-state region has experienced its best quarterly growth since the recession. While employment growth in Pennsylvania and New Jersey will most likely fall short of the national rate in 1995, employment levels should still be higher than in recent years. Employment in Delaware, however, continues to grow at a rate faster than that of the national average, and this state is a good place for job seekers to research employment opportunities in the region.

Helpful resources for job seekers:

Philadelphia Chamber of Commerce: 215/545-1234
Trenton, New Jersey Chamber of Commerce: 609/393-4143
New Jersey Department of Labor- Research Department: 609/633-6425
Atlantic City, New Jersey Chamber of Commerce: 609/345-2251
Wilmington, Delaware Chamber of Commerce: 302/655-7221
Delaware Development Office: 302/739-4271

THE JOB SEARCH

THE BASICS OF JOB WINNING:
A CONDENSED REVIEW

The best way to obtain a better professional job is to contact the employer directly. Broad-based statistical studies by the Department of Labor show that job seekers find jobs more successfully by contacting employers directly than by using any other method.

However, given the diversity and the increasingly specialized nature of both industries and job tasks, in some situations other job seeking methods may also be successful. Three of the other most commonly used methods are: relying on personal contacts, using employment services, and following up help wanted advertisements. Many professionals have been successful in finding better jobs using one of these methods. However, the Direct Contact method boasts twice the success rate of any other method, and is used successfully by many more professionals. So unless you have specific reasons to believe that another method would work best for you, the Direct Contact method should form the foundation of your job search.

The Objective

With any business task, you must develop a strategy for meeting a goal. This is especially true when it comes to obtaining a better job. First you need to clearly define your objectives.

Setting your job objectives is better known as career planning (or life planning for those who wish to emphasize the importance of combining the two). Career planning has become a field of study in and of itself. Since many of our readers are probably well-entrenched in their career path, we will touch on career planning only briefly.

The first step in beginning your job search is to clearly define your objectives

If you are thinking of choosing or switching careers, we particularly emphasize two things. First, choose a career where you will enjoy most of the day-to-day tasks. This sounds obvious, but most of us have at one point or another been attracted by a glamour industry or a prestigious job title without thinking of the most important consideration: Would we enjoy performing the everyday tasks the position entailed?

The second key consideration is that you are not merely choosing a career, but also a lifestyle. Career counselors indicate that one of the most common problems people encounter in job seeking is that they fail to consider how well-suited they are for a particular position or career. For example, some people, attracted to management consulting by good salaries, early responsibility, and high-level corporate exposure, do not adapt well to the long hours, heavy travel demands, and the constant pressure to produce. Be sure to ask yourself how you might adapt to not only the day-to-day duties and working environment that a specific position entails, but also how you might adapt to the demands of that career or industry choice as a whole.

The Strategy

Assuming that you've established your career objectives, the next step of the job search is to develop a strategy. If you don't take the time to develop a strategy and lay out a plan, you will find yourself going in circles after several weeks of random searching for opportunities that always seem just beyond your reach.

Your strategy can be thought of as having three simple elements:

1. Choosing a method of contacting employers.

2. Allocating your scarce resources. (In most job searches the key scarce resource will be time, but financial considerations will become important in some searches, too.)

3. Evaluating how the selected contact method is working and then considering adopting other methods.

We suggest you consider using the Direct Contact method exclusively. However, we realize it is human nature to avoid putting all your eggs in one basket. So if you prefer to use other methods as well, try to expend at least half your effort on the Direct Contact method, spending the rest on all of the other methods combined. Millions of other jobseekers have already proven that Direct Contact has been twice as effective in obtaining employment, so why not benefit from their effort?

Job hunting is intellectually demanding work that requires you to be at your best. So don't tire yourself out working around the clock

---

With your strategy in mind, the next step is to work out the details. The most important detail is setting up a schedule. Of course, since job searches aren't something most people do regularly, it may be hard to estimate how long each step will take. Nonetheless, it is important to have a plan so that you can see yourself progressing.

When outlining your job search schedule, have a realistic time frame in mind. If you will be job searching full-time, your search will probably take at least two months. If you can only devote part-time effort, it will probably take four months.

You probably know a few people who seem to spend their whole lives searching for a better job in their spare time. Don't be one of them. Once you begin your job search on a part-time basis, give it your whole-hearted effort. If you don't feel like devoting a lot of energy to job seeking right now, then wait. Focus on enjoying your present position, performing your best on the job, and storing up energy for when you are really ready to begin your job search.

Those of you currently unemployed should remember that job hunting is tough work physically and emotionally. It is also intellectually demanding work that requires you to be at your best. So don't tire yourself out by working on your job campaign around the clock. At the same time, be sure to discipline yourself. The most logical way to manage your time while looking for a job is to keep your regular working hours.

Try calling as early as 8 AM and as late as 6 PM. You'll be surprised how often you will be able to reach the executive you want during these times of the day

---

For those of you who are still employed, job searching will be particularly tiring because it must be done in addition to your regular duties. So don't work yourself to the point where you show up to interviews looking exhausted and start to slip behind at your current job. On the other hand, don't be tempted to quit your current job! The long hours are worth it. Searching for a job while you have one puts you in a position of strength.

If you are searching full-time and have decided to choose several different contact methods, we recommend that you divide up each week allowing some time for each method. For instance, you might devote Mondays to following up newspaper ads because most of them appear in Sunday papers. Then you might devote Tuesdays, and Wednesday mornings to working and developing the personal contacts you have, in addition to trying a few employment services. Then you could devote the rest of the week to the Direct Contact method. This is just one plan that may succeed for you.

By trying several methods at once, job-searching will be more interesting, and you will be able to evaluate how promising each of the methods seems, altering your schedule accordingly. Be very careful in your evaluation, however, and don't judge the success of a particular method just by the sheer number of interviews you obtain. Positions advertised in the newspaper, for instance, are likely to generate many more interviews per opening than positions that are filled without being advertised.

If you are searching part-time and decide to try several different contact methods, we recommend that you try them sequentially. You simply won't have enough time to put a meaningful amount of effort into more than one method at once. So estimate the length of your job search, and then allocate so many weeks or months for each contact method you will use. (We suggest that you try Direct Contact first.)

If you're expected to be in your office during the business day, then you have an additional problem to deal with. How can you work interviews into the business day? And if you work in an open office, how can you even call to set up interviews? As much as possible you should keep up the effort and the appearances on your present job. So maximize your use of the lunch hour, early mornings and late afternoons for calling. If you keep trying you'll be surprised how often you will be able to reach the executive you are trying to contact during your out-of-office hours. Also you can catch people as early as 8 AM and as late as 6 PM on frequent occasions. Jot out a plan each night on how you will be using each minute of your precious lunch break.

Your inability to interview at any time other than lunch just might work to your advantage. If you can, try to set up as many interviews as possible for your lunch hour. This will go a long way to creating a relaxed rapport. (Who isn't happy when eating?) But be sure the interviews don't stray too far from the agenda on hand.

Consider where your skills might be in demand, the degree of competition for employment, and the employment outlook at each particular firm

---

Lunchtime interviews are much easier to obtain if you have substantial career experience. People with less experience will often find no alternative to taking time off for interviews. If you have to take time off, you have to take time off. But try to do this as little as possible. Try to take the whole day off in order to avoid being blatantly obvious about your job search. Try to schedule in two to three interviews for the same day. (It is very difficult to maintain an optimum level of energy at more than three interviews in one day.) Explain to the interviewer why you might have to juggle your interview schedule -- he/she should honor the respect you're showing your current employer by minimizing your days off and will probably appreciate the fact that another prospective employer is interested in you.

We want to stress that if you are searching for a job -- especially part-time -- get out there and do the necessary tasks to the best of your ability and get it over with. Don't let your job search drag on endlessly.

And remember that all schedules are meant to be broken. The purpose of a job search schedule is not to rush you to your goal but to help you map out the road ahead, and then to periodically evaluate how you're progressing.

The Direct Contact Method

Once you have scheduled your time, you are ready to begin your search in earnest. We'll limit discussion here to the Direct Contact method.

The first step in preparing for Direct Contact is to develop a check list for categorizing the types of firms for which you'd like to work. You might categorize firms by product line, size, customer-type (such as industrial or consumer), growth prospects, or, by geographical location. Your list of important criteria might be very short. If it is, good! The shorter it is, the easier it will be to locate the company that is right for you.

DEVELOPING YOUR CONTACTS

Some career counselors feel that the best route to a better job is through somebody you already know or through somebody to whom you can be introduced. The counselors recommend that you build your contact base beyond your current acquaintances by asking each one to introduce you, or refer you, to additional people in your field of interest.

The theory goes like this: You might start with 15 personal contacts, each of whom introduces you to three additional people, for a total of 45 additional contacts. Then each of these people introduces you to three additional people, which adds 135 additional contacts. Theoretically, you will soon know every person in the industry.

Of course, developing your personal contacts does not usually work quite as smoothly as the theory suggests because some people will not be able to introduce you to anyone. The further you stray from your initial contact base, the weaker your references may be. So, if you do try developing your own contacts, try to begin with as many people you know personally as you can. Dig into your personal phone book and your holiday greeting card list and locate old classmates from school. Be particularly sure to approach people who perform your personal business such as your lawyer, accountant, banker, doctor, stockbroker, and insurance agent. These people develop a very broad contact base due to the nature of their professions.

Next, try to decide at which firms you're most likely to be able to find a job. Try matching your skills with those that a specific job demands. Consider where your skills might be in demand, the degree of competition for employment, and the employment outlook at each particular firm.

Now you'll want to assemble your list of potential employers. Build up your list to at least 100 prospects. Then separate your prospect list into three groups. The first tier of around 25 firms will be your primary target group, the second tier of another 25 firms will be your secondary group, and the remaining names you can keep in reserve.

This book will help you greatly in developing your prospect list. You'll notice that employer listings are arranged according to state. If you know of a company, but you're unsure where it's located, then refer to the state index at the rear of the book to find the company's location.

After you form your prospect list begin work on your resume. Refer to the sample resumes included in the Resumes and Cover Letters section following this chapter in order to get ideas.

You should plan to spend an average of three or four hours researching each firm

Once your resume is complete, begin researching your first batch of 25 prospective employers. You will want to determine whether you would be happy working at the firms you are researching and also get a better idea of what their employment needs might be. You also need to obtain enough information to sound highly informed about the company during phone conversations and in mail correspondence. But don't go all out on your research yet! At some of these firms you probably will not be able to arrange interviews, so save your big research effort until you start to arrange interviews. Nevertheless, you should plan to spend an average of three to four hours researching each firm. Do your research in batches to save time and energy. Use one resource at a time and find out what you can about each of the 25 firms in the batch. Start with the easiest resources to use (such as this book). Keep organized. Maintain a folder on each firm.

If you discover something that really disturbs you about the firm (they are about to close their only local office), or if you discover that your chances of getting a job there are practically nil (they have just instituted a hiring freeze), then cross them off your prospect list.

If possible, supplement your research efforts with contacts to individuals who know the firm well. Ideally you should make an informal contact with someone at the particular firm, but often a contact at a direct competitor, or a major supplier or customer will be able to supply you with just as much information. At the very least, try to obtain whatever printed information that the company has available, not just annual reports, but product brochures and any other printed material the firm may have to offer. The company might have printed information about career opportunities.

DON'T BOTHER WITH MASS MAILINGS OR BARRAGES OF PHONE CALLS

Direct Contact does not mean burying every firm within a hundred miles with mail and phone calls. Mass mailings rarely work in the job hunt. This also applies to those letters that are personalized -- but dehumanized -- on an automatic typewriter or computer. Don't waste your time or money on such a project; you will fool no one but yourself.

The worst part of sending out mass mailings -- or making unplanned phone calls to companies you have not researched -- is that you are likely to be remembered as someone with little genuine interest in the firm, who lacks sincerity, and as somebody that nobody wants to hire.

HELP WANTED ADVERTISEMENTS

Only a small fraction of professional job openings are advertised. Yet a majority of job seekers -- and a lot of people not in the job market -- spend a lot of time studying the help wanted ads. As a result, the competition for advertised openings is often very severe.

A moderate-sized employer told us about an experience advertising in the help wanted section of a major Sunday newspaper:

It was a disaster. We had over 500 responses from this relatively small ad in just one week. We have only two phone lines in this office and one was totally knocked out. We'll never advertise for professional help again.

If you insist on following up on help wanted ads, then research a firm before you reply to an ad. Preliminary research might help to separate you from all of the other professionals responding to that ad, many of whom will only have a passing interest in the opportunity, and will give you insight about a particular firm to help you determine if it is potentially a good match. That said, your chances of obtaining a job through the want-ads are still much smaller than they are if you use the Direct Contact method.

Getting The Interview

Now it is time to arrange an interview, time to make the Direct Contact. If you have read many books on job searching, you may have noticed that most of these books tell you to avoid the personnel office like the plague. It is said that the personnel office never hires people; they screen candidates. Unfortunately, this is often the case, but there are other options available to you. If you can identify the appropriate manager with the authority to hire you, contact that person directly. This will take a lot of time in each case, and often you'll be bounced back to personnel despite your efforts. So we suggest that initially you begin your Direct Contact campaign through personnel offices. If it seems that the firms on your prospect list do little hiring through personnel, you might consider some alternative courses of action. The three obvious means of initiating Direct Contact are:

-Showing up unannounced
-Mail
-Phone calls

Cross out the first one right away. You should never show up to seek a professional position without an appointment. Even if you are somehow lucky enough to obtain an interview, you will appear so unprofessional that you will not be seriously considered.

Mail contact seems to be a good choice if you have not been in the job market for a while. You can take your time to prepare a letter, say exactly what you want, and of course include your resume. Remember that employers receive many resumes every day. Don't be surprised if you do not get a response to your
inquiry, so don't spend weeks waiting for responses that may never come. If you do send a cover letter, follow it up (or precede it) with a phone call. This will increase your impact, and because of the initial research you did, will underscore both your familiarity and your interest in the firm.

Always include a cover letter with your resume even if you are not specifically asked to do so

---

Another alternative is to make a "Cover Call." Your Cover Call should be just like your cover letter: concise. Your first sentence should interest the employer in you. Then try to subtly mention your familiarity with the firm. Don't be overbearing; keep your introduction to three sentences or less. Be pleasant, self-confident, and relaxed. This will greatly increase the chances of the person at the other end of the line developing the conversation. But don't press. When you are asked to follow up "with something in the mail", don't try to prolong the conversation once it has ended. Don't ask what they want to receive in the mail. Always send your resume and a highly personalized follow-up letter, reminding the addressee of the phone conversation. Always include a cover letter if you are requested to send a resume.

Unless you are in telephone sales, making smooth and relaxed cover calls will probably not come easily. Practice them on your own and then with your friends or relatives.

If you obtain an interview as a result of a telephone conversation, be sure to send a thank you note reiterating the points you made during the conversation. You will appear more professional and increase your impact.

However, unless specifically requested, don't mail your resume once an interview has been arranged. Take it with you to the interview instead.

Preparing For The Interview

Once the interview has been arranged, begin your in-depth research. You should arrive at an interview knowing the company upside down and inside out. You need to know the company's products, types of customers, subsidiaries, the parent company, principal locations, rank in the industry, sales and profit trends, type of ownership, size, current plans, and much more. By this time you have probably narrowed your job search to one industry. If you haven't, then be familiar with the trends in the firm's industry, the firm's principal competitors and their relative performance, and the direction that the industry leaders are headed. Dig into every resource you can! Read the company literature, the trade press, the business press, and if the company is public, call your stockbroker (if you have one) and ask for additional information. If possible, speak to someone at the firm before the interview, or if not, speak to someone at a competing firm. The more time you spend, the better. Even if you feel extremely pressed for time, you should set aside at least 12 hours for pre-interview research.

You should arrive at an interview knowing the company upside down and inside out

---

If you have been out of the job market for some time, don't be surprised if you find yourself tense during your first few interviews. It will probably happen every time you re-enter the market, not just when you seek your first job after getting out of school.

Tension is natural during an interview, but if you can be relaxed you will have an advantage. Knowing you have done a thorough research job should put you more at ease. Make a list of questions that you think might be asked in an interview. Think out your answers carefully; practice reviewing

SOME FAVORITE INTERVIEW QUESTIONS

Tell me about yourself...

Why did you leave your last job?

What excites you in your current job?

What are your career goals?

Where would you like to be in 5 years?

What are your greatest strengths?

What are your greatest weaknesses?

Why do you wish to work for this firm?

Where else are you seeking employment?

Why should we hire you?

them with a friend. Tape record your responses to the problem questions. If you feel particularly unsure of your interviewing skills, arrange your first interviews at firms you are not as interested in. (But remember it is common courtesy to seem excited about the possibility of working for any firm at which you interview.) Practice again on your own after these first few interviews. Go over the difficult questions that you were asked.

How important is the proper dress for a job interview? Buying a complete wardrobe of Brooks Brothers pinstripes or Liz Claiborne suits, donning new wing tip shoes or pumps, and having your hair styled every morning is not enough to guarantee you a career position as an investment banker. But on the other hand, if you can't find a clean, conservative suit or a nice skirt and blouse, or won't take the time to wash your hair, then you are just wasting your time by interviewing at all.

Very rarely will the final selection of candidates for a job opening be determined by dress. So don't spend a fortune on a new wardrobe. But be sure that your clothes are adequate. Men applying for any professional position should wear a suit; women should either wear a dress or a suit (but not a pant suit). Your clothes should be at least as formal or slightly more formal and more conservative than the position would suggest.

Top personal grooming is more important than finding the perfect clothes for a job interview. Careful grooming indicates both a sense of thoroughness and self-confidence.

Be sure that your clothes fit well and that they are immaculate. Hair must be neat and clean. Shoes should be newly polished. Women need to avoid excessive jewelry and excessive makeup. Men should be freshly shaven, even if the interview is late in the day.

Be complete. Everyone needs a watch, a pen, and a notepad. Finally, a briefcase or a leather-bound folder (containing extra copies of your resume) will help complete the look of professionalism.

The very beginning of the interview is the most important part because it determines the rapport for the rest of it

---

Sometimes the interviewer will be running behind schedule. Don't be upset, be sympathetic. There is often pressure to interview a lot of candidates and to quickly fill a demanding position. So be sure to come to your interview with good reading material to keep yourself occupied. This will help you to relax.

The Interview

The very beginning of the interview is the most important part because it determines the rapport for the rest of it. Those first few moments are especially crucial. Do you smile when you meet? Do you establish enough eye contact, but not too much? Do you walk into the office with a self-assured and confident stride? Do you shake hands firmly? Do you make small talk easily without being garrulous? It is human nature to judge people by that first impression, so make sure it is a good one. But most of all, try to be yourself.

Often the interviewer will begin, after the small talk, by telling you about the company, the division, the department, or perhaps, the position. Because of your detailed research, the information about the company should be repetitive for you, and the interviewer would probably like nothing better than to avoid this regurgitation of the company biography. So if you can do so tactfully, indicate to the interviewer that you are very familiar with the firm. If he or she seems intent on providing you with background information, despite your hints, then acquiesce.

But be sure to remain attentive. If you can manage to generate a brief discussion of the company or the industry at this point, without being forceful, great. It will help to further build rapport, underscore your interests, and increase your impact.

If you are really unsure as to how detailed a response the interviewer is seeking, then ask

---

Soon (if it didn't begin that way) the interviewer will begin the questions. This period of the interview falls into one of two categories (or somewhere in between): either a structured interview, where the interviewer has a prescribed set of questions to ask; or an unstructured interview, where the interviewer will ask only leading questions to get you to talk about yourself, your experiences and your goals. Try to sense as quickly as possible which direction the interviewer wishes to proceed. This will make the interviewer feel more relaxed and in control of the situation.

Many of the questions will be similar to the ones that you were expecting and have practiced. Remember to keep attuned to the interviewer and make the length of your answers appropriate to the situation. If you are really unsure as to how detailed a response the interviewer is seeking, then ask.

As the interview progresses, the interviewer will probably mention some of the most important responsibilities of the position. If applicable, draw parallels between your experience and the demands of the position as detailed by the interviewer. Describe your past experience in the same manner that you did on your resume: emphasizing results and achievements and not merely describing activities. If you listen carefully (listening is a very important part of the interviewing process) the interviewer might very well imply the skills needed for the position. Don't exaggerate. Be on the level about your abilities.

Try not to cover too much ground during the first interview. This interview is often the toughest, where many candidates are screened out. If you are interviewing for a very competitive position, you will have to make an impression that will last. Focus on a few of your greatest strengths that are relevant to the position. Develop these points carefully, state them again in other words, and then try to summarize them briefly at the end of the interview.

Often the interviewer will pause towards the end and ask if you have any questions. Particularly in a structured interview, this might be the one chance to really show your knowledge of and interest in the firm. Have a list prepared of specific questions that are of real interest to you. Let your questions subtly show your research and your knowledge of the firm's activities. It is wise to have an extensive list of questions, as several of them may be answered during the interview.

YOU'RE FIRED!!

You are not the first and will not be the last to go through this traumatic experience. Thousands of professionals are fired every week. Remember, being fired is not a reflection on you as a person. It is usually a reflection of your company's staffing needs and its perception of your recent job performance. Share the fact with your relatives and friends. Being fired is not something of which to be ashamed.

Don't start your job search with a flurry of unplanned activity. Start by choosing a strategy and working out a plan. Now is not the time for major changes in your life. If possible, remain in the same career and in the same geographical location, at least until you have been working again for a while. On the other hand, if the only industry for which you are trained is leaving, or is severely depressed in your area, then you should give prompt consideration to moving or switching careers.

Register for unemployment compensation immediately. A thorough job search could take months. After all, your employers have been contributing to unemployment insurance specifically for you ever since your first job. Don't be surprised to find other professionals collecting unemployment compensation as well. Unemployment compensation is for everybody who is between jobs.

Be prepared for the question, "Why were you fired?", during job interviews. Avoid mentioning you were fired while arranging interviews. Try especially hard not to speak negatively of your past employer and not to sound particularly worried about your status of being temporarily unemployed. But don't spend much time reflecting on why you were fired or how you might have avoided it. Learn from your mistakes and then look ahead. Think positively. And be sure to follow a careful plan during your job search.

Do not turn your opportunity to ask questions into an interrogation. Avoid bringing your list of questions to the interview. Ask questions that you are fairly certain the interviewer can answer (remember how you feel when you cannot answer a question during an interview).

Even if you are unable to determine the salary range beforehand, do not ask about it during the first interview. You can always ask about it later. Above all, don't ask about fringe benefits until you have been offered a position. (Then be sure to get all the details.) You should be able to determine the company's policy on fringe benefits relatively easily before the interview.

Try not to be negative about anything during the interview. (Particularly any past employer or any previous job.) Be cheerful. Everyone likes to work with someone who seems to be happy.

Don't let a tough question throw you off base. If you don't know the answer to a question, say so simply -- do not apologize. Just smile. Nobody can answer every question -- particularly some of the questions that are asked in job interviews.

Before your first interview, you may be able to determine how many interviews there usually are for positions at your level. (Of course it may differ quite a bit even within the different levels of one firm.) Usually you can count on attending at least three or four interviews, although some firms, such as some of the professional partnerships, are well-known to give a minimum of six interviews for all professional positions. While you should be more relaxed as you return for subsequent interviews, the pressure will be on. The more prepared you are, the better.

Depending on what information you are able to obtain, you might want to vary your strategy quite a bit from interview to interview. For instance, if the first interview is a screening interview, then be sure a few of your strengths really stand out. On the other hand, if later interviews are primarily with people who are in a position to veto your hiring, but not to push it forward (and few people are weeded out at these stages), then you should primarily focus on building rapport as opposed to reiterating and developing your key strengths.

If it looks as though your skills and background do not match the position your interviewer was hoping to fill, ask him or her if there is another division or subsidiary that perhaps could profit from your talents.

After The Interview

Write a follow-up letter immediately after the interview, while it is still fresh in the interviewer's mind. Then, if you have not heard from the interviewer within seven days, call to stress your continued interest in the firm, and the position, and request a second interview.

A parting word of advice. Again and again during your job search you will be rejected. You will be rejected when you apply for interviews. You will be rejected after interviews. For every job you finally receive, you will have probably been rejected a multitude of times. Don't let rejections slow you down. Keep reminding yourself that the sooner you go out and get started on your job search, and get those rejections flowing in, the closer you will be to obtaining the job you want.

RESUMES AND COVER LETTERS

RESUMES/OVERVIEW

When filling a position, a recruiter will often have 100 plus applicants, but time to interview only the 5 or 10 most promising ones. So he or she will have to reject most applicants after a brief skimming of their resume.

Unless you have phoned and talked to the recruiter -- which you should do whenever you can -- you will be chosen or rejected for an interview entirely on the basis of your resume and cover letter. So your resume must be outstanding. (But remember -- a resume is no substitute for a job search campaign. YOU must seek a job. Your resume is only one tool.)

RESUME PREPARATION

One page, usually

Unless you have an unusually strong background with many years of experience and a large diversity of outstanding achievements, prepare a one page resume. Recruiters dislike long resumes.

8-1/2 x 11 Size

Recruiters often get resumes in batches of hundreds. If your resume is on small sized paper it is likely to get lost in the pile. If oversized, it is likely to get crumpled at the edges, and won't fit in their files.

Typesetting

Modern photocomposition typesetting gives you the clearest, sharpest image, a wide variety of type styles and effects such as italics, bold facing, and book-like justified margins. Typesetting is the best resume preparation process, but is also the most expensive.

Word Processing

The most flexible way to get your resume typed is on a good quality word processor. With word processing, you can make changes almost instantly because your resume will be stored on a magnetic disk and the computer will do all the re-typing automatically. A word processing service will usually offer you a variety of type styles in both regular and proportional spacing. You can have bold facing for emphasis, justified margins, and clear, sharp copies.

Typing

Household typewriters and office typewriters with nylon or other cloth ribbons are NOT good for typing the resume you will have printed. If you can't get word processing or typesetting, hire a professional who uses a high quality office typewriter with a plastic ribbon (usually called a "carbon ribbon").

Printing

Find the best quality offset printing process available. DO NOT make your copies on an office photocopier. Only the personnel office may see the resume you mail. Everyone else may see only a copy of it. Copies of copies quickly become unreadable. Some professionally maintained, extra-high-quality photocopiers are of adequate quality, if you are in a rush. But top quality offset printing is best.

Proofread your resume

Whether you typed it yourself or had it written, typed, or typeset, mistakes on resumes can be embarrassing, particularly when something obvious such as your name is misspelled. No matter how much you paid someone else to type or write or typeset your resume, YOU lose if there is a mistake. So proofread it as carefully as possible. Get a friend to help you. Read your draft aloud as your friend checks the proof copy. Then have your friend read aloud while you check. Next, read it letter by letter to check spelling and punctuation.

If you are having it typed or typeset by a resume service or a printer, and you can't bring a friend or take the time during the day to proof it, pay for it and take it home. Proof it there and bring it back later to get it corrected and printed.

RESUME FORMAT (See samples)

Basic data

Your name, phone number, and a complete address should be at the top of your resume. (If you are a university student, you should also show your home address and phone number.)

Separate your education and work experience

In general, list your experience first. If you have recently graduated, list your education first, unless your experience is more important than your education. (For example, if you have just graduated from a teaching school, have some business experience and are applying for a job in business you would list your business experience first.) If you have two or more years of college, you don't need to list high schools.

Reverse chronological order

To a recruiter your last job and your latest schooling are the most important. So put the last first and list the rest going back in time.

Show dates and locations

Put the dates of your employment and education on the left of the page. Put the names of the companies you worked for and the schools you attended a few spaces to the right of the dates. Put the city and state, or the city and country where you studied or worked to the right of the page.

Avoid sentences and large blocks of type

Your resume will be scanned, not read. Short, concise phrases are much more effective than long-winded sentences. Keep everything easy to find. Avoid paragraphs longer than six lines. Never go ten or more lines in a paragraph. If you have more than six lines of information about one job or school, put it in two or more paragraphs.

RESUME CONTENT

Be factual

In many companies, inaccurate information on a resume or other application material will get you fired as soon as the inaccuracy is discovered. Protect yourself.

Be positive

You are selling your skills and accomplishments in your resume. If you achieved something, say so. Put it in the best possible light. Don't hold back or be modest, no one else will. But don't exaggerate to the point of misrepresentation.

Be brief

Write down the important (and pertinent) things you have done, but do it in as few words as possible. The shorter your resume is, the more carefully it will be examined.

Work experience

Emphasize continued experience in a particular type of function or continued interest in a particular industry. De-emphasize irrelevant positions. Delete positions that you held for less than four months. (Unless you are a very recent college grad or still in school.)

Stress your results

Elaborate on how you contributed to your past employers. Did you increase sales, reduce costs, improve a product, implement a new program? Were you promoted?

Mention relevant skills and responsibilities

Be specific. Slant your past accomplishments toward the type of position that you hope to obtain. Example: Do you hope to supervise people? Then state how many people, performing what function, you have supervised.

Education

Keep it brief if you have more than two years of career experience. Elaborate more if you have less experience. Mention degrees received and any honors or special awards. Note individual courses or research projects that might be relevant for employers. For instance, if you are a liberal arts major, be sure to mention courses in such areas as: accounting, statistics, computer programming, or mathematics.

Job objective

Leave it out. Even if you are certain of exactly the type of job that you desire, the inclusion of a job objective might eliminate you from consideration for other positions that a recruiter feels are a better match for your qualifications.

Personal data

Keep it very brief. Two lines maximum. A one-word mention of commonly practiced activities such as golf, skiing, sailing, chess, bridge, tennis, etc., can prove to be good way to open up a conversation during an interview. Do not include your age, weight, height, etc.

SHOULD YOU HIRE A RESUME WRITER?

If you write reasonably well, there are some advantages to writing your resume yourself. To write it well, you will have to review your experience and figure out how to explain your accomplishments in clear, brief phrases. This will help you when you explain your work to interviewers.

If you write your resume, everything in it will be in your own words -- it will sound like you. It will say what you want it to say. And you will be much more familiar with the contents. If you are a good writer, know yourself well, and have a good idea of what parts of your background employers are looking for, you may be able to write your own resume better than anyone else can. If you write your resume yourself, you should have someone who can be objective (preferably not a close relative) review it with you.

When should you have your resume professionally written?

If you have difficulty writing in "resume style" (which is quite unlike normal written language), if you are unsure of which parts of your background you should emphasize, or if you think your resume would make your case better if it did not follow the standard form outlined here or in a book on resumes, then you should have it professionally written.

There are two reasons even some professional resume writers we know have had their resumes written with the help of fellow professionals. First, when they need the help of someone who can be objective about their background, and second, when they want an experienced sounding board to help focus their thoughts.

If you decide to hire a resume writer

The best way to choose a writer is by reputation -- the recommendation of a friend, a personnel director, your school placement officer or someone else knowledgeable in the field.

You should ask, "If I'm not satisfied with what you write, will you go over it with me and change it?"

You should ask, "How long has the person who will write my resume been writing resumes?"

There is no sure relation between price and quality, except that you are unlikely to get a good writer for less than $50 for an uncomplicated resume and you shouldn't have to pay more than $300 unless your experience is very extensive or complicated. There will be additional charges for printing.

Few resume services will give you a firm price over the phone, simply because some people's resumes are too complicated and take too long to do at any predetermined price. Some services will quote you a price that applies to almost all of their customers. Be sure to do some comparative shopping. Obtain a firm price before you engage their services and find out how expensive minor changes will be.

COVER LETTERS

Always mail a cover letter with your resume. In a cover letter you can show an interest in the company that you can't show in a resume. You can point out one or two skills or accomplishments the company can put to good use.

Make it personal

The more personal you can get, the better. If someone known to the person you are writing has recommended that you contact the company, get permission to include his/her name in the letter. If you have the name of a person to send the letter to, make sure you have the name spelled correctly and address it directly to that person. Be sure to put the person's name and title on both the letter and envelope. This will ensure that your letter will get through to the proper person, even if a new person now occupies this position. But even if you are addressing it to the "Personnel Director" or the "Hiring Partner," send a letter.

Type cover letters in full. Don't try the cheap and easy ways like photocopying the body of your letter and typing in the inside address and salutation. You will give the impression that you are mailing to a multitude of companies and have no particular nterest in any one. Have your letters fully typed and signed with a pen.

Bring extra copies of your resume to the interview

If the person interviewing you doesn't have your resume, be prepared. Carry copies of your own. Even if you have already forwarded your resume, be sure to take extra copies to the interview, as someone other than the interviewer(s) might now have the first copy you sent.

FUNCTIONAL RESUME
(Prepared on a word processor and laser printed.)

Michelle Hughes
430 Miller's Crossing
Essex Junction, VT 05452
802/555-9354

Solid background in plate making, separations, color matching, background definition, printing, mechanicals, color corrections, and personnel supervision. A highly motivated manager and effective communicator. Proven ability to:

*Create Commercial Graphic ***Produce Embossing Drawings**
*Control Quality ***Resolve Printing Problems**

Qualifications

Printing:
Black and white and color. Can judge acceptability of color reproduction by comparing it with original. Can make four or five color corrections on all media. Have long developed ability to restyle already reproduced four-color artwork. Can create perfect tone for black and white match fill-ins for resume cover letters.

Customer Relations:
Work with customers to assure specifications are met and customers are satisfied. Can guide work through entire production process and strike a balance between technical printing capabilities and need for customer approval.

Specialties:
Make silk screen overlays for a multitude of processes. Velo bind, GBC bind, perfect bind. Have knowledge to prepare posters, flyers, and personalized stationery.

Personnel Supervision:
Foster an atmosphere that encourages highly talented artists to balance high level creativity with a maximum of production. Meet or beat production deadlines. Instruct new employees, apprentices and students in both artistry and technical operations.

Experience
Graphic Arts Professor, University of Vermont, Burlington, VT (1987-present).
Assistant Manager (part time), Design Graphics, Barre, VT (1991-present).

Education
Massachusetts Conservatory of Art, Ph.D. 1987
University of Massachusetts, B.A. 1984

CHRONOLOGICAL RESUME
(Prepared on a word processor and laser printed.)

RICHARD FRAIN
412 Maple Court
Seattle, WA 98404
206/555-6584

EXPERIENCE

1992-present THE CENTER COMPANY, Seattle, WA
Systems Analyst, design systems for the manufacturing unit. Specifically, physical inventory, program specifications, studies of lease buy decisions, selection of hardware for the outside contractors and inside users. Wrote On-Site Computer Terminal Operators Manual. Adapted product mix problems to the LAPSP (Logistical Alternative Product Synthesis Program).

February 1990-February 1992
Industrial Engineer, designed computerized systems. Evaluated operations efficiency, productivity, and budget allocations. Analyzed material waste. Recommended solutions.

ADDITIONAL EXPERIENCE

1986-1990   *Graduate Research Assistant* at New York State Institute of Technology.
1984-1986   *Graduate Teaching Assistant* at Salem State University.

EDUCATION

1988-1990   NEW YORK STATE INSTITUTE OF TECHNOLOGY, Albany, NY
M.S. in Operations Research. GPA: 3.6. Graduate courses included Advanced Location and Queueing Theories, Forecasting, Inventory and Material Flow Systems, Linear and Nonlinear Determination Models, Engineering Economics and Integer Programming.

1986-1988   M.S. in Information and Computer Sciences. GPA: 3.8.
Curriculum included Digital Computer Organization & Programming. Information Structure & Process. Mathematical Logic, Computer Systems, Logic Design, and Switching Theory.

1982-1986   SALEM STATE UNIVERSITY, Salem, OR
B.A. in Mathematics. GPA: 3.6.

AFFILIATIONS

Member of the American Institute of Computer Programmers, Association for Computing Machinery and the Operations Research Society of America.

PERSONAL

Married, three dependents, able to relocate.

CHRONOLOGICAL RESUME
(Prepared on a word processor and laser printed.)

Lorraine Avakian
70 Monback Avenue
Oshkosh, WI 54901
Phone: 414/555-4629

Business Experience

NATIONAL PACKAGING PRODUCTS, Princeton, WI
1991-present **District Sales Manager**
Improved 28-member sales group from a company rank in the bottom thirty percent to the top twenty percent. Complete responsibility for personnel, including recruiting, hiring and training. Developed a comprehensive sales improvement program and advised its implementation in eight additional sales districts.

1988-1990 **Marketing Associate**
Responsible for research, analysis, and presentation of marketing issues related to long-term corporate strategy. Developed marketing perspective for capital investment opportunities and acquisition candidates, which was instrumental in finalizing decisions to make two major acquisitions and to construct a $35 million canning plant.

1986-1988 **Salesperson, Paper Division**
Responsible for a four-county territory in central Wisconsin. Increased sales from $700,000 to over $1,050,000 annually in a 15 month period. Developed six new accounts with incremental sales potential of $800,000. Only internal candidate selected for new marketing program.

AMERICAN PAPER PRODUCTS, INC., Oshkosh, WI
1985-1986 **Sales Trainee**
Completed intensive six month training program and promoted to salesperson status. Received the President's Award for superior performance in the sales training program.

HENDUKKAR SPORTING GOODS, INC., Oshkosh, WI
1985 **Assistant Store Manager**
Supervised six employees on the evening shift. Handled accounts receivable.

Education
1979-1984 **BELOIT COLLEGE**, Beloit, WI
Received Bachelor of Science Degree in Business Administration in June 1982. Varsity Volleyball. Financed 50% of educational costs through part-time and co-op program employment.

Personal Background
Able to relocate; Excellent health; Active in community activities.

CHRONOLOGICAL RESUME
(Prepared on a word processor and laser printed.)

Melvin Winter
43 Aspen Wall Lane
Wheaton, IL 60512
312/555-6923 (home)
312/555-3000 (work)

Related Experience

GREAT LAKES PUBLISHING COMPANY, Chicago, IL
<u>Operations Supervisor</u> (1990-present)
Work in the Engineering Division of large trade publishing house. Maintain on-line computerized customer files, title files, accounts receivable, inventory and sales files. Organize department activities, establish priorities and train personnel. Provide corporate accounting with monthly reports of sales, earned income from journals, samples, inventory levels/value and sales and tax data. Divisional sales average $3 million annually.

<u>Senior Customer Service Representative</u> (1988-1990)
in the Construction Division. Answered customer service inquiries regarding orders and accounts receivable, issued return and shortage credits and expedited special sales orders for direct mail and sales to trade schools.

<u>Customer Service Representative</u> (1986-1987)
in the International Division. Same duties as for construction division except that sales were to retail stores and universities in Europe.

B. DALTON, BOOKSELLER, Salt Lake City, UT
<u>Assistant Manager</u> (1984-1986)
of this retail branch of a major domestic book seller, maintained all paperback inventories at necessary levels, deposited receipts daily and created window displays.

Education

1980-1984 UNIVERSITY OF MAINE, Orono, ME
Awarded a degree of Bachelor of Arts in French Literature.

Languages

Fluent in French. Able to write in French, German and Spanish.

Personal

Willing to travel and relocate, particularly in Europe.

References available upon request.

General Model for a Cover Letter

Your address
Date

Contact Person Name
Title
Company
Address

Dear Mr./Ms._____:

Immediately explain why your background makes you the best candidate for the position that you are applying for. Keep the first paragraph short and hard-hitting.

Detail what you could contribute to this company. Show how your qualifications will benefit this firm. Remember to keep this letter short; few recruiters will read a cover letter longer than half a page.

Describe your interest in the corporation. Subtly emphasize your knowledge about this firm (the result of your research effort) and your familiarity with the industry. It is common courtesy to act extremely eager to work for any company that you interview with.

In the closing paragraph you should specifically request an interview. Include your phone number and the hours when you can be reached. Alternatively, you might prefer to mention that you will follow up with a phone call (to arrange an interview at a mutually convenient time within the next several days).

Sincerely,
(signature)
Your full name
(typed)

General Model for a Follow-Up Letter

Your Address
Date

Contact Person Name
Title
Company
Address

Dear Mr./Ms._____:

Remind the interviewer of the position for which you were interviewed, as well as the date. Thank him/her for the interview.

Confirm your interest in the opening and the organization. Use specifics to emphasize both that you have researched the firm in detail and considered how you would fit into the company and the position.

As in your cover letter, emphasize one or two of you strongest qualifications and slant them toward the various points that the interviewer considered the most important for the position. Keep the letter brief, a half-page is plenty.

If appropriate, close with a suggestion for further action, such as a desire to have additional interviews. Mention your phone number and the hours that you can best be reached. Alternatively, you may prefer to mention that you will follow up with a phone call in several days.

Sincerely yours,
(signature)
Your full name
(typed)

PRIMARY EMPLOYERS OF
GREATER PHILADELPHIA

ACCOUNTING/MANAGEMENT CONSULTING

 *Receipts for accounting and bookkeeping services have been climbing in recent years, up 5 percent from 1992 to 1993, for example. And while the Big Six generate most of the industry's revenues, their growth has been slower than the smaller accounting houses.*

In the past few years, the industry has undergone some changes. Accounting firms are dropping clients that fall into high-risk categories, like savings and loans, while other accounting houses are refusing to take new, risky clients. Auditors and accountants are being asked to play a bigger role in evaluating the way corporations are run, and to improve their data in order to evaluate and project managment's performance.

A new trend is evolving on the employment scene -- CPA firms, both large and small, are taking care of staffing needs by hiring accounting paraprofessionals. While billing rates remain the same because their skills are similar, there are significant savings between the paraprofessionals and staff professionals. The cost of fringe benefits is reduced by hiring paraprofessionals, most of whom work part-time.

ARTHUR ANDERSEN & COMPANY
1601 Market Street, Philadelphia PA 19103. 215/241-7300. **Contact:** Michael Molloy, Director of Administration. **Description:** One of the six largest certified public accounting organizations in the world, operating offices in more than 40 countries. Operates in the following divisions: Audit, Tax, and Management Information Consulting. **Corporate headquarters location:** Chicago IL.

BOWMAN & COMPANY
601 White Horse Road, Voorhees NJ 08043. 609/435-6200. **Contact:** Human Resources Department. **Description:** A certified public accounting firm. **Common positions include:** Accountant/Auditor.

COOPERS & LYBRAND
2400 Eleven Penn Center, Philadelphia PA 19103. 215/963-8000. **FAX:** 215/963-8700. **Contact:** Kelley Fish, Supervisor of Recruiting. **Description:** A large certified public accounting firm, providing a broad range of services in the areas of accounting and auditing; taxation; management consulting and actuarial; and benefits and compensation consulting. Operates 102 offices in the United States; represented in 125 countries worldwide. **Common positions include:** Accountant/Auditor; Administrative Services Manager; Mathematician. **Educational backgrounds include:** Accounting. **Corporate headquarters location:** New York NY.

ERNST & YOUNG
Two Commerce Square, 2001 Market Street, P.O. Box 4000, Philadelphia PA 19103. 215/448-5000. **Contact:** Thomas G. Elicker, Director/Human Resources. **Description:** An international partnership with a staff of over 500; a member of PCPS and SECPS. Provides accounting, auditing, tax, actuarial, and management advisory services. CPE

is offered and paid for by the firm through in-house courses. Overnight travel is less than 10% and overtime is 11-15%. Applicants are required to have a BA or BS degree and should intend to become certified as soon as possible. **Common positions include:** Accountant/Auditor. **Educational backgrounds include:** Accounting. **Benefits:** Dental Insurance; Disability Coverage; Life Insurance; Medical Insurance; Pension Plan.

HOSPITAL CENTRAL SERVICES INC.
2171 28th Street SW, Allentown PA 18103. 215/791-2222. **Contact:** Human Resources. **Description:** Provides management services.

KEPNER-TREGOE, INC.
P.O. Box 704, Research Road, Princeton NJ 08542. 609/921-2806. **Contact:** Eileen J. Hamer, Manager, Human Resources. **Description:** A worldwide management consulting firm. Product categories include strategy formulation, systems improvement, skill development, and specific issue resolution. Industry markets are automotive, information technology, chemical, financial services, and natural resources. Operates in 44 countries and in 14 languages. **Common positions include:** Accountant/Auditor; Administrator; Marketing Specialist; Operations/Production Manager; Planner. **Educational backgrounds include:** Business Administration; Education; Finance; Liberal Arts; Marketing. **Benefits:** Dental Insurance; Disability Coverage; Employee Discounts; Life Insurance; Medical Insurance; Pension Plan; Profit Sharing; Savings Plan; Tuition Assistance. **Corporate headquarters location:** This Location. **Parent company:** USF&G. **Operations at this facility include:** Administration; Sales; Service. **Listed on:** New York Stock Exchange.

MANAGED LOGISTICS SYSTEMS INC.
216 Haddon Avenue, Collingswood NJ 08108. 609/858-1818. **Contact:** Human Resources. **Description:** Offers business management services.

NATIONAL FULFILLMENT SERVICES
100 Pine Avenue, Holmes PA 19043. 215/532-4700. **Contact:** Human Resources Department. **Description:** Provides accounting and bookkeeping services.

PRICE WATERHOUSE
30 South 17th Street, Philadelphia PA 19103. 215/665-9500. **Contact:** Tom Kovell, Regional Director of Human Resources. **Description:** Provides public accounting, business advisory, management consulting, and taxation services. **Number of employees nationwide:** 13,000.

RIGHT MANAGEMENT
1818 Market Street, Philadelphia PA 19103. 215/988-1588. **Contact:** Human Resources. **Description:** Provides management consulting services.

R.M. SHOEMAKER COMPANY
1 Tower Bridge, P.O. Box 888, West Conshohocken PA 19428. 215/941-5500. **Contact:** Human Resources. **Description:** A management services firm.

TILLINGHAST COMPANY
1500 Market Street, 21st Floor, Philadelphia PA 19102. 215/246-6262. **Contact:** Human Resources Department. **Description:** A management consulting firm.

VERTEX SYSTEMS INC.
1041 Old Cassatt Road, Berwyn PA 19312. 215/640-4200. **Contact:** Human Resources. **Description:** Provides accounting and related services.

Note: Because addresses and telephone numbers of smaller companies change rapidly, we recommend you contact each company and verify the information below before contacting employers. Mass mailings are not recommended.

Additional medium sized employers: under 500

BUSINESS CONSULTING SERVICES

Conservation Management Corporation
1777 Sentry Pky W, Blue Bell PA 19422. 215/540-5800.

The Hibbert Group
400 Pennington Ave, Trenton NJ 08618-3105. 609/394-7500.

MANAGEMENT SERVICES

Sidmar Management Corporation
State Hwy No 33 & Woodside Av, Hightstown NJ 08520. 609/443-8210.

MANAGEMENT CONSULTING SERVICE

Central Telephone
920 Town Center Dr, Langhorne PA 19047-1755. 215/752-7266.

Focus Suites Of Philadelphia
1 Bala Plz, Bala Cynwyd PA 19004-1401. 610/667-1110.

GRD Inc.
444 Jacksonville Rd Ste 200, Warminster PA 18974-4898. 215/674-5660.

Hill International Inc.
1 Levitt Pky, Willingboro NJ 08046-1436. 609/871-5800.

McGettigan's Travel Bureau Inc.
100 S Penn Sq, Philadelphia PA 19107-3519. 215/422-1000.

Northwestern Corporation
906 Bethlehem Pike, Philadelphia PA 19118-1799. 215/233-2344.

PA Consulting Group
279 Princeton Hightstown Rd, Hightstown NJ 08520-1401. 609/426-4700.

Philip Crosby Associates Inc.
100-200 Village Blvd, Princeton NJ 08540. 609/452-0577.

Professional Management Service
1851 Charter Ln, Lancaster PA 17601-5873. 717/293-3223.

Quick Test Opinion Center
2200 W Broad St, Bethlehem PA 18018-3216. 610/861-8880.

Systematic Management Services
1703 Langhorne Newtown Rd # 6, Langhorne PA 19047-1008.

Universal Scheduling Company
1 Bala Cynwyd Plaza, Bala Cynwyd PA 19004. 610/667-1070.

Zenger & Miller Inc.
150 S Warner Rd, Wayne PA 19087-2126. 610/971-0880.

ACCOUNTING, AUDITING AND BOOKKEEPING

Boyanoski Halko & Co.
650 N Main St, Taylor PA 18517. 717/348-1138.

Deloitte & Touche
117 Campus Dr, Princeton NJ 08540-6400. 609/520-2300.

KPMG Peat Marwick
1600 Market St, Philadelphia PA 19103-7240. 215/299-3100.

KPMG Peat Marwick
101 Lindenwood Dr,
Malvern PA 19355-1755.
610/889-7801.

**Medical Claims
Processing Inc.**
State Hwy No 50, Ocean
View NJ 08230.
609/390-0005.

Price Waterhouse
30 S 17th St,
Philadelphia PA 19103-
4021. 215/665-9500.

**Shotz Miller & Glusman
Pc**
1601 Market Street 24th
Floor, Philadelphia PA
19103-2337. 215/665-
4000.

For more information on career opportunities in accounting/management consulting:

Associations

**AMERICAN ACCOUNTING
ASSOCIATION**
5717 Bessie Drive, Sarasota FL
34233. 813/921-7747.

**AMERICAN INSTITUTE OF CERTIFIED
PUBLIC ACCOUNTANTS**
1211 Avenue of the Americas, New
York NY 10036. 212/596-6200.

**AMERICAN MANAGEMENT
ASSOCIATION**
Management Information Service, 135
West 50th Street, New York NY
10020. 212/586-8100.

**ASSOCIATION OF GOVERNMENT
ACCOUNTANTS**
2200 Mount Vernon Avenue,
Alexandria VA 22301. 703/684-
6931.

**ASSOCIATION OF MANAGEMENT
CONSULTING FIRMS**
521 Fifth Avenue, 35th Floor, New
York NY 10175. 212/697-9693.

**COUNCIL OF CONSULTANT
ORGANIZATIONS**
521 Fifth Avenue, 35th Floor, New
York NY 10175. 212/697-8262.

**FEDERATION OF TAX
ADMINISTRATORS**
444 North Capital Street NW,
Washington DC 20001. 202/624-
5890.

INSTITUTE OF INTERNAL AUDITORS
49 Maitland Avenue, Altamont
Springs FL 32701. 407/830-7600.

**INSTITUTE OF MANAGEMENT
CONSULTANTS**
521 Fifth Avenue, 35th Floor, New
York NY 10175. 212/697-8262.

**INSTITUTE OF MANAGEMENT
ACCOUNTING**
10 Paragon Drive, Box 433, Montvale
NJ 07645-1760. 201/573-9000.

**NATIONAL ASSOCIATION OF TAX
CONSULTORS**
454 North 13th Street, San Jose CA
95112. 408/298-1458.

**NATIONAL ASSOCIATION OF TAX
PRACTITIONERS**
720 Association Drive, Appleton WI
54914. 414/749-1040.

**NATIONAL SOCIETY OF PUBLIC
ACCOUNTANTS**
1010 North Fairfax Street, Alexandria
VA 22314. 703/549-6400.

Directories

**AICPA DIRECTORY OF ACCOUNTING
EDUCATION**
American Institute of Certified Public
Accountants, 1211 Avenue of the
Americas, New York NY 10036.
212/596-6200.

ACCOUNTING FIRMS AND PRACTITIONERS

American Institute of Certified Public Accountants, 1211 Avenue of the Americas, New York NY 10036. 212/596-6200.

Magazines

CPA JOURNAL
200 Park Avenue, New York NY 10166. 212/719-8300.

CPA LETTER
American Institute of Certified Public Accountants, 1211 Avenue of the Americas, New York NY 10036. 212/575-6200.

JOURNAL OF ACCOUNTANCY
American Institute of Certified Public Accountants, 1211 Avenue of the Americas, New York NY 10036. 212/596-6200.

MANAGEMENT ACCOUNTING
Institute of Management Accounting, 10 Paragon Drive, Montvale NJ 07645. 201/573-9000.

WENDELL'S REPORT FOR CONTROLLERS
Warren, Gorham, and Lamont, Inc., 210 South Street, Boston MA 02111. 617/423-2020.

ADVERTISING, MARKETING AND PUBLIC RELATIONS

The long recession forced advertising firms to tighten their money belts as client companies slashed their advertising budgets. Now PR firms and advertising houses are keeping employment levels at a minimum, hoping to boost efficiency. The industry should improve as the economy injects more advertising dollars into American business.

Analysts point to two factors which could increase competition. One is in television, which accounts for a quarter of all advertising expenditures. A new FCC rule will allow networks to make more money from syndication of shows on cable television, reducing their dependence on advertising dollars. Another concern is that Congress, in an effort to reduce the federal deficit, may eliminate business tax deductions for the cost of advertising certain products. Loss of this tax break could force some companies to cut advertising dollars. Affected products could include tobacco, pharmaceuticals and children's products.

AMERICAN TELE-RESPONSE
401 Pilgrim Lane, Drexel Hill PA 19026. 215/789-7000. **Contact:** Personnel. **Description:** A marketing research service.

DAVIS ADVERTISING INC.
1700 Market Street, Suite 2626, Philadelphia PA 19103. **Contact:** Personnel. **Description:** An advertising company.

DONNELLEY DIRECTORY
Executive Terrace, 455 South Gulph Road, King of Prussia PA 19046. 215/962-7000. **Contact:** Personnel Services Manager. **Description:** Engaged in selling advertising space in the Yellow Pages for AT&T as well as for independent companies. Offices are located throughout the United States, including Chicago, Los Angeles, New York City, Miami, and others locations. **Corporate headquarters location:** Chicago IL. **Parent company:** Dun & Bradstreet Corporation.

EARLE PALMER BROWN & SPIRO
One Liberty Place, 1650 Market Street, 15th Floor, Philadelphia PA 19103. 215/851-9600. **Contact:** V.P./Human Resources. **Description:** An agency offering the following services: advertising; public relations; marketing research; Yellow Page advertising; recruitment advertising; direct marketing. **Common positions include:** Account Executive; Advertising Clerk; Art Director; Copywriter; Public Relations Specialist. **Benefits:** Dental Insurance; Disability Coverage; Life Insurance; Medical Insurance; Tuition Assistance. **Special Programs:** Internships. **Corporate headquarters location:** Bethesda MD.

FCB/LGK

200 South Broad Street, 10th Floor, Philadelphia PA 19102. 215/790-4132. **Contact:** Bernadette Nolan, Human Resources. **Description:** A full-service advertising agency. **Common positions include:** Advertising Clerk; Computer Programmer; Public Relations Specialist; Technical Writer/Editor. **Educational backgrounds include:** Art/Design; Business Administration; Marketing. **Benefits:** Dental Insurance; Disability Coverage; Life Insurance; Medical Insurance; Profit Sharing; Savings Plan; Tuition Assistance. **Corporate headquarters location:** Chicago IL. **Parent company:** FCB. **Operations at this facility include:** Service. **Number of employees at this location:** 150.

INTER-MEDIA MARKETING

201 Carter Drive, West Chester PA 19382. 215/696-4646. **Contact:** Human Resources Department. **Description:** Provides market research services.

KETCHUM COMMUNICATIONS

1717 Arch Street, Suite 3300, Philadelphia PA 19103. 215/656-8000. **Contact:** Sharon Jones, Director of Human Resources. **Description:** A Philadelphia advertising agency.

AL PAUL LEFTON ADVERTISING

Rohm and Haas Building, Independence Mall West, Philadelphia PA 19106. 215/923-9600. **Contact:** Claire Russakoff, Administrative Assistant. **Description:** An advertising agency.

LEVLANE ADVERTISING

One Belmont Avenue, Suite 703, Bala-Cynwyd PA 19004. 215/667-7313. **Contact:** Personnel. **Description:** An advertising agency.

LYONS, INC.

715 Orange Street, Wilmington DE 19801. 302/654-6146. **Contact:** Office Manager. **Description:** A Wilmington advertising agency.

NATIONAL MEDIA CORPORATION

1700 Walnut Street, Philadelphia PA 19103. 215/772-5000. **Contact:** Human Resources. **Description:** A direct marketing company.

PRO DIRECT INTERVIEWING

Cherry Hill One Building, Suite 700, Cherry Hill NJ 08022. 609/482-8400. **Contact:** Personnel. **Description:** A marketing research service.

Note: Because addresses and telephone numbers of smaller companies change rapidly, we recommend you contact each company and verify the information below before contacting employers. Mass mailings are not recommended.

Additional medium sized employers: 100-499

PUBLIC RELATIONS
SERVICES

Marketsource
Corporation
Ten Abeel Rd, Cranbury
NJ 08512. 609/655-
8990.

Weightman Group Inc.
100 Penn Sq E,
Philadelphia PA 19107-
3321. 215/561-6100.

RADIO, TELEVISION AND PUBLISHERS' ADVERTISING REPRESENTATIVES

The Mercury
Hanover & King Sts,
Pottstown PA 19464.
610/323-3000.

ADVERTISING

Kale Design
50 Oreland Mill Rd,
Oreland PA 19075-1305.
215/884-5400.

Kapp Advertising Service
100 E Cumberland St,
Lebanon PA 17042-
5400. 717/273-8127.

Additional small employers: under 100

ADVERTISING AGENCIES

Dorshimer Graphics Plus
612-614 Linden,
Bethlehem PA 18018.
610/866-0901.

Keystone Associates Inc.
401 Old Penllyn Pike,
Blue Bell PA 19422-
9996. 215/643-5300.

Metrobase Cable Advertising
4 Park Plz, Reading PA
19610. 610/375-1100.

OUTDOOR ADVERTISING SERVICES

Bulletin Board
1945 S Queen St, York
PA 17403-4715.
717/845-6765.

TV
1310 Holly Pike, Carlisle
PA 17013-4242.
717/258-3333.

DIRECT MAIL ADVERTISING

American Advertising Distributors
108 Fineview Rd, Camp
Hill PA 17011-8446.
717/761-7907.

Expressed Idea
336 Winding Way, Kng
Of Prussa PA 19406-
2633. 610/272-5640.

For more information on career opportunities in advertising, marketing, and public relations:

<u>Associations</u>

ADVERTISING RESEARCH FOUNDATION
641 Lexington Avenue, New York NY
10022. 212/751-5656.

AFFILIATED ADVERTISING AGENCIES INTERNATIONAL
2280 South Xanadu Way, Suite 300
Aurora CO 80014. 303/671-8551.

AMERICAN ASSOCIATION OF ADVERTISING AGENCIES
666 Third Avenue, New York NY
10017. 212/682-2500.

AMERICAN MARKETING ASSOCIATION
250 South Wacker Drive, Suite 200,
Chicago IL 60606. 312/648-0536.

BUSINESS-PROFESSIONAL ADVERTISING ASSOCIATION
901 North Washington Street, Suite
206, Alexandria VA 22314. 703/683-
2722.

DIRECT MARKETING ASSOCIATION
11 West 42nd Street, New York NY
10036. 212/768-7277

INTERNATIONAL ADVERTISING ASSOCIATION
342 Madison Avenue, Suite 2000,
New York NY 10017. 212/557-1133.

LEAGUE OF ADVERTISING AGENCIES
2 South End Avenue #4C, New York
NY 10280. 212/945-4991.

**MARKETING RESEARCH
ASSOCIATION**
2189 Silas Deane Highway, Suite #5,
Rocky Hill CT 06067. 203/257-4008.

**PUBLIC RELATIONS SOCIETY OF
AMERICA**
33 Irving Place, New York NY 10003.
212/995-2230.

**TELEVISION BUREAU OF
ADVERTISING**
850 3rd Avenue, 10th Floor, New
York NY 10022-5892. 212/486-
1111.

Directories

AAAA ROSTER AND ORGANIZATION
American Association of Advertising
Agencies, 666 Third Avenue, New
York NY 10017. 212/682-2500.

**DIRECTORY OF MINORITY PUBLIC
RELATIONS PROFESSIONALS**
Public Relations Society of America,
33 Irving Place, New York NY 10003.
212/995-2230.

**O'DWYER'S DIRECTORY OF PUBLIC
RELATIONS FIRMS**
J. R. O'Dwyer Co., 271 Madison
Avenue, New York NY 10016.
212/679-2471.

**PUBLIC RELATIONS CONSULTANTS
DIRECTORY**
American Business Directories,
Division of American Business Lists,
5711 South 86th Circle, Omaha NE
68127. 402/593-4500.

**PUBLIC RELATIONS JOURNAL
REGISTER ISSUE**
Public Relations Society of America,
33 Irving Place, New York NY 10003.
212/995-2230.

**STANDARD DIRECTORY OF
ADVERTISING AGENCIES**
National Register Publishing Company,
P.O. Box 31, New Providence NY
07974. 800/521-8110.

Magazines

ADVERTISING AGE
Crain Communications, 740 North
Rush Street, Chicago IL 60611.
312/649-5316.

ADWEEK
1515 Broadway, 12th Floor, New
York NY 10036. 212/536-5336.

BUSINESS MARKETING
Crain Communications, 740 North
Rush Street, Chicago IL 60611.
312/649-5260.

JOURNAL OF MARKETING
American Marketing Association, 250
South Wacker Drive, Suite 200,
Chicago IL 60606. 312/648-0536.

THE MARKETING NEWS
American Marketing Association, 250
South Wacker Drive, Suite 200,
Chicago IL 60606. 312/648-0536.

PR REPORTER
PR Publishing Co., P.O. Box 600,
Exeter NH 03833. 603/778-0514.

PUBLIC RELATIONS JOURNAL
Public Relations Society of America,
33 Irving Place, New York NY 10003.
212/995-2230.

PUBLIC RELATIONS NEWS
Phillips Publishing Inc., 1202 Seven
Locks Road, Suite 300, Potomac MD
20854. 301/340-1520.

AEROSPACE

Despite earlier projections that it was "well-poised" for growth in the '90s, the aerospace industry is still fighting an uphill battle. Industry shipments continue to drop due to continued cuts in the defense budget, a weak global economy, and growing competition from overseas.

The downturn in the industry is resulting in severe job losses. According to the Bureau of Labor, between 1989 and 1993, total aerospace employment fell from 912,000 to 615,000. From December 1989 to June 1993, industry employment dove at a rate of nearly 6,000 jobs a month. And the future does not look much better. In the words of the U.S. Department of Commerce, "Aerospace companies will continue to severely reduce their employment levels."

ATLANTIC AVIATION CORPORATION
P.O. Box 15000, Wilmington DE 19850. 302/322-7000. **Contact:** Rose-Marie Zappone, Manager, Personnel Resources. **Description:** Engaged in the maintenance, refurbishment, and service of corporate aircraft.

CHROMALLOY COMPANY
1400 North Cameron Street, Harrisburg PA 17103. 717/255-3478. **Contact:** Human Resources. **Description:** Manufactures aircraft engine parts.

EXECUTIVE AIRCRAFT DESIGN
2034 Green Street, Philadelphia PA 19130. 215/564-5390. **Contact:** Human Resources. **Description:** An aerospace company.

LANCASTER AERO REFINISHERS
311 Airport Drive, Smoketown PA 17576. 717/394-5805. **Contact:** Human Resources. **Description:** Provides aerospace services.

NARCO AVIONICS
270 Commerce Drive, Fort Washington PA 19034. 215/643-2900. **Contact:** Personnel Manager. **Description:** Produces a wide range of instruments and systems for general aviation users.

NAVAL AIR WARFARE CENTER/AIRCRAFT DIVISION
P.O. Box 5152, Warminster PA 18974-0591. 215/441-3960. **Contact:** Recruiting Specialist. **Description:** Involved in the research and development of aircraft systems: conceptualization of advanced systems, refinement of basic equipment, and development of resulting high performance air/sea systems. **Number of employees nationwide:** 2,500.

SMITH INDUSTRIES
255 Great Valley Parkway, Malvern PA 19355. 215/296-5000. **Contact:** Human Resources Department. **Description:** An aircraft engine and engine parts manufacturer.

Note: Because addresses and telephone numbers of smaller companies change rapidly, we recommend you contact each company and verify the information below before contacting employers. Mass mailings are not recommended.

Additional medium sized employers: 100-499

GUIDED MISSILES AND
SPACE VEHICLES

Allied Signal Aerospace
200 Gibraltar Rd,
Horsham PA 19044-
2318. 215/957-6480.

Parker Hannifan
Corporation
7 Dover Rd, Mount Holly
NJ 08060-2328.
609/267-0627.

GUIDED MISSILE AND
SPACE VEHICLE
PROPULSION UNITS

Lavelle Aircraft Company
275 Geiger Rd,
Philadelphia PA 19115-
1009. 215/673-7700.

AIRCRAFT

Agusta Aerospace
Corporation
3050 Red Lion Rd,
Philadelphia PA 19114-
1128. 215/281-1400.

Bell Helicopter Textron
627 Fairhill Rd, Hatfield
PA 19440-1106.
215/723-6195.

Boeing Helicopters
212 N 3rd St, Harrisburg
PA 17101-1505.
717/232-6820.

FST
1831 Harney Rd,
Littlestown PA 17340-
9751. 717/359-9071.

AIRCRAFT ENGINES AND
PARTS

Valley Manufacturing
Corporation
120 Hazle St, Wilkes
Barre PA 18702-4306.
717/825-4544.

AIRCRAFT PARTS AND
AUXILIARY EQUIPMENT

Bihrle Applied Research
140 Scenic Rd,
Springfield PA 19064-
1945. 610/544-6676.

Compressor Components
Textron
Rt 11 & Woodbine Ln,
Danville PA 17821.
717/275-7511.

Hexcel Corporation
Structural Division
St Clair Indl Pk, Saint
Clair PA 17970.
717/429-1741.

Tedeco Division
24 E Glenolden Ave,
Glenolden PA 19036-
2198. 610/583-9400.

Transicoil Inc.
2560 General Armistead
Ave, Norristown PA
19403-5214. 610/539-
4400.

Additional small employers: under 100

AIRCRAFT

Paraplane International
Corporation
68 Stacy Haines Rd,
Medford NJ 08055-
4106. 609/261-1234.

AIRCRAFT ENGINES AND
ENGINE PARTS

Tasco Corporation
2055 Bennett Rd,
Philadelphia PA 19116-
3019. 215/673-1350.

AIRCRAFT PARTS AND
AUXILIARY EQUIPMENT

Eaton Corporation
Control Displays
3075 Advance Ln,
Colmar PA 18915-9765.
215/822-3383.

General Aviation Manufacturing
2693 Philmont Ave, Huntingdon Vy PA 19006-5301. 215/947-4010.

Nuco Inc.
1460 Shoemaker Ave, Pittston PA 18644-1021. 717/287-0966.

Piasecki Aircraft Corporation
West Terminus Of Second St, Essington PA 19029. 610/521-5700.

For more information on career opportunities in aerospace:

Associations

AIR TRANSPORT ASSOCIATION OF AMERICA
1301 Pennsylvania Avenue NW, Suite 1100, Washington DC 20004. 202/626-4000.

AMERICAN INSTITUTE OF AERONAUTICS AND ASTRONAUTICS
555 West 57th Street, New York NY 10019. 212/247-6500.

FUTURE AVIATION PROFESSIONALS OF AMERICA
4959 Massachusetts Boulevard, Atlanta GA 30337. 404/997-8097.

NATIONAL AERONAUTIC ASSOCIATION OF USA
1815 North Fort Meyer Drive, Suite 700, Arlington VA 22209. 703/527-0226.

PROFESSIONAL AVIATION MAINTENANCE ASSOCIATION
500 NW Plaza, Suite 1016, St. Ann MO 63074. 314/739-2580.

APPAREL AND TEXTILES

 *After employment gains for four straight years in the late '80s, layoffs hit the industry hard as the '90s opened. And while shipments continued to increase in 1993, employment continued to drop. Production line work has dropped off for two reasons. First, foreign producers have increased their share of the U.S. market. Second, automation has replaced many positions, so future jobs will not consist of old-style production-line work. Those with technical and computer backgrounds have a distinct advantage.*

ABERDEEN SPORTSWEAR, INC.
P.O. Box 8413, Trenton NJ 08650. 609/587-2309. **Contact:** Personnel. **Description:** A manufacturer of quality sportswear.

ALFRED ANGELO, INC.
116 Welsh Road, Willow Grove PA 19044. 215/659-5300. **Contact:** Cynthia S. Lin, Human Resources Representative. **Description:** Designs, produces, and wholesales bridal gowns, special occasion dresses, and a wide range of related accessories. **Common positions include:** Accountant/Auditor; Computer Programmer; Credit Manager; Customer Service Representative; Department Manager; Designer; Financial Analyst; Manufacturer's/Wholesaler's Sales Rep.; Marketing Specialist; Operations/Production Manager; Purchasing Agent and Manager; Systems Analyst; Warehouse/Distribution Worker. **Educational backgrounds include:** Accounting; Business Administration; Communications; Computer Science; Finance; Liberal Arts; Marketing. **Benefits:** Dental Insurance; Disability Coverage; Flexible Benefits; Life Insurance; Medical Insurance; Profit Sharing; Tuition Assistance. **Special Programs:** Training Programs. **Corporate headquarters location:** This Location. **Operations at this facility include:** Administration; Design; Manufacturing; Sales; Service.

BARSEW
428 South Seventh Street, Leighton PA 18235. 215/377-1110. **Contact:** Renee Barson, Manager. **Description:** Manufactures women's blouses and shirts in a wide range of styles.

BOLLMAN HAT COMPANY
110 East Main Street, Adamstown PA 19501. 215/484-4361. **Contact:** Human Resource Manager. **Description:** Manufacturer of wool felt, fur felt, cloth, and straw headwear. Also cleans and processes wool. **Common positions include:** Accountant/Auditor; Administrator; Blue-Collar Worker Supervisor; Buyer; Chemical Engineer; Chemist; Department Manager; Electrical/Electronic Engineer; General Manager; Industrial Designer; Industrial Engineer; Management Trainee; Mechanical Engineer; Operations/Production Manager; Personnel/Labor Relations Specialist. **Benefits:** Daycare Assistance; Dental Insurance; Disability Coverage; Employee Discounts; Life Insurance; Medical Insurance; Pension Plan; Savings Plan; Stock Option; Tuition Assistance. **Corporate headquarters location:** This Location. **Operations at this facility include:** Administration; Manufacturing; Research and Development; Sales.

BOYERTOWN APPAREL, INC.
320 South Franklin Street, Boyerton PA 19512. 215/367-2161. **Contact:** Tony Albrecht, President. **Description:** Produces a range of lingerie.

CAPITAL PANTS COMPANY
700 East Erie Avenue, Philadelphia PA 19134. 215/291-9300. **Contact:** William Ritzman, Controller. **Description:** A local apparel company specializing in the manufacture of women's pants.

CHARMING SHOPPES
450 Winks Lane, Bensalem PA 19020. 215/245-9100. **Contact:** Karin Foreman, Associate Director/H.R. **Description:** Produces a wide range of women's specialty and retail apparel. **Common positions include:** Accountant/Auditor; Administrator; Advertising Clerk; Attorney; Blue-Collar Worker Supervisor; Buyer; Computer Programmer; Credit Manager; Department Manager; Financial Analyst; General Manager; Industrial Engineer; Personnel/Labor Relations Specialist; Purchasing Agent and Manager; Systems Analyst; Transportation/Traffic Specialist. **Educational backgrounds include:** Accounting; Business Administration; Communications; Computer Science; Finance; Liberal Arts; Marketing. **Benefits:** Medical Insurance. **Special Programs:** Internships; Training Programs.

COYNE TEXTILE SERVICES
4825 Brown Street, Philadelphia PA 19139. 215/878-0100. **Contact:** Brenda Wilson, Office Manager. **Description:** A textiles company.

CRAFTEX MILLS INC. OF PENNSYLVANIA
450 East Century Parkway, P.O. Box 3017, Blue Bell PA 19422-0795. 215/941-1212. **Contact:** Bruce Shawlis, Plant Manager. **Description:** Produces upholstery fabrics for use by furniture manufacturers.

CRYSTAL BRAND MEN'S SPORTSWEAR GROUP
P.O. Box 4440, Allentown PA 18105. 215/797-6200. **Contact:** Personnel Department. **Description:** Produces men's clothing.

CRYSTAL BRANDS
Airport Industrial Park West, Route 183, P.O. Box 15206, Reading PA 19612-5206. 215/374-4242. **Contact:** Robert Daneker, Personnel Director. **Description:** Produces a wide range of dresses sold under the David Crystal name. **Corporate headquarters location:** Minneapolis MN. **Parent company:** General Mills, Inc.

FERNBROOK & COMPANY
P.O. Box 162, Palmerton PA 18071. 215/826-2076. **Contact:** Peter Bartar, Owner. **Description:** Produces women's sportswear.

H. FREEMAN & SON, INC.
3601 Island Avenue, Philadelphia PA 19153. 215/365-7705. **Contact:** Linda Orsino, Payroll Supervisor. **Description:** A manufacturer of men's suits and coats.

GOOD LAD COMPANY
431 East Tioga Street, Philadelphia PA 19134. 215/739-0200. **Contact:** Personnel Director. **Description:** A producer of outwear and other apparel, and children's clothing.

GREGG SHIRTMAKERS/HUTSPAH
185 West Wyoming Avenue, Philadelphia PA 19140. 215/329-7700. **FAX:** 215/329-4650. **Contact:** Ken Williams, Personnel Director. **Description:** An area apparel manufacturer, specializing in shirts and nightwear. **Common positions include:** Accountant/Auditor; Clerical Supervisor; Computer Operator; Credit Manager; Order Clerk; Receptionist; Secretary; Stock Clerk. **Corporate headquarters location:** This Location. **Operations at this facility include:** Administration.

THE GREIF COMPANIES
939 Marcon Boulevard, P.O. Box 25400, Lehigh Valley PA 18002-5400. 215/266-2229. **Contact:** Bill Lagorda, Plant Relations Manager. **Description:** Manufactures and sells high-quality men's tailored clothing and tailored service industry uniforms. **Common positions include:** Blue-Collar Worker Supervisor; Computer Programmer; Customer Service Representative; Industrial Engineer; Operations/Production Manager; Personnel/Labor Relations Specialist. **Educational backgrounds include:** Business Administration; Computer Science; Engineering. **Benefits:** Dental Insurance; Disability Coverage; Employee Discounts; Life Insurance; Medical Insurance; Savings Plan. **Parent company:** Genesco, Inc. **Operations at this facility include:** Administration; Manufacturing; Service. **Listed on:** New York Stock Exchange.

HARMONY CLOTHES
W. SEITCHIK & SONS
Northeast Corner of 19th & Allegheny, 5th Floor, Philadelphia PA 19132. 215/226-0200. **Contact:** Richard Seitchik, President. **Description:** A men's apparel company.

JONES APPAREL GROUP INC.
20 Rittenhouse Circle, Bristol PA 19007. 215/785-4000. **Contact:** Human Resources Department. **Description:** Manufactures women's clothing.

K&D CLOTHING MANUFACTURING CO.
640 North Broad Street, Philadelphia PA 19130. 215/236-3223. **Contact:** Norman Katz, President. **Description:** A local apparel manufacturer.

KAHN-LUCAS-LANCASTER, INC.
P.O. Box 120, Columbia PA 17512. 717/684-6911. **Contact:** Donald McKonly, Chief Financial Officer. **Description:** Manufactures children's dresses.

KLEINERTS INCORPORATED
120 West Germantown Pike, Suite 100, Plymouth Meeting PA 19462-1420. 215/828-7261. **Contact:** Human Resources. **Description:** Manufactures women's and misses' apparel.

KRAEMER TEXTILES, INC.
240 South Main Street, P.O. Box 72, Nazareth PA 18064. 215/759-4030. **Contact:** Dave Schmidt, President. **Description:** Produces spun yarns for apparel, home furnishings, and craft fields. **Corporate headquarters location:** This Location.

MANNINGTON MILLS INC.
P.O. Box 30, Salem NJ 08079. 609/935-3000. **Contact:** Human Resources Department. **Description:** A carpets and rugs manufacturer.

H. ORITSKY, INC.
106 Grape Street, Reading PA 19602. 215/376-2971. **Contact:** Marge McNally, Personnel Manager. **Description:** Manufacturer of men's suits and sport coats.

Common positions include: Customer Service Representative; Manufacturer's/Wholesaler's Sales Rep.; Operations/ Production Manager; Quality Control Supervisor. **Educational backgrounds include:** Fashion; Textiles. **Benefits:** Dental Insurance; Medical Insurance. **Corporate headquarters location:** This Location. **Number of employees at this location:** 160.

PARIS ACCESSORIES
Building #40, Third Street, Walnutport PA 18088. 215/767-3051. **Contact:** Gary Yonker, Plant Manager. **Description:** Produces women's scarves.

PINCUS BROTHERS, INC.
Independence Mall East, Philadelphia PA 19106. 215/922-4900. **Contact:** Personnel. **Description:** Manufacturers of a variety of men's suits and coats.

SUNBURY TEXTILE MILLS INC.
Miller Street, Sunbury PA 17801. 717/286-3800. **Contact:** Nancy Bordner, Personnel Director. **Description:** Produces upholstery fabrics.

SURE FIT PRODUCTS CO.
East Broad and Wood Streets, Bethlehem PA 18016. 215/867-7581. **Contact:** Kenneth J. Guerin, Director/Human Resources. **Description:** Provides decorative home textiles including window treatments, table rounds, furniture covers, slipcovers and toss pillows. **Common positions include:** Accountant/Auditor; Blue-Collar Worker Supervisor; Computer Programmer; Credit Manager; Customer Service Representative; Industrial Engineer; Systems Analyst. **Educational backgrounds include:** Accounting; Business Administration; Computer Science; Textiles. **Benefits:** 401K; Employee Discounts; Life Insurance; Medical Insurance. **Corporate headquarters location:** New York NY. **Operations at this facility include:** Administration; Manufacturing.

TRIMFIT INC./KAYBEE MILLS
10450 Drummond Road, Philadelphia PA 19154. 215/632-3000. **Contact:** Harry Sholtz, Controller. **Description:** A distribution center for a major hosiery manufacturer.

VF CORPORATION
1047 North Park Road, Wyomissing PA 19610. 215/378-1151. **Contact:** Personnel Department. **Description:** An apparel manufacturer. **Number of employees nationwide:** 49,000.

VALERIE FASHIONS
316 Broadway, Windgap PA 18091. 215/863-6051. **Contact:** General Manager. **Description:** Produces shirts and blouses.

WILMINGTON FINISHING COMPANY
One Mill Road, Wilmington DE 19806. 302/654-5311. **Contact:** Jack McDermott, Personnel. **Description:** A Wilmington company that specializes in the dying and bleaching of fabrics.

WOOLRICH, INC.
One Mill Street, Woolrich PA 17779. 717/769-6464. **Contact:** Human Resources Department. **Description:** An apparel company.

Note: Because addresses and telephone numbers of smaller companies change rapidly, we recommend you contact each company and verify the information below before contacting employers. Mass mailings are not recommended.

Additional large employers: 500 +

HOSIERY

Danskin Division
305 N State St., York PA
17403-1316. 717/852-
6100.

KNIT APPAREL

**Springford Knitting
Company**
P.O. Box 29, Spring City
PA 19475. 610/948-
4881.

Guilford Mills Inc.
121 North Main St., Pine
Grove PA 17963-1211.
717/345-2611.

CARPETS & RUGS

Magee Carpet Company
480 W Fifth St.,
Bloomsburg PA 17815-
1564. 717/784-4100.

Masland Holdings Inc.
P.O. Box 40, Carlisle PA
17013-1974. 717/249-
1866.

SUITS AND COATS

500 Fashion Group
39 W 21st St.,
Northampton PA 18067-
1247. 610/262-5695.

BLOUSES AND SHIRTS

Scotty's Fashions
230 Ochre St., Lehighton
PA 18235-1465.
610/377-3032.

**Scotty's Fashions Cutting
Inc.**
315 W Pennsylvania
Ave., Pen Argyl PA
18072-2025. 610/863-
4157.

**UNDERWEAR AND
NIGHTWEAR**

Wundies Enterprises
1501 W 3rd St.,
Williamsport PA 17701-
7814. 717/326-2451.

**CHILDREN'S DRESSES
AND BLOUSES**

Dallco Industries Inc.
P.O. Box 2727, York PA
17405. 717/854-7875.

**LEATHER TANNING AND
FINISHING**

Garden State Tanning
16 S Franklin St.,
Fleetwood PA 19522-
1613. 610/944-7601.

Additional medium sized employers: under 500

**WOMEN'S AND
CHILDREN'S CLOTHING
WHOLESALE**

Diversified Apparel Inc.
308 York Rd, Jenkintown
PA 19046. 215/887-
8023.

**BROADWOVEN COTTON
FABRIC MILLS**

Berwick Weaving Inc.
PO Box 158, Berwick PA
18603-0158. 717/752-
4516.

**Blue Bird Fabrics
Corporation**
600 N Hartley St, York
PA 17404-2860.
717/848-2387.

Chromatex Inc.
Rotary Dr Valmont Indl
Pk, Hazleton PA 18201.
717/459-0700.

Crown Textile Co.
3 Valley Sq 512 Twp
Line Rd, Blue Bell PA
19422-2714. 215/641-
9900.

H Warshow & Sons
S Front & River Rds,
Milton PA 17847.
717/742-2200.

Keystone Weaving Mills
1320 W Market St, York
PA 17404-3468.
717/845-3621.

Richard Textiles
120 N Seneca St,
Shippensburg PA 17257-
1239. 717/532-4156.

Weave Corporation
142 Walnut & 2nd Sts,
Denver PA 17517-1606.
215/267-7577.

**BROADWOVEN SILK
AND MAN-MADE FIBER
FABRIC MILLS**

Amatex Corporation
Stanbridge & Sterigere
Sts, Norristown PA
19401. 610/277-6100.

**American Silk Mills
Corporation**
75 Stark St, Wilkes Barre
PA 18705-2906.
717/822-7147.

Beavertown Mills Inc.
R D 1 Box 3, Beavertown
PA 17813-9801.
717/658-8041.

Bloomsburg Mills Inc.
Sixth & West Sts,
Bloomsburg PA 17815.
717/784-4262.

**Jaunty Textile
Corporation**
15 Poplar St, Scranton
PA 18509-2601.
717/346-8421.

Lending Textile Inc.
300 E Church St,
Williamsport PA 17701-
5306. 717/327-1325.

McGinley Mills Inc.
100 Kuebler Rd, Easton
PA 18042-9299.
610/559-6400.

Stanwood Mills Inc.
Fairview Ave, Slatington
PA 18080. 610/767-
3881.

Sunbury Textile Mills
Miller St, Sunbury PA
17801. 717/286-3800.

Thermco Products
1409 W Broad St,
Quakertown PA 18951-
1109. 215/536-5460.

NARROW FABRIC MILLS

Bally Ribbon Mills
23 N 7th St, Bally PA
19503. 610/845-2211.

Narricot Industries Inc.
928 Jaymor Rd Ste
C150, Southampton PA
18966-3843. 215/322-
3900.

Narrow Fabric Industries
PO Box 6948, Reading
PA 19610-0948.
610/376-2891.

Trimtex Co Inc.
400 Park Ave,
Williamsport PA 17701-
4930. 717/326-9135.

WOMEN'S HOISERY

**Hosiery Corporation Of
America**
3369 Progress Dr,
Bensalem PA 19020-
5801. 215/244-1777.

HOISERY

Camp Hosiery Co Inc.
1801 N 12th St, Reading
PA 19604-1527.
610/921-0611.

**Great American Knitting
Mills**
131 S Church St, Bally
PA 19503. 610/845-
2111.

**KNIT OUTERWEAR
MILLS**

Alpha Mills Corporation
122 Margaretta St,
Shuykl Haven PA 17972.
717/385-0511.

Borwick Knit Wear
PO Box 424, Berwick PA
18603-0424.

Briar Knitting Inc.
3rd & Oak Sts 205,
Berwick PA 18603.
717/759-0325.

HL Miller & Son Inc.
15 Coal St, Port Carbon
PA 17965-1804.
717/622-6181.

Tighe Industries Inc.
RR 12 Box 251A, York
PA 17406-9643.
717/252-1578.

**Waymart Knitting
Company**
Rte 296 R D 1, Waymart
PA 18472. 717/488-
6127.

**KNIT UNDERWEAR AND
NIGHTWEAR MILLS**

Ashmore Sportswear
132 Ashmore Dr, Leola
PA 17540-2007.
717/656-2971.

Cinderella Knitting Mills
130 E Wall St, Leesport
PA 19533. 610/926-
2141.

Eagle Shirt Wear Inc.
715 W Mahanoy St,
Mahanoy City PA 17948-
2440. 717/773-0247.

Union Knitting Mills
Ten W William St, Shuykl
Haven PA 17972.
717/385-0730.

**Wright's Knitwear
Corporation**
Pine & 2nd Sts, Hamburg
PA 19526. 610/562-
3051.

**WEFT KNIT FABRIC
MILLS**

Bertha's Boys Inc.
3607 W 4th St,
Williamsport PA 17701-
4108. 717/326-7506.

Jomac Inc.
863 Easton Rd,
Warrington PA 18976-
1855. 215/343-0800.

Tricor Fabrics Inc.
20 W Mohler Church Rd,
Ephrata PA 17522-9212.
717/738-4271.

**Wright's Knitwear
Corporation**
Lincoln Ave Box 1005-A,
Orwigsburg PA 17961.
717/366-0541.

**LACE AND WARP KNIT
FABRIC MILLS**

Beaufab Mills Inc.
1901 W Main St,
Stroudsburg PA 18360-
1092. 717/421-9910.

Native Textiles Company
PO Box 130, Dallas PA
18612-0130. 717/675-
2123.

KNITTING MILLS

**Cinderella Knitting Mills
Inc.**
N 4th St, Denver PA
17517. 215/267-7555.

Pocono Knits Inc.
100 E Diamond Ave,
Hazleton PA 18201-
5241. 717/455-7706.

**FINISHERS OF
BROADWOVEN COTTON
FABRIC**

Belmont Processing
Belmont Ave & Heisters
Ln, Reading PA 19605.
610/929-0780.

Kennetex Inc.
740 W Cypress St,
Kennet Sq PA 19348-
2235. 610/444-0600.

OB Dyers Inc.
45 N Noble St, Reading
PA 19611-1641.
610/376-8161.

Penn-Tex
400 Jaycee Dr, Hazleton
PA 18201-1150.
717/455-6133.

**Pottsville Bleaching &
Dyeing**
250 Route 61 S, Shuykl
Haven PA 17972-9708.
717/385-4082.

**Printed Terry Finishing
Company**
34 N 16th St, Lebanon
PA 17042-4505.
717/273-8101.

FINISHERS OF TEXTILES

Chloe Textiles Inc.
142 Airport Dr,
Middletown PA 17057-
5046. 717/944-4036.

Globe Dye Works Co.
4500 Worth St,
Philadelphia PA 19124-
3499. 215/535-3301.

**Textile Dyeing &
Finishing Co**
2015 City Line Rd,
Bethlehem PA 18017-
2179. 610/865-6900.

CARPETS AND RUGS

**Bloomsburg Carpet
Industries**
4999 New Berwick Hwy,
Bloomsburg PA 17815-
8854. 717/784-9188.

Downs Carpet Co.
Davisville Rd & Turnpike
Dr, Willow Grove PA
19090. 215/672-1100.

General Felt Inds Inc.
2121 Wheatsheaf Ln,
Philadelphia PA 19137-
1021. 215/744-4444.

YARN MILLS

Keystone Weaving Mills
14th & Cumberland Sts,
Lebanon PA 17042.
717/272-4665.

Warp Processing Inc.
180 Courtright St #200,
Wilkes Barre PA 18702-
1802. 717/824-8316.

**Huntingdon Throwing
Mills Inc.**
PO Box 9, Mifflinburg PA
17844-0009. 717/966-
3111.

William F Groce Inc.
210 Sassafras St,
Selinsgrove PA 17870-
1422. 717/374-0141.

THREAD MILLS

Coren-Indik Inc.
4224 N Front St,
Philadelphia PA 19140-
2798. 215/329-9650.

Middleburg Yarn Processing Co
909 Orange St, Selinsgrove PA 17870-1729. 717/374-0967.

COATED FABRICS, NOT RUBBERIZED

Herculite Products Inc.
PO Box 786, York PA 17405-0786. 717/764-1191.

Stroudsburg Dyeing & Finishing
Brown & Lincoln Sts, E Stroudsburg PA 18301. 717/424-8421.

NONWOVEN FABRICS

Veratec
Rt 15 N, Lewisburg PA 17837. 717/524-2281.

CORDAGE AND TWINE

Eddington Thread Manufacturing Co.
3222 Knights Rd, Bensalem PA 19020-2819. 215/639-8900.

TEXTILE GOODS

Mutual Industries Inc.
707 W Grange Ave, Philadelphia PA 19120-2224. 215/927-6000.

MEN'S AND BOYS' SUITS AND COATS

Aneco Trousers Corporation
713 Linden Ave, Hanover PA 17331-4629. 717/632-9676.

Crown Clothing Co.
609 Paul St, Vineland NJ 08360-5699. 609/691-0343.

Jacob Siegel Co.
1843 W Allegheny Ave, Philadelphia PA 19132-1607. 215/763-8000.

Romart Inc.
717 Capouse Ave, Scranton PA 18509-3121. 717/342-9257.

Singer Manufacturing
A & Lippincott Sts, Philadelphia PA 19106. 215/423-5347.

Vista Corporation
Atlantic Ave, Minotola NJ 08341. 609/697-0600.

W Seitchik & Sons Inc.
19th & Allegheny, Philadelphia PA 19132. 215/226-0200.

MEN'S AND BOYS' SHIRTS

Ashland Shirt Inc.
2212 Center St, Ashland PA 17921-1016. 717/875-3100.

City Shirt Co.
242 Frackville Industrial Park, Frackville PA 17931. 717/874-4251.

Cressona Knit Products
87 Schuylkill St, Cressona PA 17929-1408. 717/385-3301.

Eagle Shirtmakers Inc.
2645 Mitchell Ave, Allentown PA 18103-6610. 610/797-6200.

Fleetwood Shirt Corporation
26 E Locust St, Fleetwood PA 19522-1603. 610/944-7636.

Lebro Shirt Corporation
Arch & Hannah Sts, Lykens PA 17048. 717/453-7146.

Richfield Shirt Manufacturing Co Inc.
S Walnut St, Richfield PA 17086. 717/694-3721.

Wright's Knitwear Corporation
757 W Broad St, Hazleton PA 18201-6103. 717/454-6631.

MEN'S UNDERWEAR AND NIGHTWEAR

JE Morgan Knitting Mills
E Wiconisco Ave, Tower City PA 17980. 717/647-2186.

KTC Inc.
704 E 4th St, Boyertown PA 19512-2104. 610/367-2398.

MEN'S AND BOYS' NECKWEAR

Jayo Neckwear Co Inc.
1345 E 5th St, Bethlehem PA 18015-2103. 610/691-5733.

MEN'S AND BOYS' PANTS AND TROUSERS

AG Pants Manufacturing Co Inc.
115 N 5th St, Perkasie PA 18944-1403. 215/257-6576.

Alperin Inc.
1 Maxson Dr, Old Forge PA 18518-2063. 717/457-0500.

Mayflower Manufacturing Co Inc.
PO Box 3627, Scranton PA 18505-0627.
717/457-5151.

Osan Manufacturing Co
320 S Washington St, Boyertown PA 19512-1531. 610/367-2001.

Pawnee Pants Manufacturing Co Inc.
101-05 Lackawanna Ave, Olyphant PA 18447. 717/489-7544.

MEN'S AND BOYS' WORK CLOTHING

Executive Apparel Inc.
A & Lippincott Sts, Philadelphia PA 19106. 215/634-6668.

Ippoliti Inc.
7300 Lindbergh Blvd, Philadelphia PA 19153-3022. 215/365-1600.

MEN'S AND BOYS' CLOTHING

American Argo Corp.
Margaretta & Market Sts, Shuykl Haven PA 17972. 717/385-2200.

Charles Navasky & Co
19 Water St, Philipsburg PA 16866-2201. 814/342-1160.

Darjan Co Inc.
1223-27 Lafayette St, Lebanon PA 17042. 717/273-1691.

Kaijay Pants Co Inc.
Willow St, Nesquehoning PA 18240. 717/669-9497.

Kent Sportswear Inc.
Water St, Curwensville PA 16833. 814/236-2110.

Majestic Athletic Wear
636 Pen Argyl St, Pen Argyl PA 18072-1998. 610/863-6161.

Meke Corporation
638 E Main St, New Holland PA 17557-1425. 717/354-6353.

Rennoc Corporation
3600 Southeast Blvd, Vineland NJ 08360. 609/327-5400.

Sandess Manufacturing Co Inc.
19th St & Lehigh Ave, Philadelphia PA 19132. 215/226-2900.

State Manufacturing Co
Valley & Pine Sts, New Philadelphia PA 17959. 717/277-6618.

Sun Clothes Inc.
624 Moore St, Philadelphia PA 19148-1716. 215/336-5400.

Trevorton Manufacturing
314 E Shamokin St, Trevorton PA 17881-1622. 717/797-4145.

Wright's Knitwear Corporation
800 W Market St, Auburn PA 17922. 717/754-3261.

WOMEN'S AND MISSES' BLOUSES

Alley Cat Inc.
855 Pennsylvania Blvd, Fstrvl Trvose PA 19053-7813. 215/364-3800.

Bar-Sew Inc.
428 S 7th St, Lehighton PA 18235-1824. 610/377-1110.

Dutch Miss Inc.
7th & Locust Sts, Lebanon PA 17042. 717/272-7331.

Gino & Jack Sportswear
231 Moorestown Dr, Bath PA 18014-1405. 610/837-1846.

Merry Maid Inc.
25 Messinger St, Bangor PA 18013. 610/588-0927.

Pine Shirt Co.
14th & Laurel Sts, Pottsville PA 17901. 717/622-4001.

Sportette Industries
2413 Community Dr, Bath PA 18014-8840. 610/759-4134.

Tara-Lee Sportswear
601 Water St, New Berlin PA 17855. 717/966-3817.

Valerie Fashions
316 N Broadway, Wind Gap PA 18091-1299. 610/863-6051.

WOMEN'S AND MISSES' DRESSES

Bonnell Manufacturing
Church Rd & Roland Ave, Mount Laurel NJ 08054. 609/235-2885.

Connie Sportswear
27 S Potomac St, Waynesboro PA 17268-1561. 717/762-2194.

Downing Garment Inc.
111-113 E Main St,
Plymouth PA 18651.
717/779-4615.

**Hesteco Manufacturing
Co Inc.**
443 W High St,
Elizabethtown PA 17022-
2152. 717/367-1145.

Hillside Sportswear
Pearl & Webster Sts,
Shamokin PA 17872.
717/644-0578.

Hip Industries
237 Jacksonville Rd,
Hatboro PA 19040-2689.
215/674-2400.

**Juniata Garment
Company**
101 S Juniata St, Mifflin
PA 17058-9743.
717/436-2138.

Lee Manufacturing Co
247-49 S Main St,
Pittston PA 18640.
717/654-6789.

Len-Jef Inc.
110 Maple St, Kulpmont
PA 17834-1440.
717/373-5841.

Leslie Fay Co's Inc.
Rt 315, Wilkes Barre PA
18702. 717/824-9911.

Lyon Fashion Inc.
School St, Mc Alistervle
PA 17049. 717/463-
2118.

**Meshoppen
Manufacturing Inc.**
Bridge St, Meshoppen PA
18630. 717/833-5188.

Pittston Fashions Inc.
351 S Main St, Pittston
PA 18640-2337.
717/654-0189.

**Ricky Fashions
Corporation**
101 S Main St, Wilkes
Barre PA 18701-1611.
717/822-5356.

**Summit Station
Manufacturing Inc.**
194 S Tulpehocken St,
Pine Grove PA 17963-
1035. 717/345-4191.

Throop Fashions Inc.
Charles & Center Sts,
Scranton PA 18512.
717/489-5341.

**USA Manufacturing
Corporation**
213 E Luzerne Ave,
Wilkes Barre PA 18704-
1028. 717/288-6631.

**WOMEN'S AND MISSES'
SUITS, SKIRTS AND
COATS**

Country Miss Inc.
PO Box 769, Easton PA
18044-0769.

Gailord Classics Inc.
3451 W Allegheny Ave,
Philadelphia PA 19132-
1021. 215/482-4260.

In Vogue Apparel Inc.
324 Allen St, Hazleton
PA 18201-2623.
717/455-3633.

Jean-Michaels Inc.
50 Ironside Ct,
Willingboro NJ 08046-
2533. 609/871-8888.

Julie Fashions
Cottage St, Minersville
PA 17954. 717/544-
4778.

Kalena Sports Wear
223 Pratt St,
Hammonton NJ 08037-
1719. 609/561-0066.

Kingston Fashions Inc.
144 Eley St, Wilkes Barre
PA 18704-3905.
717/288-3656.

Mount Union Sportswear
15 W Pine St, Mount
Union PA 17066-1147.
814/542-2526.

Scotty's Fashions
Rt 209, Kresgeville PA
18333. 610/681-4118.

**Tama Manufacturing Co
Inc.**
1798 Main St,
Northampton PA 18067-
1543. 610/262-7801.

**WOMEN'S AND MISSES'
OUTERWEAR**

A&H Sportswear Co.
1111 Spring Garden St,
Easton PA 18042-3243.
610/250-0804.

A&H Sportswear Co.
229 N Green St, Easton
PA 18042-1862.
610/253-4281.

A&H Sportswear Co.
500 William St, Pen
Argyl PA 18072-1772.
610/863-4176.

Bethleon Togs Inc.
120-128 W Union Blvd,
Bethlehem PA 18018.
610/867-8311.

Blough-Wagner Manufacturing Co Inc.
PO Box 396, Middleburg PA 17842-0396.
717/837-0011.

Bru-Mar Manufacturing
N 7th & W Allen Sts, Allentown PA 18102.
610/433-7559.

David Stevens Manufacturing Inc.
109 N Black Horse Pike, Blackwood NJ 08012-3043. 609/227-0655.

Dolfin International Corporation
Catherine & Sterly Sts, Reading PA 19607.
610/775-5500.

Fernbrook & Co.
PO Box 162, Palmerton PA 18071-0162.
610/826-2465.

Linden Knitwear Inc.
Main St, Mohrsville PA 19541. 610/926-4181.

Mary Fashion Manufacturing Co Inc.
380 W Main St, Bath PA 18014-1012. 610/837-6763.

Milco Industries Inc.
550 E 5th St, Bloomsburg PA 17815-2301. 717/784-0400.

New Holland Lingerie
494 W Broad St, New Holland PA 17557-1102.
717/354-2306.

Pine Grove Woolens
11-13 E Pottsville St, Pine Grove PA 17963-1506. 717/345-2628.

Progr Knitting Mills Pennsylvania Inc.
5695 Rising Sun Ave, Philadelphia PA 19120-1625. 215/725-5400.

Quartet Fashions Inc.
181 S Whitfield St, Nazareth PA 18064-2152. 610/759-6560.

Scotty's Fashions
477 Lehigh Ave, Palmerton PA 18071-1988. 610/826-2118.

Wyoming Valley Garment
237 Old River Rd, Wilkes Barre PA 18702-1616.
717/823-7720.

WOMEN'S AND MISSES' UNDERWEAR AND NIGHTWEAR

Baronol Garment Co
7th & Locust Sts, Bloomsburg PA 17815.
717/784-7071.

Colebrook-Terry Inc.
110 Carlisle Ave, York PA 17404-3253.
717/843-8071.

Donegal Industries Inc.
R D 1, Mount Joy PA 17552-9801. 717/653-1486.

JE Morgan Knitting Mills
100 S Tunnel St, Williamstown PA 17098-1527. 717/647-7125.

JK Operating Corporation
1340 Chestnut St, Kulpmont PA 17834-1112. 610/532-5522.

Liberty Lingerie Corporation
Rt 414, Liberty PA 16930. 717/324-2511.

Loungewear Mfg Corp.
978 E Main St, Ephrata PA 17522-9302.
717/738-2026.

Milco Industries Inc.
Colley St, Benton PA 17814. 717/925-6321.

NQ II Limited
7 Indl Pk, Mifflinburg PA 17844. 717/966-3195.

Ocello Inc.
300 Poplar St, Richland PA 17087-9715.
717/866-5778.

Sayre Lingerie Inc.
701-11 S Elmer Ave, Sayre PA 18840.
717/888-2286.

Sylray Inc.
216 W Independence St, Orwigsburg PA 17961-2102. 717/366-0537.

The Kaydette Corporation
2100 Dickson St, Berwick PA 18603-1131. 717/759-0327.

Val Mode Lingerie Inc.
45 Rosenhayn Ave, Bridgeton NJ 08302-1216. 609/451-7800.

Wundies Enterprises
RR 3 Box 250, Wellsboro PA 16901-9426.
717/724-3755.

BRASSIERES, GIRDLES AND ALLIED GARMENTS

Reach Road Manufacturing Corporation
2729 Reach Rd, Williamsport PA 17701-4179. 717/322-7806.

True Form Foundations Corporation
2009 Elmwood Ave,
Sharon Hill PA 19079-
1041. 610/522-9201.

HATS, CAPS AND MILLINERY

F&M Hat Co Inc.
103 Walnut St, Denver
PA 17517-1605.
215/267-5505.

GIRLS' AND CHILDREN'S DRESSES AND BLOUSES

Hartstrings Inc.
270 E Conestoga Rd,
Wayne PA 19087-2565.
610/687-6900.

Seibel & Stern Corporation
Walnut and Orchard Sts,
Bridgeton NJ 08302.
609/451-4200.

Seven Valleys Garment Co Inc.
Cherry St, Seven Valleys
PA 17360. 717/428-
1943.

Stitches Inc.
300 Race St, Sunbury PA
17801-1912. 717/286-
5745.

GIRLS' AND CHILDREN'S OUTWEAR

Demford Manufacturing
N 7th & Reinoehl Sts,
Lebanon PA 17042.
717/272-5688.

ROBES AND DRESSING GOWNS

Katz Inc.
120 Sunrise Ave,
Honesdale PA 18431-
1028. 717/253-2544.

APPAREL AND BELTS

American Belt Co.
1355 Adams Rd,
Bensalem PA 19020-
3912. 215/639-8000.

APPAREL AND ACCESSORIES

Lending Textile Co Inc.
169 Miller Ave,
Montgomery PA 17752-
1419. 717/547-6636.

CURTAINS AND DRAPERIES

Avante Bedspreads Company
St Johns & Philadelphia
Rd, Easton PA 18042.
610/258-2320.

Haleyville Drapery Manufacturing
7040 New Berwick Hwy,
Bloomsburg PA 17815-
8634. 717/784-8350.

Merrill Y Landis Ltd
PO Box 249, Telford PA
18969-0249. 215/723-
8177.

HOMEFURNISHINGS

Bess Manufacturing Company
1807-27 E Huntingdon
St, Philadelphia PA
19125. 215/425-9450.

Lincoln Textile Products Co Inc.
Belvidere & Whitfield,
Nazareth PA 18064.
610/759-6211.

Pressing Supply Co.
5400 N 6th St,
Philadelphia PA 19120-
2738. 215/324-7600.

Quickie Manufacturing Corporation
1150 Taylors Ln,
Riverton NJ 08077-
2506. 609/829-7900.

Town & Country Linen Corporation
475 Oberlin Ave S,
Lakewood NJ 08701-
6904. 908/364-2000.

TEXTILE BAGS

A Rifkin Co.
1400 Sans Souci Pky,
Wilkes Barre PA 18702-
2097. 717/825-9551.

Philadelphia Insulated Wire Co.
333 New Albany Rd,
Moorestown NJ 08057-
1120. 609/235-6700.

PLEATING, DECORATIVE AND NOVELTY STITCHING

Aureus Adidas
330 Philadelphia Ave,
Pittston PA 18643-2147.
717/655-6811.

Needleworks Inc.
453 E Pine St,
Millersburg PA 17061-
1453. 717/692-2144.

Penn Company
10909 Dutton Rd,
Philadelphia PA 19154-
3203. 215/632-7800.

Swiss Maid Emblem Co Inc.
RR 1 Box 58, Greentown
PA 18426-9714.

The Kimberton Co.
Lincoln & Hall Aves,
Phoenixville PA 19460.
610/933-8985.

AUTOMOTIVE TRIMMINGS AND APPAREL FINDINGS

Fasco Product Indentification
1 Wilcox St, Sayre PA 18840-2929. 717/888-6641.

Fit-Rite Headwear Inc.
92 S Empire St, Wilkes Barre PA 18702-6696. 717/825-3459.

Penn Pad Company
300 E Clearfield Sts, Philadelphia PA 19134-2953. 215/426-2000.

FABRICATED TEXTILE PRODUCTS

Budge Industries Inc.
821 Tech Dr, Telford PA 18969-1183.

Collegeville Flag & Manufacturing Co.
4th & Walnut, Collegeville PA 19426. 610/489-4131.

Ritztek Manufacturing Company
S Main St, Montrose PA 18801. 717/278-3707.

Switlik Parachute Co
1325 E State St, Trenton NJ 08609-1696. 609/587-3300.

Valley Forge Flag Co
150 N Main St, Spring City PA 19475-1828. 610/948-4900.

Valley Forge Flag Co
1700 Conrad Weiser Pky, Womelsdorf PA 19567-9759. 610/589-2400.

Victoria Vogue Inc.
90 Southland Dr, Bethlehem PA 18017-8925. 610/865-1500.

LEATHER TANNING AND FINISHING

Loewengart & Co Inc.
209 Oregon St, Mercersburg PA 17236-1629. 717/328-3111.

Westfield Tanning Co.
360 Church St, Westfield PA 16950-1593. 814/367-5951.

HOUSE SLIPPERS

Columbia Footwear Corporation
Fulton Ct & Spring St, Hazleton PA 18201. 717/455-4742.

MEN'S FOOTWEAR

Country Cousins Shoes
Jeannette St, Shickshinny PA 18655. 717/824-2434.

Fairfield Shoe Co.
Balder St, Fairfield PA 17320. 717/642-8201.

Johnson-Baillie Shoe Company
Wiconisco St, Millersburg PA 17061. 717/692-2102.

Richland Shoe Company
30 N 3rd St, Womelsdorf PA 19567-1404. 610/589-4586.

WOMEN'S FOOTWEAR

B Levy & Sons
700 N South Rd, Scranton PA 18504-1432. 717/346-4601.

Beaver Shoe Corporation
Snider Ave, Beaver Sprgs PA 17812. 717/658-2473.

Bedford Shoe Co.
Orange St, Carlisle PA 17013. 717/249-1131.

Carter Footwear Inc.
1167 N Washington St, Wilkes Barre PA 18705-1837. 717/824-2434.

Milton Shoe Manufacturing Co Inc.
700 Hepburn St, Milton PA 17847-2422. 717/742-9621.

Penn Footwear Company
Line & Grove Sts, Nanticoke PA 18634. 717/735-3200.

FOOTWEAR

Ephrata Shoe Co Inc.
18 N State St, Ephrata PA 17522-2737. 717/733-2215.

Newville Division
14-16 S Washington St, Newville PA 17241. 717/776-3141.

Walkin Shoe Co Inc.
Columbia & Pkwy Sts, Shuykl Haven PA 17972. 717/385-0100.

Willits Shoe Co.
North Second Ave, Halifax PA 17032. 717/896-3411.

For more information on career opportunities in the apparel and textiles industries:

Associations

AFFILIATED DRESS MANUFACTURERS
225 West 39th, 5th Floor, New York NY 10018.

AMERICAN APPAREL MANUFACTURERS ASSOCIATION
2500 Wilson Boulevard, Suite 301, Arlington VA 22201. 703/524-1864.

AMERICAN CLOAK AND SUIT MANUFACTURERS ASSOCIATION
450 Seventh Avenue, New York NY 10123. 212/244-7300.

THE FASHION GROUP
597 5th Avenue, 8th Floor, New York NY 10017. 212/593-1715.

INTERNATIONAL ASSOCIATION OF CLOTHING DESIGNERS
475 Park Avenue South, 17th Floor, New York NY 10016. 212/685-6602.

Directories

AAMA DIRECTORY
American Apparel Manufacturers Association, 2500 Wilson Boulevard, Suite 301, Arlington VA 22201. 703/524-1864.

APPAREL TRADES BOOK
Dun & Bradstreet Inc., 430 Mountain Avenue, New Providence NJ 07974. 908/665-5000.

FAIRCHILD'S MARKET DIRECTORY OF WOMEN'S AND CHILDREN'S APPAREL
Fairchild Publications, 7 West 34th Street, New York NY 10001. 212/630-4000.

Magazines

AMERICA'S TEXTILES
Billiam Publishing, 37 Villa Road, Suite 111, P.O. Box 103 Greenville SC 29615. 803/242-5300.

APPAREL INDUSTRY MAGAZINE
Shore Communications Inc., 6255 Barfield Road, Suite 200, Atlanta GA 30328-4893. 404/252-8831.

ACCESSORIES
Business Journals, 50 Day Street, P.O. Box 5550, Norwalk CT 06856. 203/853-6015.

BOBBIN
Bobbin Publications, P.O. Box 1986, 1110 Shop Road, Columbia SC 29202. 803/771-7500.

WOMEN'S WEAR DAILY (WWD)
Fairchild Publications, 7 West 34th Street, New York NY 10001. 212/630-4000.

ARCHITECTURE, CONSTRUCTION AND ENGINEERING

 *In the construction industry, home building is expected to stabilize, but commercial real estate construction -- particularly office buildings and hotels -- will continue to decline. Home improvement, hospitals, schools, water supply buildings, and public service buildings construction should offer the best opportunities.*

Job prospects for engineers have been good for a number of years, and will continue to improve into the next century. Employers will need more engineers as they increase investment in equipment in order to expand output. In addition, engineers will find work improving the nation's deteriorating infrastructure.

BUCKLEY & COMPANY, INC.
3401 Moore Street, Philadelphia PA 19145. 215/334-7500. **Contact:** Joseph Martosella, Vice President. **Description:** A heavy construction firm, involved in projects such as highways, bridges, tunnels, and other large-scale construction projects.

BUILDING CORPORATION
One Vala Avenue, Bala Cynwyd PA 19004. 215/668-4100. **Contact:** Lou Parise, Vice President. **Description:** An area construction firm.

THE CONDUIT AND FOUNDATION CORPORATION
33 Rock Hill Road, Bala Cynwyd PA 19004. 215/668-8400. **Contact:** Joe Kapalko, Controller. **Description:** A general construction firm engaged in large project construction and related services, including the construction of highways, bridges, tunnels, wastewater treatment plants; dams; power generation stations; and similar projects. **Common positions include:** Accountant/Auditor; Civil Engineer; Computer Programmer; Construction Superintendent; Management Trainee; Mechanical Engineer; Purchasing Agent and Manager. **Educational backgrounds include:** Accounting; Business Administration; Computer Science; Engineering; Mathematics. **Benefits:** Disability Coverage; Life Insurance; Medical Insurance; Pension Plan; Profit Sharing; Tuition Assistance. **Special Programs:** Internships; Training Programs. **Corporate headquarters location:** This Location. **Other U.S. locations:** Orlando FL; Parsippany NJ. **Operations at this facility include:** Administration; Regional Headquarters; Sales; Service.

CORRADO AMERICAN, INC.
200 Marsh Lane, New Castle DE 19720. 302/655-6501. **Contact:** Marty Bienowski, Controller. **Description:** A Delaware construction company.

FACTORY MUTUAL ASSOCIATION
401 City Avenue, Suite 420, Bala Cynwyd PA 19004. 215/668-2250. **Contact:** District Office. **Description:** A loss control services organization owned by Allendale Insurance, Arkwright, and Protection Mutual Insurance, with 17 district offices strategically located throughout the United States and Canada. Research facilities are

located in Norwood, MA, and West Gloucester, RI. Primary objective is to help owner company policyholders to protect their properties and occupancies from damage from fire, wind, flood, and explosion; from boiler, pressure vessel, and machinery accidents; and from many other insured hazards. To accomplish this objective, a wide range of engineering, research, and consulting services are provided, primarily in the field of loss control. **Common positions include:** Chemical Engineer; Civil Engineer; Electrical/Electronic Engineer; Fire Science Engineer; Mechanical Engineer. **Benefits:** Dental Insurance; Disability Coverage; Employee Discounts; Life Insurance; Medical Insurance; Pension Plan; Savings Plan; Tuition Assistance. **Corporate headquarters location:** Norwood MA.

FLUOR DANIEL INC.
P.O. Box 950, Marlton NJ 08053. 609/985-6587. **Contact:** Daphne Grabowski, College Relations Coordinator. **Description:** An engineering firm.

GLASGOW, INC.
P.O. Box 1089, Glenside PA 19038-1089. 215/884-8800. **Contact:** Bruce Rambo, President. **Description:** An area construction firm. **Corporate headquarters location:** This Location.

JOHN E. HEALY AND SONS, INC.
P.O. Box 470, New Castle DE 19720. 302/322-9600. **Contact:** Mike Healy, President. **Description:** A Philadelphia area construction company.

HENKELS & McCOY, INC.
985 Jolly Road, Blue Bell PA 19422-0900. 215/283-7688. **Contact:** Vince Benedict, Jr., Senior Director. **Description:** Engineers and contractors for the electric, gas, and telephone utilities and for industrial and commercial process plants. **Common positions include:** Accountant/Auditor; Administrator; Architect; Buyer; Civil Engineer; Computer Programmer; Credit Manager; Department Manager; Draftsperson; Editor; Electrical/Electronic Engineer; Financial Analyst; General Manager; Management Trainee; Marketing Specialist; Mechanical Engineer; Personnel/Labor Relations Specialist; Purchasing Agent and Manager; Reporter; Sales Associate; Technical Writer/Editor. **Educational backgrounds include:** Accounting; Business Administration; Computer Science; Engineering; Finance; Liberal Arts; Marketing. **Benefits:** Disability Coverage; Life Insurance; Medical Insurance; Profit Sharing; Savings Plan; Tuition Assistance. **Corporate headquarters location:** This Location.

HIGH INDUSTRIES, INC.
P.O. Box 10008, Lancaster PA 17605-0008. 717/293-4486. **Contact:** Vincent F. Mizeras, Director of Human Resources. **Description:** Products and services include: steel fabrication; real estate development and management; design/build construction services; prestress/precast concrete products; food services; hotel management; and cable TV system and radio station ownership and management. **Common positions include:** Accountant/Auditor; Architect; Civil Engineer; Computer Programmer; Customer Service Representative; Draftsperson; Hotel Manager/Assistant Manager; Personnel/Labor Relations Specialist; Services Sales Representative; Systems Analyst. **Educational backgrounds include:** Accounting; Business Administration; Computer Science; Engineering; Finance; Marketing. **Benefits:** Credit Union; Dental Insurance; Disability Coverage; Life Insurance; Medical Insurance; Pension Plan; Profit Sharing; Savings Plan; Tuition Assistance. **Corporate headquarters location:** This Location. **Operations at this facility include:** Administration; Manufacturing.

IREX CORPORATION
P.O. Box 1268, Lancaster PA 17608. 717/397-3633. **Contact:** Human Resources. **Description:** A special trade contractor.

IRWIN & LEIGHTON, INC.
460 North Gulph Road, King of Prussia PA 19406. 215/265-7300. **Contact:** Personnel. **Description:** An area construction services firm.

JOY ENVIRONMENTAL EQUIPMENT COMPANY
One Countryview Road, P.O. Box 3006, Malvern PA 19355-0706. 215/647-9900. **Contact:** Mary Sue Good, Human Resources Coordinator. **Description:** Engaged in the design engineering of material handling systems for power plants (fossil fuel) and industrial applications. **Common positions include:** Buyer; Department Manager; Draftsperson; Electrical/Electronic Engineer; Industrial Engineer; Marketing Specialist; Mechanical Engineer; Mining Engineer; Purchasing Agent and Manager; Technical Writer/Editor. **Educational backgrounds include:** Business Administration; Computer Science; Engineering. **Benefits:** Dental Insurance; Disability Coverage; Life Insurance; Medical Insurance; Pension Plan; Tuition Assistance. **Corporate headquarters location:** Pittsburgh PA. **Parent company:** Joy Technology. **Operations at this facility include:** Divisional Headquarters.

THE KLING-LINDQUIST PARTNERSHIP, INC.
2301 Chestnut Street, Philadelphia PA 19103. 215/569-2900. **Contact:** Steve Huston, Technical Recruiter. **Description:** An architectural and engineering firm. **Common positions include:** Architect; Civil Engineer; Computer-Aided Designer; Draftsperson; Electrical/Electronic Engineer; Interior Designer; Marketing Specialist; Mechanical Engineer; Public Relations Specialist; Security Manager; Structural Engineer. **Educational backgrounds include:** Architecture; Engineering; Interior Design. **Benefits:** Dental Insurance; Disability Coverage; Life Insurance; Medical Insurance; Pension Plan; Savings Plan; Tuition Assistance. **Special Programs:** Internships; Training Programs. **Corporate headquarters location:** This Location.

THE KORMAN COMPANY
2 Neshaminy Interplex, Trevose PA 19053. 215/245-0700. **Contact:** Personnel Department. **Description:** An area developer and construction firm. **Corporate headquarters location:** This Location.

KRAPF CAN DO IT
307 A Street, Wilmington DE 19801. 302/656-6686. **Common positions include:** **Contact:** Tom Devlin, Personnel Director. **Description:** A general contracting company.

M&T COMPANY
Valley Forge Park Office Building, 1018 West 9th Avenue, P.O. Box 61886, King of Prussia PA 19406. 215/337-8200. **Contact:** Personnel Department. **Description:** Provides a wide range of technical services, including engineering, designing, drafting, and graphic arts services.

JAMES D. MORRISSEY, INC.
9119 Frankford Avenue, Philadelphia PA 19114. **Contact:** Employment Manager. **Description:** A heavy construction firm working on large-scale projects such as highways, buildings, etc. **Common positions include:** Civil Engineer; Computer Programmer; Draftsperson; Management Trainee; Mining Engineer; Purchasing Agent and Manager; Systems Analyst. **Educational backgrounds include:** Engineering. **Benefits:** Dental Insurance; Life Insurance; Medical Insurance; Pension Plan; Tuition

Assistance. **Corporate headquarters location:** This Location. **Operations at this facility include:** Regional Headquarters.

NANTICOKE HOMES, INC.
P.O. Box F, Greenwood DE 19950. 302/349-4561. **Contact:** Ed Moore, Personnel Manager. **Description:** Produces quality sectional homes. **Common positions include:** Accountant/Auditor; Administrator; Architect; Blue-Collar Worker Supervisor; Buyer; Computer Programmer; Customer Service Representative; Department Manager; Draftsperson; General Manager; Industrial Engineer; Mechanical Engineer; Operations/Production Manager; Personnel/Labor Relations Specialist; Purchasing Agent and Manager; Quality Control Supervisor; Services Sales Representative. **Educational backgrounds include:** Accounting; Business Administration; Engineering; Sales. **Benefits:** Disability Coverage; Employee Discounts; Eye Care; Life Insurance; Medical Insurance; Pension Plan; Profit Sharing; Savings Plan; Tuition Assistance. **Corporate headquarters location:** This Location.

TARKETT INC.
1139 Lehigh Avenue, Whitehall PA 18052. 215/266-5500. **Contact:** Sylvia A. Hajewski, Human Resources. **Description:** Manufacturer of sheet vinyl flooring. **Common positions include:** Accountant/Auditor; Administrator; Blue-Collar Worker Supervisor; Chemist; Commercial Artist; Computer Programmer; Customer Service Representative; Department Manager; Draftsperson; Mechanical Engineer; Operations/Production Manager; Purchasing Agent and Manager; Quality Control Supervisor; Statistician; Systems Analyst. **Educational backgrounds include:** Accounting; Art/Design; Business Administration; Chemistry; Computer Science; Engineering; Marketing. **Benefits:** 401K; Dental Insurance; Disability Coverage; Employee Discounts; Life Insurance; Medical Insurance; Pension Plan; Savings Plan; Tuition Assistance. **Corporate headquarters location:** Parsippany NJ. **Operations at this facility include:** Administration; Manufacturing; Research and Development. **Number of employees at this location:** 387.

TOLL BROTHERS INC.
3103 Philmont Avenue, Huntington Valley PA 19006-4298. 215/938-8000. **Contact:** Human Resources. **Description:** Designs, builds, markets, and finances single-family detached homes, townhouses, and low-rise condominiums in middle and high income residential communities. **Number of employees at this location:** 650.

UNITED ENGINEERS & CONSTRUCTORS INC.
30 S. 17th Street, Philadelphia PA 19103. 215/422-3000. **Contact:** Personnel Department. **Description:** Provides a broad range of engineering and construction services, including maintenance and management services.

WILLIARD INC.
375 Highland Avenue, Jenkintown PA 19046. 215/885-5000. **Contact:** Ellen Slusarczyk, Personnel Administrator. **Description:** A mechanical-electrical construction firm. **Corporate headquarters location:** This Location.

Note: Because addresses and telephone numbers of smaller companies change rapidly, we recommend you contact each company and verify the information below before contacting employers. Mass mailings are not recommended.

Additional large employers: 500 +

ENGINEERING SERVICES

STV Group Incorporated
11 Robinson St.,
Pottstown PA 19464-
6439. 610/326-4600.

Allstates Design & Dev.
Company
1210 Northbrook Dr
Suite 150, Fstrvl Trvose

PA 19053-8406.
215/953-5100.

STONE WORK
CONTRACTORS

John B. Kelly Inc. of PA
1436 Lancaster Ave.
Ste. 210, Berwyn PA
19312-1288. 610/251-
0888.

PREFABRICATED
WOODEN BUILDINGS

Muncy Homes Inc.
P.O. Box 325, Muncy PA
17756. 717/546-2261.

Additional medium sized employers: under 500

ENGINEERING SERVICES

Andrews Bettigole &
Clark Inc.
310 Main St, Toms River
NJ 08753-7440.
908/349-3446.

Blasland & Bouck
Engineers
1 E Uwchlan Ave, Exton
PA 19341-1271.
610/524-9340.

C-Cor Electronics Inc.
60 Decibel Rd, State
College PA 16801-7530.
814/238-2461.

Camp Dresser & McKee
Inc.
280 Granite Run Dr,
Lancaster PA 17601-
6820. 717/560-7500.

Clarke & Rapuano
510 Heron Dr,
Swedesboro NJ 08085-
1740. 609/467-5223.

Commec Inc.
1480 Valley Center Pky,
Bethlehem PA 18017-
2264. 610/758-7500.

Engineered Systems
Division
2550 Market St, Aston
PA 19014-3426.
610/494-8000.

ERM - Environmental
Resources Management
Inc.
300 Phillips Blvd, Trenton
NJ 08618-1427.
609/895-0050.

Ewing Cole Cherry Inc.
100 N 6th St,
Philadelphia PA 19106-
1529. 215/923-2020.

Liberty Technology
Center Inc.
555 North Lane,
Conshohocken PA
19428. 610/834-0330.

McCormick Taylor &
Assoc Inc.
900 Haddon Ave,
Collingswood NJ 08108-
2101. 609/854-1493.

NTH Consultants Ltd
860 Springdale Dr, Exton
PA 19341-2847.
610/524-2300.

Quasar Engineering
300 Phillips Blvd, Trenton
NJ 08618-1427.
609/844-1200.

Raytheon Service
Company Inc.
200 Scarborough Dr,
Pleasantville NJ 08232-
4856. 609/641-5544.

Richard A Alaimo
Associates
200 High St, Mount Holly
NJ 08060-1404.
609/267-8310.

Sega Inc.
3l Bewers La, Jackson
NJ 08527. 908/905-
6323.

SSM - Spotts Stevens & McCoy Inc.
345 N Wyomissing Blvd
Box 6307, Reading PA
19610-2935. 610/376-
6581.

Stone & Webster Engineering Corporation
State Hwy No 70 &
Cuthbert Blv, Cherry Hill
NJ 08002. 609/482-
3000.

The Sigel Group
Sabine & Essex Av,
Narberth PA 19072.
215/839-3200.

Veda Inc.
730 Louis Dr, Warminster
PA 18974-2854.
215/672-3200.

Whitman Requardt & Associates
2200 S George St Ste D,
York PA 17403-4594.
717/741-5057.

ARCHITECTURAL SERVICES

Basco Assocs Architects & Engineers
Eves Dr, Marlton NJ
08053. 609/983-0110.

Hillier Group Architects & Planners
500 Alexander Park,
Princeton NJ 08540-
6307. 609/452-8888.

Acer Engineers & Cnslt Inc.
270 Granite Run Dr,
Lancaster PA 17601-
6804. 717/569-7021.

CONSTRUCTION MATERIALS WHOLESALE

Lumbermens Merchandising Corporation
PO Box 6790, Wayne PA
19087-8790. 610/293-
7000.

Speciality Products & Insltn
992 N Peifers Ln,
Harrisburg PA 17109-
5907. 717/558-2072.

MOBILE HOME MANUFACTURING

Fleetwood Homes Of Pennsylvania Inc.
48 Indl Rd Conewago
Indl Pk, Elizabethtown PA
17022. 717/367-8222.

Imperial Homes Corporation
PO Box 157, Hegins PA
17938-0157. 717/682-
9001.

Marlette Homes Inc.
30 Indl Pk Rd, Lewistown
PA 17044. 717/248-
3947.

Pine Grove Manufactured Homes
Rte 443, Pine Grove PA
17963. 717/345-2011.

Redman Homes Inc.
101 Garden Spot Rd,
Ephrata PA 17522-9760.
717/733-7941.

Skyline Corporation
465 N Reading Rd,
Ephrata PA 17522-9606.
717/733-4171.

Skyline Homes Corporation
99 Horseshoe Rd, Leola
PA 17540-1763.
717/656-2071.

Sturbridge Homes Inc.
1124 Eagle St,
Allentown PA 18106-
9506. 610/391-0373.

PREFABRICATED WOOD BUILDINGS AND COMPONENTS

Advanced Building Tech
1 American Dr, Tamaqua
PA 18252. 717/668-
5670.

Contempri Homes Inc.
Stauffer Indl Pk, Taylor
PA 18517. 717/562-
0110.

Delair Group Inc.
8600 River Rd,
Pennsauken NJ 08110-
3300. 609/663-2900.

Deluxe Homes Of Pennsylvania Inc.
499 W 3rd St, Berwick
PA 18603-2999.
717/752-5914.

Excel Homes Inc.
RR 2 Box 683, Liverpool
PA 17045-9516.
717/444-3395.

Foremost Industries
2375 Buchanan Trl W,
Greencastle PA 17225-
9499. 717/597-7166.

Haven Homes Inc.
Rte 150, Beech Creek PA
16822. 717/962-2111.

Lifestyle Homes Inc.
RR 1 Box 1660, Berwick
PA 18603-9738.
717/752-6990.

Penn Lyon Homes Inc.
Airport Rd, Selinsgrove
PA 17870. 717/374-
4004.

**Ritz Craft Corporation Of
Pennsylvania Inc.**
15 Industrial Park Rd,
Mifflinburg PA 17844.
717/966-1053.

Simplex Industries Inc.
Simplex Dr, Scranton PA
18504. 717/346-5113.

**GENERAL
CONTRACTORS--SINGLE
FAMILY HOUSES**

**Brad R Hemmerle &
Associates**
334 Park Ave, Chalfont
PA 18914-2106.
215/822-6882.

Harold H Hogg Inc.
2350 Springwood Rd,
York PA 17402-8873.
717/741-0839.

Orrino Builders Inc.
36 Remington Pl,
Warminster PA 18974-
1272. 215/355-8728.

**Richard E Pierson
Construction Co.**
Industrial Dr,
Williamstown NJ 08094.
609/728-2703.

Ritter Bros Inc.
1511 N Cameron St,
Harrisburg PA 17103-
1015. 717/234-3061.

**Sordoni Construction
Service Inc.**
45 Owen St, Wilkes
Barre PA 18704-4339.
717/287-3161.

The Canuso Group
Bustleton Pike & Stump
Rd, Langhorne PA
19047. 215/322-2700.

Whitting-Turner Co
State Hwy No 72,
Manahawkin NJ 08050.
609/597-1780.

Woods At Millbrook
6 Newport Dr, Princeton
Jct NJ 08550-2224.
609/490-0220.

**GENERAL
CONTRACTORS--
INDUSTRIAL BUILDINGS
AND WAREHOUSES**

Lundy Construction
Arch St & Reach Rd,
Williamsport PA 17701.
717/323-8451.

Nason and Cullen Inc.
150 S Warner Rd, Wayne
PA 19087-2126.
610/687-6100.

**GENERAL
CONTRACTORS--
NONRESIDENTIAL
BUILDINGS**

Radnor Corporation
1 Radnor Corporate Ctr,
Wayne PA 19087-4515.
610/293-6994.

**HIGHWAY AND STREET
CONSTRUCTION**

Giza Associates Inc.
1637 Westwood Rd,
Reading PA 19610-1141.
610/678-0181.

**WATER, SEWER,
PIPELINE,
COMMUNICATIONS AND
POWER LINE
CONSTRUCTION**

R&T Group Inc.
Ellis & Sewell Sts,
Glassboro NJ 08028.
609/881-2511.

HEAVY CONSTRUCTION

JE Brenneman Company
800 Hudson Sq, Camden
NJ 08102-1155.
609/966-8400.

WE Yoder Inc.
41 S Maple St, Kutztown
PA 19530-1520.
610/683-7383.

**PLUMBING, HEATING
AND AIR-CONDITIONING**

**Dual Temp Fuels-
Holtzman**
326 N 2nd St, Allentown
PA 18102-3510.
610/791-1151.

**Harvey Sid Of
Pennsylvania**
390 Chestnut St, York
PA 17403-1347.
717/845-2608.

RE Michel Company
641 N Pennsylvania Ave,
Wilkes Barre PA 18705-
2421. 717/829-0383.

ELECTRICAL WORK

BJ Baldiin Electric Inc.
114 Market St, Auburn
PA 17922. 717/754-
3118.

CC Kottcamp & Son
515 W Market St, York
PA 17404-3710.
717/845-7611.

Denca Communications
1222 Ridge Ave,
Philadelphia PA 19123-
3205. 610/825-2272.

Harry F Ortlip Co.
780 Lancaster Ave, Bryn
Mawr PA 19010-3415.
610/527-7000.

M Newmark & Bro Inc.
1924 Arch St,
Philadelphia PA 19103-
1404. 215/567-0547.

Tri-M Corporation
7584 Morris Ct,
Allentown PA 18106-
9250. 610/398-3663.

WV Pangborne & Co
150 Rock Hill Rd, Bala
Cynwyd PA 19004-
2133. 610/668-2711.

**PLASTERING, DRYWALL
AND INSULATION**

**Benner-White
Construction**
185 Ruth Rd, Harleysville
PA 19438-1823.
610/272-2797.

JB Acoustical Supply
102 Park Rd, Ambler PA
19002-1120. 215/628-
9090.

**FLOOR LAYING AND
OTHER FLOOR WORK**

**Drehmann Paving &
Flooring Co**
2101 Byberry Rd,
Philadelphia PA 19116-
3068. 215/464-7700.

Herre Bros Inc.
4417 Valley St, Enola PA
17025. 717/732-4454.

**ROOFING, SIDING AND
SHEET METAL WORK**

**American Aluminum &
Insulation Inc.**
5 Highland Ave,
Bethlehem PA 18017-
8967. 610/694-9958.

Centimark Corporation
25 Utley Dr, Camp Hill
PA 17011-8032.
717/731-4750.

Centimark Corporation
57 S Commerce Way,
Bethlehem PA 18017-
8964. 610/758-9880.

George H Duross Inc.
7921 Oxford Ave,
Philadelphia PA 19111-
2298. 215/725-6400.

NRC Roofing Co.
404 S 29th St,
Harrisburg PA 17103-
2110. 717/232-0597.

CONCRETE WORK

Rogele Inc.
1025 S 21st St,
Harrisburg PA 17104-
2706. 717/564-0478.

**STRUCTURAL STEEL
ERECTION**

RA Marker & Sons Inc.
2101 U S Hwy 522 N,
Lewistown PA 17044-
2761. 717/242-2529.

VPF Corporation
RR 1, Lehighton PA
18235-9801. 717/386-
5956.

EXCAVATION WORK

**Harvey M Fisher
Excavating**
RR 1 Box 36,
Hummelstown PA
17036-9801. 717/533-
3031.

**INSTALLATION AND
ERECTION OF BUILDING
EQUIPMENT**

**General Elevator
Company Inc.**
2106 New Rd, Linwood
NJ 08221-1046.
609/653-0939.

United Ropes
120 Keystone Dr # B,
Montgomeryvle PA
18936-9637. 215/641-
4850.

**SPECIAL TRADE
CONTRACTORS**

Aycock Inc.
8261 Derry St,
Hummelstown PA
17036-9308. 717/737-
6718.

**Culbertson Restoration
Ltd**
Snyder Av, West Chester
PA 19382. 610/436-
4455.

**Environmental Control
Group Inc.**
115 Twinbridge Dr,
Pennsauken NJ 08110-
4206. 609/488-2000.

KDI Sylvan Pools Inc.
Rte 611, Doylestown PA
18901. 215/348-9011.

For more information on career opportunities in architecture, construction and engineering:

Associations

AMERICAN ASSOCIATION OF COST ENGINEERS
209 Prairie Avenue, Suite 100, P.O. Box 1557, Morgantown WV 26507-1550. 304/296-8444. 800/858-2678. Toll-free number provides information on scholarships for undergraduates.

AMERICAN CONSULTING ENGINEERS COUNCIL
1015 15th Street NW, Suite 802, Washington DC 20005. 202/347-7474.

AMERICAN INSTITUTE OF ARCHITECTS
1735 New York Avenue NW, Washington DC 20006. 202/626-7300. 800/365-2724. Toll-free number for brochures.

AMERICAN SOCIETY FOR ENGINEERING EDUCATION
1818 N Street NW, Suite 600, Washington DC 20036. 202/331-3500.

AMERICAN SOCIETY OF CIVIL ENGINEERS
345 East 47th Street, New York NY 10017. 212/705-7496.

AMERICAN SOCIETY OF HEATING, REFRIGERATING AND AIR CONDITIONING ENGINEERS
1791 Tullie Circle NE, Atlanta GA 30329. 404/636-8400.

AMERICAN SOCIETY OF LANDSCAPE ARCHITECTS
4401 Connecticut Avenue NW, Fifth Floor, Washington DC 20008. 202/686-2752.

AMERICAN SOCIETY OF MECHANICAL ENGINEERS
345 East 47th Street, New York NY 10017. 212/705-7722.

AMERICAN SOCIETY OF NAVAL ENGINEERS
1452 Duke Street, Alexandria VA 22314. 703/836-6727.

AMERICAN SOCIETY OF PLUMBING ENGINEERS
3617 Thousand Oaks Boulevard, Suite 210, Westlake CA 91362. 805/495-7120.

AMERICAN SOCIETY OF SAFETY ENGINEERS
1800 East Oakton Street, Des Plaines IL 60018-2187. 708/692-4121.

ILLUMINATING ENGINEERING SOCIETY OF NORTH AMERICA
120 Wall Street, 17th Floor, New York NY 10005. 212/248-5000.

INSTITUTE OF INDUSTRIAL ENGINEERS
25 Technology Park, Norcross GA 30092. 404/449-0460.

NATIONAL ACTION COUNCIL FOR MINORITIES IN ENGINEERING
3 West 35th Street, New York NY 10001. 212/279-2626.

NATIONAL ASSOCIATION OF MINORITY ENGINEERING
435 North Michigan Avenue, Suite 1115, Chicago IL 60611. 312/661-1700, ext. 744.

JUNIOR ENGINEERING TECHNICAL SOCIETY
1420 King Street, Suite 405, Alexandria VA 22314. 703/548-JETS.

NATIONAL INSTITUTE OF CERAMIC ENGINEERS
735 Ceramic Place, Westerville OH 43081. 614/890-4700.

NATIONAL SOCIETY OF BLACK ENGINEERS
1454 Duke Street, Alexandria VA 22314. 703/549-2207.

NATIONAL SOCIETY OF PROFESSIONAL ENGINEERS
1420 King Street, Alexandria VA 22314-2715. 703/684-2800. 703/684-2830. Number provides scholarship information for students.

SOCIETY OF FIRE PROTECTION ENGINEERS
1 Liberty Square, Boston MA 02109-4825. 617/482-0686.

SOCIETY OF MANUFACTURING ENGINEERS
P.O. Box 930, One SME Drive, Dearborn MI 48121. 313/271-1500.

UNITED ENGINEERING TRUSTEES
345 East 47th Street, New York NY 10017. 212/705-7000.

Directories

DIRECTORY OF ENGINEERING SOCIETIES
American Association of Engineering Societies, 1111 19th Street NW, Suite 608, Washington DC 20036. 202/296-2237.

DIRECTORY OF ENGINEERS IN PRIVATE PRACTICE
National Society of Professional Engineers, 1420 King Street, Alexandria VA 22314. 703/684-2800.

ENCYCLOPEDIA OF PHYSICAL SCIENCES & ENGINEERING INFORMATION SOURCES
Gale Research Inc., 835 Penobscot Building, Detroit MI 48226. 313/961-2242.

Magazines

CAREERS AND THE ENGINEER
Bob Adams, Inc., 260 Center Street, Holbrook MA 02343. 617/767-8100.

COMPUTER-AIDED ENGINEERING
Penton Publishing, 1100 Superior Avenue, Cleveland OH 44114. 216/696-7000.

EDN CAREER NEWS
Cahners Publishing Co., 275 Washington Street, Newton MA 02158. 617/964-3030.

ENGINEERING TIMES
National Society of Professional Engineers, 1420 King Street, Alexandria VA 22314. 703/684-2800.

ARTS AND ENTERTAINMENT/RECREATION

Things are looking up for the entertainment industry. Revenues for the different sectors of the industry have improved since 1991, when the recession slumped sales of movie tickets and prerecorded music. Technological advances continues to be a major variable in the industry's future -- multimedia interactive entertainment, the use of digital technology to integrate audio, video, computers and telecommunications, has attracted investment from four major movie houses and companies from related industries.

Movie attendance continues to grow in the U.S., despite a decline in the number of new releases. Abroad, growth of U.S. exports has practically stopped. American films, however, continue to dominate the international film industry.

Prerecorded music sales are soaring. Some of the fastest sales have been of CD singles, which has shown faster sales than full-length CD's. Sales of cassette tapes are expected to slow, and cassette singles generate faster sales growth than full-length tapes.

COMMUNITY Y
2110 Garrett Road, Landsdowne PA 19050. 215/259-1661. **Contact:** Personnel. **Description:** A recreation center.

DELAWARE RACING ASSOCIATION
P.O. Box 6008, Stanton DE 19804. 302/994-2521. **Contact:** Eileen O'Neil, Personnel Director. **Description:** An association dedicated to serving the needs of the professional racing industry.

THE FRANKLIN INSTITUTE ✓
SCIENCE MUSEUM
20th and The Benjamin Franklin Parkway, Philadelphia PA 19103. 215/448-1200. **Contact:** Suzzette Graves, Human Resources Assistant Director. **Description:** A not-for-profit scientific and educational corporation, founded in 1824. The Franklin Institute Science Museum consists of The Science Center, The Mandel Futures Center, The Fels Planetarium and The Tuttleman Omniverse Theater, with a wide range of interactive and educational exhibits in many different scientific areas. **Common positions include:** Accountant/Auditor; Blue-Collar Worker Supervisor; Customer Service Representative; Designer; Education Administrator; Graphic Artist; Sales Associate; Teacher. **Educational backgrounds include:** Accounting; Chemistry; Communications; Education; Finance; Geology. **Benefits:** Dental Insurance; Disability Coverage; Life Insurance; Medical Insurance; Savings Plan; Tuition Assistance.

GARDEN STATE RACE TRACK INC.
P.O. Box 4274, Cherry Hill NJ 08034-0649. 609/488-8400. **Contact:** Human Resources Department. **Description:** A race track.

LONGWOOD GARDENS
P.O. Box 501, Kennett Square PA 19348. 215/388-6741. **FAX:** 215/388-2078.
Contact: Human Resources. **Description:** Horticultural display garden for the education
and enjoyment of the public.

McCARTER THEATRE
CENTER FOR THE PERFORMING ARTS
91 University Place, Princeton NJ 08540. 609/683-9100. **FAX:** 609/497-0369.
Contact: General Manager. **Description:** Performing arts center producing and
presenting artists in drama, music, dance, and special events. Established in 1963.

PENNSYLVANIA NATIONAL TURF CLUB, INC.
P.O. Box 32, Grantville PA 17028-0032. 717/469-2211. **Contact:** Human Resources.
Description: Operates a race track.

PHILADELPHIA MUSEUM OF ART
P.O. Box 7646, Philadelphia PA 19101. 215/684-7925. **FAX:** 215/236-4465.
Contact: Human Resources. **Description:** Art museum housing a collection of European
and American paintings and decorative arts as well as Indian and East Asian Art.
Established in 1876.

PHILADELPHIA PARK
3001 Street Rd, Bensalem PA 19020. 215/639-9000. **Contact:** Personnel.
Description: A race track.

Ned Horner - Die of

SONY MUSIC
400 North Woodbury Road, Pitman NJ 08071. 609/589-8000. **Contact:** Human
Resources Department. **Description:** Offices of the major record company.

SPECTACOR ✓ *Alice Marini   V.P.*
1804 Rittenhouse Square, Philadelphia PA 19102. 215/875-2161. **Contact:** Human
Resources Department. **Description:** A sports/entertainment firm operating in the
following divisions: Philadelphia Flyers, which operates the National Hockey League
franchise; the Spectrum, which operates the arena in Philadelphia, PA; SpectaGuard,
which operates industrial, event, and industrial electronic security services with offices
in Wynnewood, PA and Waltham, MA; SpectAthelete, which operates a chain of retail
outlets offering authentic and replica sports merchandise; and Ticketmaster of
Delaware Valley, Inc., a computerized ticketing agency. **Common positions include:**
Accountant/Auditor; Administrator; Blue-Collar Worker Supervisor; General Manager;
Marketing Specialist; Operations/Production Manager; Personnel/Labor Relations
Specialist; Public Relations Specialist; Services Sales Representative. **Educational
backgrounds include:** Accounting; Business Administration; Communications; Finance;
Marketing. **Benefits:** Dental Insurance; Disability Coverage; Employee Discounts; Life
Insurance; Medical Insurance; Pension Plan; Tuition Assistance. **Special Programs:**
Internships. **Operations at this facility include:** Administration.

Note: Because addresses and telephone numbers of smaller companies change rapidly, we recommend you contact each company and verify the information below before contacting employers. Mass mailings are not recommended.

Additional medium sized employers: 100-499

AMUSEMENT AND RECREATION SERVICES

Top Dog
Pine Mall, Wilkes Barre PA 18702. 717/822-9999.

Breakers Billiard Center
1536 Kings Hwy N, Cherry Hill NJ 08034-2307. 609/795-5458.

Fair Lanes Edgewater Park
2330 Route 130, Beverly NJ 08010-3015. 609/877-1100.

Additional small employers: under 100

MOTION PICTURE AND VIDEO TAPE PRODUCTION

Accent Video Productions
519 W Diamond Ave, Hazleton PA 18201-4916. 717/455-1258.

Grauf Productions
2360 High St, Reading PA 19605-2829. 610/921-9327.

MOTION PICTURE THEATERS

Peoples Light & Theatre Co.
39 Conestoga Rd, Malvern PA 19355-1737. 610/647-1900.

Stroud Mall Cinema
Rt 611 and Bridge St, Stroudsburg PA 18360-1198. 717/421-5700.

VIDEO TAPE RENTAL

Bally Video
632 Main St, Bally PA 19503. 610/845-2561.

Choices Movies & Music
1411 Blackwood Clementon Rd, Clementon NJ 08021-5662. 609/784-0202.

Fox Video
702 Exeter Ave, Pittston PA 18643-1727. 717/883-1110.

Gateway Video
165 Nutt Rd, Phoenixville PA 19460-3905. 610/933-2750.

Powell Video
1500 Powell St, Norristown PA 19401-3336. 610/279-5210.

DANCE STUDIOS, SCHOOLS AND HALLS

Mari-Anne Dance School
Oxford Plza Shopping Ctr, Philadelphia PA 19111. 215/288-5200.

THEATRICAL PRODUCERS AND MISCELLANEOUS THEATRICAL SERVICES

McCarter Theatre Co.
91 University Pl, Princeton NJ 08540-5121. 609/683-9100.

The Pennsylvania Ballet
1101 S Broad St, Philadelphia PA 19147-4410. 215/551-7000.

Womans World International Inc.
3185 Manor Rd, Huntingdon Vy PA 19006-4137. 215/938-7116.

RACING, INCLUDING TRACK OPERATION

Atco Raceway
245 E Atlantic Ave, Atco NJ 08004-1522. 609/768-0900.

Pocono Intl. Raceway
PO Box 500, Long Pond PA 18334-0500. 717/646-2300.

The Breeders Crown
7250D Westfield Ave,
Pennsauken NJ 08110-
4010. 609/665-4454.

PUBLIC GOLF COURSES

Green Hills Golf Course
RR 1, Birdsboro PA
19508-9801. 610/856-
7672.

Rolling Turf Golf Course
Smith Rd, Schwenksville
PA 19473. 610/287-
7297.

**COIN OPERATED
AMUSMENT DEVICES**

Terminal Amusement Co.
301 W Clinton Ave,
Oaklyn NJ 08107-1524.
609/854-2100.

**AMUSEMENT PARKS
AND ARCADES**

**Barnacle Bill's
Amusements**
1968 Grand Central Av,
Seaside Hgts NJ 08751.
908/793-9345.

Belle Freeman Estate
Dupont Av & Bdwk,
Seaside Hgts NJ 08751.
908/793-1046.

Big Hearted John
617 Boardwalk, Seaside
Hgts NJ 08751-2103.
908/793-2223.

Casey's Amusements
Boardwalk & Arnold Av,
Pt Pleas Bch NJ 08742.
908/899-6864.

Central Arcade
401 Boardwalk, Seaside
Hgts NJ 08751-2509.
908/793-0131.

Coin Castle Amusements
500 Boardwalk, Seaside
Hgts NJ 08751-2512.
908/793-1500.

Dotty's
101 Boardwalk, Seaside
Hgts NJ 08751-2503.
908/793-6816.

**Fantasy Island
Amusement Park**
320 7th St, Beach Haven
NJ 08008-1980.
609/492-4000.

Fun Town Amusements
1802 Boulevard, Seaside
Park NJ 08752-1209.
908/830-1591.

Fun-N-Games Inc.
US Hwy No 9 &
Bayshore Dr, Barnegat
NJ 08005. 609/698-
5200.

Gameland
New Prospect Rd,
Jackson NJ 08527.
908/363-9573.

Great Adventure
Route No 537, Jackson
NJ 08527. 908/928-
2000.

Haven Beach
409 Boardwalk, Pt Pleas
Bch NJ 08742-3280.
908/899-0142.

**Jenkinson's Beach &
Boardwalk**
3 Broadway, Pt Pleas Bch
NJ 08742-2605.
908/892-3274.

Log Flume Ride
Boardwalk, Seaside Park
NJ 08752. 908/830-
5481.

Lucky Arcade
1215 Kearney Av,
Seaside Hgts NJ 08751.
908/793-1565.

Lucky Games Inc.
612 Boardwalk, Pt Pleas
Bch NJ 08742. 908/899-
1808.

Lucky Leo's
215 Boardwalk, Seaside
Hgts NJ 08751-2505.
908/793-1323.

Lucky's Fascination
417 Ocean Ter, Seaside
Hgts NJ 08751-2541.
908/830-2225.

Lucky's Games Inc.
610 Boardwalk, Pt Pleas
Bch NJ 08742. 908/899-
1888.

PW Candy's Playland
240 Chambersbridge Rd,
Brick NJ 08723-2888.
908/262-0600.

Playday Distributors
116 Sumner Ave,
Seaside Hgts NJ 08751-
2326. 908/830-8756.

Seabreeze Baths
617 Boardwalk, Seaside
Hgts NJ 08751-2103.
908/830-4726.

Seaside Amusements
359 E Granada Ave,
Hershey PA 17033-
1346.

Shermat Arcade
1706 Long Beach Blvd,
Beach Haven NJ 08008-
5459. 609/492-0101.

Slot Car Raceway
1200 Route 88,
Lakewood NJ 08701-
4516. 908/370-5344.

South Beach Arcade
610 Ocean Ave, Pt Pleas
Bch NJ 08742-3266.
908/892-5211.

Sports Central
1904 Promenade # A,
Seaside Park NJ 08752-
1241. 908/793-4112.

Strand Skilo
1904 Boardwalk, Seaside
Park NJ 08752-1202.
908/793-0432.

Time-Out
5112 Jonestown Rd,
Harrisburg PA 17112-
4908. 717/540-5423.

Trader Tom's
Boardwalk, Seaside Hgts
NJ 08751. 908/793-
3020.

Water Works
Sherman Av &
Boardwalk, Seaside Hgts
NJ 08751. 908/793-
6495.

**MEMBERSHIP SPORTS
AND RECREATION
CLUBS**

**Atlantic City Country
Club**
Shore Rd, Northfield NJ
08225. 609/641-7575.

Country Club Of York
Country Club Rd Ext,
York PA 17404.
717/843-8078.

Pine Valley Golf Club
Atlantic Av, Clementon
NJ 08021. 609/783-
3000.

**Whitemarsh Valley
Country Club**
Thomas Rd &
Germantown Pke,
Lafayette HI PA 19444.
215/233-3901.

**AMUSEMENT AND
RECREATION SERVICES**

Amber Hill Farms
RR 3, Honey Brook PA
19344-9803. 610/857-
3869.

Casino II Billiards
223 N 2nd St, Harrisburg
PA 17101-1442.
717/234-1650.

**Challenge Miniature Golf
Course**
366 Middletown Rd,
Hummelstown PA
17036-8815. 717/566-
6322.

Doc's Roller Review
1733 E Harrisburg Pike,
Middletown PA 17057-
3825. 717/944-7866.

Ed's Buggys
Rt 896, Strasburg PA
17579. 717/687-0360.

**Great Golf Learning
Center**
600 Righters Ferry Rd,
Bala Cynwyd PA 19004-
1306. 610/667-4450.

Ocean Lottery
44 Brick Plz, Brick NJ
08723-4045. 908/477-
7214.

Scranton Karate School
1702 Pittston Ave,
Scranton PA 18505-
1630. 717/344-0551.

Tilton Billiards
London Square Mall,
Northfield NJ 08225.
609/645-1181.

**ARBORETA AND
BOTANICAL OR
ZOOLOGICAL GARDENS**

**City Parks Association
Inc.**
3201 W Girard Ave,
Philadelphia PA 19130-
1141. 215/763-7901.

**Zoological Society Of
Philadelphia**
34 W Girard Ave,
Philadelphia PA 19123-
1721. 215/387-6400.

For more information on career opportunities in arts, entertainment and recreation:

Associations

ACTOR'S EQUITY ASSOCIATION
165 West 46th Street, New York NY
10036. 212/869-8530.

AFFILIATE ARTISTS
45 West 60th Street, New York NY
10023. 212/246-3889.

**AMERICAN ALLIANCE FOR THEATRE
AND EDUCATION**
Division of Performing Arts, Virginia
Tech, Blacksburg VA 24061-0141.
703/231-5335.

AMERICAN ASSOCIATION OF MUSEUMS
1225 I Street NW, Suite 200, Washington DC 20005. 202/289-1818.

AMERICAN ZOO AND AQUARIUM ASSOCIATION
Oglebay Park, Wheeling WV 26003. 304/242-2160.

AMERICAN COUNCIL FOR THE ARTS
1 East 53rd Street, New York NY 10022. 212/223-2787.

AMERICAN CRAFTS COUNCIL
72 Spring Street, New York NY 10012. 212/274-0630.

AMERICAN DANCE GUILD
31 West 21st Street, New York NY 10010. 212/627-3790.

AMERICAN FEDERATION OF MUSICIANS
1501 Broadway, Suite 600, New York NY 10036. 212/869-1330.

AMERICAN FEDERATION OF TELEVISION AND RADIO ARTISTS
260 Madison Avenue, New York NY 10016. 212/532-0800. Membership required.

AMERICAN FILM INSTITUTE
John F. Kennedy Center for the Performing Arts, Washington DC 20566. 202/828-4000.

AMERICAN GUILD OF MUSICAL ARTISTS
1727 Broadway, New York NY 10019. 212/265-3687.

AMERICAN MUSIC CENTER
30 West 26th Street, Suite 1001, New York NY 10010. 212/366-5260.

AMERICAN SOCIETY OF COMPOSERS, AUTHORS, AND PUBLISHERS
1 Lincoln Plaza, New York NY 10023. 212/595-3050.

AMERICAN SYMPHONY ORCHESTRA LEAGUE
777 14th Street NW, Suite 500, Washington DC 20005. 202/628-0099.

ASSOCIATION OF INDEPENDENT VIDEO AND FILMMAKERS
625 Broadway, 9th Floor, New York NY 10012. 212/473-3400.

NATIONAL ARTISTS' EQUITY ASSOCIATION
P.O. Box 28068, Central Station, Washington DC 20038-8068. 202/628-9633.

NATIONAL DANCE ASSOCIATION
1900 Association Drive, Reston VA 22091. 703/476-3436.

NATIONAL ENDOWMENT FOR THE ARTS
1100 Pennsylvania Avenue NW, Washington DC 20506. 202/682-5400.

NATIONAL ORGANIZATION FOR HUMAN SERVICE EDUCATION
Brookdale Community College, Newman Springs Road, Lyncroft NJ 07738. 908/842-1900, ext. 546.

NATIONAL RECREATION AND PARK ASSOCIATION
2775 South Quincy Street, Suite 300, Arlington VA 22206. 703/820-4940.

PRODUCERS GUILD OF AMERICA
400 South Beverly Drive, Suite 211, Beverly Hills CA 90212. 310/557-0807.

SCREEN ACTORS GUILD
5757 Wilshire Boulevard, Hollywood CA 90036-3600. 213/954-1600.

THEATRE COMMUNICATIONS GROUP
355 Lexington Avenue, New York NY 10017. 212/697-5230.

WOMEN'S CAUCUS FOR ART
Moore College of Art, 20th & The
Parkway, Philadelphia PA 19103.
215/854-0922.

Directories

ARTIST'S MARKET
Writer's Digest Books, 1507 Dana
Avenue, Cincinnati OH 45207.
513/531-2222.

CREATIVE BLACK BOOK
866 3rd Avenue, 3rd Floor, New York
NY 10022. 212/254-1330.

PLAYERS GUIDE
165 West 46th Street, New York NY
10036. 212/869-3570.

ROSS REPORTS TELEVISION
Television Index, Inc., 40-29 27th
Street, Long Island City NY 11101.
718/937-3990.

Magazines

AMERICAN ARTIST
One Astor Place, 1515 Broadway,
New York NY 10036. 212/764-7300.
800/346-0085, ext. 477.

AMERICAN CINEMATOGRAPHER
American Society of
Cinematographers, P.O. Box 2230,
Hollywood CA 90028. 213/969-
4333.

ART BUSINESS NEWS
Myers Publishing Co., 19 Old Kings
Highway South, Darien CT 06820.
203/656-3402.

ART DIRECTION
10 East 39th Street, 6th Floor, New
York NY 10016. 212/889-6500.

ARTFORUM
65 Bleecker Street, New York NY
10012. 212/475-4000.

ARTWEEK
12 South First Street, Suite 520, San
Jose CA 95113. 408/279-2293.

AVISO
American Association of Museums,
1225 I Street NW, Suite 200,
Washington DC 20005. 202/289-
1818.

BACK STAGE
1515 Broadway, New York NY
10036. 212/764-7300.

BILLBOARD
Billboard Publications, Inc., 1515
Broadway, New York NY 10036.
212/764-7300.

CASHBOX
157 West 57th Street, Suite 503,
New York NY 10019. 212/245-4224.

CRAFTS REPORT
300 Water Street, Wilmington DE
19801. 302/656-2209.

DRAMA-LOGUE
P.O. Box 38771, Los Angeles CA
90038. 213/464-5079.

HOLLYWOOD REPORTER
5055 Wilshire Boulevard, 6th Floor,
Los Angeles CA 90036. 213/525-
2000.

VARIETY
249 West 17th Street, New York NY
10011. 212/779-1100.800/323-
4345. Customer Service.

WOMEN ARTIST NEWS
300 Riverside Drive, New York NY
10025. 212/666-6990.

AUTOMOTIVE

 *Because the market for new passenger cars and light trucks in the U.S. is essentially saturated, sales from year to year shouldn't grow much faster than 1 or 2 percent. This saturation level has spurred intense competition. "The severity of the competition has taken its toll on domestic profits," writes the U.S. Department of Commerce. "It also has propelled the industry on a painful, but beneficial, journey to reduce operating expenditures through improvements in manufacturing technology and productivity and reductions in overhead expenses."*

The motor vehicle and parts industry is a key component of the U.S. economy, and makes up a large percentage of direct and indirect employment and industrial output. Over six million people were employed directly and in allied automotive industries in 1991, accounting for 6.2 percent of the nation's nonfarm employment.

ALDERMAN AUTOMOTIVE SERVICE, INC.
2317 North Du Pont Highway, New Castle DE 19720. 302/652-3068. **Contact:** Jane Savino, Personnel Director. **Description:** A Delaware automotive service company.

BANGOR AUTOMOTIVE DIAGNOSTICS
100 Werner Street, Bangor PA 18013-2895. 215/588-4400. **Contact:** John McCoy, Plant Manager. **Description:** Produces a wide range of automotive test equipment. **Corporate headquarters location:** This Location.

CARDONE INDUSTRIES
5670 Rising Sun Avenue, Philadelphia PA 19120. 215/722-9700. **Contact:** Personnel Manager. **Description:** Engaged in automotive reconditioning and rebuilding.

CATERPILLAR INC.
P.O. Box 787, York PA 17402. 717/751-5123. **Contact:** Julie McQuay, Director of Personnel. **Description:** A multinational company which designs, manufactures, and markets products in two principal categories: Earthmoving Equipment, such as bulldozers, graders, and off-highway trucks; and Engines, primarily diesel and gas engines for the company's earthmoving equipment. Maintains 15 plants in the United States, with international operations in Australia, Belgium, Brazil, Canada, France, Mexico, Great Britain, Japan, and India. **Corporate headquarters location:** Peoria IL. **Listed on:** New York Stock Exchange.

CHRYSLER CORPORATION
550 South College Avenue, Newark DE 19713-1302. 302/453-5635. **Contact:** David E. Stepaniak, Personnel Administrator. **Description:** An auto parts warehouse for Chrysler. **Corporate headquarters location:** Detroit MI.

COOPER INDUSTRIES/WAGNER DIVISION
2nd and Jefferson Streets, Boyertown PA 19512. 215/367-2604. **Contact:** Personnel Manager. **Description:** Designs, develops, manufactures, and markets automotive products which are sold to OEMs and auto parts distributors, as well as retailers of replacement parts and equipment. The Boyertown plant manufactures sealed beam headclamps. **Corporate headquarters location:** Parsippany NJ.

DANA CORPORATION
125 South Keim Street, Pottstown PA 19464. 215/323-4200. **Contact:** Human Resources Department. **Description:** Produces motor vehicles and passenger car bodies.

DANA CORPORATION/PARISH DIVISION
P.O. Box 13459, Reading PA 19612-3459. 215/371-7193. **Contact:** Lou Benien, Human Resource Manager. **Description:** Stamps, forms, and bends metal parts used in the assembly of vehicular frames for OEM customers. **Common positions include:** Accountant/Auditor; Blue-Collar Worker Supervisor; Buyer; Computer Programmer; Department Manager; Draftsperson; Electrical/Electronic Engineer; Industrial Engineer; Mechanical Engineer; Operations/Production Manager; Personnel/Labor Relations Specialist; Quality Control Supervisor; Systems Analyst; Transportation/Traffic Specialist. **Educational backgrounds include:** Accounting; Business Administration; Computer Science; Engineering; Finance; Geology. **Benefits:** Dental Insurance; Disability Coverage; Employee Discounts; Life Insurance; Medical Insurance; Pension Plan; Savings Plan; Tuition Assistance. **Special Programs:** Training Programs. **Corporate headquarters location:** Toledo OH. **Operations at this facility include:** Administration; Divisional Headquarters; Manufacturing; Research and Development. **Listed on:** New York Stock Exchange.

GENERAL MOTORS CORPORATION
P.O. Box 1512, Wilmington DE 19899. 302/428-7000. **Contact:** Larry Hayes, Personnel Director. **Description:** An auto assembly plant.

HARLEY-DAVIDSON MOTOR COMPANY, INC.
1425 Eden Road, York PA 17402. 717/848-1177. **Contact:** Carolyn Boyer, Manager of Human Resources. **Description:** Designs, manufactures, and distributes the world-recognized line of motorcycles. **Common positions include:** Accountant/Auditor; Administrator; Buyer; Chemist; Computer Programmer; Electrical/Electronic Engineer; Financial Analyst; General Manager; Industrial Engineer; Mechanical Engineer; Metallurgical Engineer; Operations/Production Manager; Personnel/Labor Relations Specialist; Production Manager; Purchasing Agent and Manager; Statistician; Systems Analyst; Transportation/Traffic Specialist. **Educational backgrounds include:** Accounting; Business Administration; Chemistry; Communications; Computer Science; Engineering; Finance. **Benefits:** Dental Insurance; Disability Coverage; Employee Discounts; Life Insurance; Medical Insurance; Pension Plan; Savings Plan; Tuition Assistance. **Corporate headquarters location:** Milwaukee WI.

JOHNSON MATTHEY INC.
456 Devon Park Drive, Wayne PA 19087. 215/341-8300. **Contact:** Human Resources Department. **Description:** Produces motor vehicle parts and accessories.

MACK TRUCKS, INC.
P.O. Box M, Allentown PA 18105-5000. 215/439-3011. **Contact:** William J. Gmitter, Manager/Employment. **Description:** Manufactures and sells heavy-duty trucks, truck tractors, and truck replacement parts; and provides repair and maintenance service for

these products. One of the largest producers of oversize (over 33,000 pounds) trucks in the United States. **Common positions include:** Accountant/Auditor; Attorney; Blue-Collar Worker Supervisor; Branch Manager; Buyer; Computer Programmer; Department Manager; Draftsperson; Electrical/Electronic Engineer; General Manager; Industrial Engineer; Manufacturer's/ Wholesaler's Sales Rep.; Mechanical Engineer; Operations/Production Manager; Personnel/Labor Relations Specialist; Purchasing Agent and Manager; Quality Control Supervisor; Systems Analyst. **Educational backgrounds include:** Accounting; Business Administration; Communications; Computer Science; Economics; Engineering; Finance; Liberal Arts; Marketing. **Benefits:** Dental Insurance; Disability Coverage; Life Insurance; Medical Insurance; Pension Plan; Savings Plan; Tuition Assistance. **Corporate headquarters location:** This Location. **Operations at this facility include:** Administration. **Number of employees at this location:** 5,400.

NEAPCO, INC.

Queen and Bailey Streets, Pottstown PA 19464. 215/323-6000. **Contact:** Nina Slaybaugh, Personnel Manager. **Description:** Manufactures power driveline components, u-joints, and front wheel drive products. Competes in a worldwide marketplace in the OEM and Aftermarket with customers in automotive, heavy duty, and agricultural lines. Operates a manufacturing facility in Nebraska with distribution centers in Missouri and California. **Common positions include:** Customer Service Representative; Manufacturer's/Wholesaler's Sales Rep.; Mechanical Engineer. **Educational backgrounds include:** Accounting; Business Administration; Engineering. **Benefits:** Dental Insurance; Disability Coverage; Life Insurance; Medical Insurance; Pension Plan; Tuition Assistance. **Corporate headquarters location:** This Location. **Parent company:** UIS, Inc. (New York, NY). **Operations at this facility include:** Manufacturing; Research and Development; Sales.

SUBARU OF AMERICA

Subaru Plaza, P.O. Box 6000, Cherry Hill NJ 08034. 609/488-8500. **Contact:** Monica D. Haley, Vice President of Human Resources. **Description:** Corporate office for the well-known manufacturers for cars and trucks.

UNITED DEFENSE

S.M.C.
P.O. Box 15512, York PA 17405-1512. 717/225-4781. **Contact:** Supervisor/Employee Services. **Description:** Manufactures military tracked-vehicles and personnel carriers. **Common positions include:** Accountant/Auditor; Electrical/Electronic Engineer; Financial Analyst; Mechanical Engineer; Systems Analyst; Technical Writer/Editor. **Educational backgrounds include:** Engineering; Finance. **Corporate headquarters location:** Camp Hill PA. **Operations at this facility include:** Manufacturing. **Listed on:** New York Stock Exchange. **Number of employees nationwide:** 2,000. **Projected hires for the next 12 months (Nationwide):** 12 hires.

Note: Because addresses and telephone numbers of smaller companies change rapidly, we recommend you contact each company and verify the information below before contacting employers. Mass mailings are not recommended.

Additional medium sized employers: under 500

AUTO SUPPLIES AND NEW PARTS WHOLESALE	R&B Inc. 3400 E Walnut St Box 1800, Colmar PA 18915-9768. 215/997-1800.

TRAVEL TRAILERS AND CAMPERS

Skyline Corporation
77 Horseshoe Rd, Leola
PA 17540-1763.
717/656-2111.

Sunline Coach Company
S Muddy Creek Rd,
Denver PA 17517.
215/267-2858.

Thor Industries Of Pennsylvania Inc.
R D 3, Middleburg PA
17842-9803. 717/837-1663.

TANK AND TANK COMPONENTS

General Dynamics Inc.
175 East St, Archbald PA
18403-1326. 717/876-2121.

MOTOR VEHICLES AND PASSENGER CAR BODIES

Edwin L Heim Company
1918 Greenwood St,
Harrisburg PA 17104-2328. 717/233-8711.

Kovatch Mobile Equipment Corporation
One Industrial Complex,
Nesquehoning PA 18240.
717/669-9461.

TRUCK AND BUS BODIES

Accurate Industries
New Brooklyn and
Filbert, Williamstown NJ
08094. 609/629-9222.

Dayton Parts
3500 Indl Pkwy,
Harrisburg PA 17110.
717/255-8500.

Dorsey Trailers Inc.
R D 1, Northumberlnd PA
17857-9801. 717/275-5006.

Grumman-Olson Mayfield
400 Penn Ave, Jermyn
PA 18433-1813.
717/876-4560.

Jerr-Dan Corporation
1080 Hykes Rd,
Greencastle PA 17225-9699. 717/597-7111.

Reading Body Works
Hancock Blvd & Gerry St
Box 14, Reading PA
19611. 610/775-3301.

Simon Ladder Towers
64 Cocalico Creek Rd,
Ephrata PA 17522-9403.
717/859-1176.

TRUCK TRAILERS

Delta Truck Body Co.
PO Box 295, Spring
House PA 19477-0295.
610/584-6800.

Florig Equipment Co
906 W Ridge Pike,
Conshohocken PA
19428-1098. 610/825-0900.

For more information on career opportunities in the automotive industry:

Associations

ASSOCIATION OF INTERNATIONAL AUTOMOBILE MANUFACTURERS
1001 19th Street North, Suite 1200,
Arlington VA 22209. 703/525-7788.

AUTOMOTIVE AFFILIATED REPRESENTATIVES
25 Northwest Point Boulevard, Suite
425, Elk Grove Village IL 6007-1035.
708/228-1310

AUTOMOTIVE SERVICE ASSOCIATION
1901 Airport Freeway, Suite 100,
P.O. Box 929, Bedford TX 76095.
817/283-6205

MOTOR VEHICLE MANUFACTURERS ASSOCIATION
7430 2nd Avenue, Suite 300, Detroit
MI 48202. 313/872-4311.

NATIONAL AUTOMOTIVE PARTS ASSOCIATION
2999 Circle 75 Parkway, Atlanta GA
30339. 404/956-2200.

**NATIONAL INSTITUTE FOR
AUTOMOTIVE SERVICE EXCELLENCE**
13505 Dulles Technology Drive,
Herndon VA 22071. 703/713-3800.

Directories

**AUTOMOTIVE NEWS MARKET DATA
BOOK**
Automotive News, 1400 Woodbridge
Avenue, Detroit MI 48207-3187.
313/446-6000.

WARD'S AUTOMOTIVE YEARBOOK
Ward's Communications, 3000 Town
Center, Suite 2750, Southville, MI
48075. 810/357-0800.

Magazines

AUTOMOTIVE INDUSTRIES
Chilton Book Co., 201 King of Prussia
Road, Radnor PA 19089. 800/695-
1214.

AUTOMOTIVE NEWS
1400 Woodbridge Avenue, Detroit MI
48207. 313/446-6000.

WARD'S AUTO WORLD
Ward's Communications, Inc., 3000
Town Center, Suite 2750, Southville
MI 48075. 810/357-0800.

WARD'S AUTOMOTIVE REPORTS
Ward's Communications, Inc., 3000
Town Center, Suite 2750, Southville
MI 48075. 810/357-0800.

BANKING/SAVINGS AND LOAN

Heading into the mid-1990s, the banking industry is continuing to evolve. The industry began the decade with a series of mega-mergers aimed at solidifying its strongest institutions, and resulting in a series of major layoffs. By the end of 1991, however, commercial banks had rebounded strongly, and the recovery continued through 1992 and 1993. Even so, there is still pressure on legislators and regulators alike to address the banking industry's problems.

Increasingly, banks are facing new competition from mutual funds and other financial services. Competition will most likely take the form of innovation, such as new products and delivery systems; of securitization, such as converting assets into marketable certificates; and of internationalization, such as the elimination of geographic barriers.

BANK AND TRUST COMPANY OF OLD YORK
York & Easton Road, P.O. Box W, Willow Grove PA 19090. 215/659-3400. **Contact:** Human Resources. **Description:** A bank.

BENEFICIAL CORPORATION
301 North Walnut, P.O. Box 911, Wilmington DE 19899-0911. 302/798-0800. **Contact:** Nicki Paloni, Personnel Manager. **Description:** A provider of statewide banking and other financial services. **Corporate headquarters location:** This Location.

BENEFICIAL SAVINGS BANK
White Building, 105 South 12th Street, Philadelphia PA 19107. 215/864-6000. **Contact:** Joseph Vetter, Personnel Manager. **Description:** A full-service savings bank, also offering home mortgaging.

BRYN MAWR BANK CORPORATION
801 Lancaster Avenue, Bryn Mawr PA 19010-3396. 215/526-2300. **Contact:** Human Resources. **Description:** A bank.

CHASE USA
802 Delaware Avenue, Wilmington DE 19801. 302/575-5000. **Contact:** Human Resources. **Description:** A consumer credit bank.

CHELTENHAM BANK
50 Huntingdon Pike, Philadelphia PA 19111. 215/379-1800. **Contact:** Human Resources. **Description:** A bank.

CHESTER VALLEY BANCORP
100 East Lancaster Avenue, Downington PA 19335. 215/269-9700. **Contact:** Human Resources. **Description:** A savings bank.

CITICORP BANKING CORP.
1 Penns Way, New Castle DE 19720. 302/323-3142. **Contact:** Human Resources.
Description: Engaged in mortgage banking.

COLLECTIVE FEDERAL SAVINGS BANK
158 Philadelphia Avenue, Egg Harbor NJ 08215. 609/625-1110. **Contact:** Human Resources. **Description:** A savings and loan.

COMMERCE BANK
17000 Horizon Way, Mt. Laurel NJ 08054. 609/778-1800. **Contact:** Human Resources Department. **Description:** An area bank.

COMMERCE BANK, NA
1701 Route 70 East, Cherry Hill NJ 08034. 609/751-9000. **Contact:** Human Resources. **Description:** A bank.

COMMONWEALTH FEDERAL SAVINGS BANK
70 Valley Stream Parkway, P.O. Box 2100, Valley Forge PA 19482-2100. 215/677-2500. **Contact:** Human Resources. **Description:** A savings bank.

CONTINENTAL BANCORP, INC.
1500 Market Street, Philadelphia PA 19102. 215/564-7000. **Contact:** Personnel Department. **Description:** Operates a bank holding company. **Parent company:** Midlantic Corporation. **Number of employees nationwide:** 3,000.

CORESTATES BANK
P.O. Box 7618, Philadelphia PA 19101. 215/973-7399. **Contact:** Assistant Vice President. **Description:** A banking and financial services company. **Common positions include:** Accountant/Auditor; Bank Officer/Manager; Financial Analyst. **Educational backgrounds include:** Accounting; Business Administration; Finance. **Benefits:** Daycare Assistance; Dental Insurance; Disability Coverage; Employee Discounts; Life Insurance; Medical Insurance; Pension Plan; Savings Plan; Tuition Assistance. **Special Programs:** Training Programs. **Corporate headquarters location:** This Location. **Listed on:** American Stock Exchange.

CORESTATES HAMILTON BANK
1097 Commercial Avenue, Lancaster PA 17601. 717/569-8731. **Contact:** Linda Dellinger, Employment Administrator. **Description:** A full-service commercial banking institution. **Parent company:** Core State Financial Corporation.

DELAWARE TRUST COMPANY
900 Market Street, Wilmington DE 19801. 302/421-7490. **Contact:** Joyce Ackerman, Recruitment. **Description:** Provides statewide banking services. **Common positions include:** Bank Officer/Manager; Branch Manager; Management Trainee. **Educational backgrounds include:** Accounting; Business Administration; Communications; Economics; Finance; Liberal Arts; Marketing. **Benefits:** Dental Insurance; Disability Coverage; Life Insurance; Medical Insurance; Pension Plan; Savings Plan; Tuition Assistance. **Special Programs:** Internships; Training Programs. **Corporate headquarters location:** Reading PA. **Parent company:** Meridian Bancorp.

FARMERS BANK & TRUST
13 Baltimore Street, Hanover PA 17331. 717/637-2291. **Contact:** Human Resources.
Description: A bank holding company.

FEDERAL RESERVE BANK OF PHILADELPHIA

100 North Sixth Street, Philadelphia PA 19106. 215/574-6000. **Contact:** Personnel Department. **Description:** One of 12 banks which, along with the Board of Governors in Washington DC, form the Federal Reserve System, the nation's central bank. Three major responsibilites include formulating and executing monetary policy; maintaining a safe, sound, and competitive banking system; and ensuring the safety, solvency and certainty of the nation's payment mechanism. Major organizational units include Bank Supervision; Economic Research; Operations; and Management Planning and Support. **Number of employees nationwide:** 1,179.

FIDELITY BANK

123 South Broad Street, 19th Floor, Philadelphia PA 19109. 215/985-8777. **Contact:** Marlene A. Prolejko, Human Resources Representative. **Description:** Provides a wide range of banking and related financial services. **Common positions include:** Accountant/Auditor; Computer Programmer; Customer Service Representative; Financial Analyst; Management Trainee. **Educational backgrounds include:** Accounting; Business Administration; Liberal Arts. **Benefits:** Dental Insurance; Disability Coverage; Employee Discounts; Life Insurance; Medical Insurance; Pension Plan; Savings Plan; Tuition Assistance. **Special Programs:** Training Programs. **Corporate headquarters location:** This Location. **Parent company:** First Fidelity Bancorporation. **Listed on:** New York Stock Exchange.

FIRST FIDELITY BANK

667 Welsh Road, Huntingdon Valley PA 19006. 215/572-2727. **Contact:** Human Resources. **Description:** A bank.

FIRST VALLEY BANK

One Bethlehem Plaza, Bethlehem PA 18018. 215/865-8752. **FAX:** 215/865-8829. **Contact:** E. Kent Frazier, Assistant V.P./Human Resources. **Description:** A holding company with $12.9 billion in assets; banking offices are located in New Jersey and in eastern Pennsylvania. A subsidiary of UJB Financial Corporation, which provides financial services to individuals, businesses, non-profit organizations, government offices, and other financial institutions. **Number of employees nationwide:** 1,200.

FRANKFORD BANK

601 Dresher Road, Horsham PA 19044. 215/956-7016. **Contact:** Ms. Christiann Griffith, Human Resources Administrator. **Description:** A full-service banking institution. **Common positions include:** Accountant/Auditor; Bank Officer/Manager; Customer Service Representative. **Educational backgrounds include:** Accounting; Finance. **Benefits:** Employee Discounts; Life Insurance; Medical Insurance; Pension Plan; Tuition Assistance. **Special Programs:** Training Programs. **Corporate headquarters location:** This Location.

FULTON BANK

One Penn Square, Lancaster PA 17602. 717/291-2411. **Contact:** Human Resources. **Description:** A bank.

GERMANTOWN SAVINGS BANK

4275 County Line Road, Chalfont PA 18914. 215/997-8510. **Contact:** Human Resources. **Description:** A savings bank.

GERMANTOWN SAVINGS BANK

One Belmont Avenue, Bala Cynwyd PA 19004-1646. 215/667-9300. **Contact:** Human Resources. **Description:** A savings bank.

INDEPENDENCE BANCORP INCORPORATED
1 Hillendale Road, Perkasie PA 18944. 215/453-3000. **Contact:** Human Resources. **Description:** A bank.

JEFFERSON BANK
Independence Square, 5th & Chestnut Street, Philadelphia PA 19106. 215/627-1400. **Contact:** Human Resources. **Description:** A bank.

JEFFERSON BANK
31 South 18th Street, Philadelphia PA 19103. 215/564-2095. **Contact:** Human Resources. **Description:** A bank.

LEBANON VALLEY NATIONAL BANK
P.O. Box 1285, 555 Willow Street, Lebanon PA 17042-1285. 717/274-6800. **Contact:** Human Resources. **Description:** A bank.

MBNA AMERICA
400 Christiana Road, Newark DE 19713. 302/453-6244. **Contact:** Employment Office. **Description:** A national banking institution offering credit card services. **Common positions include:** Bank Officer/Manager; Collections Agent; Customer Service Representative; Financial Analyst. **Educational backgrounds include:** Business Administration; Liberal Arts. **Benefits:** 401K; Daycare Assistance; Dental Insurance; Disability Coverage; Employee Discounts; Life Insurance; Medical Insurance; Pension Plan; Savings Plan; Tuition Assistance. **Special Programs:** Internships; Training Programs. **Corporate headquarters location:** This Location. **Operations at this facility include:** Administration; Service. **Listed on:** New York Stock Exchange.

MELLON BANK
P.O. Box 7899, Mellon Bank East, Mellon Independence Center, Philadelphia PA 19101-7899. 215/553-3000. **Contact:** Human Resources. **Description:** Operates a full-service bank. **Corporate headquarters location:** This Location.

MELLON BANK
5607 Vine Street, Philadelphia PA 19139. 215/472-6020. **Contact:** Human Resources. **Description:** A bank.

MELLON BANK
Eight West Market Street, Wilkes Barre PA 18711. 717/826-2611. **Contact:** Human Resources. **Description:** A bank.

MELLON BANK/DELAWARE
4500 New Linden Hill Road, Wilmington DE 19808. **Contact:** Truee Jennings, Employment Recruiter. **Description:** Provides statewide banking services.

MELLON P.S.F.S.
330 Oregon, Philadelphia PA 19148. 215/336-4104. **Contact:** Human Resources. **Description:** A savings bank.

MELLON P.S.F.S.
55 Franklin Boulevard, Philadelphia PA 19154. 215/637-7419. **Contact:** Human Resources. **Description:** A savings bank.

MERIDIAN BANCORP, INC.
P.O. Box 7588, Penn Center 1605, Philadelphia PA 19101. 215/854-3300. **Contact:** Christopher A. Cardarelli, Human Resources Officer. **Description:** A diversified multi-state, multi-bank financial services company which primarily serves the southeastern/south-central part of Pennsylvania. Meridian offers a Management Training program that consists of 18 to 24 months of on-the-job training. The company offers an array of entry-level opportunities primarily in the areas of Retail Branch Management, Corporate Lending, and Data Processing. **Common positions include:** Bank Officer/Manager; Branch Manager; Computer Programmer; Customer Service Representative; Department Manager; Financial Analyst; Management Trainee; Systems Analyst. **Educational backgrounds include:** Accounting; Business Administration; Computer Science; Economics; Finance; Liberal Arts; Mathematics. **Benefits:** Daycare Assistance; Dental Insurance; Disability Coverage; Employee Discounts; Life Insurance; Medical Insurance; Pension Plan; Savings Plan; Tuition Assistance. **Special Programs:** Internships; Training Programs. **Operations at this facility include:** Divisional Headquarters.

MERIDIAN BANCORP, INC.
1 Meridan Boulevard, Wyomissing PA 19610. 215/655-2000. **Contact:** Human Resources. **Description:** A bank.

MERIDIAN BANCORP, INC.
Route 512 & Jacobsburg Road, Wind Gap PA 18091. 215/759-2977. **Contact:** Human Resources. **Description:** A bank.

J.P. MORGAN DELAWARE
A SUBSIDIARY OF J.P. MORGAN CO. INC.
500 Stanton Christiana Road, Newark DE 19713-2107. 302/634-1040. **Contact:** Colette C. Matsanka, Human Resources Department. **Description:** Engaged in money center banking. **Common positions include:** Customer Service Representative. **Benefits:** Dental Insurance; Disability Coverage; Employee Discounts; Life Insurance; Medical Insurance; Profit Sharing; Tuition Assistance. **Special Programs:** Internships; Training Programs. **Number of employees at this location:** 1,000. **Projected hires for the next 12 months (This location):** 100 hires.

NATIONAL PENN BANK
P.O. Box 547, Boyertown PA 19512. 215/367-6001. **Contact:** Human Resources. **Description:** A bank.

NATWEST
200 East State Street, Trenton NJ 08608. **Contact:** Louis J. Foery, Branch Manager. **Description:** Toll free phone: 800/333-5922. A full-service bank.

PNC BANK
Penn Avenue & Spruce Street, Scranton PA 18503. 717/961-6520. **Contact:** Human Resources. **Description:** A bank.

PNC BANK
18 South Bryn Mawr, Bryn Mawr PA 19010. 215/527-3165. **Contact:** Human Resources. **Description:** A bank.

PNC BANK
Airport Business Center, 200 Stevens Drive, Suite 110, Lester PA 19113. 215/521-7800. **Contact:** Maureen Crawford, Human Resources Manager. **Description:** A bank.

PNC BANK
505 Wilmington-Westchester Pike, Glen Mills PA 19342. 215/558-2630. **Contact:** Human Resources. **Description:** A bank.

PNC BANK/DELAWARE
222 Delaware Avenue, Wilmington DE 19801. 302/429-1679. **Contact:** Catherine W. Ford, Assistant V.P./Human Resources. **Description:** A commercial banking institution. **Common positions include:** Accountant/Auditor; Administrator; Advertising Clerk; Bank Officer/Manager; Branch Manager; Claim Representative; Credit Manager; Customer Service Representative; Department Manager; Economist/Market Research Analyst; Financial Analyst; Management Trainee; Marketing Specialist; Public Relations Specialist; Purchasing Agent and Manager; Services Sales Representative. **Educational backgrounds include:** Accounting; Business Administration; Economics; Finance; Marketing. **Benefits:** Dental Insurance; Disability Coverage; Life Insurance; Medical Insurance; Pension Plan; Savings Plan; Tuition Assistance. **Corporate headquarters location:** This Location.

PENNSYLVANIA NATIONAL BANK & TRUST COMPANY
P.O. Box 1150, Pottsville PA 17901. 717/622-4200. **Contact:** Human Resources. **Description:** A bank.

PHILADELPHIA NATIONAL BANK/CORESTATES
P.O. Box 7558, 1500 Market Street, Philadelphia PA 19101. 215/973-7399. **Contact:** Vickie Passfeld, Assistant Vice President. **Description:** A full-service bank, managing $22 billion in assets. **Parent company:** CoreStates, N.A. **Number of employees at this location:** 12,000.

PROVIDENT NATIONAL BANK
P.O. Box 7648, Philadelphia PA 19101. 215/585-6588. **Contact:** George T. Huddleston, Jr., Vice President. **Description:** Job Line: 800/PNC-JOBS. Offers complete banking services. **Common positions include:** Accountant/Auditor; Branch Manager; Financial Analyst; Lender; Management Trainee. **Educational backgrounds include:** Accounting; Business Administration; Finance; Marketing. **Benefits:** Dental Insurance; Disability Coverage; Employee Discounts; Life Insurance; Medical Insurance; Pension Plan; Profit Sharing; Savings Plan; Tuition Assistance. **Corporate headquarters location:** Pittsburgh PA. **Parent company:** PNC Corporation. **Operations at this facility include:** Administration; Divisional Headquarters; Regional Headquarters. **Listed on:** NASDAQ.

ROYAL BANK OF PENNSYLANIA
732 Montgomery Avenue, Narberth PA 19072. 215/668-4700. **Contact:** Human Resources. **Description:** A bank.

SOUTHERN OCEAN STATE BANK
P.O. Box 337, Manahawkin NJ 08050. 609/597-1800. **Contact:** Human Resources. **Description:** A bank.

SOVEREIGN BANK
P.O. Box 37, Reading PA 19603. 215/320-8400. **Contact:** Human Resources. **Description:** A savings and loan.

UNION NATIONAL BANK AND TRUST COMPANY
14 Main Street, Souderton PA 18964. 215/242-4814. **Contact:** Human Resources. **Description:** A bank.

UNITED JERSEY BANKS
P.O. Box 2066, Princeton NJ 08543. 609/987-3200. **Contact:** James N. Ferrier, Manpower Planning/Staffing Manager. **Description:** A multi-bank holding company with 115 branch banking offices located throughout the state. **Corporate headquarters location:** This Location.

WILMINGTON SAVINGS FUND SOCIETY, FSB
838 Market Street, Wilmington DE 19801. 302/571-7227. **Contact:** Donna Agnew, Human Resources Generalist. **Description:** A Wilmington savings bank with two subsidiaries. Manages $1.2 billion in assets. **Common positions include:** Accountant/Auditor; Administrator; Bank Officer/Manager; Branch Manager; Credit Manager; Customer Service Representative; Department Manager; General Manager; Purchasing Agent and Manager; Services Sales Representative. **Educational backgrounds include:** Accounting; Business Administration; Communications; Economics; Liberal Arts. **Benefits:** Daycare Assistance; Dental Insurance; Disability Coverage; Life Insurance; Medical Insurance; Savings Plan; Tuition Assistance. **Corporate headquarters location:** This Location. **Parent company:** WSFS Financial Corporation. **Listed on:** NASDAQ. **Number of employees nationwide:** 400. **Projected hires for the next 12 months (Nationwide):** 25 hires.

WILMINGTON TRUST CORPORATION
Wilmington Trust Center, Wilmington DE 19890. 302/651-1000. **Contact:** Human Resources. **Description:** Wilmington Trust Corporation is the holding company for Wilmington Trust Company, a provider of banking and related financial services to businesses in the state of Delaware and the surrounding region. The Trust Company provides services including commercial lending, cash management systems, and investment management. Wilmington is among the largest precious metals depositories in the U.S.

YORK FEDERAL SAVINGS & LOAN ASSOCIATION
P.O. Box 15068, York PA 17405. 717/846-8777. **Contact:** Human Resources. **Description:** A savings and loan.

Note: Because addresses and telephone numbers of smaller companies change rapidly, we recommend you contact each company and verify the information below before contacting employers. Mass mailings are not recommended.

Additional large employers: 500 +

BANKS

Hamilton Bank
100 N Queen St., Lancaster PA 17603-3500. 717/569-8731.

Merchants Bank
702 Hamilton Mall, Allentown PA 18101-2419. 610/821-7322.

New Jersey Nat'l Bank
370 Scotch Rd., Trenton NJ 08628-1301. 609/771-5700.

Northeastern Bank
Penn Ave. & Spruce St., Scranton PA 18503. 717/961-6520.

Bucks County Bank & Trust Co.
7th & Chestnut, Perkasie PA 18944. 215/453-3000.

Dauphin Deposit Bank & Trust Co.
P.O. Box 2961,
Harrisburg PA 17105-2961. 717/255-2121.

Northern Central Bank
102 W 4th St.,
Williamsport PA 17701-6132. 717/326-2611.

Philadelphia Depository Trust Company
1900 Market St.,
Philadelphia PA 19103-3527. 215/496-5005.

CREDIT UNIONS

Bachman Employees Credit Union
P.O. Box 15053, Reading PA 19612-5053.
610/929-6885.

Corning Greencastle Credit Union
6775 Antrim Way,
Greencastle PA 17225.
717/597-6206.

Ingersoll Rand Fed. Credit Union
199 N Main St., Athens PA 18810-1707.
717/888-7121.

Mobil Fed. Credit Union 1166
Billingsport Rd.,
Paulsboro NJ 08066.
609/423-1456.

Topps Employees Credit Union
401 York Ave., Pittston PA 18642-2025.
717/457-6761.

WFAS Employees Credit Union
780 5th Ave., Kng Of Prussa PA 19406-1437.
610/337-3855.

Whitehall Hammonton Credit Union
999 S Grand St.,
Hammonton NJ 08037-8434. 609/561-2200.

Flinchbaugh Credit Union
200 E High St., Red Lion PA 17356-1426.
717/244-4551.

Additional medium sized employers: under 500

OFFICES OF BANK HOLDING COMPANIES

Commerce Bancorp
PO Box 129, Forest City PA 18421-0129.
717/785-3181.

Commerce Bancorp Incorporated
1701 Rte 70 E, Cherry Hill NJ 08003-2306.
609/751-9000.

Drovers Bancshares Corporation
30 S George St, York PA 17401-1440. 717/843-1586.

Execufirst Bancorp Inc.
1513 Walnut St,
Philadelphia PA 19102-3001. 610/861-2811.

FB&T Corporation
13 Baltimore St, Hanover PA 17331-3109.
717/637-2291.

First Jermyn Corporation
645 Washington Ave,
Jermyn PA 18433-1612.
717/876-1050.

Fms Financial Corporation
Sunset & Salem Rds,
Burlington NJ 08016.
609/386-2400.

Glendale Bancorporation
1099 White Horse Rd,
Voorhees NJ 08043-4405. 609/346-8400.

Harmonia Bancorp Inc.
36 Washington St, Toms River NJ 08753-7643.

Pioneer American Holding Co Corporation
41 N Main St,
Carbondale PA 18407-2357. 717/282-2662.

Regent Bancshares Corporation
1430 Walnut St,
Philadelphia PA 19102-4016. 215/546-6500.

United Federal Bancorp
1631 S Atherton St,
State College PA 16801-6210. 814/231-1600.

OFFICES OF HOLDING COMPANIES

Community Banks Inc. Pennsylvania
150 Market St,
Millersburg PA 17061-1330. 717/692-4781.

MC Enterprises Inc.
6722 Bustleton Ave,
Philadelphia PA 19149-
2301. 215/624-6000.

Penn Fuel Gas Inc.
55 S 3rd St, Oxford PA
19363-1602. 610/932-
2000.

Sovereign Bancorp Inc.
1130 Berkshire Blvd Box
37, Reading PA 19610-
1200. 610/320-8400.

Thomas Cook Inc.
3 Independence Way,
Princeton NJ 08540-
6667. 609/987-7200.

Turtle Industries
1903 N Keim St,
Pottstown PA 19464-
2015. 610/327-2332.

**NATIONAL
COMMERCIAL BANKS**

Bank Hapoalim
3 Penn Center Plz,
Philadelphia PA 19102-
1957. 215/665-0930.

**Borinquen Federal Credit
Union**
2757 N 5th St,
Philadelphia PA 19133-
2702. 215/425-8119.

**Chestnut Hill National
Bank**
9 W Evergreen Ave,
Philadelphia PA 19118-
3314. 215/247-4800.

**Chestnut Hill National
Bank**
3617 Midvale Ave,
Philadelphia PA 19129-
1712. 215/848-3100.

Constitution Bank
1100 Walnut St,
Philadelphia PA 19107-
5502. 215/627-5666.

Continental Bank
17 St & J F Kennedy
Blvd, Philadelphia PA
19103. 215/563-9027.

Fidelity Bank
1601 Walnut St,
Philadelphia PA 19102-
2916. 215/496-4200.

Fidelity Bank
1700 Market St Bldg
1stfl, Philadelphia PA
19103-3913. 215/496-
4120.

Fidelity Bank
417 W Olney Ave,
Philadelphia PA 19120-
2381. 215/549-9600.

Fidelity Bank
136 W Girard Ave,
Philadelphia PA 19123-
1623. 215/922-7770.

Fidelity Bank
2401 Pennsylvania Ave,
Philadelphia PA 19130-
3061. 215/763-6225.

Fidelity Bank
18 E Walnut Ln,
Philadelphia PA 19144-
2003. 215/985-8281.

First National Trust Bank
400 Market St, Sunbury
PA 17801-2336.
717/286-6781.

Firstrust Savings Bank
9309 Krewstown Rd,
Philadelphia PA 19115-
3734. 215/673-6673.

Frankford Corporation
601 Dresher Rd,
Horsham PA 19044-
2202. 215/956-7006.

Hazleton National Bank
101 W Broad St Box
518, Hazleton PA
18201-6397. 717/459-
4211.

Jefferson Bank
31 S 18th St,
Philadelphia PA 19103-
4138. 215/564-3755.

Jefferson Bank
5th & Chestnut,
Philadelphia PA 19123-
2896. 215/627-1400.

Keystone Heritage Group
555 Willow St, Lebanon
PA 17046-4869.
717/274-6800.

Knoblauch Private Bank
1631 Locust St,
Philadelphia PA 19103-
6304. 215/546-0555.

Miners National Bancorp
120 S Centre St,
Pottsville PA 17901-
3002. 717/622-2320.

**National Bank Of
Boyertown**
PO Box 547, Boyertown
PA 19512-0547.
610/367-6001.

**Nazareth National Bank &
Trust Co.**
76 S Main St, Nazareth
PA 18064-2053.
610/746-7300.

Ocean National Bank
501 Arnold Ave, Pt Pleas
Bch NJ 08742-2501.
908/892-1900.

Pennsylvania Savings Bank
10 & Catherine Sts,
Philadelphia PA 19147.
215/922-0700.

Prime Bancorp Inc.
6425 Rising Sun Ave,
Philadelphia PA 19111-5228. 215/742-5300.

Prime Savings Bank
723 Street Rd,
Southampton PA 18966-3989. 215/357-9090.

Progress Federal Savings Bank
600 W Germantown Pike, Plymouth Mtng PA 19462-1046. 610/825-8800.

Sigma American Corporation
PO Box 7378,
Philadelphia PA 19101-7378.

The Yardville National Bank
PO Box 8487, Trenton NJ 08650-0487.
609/585-5100.

Third Natl Bank & Trust Co Scranton
130 Wyoming Ave,
Scranton PA 18503-2020. 717/348-8230.

United Hands Community Land Trust
2200 N 2nd St,
Philadelphia PA 19133-3301. 215/425-7602.

Univest Corporation Of Pennsylvania
Univest Plaza Broad & Main Sts, Souderton PA 18964. 215/721-2400.

Valley Bank & Trust Company
55 S Main St,
Chambersburg PA 17201-2262. 717/263-2265.

1st Nationwide Bank
900 Orthodox St,
Philadelphia PA 19124-3128. 215/288-2802.

1st Nationwide Bank
8801 Torresdale Ave,
Philadelphia PA 19136-1510. 215/332-5548.

STATE COMMERCIAL BANKS

A Midlantic Bank
1201 Chestnut St,
Philadelphia PA 19107-4123.

A Midlantic Bank
Broad & Tasker Sts,
Philadelphia PA 19110-1083.

A Midlantic Bank
510 West Marshall St,
Philadelphia PA 19123-3504.

A Midlantic Bank
205 E High St,
Philadelphia PA 19144-1101.

A Midlantic Bank
1544 Packer Ave,
Philadelphia PA 19145-5407.

A Midlantic Bank
1740 South St,
Philadelphia PA 19146-1529.

A Midlantic Bank
6735 Harbison Ave,
Philadelphia PA 19149-2305.

A Midlantic Bank
8344 Bustleton Ave,
Philadelphia PA 19152-1909.

A Midlantic Bank
12300 Academy Rd,
Philadelphia PA 19154-1928.

ACNB Corporation
675 Old Harrisburg Rd,
Gettysburg PA 17325-3400. 717/334-3161.

BMJ Financial Corporation
PO Box 1001,
Bordentown NJ 08505-1001. 609/298-5500.

Bank and Trust Co Old York Rd
235 S 15th St,
Philadelphia PA 19102-5033. 215/985-4446.

Bank and Trust Co Old York Rd
5031 Tacony St,
Philadelphia PA 19137.
215/535-0330.

Bank Hapoalim
1515 Market Street,
Philadelphia PA 19102-1957. 215/665-2200.

Bank Leumi
1511 Walnut St,
Philadelphia PA 19102-3089.

Brown Brothers Harriman & Co
1531 Walnut St,
Philadelphia PA 19102-3001.

Central Pennsylvania Savings Assn.
2820 W Girard Ave, Philadelphia PA 19130-1215. 215/769-2826.

Citizens & Northern Bank
PO Box 10, Ralston PA 17763-0010. 717/724-3411.

Commonwealth Federal Savings Bank
2501 Welsh Rd, Philadelphia PA 19114-3203. 215/677-2500.

Commonwealth Federal Savings Bank
7149 Frankford Ave, Philadelphia PA 19135-1008. 215/333-9300.

Constitution Bank
110-20 N 17th St, Philadelphia PA 19103. 215/977-9500.

Constitution Bank
1608 Walnut St, Philadelphia PA 19103-5457. 215/545-5450.

Crusader Savings Bank
6526 Castor Ave, Philadelphia PA 19149-2709.

Daiwa Bank
1650 Market St Ste 2860, Philadelphia PA 19103-7301. 215/636-4440.

Farmers Trust Bank
817 Cumberland Street, Lebanon PA 17042-5238. 717/274-6500.

Fidelity Fed Savings & Loan Assn.
7425 Frankford Ave, Philadelphia PA 19136-3932.

Financial Trust Corporation
1 W High St, Carlisle PA 17013-2951. 717/243-3212.

First Bank Of Philadelphia
1760 Market St, Philadelphia PA 19103-4134. 215/568-4700.

First Commercial Bank Of Philadelphia
1027 Arch St, Philadelphia PA 19107-2317. 215/592-0700.

First Executive Bank
1513 Walnut St, Philadelphia PA 19102-3001. 215/564-3300.

First Fidelity Bank Natl Assn. Pennsylvania
1601 Walnut St, Philadelphia PA 19102-2916. 215/985-6000.

First Fidelity Bank Natl Assn. Pennsylvania
8580 Verree Rd, Philadelphia PA 19111-1370. 215/985-6000.

First Fidelity Bank Natl Assn. Pennsylvania
11730 Bustleton Ave, Philadelphia PA 19116-2516. 215/985-6000.

First Fidelity Bank Natl Assn. Pennsylvania
417 W Olney Ave, Philadelphia PA 19120-2311. 215/985-6000.

First Fidelity Bank Natl Assn. Pennsylvania
136 W Girard Ave, Philadelphia PA 19123-1623. 215/985-6000.

First Fidelity Bank Natl Assn. Pennsylvania
600 E Cathedral Rd, Philadelphia PA 19128-1933. 215/985-6000.

First Fidelity Bank Natl Assn. Pennsylvania
2401 Pennsylvania Ave, Philadelphia PA 19130-3061. 215/985-6000.

First Fidelity Bank Natl Assn. Pennsylvania
2120 E Allegheny Ave, Philadelphia PA 19134-3802. 215/985-6000.

First Fidelity Bank Natl Assn. Pennsylvania
8423 Frankford Ave, Philadelphia PA 19136-2420. 215/985-6000.

First Fidelity Bank Natl Assn. Pennsylvania
16th St & J F K Blvd, Philadelphia PA 19146-1596. 215/985-6000.

First Fidelity Bank Natl Assn. Pennsylvania
7048 Castor Ave, Philadelphia PA 19149-1713. 215/985-6000.

First Fidelity Bank Natl Assn. Pennsylvania
1620 Wadsworth Ave, Philadelphia PA 19150-1020. 215/985-6000.

First Fidelity Bank Natl Assn. Pennsylvania
7636 City Ave, Philadelphia PA 19151-2007. 215/985-6000.

First Fidelity Bank Natl Assn. Pennsylvania
8200 Castor Ave, Philadelphia PA 19152-2719. 215/985-6000.

First Fidelity Bank Natl Assn. Pennsylvania
4170 Woodhaven Rd,
Philadelphia PA 19154-2821. 215/985-6000.

First Pennsylvania Bank
PO Box 13616,
Philadelphia PA 19101-3616. 215/786-8014.

First Pennsylvania Bank
1835 Market St,
Philadelphia PA 19103-2968. 215/972-7048.

First Pennsylvania Bank
2005 Market St,
Philadelphia PA 19103-7042. 215/569-1803.

First Pennsylvania Bank
10168 Bustleton Ave,
Philadelphia PA 19116-3704. 215/676-5566.

First Pennsylvania Bank
8527 Germantown Ave,
Philadelphia PA 19118-3375. 215/242-4110.

First Pennsylvania Bank
6740 Germantown Ave,
Philadelphia PA 19119-2192. 215/843-3266.

First Pennsylvania Bank
2 W Girard Ave,
Philadelphia PA 19123-1798. 215/739-4300.

First Pennsylvania Bank
2627 Germantown Ave,
Philadelphia PA 19133-1618. 215/223-3066.

First Pennsylvania Bank
861 E Allegheny Ave,
Philadelphia PA 19134-2493. 215/425-8000.

First Pennsylvania Bank
101 E Allegheny Ave,
Philadelphia PA 19134-2206. 215/425-9500.

First Pennsylvania Bank
7157 Frankford Ave,
Philadelphia PA 19135-1008. 215/624-7900.

First Pennsylvania Bank
8001 Frankford Ave,
Philadelphia PA 19136-2736. 215/624-1000.

First Pennsylvania Bank
1444 W Passyunk Ave,
Philadelphia PA 19145-2399. 215/336-5700.

First Pennsylvania Bank
420 Bainbridge St,
Philadelphia PA 19147-1587. 215/923-9065.

First Pennsylvania Bank
7345 Bustleton Ave,
Philadelphia PA 19152-4310. 215/335-0700.

First Valley Bank
9501 Bustleton Ave,
Philadelphia PA 19115-3801. 215/464-6431.

Firstrust Savings Bank
21 S 5th St, Philadelphia
PA 19106-2515.
215/592-0130.

Firstrust Savings Bank
1332 Point Breeze Ave,
Philadelphia PA 19146-4317. 215/468-3300.

Fox Chase Federal Savings Bank
401 Rhawn St,
Philadelphia PA 19111-2295. 215/342-3700.

Frankford Trust Co.
4400 Frankford Ave,
Philadelphia PA 19124-3637. 215/831-6400.

Frankford Trust Company
2417 Welsh Rd,
Philadelphia PA 19114-2213. 215/552-9848.

Frankford Trust Company
9375 Bustleton Ave,
Philadelphia PA 19115-4606. 215/673-5200.

Frankford Trust Company
7121 Frankford Ave,
Philadelphia PA 19135-1008. 215/331-1910.

Glendale Bank Of Pennsylvania
230 S Broad St,
Philadelphia PA 19102-4121. 610/352-1500.

Gorgas Savings Association
1515 Market St 1806,
Philadelphia PA 19102-1918. 215/568-5340.

Hometown Building & Loan Assn.
4384 Manayunk Ave,
Philadelphia PA 19128-4831. 215/483-9630.

Jefferson Bank
1607 Walnut St,
Philadelphia PA 19103-5402.

Jefferson Bank
4312 Main St,
Philadelphia PA 19127-1529.

Jefferson Bank
2300 S Broad St,
Philadelphia PA 19145-4417.

Jefferson Bank
Second & South St,
Philadelphia PA 19147.

**Jefferson Bank
Downingtown
Pennsylvania**
250 S 18th St,
Philadelphia PA 19103.
215/564-2095.

Juniata Valley Bank
2 S Main St, Mifflintown
PA 17059-1313.
717/436-8211.

Metro Bank
1528 Walnut St,
Philadelphia PA 19102-
3685. 215/545-9000.

**Osla Savings and Loan
Assn**
414 Walnut St 4th Floor,
Philadelphia PA 19106-
3748. 215/592-1713.

**Penn Security Bank &
Trust Co**
150 N Washington Ave,
Scranton PA 18503-
1848. 717/346-7741.

**Pennsylvania Savings
Bank**
Broad & Porter Sts,
Philadelphia PA 19110-
1083.

**Pennsylvania Savings
Bank**
1210 Tasker St,
Philadelphia PA 19148-
1019. 215/465-3000.

**Pennsylvania Savings
Bank**
1833 E Passyunk Ave,
Philadelphia PA 19148-
2127.

**Peoples National Bank
Central Pennsylvania**
117 S Allen St, State
College PA 16801-4752.
814/237-7641.

**PNC Bank National
Association**
4242 Carlisle Pike, Camp
Hill PA 17011. 717/730-
2300.

**PNC Bank National
Association**
1818 Market St,
Philadelphia PA 19103-
3638.

**PNC Bank National
Association**
Broad & Chestnut Sts,
Philadelphia PA 19110-
1083.

**PNC Bank National
Association**
6500 Tabor Rd,
Philadelphia PA 19111-
5332. 215/697-8013.

**PNC Bank National
Association**
9906 Roosevelt Blvd,
Philadelphia PA 19115-
1705. 215/934-6300.

**PNC Bank National
Association**
11830 Bustleton Ave,
Philadelphia PA 19116-
2538.

**PNC Bank National
Association**
8705 Germantown Ave,
Philadelphia PA 19118-
2716.

**PNC Bank National
Association**
401 W Tabor Rd,
Philadelphia PA 19120-
2809. 215/224-6100.

**PNC Bank National
Association**
Erie & I, Philadelphia PA
19124.

**PNC Bank National
Association**
150 W Chelten Ave,
Philadelphia PA 19144-
3302.

**PNC Bank National
Association**
326 S St, Philadelphia PA
19147-1536.

**PNC Bank National
Association**
2200 Cottman Ave,
Philadelphia PA 19149-
1203.

Port Richmond Savings
2522 E Allegheny Ave,
Philadelphia PA 19134-
5197. 215/634-7000.

Prime Bank
1000 Cottman Ave,
Philadelphia PA 19111-
3644. 215/342-2425.

Prime Bank
1695 Grant Ave,
Philadelphia PA 19115-
3149. 215/673-9600.

Prime Bank
14425 Bustleton Ave,
Philadelphia PA 19116.
215/671-1232.

Prime Bank
423 E Girard Ave,
Philadelphia PA 19125-
3305. 215/426-3303.

**Progress Federal Savings
Bank**
Andora Shpg Center,
Philadelphia PA 19128.
215/483-0450.

**Prudential Savings
Association**
112 S 19th St,
Philadelphia PA 19103-
4629.

**Prudential Savings
Association**
1834 W Oregon Ave,
Philadelphia PA 19145-
4725. 215/755-1500.

**Prudential Savings
Association**
238 Moore St,
Philadelphia PA 19148-
1925.

**Prudential Savings
Association**
1903 S Broad St,
Philadelphia PA 19148-
2297.

Republic Bank
1515 Market St,
Philadelphia PA 19102-
2094. 215/563-3600.

**Roxborough Manayunk
Fed Savings**
4349 Main St,
Philadelphia PA 19127-
1415. 215/483-1500.

**Roxborough Manayunk
Fed Savings**
6060 Ridge Ave,
Philadelphia PA 19128-
1696. 215/483-2800.

**Roxborough Manayunk
Fed Savings**
8345 Ridge Ave,
Philadelphia PA 19128-
2113. 215/483-1200.

**Roxborough Manayunk
Fed Savings**
6503-15 Haverford Ave,
Philadelphia PA 19151.
215/748-6312.

**Royal Bank Of
Pennsylvania**
30 S 15th St,
Philadelphia PA 19102-
4826. 215/972-5300.

**Second National Fed
Savings Assn**
18th & Jfk Blvd,
Philadelphia PA 19103.
215/972-7072.

**Susquehanna Bancshares
Inc.**
26 N Cedar St, Lititz PA
17543-1514. 717/626-
4721.

**The Ephrata National
Bank**
935 N Railroad Ave, New
Holland PA 17557-9752.
717/354-4951.

**The Glenmede Trust
Company**
229 S 18th St,
Philadelphia PA 19103-
6144. 215/875-3200.

The Marian State Bank
401 Fairmount Ave,
Philadelphia PA 19123-
2807. 215/627-1191.

The York Bank
107 E Market St, York
PA 17401-1221.
717/843-8651.

**Trident Savings and Loan
Assn.**
2325 Brown St,
Philadelphia PA 19130-
1957. 215/236-2280.

**Ukrainian Fed Savings &
Loan Assn.**
1321 Lindley Ave,
Philadelphia PA 19141-
2746. 215/329-7080.

**United Bank Of
Philadelphia**
Two Penn Center,
Philadelphia PA 19102-
1502. 215/751-9321.

**United Bank Of
Philadelphia**
714 Market St,
Philadelphia PA 19106-
2397. 215/829-2265.

**United Bank Of
Philadelphia**
4806 Frankford Ave,
Philadelphia PA 19124-
2606. 215/831-0207.

United Savings Bank
1510 Packer Ave,
Philadelphia PA 19145-
5407. 215/467-4300.

United Savings Bank
732 S 10th St,
Philadelphia PA 19147-
2742. 215/923-8490.

**Vanguard Savings and
Loan Assn**
1003 Walnut St,
Philadelphia PA 19107-
5001. 215/564-6066.

**Washington Savings
Association**
2458 E Lehigh Ave,
Philadelphia PA 19125-
2347.

**3rd Fed Savings & Loan
Assn. Philadelphia**
4625 Frankford Ave,
Philadelphia PA 19124-
5889. 215/289-1400.

**3rd Fed Savings & Loan
Assn. Philadelphia**
York & Memphis Sts,
Philadelphia PA 19125.
215/423-2314.

3rd Fed Savings & Loan Assn. Philadelphia
Knights Road Center
Knights &, Philadelphia
PA 19154. 215/824-0151.

FEDERALLY CHARTERED SAVINGS INSTITUTIONS

Berean Federal Savings Bank
5228 Chestnut St,
Philadelphia PA 19139-3414. 215/472-4545.

First American Savings
500 Old York Rd,
Jenkintown PA 19046-2835. 215/576-5900.

First American Savings
4710 Rising Sun Ave,
Philadelphia PA 19120-4221. 215/324-5535.

Franklin First Savings Bank
Rte 6, E Stroudsburg PA
18301-9806. 717/779-5351.

Home Building Society
5018 Ditman St,
Philadelphia PA 19124-2231. 215/743-8734.

Home Unity Fed Savings & Loan Assoc
618 Germantown Pike,
Lafayette Hl PA 19444-1810. 610/825-8040.

SAVINGS INSTITUTIONS, NOT FEDERALLY CHARTERED

Security Federal Savings Bank
818 Landis Ave, Vineland
NJ 08360-8019.
609/691-2400.

FEDERALLY CHARTERED CREDIT UNIONS

Airwork Employees Fed Credit Union
PO Box 1187, Millville NJ
08332-8187. 609/327-5755.

Allstéel Employees Credit Union
425 Jaycee Dr, Hazleton
PA 18201-1151.
717/454-0862.

CA Reed Employees Credit Union
99 Chestnut St,
Williamsport PA 17701-5473. 717/326-9021.

Coastal Eagle Point Credit Union
P O Box 1000, Westville
NJ 08093-1000.
609/853-3100.

General Foam Credit Union
25 Jaycee Dr, Hazleton
PA 18201-1143.
717/455-4931.

Glidco Credit Union
3rd & Bern Sts, Reading
PA 19601. 610/373-4111.

Honeywell Philadelphia Div Fed Credit Union
1100 Virginia Dr, Ft
Washington PA 19034-3204. 215/641-3490.

ICC Rdg Credit Union
Grace & Meade Streets,
Reading PA 19611.
610/376-7123.

Liberty Credit Union
303 N Plum St,
Lancaster PA 17602-2401. 717/392-4125.

Lower Bucks Hospital Credit Union
Bath Road & Orchard Av,
Bristol PA 19007.
215/785-9488.

PNC Employees Credit Union
2111 Eastburn Ave,
Philadelphia PA 19138-2611. 215/549-9200.

Pillowtex Credit Union
Rd 3 Moulstown Road,
Hanover PA 17331-9803. 717/637-7116.

PVC Credit Union
Crestwood Industrial P,
Mountain Top PA 18707.
717/474-6741.

S&S MH Employee Credit Union
Solders & Sailors Memo,
Wellsboro PA 16901.
717/724-1631.

Schnadig Montoursville Credit Union
Streibeigh Lane,
Montoursville PA 17754.
717/368-8382.

Science Press Credit Union
300 W Chestnut St,
Ephrata PA 17522-2002.
717/733-7981.

Scranton Times Employe Credit Union
129 Penn Ave, Scranton
PA 18503-2015.
717/348-9192.

Sup Tube Employees Credit Union
Germantown Pike,
Collegeville PA 19426.
610/489-7239.

Tarkett Whitehall Credit Union
1139 Lehigh Ave,
Whitehall PA 18052-5515. 610/264-0547.

Teleflex Credit Union
205 Church Rd, North Wales PA 19454-4137. 215/699-4861.

Win-Glen Credit Union
400 W Stoever Ave, Myerstown PA 17067-1418. 717/866-2141.

York Sylvania Employee Credit Union
1128 Roosevelt Ave, York PA 17404-2348. 717/848-8080.

For more information on career opportunities in the banking/savings and loan industry:

Associations

AMERICAN BANKERS ASSOCIATION
1120 Connecticut Avenue NW, Washington DC 20036. 202/663-5221.

INDEPENDENT BANKERS ASSOCIATION OF AMERICA
One Thomas Circle NW, Suite 950, Washington DC 20005. 202/659-8111.

U.S. LEAGUE OF SAVINGS AND LOAN INSTITUTIONS
900 19th Street NW, Suite 400, Washington DC 20006. 202/857-3100.

Directories

AMERICAN BANK DIRECTORY
Thomson Financial Publications, 6195 Crooked Creek Road, Norcross GA 30092. 404/448-1011.

AMERICAN SAVINGS DIRECTORY
McFadden Business Publications, 6195 Crooked Creek Road, Norcross GA 30092. 404/448-1011.

BUSINESS WEEK/TOP 200 BANKING INSTITUTIONS ISSUE
McGraw-Hill, Inc., 1221 Avenue of the Americas, 39th Floor, New York NY 10020. 212/512-4776.

MOODY'S BANK AND FINANCE MANUAL
Moody's Investors Service, Inc., 99 Church Street, First Floor, New York NY 10007. 212/553-0300.

POLK'S BANK DIRECTORY
R.L. Polk & Co., P.O. Box 305100, Nashville TN 37320-5100. 615/889-3350.

RANKING THE BANKS/ THE TOP NUMBERS
American Banker, Inc., 1 State Street Plaza, New York NY 10004. 212/943-6700.

Magazines

ABA BANKING JOURNAL
American Bankers Association, 1120 Connecticut Avenue NW, Washington DC 20036. 202/663-5221.

BANK ADMINISTRATION
1 North Franklin, Chicago IL 60606. 800/323-8552.

BANKERS MAGAZINE
Warren, Gorham & Lamont, Park Square Building, 31 St. James Avenue, Boston MA 02116-4112. 617/423-2020.

JOURNAL OF COMMERCIAL BANK LENDING
Robert Morris Associates, P.O. Box 8500 S-1140, Philadelphia PA 19178. 215/851-9100. Cover letter required.

BIOTECHNOLOGY, PHARMACEUTICALS, AND SCIENTIFIC R&D

Biotechnology continues to move forward, and industry analysts expect it to be a $50 billion industry by the year 2000. Most biotech firms are relatively small -- 99 percent employ fewer than 500 people, and 76 percent have fewer than 50 employees.

Observers expected the pharmaceutical industry to sustain steady real growth of roughly 2 percent during 1994.
The long-term outlook will depend on the level of research and development, further expansion into foreign markets, and the result of the current national health care reform.

Skilled science technicians should find excellent employment opportunities in the '90s, largely due to the increased emphasis on the research and development of technical products.

BRISTOL-MYERS SQUIBB CORPORATION
P.O. Box 4000, Princeton NJ 08543. 609/252-4000. **Contact:** Human Resources. **Description:** A diversified company whose products include pharmaceuticals, healthcare and personal care products.

ELKINS-SINN INC.
2 Esterbrook Lane, Cherry Hill NJ 08003. 609/424-3700. **Contact:** Human Resources. **Description:** A pharmaceuticals company.

MARSAM PHARMACEUTICALS
Building 31, 24 Olney Avenue, Cherry Hill NJ 08003. 609/424-5600. **Contact:** Human Resources. **Description:** Produces generic drugs.

McNEIL CONSUMER PRODUCTS COMPANY
7050 Camp Hill Road, Fort Washington PA 19034-2292. 215/233-7000. **Contact:** Human Resources. **Description:** Manufactures and markets a wide range of consumer pharmaceutical products, including Tylenol and many other well-known products. A division of McNeil Laboratories. **Common positions include:** Accountant/Auditor; Buyer; Chemical Engineer; Chemist; Claim Representative; Computer Programmer; Credit Manager; Customer Service Representative; Industrial Engineer; Manufacturer's/Wholesaler's Sales Rep.; Marketing Specialist; Mechanical Engineer; Operations/Production Manager; Personnel/Labor Relations Specialist; Purchasing Agent and Manager; Quality Control Supervisor; Statistician; Systems Analyst; Transportation/Traffic Specialist. **Educational backgrounds include:** Business Administration; Chemistry; Computer Science; Engineering; Finance; Marketing. **Benefits:** Dental Insurance; Disability Coverage; Employee Discounts; Life Insurance; Medical Insurance; Pension Plan; Savings Plan; Tuition Assistance. **Corporate headquarters location:** Spring House PA. **Parent company:** Johnson & Johnson (New Brunswick, NJ).

McNEIL PHARMACEUTICAL

Walsh and McKean Road, Spring House PA 19477-0776. 215/628-5000. **Contact:** JoAnn Stehr, Employment Manager. **Description:** Producers of ethical pharmaceuticals. **Common positions include:** Accountant/Auditor; Chemical Engineer; Computer Programmer; Electrical/Electronic Engineer; Financial Analyst; Industrial Engineer; Manufacturer's/Wholesaler's Sales Rep.; Mechanical Engineer; Personnel/Labor Relations Specialist; Statistician; Technical Writer/Editor. **Educational backgrounds include:** Accounting; Business Administration; Computer Science; Engineering; Finance. **Benefits:** 401K; Dental Insurance; Disability Coverage; Employee Discounts; Life Insurance; Medical Insurance; Pension Plan; Savings Plan; Tuition Assistance. **Corporate headquarters location:** This Location. **Parent company:** Johnson & Johnson. **Operations at this facility include:** Administration; Manufacturing; Research and Development.

MERCK & COMPANY, INC.

P.O. Box 4, West Point PA 19486. 215/661-5000. **Contact:** Human Resources. **Description:** A worldwide corporation engaged primarily in the business of discovering, developing, producing, and marketing products and services for the maintenance or restoration of health and the environment.

RHONE POULENC RORER INC.

500 Arcola Road, Collegeville PA 19426. 215/454-8200. **Contact:** Human Resources Department. **Description:** A pharmaceutical preparations company.

SETON COMPANY

2500 Monroe Boulevard, Norristown PA 19403. 215/666-9600. **Contact:** Human Resources Department. **Description:** A pharmaceutical preparations company.

SMITHKLINE BEECHAM CLINICAL LABORATORIES

400 Egypt Road, Norristown PA 19403. 215/631-4200. **Contact:** Human Resources Department. **Description:** A clinical testing laboratory. **Common positions include:** Customer Service Representative; Laboratory Technician; Medical Technologist. **Educational backgrounds include:** Biology; Chemistry; Medical Technology. **Corporate headquarters location:** King of Prussia PA. **Parent company:** Smithkline Beecham. **Operations at this facility include:** Administration; Sales; Service. **Listed on:** New York Stock Exchange.

SMITHKLINE BEECHAM CORPORATION

1 Franklin Plaza, P.O. Box 7929, Philadelphia PA 19101. 215/751-4000. **Contact:** Personnel Department. **Description:** A health care company engaged in the research, development, manufacture and marketing of ethical pharmaceuticals, animal health products, ethical and proprietary medicines, and ethical and proprietary eye care products. Company is also engaged in many other aspects of the health care field, including the production of medical instruments and electronic instruments used in the health care field. Manufactures proprietary medicines through its subsidiary, Menley & James Laboratories (same address), including such nationally-known products as Contac Cold Capsules, Sine-Off sinus medicine, Love cosmetics, and Sea & Ski outdoor products. **Corporate headquarters location:** This Location. **Number of employees nationwide:** 20,000.

WARNER-LAMBERT COMPANY

400 West Lincoln Avenue, Lititz PA 17543. 717/626-2011. **Contact:** Human Resources. **Description:** A pharmaceuticals company.

WISTAR INSTITUTE OF ANATOMY AND BIOLOGY
3601 Spruce Street, Philadelphia PA 19104. 215/898-3700. **Contact:** Victoria Mulhern, Director of Human Resources. **Description:** A non-profit biomedical research facility devoted to the study of cellular and molecular characteristics and functions in both healthy and diseased organisms. The general areas of research include: molecular genetics, immunology, molecular and cellular biology, structural biology, and virology. **Common positions include:** Research Technician. **Educational backgrounds include:** Biochemistry; Biology; Chemistry. **Benefits:** Dental Insurance; Disability Coverage; Life Insurance; Medical Insurance; Pension Plan; Spending Account; Tuition Assistance. **Operations at this facility include:** Administration; Research and Development.

WYETH-AYERST LABORATORIES
611 East Nield, West Chester PA 19382. 215/696-3100. **Contact:** Personnel Director. **Description:** Produces a wide range of well-known pharmaceutical products and proprietary medicines.

WYETH-AYERST LABORATORIES
145 King of Prussia Road, Radnor PA 19087. 215/688-4400. **Contact:** Human Resources Department. **Description:** A pharmaceutical preparations company.

Note: Because addresses and telephone numbers of smaller companies change rapidly, we recommend you contact each company and verify the information below before contacting employers. Mass mailings are not recommended.

Additional large employers: 500+

PHARMACEUTICALS

Armour Pharmaceutical
500 Arcola Rd.,
Collegeville PA 19426-
3930. 610/454-8000.

Packaging Coordinators
1200 E Erie Ave.,
Philadelphia PA 19124-
5526. 215/537-8100.

Paco Pharmaceutical Service Inc.
1200 Paco Way,
Lakewood NJ 08701-
5938. 9083679000.

BIOLOGICAL PRODUCTS

Connaught Labs Inc.
Rt. 611, Swiftwater PA
18370. 717/839-7187.

Additional medium sized employers: under 500

RESEARCH ORGANIZATIONS

AT&T Bell Labs
1247 S Cedar Crest Blvd,
Allentown PA 18103-
6209. 610/770-2200.

Biopore Inc.
123 Coal Aly, State
College PA 16801-3812.
814/234-4664.

DNA Plant Technology Corporation
2611 Branch Pike,
Riverton NJ 08077-
3723. 609/829-0110.

Du Pont Merck Pharmaceuticals
500 S Ridgeway Ave,
Glenolden PA 19036-
2307. 610/237-7700.

Lancaster Labs Inc.
2425 New Holland Pike,
Lancaster PA 17601-
5946. 717/656-2301.

Nittany Geoscience
120 Radnor Rd, State
College PA 16801-7970.
814/231-2170.

Paragon Technology
820 N University Dr,
Univ Park PA 16802-
1012. 814/234-3335.

RE Wright Associates
3240 Schoolhouse Rd,
Middletown PA 17057-
3595. 717/944-5501.

Solarex Corporation
826 Newtown-Yardley
Rd, Newtown PA 18940-
1721. 215/860-0902.

Valley Biologics
735 Westerly Pky, State
College PA 16801-4227.
814/234-2876.

Zynaxis Inc.
371 Phoenixville Pike,
Malvern PA 19355-9603.
610/889-2200.

**Opinion Research
Corporation**
PO Box 183, Princeton
NJ 08542-0183.
609/924-5900.

The Wefa Group
401 City Avenue 300,
Bala Cynwyd PA 19004-
1122. 610/667-6000.

**Advance Research
System**
1942 Riverbend Rd,
Allentown PA 18103-
9687. 610/439-8022.

**Juvenile Diabetes
Foundation**
539 N 16th St,
Allentown PA 18102-
2039. 610/820-6333.

United States Bioscience
PO Box 851,
Conshohocken PA
19428-0851. 610/832-
0570.

**TESTING
LABORATORIES**

Metpath Inc.
900 Business Center Dr
Ste 100, Horsham PA
19044-3408. 215/957-
9300.

Pelmor Laboratories
401 Lafayette St,
Newtown PA 18940-
2151. 215/968-3826.

QC Inc.
1205 Indl Hwy,
Southampton PA 18966.
215/355-3900.

**DRUGS AND DRUG
PROPRIETARIES
WHOLESALE**

James F Havice Inc.
Five Industrial Park Rd,
Lewistown PA 17044-
9342. 717/242-1427.

Kay Wholesale Drug Co
1 Alta Rd, Wilkes Barre
PA 18702-2070.
717/823-5177.

**PHARMACEUTICAL
PRODUCTS**

GPS Health Care
1515 Mount Hope Ave,
Pottsville PA 17901-
1412. 717/622-3558.

Herbalife Distributor
805 E Mountain Rd,
Scranton PA 18505-
2764. 717/346-1124.

IGI Inc.
2285 E Landis Ave,
Vineland NJ 08360-
2959. 609/691-2411.

Lemmon Company
PO Box 630, Sellersville
PA 18960-0630.
215/256-8400.

Medical Products Labs
9990 Global Rd,
Philadelphia PA 19115-
1015. 215/677-5200.

Menley & James Inc.
100 Tournament Dr,
Horsham PA 19044-
3602. 215/441-6500.

**Mutual Pharmaceutical
Co Inc.**
1100 Orthodox St,
Philadelphia PA 19124-
3199. 215/288-6500.

**IN VITRO AND IN VIVO
DIAGNOSTIC
SUBSTANCES**

Drug Screening Systems
1001 Lower Landing Rd,
Blackwood NJ 08012-
3124. 609/228-8500.

For more information on career opportunities in biotechnology, pharmaceuticals, and scientific R&D:

Associations

AMERICAN ASSOCIATION FOR CLINICAL CHEMISTRY
2029 K Street NW, 7th Floor, Washington DC 20006. 202/857-0717.

AMERICAN ASSOCIATION OF COLLEGES OF PHARMACY
1426 Prince Street, Alexandria VA 22314. 703/739-2330.

AMERICAN COUNCIL ON PHARMACEUTICAL EDUCATION
311 West Superior Street, Chicago IL 60610. 312/664-3575.

AMERICAN PHARMACEUTICAL ASSOCIATION
2215 Constitution Avenue NW, Washington DC 20037. 202/628-4410.

AMERICAN SOCIETY FOR BIOCHEMISTRY AND MOLECULAR BIOLOGY
9650 Rockville Pike, Bethesda MD 20814. 301/530-7145.

AMERICAN SOCIETY OF HOSPITAL PHARMACISTS
7272 Wisconsin Avenue, Bethesda MD 20814. 301/657-3000.

BIOMEDICAL INDUSTRY COUNCIL
225 Broadway, Suite 1600, San Diego, CA 92101. 619/236-1322.

BIOTECHNOLOGY INDUSTRY ORGANIZATION
1625 K Street NW, Suite 1100, Washington DC 20006-1604. 202/857-0244.

NATIONAL ASSOCIATION OF PHARMACEUTICAL MANUFACTURERS
747 Third Avenue, New York NY 10017. 212/838-3720.

NATIONAL PHARMACEUTICAL COUNCIL
1894 Preston White Drive, Reston VA 22091. 703/620-6390.

Directories

DRUG TOPICS RED BOOK
Medical Economics Company, 5 Paragon Drive, Montvale, NJ 07645. 201/358-7200.

Magazine

DRUG TOPICS
Medical Economics Co., 5 Paragon Drive, Montvale NJ 07645. 201/358-7200.

PHARMACEUTICAL ENGINEERING
International Society of Pharmaceutical Engineers, 3816 West Linebaugh Avenue, Suite 412, Tampa FL 33624. 813/960-2105.

BUSINESS SERVICES AND NON-SCIENTIFIC RESEARCH

This industry covers a broad spectrum of services and careers. Here's a sampling:

Guards and Security Officers: Openings for applicants should be plentiful through the year 2005. Most of these openings can be attributed to the high turnover within the industry. The greatest competition will be for the full-time, in-house positions, which are generally the higher paying positions.

Data Processing Services: Performing such services as credit card authorization, data entry and payroll processing, revenues of data processing companies have grown as other companies choose not to maintain staff to provide these services in-house.

ADP (AUTOMATIC DATA PROCESSING)
1125 Virginia Drive, Fort Washington PA 19034. 215/283-4113. **Contact:** Personnel. **Description:** A payroll preparation service. **Number of employees at this location:** 250.

ACXIOM MAILING SERVICE
11500 Roosevelt Boulevard D, Philadelphia PA 19116. 215/464-5400. **Contact:** Human Resources Department. **Description:** A data processing service.

BERLITZ INTERNATIONAL, INC.
293 Wall Street, Princeton NJ 08540-1555. 609/924-8500. **Contact:** David Horn, Personnel Director, North America. **Description:** Berlitz International, Inc. is the premier language services firm providing instruction and translation services throughout 298 language centers in 28 countries throughout the world. The company also publishes Berlitz Pocket Travel Guides, foreign language phrase books and home study materials. Benefits dependent on hours worked. **Common positions include:** Accountant/Auditor; Director; Instructor/Trainer; Services Sales Representative. **Educational backgrounds include:** Accounting; Business Administration; Finance; Foreign Languages; Liberal Arts. **Corporate headquarters location:** This Location. **Operations at this facility include:** Administration. **Listed on:** New York Stock Exchange. **Number of employees nationwide:** 3,500.

CDI CORPORATION
1717 Arch Street 35th, Philadelphia PA 19103-2768. 215/569-2200. **Contact:** Corporate Personnel Department. **Description:** If calling from outside PA, use the following number: 800/562-5463. Provides contract technical services to aerospace, electronics, industrial, marine, power, and transportation firms. Services include engineering, design, and drafting. Branch offices nationwide. **Common positions include:** Aerospace Engineer; Chemical Engineer; Civil Engineer; Computer Programmer; Draftsperson; Electrical/Electronic Engineer; Industrial Engineer; Manufacturing Engineer; Mechanical Engineer; Metallurgical Engineer; Petroleum Engineer; Physicist/Astronomer; Quality Control Supervisor; Systems Analyst; Technical Writer/Editor. **Educational backgrounds include:** Chemistry; Computer Science; Engineering; Mathematics; Physics. **Benefits:** Life Insurance; Medical

Insurance. **Corporate headquarters location:** This Location. **Operations at this facility include:** Administration.

OLIVER B. CANNON & SONS
5600 Woodland Avenue, Philadelphia PA 19143. 215/729-4600. **Contact:** Michael Olsen, Vice President. **Description:** Offices of an industrial and commercial painting company.

CANTERBURY EDUCATIONAL SERVICES, INC.
1600 Medford Plaza, Route 70, Hartford Road, Medford NJ 08055-3503. 609/953-0044. **Contact:** Human Resources. **Description:** Develops, markets, and teaches courses that focus upon job-related skills in vocations such as hotel/motel management building maintenance, bartending, food and beverage management, word processing, and medical secretary. **Number of employees at this location:** 197.

DANAHER TOOL GROUP
805 Estelle Drive, Lancaster PA 17601. 717/898-6577. **Contact:** Yvonne Carey, Personnel Administrator. **Description:** Engaged in the development, promotion, and service of a line of automotive, hardware, and tool products. **Common positions include:** Accountant/Auditor; Administrator; Computer Programmer; Customer Service Representative; Draftsperson; Sales Associate; Systems Analyst. **Educational backgrounds include:** Accounting; Business Administration; Finance; Marketing. **Benefits:** Dental Insurance; Disability Coverage; Life Insurance; Medical Insurance; Savings Plan. **Parent company:** Danaher Corporation. **Operations at this facility include:** Administration; Manufacturing; Research and Development; Sales; Service.

ENVIRONMENTAL TECTONICS (ETC)
County Line Industrial Park, Southampton PA 18966. 215/355-9100. **Contact:** Human Resources. **Description:** Provides training systems.

HAY GROUP INCORPORATED
Nancy Panetta - HR Administrator

229 South 18th Street, Philadelphia PA 19103. 215/875-2300. **Contact:** Personnel. **Description:** An international human resources and management consulting firm. Other U.S. locations: 18 field offices throughout the United States. **Common positions include:** Accountant/Auditor; Actuary; Computer Programmer; Customer Service Representative; Marketing Specialist; Personnel/Labor Relations Specialist; Systems Analyst. **Educational backgrounds include:** Business Administration; Computer Science; Economics; Human Resources. **Corporate headquarters location:** This Location.

ISS
101 Webster Building, Concord Plaza, 3411 Silverside Rd., Wilmington DE 19810. 302/478-7225. **Contact:** Linda Miller, Administrative Assistant. **Description:** A Wilmington janitorial service. **Common positions include:** Administrator; Branch Manager; Department Manager. **Special Programs:** Training Programs. **Corporate headquarters location:** New York NY. **Operations at this facility include:** Service. **Listed on:** New York Stock Exchange.

MATHEMATICA POLICY RESEARCH, INC.
P.O. Box 2393, Princeton NJ 08543-2393. 609/936-2767. **Contact:** Linda Sigafoos, Personnel Specialist. **Description:** An employee-owned company which conducts social policy research (both data collection and data analysis) for government agencies, foundations, and private sector clients. The areas studied include health, labor, welfare, education, child care and food and nutrition. **Common positions include:**

Economist/Market Research Analyst; Statistician. **Educational backgrounds include:** Economics. **Benefits:** Dental Insurance; Disability Coverage; Life Insurance; Medical Insurance; Pension Plan; Profit Sharing; Savings Plan; Tuition Assistance. **Corporate headquarters location:** This Location. **Other U.S. locations:** Washington DC. **Operations at this facility include:** Service. **Number of employees at this location:** 200. **Projected hires for the next 12 months (This location):** 10 hires.

NATIONAL ANALYSTS
1700 Market Street, 17th Floor, Philadelphia PA 19103. 215/496-6800. **Contact:** Manager/Human Resources. **Description:** Performs a wide range of marketing and social sciences research as a division of an international management consulting firm. **Parent company:** Booz, Allen & Hamilton (New York, NY).

NIXON UNIFORM
2925 Northeast Boulevard, Wilmington DE 19802. 302/764-7550. **Contact:** Frank O'Donnell, Manager, Human Resources. **Description:** A uniform rental operation. **Common positions include:** General Manager; Operations/Production Manager. **Benefits:** Dental Insurance; Life Insurance; Medical Insurance; Pension Plan; Tuition Assistance. **Special Programs:** Internships; Training Programs. **Corporate headquarters location:** This Location. **Other U.S. locations:** Washington DC; Baltimore MD; Newark NJ; Lancaster PA. **Number of employees at this location:** 300. **Projected hires for the next 12 months (This location):** 10 hires.

PROTECTION TECHNOLOGY
280 King Prussia Road, 1st Floor, Radnor PA 19087. 215/341-3605. **Contact:** Human Resources Department. **Description:** A security service.

SERVICELINK, INC.
SECURITY SERVICE/INVESTIGATIONS
University Office Plaza, Commonwealth Building, Suite 200, Newark DE 19702. 302/328-3137. **Contact:** Arthur Kitchen, Operations Manager. **Description:** A provider of security guard services. **Benefits:** Dental Insurance; Medical Insurance. **Special Programs:** Training Programs. **Corporate headquarters location:** New York NY. **Other U.S. locations:** DC; MD; NJ; NY; PA. **Listed on:** London Stock Exchange.

STAR BUILDING SERVICES
34 Blevins Drive, Wilmington DE 19850. 302/324-1600. **Contact:** Human Resources. **Description:** Provides building cleaning and maintenance services.

UNISYS CORPORATION
P.O. Box 500, Blue Bell PA 19424. 215/986-2766. **Contact:** Human Resources. **Description:** A nationally-known information management company. **Number of employees nationwide:** 78,000.

Note: Because addresses and telephone numbers of smaller companies change rapidly, we recommend you contact each company and verify the information below before contacting employers. Mass mailings are not recommended.

Additional large employers: 500+

**DATA PROCESSING
SERVICES**

Pace Resources Inc.
40 S Richland Ave., York
PA 17404-3425.
717/854-5564.

**SECURITY SYSTEMS
SERVICES**

Day & Zimmermann Inc.
280 King Of Prussia Rd.,
Wayne PA 19087-5110.
610/975-6875.

Additional medium sized employers: under 500

**MISCELLANEOUS
SERVICES**

Beacon Research Inc.
Beaver College, Glenside
PA 19038. 215/572-
8977.

**FACILITIES SUPPORT
MANAGEMENT
SERVICES**

Nuclear Support Services
PO Box 3120, Hershey
PA 17033-3120.
717/838-8125.

**DETECTIVE, GUARD
AND ARMORED CAR
SERVICES**

Allied Security Inc.
7900-02 Bustleton Av,
Philadelphia PA 19152.
215/745-3010.

**SECURITY SYSETEMS
SERVICES**

**Sentry Security
Corporation**
1510 Gary Ave,
Bethlehem PA 18018-
2268. 610/758-8818.

**PHOTOFINISHING
LABORATORIES**

Big Picture Co.
4518 Church Rd, Mount
Laurel NJ 08054-2210.
609/866-1110.

BUSINESS SERVICES

**AAA Exec
Communication Service**
514 W Washington Ave,
Pleasantville NJ 08232-
2326. 609/645-7331.

APS Inc.
325 Andrews Rd, Fstrvl
Trvose PA 19053-3429.
215/364-0211.

Ballinger
Curtis Center Ind Sq W,
Philadelphia PA 19106.
215/592-0900.

Brunswick Hotel
160 Saint James Pl,
Atlantic City NJ 08401-
7106. 609/344-8098.

**Camelback Ski
Corporation**
PO Box 168, Tannersville
PA 18372-0168.
717/629-1661.

Carson Services Inc.
32-H Blooming Glen Rd,
Perkasie PA 18944.
215/249-3535.

Delcor Labs Inc.
Rt 447 N, E Stroudsburg
PA 18301. 717/424-
9512.

Envirofil Inc.
150 Radnor Chester Rd,
Wayne PA 19087-5221.
610/254-4997.

**Horsehead Resource
Development Co.**
613 3rd St, Palmerton
PA 18071-1520.
610/826-8608.

IKEA Pennsylvania Inc.
Plymouth Commons,
Plymouth Mtng PA
19462. 610/834-0150.

Marlton Technologies
111 Presidential Blvd,
Bala Cynwyd PA 19004-
1008. 610/664-6900.

**Schiff's Restaurant
Service**
3410 N Main Ave,
Scranton PA 18508-
1439. 717/343-1294.

COMMERCIAL PHOTOGRAPHY

Micor
458 Pike Rd, Huntingdon Vy PA 19006-1610.
215/322-8100.

SECRETERIAL AND COURT REPORTING SERVICES

My Office Inc.
40 Irons St, Toms River NJ 08753-6534.
908/341-9797.

DISINFECTING AND PEST CONTROL SERVICES

Terminix International
South Main St & Easton Rd, Nazareth PA 18064.
610/746-3720.

BUILDING CLEANING AND MAINTENANCE SERVICES

Community Building Service
954 Main St, Peckville PA 18452-2159.
717/489-5531.

Cons Building Maintenance & Supply
2377 Mill Rd, Jamison PA 18929-1705.
215/343-5550.

Coverall Of Philadelphia
150 S Warner Rd, Kng Of Prussa PA 19406-2826.
610/293-9500.

EQUIPMENT RENTAL AND LEASING

Blue Valley Welding Supply Inc.
919 Jefferson Ave, Scranton PA 18510-1006. 717/344-9353.

MECO Excavating
4 E Roseville Rd, Lancaster PA 17601-3835. 717/569-5657.

Morris Kreitz & Sons
220 Park Rd N, Reading PA 19610-2908.
610/376-7187.

O'Brien Environmental Energy Inc.
225 S 8th St, Philadelphia PA 19106-3519. 215/627-5500.

Ryder Truck Rental-One-Way Inc.
Delilah Rd, Pleasantville NJ 08232. 609/645-1520.

Tokai Financial Services
1055 Westlakes Dr, Berwyn PA 19312-2410.
610/651-5000.

U-Haul Center Of MacArthur Road
3001 MacArthur Rd, Whitehall PA 18052-3424. 610/770-0240.

LINEN SUPPLY

KK Linen Supply
224 Vine St, Hammonton NJ 08037-1450.
609/567-8251.

Mary MacIntosh Service Inc.
515 N 12th St, Allentown PA 18102-2795. 610/437-5435.

Mary MacIntosh Services
165 Main St, Wilkes Barre PA 18702-2706.
717/822-1121.

For more information on career opportunities in business services:

Associations

AMERICAN SOCIETY OF APPRAISERS
P.O. Box 17265, Washington DC 20041. 703/478-2228.

EQUIPMENT LEASING ASSOCIATION OF AMERICA
1300 17th Street, North Arlington VA 22209. 703/527-8655.

INTERACTIVE SERVICES ASSOCIATION
Suite 865, 8403 Colesville Road, Silver Springs MD 20910. 301/495-4955.

Directories

WORLD LEASING YEARBOOK
Euromoney, Inc., 145 Hudson Street, 7th Floor, New York NY 10012. 212/941-5880.

CHARITIES/SOCIAL SERVICES/MEMBERSHIP ORGANIZATIONS

The outlook for social services workers is better than average. In fact, opportunities for qualified applicants are expected to be excellent, partly due to the rapid turnover in the industry, the growing number of older citizens, and an increased awareness of the needs of the mentally and physically handicapped.

DELAWARE NATURE SOCIETY
P.O. Box 700, Hockessin DE 19707. **Contact:** Human Resources. **Description:** A private nonprofit membership organization dedicated to environmental education and the preservation of natural areas. Operates the Ashland and Abbott's Mill, offering year-round programming for all age groups.

SOUTHERN HOME SERVICES
3200 South Broad Street, Philadelphia PA 19145. 215/334-4319. **Contact:** Ellen Giunta, Assistant Director/Operations. **Description:** Operates a child and family treatment center.

WOODSIDE HALL ADDICTION CENTER
4200 Monument Road, Philadelphia PA 19131. 215/877-2000. **Contact:** Human Resources Department. **Description:** A drug abuse/addiction information and treatment center.

Note: Because addresses and telephone numbers of smaller companies change rapidly, we recommend you contact each company and verify the information below before contacting employers. Mass mailings are not recommended.

Additional medium sized employers: under 500

INDIVIDUAL AND FAMILY SOCIAL SERVICES

B'nai Brith Youth Organization
537 Center St,
Bethlehem PA 18018-5910. 610/866-2441.

Center For Industrial Training
262 Silver Springs Rd,
Mechanicsburg PA

17055-8120. 717/243-2397.

Comprehensive Rehabilitaion Assocs
550 American Ave, Kng Of Prussa PA 19406-1441. 610/337-8733.

Creative Health Systems Inc.
1 Mennonite Church Rd,
Spring City PA 19475-1518. 610/948-6490.

Crisis Service
N 21st, Camp Hill PA 17011. 717/834-3326.

Eagleville Hospital
100 Eagleville Rd,
Norristown PA 19403-1800. 610/539-6000.

Early Intervention Programs
51 Banks St, Harrisburg PA 17103-2016.
717/232-8382.

General Rehabilitation Service
1210 Northbrook Dr, Fstrvl Trvose PA 19053-8406. 215/322-3988.

Habitat Mid-Atlantic
736 Columbia Ave, Lancaster PA 17603-3635. 717/399-9592.

Help Counseling Center
Barnard & S Adams St, West Chester PA 19382. 610/436-5388.

Horsham Clinic
722 E Butler Pike, Ambler PA 19002-2310. 215/643-7800.

Muhlenberg Rehab Care Center
2855 Schoenersville Rd, Bethlehem PA 18017-7306. 610/861-1220.

Newtown Sports Therapy Center
3 Cambridge Ln, Newtown PA 18940-3326. 215/968-7500.

Northwestern Institute
450 S Bethlehem Pike, Ft Washington PA 19034-2312. 215/641-5300.

Remed Recovery Care Center
625 Ridge Pike, Conshohocken PA 19428-3204. 610/834-1300.

Ridge Crest
22 Almont Rd, Sellersville PA 18960-1596. 215/257-1155.

Sub Acute Care Facility
4950 Wilson Ln, Mechanicsburg PA 17055-4442. 717/697-7706.

JOB TRAINING AND VOCATIONAL REHABILITIATION SERVICES

Competitive Supported Employment
1057 Main Av, Dickson City PA 18519. 717/383-4140.

Delco Blind/Sight Center
100 W 15th St, Chester PA 19013-5314. 610/874-1476.

Developmental Enterprises Corporation
333 E Airy St, Norristown PA 19401-5039. 610/277-3122.

Good Shepherd Work Services
1901 Lehigh St, Allentown PA 18103-4731. 610/791-2230.

Hart Center
450 E Golden Ln, New Oxford PA 17350. 717/624-4323.

Hope Enterprises Inc.
136 Catawissa Ave, Williamsport PA 17701-4114. 717/326-3745.

Suncom Inds Inc.
128 Water St, Northumberlnd PA 17857-1907. 717/473-8352.

Threshold Rehabilitation Service
1000 Lancaster Ave, Reading PA 19607-1610. 610/777-7691.

CHILD DAY CARE SERVICES

Breezy Point Nursery & Kindergarten
1126 Bridgetown Pike, Fstrvl Trvose PA 19053-7233. 215/741-4288.

Children's Choice Inc.
5 Courtyard Ofc, Selinsgrove PA 17870. 717/743-0505.

Early Learning Center
General Delivery, Immaculata PA 19345-9999. 610/647-4400.

Magic Years Child Care
532 E Main St, Wilkes Barre PA 18702-6958. 717/825-5437.

Northern Hebrew Day Nursery
10800 Jamison Ave, Philadelphia PA 19116-3859. 215/677-7191.

Salem Head Start Center
325 Keasbey St, Salem NJ 08079-1230. 609/935-5444.

Sally Watson House Crisis
5128 Wayne Ave, Philadelphia PA 19144-3526. 215/844-6931.

William Penn Adolescent Dc
101 W College Ave, York PA 17403-5403. 717/845-3571.

RESIDENTAL CARE

Crystal Stables
5413 Dante Ave, Vineland NJ 08360-6880. 609/692-3435.

Glen Regent's
96 S George St, York PA
17401-1426. 717/854-
0160.

Holly Commons
54 Sharp St, Millville NJ
08332-2474. 609/327-
4400.

Mennonite Home
1520 Harrisburg Pike,
Lancaster PA 17601-
2697. 717/393-1301.

**Wiley Christian
Retirement Community**
99 E Main St, Marlton NJ
08053-2122. 609/983-
0411.

SOCIAL SERVICES

American Cancer Society
280 N Providence Rd,
Media PA 19063-3525.
610/565-1009.

American Cancer Society
1681 Crown Ave,
Lancaster PA 17601-
6300. 717/397-3744.

Carefree Learning Center
101 Tanner Dr, Exton PA
19341-1250. 610/524-
9424.

Children's Choice Inc.
600 W Harvey St,
Philadelphia PA 19144-
4306. 215/848-6350.

Children's Home Of York
3299 N Susquehanna Trl,
York PA 17402-9738.
717/764-9253.

Children's Home Of York
441 Linden Ave, York PA
17404-2960. 717/846-
1135.

**Community Council For
Mental Health**
4900 Wyalusing Ave,
Philadelphia PA 19131-
5127. 215/473-7033.

**Community Action
Agency**
862 Main St, Darby PA
19023-2109. 610/583-
9133.

Concern Group Home
1 W Main St, Fleetwood
PA 19522-1314.
717/386-2990.

**Concern Pro Service For
Child Youth**
1 W Main St, Fleetwood
PA 19522-1314.
610/944-0445.

**Development Resources
Corporation**
650 White Horse Pike S,
Hammonton NJ 08037-
2014. 609/567-9055.

**Developmental
Enterprises Corporation**
950 High St, Pottstown
PA 19464. 610/326-
5257.

**Easter Seal Society For
Crippled Children**
468 N Middletown Rd,
Media PA 19063-5506.
610/565-2353.

First Step
Union & Sickle Sts,
Kennet Sq PA 19348.
610/444-1023.

Gaudenzia Inc.
607 E Church Ln,
Philadelphia PA 19144-
1420. 215/848-0280.

**Ken Crest-River Crest
Center**
Rt 29, Mont Clare PA
19453. 610/935-1581.

Lutheran Social Services
1000 Quentin Rd,
Lebanon PA 17042-
6947. 717/272-5641.

Lutheran Social Service
4-6 Sturgis Lane, Lititz
PA 17543. 717/627-
2075.

**McConnellsburg Goodwill
Store**
Hc 80, Mc Connellsbg PA
17233-9804. 717/485-
3011.

**NJARC
Mercer County Unit**
1018 Brunswick Ave,
Trenton NJ 08638-3944.
609/695-3820.

Perry Cumberland Assn
117 N Hanover St,
Carlisle PA 17013-2442.
717/697-8343.

Pomfret Place
152 E Pomfret St,
Carlisle PA 17013-3314.
717/245-2254.

Project Sted
91 Progress Ave,
Pottsville PA 17901-
2976. 717/628-9090.

Respond Inc.
530 State St, Camden
NJ 08102-1919.
609/365-4400.

**Resources For Human
Development Inc.**
504 Washington Ave,
Philadelphia PA 19147-
4028. 215/462-5041.

Vision Quest Inc.
179 White Horse Rd W,
Voorhees NJ 08043-
3664. 609/435-4389.

BUSINESS ASSOCIATIONS

Assn For Retarded Citzns
1555 Gateway Blvd,
Woodbury NJ 08096-
1018. 609/848-8648.

**Assocd Unionized Empl
Pennsylvania Inc.**
3031 B Walton Rd, Blue
Bell PA 19422. 610/941-
9400.

**Associated Builders &
Contractors Inc.**
801 E Germantown Pike,
Norristown PA 19401-
2480. 610/279-6666.

Boy Scouts Of America
1 Badden Powell Ln,
Mechanicsburg PA
17055-2344. 717/766-
1591.

**Delaware County
Inspection Assn.**
144 W Eagle Rd,
Havertown PA 19083-
1110. 610/853-2340.

**Kutztown Area Historical
Society**
Normal & White,
Kutztown PA 19530.
610/683-7697.

**Pennsylvania State
Education Assn**
400 N 3rd St, Harrisburg
PA 17101-1346.
717/255-7000.

**Pike County Chamber Of
Commrce**
305 Broad St, Milford PA
18337-1322. 717/296-
8700.

PROFESSIONAL MEMBERSHIP ORGANIZATIONS

Penna Medical Society
212 N 3rd St, Harrisburg
PA 17101-1505.
717/232-8904.

LABOR UNIONS

**Natl PO Mailhandlers Lcl
308**
5124 Walnut St,
Philadelphia PA 19139-
4129. 215/474-9700.

**Pennsylvania State
Education Assn.**
1005 Penllyn Pike, Spring
House PA 19477.
215/643-6721.

CIVIC, SOCIAL AND FRATERNAL ASSOCIATIONS

**Chesapeake Bay
Foundation**
214 State St, Harrisburg
PA 17113-1376.
717/234-5550.

Hokendauqua Fire Co.
3022 S 2nd St, Whitehall
PA 18052-3204.
610/264-3292.

Techlaw Inc.
940 W Valley Rd, Wayne
PA 19087-1829.
610/687-2244.

MEMBERSHIP ORGANIZATIONS

AML Development
520 W 4th St Ste 1A,
Williamsport PA 17701-
6038. 717/326-7937.

**Lafayette College Alumni
Assoc**
Lafayette College
Campus, Easton PA
18042. 610/250-5040.

CHEMICALS/RUBBER AND PLASTICS

Historically, the chemicals industry has been a cyclical one and is currently coming out of the low end of its cycle. The U.S. Commerce Department reports that an upturn in the domestic and foreign economies is needed to stimulate the chemical industry, so over the next five years the American chemical industry is expected to grow at a rate just above GNP. Jobseekers with chemical engineering experience will benefit from the current shortage of workers in the industry.

The rubber and plastic industries will do better as well -- growth will be in the 4 to 5 percent range. The highest growth rates will be for high-value, small-volume elastomers. In fabricated rubber, the big trend is toward customized production. Jobseekers with experience in Computer Aided Design for Manufacturing will reap the benefits of this trend. Demand for commodity plastics is expected to rise, as the market grows in North America but shrinks overseas. Competition in Europe, for example, is forcing many companies there to close their doors.

AIR PRODUCTS AND CHEMICALS, INC.

7201 Hamilton Boulevard, Allentown PA 18195-1501. 215/481-7050. **Contact:** University Relations. **Description:** A manufacturer of industrial gases, process equipment, and chemicals. In addition, company is also a provider of engineering services. **Common positions include:** Chemical Engineer; Financial Analyst; Mechanical Engineer. **Educational backgrounds include:** Engineering; Finance; Marketing; MBA. **Benefits:** Dental Insurance; Disability Coverage; Life Insurance; Pension Plan; Savings Plan; Stock Option; Tuition Assistance. **Special Programs:** Internships; Training Programs.

AIRGAS, INC.

100 Matsonford Road, Suite 550, 5 Radnor Corporate Center, Radnor PA 19087. 215/687-5253. **Contact:** Human Resources. **Description:** Airgas, Inc. distributes industrial, medical and specialty gases, protective equipment and welding accessories, and to a much lesser extent, has interests in the manufacture of certains carbon and other products. **Number of employees nationwide:** 2,800.

AKZO SALT INC.

P.O. Box 352, Abington Executive Park, Clarks Summit PA 18411. 717/587-5131. **Contact:** Human Resources. **Description:** A chemicals manufacturer.

ALLIEDSIGNAL CORPORATION

Margaret and Bermuda Streets, Philadelphia PA 19137. 215/533-3000. **Contact:** Personnel Department. **Description:** A producer of a variety of chemical products, including synthetic phenol, acetone, alpha methylstyrene, and cumene hydroperoxide. Other facilities are in Pottsville and Marcus Hook. Parent company, AlliedSignal Corporation serves a broad spectrum of industries through its more than 40 strategic businesses, which are grouped into three sectors: Aerospace; Automotive; and

Engineered Materials. AlliedSignal is one of the nation's largest industrial organizations.

AMERICAN TIRE & SERVICE CO.
DIVISION OF BRIDGESTONE/FIRESTONE, INC.
656 East Swedesford Road, Suite 224, Wayne PA 19087. 215/687-6707. **Contact:** Bob Pierce, Human Resources Manager. **Description:** Zone office responsible for supporting and directing more than 250 retail stores, marketing tires and automotive services, throughout the Northeast. Other U.S. locations: Nationwide. **Common positions include:** Automotive Mechanic/Body Repairer; Retail Sales Worker. **Educational backgrounds include:** Marketing; Sales. **Special Programs:** Training Programs. **Corporate headquarters location:** Rolling Meadows IL. **Operations at this facility include:** Administration; Service.

ANZON, INC.
2545 Aramingo Avenue, Philadelphia PA 19125. 215/427-3000. **Contact:** Personnel. **Description:** A producer of industrial organic chemicals.

ARCO CHEMICAL COMPANY
3801 West Chester Pike, Newton Square PA 19073. 215/359-2000. **Contact:** Human Resources Department. **Description:** A chemical manufacturer and marketer specializing in plastics, foams, fuel additives, and other intermediate chemicals. **Common positions include:** Chemical Engineer; Chemist; Electrical/Electronic Engineer; Metallurgical Engineer. **Listed on:** New York Stock Exchange.

BEMIS
P.O. Box 557, Hazleton PA 18201. 717/455-7741. **Contact:** Human Resources. **Description:** Manufactures plastic products.

BETZ LABORATORIES
4636 Somerton Road, Trevose PA 19053. 215/355-3300. **Contact:** Manager of Human Resources. **Description:** Company is engaged in the engineered chemical treatment of water, wastewater, and process systems. Operates in a wide variety of industrial and commercial applications, with particular emphasis on the chemical, petroleum refining, paper, automotive, electrical utility, and steel industries. Company produces and markets a wide variety of specialty chemical products, including the technical and laboratory services necessary to utilize Betz products effectively. Chemical treatment programs are applied for and used in boilers, cooling towers, heat exchangers, paper and petroleum process streams, and both influent and effluent systems. The company has 15 production plants in the United States and seven in foreign countries, and employs approximately 2,840 persons, of which 1,055 represent a highly technical sales force.

M.A. BRUDER & SONS INC.
600 Reed Road, P.O. Box 600, Broomall PA 19008. 215/353-5100. **Contact:** Joseph Flaherty, Personnel Manager. **Description:** Manufactures paints, lacquers, and similar products.

CARLISLE SYNTEC SYSTEMS
P.O. Box 7000, Carlisle PA 17013. 717/245-7000. **Contact:** Human Resources. **Description:** Manufactures fabricated rubber products.

DU PONT DE NEMOURS EI & COMPANY
U.S. Highway 130 and Canal Road, Deepwater NJ 08023. 609/299-5000. **Contact:** Human Resources Department. **Description:** Produces plastics materials and synthetic resins.

E.I. DuPONT DeNEMOURS & COMPANY
3401 Grays Ferry Avenue, Philadelphia PA 19146. 215/339-6000. **Contact:** Employee Relations Manager. **Description:** .Engaged principally in the manufacturing and marketing of a diversified line of chemicals, plastics, specialty products, and fibers. Principal manufacturing and marketing activities are conducted through various independent operating subsidiaries. Company sells some 1,700 product lines to other industries. **Common positions include:** Chemist; Civil Engineer; Electrical/Electronic Engineer; Mechanical Engineer. **Educational backgrounds include:** Chemistry; Computer Science; Engineering; Mathematics; Physics. **Benefits:** Dental Insurance; Disability Coverage; Life Insurance; Medical Insurance; Pension Plan; Savings Plan; Tuition Assistance. **Special Programs:** Training Programs. **Corporate headquarters location:** Wilmington DE. **Operations at this facility include:** Research and Development. **Listed on:** New York Stock Exchange.

DYNASIL CORPORATION OF AMERICA
195 North Cooper Road, Berlin NJ 08009. 609/767-4600. **Contact:** Charlene Menard, Office Manager. **Description:** Manufacturers of synthetic fused silicon.

FMC CORPORATION
1735 Market Street, Philadelphia PA 19103. 215/299-6000. **Contact:** Human Resources. **Description:** Manufactures chemicals.

GENERAL CHEMICAL CORPORATION
6300 Philadelphia Pike, Claymont DE 19703. 302/792-8500. **Contact:** Dave Bona, Manager/Human Resources. **Description:** Manufactures and distributes sulfuric acid.

GENERAL FOAM CORPORATION (GFC)
Valmont Industrial Park, 25 Jaycee Drive, West Hazleton PA 18201. 717/455-4931. **Contact:** Mary Murray, Personnel Director. **Description:** Produces polyurethane products. **Educational backgrounds include:** Business Administration; Chemistry; Engineering. **Corporate headquarters location:** Paramus NJ. **Operations at this facility include:** Manufacturing; Research and Development.

THE GLIDDEN COMPANY
P.O. Box 15049, Reading PA 19612. 215/373-4111. **Contact:** Gary Knoll, Human Resources Manager. **Description:** A well-known manufacturer of paints, coatings, resins, and lacquers. Parent company is a diversified corporation with interests in paper, consumer goods, chemicals, metals, foods, and other areas. **Common positions include:** Accountant/Auditor; Administrator; Blue-Collar Worker Supervisor; Branch Manager; Buyer; Chemical Engineer; Chemist; Civil Engineer; Claim Representative; Credit Manager; Customer Service Representative; Financial Analyst; General Manager; Industrial Engineer; Management Trainee; Manufacturer's/Wholesaler's Sales Rep.; Marketing Specialist; Mechanical Engineer; Operations/Production Manager; Personnel/Labor Relations Specialist; Purchasing Agent and Manager; Quality Control Supervisor; Transportation/Traffic Specialist. **Educational backgrounds include:** Accounting; Business Administration; Chemistry; Engineering; Finance; Marketing. **Benefits:** Dental Insurance; Disability Coverage; Employee Discounts; Life Insurance; Medical Insurance; Pension Plan; Profit Sharing; Savings Plan; Tuition Assistance. **Parent company:** ICI, Inc. **Operations at this facility include:** Regional Headquarters.

GOODALL RUBBER COMPANY
Quaker Bridge Executive Center, Suite 203, Grovers Mill Road, Lawrenceville NJ 08648. 609/799-2000. **Contact:** Bonnie Gessner, Personnel. **Description:** A rubber manufacturer, and distribution and sales company, with 45 United States and Canadian sales and service centers. **Common positions include:** Accountant/Auditor; Blue-Collar Worker Supervisor; Computer Programmer; Customer Service Representative. **Educational backgrounds include:** Accounting; Business Administration; Chemistry; Engineering; Finance; Marketing. **Benefits:** Disability Coverage; Life Insurance; Medical Insurance; Pension Plan; Profit Sharing; Savings Plan; Tuition Assistance. **Corporate headquarters location:** This Location. **Operations at this facility include:** Administration; Sales; Service.

GOODALL RUBBER COMPANY
P.O. Box 206, Folcroft PA 19032. 215/534-2100. **Contact:** Thomas Windle, Service Manager. **Description:** Produces a broad range of industrial rubber products, including hose and belting products, lined pipe and fittings. **Common positions include:** Blue-Collar Worker Supervisor; Branch Manager; Buyer; Manufacturer's/Wholesaler's Sales Rep. **Educational backgrounds include:** Business Administration; Marketing; Mathematics. **Benefits:** Disability Coverage; Life Insurance; Medical Insurance; Pension Plan; Savings Plan. **Corporate headquarters location:** Trenton NJ. **Parent company:** Goodall. **Operations at this facility include:** Administration; Regional Headquarters; Sales; Service.

GOODYEAR TIRE & RUBBER COMPANY
Scott Plaza #2, Philadelphia PA 19113-1513. 215/521-4000. **Contact:** Kathy Remaley, District Operations Manager. **Description:** The well-known manufacturer of tire and rubber products. Engaged in operations throughout the United States and over 45 plants in some 27 foreign countries. An average of 140,000 people are employed worldwide, including more than 70,000 in the United States. Goodyear's principal business is the development, manufacture, distribution, and sale of tires of every type. It also manufactures and sells thousands of other products including metal, rubber, plastic products for the transportation industry and various industrial consumer markets; and synthetic rubber and numerous high-technology products for aerospace, defense, and nuclear energy applications. **Corporate headquarters location:** Akron OH. **Listed on:** New York Stock Exchange.

W.R. GRACE & CO./FORMPAC
P.O. Box 295, Tuckerton Road, Reading PA 19603. 215/926-7551. **Contact:** Timothy Reich, Human Resources Manager. **Description:** Produces foam trays for meat, poultry, and produce. Parent company is a diversified worldwide enterprise consisting of specialty and agricultural chemicals; energy production and services; retailing, restaurants, and other businesses. The firm operates over 2,500 facilities in 47 states and 42 foreign countries. **Corporate headquarters location:** New York NY. **Parent company:** W.R. Grace & Co. **Number of employees at this location:** 80,000.

GRAPHIC PACKAGING CORPORATION
Matthews & Cedar Hollow Roads, Paoli PA 19301. 215/647-0500. **Contact:** Human Resources. **Description:** Manufactures plastic products.

HARGRO FLEXIBLE PACKAGING CORPORATION
P.O. Box 588, Boyertown PA 19512. 215/367-2991. **Contact:** Scott Haden, Personnel Manager. **Description:** Produces polyethylene.

HERCULES INCORPORATED

Hercules Plaza, Wilmington DE 19894. 302/594-5000. **Contact:** Manager/Professional Staffing. **Description:** Produces a broad line of materials and products, including cellulose and natural gum thickeners, flavors and fragrances, natural and hydrocarbon rosins and resins, polypropylene fibers and films, graphite fibers and products for aerospace. Incorporated in 1913, Hercules employs over 23,000 at its more than 80 domestic and international locations, and at its Research Center and headquarters in Wilmington, DE. Opportunities for entry level candidates exist in the following areas: Operations- Plant locations seek Engineers (all disciplines) for process and project work, maintenance, trouble-shooting, and power work; Research and Development- Chemists (analytical, organic) and Engineers (chemical, mechanical) to work in main research facility or at plant locations to discover new products and maintain quality existing of products; Technical Sales and Service- Positions for Chemists and Chemical and Mechanical Engineers involving extensive customer contacts in sales and service of chemical products. **Common positions include:** Chemical Engineer; Chemist; Mechanical Engineer. **Educational backgrounds include:** Chemistry; Engineering. **Benefits:** Dental Insurance; Disability Coverage; Life Insurance; Medical Insurance; Pension Plan; Savings Plan; Tuition Assistance. **Special Programs:** Internships; Training Programs. **Corporate headquarters location:** This Location. **Operations at this facility include:** Regional Headquarters; Research and Development; Sales. **Listed on:** New York Stock Exchange.

HERCULES INDUSTRIAL CHEMICALS

P.O. Box 249, Burlington NJ 08016. 609/386-1300. **Contact:** Personnel. **Description:** Manufacturer of synthetic resins.

HIMONT INC.

2801 Centerville Rd., Box 15439, Wilmington DE 19850-5439. 302/996-6000. **Contact:** Manager, Staffing. **Description:** A company that produces and markets polypropylene and a broad range of polymer-based specialty composites and alloys. **Parent company:** Feruzzi/Montedison Group. **Number of employees nationwide:** 4,500.

ICI/ATLAS POINT

315 Cherry Lane, Atlas Point, New Castle DE 19720. 302/427-1400. **Contact:** Personnel Department. **Description:** Area chemical manufacturing plant, wholly owned by Imperial Chemical Industries PLC of London England, one of the top four chemical companies in the world. Products include a broad line of pharmaceuticals, agricultural chemicals, plastics, polyester films, paints, specialty chemicals, dyes and colorants, advanced materials/composites, fibers, security devices, and aerospace components. **Parent company:** Imperial Chemical Industries PLC.

ILC DOVER, INC.

P.O. Box 266, Frederica DE 19946. 302/335-3911. **Contact:** Frank Mossnan, Director of Human Resources. **Description:** Manufactures NASA spacesuits, inflatable products, and protective equipment. **Common positions include:** Accountant/Auditor; Aerospace Engineer; Biomedical Engineer; Buyer; Chemical Engineer; Chemist; Computer Programmer; Designer; Draftsperson; Financial Analyst; Industrial Engineer; Manufacturing Engineer; Mechanical Engineer; Operations/Production Manager; Purchasing Agent and Manager; Quality Assurance Engineer; Quality Control Supervisor; Systems Analyst; Technical Writer/Editor. **Educational backgrounds include:** Accounting; Business Administration; Chemistry; Computer Science; Engineering; Mathematics; Physics; Textiles. **Benefits:** Dental Insurance; Disability Coverage; Employee Discounts; Life Insurance; Medical Insurance; Pension Plan; Savings Plan; Tuition Assistance. **Corporate headquarters location:** Bohemia NY.

Parent company: ILC Industries. **Operations at this facility include:** Administration; Divisional Headquarters; Manufacturing; Research and Development; Sales; Service.

INOLEX CHEMICAL COMPANY
Jackson and Swanson, Philadelphia PA 19148. 215/271-0800. **Contact:** Rita Stishock, Personnel Director. **Description:** An area chemical company.

JAMES RIVER CORPORATION
P.O. Box 110, New Castle DE 19720. 302/323-4000. **Contact:** Deborah Stauffer, Human Resources Manager. **Description:** A manufacturer of plastic films.

NVF COMPANY
P.O. Box 0516, Kennett Square PA 19348. 215/444-2800. **Contact:** Industrial Relations Supervisor. **Description:** Produces a wide range of laminated plastics and filament wound tubes. **Common positions include:** Accountant/Auditor; Blue-Collar Worker Supervisor. **Educational backgrounds include:** Accounting. **Benefits:** Dental Insurance; Disability Coverage; Life Insurance; Medical Insurance; Pension Plan; Tuition Assistance. **Corporate headquarters location:** Yorklyn DE. **Operations at this facility include:** Divisional Headquarters; Manufacturing; Research and Development; Sales.

NOR-AM CHEMICAL COMPANY
P.O. Box 7495, 3509 Silverside Road, Wilmington DE 19803. 302/477-3020. **Contact:** Mary Regan, Human Resources Director. **Description:** A producer of agricultural chemicals. **Common positions include:** Chemist. **Educational backgrounds include:** Biology; Chemistry. **Corporate headquarters location:** This Location.

OCCIDENTAL CHEMICAL PVC DIVISIONS
P.O. Box 699, Pottstown PA 19464. 215/327-6400. **Contact:** Vern Davis, Human Resources Manager. **Description:** Manufactures a wide range of PVC resins, compounds, and fabricated products as a division of Occidental Chemical Corporation. OCC is a part of Occidental Petroleum Company, a natural resources company engaged in the exploration for and the development of oil and natural gas in the United States. **Corporate headquarters location:** Los Angeles CA.

THE POLYMER CORPORATION
P.O. Box 14235, Reading PA 19612-4235. 215/320-6600. **Contact:** Supervisor/Personnel. **Description:** A manufacturer of engineering plastic products. **Common positions include:** Accountant/Auditor; Chemical Engineer; Computer Programmer; Customer Service Representative; Manufacturer's/Wholesaler's Sales Rep.; Operations/ Production Manager. **Educational backgrounds include:** Business Administration; Chemistry; Engineering; Finance. **Benefits:** Disability Coverage; Life Insurance; Medical Insurance; Pension Plan; Tuition Assistance. **Corporate headquarters location:** This Location. **Parent company:** DSM.

QUAKER CHEMICAL CORPORATION
Elm & Lee Streets, Conshohocken PA 19428. 215/832-4000. **Contact:** Ann Williams, Employment Manager. **Description:** Manufactures rolling lubricants for steel and non-ferrous metals, corrosion preventives, machining, grinding and drawing compounds, hydraulic fluids, metal finishing compounds, and other products.

RHEOX, INC.
P.O. Box 700, Wyckoffs Mill Road, Highstown NJ 08520. 609/443-2467. **Contact:** Human Resources. **Description:** A chemical manufacturer.

ROHM & HAAS COMPANY
727 Norristown Road, P.O. Box 904, Spring House PA 19477. 215/641-7000.
Contact: Human Resources Department. **Description:** A chemicals company.

ROHM & HAAS COMPANY
Independence Mall West, Philadelphia PA 19105. 215/592-3000. **Contact:** Corporate
Staffing. **Description:** A specialty chemicals company operating in four industry
segments: Polymers, Resins, and Monomers; Plastics; Industrial Chemicals; and
Agricultural Chemicals. Also engaged in non-chemical industries such as forestry
products, carpet production, and biomedical testing. **Corporate headquarters location:**
This Location. **Listed on:** New York Stock Exchange.

SUN CHEMICAL/GENERAL PRINTING INC.
3301 Hunting Park Avenue, Philadelphia PA 19129. 215/223-8220. **Contact:** Louis A.
Schiliro, Personnel. **Description:** A manufacturer of printing ink.

SYBRON CHEMICALS INC.
P.O. Box 66, Birmingham Road, Birmingham NJ 08011. 609/893-1100. **Contact:**
Human Resources. **Description:** Manufactures chemicals.

*Note: Because addresses and telephone numbers of smaller companies change rapidly, we
recommend you contact each company and verify the information below before contacting
employers. Mass mailings are not recommended.*

Additional large employers: 500 +

CHEMICALS

Bulova Technologies
P.O. Box 4787,
Lancaster PA 17604-
4787. 717/299-2581.

**Elf Atochem North
America Inc.**
3 Parkway #619,
Philadelphia PA 19102-
1306. 215/419-7000.

Centocor Inc.
200 Great Valley Pkwy,
Malvern PA 19355-1307.
610/651-6000.

SOAP AND DETERGENTS

Herco Inc.
300 Park Blvd., Hershey
PA 17033-2737.
717/534-3131.

**PAINTS AND RELATED
CHEMICALS**

Stonhard Inc.
Park Ave., Maple Shade
NJ 08052. 609/779-
7500.

FERTILIZERS

Kaolin Mushroom Farms
649 W South St., Kennet
Sq PA 19348-3417.
610/444-4800.

**PESTICIDES AND
AGRICULTURAL
CHEMICALS**

**American Cyanamid
Company Inc.**
P.O. Box 400, Princeton
NJ 08543-0400.
609/799-0400.

PLASTICS PRODUCTS

AC&S Inc.
120 N Lime St.,
Lancaster PA 17602-
2951. 717/397-3631.

Wheaton Industries
Mill Street and
Weymouth Rd., Mays
Landing NJ 08330.
609/625-4811.

Additional medium sized employers: under 500

CHEMICALS AND ALLIED PRODUCTS WHOLESALE

Atochem North America
900 1st Ave, Kng Of Prussa PA 19406-1353. 610/337-6500.

Soco Chemical Inc.
Pottsville Pike & Huller Lane, Reading PA 19605. 610/926-6100.

Thomas Scientific
PO Box 99, Swedesboro NJ 08085-6099. 609/467-2000.

PETROLEUM AND PETROLEUM PRODUCTS WHOLESALE

Petroleum Products Corporation
900 Eisnhwr Blvd, Highspire PA 17034. 717/939-0466.

Shipley Oil Company
550 E King St, York PA 17403-1720. 717/848-4100.

The Sico Company
PO Box 302, Mount Joy PA 17552-0302. 717/653-1411.

INDUSTRIAL INORGANIC CHEMICALS

Ashland Chemical Co
400 Island Park Rd, Easton PA 18042-6899. 610/258-9135.

Cyprus Foote Mineral
301 Lindenwood Dr #301, Malvern PA 19355-1757. 610/889-9605.

EM Diagnostics Systems
480 S Democrat Rd, Gibbstown NJ 08027-1239. 609/423-6300.

EM Science Div
480 S Democrat Rd, Gibbstown NJ 08027-1239. 609/354-9200.

Owens-Corning Fiberglass Corporation
Jackson Rd, Berlin NJ 08009. 609/767-3300.

Polysciences Inc.
Paul Vly Indl Pk, Warrington PA 18976. 215/343-6484.

Pottsville Bleaching & Dyeing
6 Coal St, Port Carbon PA 17965-1805. 717/622-0277.

Rhein Chemie Corp.
1008 Whitehead Rd Ext, Trenton NJ 08638-2406. 609/882-5405.

Rhone-Poulenc Basic Chemicals
2300 S Pennsylvania Ave, Morrisville PA 19067-2504. 215/295-7132.

Scientific Emulation
84 Roper Rd, Princeton NJ 08540-4069. 609/497-3385.

PLASTICS MATERIALS AND SYNTHETIC RESINS

Bunnell Plastics Div
I-295 & Harmony Rd, Mickleton NJ 08056-1203. 609/423-6630.

Crest Polymers Inc.
914 Town Ctr, Doylestown PA 18901-5191. 215/340-0279.

Customill
Locust & Spruce, Camden NJ 08103. 609/541-3663.

Elf Atochem North America Inc.
1112 Lincoln Rd, Birdsboro PA 19508-1804. 610/582-1551.

Foamex Lp
1500 E 2nd St, Crum Lynne PA 19022-1589. 610/876-2551.

General Polymers
3 S Middlesex Ave, Cranbury NJ 08512-9557. 609/860-0200.

Huntsman Polypropylene Corporation
Mantua Grove Rd, Paulsboro NJ 08066. 609/423-7900.

Interplast Inc.
1 Connecticut Dr, Burlington NJ 08016-4101. 609/386-4990.

LNP Engineering Plastics
251 S Bailey Rd, Downingtown PA 19335-2003. 610/383-8900.

Modern Packaging Inc.
PO Box 15, Mount Holly NJ 08060-0015. 609/267-5900.

Monsanto Company
PO Box 309, Bridgeport
NJ 08014-0309.
609/467-3000.

**Plascom Trading
Company**
1800 E State St, Trenton
NJ 08609-2020.
609/587-9522.

Polycom Huntsman
Smithtown Rd, Pipersville
PA 18947. 215/766-
0760.

Purolite Company
150 Monument Rd, Bala
Cynwyd PA 19004-
1725. 610/668-9090.

Reneer Films Corporation
Hickory Dr, Auburn PA
17922. 717/366-1051.

**Ricard Plastic Products
Co Inc.**
40 Enterprise Ave,
Trenton NJ 08638-4402.
609/695-7276.

**The BF Goodrich
Company**
Rte 130 Salem P O Box
400, Pedricktown NJ
08067. 609/299-5400.

**CELLULOSIC MAN-MADE
FIBERS**

Celotex Corporation
1400 Susquehanna Ave,
Sunbury PA 17801-
1160. 717/286-5831.

**GASKETS, PACKING
AND SEALING DEVICES**

**Durabla Manufacturing
Company**
140 Sheree Blvd, Exton
PA 19341-1231.
610/363-8900.

Garlock Bearings Division
700 Mid-Atlantic Pkwy,
Thorofare NJ 08086.
609/848-3200.

Greene Tweed & Co
PO Box 305, Kulpsville
PA 19443-0305.
215/256-9521.

**The Home Rubber
Company**
31 Woolverton Ave,
Trenton NJ 08611-2429.
609/394-1176.

**FABRICATED RUBBER
PRODUCTS**

Aldan Rubber Co.
Salmon & Tioga Sts,
Philadelphia PA 19134.
215/739-6500.

Carter-Wallace
PO Box 5147, Trenton
NJ 08638-0147.
609/392-5134.

**National Sponge Cushion
Co.**
1936 E State St Ext,
Trenton NJ 08619-3393.
609/587-5800.

**Tompkins Rubber
Company**
550 Township Line Rd,
Blue Bell PA 19422-
2701. 610/825-3400.

**UNSUPPORTED PLASTIC
FILMS AND SHEETS**

Kama Corporation
666 Dietrich Ave,
Hazleton PA 18201-
7754. 717/455-2021.

O'Sullivan Corporation
1507 Willow St, Lebanon
PA 17042-4585.
717/274-2851.

**UNSUPPORTED PLASTIC
PROFILES**

**Mercury Tool &
Manufacturing**
180 N Hurffville Rd,
Woodbury NJ 08096-
3868. 609/228-6166.

LAMINATED PLASTIC

Dee Paper Co Inc.
Front & Broomall,
Chester PA 19013.
610/876-9285.

PLASTIC BOTTLES

**Bercon Packaging
Company**
910 7th Ave, Berwick PA
18603-1127. 717/759-
6200.

**Drug Plastics & Glass
Company Inc.**
One Bottle Dr, Boyertown
PA 19512. 610/367-
5000.

Silgan PET Corporation
121 Wheeler Ct,
Langhorne PA 19047-
1701. 215/757-2676.

**PLASTIC FOAM
PRODUCTS**

Cartex Corporation
200 Rock Run Rd,
Fairless Hls PA 19030-
4391. 215/736-0970.

PLASTIC PRODUCTS

A&E Products Group
W Main St, Ringtown PA
17967. 717/889-3131.

AL Hyde Co.
1 Main St, Grenloch NJ
08032. 609/227-0500.

Allied Signal Inc.
Westwood Rd, Pottsville
PA 17901. 717/622-
3384.

Brentwood Inds Inc.
610 Morgantown Rd,
Reading PA 19611.
610/374-5109.

**Canton Manufacturing
Corporation**
120 E 2nd St, Canton PA
17724-1912. 717/673-
5145.

Clifton Plastics Inc.
557 E Baltimore Ave,
Clifton Hgts PA 19018-
2402. 610/622-3900.

**Cyklop Strapping
Corporation**
Boot Rd, Downingtown
PA 19335. 610/873-
0290.

Data Card Corporation
207 Progress Dr,
Montgomeryvle PA
18936-9618. 215/699-
7041.

Double H Plastics Inc.
50 W State Rd,
Warminster PA 18974.
215/674-4100.

Fabri-Kal Corporation
Valmont Industrial Park,
Hazleton PA 18201.
717/454-6672.

Forbo Industries Inc.
PO Box 667, Hazleton PA
18201-0673.
2013662020.

Fypon Inc.
22 E Pennsylvania Ave,
Stewartstown PA
17363-4096. 717/993-
2593.

Helvoet Pharma Inc.
9012 Pennsauken Hwy,
Pennsauken NJ 08110-
1204. 609/663-2202.

ICI Americas Inc.
Mantua Grove Rd,
Paulsboro NJ 08066.
609/423-8300.

**Jamison Plastic
Corporation**
5001 Crackersport Rd,
Allentown PA 18104-
9553. 610/391-1400.

Jet Plastica Industries
1100 Schwab Rd,
Hatfield PA 19440-3231.
215/362-1501.

**Kerr-Plastic Products
Division**
500 New Holland Ave,
Lancaster PA 17602-
2104. 717/299-6511.

Lasco Bathware
40 Indl Rd, Elizabethtown
PA 17022. 717/367-
1100.

LNP Engineering Plastics
475 Creamery Way,
Exton PA 19341-2546.
610/363-4500.

M&Q Plastic Products
1364 Welsh Rd # 1A,
North Wales PA 19454-
1913.

MCS Industries Inc.
110 Main St, Easton PA
18042-6187. 610/253-
6268.

**Metamora Products
Corporation**
Elkland Indl Pk, Elkland
PA 16920. 814/258-
7122.

Moldamatic Inc.
29 Noeland Ave,
Langhorne PA 19047-
5288. 215/757-4819.

**Easton Molded
Acoustical Products**
1 Danforth Dr, Easton PA
18042-8992. 610/253-
7135.

Nursery Supplies Inc.
1415 Orchard Dr,
Chambersburg PA
17201-4810.

Nylomatic Division
Ten Headley Pl,
Levittown PA 19054.
215/736-0961.

**Oppenheimer Precision
Products**
169 Centennial Plz,
Horsham PA 19044.
215/659-6000.

Pac Tec Division
8425 Executive Ave,
Philadelphia PA 19153-
3805. 215/365-8400.

Packaging Resources
Locust Gap Hwy, Mount
Carmel PA 17851.
717/339-1210.

**Paramount Packaging
Corporation**
202 Oak Ave, Chalfont
PA 18914. 215/822-
2911.

Poly-Hi
900 N South Rd,
Scranton PA 18504-
1412. 717/348-6800.

Polychem Division
Franklin Ave & Grant St,
Phoenixville PA 19460.
610/935-0225.

Portion Packaging Inc.
2558 Pearl Buck Rd,
Bristol PA 19007-6896.
215/781-8200.

Quaker Plastic Corporation
103 S Manor St,
Mountville PA 17554-1615. 717/285-4571.

Scranton Lace Company
1313 Meylert Ave,
Scranton PA 18509-2224. 717/344-1121.

Shaw Plastics Corporation
201 N 1st St,
Stroudsburg PA 18360-2531. 717/421-8282.

Specialty Plastic Products Inc.
Sherwood & Reeves Sts,
Scranton PA 18512.
717/961-2042.

Superior Inc.
R D 1, Felton PA 17322-9801. 717/244-4581.

Topcraft Precision Molders Inc.
1099 Mearns Rd,
Warminster PA 18974-2213. 215/441-4700.

Tray-Pak Corporation
PO Box 244, Reading PA 19603-0244. 610/926-5800.

Warminster Fiberglass Company
725 County Line Rd,
Southampton PA 18966.
215/953-1260.

Wheaton Injection Molding
P O Box 5006, Millville NJ 08332-5006.
609/327-1540.

CYCLIC ORGANIC CRUDES AND ORGANIC DYES

Ciba-Geigy Corporation
RR 37, Toms River NJ 08753. 908/349-5200.

Crompton & Knowles Corporation
Rt 724, Birdsboro PA 19508. 610/582-8765.

INDUSTRIAL ORGANIC CHEMICALS

Allied Signal Inc.
Margaret & Bermuda Sts,
Philadelphia PA 19137.
215/533-3000.

Firmenich Inc.
PO Box 5880, Princeton NJ 08543-5880.
609/452-1000.

Glyco Inc.
Trenton Ave,
Williamsport PA 17701.
717/322-4681.

Organon Teknika Corporation
1230 Wilson Dr, West Chester PA 19380-4254.
610/431-8500.

Ruetgers-Nease Chemical Co.
201 Struble Rd, State College PA 16801-7499.
814/238-2424.

NITROGENOUS FERTILIZERS

Castle Energy Corporation
512 Township Line Rd,
Blue Bell PA 19422-2703. 215/542-0610.

Scotts Hyponex Corporation
250 Reedville Rd, Oxford PA 19363-2108.
610/932-4200.

PESTICIDES AND AGRICULTURAL CHEMICALS

Lebanon Chemical Corporation
1600 E Cumberland St,
Lebanon PA 17042-8386. 717/273-1685.

ADHESIVES AND SEALANTS

NL Chemicals Inc.
PO Box 700, Hightstown NJ 08520-1007.
609/443-2000.

Topflight Corporation
160 E 9th Ave, York PA 17404-2145. 717/843-9901.

EXPLOSIVES

Atlas Powder Co.
PO Box 271, Tamaqua PA 18252-0271.
717/386-4121.

PRINTING INK

American Inks & Coating Corporation
P O Box 803, Valley Forge PA 19482-0803.
610/272-8866.

CHEMICALS AND CHEMICAL PREPARATIONS

Lonza Inc.
900 River Rd,
Conshohocken PA 19428-2647. 610/292-4300.

Pfizer Specialty Minerals
640 N 13th St, Easton
PA 18042-1431.
610/250-3000.

INORGANIC PIGMENTS

Harcras Pigments Inc.
1525 Wood Ave, Easton
PA 18042-3186.
610/250-3700.

Sartomer Co Inc.
468 Thomas Jones Way,
Exton PA 19341-2528.
610/363-4100.

For more information on career opportunities in the chemicals/rubber and plastics industries:

Associations

AMERICAN CHEMICAL SOCIETY
Career Services, 1155 16th Street
NW, Washington DC 20036.
202/872-4600.

AMERICAN INSTITUTE OF CHEMICAL ENGINEERING
345 East 47th Street, New York NY
10017. 212/705-7338.

AMERICAN INSTITUTE OF CHEMISTS
7315 Wisconsin Avenue, Suite 502 E,
Bethesda MD 20814. 301/652-2447.

CHEMICAL MANUFACTURERS ASSOCIATION
2501 M Street NW, Washington DC
20037. 202/887-1100.

CHEMICAL MARKETING RESEARCH ASSOCIATION
60 Bay Street, Suite 702, Staten
Island NY 10301. 718/876-8800.

SOCIETY OF PLASTICS ENGINEERS
14 Fairfield Drive, P.O. Box 0403,
Brookfield CT 06804-0403. 203/775-
0471.

SOCIETY OF PLASTICS INDUSTRY
1275 K Street NW, Suite 400,
Washington DC 20005. 202/371-
5200.

Directories

CHEMICAL INDUSTRY DIRECTORY
State Mutual Book and Periodical
Service, Order Department, 17th

Floor, 521 5th Avenue, New York NY
10175. 516/537-1104.

CHEMICALS DIRECTORY
Cahners Publishing, 275 Washington
Street, Newton MA 02158. 617/964-
3030.

DIRECTORY OF CHEMICAL ENGINEERING CONSULTANTS
American Institute of Chemical
Engineering, 345 East 47th Street,
New York NY 10017. 212/705-7338.

DIRECTORY OF CHEMICAL PRODUCERS
SRI International, 333 Ravenswood
Avenue, Menlo Park CA 94025.
415/326-6200.

Magazines

CHEMICAL & ENGINEERING NEWS
1155 16th Street NW, Washington
DC 20036. 202/872-4600.

CHEMICAL MARKETING REPORTER
Schnell Publishing Co., 80 Brot Street,
23rd Floor, New York NY 10004.
212/248-4177.

CHEMICAL PROCESSING
Putnam Publishing Co., 301 East Erie
Street, Chicago IL 60611. 312/644-
2020.

CHEMICAL WEEK
888 7th Avenue, 26th Floor, New
York NY 10106. 212/621-4900.

COMMUNICATIONS: TELECOMMUNICATIONS & BROADCASTING

Broadcasting: Competition for jobs in broadcasting, especially announcers and newscasters, is extremely intense because there are often more people looking to enter the field than there are positions. The smaller the station, the more duties an announcer has, while many specialize in weather, sports or news once they get to larger stations. Broadcasting technicians face a tough labor market because of technical advances. Computer controlled programming and remote control of transmitters are two examples of advances which cut directly into the job of a technician. The U.S. Department of Labor expects employment in radio and television broadcasting to decline for broadcast technicians in the future.

Telecommunications: While the demand for telecommunications equipment was sluggish in 1993, shipments should slowly start to takeoff again. Product areas leading this growth will be network equipment, wireless communications equipment and satellite communications. The telecommunications services industry should continue to expand. Revenues generated from international services are expected to climb by 20 percent.

BELL ATLANTIC CORPORATION   *Charles Crist*
1717 Arch Street, Philadelphia PA 19103. 215/963-6000. **Contact:** Vice President/Human Resources. **Description:** A Philadelphia telecommunications corporation. **Listed on:** Midwest Stock Exchange; New York Stock Exchange; Pacific Exchange; Philadelphia Exchange. **Number of employees at this location:** 80,950.

BELL ATLANTIC STAR
P.O. Box 17505, Code EVRU, Arlington VA 22201. 215/466-2678. **Contact:** Manager of Employment. **Description:** A subsidiary operation of Bell Atlantic, the telecommunications firm.

COMCAST CORPORATION
1234 Market Street, 16th Floor, Philadelphia PA 19107-3723. 215/665-1700. **Contact:** Human Resources. **Description:** A cable TV system operator, which also distributes Muzak and provides cellular phone service. **Common positions include:** Accountant/Auditor; Administrator; Customer Service Representative; Financial Analyst; General Manager; Operations/Production Manager; Purchasing Agent and Manager. **Educational backgrounds include:** Accounting; Business Administration; Engineering; Finance; Marketing; Mathematics. **Special Programs:** Training Programs. **Corporate headquarters location:** This Location. **Operations at this facility include:** Administration; Divisional Headquarters; Regional Headquarters. **Number of employees nationwide:** 3,478.

GARDEN STATE CABLE TV
1250 Haddonfield-Berlin Road, P.O. Box 5025, Cherry Hill NJ 08034. 609/354-1880.
Contact: Human Resources. **Description:** A cable broadcaster.

GILBERT COMMONWEALTH, INC.
P.O. Box 1498, Reading PA 19603. 215/775-2600. **Contact:** Ross Tierno,
Employment Relations Manager. **Description:** Engaged in the manufacture of
telecommunication simulation systems.

ms. Iona Harper - Dir of HR.

KYW-TV NEWS
5th and Market Streets, Philadelphia PA 19106. 215/233-3333. **Contact:** Human
Resources Department. **Description:** A television station.

QVC NETWORK, INC. & SUBSIDIARIES
1365 Enterprise Drive, West Chester PA 19380. 215/431-8456. **Contact:** Mike
Cavanaugh, Manager of Staffing. **Description:** The well-known nationwide cable TV
home shopping network. **Corporate headquarters location:** This Location. **Listed on:**
NASDAQ. **Annual Revenues:** $1,200,000,000. **Number of employees at this location:**
2,500. **Number of employees nationwide:** 6,000. **Projected hires for the next 12
months (Nationwide):** 200 hires.

REGAL COMMUNICATIONS CORPORATION
1250 Virginia Drive, Fort Washington PA 19034-2801. 215/643-2100. **Contact:**
Human Resources. **Description:** Develops and markets informational and entertainment
phone programs for the consumer market, offering passive recordings, interactive
recordings, and line programs on a pay-per-call basis. **Number of employees at this
location:** 227.

WCAU-TV CHANNEL 10 *ms. Bernadette Prudente - manager*
City and Monument Avenue, Philadelphia PA 19131. 215/668-5510. **Contact:** Human
Resources Department. **Description:** A television station.

WILM NEWS RADIO
1215 French Street, Wilmington DE 19801. 302/656-9800. **Contact:** Human
Resources. **Description:** An all news AM radio station.

*Note: Because addresses and telephone numbers of smaller companies change rapidly, we
recommend you contact each company and verify the information below before contacting
employers. Mass mailings are not recommended.*

Additional large employers: 500+

**BROADCASTING
EQUIPMENT**

**TELEPHONE
COMMUNICATIONS**

**CABLE/PAY TELEVISION
SERVICES**

Gai-Tronics Corporation
P.O. Box 31, Reading PA
19603-0031. 610/777-
1374.

AT&T Company
2525 N 12th St.,
Reading PA 19605-2749.
610/939-7011.

Mercom Inc.
P.O. Box 3000, Wilkes
Barre PA 18703-3000.
717/825-1100.

Additional medium sized employers: under 500

RADIOTELEPHONE COMMUNICATIONS

A&A Connections Inc.
705 W Montgomery Ave,
Philadelphia PA 19122-
2905. 610/667-8353.

AT&T
2401 Reach Rd,
Williamsport PA 17701-
4193. 717/327-9142.

AT&T Marketing Sales Office
214 Senate Av Ste 401,
Camp Hill PA 17011-
2336. 717/731-6600.

ATX Telecommunication Service
39 E Chestnut Hill Ave,
Philadelphia PA 19118-
2728. 215/386-4900.

Advanced Telecom Services Inc.
996 Old Eagle School Rd
Ste 11, Wayne PA
19087-1806. 610/964-
9146.

Advanced Telecommunications Network
522 S Broadway,
Gloucester Cy NJ 08030-
2428. 609/742-8096.

AIM Telephone Inc.
75 Utley Dr, Camp Hill
PA 17011-8000.
717/731-9500.

All Type Wire
54 State Ave, Clementon
NJ 08021-3215.
609/783-7452.

Allnet Communication Service Inc.
1528 Walnut St,
Philadelphia PA 19102-
3604. 215/546-1100.
Mathew Thatcher Salesman

Allnet Communications
130 N Broadway,
Camden NJ 08102-
1122. 609/964-8161.

Alltel Pennsylvania Inc.
211 Mulberry St,
Harrisburg PA 17104-
3509. 717/232-6501.

Alltel Pennsylvania Inc.
E Penn, Muncy PA
17756. 717/546-8123.

American Long Lines
2401 Locust St,
Philadelphia PA 19103-
5553. 215/568-7300.

American Telephone & Telegraph
7000 Lincoln Dr E,
Marlton NJ 08053-3128.
609/273-4600.

Amnex Inc.
2300 Computer Rd,
Willow Grove PA 19090-
1732. 215/657-5722.

Associated Phone & Data Service
431 High St, Easton PA
18042-7630. 610/559-
1019.

Async
421 Chestnut St,
Philadelphia PA 19106-
2415. 215/440-4000.

BBC International
124 E Main St,
Norristown PA 19401-
4917. 610/277-7830.

Bell Telephone Of Pennsylvania
59 N 4th St, Easton PA
18042-3530. 610/250-
5986.

Bell Telephone Of Pennsylvania
404 W 4th St,
Williamsport PA 17701-
6002. 717/327-7801.

Bell Telephone Of Pennsylvania
351 Market St,
Williamsport PA 17701-
6329. 717/327-7984.

Bell Telephone Of Pennsylvania
121 Adams Av 1st Fl,
Scranton PA 18503-
1805. 717/348-5851.

Bell Telephone Of Pennsylvania
125 S 30th St, Camp Hill
PA 17011-4507.
717/761-0021.

Bell Telephone Of Pennsylvania
14 N High St,
Mechanicsburg PA
17055-6258. 717/766-
0207.

Bell Telephone Of Pennsylvania
126 N Duke St,
Lancaster PA 17602-
2843. 717/299-8401.

Bell Telephone of Pennsylvania
409 Washington St,
Reading PA 19601-3907.
610/371-4050.

CS Telcom
1120 Napfle Ave,
Philadelphia PA 19111-
2743. 215/722-5552.

**Capital
Telecommunications**
301 Chestnut St,
Harrisburg PA 17101-
2755. 717/234-4900.

**Capital
Telecommunications**
96 S George St Fl 4,
York PA 17401-1426.
717/848-8800.

**Capital
Telecommunications**
108 N Washington Ave
Ste 802, Scranton PA
18503-1818. 717/963-
9350.

Catsco
61 Waller St, Wilkes
Barre PA 18702-3428.
717/823-8302.

Coastcom Inc.
3 Johns Dr,
Mechanicsburg PA
17055-1550. 717/691-
9669.

**Colonial Communications
Inc.**
1655 N Olden Ave,
Trenton NJ 08638-3205.
609/883-2787.

**Corporate
Communications
Consultants**
610 Jackson Rd, Atco
NJ 08004-1232.
609/753-9339.

**Corporate
Telecommunications Plan**
620 Baron Dekalb Ln,
Wayne PA 19087-1302.
610/688-2333.

**Crew Communications
Management**
1243 Victoria Ln, West
Chester PA 19380-4046.
610/431-1675.

**Denca Communications
Inc.**
1222 W Ridge Pike,
Conshohocken PA
19428-1059. 610/825-
2272.

Dennison Group Limited
621 Orchard Way, Mount
Laurel NJ 08054-1313.
609/778-0144.

Dicomm Inc.
430 Kelham Ct, Mount
Laurel NJ 08054-3724.
609/273-1496.

Digitel Long Distance
1301 Whitehorse Merc
Rd, Trenton NJ 08619-
3826. 609/581-8666.

**Diversified
Communication Service
Inc.**
112 E King St, York PA
17403-2036. 717/852-
7590.

**Diversified Telecom
Services**
1613 Newton Ransom
Blvd, Clarks Summit PA
18411-9606. 717/586-
8441.

**Eastern Business Alliance
Inc.**
52 S Memorial Hwy,
Shavertown PA 18708-
1458. 717/696-0142.

**Eastern Telephone Long
Distance**
1300 Virginia Dr Fl 220,
Ft Washington PA
19034-3223. 215/628-
4111.

✓ sent

**Eastern Telelogic
Corporation**
630 Freedom Business
Ctr Dr, Kng Of Prussa PA
19406-1331. 610/337-
8899.

Econo-Tel
2690 Commerce Dr,
Harrisburg PA 17110-
9370. 717/541-8140.

Eggbert Communications
440 Harvest Dr,
Harrisburg PA 17111-
5652. 717/236-1915.

Emerald Communications
1703 Grant Rd, Lansdale
PA 19446-6036.
215/699-8877.

**EMI Communications
Corporation**
24 Northeast Dr, Hershey
PA 17033-2732.
717/533-6314.

**Enterprise Telephone
Company**
5 N Maple Ave, Leola PA
17540-1414. 717/656-
2611.

Execom
340 E Maple Ave,
Langhorne PA 19047-
2850. 215/750-5218.

Execom
340 Maple Ave,
Philadelphia PA 19116-
1042. 215/750-5218.

**Executone Of
Williamsport**
36 W 4th St # 3,
Williamsport PA 17701-
6213. 717/322-6300.

Ferraro & Associates
235 E Elizabeth St,
Landisville PA 17538-
1222. 717/898-1789.

**Fiberlink Communications
Corporation**
11 Bala Ave, Bala
Cynwyd PA 19004-
3210. 610/668-7950.

**First Choice
Communications Inc.**
PO Box 476, Quakertown
PA 18951-0476.

**First Federated
Communications Inc.**
2500 Maryland Rd,
Willow Grove PA 19090-
1216. 215/784-9755.

**Fujitsu Business
Communication Systems**
1001 Briggs Rd, Mount
Laurel NJ 08054-4100.
609/727-9494.

**Fujitsu Business
Communications
Systems**
5060 Ritter Rd,
Mechanicsburg PA
17055-6918. 717/790-
9880.

GTE
409 Railroad St, Emmaus
PA 18049-3826.
610/965-8888.

Image Technology Inc.
108 Park Rd, Ambler PA
19002-1120. 215/641-
1470.

**Innovative
Communications**
1919 Chestnut St,
Philadelphia PA 19103-
3401. 215/567-7868.

Integra Trak
9 Hilltop Ln, Medford NJ
08055-2362. 609/953-
7661.

**ISB Information Service
Bur Inc.**
5832 Tulip St,
Philadelphia PA 19135-
4208. 215/537-0505.

**JWP Info Systems
Network Service**
4627 W Chester Pike,
Newtown Sq PA 19073-
2225. 610/325-0300.

Keystone Telecom
205 N Main Ave,
Scranton PA 18504-
3303. 717/344-7748.

LED Communications
908 S Franklin St, Wilkes
Barre PA 18702-3463.
717/825-9399.

Larse Corporation
2116 Chapman Cir,
Jamison PA 18929-
1542. 215/343-8010.

**Lehigh Valley
Communications**
618 2nd Ave, Bethlehem
PA 18018-5516.
610/974-9479.

Lightnet
2401 Locust St,
Philadelphia PA 19103-
5553. 215/854-8455.

Listco Inc.
325 Westtown Rd, West
Chester PA 19382-4556.
610/429-3300.

Local Area Telecom
216 Paoli Ave,
Philadelphia PA 19128-
4340. 215/483-8769.

**Management Resource
Tech Inc.**
2306 Aspen Cir,
Springfield PA 19064-
1013. 610/328-9558.

**Markussen Business
Products**
146 Cambridge Dr, Glen
Mills PA 19342-1538.
610/558-9197.

**MCI Telecommunications
Corporation**
3 Independence Way,
Princeton NJ 08540-
6626. 609/520-1080.

**MCI Telecommunications
Corporation**
1125 Atlantic Ave,
Atlantic City NJ 08401-
4806. 609/348-4963.

**Metromedia
Communications
Corporation**
8 N Queen St, Lancaster
PA 17603-3829.
717/299-1260.

**Metromedia
Communications Inc.**
301 Chestnut St,
Harrisburg PA 17101-
2755. 717/234-2633.

Metromedia Company
214 Carnegie Ctr,
Princeton NJ 08540-
6237. 609/452-8100.

Montallo Contracting
454 16th Ave, Brick NJ
08724-2659. 908/840-
6889.

Nationwide Telecom
3747 Church Rd Ste
106, Mount Laurel NJ
08054-1151. 609/727-
4929.

Net-Tel
1358 Hooper Ave # 277,
Toms River NJ 08753-
2856.

**Network Analysis Group
Inc.**
7540 Windsor Dr,
Allentown PA 18195-
1015. 610/391-1434.

Network Cable Inc.
9958 Bridle Rd,
Philadelphia PA 19115-
1303. 215/464-1517.

Network Fax Inc.
230 Moore St,
Philadelphia PA 19148-
1925. 215/271-1289.

**Network
Telemanagement Service
Inc.**
183 Old Belmont Ave,
Bala Cynwyd PA 19004-
1934. 610/660-8000.

**North American
Communications**
887 Wyoming Ave Ste 5,
Pittston PA 18644-1358.
717/693-4500.

**NTE National Phone
Exchange Inc.**
36 N Main St,
Chambersburg PA
17201-1811. 717/267-
3100.

**NTE National Phone
Exchange Inc.**
1770 E Market St, York
PA 17402-2874.
717/840-4225.

OTS Inc.
403 Essex Ct, Lansdale
PA 19446-6393.
215/368-9712.

Publicall Corporation
325 Chestnut St,
Philadelphia PA 19106-
2614. 215/625-0050.

Pulse
202 E 1st St, Birdsboro
PA 19508-2349.
610/369-2333.

Quadis Inc.
350 S Main St,
Doylestown PA 18901-
4871. 215/345-9229.

**Rainbow
Communications Inc.**
700 Riverview Dr, Brielle
NJ 08730-1419.
908/528-6221.

RCI Corporation
200 Stevens Dr,
Philadelphia PA 19113-
1522. 610/595-3300.

Ridge Electric
454 16th Ave, Brick NJ
08724-2659. 908/840-
0398.

Shamus Associates
1548 Ford Rd, Bensalem
PA 19020-4506.
215/638-7990.

spook w/Lou

**Shared Communications
Services** *suite 219*
1800 J F Kennedy Blvd,
Philadelphia PA 19103. *news*
215/587-1500. *admin asst*
Ms. Paula Brown-Pres.

**Shared Network Services
Inc.**
354 Winding Way,
Merion Sta PA 19066-
1534. 610/664-6228.

Sprint
5 Independence Way,
Princeton NJ 08540-
6627. 609/452-7750.

Sprint
214 Senate Ave, Camp
Hill PA 17011-2336.
717/731-4300.

Starplex Communications
1508 Almond St,
Williamsport PA 17701-
2508. 717/326-1199.

**Strategic
Telecommunications**
5239 Hamilton Blvd,
Allentown PA 18106-
9113. 610/391-8999.

Sun Telecommunications
623 S 19th St,
Philadelphia PA 19146-
1438. 215/875-1500. *397-0200*

Tel-Advantage
126 N Merion Ave, Bryn
Mawr PA 19010-2810.
610/520-9696.

Tel-Save Inc.
1017 York Rd, Willow
Grove PA 19090-1317.
215/659-5927.

Telcom Systems Services
9071 Mill Creek Rd,
Levittown PA 19054-
4204. 215/547-6950.

Telcom United
219 Country Gate Rd,
Wayne PA 19087-5321.
610/688-0801.

Tele Consult
257 W King St,
Lancaster PA 17603-
3720. 717/394-3934.

Telecom Managers
50 Birchwood Dr,
Doylestown PA 18901-
2407. 215/340-0495.

Telecommunication Management Service
53 Ramsgate Ct, Blue Bell PA 19422-2549.
610/834-1280.

Teleconcern Inc.
1616 Walnut St, Philadelphia PA 19103-5313. 215/732-4960.

Telemutual Services
661 Moore Rd, Kng Of Prussa PA 19406-1317.
610/768-5600.

Teleshare Communucations
113 Cobblestone Dr, Mount Laurel NJ 08054-2417. 609/866-1326.

Televoice Information Services
1018 N Christian St, Lancaster PA 17602-1900. 717/399-9477.

Telshare Associates
1200 Lincoln Ave Ste 2A, Prospect Park PA 19076-2034. 610/461-1100.

TFC Telecommunications
420 N 9th Ave, Scranton PA 18504-2002.
717/342-9480.

Tri America Inc.
2020 Downyflake Ln, Allentown PA 18103-4776. 610/791-4939.

Tricomm Services Corporation
86 Beverly Rancocas Rd, Willingboro NJ 08046-2597. 609/871-2401.

Union Brotherhood Assocs Inc.
17 Front St, Camp Hill PA 17011-6303.
717/731-0395.

United Telephone Company Of Pennsylvania
40 N 3rd St, Columbia PA 17512-1104.
717/684-2101.

United Telephone Long Distance
401 E Louther St, Carlisle PA 17013-2657.
717/245-2002.

Utility Research Associates
110 Roosevelt Blvd, Marmora NJ 08223-1403. 609/390-9388.

Valet Phone
1237 Clearview St, Forked River NJ 08731-4534. 609/971-5976.

Voice Tel Of Northeast Pennsylvania
7 Broad St, Pittston PA 18640-1802. 717/883-4660.

Voicecom Systems
400 Glover St, Woodbury NJ 08096-2624.
609/384-0020.

Walsh Communication Group
312 S 24th St, Philadelphia PA 19103-6436. 215/735-5919.

Wats International
12 Executive Campus, Cherry Hill NJ 08002-2956. 609/662-4000.

Xtend Communications Corporation
1026 W Airy St, Norristown PA 19401-4402. 610/277-5552.

RADIO BROADCAST STATIONS

Entertainment Communications Inc.
100 Presidential Blvd, Bala Cynwyd PA 19004-1103. 610/667-1226.

TELEVISION BROADCAST STATIONS

WHTM-TV Inc.
3235 Hoffman St, Harrisburg PA 17110-2226. 717/236-2727.

WGAL TV
333 Market St, Harrisburg PA 17101-2213. 717/236-5549.

WGAL-TV
PO Box 7127, Lancaster PA 17604-7127.
717/393-5851.

WGTW TV-48
642 N Broad St, Philadelphia PA 19130-3409. 215/765-4800.

WNEP-TV
16 Montage Mountain Rd, Moosic PA 18507-1753. 717/346-7474.

WPHL TV-17
5001 Wynnefield Ave, Philadelphia PA 19131-2598. 215/878-1700.

WPVI-TV CHANNEL 6
333 Market St, Harrisburg PA 17101-2210. 717/234-6668.

WPVI-TV CHANNEL 6
4100 City Ave,
Philadelphia PA 19131-
1610. 215/878-9700.

WTGI-TV CHANNEL 61
520 N Delaware Ave,
Philadelphia PA 19123-
4214. 215/923-2661.

WTXF-TV CHANNEL 29
4 & Market, Philadelphia
PA 19106. 215/925-
2929.

WYBE TV 35
6070 Ridge Ave,
Philadelphia PA 19128-
1647. 215/483-3900.

**CABLE AND OTHER PAY
TELEVISION SERVICES**

Instructional
216 Paoli Ave,
Philadelphia PA 19128-
4340. 215/483-2150.

It's The Law
1927 Hamilton St,
Philadelphia PA 19130-
3817. 215/568-7967.

Pennsylvania Pay TV
300 Domino Ln,
Philadelphia PA 19128-
4352. 215/483-4550.

Service Electric Cable TV
1045 W Hamilton St,
Allentown PA 18101-
1095. 610/434-7833.

Blue Ridge Cable TV
463 Delaware Ave,
Palmerton PA 18071-
1908. 610/826-2555.

**TELEPHONE AND
TELEPHONE APPARATUS**

**Communications Test
Design Inc.**
1373 Enterprise Dr, West
Chester PA 19380-5959.
610/436-5203.

**Interdigital
Communication
Corporation**
2200 Renaissance Blvd,
Kng Of Prussa PA
19406-2755. 610/278-
7800.

Metrologic Instruments
Rte 42, Blackwood NJ
08012-9805. 609/228-
8100.

Rolm
3 Computer Dr, Cherry
Hill NJ 08003-4007.
609/424-2400.

**RADIO AND TELEVISION
BROADCASTING AND
COMMUNICATIONS
EQUIPMENT**

Base Ten Systems Inc.
1 Electronics Dr, Trenton
NJ 08619-2054.
609/586-7010.

Commonwealth Comm
5000 W Tilghman St,
Allentown PA 18104-
9109. 610/395-2020.

Drexelbrook Engineering
205 Keith Valley Rd,
Horsham PA 19044-
1499. 215/674-1234.

Uni Source Ltd
120 E 3rd St,
Williamsport PA 17701-
6623. 717/322-2682.

**COMMUNICATIONS
EQUIPMENT**

Crestek Inc.
PO Box 7266, Trenton
NJ 08628-0266.
609/883-4000.

GAI-Tronics Corporation
400 E Wyomissing Ave,
Mohnton PA 19540-
1503. 610/777-1374.

**General Atronics
Corporation**
1200 E Mermaid Ln,
Philadelphia PA 19118-
1635. 215/233-4100.

**Marlee Electronics
Corporation**
2501 S Front St,
Philadelphia PA 19148-
4107. 215/463-6243.

Patrick & Wilkins Co.
P O Box 28008 W Park
Station, Philadelphia PA
19131-8008. 215/473-
8300.

For more information on career opportunities in the communications industries:

Associations

ACADEMY OF TELEVISION ARTS & SCIENCES
5220 Lankershim Boulevard, North Hollywood CA 91601. 818/752-1870 (Research Library).

AMERICAN WOMEN IN RADIO AND TV, INC.
1650 Tysons Boulevard, Suite 200, McLean VA 22102. 703/506-3290.

BROADCAST PROMOTION AND MARKETING EXECUTIVES
6255 Sunset Boulevard, Suite 624, Los Angeles CA 90028. 213/465-3777.

INTERNATIONAL TELEVISION ASSOCIATION
6311 North O'Connor Road, LB51, Suite 236, Irving TX 75309. 214/869-1112. Membership required.

NATIONAL ASSOCIATION OF BROADCASTERS
1771 N Street NW, Washington DC 20036. 202/429-5300, ext. 5490

(Research Library). 202/429-5497. Provides further employment information.

NATIONAL CABLE TELEVISION ASSOCIATION
1724 Massachusetts Avenue NW, Washington DC 20007. 202/775-3550.

UNITED STATES TELEPHONE ASSOCIATION
900 19th Street NW, Suite 800, Washington DC 20006. 202/326-7300.

Magazines

BROADCASTING AND CABLE
Broadcasting Publications Inc., 1705 DeSales Street NW, Washington DC 20036. 202/659-2340.

ELECTRONIC MEDIA
Crain Communications, 220 East 42nd Street, New York NY 10017. 212/210-0100.

COMPUTER HARDWARE, SOFTWARE AND SERVICES

Computer and Information Services: Information services are expected to remain among the most active sectors of the U.S. economy. Computer professional services include three activities: systems integration, custom programming and consulting/training. During both 1992 and 1993, most companies failed to meet their own growth expectations, so many were more willing to reduce both inventory and employment. The recent shortage of venture capital has continued to reduce the size of start-up firms offering computer professional services.

Equipment and Software: The U.S. computer industry continues it road to recovery from the 1989-91 recession, led by an increase in domestic demand. The U.S. Department of Commerce notes the "mix of shipments was towards cheaper and increasingly more powerful workstations and personal computers, as users continue to shift many of their applications from mainframes and minicomputers." The department also added that revenues of the U.S. software industry should continue to grow strongly, benefitting from its leading position in the world market and the continuing demand from users to more effectively harness the power of their PCs.

AW COMPUTER SYSTEMS INC.
9000A Commerce Parkway, Mount Laurel NJ 08054. 609/234-3939. **Contact:** Bradford Smith III, Chief Financial Officer. **Description:** A designer, developer, and marketer of high-performance computer-based point-of-sale systems for large retail chains. **Common positions include:** Computer Programmer; Electrical/Electronic Engineer; Systems Analyst. **Educational backgrounds include:** Computer Science; Engineering; Liberal Arts. **Benefits:** Dental Insurance; Disability Coverage; Life Insurance; Medical Insurance; Stock Option. **Corporate headquarters location:** This Location. **Operations at this facility include:** Administration; Research and Development; Sales; Service.

AMETEK, INC.
U.S. GAUGE DIVISION
900 Clymer Avenue, Sellersville PA 18960. 215/257-6531. **Contact:** Human Resources Department. **Description:** An electronic computer manufacturer.

BELL ATLANTIC BUSINESS SYSTEMS SERVICES, INC.
50 E. Swedesford Road, Frazer PA 19355. 215/296-6000. **Contact:** Human Resources Department. **Description:** A computer service and repair company.

COMMODORE INTERNATIONAL, LTD.
1200 Wilson Drive, West Chester PA 19380. 215/431-9100. **Contact:** Personnel Department. **Description:** A microcomputer systems company. **Number of employees nationwide:** 3,067.

COMMUNICATION CONCEPTS INC.
1010 Pulinski Road, Ivyland PA 18974. 215/672-6900. **Contact:** Rita Chrismer, Personnel Administrator. **Description:** A data processing company.

CORPORATE DATA SYSTEMS
3700 Market Street, Philadelphia PA 19104. 215/222-7046. **Contact:** Human Resources. **Description:** A computer-integrated systems design company.

DECISION DATA COMPUTER CORPORATION
One Progress Avenue, Horsham PA 19044. 215/674-3300. **Contact:** Director of Employee Relations. **Description:** A high-tech marketer and servicer of computer peripheral equipment made compatible with the IBM mid-range systems (AS400, S/38, S/36, S/34). **Common positions include:** Computer Programmer; Customer Service Representative; Electrical/Electronic Engineer; Personnel/Labor Relations Specialist; Services Sales Representative. **Educational backgrounds include:** Business Administration; Computer Science; Engineering; Marketing. **Benefits:** Dental Insurance; Disability Coverage; Employee Discounts; Life Insurance; Medical Insurance; Pension Plan; Savings Plan; Tuition Assistance. **Corporate headquarters location:** This Location. **Operations at this facility include:** Administration; Divisional Headquarters; Regional Headquarters; Research and Development; Sales; Service.

FORMATION, INC.
121 Whittendale Drive, Moorestown NJ 08057. 609/234-5020. **FAX:** 609/234-8543. **Contact:** Kathy Cava, Manager of Human Resources. **Description:** Engaged in the design and manufacture of custom-designed systems and peripheral subsystems; plug compatible controllers and peripherals; market-specific communications servers; and off-the-shelf board-level hardware and software products. Products are generated from two distinct core businesses: mass storage solution and network interoperability. Established in 1970, Formation is a privately-held, employee-owned company. **Common positions include:** Computer Engineer; Electrical/Electronic Engineer; Mechanical Engineer; Software Engineer. **Educational backgrounds include:** Engineering. **Benefits:** Dental Insurance; Disability Coverage; Flextime Plan; Investment Plan; Life Insurance; Medical Insurance; Profit Sharing; Savings Plan; Tuition Assistance. **Corporate headquarters location:** This Location. **Operations at this facility include:** Administration; Manufacturing; Regional Headquarters; Research and Development; Sales; Service. **Number of employees at this location:** 300.

GBC/VITEK
100 GBC Court, Berlin NJ 08009. 609/767-2500. **Contact:** Human Resources. **Description:** Sells microcomputer systems, peripherals, and support products. Provides systems support, services, and network systems training. **Number of employees at this location:** 132.

INTERMETRICS INC.
607 Louis Drive, Warminster PA 18974. 215/674-2913. **Contact:** Margaret Ulrich, Personnel/Defense Electronics. **Description:** Design, development, and marketing of state-of-the-art computer software products and services: compilers, support software, and real-time applications software. **Number of employees at this location:** 580.

ROBEC INCORPORATED
425 Privet Road, Horsham PA 19044. 215/675-9300. **Contact:** Human Resources. **Description:** A wholesaler of computer equipment.

SEI
680 East Swedesford Road, Wayne PA 19087. 215/254-1000. **Contact:** Personnel. **Description:** A diversified software products company. The company's core business is to provide investment accounting software to over 400 banking institution customers. **Common positions include:** Information Systems Consultant; Technician. **Benefits:** Dental Insurance; Disability Coverage; Life Insurance; Medical Insurance; Profit Sharing; Savings Plan; Tuition Assistance. **Operations at this facility include:** Administration; Research and Development; Sales; Service. **Listed on:** American Stock Exchange. **Annual Revenues:** $210,000,000.

SAFEGUARD SCIENTIFICS, INC.
800 The Safeguard Building, Wayne PA 19087-1945. 215/293-0600. **Contact:** Personnel. **Description:** A diversified entrepreneurial technology firm that acquires interests in young and growing businesses in high-growth markets.

SHARED MEDICAL SYSTEMS CORPORATION
51 Valley Stream Parkway, Malvern PA 19355. 215/219-6300. **Contact:** Noreen Becci, Human Resources Manager. **Description:** Specializes in computer-based information systems for the health care industry. **Number of employees nationwide:** 4,000.

SUNGARD DATA SYSTEMS
1285 Drummers Lane, Wayne PA 19087. 215/341-8700. **Contact:** Human Resources. **Description:** SunGard Data Systems provides specialized computer services, mainly proprietary investment support systems for the financial services industry and disaster recovery services. **Number of employees at this location:** 2,090.

TSENG LABS
6 Terry Drive, Newtown PA 18940-1831. 215/968-0502. **Contact:** Human Resources. **Description:** Manufactures and sells hardware/software peripheral enhancement packages and custom-designed integrated circuits for personal computers. **Number of employees at this location:** 59.

Note: Because addresses and telephone numbers of smaller companies change rapidly, we recommend you contact each company and verify the information below before contacting employers. Mass mailings are not recommended.

Additional medium sized employers: 100-499

COMPUTER PROGRAMMING SERVICES

Primavera Systems
2 Bala Plz Ste 925, Bala Cynwyd PA 19004-1511. 610/667-8600.

RMS Technologies Inc.
6725 Delilah Rd, Pleasantville NJ 08232-9798. 609/485-0615.

COMPUTER PROCESSING AND DATA PROCESSING SERVICES

Paychex Inc.
7660 Imperial Way # C-103, Allentown PA 18195-1016. 610/398-7518.

INFORMATION RETRIEVAL SERVICES

Biosciences Information Service
2100 Arch St, Philadelphia PA 19103-1308. 215/587-4800.

COMPUTER RELATED SERVICES

Applied Color Systems
5 Princess Rd, Trenton NJ 08648-2380. 609/896-3620.

Applied Systems Technologies
100 Highpoint Dr, Chalfont PA 18914-3926. 215/822-8888.

ELECTRONIC COMPUTERS

Datamedia Corporation
7401 Central Hwy, Merchantville NJ 08109-4310. 609/665-5400.

Mikros Systems Corporation
3490 US Highway 1 Ste 5, Princeton NJ 08540-5920. 609/987-1513.

Okidata
532 Fellowship Rd, Mount Laurel NJ 08054-3499. 609/235-2600.

Swan Technologies
3075 Research Dr, State College PA 16801-2783. 814/238-1820.

COMPUTER PERIPHERAL EQUIPMENT

Dataram Corporation
PO Box 7528, Princeton NJ 08543-7528. 609/799-0071.

Franklin Electronic Publishers
122 Burrs Rd, Mount Holly NJ 08060-4405. 609/261-4800.

National Computer Systems Inc.
3975 Continental Dr, Columbia PA 17512-9779. 717/684-4600.

Numonics Corporation
101 Commerce Dr, Montgomeryvle PA 18936-9628. 215/362-2766.

Telenex Corporation
13000 Midlantic Dr, Mount Laurel NJ 08054-1529. 609/234-7900.

World-Wide Technology
Fdlty Ct 259 Radnor Chester Rd, Wayne PA 19087. 610/964-0652.

Additional small employers: under 100

COMPUTERS AND COMPUTER PERIPHERAL EQUIPMENT

Office Automation Systems Inc.
811 Blakeslee Boulevard Dr E #, Lehighton PA 18235-8712.

COMPUTER PROGRAMMING SERVICES

Data Systems Analysts
4300 Haddonfield Rd Ste 113, Merchantville NJ 08109-3376. 609/665-6800.

Tangram Ent Solutions
7 Great Valley Pky, Malvern PA 19355-1425. 610/647-0440.

COMPUTER PROCESSING AND DATA PREPARATION

Teradyne Inc.
1259 S Cedar Crt Blvd Ste 328 , Allentown PA 18103-6259. 610/776-1671.

COMPUTER RENTAL AND LEASING

Dan Perrin
119 Fayette St, Conshohocken PA 19428-1817. 610/825-9184.

Rent-A-Center
Pottstown Plaza, Pottstown PA 19464. 610/323-9526.

COMPUTER RELATED SERVICES

Lyco Computer Marketing & Consulting
2595 Lycoming Creek Rd, Williamsport PA 17701-1139. 717/494-0722.

Macro Corporation
700 Business Center Dr, Horsham PA 19044-3471. 215/674-2000.

COMPUTERS

Human Designed Systems Inc.
421 Feheley Dr, Kng Of Prussa PA 19406-2658. 215/382-5000.

For more information on career opportunities in the computer industry:

Associations

ASSOCIATION FOR COMPUTING MACHINERY
1515 Broadway, 17th Floor, New York NY 10036. 212/869-7440. Membership required.

INFORMATION AND TECHNOLOGY ASSOCIATION OF AMERICA
1616 North Fort Myer Drive, Suite 1300, Arlington VA 22209. 703/522-5055.

Directories

INFORMATION INDUSTRY DIRECTORY
Gale Research Inc., 835 Penobscot Building, Detroit MI 48226. 313/961-2242.

Magazines

COMPUTER-AIDED ENGINEERING
Penton Publishing, 1100 Superior Avenue, Cleveland OH 44114. 216/696-7100

COMPUTERWORLD
CW Communications, 375 Cochituate Road, P.O. Box 01701-9171. 508/879-0700.

DATA COMMUNICATIONS
McGraw-Hill, 1221 Avenue of the Americas, New York NY 10020. 212/512-2000.

DATAMATION
Cahners Publishing, 275 Washington Street, Newton MA 02158. 617/964-3030.

IDC REPORT
International Data Corporation, Five Speen Street, Framingham MA 01701. 508/872-8200.

EDUCATIONAL SERVICES

Job prospects for college faculty will increase at average speed during the '90s. Most openings will result from retirements. The best prospects are in business, engineering, health sciences, physical sciences, and mathematics. Among kindergarten and elementary school teachers, the best opportunities await those with training in special education. Among high school teachers, opportunities will increase rapidly. Increased teacher involvement and higher salaries will attract new applicants.

ALLENTOWN COLLEGE
18043 Bushkill Drive, Easton PA 18043-3639. 215/253-9999. **Contact:** Personnel. **Description:** A college.

BLOOMSBURG UNIVERSITY OF PENNSYLVANIA
Waller Administration Building, Bloomsburg PA 17815. 717/389-4415. **Contact:** Human Resources. **Description:** A university.

CAMDEN COLLEGE
P.O. Box 200, Blackwood NJ 08012. 609/227-7200. **Contact:** Human Resources. **Description:** A college.

COMMUNITY COLLEGE/PHILADELPHIA
1700 Spring Garden Street, Philadelphia PA 19130. 215/751-8000. **Contact:** Human Resources Department. **Description:** A community college.

DREXEL UNIVERSITY
32nd & Chestnut Street, Philadelphia PA 19104. 215/895-2775. **Contact:** Personnel Department. **Description:** A university.

HAHNEMANN UNIVERSITY
Broad & Vine, Philadelphia PA 19102. 215/762-7114. **Contact:** Human Resources. **Description:** A university.

LA SALLE UNIVERSITY
1900 West Olney Avenue, Philadelphia PA 19141. 215/951-1013. **Contact:** Personnel Department. **Description:** A university.

LEHIGH UNIVERSITY
Office of Human Resources, 428 Brodhead Avenue, Bethlehem PA 18015. 215/758-3900. **Contact:** Rebecca Bowen, Manager of Employee Relations and Training. **Description:** A university. **Common positions include:** Accountant/Auditor; Administrator; Biological Scientist/ Biochemist; Buyer; Civil Engineer; Computer Programmer; Draftsperson; Electrical/Electronic Engineer; Geologist/Geophysicist; Industrial Engineer; Mechanical Engineer; Metallurgical Engineer; Personnel/Labor Relations Specialist; Reporter; Systems Analyst; Technical Writer/Editor; Transportation/Traffic Specialist. **Educational backgrounds include:** Accounting;

Biology; Business Administration; Chemistry; Computer Science; Economics; Engineering; Finance; Geology; Liberal Arts; Marketing; Mathematics; Physics. **Benefits:** Daycare Assistance; Disability Coverage; Employee Discounts; Life Insurance; Medical Insurance; Pension Plan; Savings Plan; Tuition Assistance. **Corporate headquarters location:** This Location. **Operations at this facility include:** Service.

MILLERSVILLE UNIVERSITY OF PENNSYLVANIA
Human Resources Department, Dilworth Building, Millersville PA 17551. 717/872-3011. **Contact:** Human Resources. **Description:** A university.

MORAVIAN COLLEGE
1200 Main Street, Bethlehem PA 18018. 215/861-1300. **Contact:** Personnel. **Description:** A college.

PHILADELPHIA COLLEGE OF TEXTILES & SCIENCE
4201 Henry Avenue, Philadelphia PA 19144. 215/951-2700. **Contact:** Human Resources. **Description:** A college.

PRINCETON UNIVERSITY
Clio Hall, Princeton NJ 08544-5264. 609/258-6130. **Contact:** Employment: Office of Human Resources. **Description:** A private university.

ROWAN COLLEGE
201 Mullica Hill Road, Glassboro NJ 08028. 609/863-5201. **Contact:** Human Resources Department. **Description:** A state college.

SHIPPENSBURG UNIVERSITY
1871 Old Main Drive, Shippensburg PA 17257-2299. 717/532-1124. **Contact:** Personnel Department. **Description:** A university.

TEMPLE UNIVERSITY
University Services Building, 1601 N. Broad Street, Philadelphia PA 19122. 215/204-7174. **Contact:** Personnel Department. **Description:** A university. **Common positions include:** Clinical Lab Technician; Computer Programmer; Counselor; Dental Assistant/Dental Hygienist; Education Administrator; Health Services Manager; Librarian; Library Technician; Licensed Practical Nurse; Nuclear Medicine Technologist; Occupational Therapist; Physical Therapist; Registered Nurse; Secretary; Typist/Word Processor. **Educational backgrounds include:** Biology; Chemistry; Computer Science. **Benefits:** Dental Insurance; Disability Coverage; Employee Discounts; Life Insurance; Medical Insurance; Pension Plan; Savings Plan; Tuition Assistance. **Corporate headquarters location:** This Location. **Operations at this facility include:** Administration; Research and Development. **Number of employees at this location:** 9,000.

THOMAS EDISON STATE COLLEGE
101 West State Street, Trenton NJ 08608-1176. 609/984-1114. **Contact:** Carron M. Albert, Director of Human Resources. **Description:** A state university. **Benefits:** Dental Insurance; Disability Coverage; Life Insurance; Medical Insurance; Pension Plan; Tuition Assistance. **Corporate headquarters location:** This Location.

TRENTON STATE COLLEGE
Hillwood Lakes, P.O. Box 4700, Trenton NJ 08650-4700. 609/771-1855. **Contact:** Personnel Department. **Description:** A state university.

UNIVERSITY OF DELAWARE

Academy Building, Main & Academy Street, Newark DE 19716. 302/831-2000. **Contact:** James D. Doctson, Employment Coordinator. **Description:** For professional staffing hotline: 302/831-2100; for salaried staffing hotline: 302/4831-6612. A university. **Educational backgrounds include:** Accounting; Art/Design; Biology; Business Administration; Chemistry; Communications; Computer Science; Economics; Engineering; Finance; Geology; Liberal Arts; Marketing; Mathematics; Physics. **Benefits:** Dental Insurance; Disability Coverage; Life Insurance; Medical Insurance; Pension Plan; Tuition Assistance. **Corporate headquarters location:** This Location. **Number of employees at this location:** 4,500.

UNIVERSITY OF PENNSYLVANIA

418 Guardian Drive, Philadelphia PA 19104-6021. 215/898-7285. **Contact:** Human Resources. **Description:** A prestigious and well-known university.

UNIVERSITY OF SCRANTON

Linden and Monroe, Scranton PA 18510. 717/941-7400. **Contact:** Human Resources. **Description:** A university.

WEST CHESTER UNIVERSITY OF PENNSYLVANIA

201 Carter Drive, West Chester PA 19383. 215/436-2800. **Contact:** Personnel. **Description:** A university.

WIDENER UNIVERSITY

University Place, Chester PA 19013. 215/499-4278. **Contact:** Personnel Director. **Description:** A university.

YORK COLLEGE OF PENNSYLVANIA

Human Resources Department, York PA 17405. 717/846-7788. **Contact:** Human Resources Manager. **Description:** A college.

Note: Because addresses and telephone numbers of smaller companies change rapidly, we recommend you contact each company and verify the information below before contacting employers. Mass mailings are not recommended.

Additional large employers: 500 +

COLLEGES AND UNIVERSITIES

Marywood College
2300 Adams Ave.,
Scranton PA 18509-1598. 717/348-6211.

Penn State Univ. Harrisburg
777 W Harrisburg Pike,
Middletown PA 17057-4846. 717/948-6000.

Penn State Univ. Main
201 Old Main, Univ. Park
PA 16802-1503.
8148654700.

Philadelphia College Of Textiles
Schlhse Lane and Henry
Ave., Philadelphia PA
19144. 215/951-2700.

Rider College
2083 Lawrenceville Rd.,
Trenton NJ 08648-3099.
609/896-5000.

St. Joseph's University
5600 City Ave.,
Philadelphia PA 19131-1376. 610/660-1000.

Wilkes College
170 S Franklin St.,
Wilkes Barre PA 18766-0001. 717/824-4651.

Additional medium sized employers: under 500

**ELEMENTARY AND
SECONDARY SCHOOLS
AND SCHOOL
DISTRICTS**

Abington Friends School
575 Washington Ln,
Jenkintown PA 19046-
2999. 215/886-4350.

**Abington Junior High
School**
2056 Susquehanna St,
Abington PA 19001-
4406. 215/884-4700.

Abington School District
970 Highland Ave,
Abington PA 19001-
4535. 215/884-4700.

Absegami High School
201 S Wrangleboro Rd,
Absecon NJ 08201-
9554. 609/652-1372.

Allen High School
126 N 17th St,
Allentown PA 18104-
5673. 610/820-2223.

Atlantic City High School
3701 Atlantic Ave,
Atlantic City NJ 08401-
6005. 609/343-7300.

**Bangor Area School
District**
44 S 3rd St, Bangor PA
18013-2594. 610/588-
2163.

**Bensalem Township High
School**
4319 Hulmeville Rd,
Bensalem PA 19020-
3838. 215/244-2881.

Camden High School
1700 Park Blvd, Camden
NJ 08103-2897.
609/966-5100.

**Cardinal Dougherty High
School**
6301 N 2nd St,
Philadelphia PA 19120-
1599. 215/276-2300.

**Cardinal O'Hara High
School**
1701 Sproul Rd,
Springfield PA 19064-
1137. 610/544-3800.

**Chambersburg Area Sr
High School**
511 S 6th St,
Chambersburg PA
17201-3405. 717/261-
3328.

Cheltenham High School
500 Rices Mill Rd,
Wyncote PA 19095-
1998. 215/881-6400.

**Cherry Hill High School
East**
1750 Kresson Rd, Cherry
Hill NJ 08003-2590.
609/424-2222.

**Cherry Hill High School
West**
2101 Chapel Ave W,
Cherry Hill NJ 08002-
2099. 609/663-8006.

Chester High School
200 W 9th St, Chester
PA 19013-4288.
610/447-3772.

Conestoga High School
200 Irish Rd, Berwyn PA
19312-1260. 610/644-
1440.

**Cumberland Regional
High School**
PO Box 5115, Bridgeton
NJ 08302-5115.
609/451-9400.

**Cumberland Valley
School District**
6746 Carlisle Pike,
Mechanicsburg PA
17055-1796. 717/697-
8261.

Dieruff High School
815 N Irving St,
Allentown PA 18103-
1894. 610/820-2200.

Don Guanella School
1797 Sproul Rd,
Springfield PA 19064-
1195. 610/543-1418.

**Downingtown Senior
High School**
445 Manor Ave,
Downingtown PA 19335-
2544. 610/269-4400.

East High School
450 Ellis Ln, West
Chester PA 19380-5123.
610/436-7204.

**East Stroudsburg Area
School District**
298 N Courtland St, E
Stroudsburg PA 18301-
2124. 717/424-8500.

Edison High School
151 W Luzerne St,
Philadelphia PA 19140-
2795. 215/324-9440.

**Egg Harbor Township
High School**
24 High School Dr,
Pleasantville NJ 08232-
9450. 609/653-0100.

Emmaus High School
851 North St, Emmaus
PA 18049-2296.
610/967-3101.

Episcopal Academy
376 N Latches Ln,
Merion Sta PA 19066.
610/667-9612.

**Frankford Senior High
School**
5000 Oxford Ave,
Philadelphia PA 19124-
2699. 215/537-2519.

**Freedom Senior High
School**
3149 Chester Ave,
Bethlehem PA 18017-
2866. 610/867-5843.

Germantown Academy
PO Box 287, Ft
Washington PA 19034-
0287. 215/646-3300.

Germantown High School
Germantown Ave and
High, Philadelphia PA
19144. 215/951-4004.

**Hamburg Area School
District**
Windsor Street, Hamburg
PA 19526. 610/562-
2241.

**Hamilton Township
School District**
5801 3rd Street, Mays
Landing NJ 08330.
609/625-9393.

Harrisburg High School
2451 Market St,
Harrisburg PA 17103-
2497. 717/255-2617.

**Harry S Truman Sr High
School**
3001 Green Ln,
Levittown PA 19057-
3105. 215/547-3000.

**Hatboro Horsham Sr High
School**
899 Horsham Rd,
Horsham PA 19044-
1209. 215/441-7900.

**Havertown Township Sr
High School**
200 Mill Rd, Havertown
PA 19083-3718.
610/853-5955.

Hazle Area High School
1601 W 23rd St,
Hazleton PA 18201-
1646. 717/459-3221.

**Hempfield Senior High
School**
200 Stanley Ave,
Landisville PA 17538-
1220. 717/898-5500.

Hightstown High School
25 Leshin Ln, Hightstown
NJ 08520-4099.
609/443-7738.

**Indian Mills Elementary
School**
99 Medford Indian Mills
Rd, Vincentown NJ
08088-8918. 609/268-
0440.

King Senior High School
6100 Stenton Ave,
Philadelphia PA 19138-
1625. 215/927-7200.

Lakewood High School
855 Somerset Ave,
Lakewood NJ 08701-
2195. 908/905-3502.

**Lenape Regional High
School District**
235 Hartford Rd,
Medford NJ 08055-
4001. 609/654-5111.

**Liberty Senior High
School**
1115 Linden St,
Bethlehem PA 18018-
2903. 610/691-7200.

Lincoln High School
3201 Ryan Ave,
Philadelphia PA 19136-
4399. 215/335-5653.

**Mainland Regional High
School**
1301 Oak Ave, Linwood
NJ 08221-1653.
609/927-4151.

**Mastbaum Tech High
School**
3116 Frankford Ave,
Philadelphia PA 19134-
3893. 215/291-4703.

**McCaskey Senior High
School**
445 N Reservoir St,
Lancaster PA 17602-
2447. 717/291-6211.

**Millville Senior High
School**
200 N Wade Blvd,
Millville NJ 08332-2206.
609/327-6040.

Neshaminy High School
2001 Old Lincoln Hwy,
Langhorne PA 19047-
3240. 215/752-6451.

**Norristown Area High
School**
1900 Eagle Dr,
Norristown PA 19403-
2720. 610/630-5096.

**North Pennsylvania
School District**
401 E Hancock St,
Lansdale PA 19446-
3960. 215/368-0400.

North Pennsylvania Sr High School
1340 S Valley Forge Rd, Lansdale PA 19446-4718. 215/368-9800.

Notre Dame High School
601 Lawrenceville Rd, Trenton NJ 08648-4298. 609/882-7900.

Olney High School
100 W Duncannon Ave, Philadelphia PA 19120-3410. 215/456-3014.

Overbrook Regional Sr High School
1200 Turnerville Rd, Clementon NJ 08021-6626. 609/767-8000.

Pennsylvania Manor School District
PO Box 1001, Millersville PA 17551-0301. 717/872-9500.

Pennsbury High School
705 Hood Blvd, Fairless Hls PA 19030-3199. 215/949-6700.

Princeton Day School
PO Box 75, Princeton NJ 08542-0075. 609/924-6700.

Rancocas Valley Regional High School District
520 Jacksonville Rd, Mount Holly NJ 08060-1212. 609/267-0830.

Reading Senior High School
801 N 13th St, Reading PA 19604-2449. 610/371-5710.

Red Land High School
560 Fishing Creek Rd, Lewisberry PA 17339-9509. 717/938-6561.

Scott Intermediate School
1901 Wayne Ave, Harrisburg PA 17109-6020. 717/257-8760.

Shawnee High School
600 Tabernacle Rd, Medford NJ 08055-9712. 609/654-7544.

South Philadelphia High School
Broad St and Snyder Ave, Philadelphia PA 19110-1083. 215/952-6220.

Southern Regional High School
600 N Main St, Manahawkin NJ 08050-3022. 609/597-9481.

St Hubert High School
7320 Torresdale Ave, Philadelphia PA 19136-4198. 215/624-6840.

The Lawrenceville School
Main Street, Trenton NJ 08648. 609/896-0400.

Toms River Inter East School
Hooper Ave, Toms River NJ 08753-8399. 908/505-5777.

Toms River North High School
1295 Old Freehold Rd, Toms River NJ 08753-4201. 908/505-5702.

Trenton Central High School
400 Chambers St, Trenton NJ 08609-2606. 609/989-2496.

Tunkhannock Area School Dist
200 Franklin Ave, Tunkhannock PA 18657-1229. 717/836-3111.

Upper Darby Senior High School
601 N Lansdown Ave, Havertown PA 19083-4107. 610/622-7000.

Vineland North High School
3010 E Chestnut Ave, Vineland NJ 08360-6196. 609/794-6800.

Vineland South Sr High School
2880 E Chestnut Ave, Vineland NJ 08360-6144. 609/794-6800.

W. Windsor-Plainsboro Elementary School
PO Box 869, Plainsboro NJ 08536-0869. 609/799-0087.

W. Windsor-Plainsboro Middle School
PO Box 410, Plainsboro NJ 08536-0410. 609/799-9600.

Washington Township High School
529 Hurffville Crosskeys Rd, Sewell NJ 08080-2746. 609/589-8500.

West Catholic High School
4501 Chestnut St, Philadelphia PA 19139-3699. 215/386-2244.

William Tennent High School
333 Centennial Rd, Warminster PA 18974-5400. 215/441-6166.

Williamsport High School
2990 W 4th St,
Williamsport PA 17701-
4141. 717/323-8411.

**Woodrow Wilson High
School**
3100 Federal St, Camden
NJ 08105-2397.
609/966-5300.

**Wyoming Valley West
High School**
150 Wadham St,
Plymouth PA 18651-
2111. 717/779-5361.

**COLLEGES,
UNVERSITIES AND
PROFESSIONAL
SCHOOLS**

Alvernia College
400 Saint Bernadine St,
Reading PA 19607-1756.
610/777-5411.

**Baptist Bible College Of
Pennsylvania**
538 Venard Rd, Clarks
Summit PA 18411-1297.
717/587-1172.

Beth Medrash Govoha
617 6th St, Lakewood
NJ 08701-2709.
908/367-1060.

Cabrini College
610 King Of Prussia Rd,
Wayne PA 19087-3698.
610/971-8100.

Cedar Crest College
100 College Dr,
Allentown PA 18104-
6196. 610/437-4471.

College Of Misericordia
301 Lake St, Dallas PA
18612-1098. 717/674-
6400.

Eastern College
10 Fairview Dr, Wayne
PA 19087-3696.
610/341-5800.

Elizabethtown College
1 Alpha Dr,
Elizabethtown PA 17022-
2298. 717/367-1151.

**Franklin and Marshall
College**
PO Box 3003, Lancaster
PA 17604-3003.
717/291-3911.

Georgian Court College
900 Lakewood Ave,
Lakewood NJ 08701-
2600. 908/364-2200.

Haverford College
370 Lancaster Ave,
Haverford PA 19041-
1392. 610/896-1000.

King's College
133 N River St, Wilkes
Barre PA 18711.
717/826-5900.

Lebanon Valley College
N College Ave, Annville
PA 17003. 717/867-
6100.

Lycoming College
700 College Pl,
Williamsport PA 17701-
5192. 717/321-4000.

Muhlenberg College
2400 W Chew St,
Allentown PA 18104-
5586. 610/821-3100.

**Pennsylvania College Of
Optometry**
1200 W Godfrey Ave,
Philadelphia PA 19141-
3323. 215/276-6200.

**Philadelphia College Of
Pharmacy**
600 S 43rd St,
Philadelphia PA 19104-
4495. 215/596-8800.

**Philadelphia College Of
The Bible**
200 Manor Ave,
Langhorne PA 19047-
2990. 215/752-5800.

Rosemont College
1400 Montgomery Ave,
Bryn Mawr PA 19010-
1699. 610/527-0200.

Spring Garden College
7309 Sommers Rd,
Philadelphia PA 19138-
1329. 215/248-7900.

Susquehanna University
University Ave,
Selinsgrove PA 17870.
717/374-0101.

Swarthmore College
500 College Ave,
Swarthmore PA 19081-
1390. 610/328-8000.

**The University Of The
Arts**
320 S Broad St,
Philadelphia PA 19102-
4901. 215/875-4800.

Ursinus College
PO Box 1000,
Collegeville PA 19426-
1000. 610/489-4111.

Wilson College
1015 Philadelphia Ave,
Chambersburg PA
17201-1285. 717/264-
4141.

JUNIOR COLLEGES AND TECHNICAL INSTITUTES

Burlington County College
Pemberton-Browns Mills Rd, Pemberton NJ 08068. 609/894-9311.

Cumberland County College
PO Box 517, Vineland NJ 08360-0517. 609/691-8600.

Delaware County Community College
901 Media Line Rd, Media PA 19063-1094. 610/359-5000.

Harrisburg Area Community College
1 Hacc Dr, Harrisburg PA 17110-2903. 717/780-2300.

Lehigh County Community College
4525 Education Park Dr, Schnecksville PA 18078-2502. 610/799-2121.

Luzerne County Community College
1333 S Prospect St, Nanticoke PA 18634-3899. 717/829-7300.

Montgomery County Community College
340 Dekalb Pike, Blue Bell PA 19422-1400. 215/641-6300.

Northampton County Area Community College
3835 Green Pond Rd, Bethlehem PA 18017-7568. 610/861-5300.

Ocean Cty College
College Dr, Toms River NJ 08753-2102. 908/255-0400.

Pennsylvania College Of Technology
1 College Ave, Williamsport PA 17701-5799. 717/326-3761.

Penn State University Ogontz
1600 Woodland Rd, Abington PA 19001-3918. 215/886-9400.

Penn State University York
1031 Edgecombe Ave, York PA 17403-3326. 717/771-4000.

Reading Area Community College
PO Box 1706, Reading PA 19603-1706. 610/372-4721.

Williamsport Area Cmty College
1005 W 3rd St, Williamsport PA 17701-5707. 717/326-3761.

DATA PROCESSING SCHOOLS

Delaware Valley College of Science & Agriculture
Rt 202 & New Britain Rd, Doylestown PA 18901. 215/345-1500.

TTS Inc.
1 Sentry Pky E, Blue Bell PA 19422-2310. 610/828-8127.

BUSINESS AND SECRETARIAL SCHOOLS

Atlantic Community College
5100 Black Horse Pike, Mays Landing NJ 08330-2699. 609/343-5000.

For more information on career opportunities in educational services:

Associations

AMERICAN ASSOCIATION OF SCHOOL ADMINISTRATORS
1801 North Moore Street, Arlington VA 22209. 703/528-0700.

AMERICAN FEDERATION OF TEACHERS
555 New Jersey Avenue NW, Washington DC 20001. 202/879-4400.

COLLEGE AND UNIVERSITY PERSONNEL ASSOCIATION
1233 20th Street NW, Suite 301, Washington DC 20036. 202/429-0311. Membership required.

NATIONAL ASSOCIATION OF BIOLOGY TEACHERS
11250 Roger Bacon Drive, #19, Reston VA 22090. 703/471-1134.

NATIONAL ASSOCIATION OF COLLEGE AND UNIVERSITY BUSINESS OFFICERS
1 DuPont Circle, Suite 500, Washington DC 20036. 202/861-2500. Membership required.

NATIONAL ASSOCIATION OF COLLEGE ADMISSION COUNSELORS
1631 Prince Street, Alexandria VA 22314. 703/836-2222.

NATIONAL SCIENCE TEACHERS ASSOCIATION
8240-1840 Wilson Boulevard, Arlington VA 22201-3000. 703/243-7100.

<u>Directories</u>

WASHINGTON HIGHER EDUCATION ASSOCIATION DIRECTORY
Council for Advancement and Support of Education, 11 DuPont Circle NW, Suite 400, Washington DC 20036 202/328-5900.

<u>Books</u>

ACADEMIC LABOR MARKETS
Falmer Press, Taylor & Francis, Inc., 1900 Frost Road, Suite 101, Bristol PA 19007. 800/821-8312.

HOW TO GET A JOB IN EDUCATION
Bob Adams, Inc., 260 Center Street, Holbrook MA 02343. 617/787-8100.

ELECTRONIC/INDUSTRIAL ELECTRICAL EQUIPMENT

Shipments for the electrical component industry were expected to jump almost 9 percent in 1994, due to an increased demand for computers, communications equipment, and electronic automotive products. Semiconductors should lead the way, sporting an estimated 25 percent growth rate in 1994. Jobseekers should seek out companies that can anticipate which technologies and product variants will be among industry standards.

Electric lighting and wiring equipment shipments rose more than 4 percent in 1993, and were expected to climb 5 percent in 1994. Shipment growth will continue to be led by the rejuvenated market for residential and commercial construction. Electrical equipment shipments were also in the 4 percent range for 1994, while renewable energy equipment -- like wind and hydro-electric turbines -- are expected to grow at different rates.

AEL INDUSTRIES, INC.
305 Richardson Road, Landsdale PA 19446. 215/822-2929. **Contact:** Matt Ludlow, Human Resources. **Description:** A defense design and development firm with many area locations. Products include communication equipment, defense electronics, microwave equipment, hybrid microcircuits; and antennas. **Common positions include:** Accountant/Auditor; Blue-Collar Worker Supervisor; Commercial Artist; Computer Programmer; Electrical/Electronic Engineer; Financial Analyst; Mechanical Engineer; Technical Writer/Editor. **Educational backgrounds include:** Business Administration; Computer Science; Engineering; Physics. **Benefits:** 401K; Dental Insurance; Disability Coverage; Employee Discounts; Life Insurance; Medical Insurance; Savings Plan; Tuition Assistance. **Special Programs:** Training Programs. **Corporate headquarters location:** This Location. **Operations at this facility include:** Administration; Research and Development. **Listed on:** NASDAQ.

AMP INCORPORATED
P.O. Box 3608, Harrisburg PA 17105. 717/564-0100. **Contact:** Human Resources. **Description:** A producer of electrical wiring devices.

ACTION MANUFACTURING COMPANY
100 East Erie Avenue, Philadelphia PA 19134. 215/739-6400. **Contact:** Manager Human Resources. **Description:** Manufacturer of precision electromechanical instruments and precision ordnance products. **Common positions include:** Accountant/Auditor; Administrator; Chemist; Computer Programmer; Financial Analyst; Geologist/ Geophysicist; Mechanical Engineer. **Educational backgrounds include:** Accounting; Chemistry; Engineering; Finance; Geology. **Benefits:** Dental Insurance; Disability Coverage; Life Insurance; Medical Insurance; Savings Plan; Tuition Assistance. **Corporate headquarters location:** This Location. **Operations at this facility include:** Administration; Manufacturing; Regional Headquarters.

ASTROPOWER INC.

30 Lovett Avenue, Newark DE 19711. 302/366-0400. **Contact:** Human Resources. **Description:** Develops and manufactures high performance semiconductor energy conversion products. A major market for these products is underdeveloped countries. The company's operations are located in Newark, DE, and in Canada, where the company's subsidiary, AstroPower Canada, is located. **Number of employees at this location:** 80.

AYDIN CONTROLS

414 Commerce Drive, Fort Washington PA 19034-2699. 215/542-7800. **Contact:** Sheldon Berkowitz, Personnel Manager. **Description:** A high-technology company which supplies sophisticated electronic equipment systems, principally for the telecommunications, computer control systems, and fusion experimentation fields. Four product lines include telecommunications, color display terminals, fusion electronics, and support components. Two facilities located in Fort Washington: Aydin Controls; and Aydin Monitors. **Common positions include:** Accountant/Auditor; Blue-Collar Worker Supervisor; Buyer; Computer Programmer; Credit Manager; Customer Service Representative; Department Manager; Draftsperson; Electrical/Electronic Engineer; Manufacturer's/Wholesaler's Sales Rep.; Marketing Specialist; Operations/Production Manager; Personnel/Labor Relations Specialist; Purchasing Agent and Manager; Quality Control Supervisor; Technical Writer/Editor. **Educational backgrounds include:** Business Administration; Communications; Computer Science; Engineering; Marketing. **Benefits:** Credit Union; Dental Insurance; Disability Coverage; Life Insurance; Medical Insurance; Profit Sharing; Tuition Assistance. **Corporate headquarters location:** Horsham PA. **Operations at this facility include:** Administration; Divisional Headquarters; Manufacturing; Research and Development; Sales; Service. **Listed on:** New York Stock Exchange.

C.W. INDUSTRIES, INC.

130 Jamesway, Southhampton PA 18966. 215/355-7080. **Contact:** Marty Mikelberg, Treasurer. **Description:** Produces a wide range of electronic components.

CONSOLIDATED ELECTRIC SUPPLY COMPANY

600 West Second Street, Wilmington DE 19801. 302/656-6651. **Contact:** Alan Johnson, Office Manager. **Description:** An electrical supply company.

CONTINENTAL WIRE & CABLE COMPANY

P.O. Box 1863, York PA 17405. 717/792-2644. **Contact:** Employee Relations Manager. **Description:** Produces insulated wire and cable power for power control applications. **Common positions include:** Accountant/Auditor; Computer Programmer; Customer Service Representative; Electrical/Electronic Engineer; Mechanical Engineer. **Educational backgrounds include:** Engineering. **Benefits:** Dental Insurance; Disability Coverage; Employee Discounts; Life Insurance; Medical Insurance; Tuition Assistance. **Corporate headquarters location:** New York NY. **Operations at this facility include:** Administration; Divisional Headquarters; Manufacturing; Research and Development; Sales; Service.

FERRANTI INTERNATIONAL, INC.

P.O. Box 3025, 3725 Electronics Way, Lancaster PA 17604. 717/285-3113. **Contact:** Human Resources Department. **Description:** An electronics company.

FETRONIC INDUSTRIES, INC.

4200 Mitchell Street, Philadelphia PA 19128. 215/482-7660. **Contact:** Daniel Kursman, President. **Description:** An electronics firm.

FINCOR ELECTRONICS DIVISION
IMO INDUSTRIES, INC.
3750 East Market Street, York PA 17402. 717/751-4200. **Contact:** Charles M. Emswiler, Jr., Personnel Manager. **Description:** Produces electronic controls for industrial and graphic arts uses. **Common positions include:** Electrical/Electronic Engineer. **Corporate headquarters location:** Lawrenceville NJ.

FISCHBACH AND MOORE
150 Rock Hill Road, Bala-Cynwyd PA 19004. 215/668-2711. **Contact:** Personnel. **Description:** An electrical contracting firm.

FISCHER & PORTER COMPANY
125 East County Line Road, Warminster PA 18974. 215/674-6205. **Contact:** Robert Austin, Human Resources. **Description:** Engaged in the design, manufacture, sales, and service of electronic and pneumatic instruments, specific process analyzers, and analog and digital systems that measure and control flow temperatures, pressure, and level.

GENERAL ELECTRIC/SWITCHGEAR DIVISION
6901 Elmwood Avenue, Philadelphia PA 19142. 215/726-2626. **Contact:** Joanne McGroarty, Personnel Specialists. **Description:** Switchgear division of the international corporation. Parent company researches, develops, manufactures, and markets electrical, electronic, chemical, and microelectronic products for business, industry, and home use. Employs 330,000 worldwide.

HONEYWELL INC.
2600 Eisenhower Avenue, Norristown PA 19403. 215/666-8269. **Contact:** Human Resources Department. **Description:** Honeywell's service division.

HONEYWELL INC.
INDUSTRIAL CONTROL DIVISION
1100 Virginia Drive, Fort Washington PA 19034-3260. 215/641-3000. **Contact:** Terrie Ferguson, Manager/Staffing. **Description:** The Process Control Division develops, manufactures, and markets instrumentation worldwide. Products are designed to increase productivity and save energy in industrial processes. Industries served include the processing and manufacturing industry as well as the OEM machinery equipment industry. **Common positions include:** Accountant/Auditor; Electrical/Electronic Engineer; Industrial Engineer; Mechanical Engineer; Personnel/Labor Relations Specialist; Purchasing Agent and Manager; Systems Analyst; Technical Writer/Editor. **Educational backgrounds include:** Accounting; Computer Science; Engineering. **Benefits:** Dental Insurance; Disability Coverage; Life Insurance; Medical Insurance; Pension Plan; Tuition Assistance. **Corporate headquarters location:** This Location. **Operations at this facility include:** Divisional Headquarters. **Listed on:** New York Stock Exchange.

HONEYWELL/IAC
P.O. Box 934, York PA 17405-0934. 717/771-8100. **Contact:** Leslie Reamer, Human Resources Representative. **Description:** Produces industrial and programmable controls for a wide range of users.

ITT ELECTRON TECHNOLOGY DIVISION
3100 Charlotte Avenue, P.O. Box 100, Easton PA 18044-0100. 215/252-7331. **Contact:** Cecelia Feichtel, Director of Human Resources. **Description:** Electron

Technology Division manufactures and markets special purpose electron tubes and integrated microwave sub-systems for use in communications, defense, industrial, scientific and medical applications. **Common positions include:** Accountant/Auditor; Buyer; Ceramics Engineer; Department Manager; Draftsperson; Electrical/Electronic Engineer; General Manager; Industrial Engineer; Manufacturer's/Wholesaler's Sales Rep.; Marketing Specialist; Mechanical Engineer; Operations/Production Manager; Personnel/Labor Relations Specialist; Purchasing Agent and Manager; Quality Control Supervisor; Systems Analyst. **Educational backgrounds include:** Accounting; Business Administration; Computer Science; Engineering; Finance; Marketing. **Benefits:** Dental Insurance; Disability Coverage; Life Insurance; Medical Insurance; Pension Plan; Savings Plan; Tuition Assistance. **Corporate headquarters location:** New York NY. **Operations at this facility include:** Administration; Manufacturing. **Listed on:** New York Stock Exchange.

INTEGRATED CIRCUIT SYSTEMS, INC.
2626 Van Bureau Avenue, Norristown PA 19403. 215/666-1900. **Contact:** Human Resources. **Description:** Integrated Circuit Systems, Inc., designs, develops and markets innovative very large-scale integrated (USLI) circuits, including standard and custom and applicational specific integrated circuit (ASIC) products, using mixed analog/digital technology. Products are marketed to original equipment manufacturers for use in video graphics display products, central processing unit (CPU) systems, PC multimedia and portable device battery charging applications. **Number of employees at this location:** 143.

JERROLD GENERAL INSTRUMENTS
2200 Byberry Road, Hatboro PA 19040. 215/674-4800. **Contact:** Senior Technical Recruiter. **Description:** A manufacturer of electronic equipment for the cable television industry.

KETEMA INC.
2233 State Road, Bensalem PA 19020. 215/639-2255. **Contact:** Human Resources Department. **Description:** Manufactures search detection systems and instruments. Send resume to: 1 Cherry Center, 501 South Cherry Street, Suite 600, Denver, CO 80022. Attn: Executive offices, Personnel.

LASKO METAL PRODUCTS
820 Lincoln Avenue, West Chester PA 19380-0294. 215/692-7400. **Contact:** Bernie Eisman, Personnel Manager. **Description:** Manufactures a wide variety of small electrical appliances.

LEEDS & NORTHRUP
351 Sumneytown Pike, P.O. Box 2000, North Wales PA 19454-0906. 215/699-2000. **Contact:** Betsy Leatherman, Secretary. **Description:** Manufactures electronic equipment and instruments, computers, and process control equipment. International facilities. **Corporate headquarters location:** This Location. **Parent company:** General Signal Corporation.

PEI-GENESIS
2180 Hornit Road, Philadelphia PA 19116. 215/673-0400. **Contact:** Personnel. **Description:** A distributor of a variety of electronic parts.

PENN VENTILATOR
Red Lion & Gantry Roads, Philadelphia PA 19115. 215/464-8900. **Contact:** Johanna Corey, Manager of Human Resources. **Description:** Company sells and manufactures

industrial fans and ventilators. **Common positions include:** Accountant/Auditor; Administrator; Advertising Clerk; Buyer; Commercial Artist; Computer Programmer; Credit Manager; Customer Service Representative; Department Manager; Draftsperson; Electrical/Electronic Engineer; General Manager; Industrial Engineer; Management Trainee; Manufacturer's/Wholesaler's Sales Rep.; Marketing Specialist; Mechanical Engineer; Operations/Production Manager; Personnel/Labor Relations Specialist; Purchasing Agent and Manager; Quality Control Supervisor. **Educational backgrounds include:** Communications; Computer Science; Engineering; Liberal Arts; Marketing. **Benefits:** Life Insurance; Medical Insurance; Pension Plan; Profit Sharing; Tuition Assistance. **Corporate headquarters location:** This Location. **Operations at this facility include:** Administration; Research and Development; Sales; Service.

POLY PLANAR
1927 Stout Drive, Unit 4, Warminster PA 18974. 215/675-7805. **Contact:** Personnel Director. **Description:** Produces and distributes portable electronics products, including all-weather loudspeakers for communications systems, transistorized power packs, frequency changers and converters. Also manufactures consumer audio products, primarily speakers. **Corporate headquarters location:** This Location.

SPD TECHNOLOGIES
13500 Roosevelt Boulevard, Philadelphia PA 19116. 215/677-4900. **Contact:** Larry Wasnock, Employee Relations Specialist. **Description:** SPD Technologies is a leader in the design, development, and manufacture of circuit breakers, switchgear and related electrical protection systems for naval applications in the United States and around the world. Corporate headquarters and primary manufacturing facility located in Philadelphia, PA. Other wholly owned subsidiaries include: SPD Switchgear, Montgomeryville, PA; Pac Ord, San Diego, CA; and Henschel, Newburyport, MA. **Common positions include:** Accountant/Auditor; Blue-Collar Worker Supervisor; Buyer; Computer Programmer; Department Manager; Draftsperson; Electrical/Electronic Engineer; Financial Analyst; Industrial Engineer; Manufacturer's/Wholesaler's Sales Rep.; Marketing/Advertising/PR Manager; Mechanical Engineer; Operations/Production Manager; Personnel/Labor Relations Specialist; Public Relations Specialist; Purchasing Agent and Manager; Quality Control Supervisor; Systems Analyst; Technical Writer/Editor. **Educational backgrounds include:** Business Administration; Computer Science; Engineering; Finance. **Benefits:** Dental Insurance; Disability Coverage; Life Insurance; Medical Insurance; Pension Plan; Profit Sharing; Tuition Assistance. **Corporate headquarters location:** This Location. **Operations at this facility include:** Administration; Divisional Headquarters; Manufacturing; Research and Development; Sales.

SPS TECHNOLOGIES
Highland Avenue, Jenkintown PA 19046. 215/572-3401. **Contact:** Employment Representative. **Description:** Engaged in the design, manufacture and marketing of high-technology fastener products, including precision components and computer-controlled tightening equipment and special materials. Maintains more than 15 manufacturing plants and sales offices located throughout the world, including Great Britain, Mexico, and Australia. **Common positions include:** Accountant/Auditor; Computer Programmer; Electrical/Electronic Engineer; Financial Analyst; Industrial Engineer; Marketing Specialist; Mechanical Engineer; Metallurgical Engineer; Operations/Production Manager. **Educational backgrounds include:** Business Administration; Engineering; Finance; Marketing. **Benefits:** Dental Insurance; Disability Coverage; Life Insurance; Medical Insurance; Pension Plan; Savings Plan; Tuition Assistance. **Corporate headquarters location:** Newtown PA. **Operations at this facility**

include: Administration; Divisional Headquarters; Manufacturing; Research and Development; Sales; Service. **Listed on:** New York Stock Exchange.

TRIBORO ELECTRIC CORPORATION
539 Jacksonville Road, Warminster PA 18974. 215/345-6000. **Contact:** Cathy Neidhardt, Human Resources Manager. **Description:** Produces a wide range of electrical wiring devices. **Common positions include:** Accountant/Auditor; Buyer; Computer Programmer; Credit Manager; Customer Service Representative; Industrial Engineer; Quality Control Supervisor. **Benefits:** 401K; Disability Coverage; Life Insurance; Medical Insurance. **Corporate headquarters location:** This Location. **Operations at this facility include:** Administration; Management Consulting; Sales; Service.

V.I.Z. MANUFACTURING COMPANY
335 East Price Street, Philadelphia PA 19144. 215/844-2626. **Contact:** Alex Ahmed, Personnel Manager. **Description:** Manufactures precision weather instruments and electronic test equipment.

XEROX CORPORATION/WILMINGTON
200 Belleview Parkway, Park Corporate Center, Wilmington DE 19809. 302/792-5100. **Contact:** Human Resources. **Description:** One of the world's largest manufacturers of business machines.

Note: Because addresses and telephone numbers of smaller companies change rapidly, we recommend you contact each company and verify the information below before contacting employers. Mass mailings are not recommended.

Additional large employers: 500+

TRANSFORMERS

Challenger Elec. Equip. Corp.
508 Lapp Rd., Malvern PA 19355-1214. 610/647-5000.

WIRING DEVICES

SI Industries Inc.
8000 Midlantic Dr., Ste. 110, Mount Laurel NJ 08054-1518. 609/727-1500.

ELECTRIC LIGHTING FIXTURES AND RELATED PRODUCTS

Progress Lighting
G Street & Erie Ave., Philadelphia PA 19107. 215/289-1200.

Wagner Lighting
Jefferson & 2nd Sts., Boyertown PA 19512. 610/367-2604.

SEMICONDUCTORS AND RELATED DEVICES

AT&T Microelectronics
555 Union Blvd., Allentown PA 18103-1229. 610/439-6011.

Microwave Semiconductor
P.O. Box 1002, Montgomeryvle PA 18936-1002.

Struthers-Dunn/Hi-G Company
Lambs Road, Pitman NJ 08071. 609/589-7500.

ELECTRONIC COMPONENTS

HRB Systems Inc.
300 S Science Park Rd., State College PA 16801-2408. 8142384311.

Harris Corp.
125 Crestwood Rd., Mountain Top PA 18707-2107. 717/474-6761.

ELECTRICAL EQUIPMENT

GS Electric
Ritner Highway, Carlisle PA 17013. 717/243-4041.

Additional medium sized employers: under 500

**ELECTRONIC PARTS
AND EQUIPMENT
WHOLESALE**

Check Point Systems
550 Grove Rd, Thorofare
NJ 08086. 609/848-
1800.

**Gandall Systems
Corporation**
Olney Av, Cherry Hill NJ
08003. 609/424-9400.

**Holloway Security
Company**
2501 S Front St,
Philadelphia PA 19148-
4107. 215/463-8500.

Powell Electronics Inc.
PO Box 8765,
Philadelphia PA 19101-
8765. 215/365-1900.

Reliance Merchandizing
Expressway 95 Industrial
Park, Bensalem PA
19020. 215/638-8200.

**Thomas & Betts
Pennsylvania Inc.**
Commerce Drive,
Montgomeryvle PA
18936. 215/368-4800.

**Westinghouse Security
Elec Inc.**
601 Ewing St, Princeton
NJ 08540-2757.
609/921-3833.

**ELECTRICAL
APPARATUS AND
EQUIPMENT
WHOLESALE**

Bright Star Industries
380 Stewart Rd, Wilkes
Barre PA 18706-1459.
717/825-1900.

Rumsey Electric Co.
3rd & Hunting Park Ave,
Philadelphia PA 19140.
215/456-2525.

ELECTRON TUBES

Electro-Space Fabricators
300 W High St, Topton
PA 19562-1420.
610/682-7181.

**Thomson Consumer
Electronics**
1002 New Holland Ave,
Lancaster PA 17601-
5606. 717/295-6100.

Unique Recoveries
Rt 81 Exit 68, Hallstead
PA 18822. 717/879-
4200.

**SEMICONDUCTORS AND
RELATED DEVICES**

Assembly Technology
795 Horsham Rd,
Horsham PA 19044-
4202. 215/672-9000.

BF Goodrich Co.
2321 Topaz Dr, Hatfield
PA 19440-1936.
215/822-6090.

**GE Company
Meter & Control Division**
205 Great Valley Pky,
Malvern PA 19355-1308.
610/251-7000.

**ITT Electron
Tech Division**
3100 Charlotte Ave,
Easton PA 18042-3786.
610/252-7331.

**Melcor Materials
Electronic**
1040 Spruce St, Trenton
NJ 08648-4534.
609/393-4178.

**Thomson Consumer
Electronics**
2000 Clements Bridge
Rd, Woodbury NJ
08096-2011. 609/853-
2525.

**ELECTRONIC
CAPACITORS**

Centre Engineering Inc.
2820 E College Ave,
State College PA 16801-
7515. 814/237-0321.

**ELECTRONIC
RESISITORS**

**Charles T Gamble
Industries**
605 Perkins Ln, Riverside
NJ 08075-5034.
609/461-1900.

**ELECTRONIC COILS,
TRANSFORMERS AND
INDUCTORS**

Everson Electric Co.
2000 City Line Rd,
Bethlehem PA 18017-
2126. 610/264-8611.

**ELECTRONIC
CONNECTORS**

Burndy Corporation
504 Fame Ave, Hanover
PA 17331-9476.
717/632-9562.

Intercon Systems Inc.
1000 Rosedale Ave,
Middletown PA 17057-
4834. 717/540-5660.

Milton Ross Company
511 2nd Street Pike,
Southampton PA 18966-
3804. 215/355-0200.

ELECTRONIC
COMPONENTS

Allegro Microsystems
3900 Welsh Rd, Willow
Grove PA 19090-2909.
215/657-8400.

ASEA Brown Boveri
7036 Snowdrift Rd Ste
2, Allentown PA 18106-
9274. 610/395-7333.

Cardinal Technology
1827 Freedom Rd,
Lancaster PA 17601-
6759. 717/293-3000.

Deltron Inc.
Wissahickon Ave, North
Wales PA 19454.
215/699-9261.

Dialight Co.
1913 Atlantic Ave,
Manasquan NJ 08736-
1005. 908/223-9400.

**GTE Elex Components &
Materials**
2333 Reach Rd,
Williamsport PA 17701-
5579. 717/326-6591.

Glasseal Products Inc.
485 Oberlin Ave S,
Lakewood NJ 08701-
6904. 908/370-9100.

Gusmer
PO Box 110, Lakewood
NJ 08701-0110.
908/370-9000.

**Instrument Specialties
Company Inc.**
PO Box A, De Water Gap
PA 18327-0136.
717/424-8510.

JPM Company
Rte 15 N, Lewisburg PA
17837. 717/523-1101.

Kanson Electronics Inc.
4700 Raycom Rd, Dover
PA 17315-1303.
717/292-5631.

**Magnetic Metals
Corporation**
P O Box 351, Camden
NJ 08101-0351.
609/964-7842.

McCoy Electronics Co.
100 Watts St, Mt Holly
Spgs PA 17065-1821.
717/486-3411.

Methode Electronics
1 Industrial Dr,
Willingboro NJ 08046-
4030. 609/871-3500.

Piezo Crystal Company
100 K St, Carlisle PA
17013-1448. 717/249-
2151.

Raycom Electronics
1 Raycom Rd, Dover PA
17315. 717/292-3641.

Reeves-Hoffman
400 W North St, Carlisle
PA 17013-2248.
717/243-5929.

Sechan Electronics Inc.
525 Furnace Hills Pike,
Lititz PA 17543-8954.
717/627-4141.

Torwico Electronics
410 Oberlin Ave S,
Lakewood NJ 08701-
6903. 908/364-1800.

Viz Manufacturing Co.
335 E Price St,
Philadelphia PA 19144-
5782. 215/844-2626.

WPI
23 S Front St, Salem NJ
08079-1342. 609/935-
7560.

PRIMARY BATTERIES

Alliant Techsystems
104 Rock Rd, Horsham
PA 19044-2311.
215/674-3800.

GNB Inc.
1 Dunham Dr, Scranton
PA 18512-2664.
717/961-8700.

ELECTRICAL EQUIPMENT
FOR INTERNAL
COMBUSTION ENGINES

Dill Products Inc.
1001 W Washington St,
Norristown PA 19401-
4437. 610/272-6850.

Kalas Manufacturing
25 Main St, Denver PA
17517-1609. 215/267-
5575.

ELECTRICAL
MACHINERY AND
EQUIPMENT

Amerace
68 Oxford Rd, Brick NJ
08723-5449. 908/477-
5669.

Bitrek Corporation
PO Box 510,
Waynesboro PA 17268-
0510. 717/762-5313.

Carol Cable Co Inc.
1050 E Broad St,
Montoursville PA 17754-
2502. 717/368-3100.

**Challenger Electric Equip
Corporation**
116 S Humer St, Enola
PA 17025-2618.
717/732-8815.

Da-Tech Corporation
141 Railroad Dr,
Warminster PA 18974-
1448. 215/322-9410.

Dictaphone Corporation
520 Fellowship Rd Unit
D402, Mount Laurel NJ
08054-3406. 609/234-
6363.

**Electri Cord
Manufacturing Co Inc.**
312 E Main St, Westfield
PA 16950-1609.
814/367-2265.

Greentree Distributors
38 W Scott St, Riverside
NJ 08075-3602.
609/461-0855.

Heintz Corporation
11000 Roosevelt Blvd,
Philadelphia PA 19116-
3961. 215/677-3600.

Herley Industries Inc.
10 Industry Dr, Lancaster
PA 17603-4092.
717/397-2777.

**M&G Electrical Supply
Company Inc.**
756 Pearl St N, Bridgeton
NJ 08302-1210.
609/451-2291.

Mid-Atlantic Cartridge
876 N Lenola Rd,
Moorestown NJ 08057-
1046. 609/235-6550.

Rofin-Sinar Inc.
1068 S Keim St,
Pottstown PA 19464-
7785. 610/326-4866.

S&C Electric Co.
2410 Highway 34,
Manasquan NJ 08736-
1809. 908/223-5050.

**SGS Thomson
Microelectronics**
211 Commerce Dr,
Montgomeryvle PA
18936-9641. 215/362-
8500.

Total Control Products
24 Country Way, Mount
Holly NJ 08060-9779.
609/835-2424.

**COMMERCIAL,
INDUSTRIAL AND
INSTITUTIONAL
ELECTRIC LIGHTING
FIXTURES**

Craftlite
100 Craftway Dr,
Littlestown PA 17340-
1651. 717/359-7131.

**Crescent Lighting
Corporation**
PO Box 99, Barrington
NJ 08007-0099.
609/546-5500.

**Keystone Lighting
Corporation**
U S Rt 13 & Beaver St,
Bristol PA 19007.
215/788-0811.

**VEHICULAR LIGHTING
EQUIPMENT**

Embacee Inc.
East Ave R R 6,
Wellsboro PA 16901-
9806. 717/724-6400.

LIGHTING EQUIPMENT

Streamlight Inc.
1030 W Germantown
Pike, Norristown PA
19403-3996. 610/631-
0600.

**CURRENT-CARRYING
WIRING DEVICES**

Brooks Electronics Inc.
4001 N American St,
Philadelphia PA 19140-
2604. 215/228-4433.

Gettig Technologies
1 Stream Side Pl E,
Spring Mills PA 16875.
814/422-8892.

HH Fluorescent Parts
104 Beecher Ave,
Cheltenham PA 19012-
2295. 215/379-2750.

Hubbell-Bell Inc.
1035 Mill Rd, Allentown
PA 18103-3177.
610/398-9700.

Malco
201 Progress Dr,
Montgomeryvle PA
18936-9618. 215/699-
5373.

**Stewart Connector
Systems Inc.**
RR 2 Box 2020, Glen
Rock PA 17327-9516.
717/235-7512.

**Stores Automated
Systems Inc.**
311 Sinclair Rd, Bristol
PA 19007-1524.
215/638-7744.

Arlington Industries
Stauffer Indl Pk, Taylor
PA 18517. 717/562-
0270.

Bentley Harris Manufacturing Co.
241 Welsh Pool Rd, Exton PA 19341-1316. 610/363-2600.

SL Waber Inc.
520 Fellowship Rd, Mount Laurel NJ 08054-3403. 609/866-8888.

RELAYS AND INDUSTRIAL CONTROLS

Eaton Corporation
2225 Avenue A, Bethlehem PA 18017-2107. 610/866-0751.

Harold Beck & Sons
2300 Terry Dr, Newtown PA 18940-1830. 215/968-4600.

Heinemann Prod Commerical Controls
11 Princess Rd, Trenton NJ 08648-2301. 609/896-0009.

RCA Distributor & Special
2000 Clements Bridge Rd, Woodbury NJ 08096-2011. 609/541-3636.

The Simco Company
2257 N Penn Rd, Hatfield PA 19440-1906. 215/822-2171.

POWER, DISTRIBUTION AND SPECIALTY TRANSFORMERS

Keystone Transformer Company
Pottstown Ave & Dotts St, Pennsburg PA 18073-1420. 215/679-4114.

Lucas Schaevitz Inc.
7905 N Rte 130, Pennsauken NJ 08110-1402. 609/662-8000.

Neshaminy Transformer Corporation
Edison-Furlong Rd, Furlong PA 18925. 215/794-7411.

NWL Transformers
Rising Sun Rd, Bordentown NJ 08505. 609/298-7300.

SWITCHGEAR AND SWITCHBOARD APPARATUS

CRL Components Inc.
1913 Atlantic Ave, Manasquan NJ 08736-1005.

GE Company Breaker Plant
6901 Elmwood Ave, Philadelphia PA 19142-1815. 215/726-3550.

Silver Cloud Manufacturing Co
525 Orange St, Millville NJ 08332-4030. 609/825-8900.

MOTORS AND GENERATORS

Flight Systems Inc.
Hempt Rd, Mechanicsburg PA 17055. 717/697-0333.

McLean Engineering Division
70 Washington Rd, Princeton Jct NJ 08550-1097. 609/799-0100.

Penn Detroit Diesel Allison
8330 State Rd, Philadelphia PA 19136-2986. 215/335-0500.

Pittman
343 Godshall Dr, Harleysville PA 19438-2007. 215/256-6601.

Plasma-Therm Inc.
136 Route 73, Voorhees NJ 08043-9539. 609/767-6120.

R&S Manufacturing
525 Mill St, Columbia PA 17512. 717/684-9599.

For more information on career opportunities in the electronic/industrial electrical equipment industry:

Associations

AMERICAN CERAMIC SOCIETY
735 Ceramic Place, Westerville OH 43081. 614/890-4700. 800/837-1804. (Ceramics futures information) Membership required.

ELECTROCHEMICAL SOCIETY
10 South Main Street, Pennington NJ 08534-2896. 609/737-1902

ELECTRONIC INDUSTRIES ASSOCIATION
2001 Pennsylvania Avenue NW, Washington DC 20006. 202/457-4900

ELECTRONICS TECHNICIANS ASSOCIATION
602 North Jackson Street, Greencastle IN 46135. 317/653-8262

INSTITUTE OF ELECTRICAL AND ELECTRONICS ENGINEERS
345 East 47th Street, New York NY 10017. 212/705-7900

INTERNATIONAL BROTHERHOOD OF ELECTRICAL WORKERS
1125 15th Street NW, Washington DC 20005. 202/833-7000

INTERNATIONAL SOCIETY OF CERTIFIED ELECTRONICS TECHNICIANS
2708 West Berry Street, Fort Worth TX 76109. 817/921-9101

NATIONAL ELECTRICAL MANUFACTURERS ASSOCIATION
2101 L Street NW, Suite 300, Washington DC 20037. 202/457-8400

NATIONAL ELECTRONICS SALES AND SERVICES ASSOCIATION
2708 West Berry, Fort Worth TX 76109. 817/921-9061

ROBOTICS INTERNATIONAL OF THE SOCIETY OF MANUFACTURING ENGINEERS
P.O. Box 930, One SME Drive, Dearborn MI 48121. 313/271-1500

ENVIRONMENTAL SERVICES

 *The environmental services sector is expected to continue growing, but according to industry observers, it will probably not have the "double-digit growth rate of the last decade." Amendments made to the Clean Air Act in 1990 will continue to drive domestic demand for environmental services, as clients try to meet tougher environmental standards. The continued closing of municipal landfills will generate new technology in the waste treatment, recycling, and disposal markets. Internationally, the industry's greatest potential lies in Eastern Europe, Mexico, Latin America, the former Soviet Union, and Southeast Asia.*

CONVERSION SYSTEMS, INC.
200 Welsh Road, Horsham PA 19044. 215/784-0990. **Contact:** Personnel. **Description:** Provides a wide range of design, engineering, and implementation services which convert specific industrial wastes into environmentally acceptable substances. **Common positions include:** Accountant/Auditor; Administrator; Buyer; Civil Engineer; Computer Programmer; Department Manager; Draftsperson; Electrical/Electronic Engineer; Geologist/Geophysicist; Industrial Designer; Purchasing Agent and Manager; Sales Associate. **Educational backgrounds include:** Accounting; Business Administration; Chemistry; Engineering; Finance; Geology; Marketing. **Benefits:** Dental Insurance; Disability Coverage; Life Insurance; Medical Insurance; Pension Plan. **Corporate headquarters location:** Philadelphia PA. **Parent company:** IU International. **Operations at this facility include:** Administration; Divisional Headquarters; Sales; Service.

ENVIRONMENTAL RESOURCES MANAGEMENT GROUP
855 Springdale Drive, Exton PA 19341. 610/524-3500. **Contact:** Human Resources. **Description:** An environmental consulting firm.

ENVIROSAFE SERVICES INCORPORATED
200 Welsh Road, Horsham PA 19044. 215/784-0750. **Contact:** Human Resources. **Description:** Provides environmental services.

ROY F. WESTON, INC.
1 Weston Way, West Chester PA 19380. 215/692-3030. **Contact:** Paula J. Gill, Employment Manager. **Description:** A full-service environmental engineering consulting services firm, providing related design and laboratory services. **Common positions include:** Accountant/Auditor; Biological Scientist/Biochemist; Chemical Engineer; Chemist; Civil Engineer; Computer Programmer; Geologist/Geophysicist; Systems Analyst. **Educational backgrounds include:** Biology; Chemistry; Computer Science; Engineering; Geology. **Benefits:** Disability Coverage; Life Insurance; Medical Insurance; Pension Plan; Profit Sharing; Savings Plan; Tuition Assistance. **Operations at this facility include:** Service. **Listed on:** NASDAQ. **Number of employees nationwide:** 3,500.

Additional small employers: under 100

American Waste Services
455 Business Center Dr, Horsham PA 19044-3415.
215/674-2747.

Canonie Environmental Service Inc.
500 North Gulph Rd Ste 315, Kng Of Prussa PA 19406-2816. 610/337-2551.

Coastal Environmental Service Inc.
2 Research Way, Princeton NJ 08540-6628. 609/987-0966.

Contamination Control Engineering
1224 Hamilton Ave, Trenton NJ 08629-1401. 609/392-1070.

Crystal Environmental Service Inc.
805 Longfield Dr, Blue Bell PA 19422-1263.
610/277-7727.

DCR Environmental Services
2300 Computer Rd, Willow Grove PA 19090-1732.
215/659-8066.

DCR Environmental Services
118 E 9th Ave, Conshohocken PA 19428-1504.
610/828-7240.

Envirite Corporation
1600 Pennsylvania Ave, York PA 17404-1754. 717/846-1900.

Envirogen Inc.
4100 Quakerbridge Rd, Trenton NJ 08648-4702.
609/936-9300.

EnvironProtect Inspection Inc.
284 Horsham Rd, Horsham PA 19044-2559. 215/674-5200.

Environmental Liability Management
218 Wall St, Princeton NJ 08540-1512. 609/683-4848.

Environmental Professionals
328 Morris Rd, Harleysville PA 19438-2638.
215/256-1339.

Environmental Science & Engineering Inc.
5219 Militia Hill Rd, Plymouth Mtng PA 19462-9918.
610/941-9700.

Healthy Habitat Inc.
4570 Province Line Rd, Princeton NJ 08540-2212.
609/924-1888.

Integrated Environmental Service
10 E 6th Ave, Conshohocken PA 19428-1784.
610/828-3078.

Judy Dockstder Environ Intl
4 Sentry Pky, Blue Bell PA 19422-2311.
610/834-0650.

Land Tech Remedial
435 Pennsylvania Ave, Ft Washington PA 19034-3414.
215/646-5855.

Ohara Environmental Service Inc.
372 S Henderson Rd, Kng Of Prussa PA 19406-2453.
610/265-1866.

P&W Land Consultants Inc.
671 Lamberton St, Trenton NJ 08611-2920. 609/695-4520.

Saint Environmental Pro Inc.
2505 Finn Rd, Perkiomenvlle PA 18074-9503.
610/754-9444.

Seed Society For Environ & Economic
50 W State St, Trenton NJ 08608-1220. 609/695-7007.

Self-Test Services
6 Lindenwald Ter, Ambler PA 19002-4912. 215/628-9700.

Soil Tech Inc.
500 Gulph Rd, Kng Of Prussa PA 19406.
610/992-0800.

**St Environmental
Services Inc.**
649 N Lewis Rd,
Royersford PA 19468-
1234. 610/495-3098.

TTI Environmental Inc.
514 Lamplighter Way,
Lansdale PA 19446-
4055. 215/393-9276.

For more information on career opportunities in environmental services:

Associations

**AIR AND WASTE MANAGEMENT
ASSOCIATION**
One Gateway Center, Third Floor,
Pittsburgh PA 15222. 412/232-3444.

**ASSOCIATION OF STATE &
INTERSTATE WATER POLLUTION
CONTROL ADMINISTRATORS**
750 First Street NE, Suite 910,
Washington DC 20002. 202/898-
0905.

**INSTITUTE OF CLEAN AIR
COMPANIES**
1707 L Street NW, Washington DC
20036. 202/457-0911

**NATIONAL SOLID WASTE
MANAGEMENT ASSOCIATION**
1730 Rhode Island Avenue NW, Suite
1000, Washington DC 20036.
202/659-4613.

**U.S. ENVIRONMENTAL PROTECTION
ASSOCIATION**
401 M Street SW, Washington DC
20460. 202/260-2090.

WATER ENVIRONMENT FEDERATION
601 Wythe Street, Alexandria VA
22314. 703/684-2400. Subscription
to federation's jobs newsletter
required for career information.

Magazines

**JOURNAL OF AIR AND WASTE
MANAGEMENT ASSOCIATION**
One Gateway Center, Third Floor,
Pittsburgh PA 15222. 412/232-3444

FABRICATED/PRIMARY METALS AND PRODUCTS

For steel manufacturers, the late '80s were a nightmare, with prices falling to ten-year lows. During 1992 and 1993, however, the industry began a modest recovery which should continue with an improving economy. A stronger economy will spur shipments of consumer goods and automobiles. Foreign companies will become more and more important; look for more joint ventures between the U.S. and overseas firms. Big Steel's toughest competition is now the increasing number of mini-mills that have spun off from rival companies in an attempt to strike out on their own.

Overall, employment prospects are weak, although metallurgical engineers are in demand.

A.I.M.S. COMPANY
2705 Black Lake Place, Philadelphia PA 19154. 215/365-6106. **Contact:** Human Resources. **Description:** A fabricated metals company.

ACME MANUFACTURING COMPANY
7500 State Road, Philadelphia PA 19136. 215/338-2850. **Contact:** Don Gray, Vice President of Operations. **Description:** A local Philadelphia sheet metal foundry.

ALL-STEEL
Valmont Industrial Park, 425 Jaycee Drive, West Hazelton PA 18201. 717/454-0862. **Contact:** Robert Gaynor, Personnel Manager. **Description:** Manufactures a broad line of steel office furniture. International facilities. **Corporate headquarters location:** Aurora IL. **Parent company:** RCA Corporation.

ALUMINUM SHAPES INC.
P.O. Box 397, Delair NJ 08110. 609/662-5500. **Contact:** Human Resources Department. **Description:** An aluminum rolling and drawing company.

AMERICAN WIRE WORKS
P.O. Box 12740, Philadelphia PA 19134. **Contact:** Personnel Department. **Description:** A wire manufacturer and processor. **Number of employees at this location:** 15.

BABCOCK INDUSTRIES INC.
ACCO CHAIN & LIFTING PRODUCTS DIVISION
76 Acco Drive, P.O. Box 792, York PA 17405. 717/741-4863. **Contact:** Human Resources Manager. **Description:** Produces welded and weldless chains, hooks, slings, tire chains, load binders, hoists, and other lifting equipment. **Common positions include:** Accountant/Auditor; Blue-Collar Worker Supervisor; Buyer; Computer Programmer; Credit Manager; Customer Service Representative; Draftsperson; Electrical/Electronic Engineer; General Manager; Industrial Designer; Industrial

Engineer; Manufacturer's/Wholesaler's Sales Rep.; Mechanical Engineer; Metallurgical Engineer; Operations/Production Manager; Personnel/Labor Relations Specialist; Purchasing Agent and Manager; Quality Control Supervisor; Systems Analyst. **Educational backgrounds include:** Accounting; Business Administration; Computer Science; Engineering; Marketing. **Benefits:** 401K; Dental Insurance; Disability Coverage; Employee Discounts; Life Insurance; Medical Insurance; Pension Plan; Profit Sharing; Tuition Assistance. **Corporate headquarters location:** Fairfield CT. **Operations at this facility include:** Administration; Design; Divisional Headquarters; Manufacturing; Sales; Service.

BIRDSBORO INDUSTRIES
31 Stonetown Road, Birdsboro PA 19508. 215/582-3000. **Contact:** Personnel. **Description:** Produces steel fabricating machinery, rolling mills, crushers, hydraulic presses, and side frames for railroad cars. **Corporate headquarters location:** This Location. **Parent company:** Pennsylvania Engineering Corporation.

BUCK COMPANY, INC.
897 Lancaster Pike, Quarryville PA 17566. 717/284-4114. **Contact:** Ron Pennington, Personnel Manager. **Description:** Produces malleable aluminum and related products, and brass alloy and gray iron castings.

CABOT
County Line Road, P.O. Box 1608, Boyertown PA 19512-1608. 215/367-2181. **Contact:** Terry R. Mest, Personnel Manager. **Description:** Produces aluminum master alloys, and tantalum metal products. **Corporate headquarters location:** Boston MA. **Parent company:** Cabot Corporation.

G.O. CARLSON, INC.
P.O. Box 526, Thorndale PA 19372-0526. 215/384-2800. **Contact:** Personnel Department. **Description:** A producer of stainless steel, nickel alloys, and titanium plate and plate products. **Common positions include:** Computer Programmer; Credit Manager; Customer Service Representative; Electrical/Electronic Engineer; Mechanical Engineer; Personnel/Labor Relations Specialist. **Benefits:** Dental Insurance; Life Insurance; Medical Insurance; Pension Plan; Tuition Assistance. **Corporate headquarters location:** This Location. **Operations at this facility include:** Administration. **Number of employees at this location:** 170.

CARPENTER TECHNOLOGY CORPORATION
P.O. Box 14662, Reading PA 19612-4662. 215/208-3118. **Contact:** Jerome T. Simcik, Employee Relations/Employment Specialist. **Description:** Engaged in the manufacture and marketing of specialty metals in a wide range of types, forms, and sizes for a variety of end-use markets. Produces stainless steel, tool steels, high-temperature and electronic alloys; and other special purpose metals. International facilities. **Common positions include:** Accountant/Auditor; Attorney; Buyer; Chemist; Computer Programmer; Draftsperson; Electrical/Electronic Engineer; Financial Analyst; Manufacturer's/Wholesaler's Sales Rep.; Mechanical Engineer; Personnel/Labor Relations Specialist; Purchasing Agent and Manager; Quality Control Supervisor; Systems Analyst. **Educational backgrounds include:** Accounting; Business Administration; Chemistry; Communications; Computer Science; Engineering; Finance; Marketing. **Benefits:** Daycare Assistance; Dental Insurance; Disability Coverage; Life Insurance; Medical Insurance; Pension Plan; Profit Sharing; Savings Plan; Tuition Assistance. **Special Programs:** Internships; Training Programs. **Corporate headquarters location:** This Location. **Operations at this facility include:** Administration;

Manufacturing; Research and Development; Sales; Service. **Listed on:** New York Stock Exchange.

CITY STEEL USA

4001 Philadelphia Pike, Claymont DE 19703. **Contact:** Jim Ryan, Manager of Employee Relations. **Description:** A steel foundry. **Corporate headquarters location:** This Location.

COLONIAL METALS COMPANY

P.O. Box 311, Columbia PA 17512. 717/684-2311. **Contact:** Jim Rowe, Personnel Manager. **Description:** Manufactures bronze, brass, and aluminum ingots. **Common positions include:** Administrator; Blue-Collar Worker Supervisor; Buyer; Chemist; Claim Representative; Department Manager; Manufacturer's/Wholesaler's Sales Rep.; Purchasing Agent and Manager; Transportation/Traffic Specialist. **Educational backgrounds include:** Accounting; Business Administration; Chemistry; Finance. **Benefits:** Disability Coverage; Life Insurance; Medical Insurance; Pension Plan; Savings Plan; Tuition Assistance. **Corporate headquarters location:** This Location. **Operations at this facility include:** Administration; Manufacturing; Sales.

CONTAINER RESEARCH CORPORATION

P.O. Box 159, Glen Riddle PA 19037. 215/459-2160. **Contact:** Hank Kalinowsky, Personnel Manager. **Description:** Engaged in sheet metal fabrication.

CROWN CORK & SEAL COMPANY, INC.

9300 Ashton Road, Philadelphia PA 19136. 215/698-5100. **Contact:** Gary L. Burgess, Vice President/Human Resources. **Description:** Manufactures and distributes cans and seals, including aerosol cans, beverage cans used by a wide range of customers, and two- and three-piece cans. International facilities. **Corporate headquarters location:** This Location. **Listed on:** New York Stock Exchange.

DOOLAN STEEL CORPORATION

2 Eves Drive, Suite 220, Marltown NJ 08053. 609/988-8100. **Contact:** Juergen Weberbauer, Personnel. **Description:** A steel company.

FLAGG BRASS

1020 West High Street, Stowe PA 19464. 215/326-9000. **Contact:** Human Resources. **Description:** Manufactures brass products.

FORBES STEEL AND WIRE CORPORATION

800 New Castle Avenue, Wilmington DE 19801. 302/656-3121. **Contact:** William H. Lotter, Jr., Vice President. **Description:** A fabricated wire company.

GRINNELL CORPORATION

1411 Lancaster Avenue, Columbia PA 17512. 717/684-4400. **Contact:** Andrea Pratt, Manager, Human Relations. **Description:** Produces specialty castings, malleable iron pipe fittings, and hangars. Divisional headquarters: Statesboro, GA.

HOFMANN INDUSTRIES, INC.

3145 Shillington Road, Sinking Spring PA 19608. 215/678-8051. **Contact:** Director of Human Resources. **Description:** Manufactures and fabricates electric-welded steel tubing. Products are used primarily by manufacturers of housewares, indoor and outdoor furniture; toys; playground equipment; automotive equipment; hardware; and sporting goods. **Common positions include:** Accountant/Auditor; Buyer; Computer Programmer; Credit Manager; Industrial Engineer; Manufacturer's/Wholesaler's Sales

Rep.; Operations/Production Manager; Quality Control Supervisor. **Educational backgrounds include:** Accounting; Business Administration; Liberal Arts; Marketing. **Benefits:** Disability Coverage; Life Insurance; Medical Insurance; Pension Plan; Tuition Assistance. **Corporate headquarters location:** This Location. **Operations at this facility include:** Administration; Manufacturing; Sales.

INTERNATIONAL MILL SERVICE INC.
Horsham Business Center, 1155 Business Center Drive, Suite 200, Horsham PA 19044. 215/956-5500. **Contact:** Personnel Director. **Description:** A steel slag recovery company.

KING FIFTH WHEEL COMPANY
P.O. Box 68, Crestwood Industrial Park, Mountain Top PA 18707. 717/474-6371. **Contact:** Peter Wright, General Manager. **Description:** Manufactures welded rings, industrial furnaces, and other steel products. Other Pennsylvania facilities located in Feasterville Mountain Top.

LA FRANCE CORPORATION
8425 Executive Avenue, Philadelphia PA 19153. 215/365-8000. **Contact:** Bill Poiesz, Personnel. **Description:** A manufacturer of die-castings.

LUKENS STEEL COMPANY
A.R.C. Building, Modena Road, Coatesville PA 19320. 215/383-2000. **Contact:** Tracy Schindler, Human Resources Supervisor. **Description:** Primarily in the business of producing and marketing carbon, alloy, and clad plate steel shapes. The leading markets for these products are steel service centers, metalworking equipment companies, and shipbuilding companies. **Corporate headquarters location:** This Location. **Listed on:** New York Stock Exchange.

LYON METAL PRODUCTIONS, INC.
P.O. Box 51235, Philadelphia PA 19115. 215/671-0300. **Contact:** Personnel Department. **Description:** Manufactures and sells steel products for industrial, commercial, office, and institutional use. Products include such items as shelving, lockers, desk tops, work benches, office furniture, and custom products. Products are distributed nationally, primarily through dealers and direct sales. **Corporate headquarters location:** Montgomery IL.

METAL INDUSTRIES INC.
Route 209, Elizabethville PA 17023. 717/362-8196. **Contact:** Human Resources. **Description:** Manufactures metal doors and frames.

OVERHEAD DOOR CORPORATION
P.O. Box 110, Lewistown PA 17044. 717/248-0131. **Contact:** Human Resources. **Description:** Manufactures metal doors and frames.

PENCO PRODUCTS, INC.
Brower Avenue, P.O. Box 378, Oaks PA 19456-0378. 215/666-0500. **Contact:** Howard Easton, Personnel Manager. **Description:** Manufactures steel storage products, such as lockers, shelves, and cabinets.

PENNSYLVANIA STEEL FOUNDRY & MACHINE CO.
Third & Arch Streets, P.O. Box 128, Hamburg PA 19526. 215/562-7533. **Contact:** Personnel. **Description:** Operates an area steel foundry.

RAHN'S SPECIALITY METALS (RSM)
Route 113, Rahns PA 19426. 215/489-7211. **Contact:** Daniel Rico, Vice President. **Description:** Rerollers of stainless steel and high nickel alloys. **Common positions include:** Accountant/Auditor; Administrator; Buyer; Credit Manager; General Manager; Marketing Specialist; Operations/Production Manager; Purchasing Agent and Manager; Systems Analyst. **Educational backgrounds include:** Accounting; Business Administration; Marketing. **Benefits:** Medical Insurance; Tuition Assistance. **Special Programs:** Internships; Training Programs.

TALCO METALS
5201 Unruh Ave, Philadelphia PA 19135. 215/333-6800. **Contact:** Mae Swain-Baronofsky, Personnel Manager. **Description:** A local metals refinery also engaged in the distribution of both metals and chemicals. **Common positions include:** Administrator; Advertising Clerk; Blue-Collar Worker Supervisor; Claim Representative; Credit Manager; Customer Service Representative; Manufacturer's/Wholesaler's Sales Rep.; Marketing Specialist; Metallurgical Engineer; Operations/Production Manager; Personnel/Labor Relations Specialist; Purchasing Agent and Manager; Quality Control Supervisor; Transportation/Traffic Specialist. **Educational backgrounds include:** Business Administration; Communications; Computer Science; Economics; Engineering; Finance; Geology; Liberal Arts; Marketing. **Benefits:** Life Insurance; Medical Insurance. **Corporate headquarters location:** This Location. **Operations at this facility include:** Administration; Divisional Headquarters; Manufacturing; Regional Headquarters; Sales; Service.

UNICAST COMPANY
P.O. Box 248, Boyertown PA 19512. **Contact:** Personnel Manager. **Description:** A producer of gray iron and aluminum castings. **Common positions include:** Industrial Engineer; Metallurgical Engineer; Operations/Production Manager; Quality Control Supervisor. **Educational backgrounds include:** Engineering. **Benefits:** 401K; Dental Insurance; Disability Coverage; Life Insurance; Medical Insurance. **Corporate headquarters location:** This Location. **Operations at this facility include:** Administration; Manufacturing; Sales. **Number of employees at this location:** 120.

WARD MANUFACTURING INC.
P.O. Box 9, Blossburg PA 16912. 717/638-2131. **Contact:** Human Resources. **Description:** Manufactures fabricated metal products.

WORTHINGTON STEEL AND WAVE
P.O. Box 3050, Malvern PA 19355. 215/644-6700. **Contact:** Joe Griesbaum, Personnel Director. **Description:** Operates a steel rolling mill.

YARWAY CORPORATION
480 Norristown Road, Blue Bell PA 19422. 215/825-2100. **Contact:** Tony Kratowicz, Personnel Director. **Description:** A metal manufacturer engineering products for the power and process industries. Products include gauges, valves, stream traps, and indicators. Also provides steam service. International facilities. **Corporate headquarters location:** This Location.

Note: Because addresses and telephone numbers of smaller companies change rapidly, we recommend you contact each company and verify the information below before contacting employers. Mass mailings are not recommended.

Additional large employers: 500+

STEEL PRODUCTS
Standard Steel Company
500 N Walnut St.,
Burnham PA 17009-
1644. 717/248-4911.

Walker Wire & Steel Corp.
10 W Market St.,
Bethlehem PA 18018-
5703. 610/868-2777.

William J Maier Inc.
2735 Briarwood Place,
Bethlehem PA 18017-
3801. 610/868-4616.

USS/Unit USX
U S S Fairless Works,
Fairless Hls PA 19030.
215/736-4203.

WG Corp.
Hemlock & Mountainview
Rds, Morgantown PA
19543. 610/286-9191.

COPPER

NGK Metals Corp.
Tuckerton Rd., Temple
PA 19560. 610/921-
5000.

ALUMINUM PRODUCTS

Cressona Aluminum Company
Pottsville St., Cressona
PA 17929. 717/385-
5000.

PRIMARY METAL PRODUCTS

Hoeganaes Corp.
River Road & Taylor's
Lane, Riverton NJ
08077. 609/829-2220.

FABRICATED PLATE WORK

Precision Components
500 Lincoln St., York PA
17404-3367. 717/848-
1126.

PREFABRICATED METAL BUILDINGS

Gichner Shelter Systems
E Locust St., Dallastown
PA 17313. 717/244-
7611.

Lord & Burnham
1241 Harrisburg Ave.,
Lancaster PA 17603-
2515.

IRON AND STEEL FORGING

Campbell-Cooper Tools
3990 E Market St., York
PA 17402-2769.
717/755-2933.

METAL PRODUCTS

Cerro Metal Products Company
P.O. Box 388, Bellefonte
PA 16823-0388.
8143556217.

METAL STAMPINGS

Jade Tool & Die
3063 Philmont Ave.,
Huntingdon Vy PA
19006-4243. 215/947-
3333.

FABRICATED WIRE PRODUCTS

Andritz Sprout Bauer Inc.
Sherman St., Muncy PA
17756. 717/546-8211.

Bridon American Corp.
280 New Commerce
Blvd., Wilkes Barre PA
18706-1497. 717/822-
3349.

Additional medium sized employers: under 500

METALS SERVICE CENTERS WHOLESALE

Edgcomb Metals Co.
420 Memory Ln, York PA
17402-2204. 717/755-
1923.

Edgcomb Metals Co.
555 State Rd, Bensalem
PA 19020-7795.
215/639-4000.

Joseph T Ryerson & Sons
5200 Grays Ave,
Philadelphia PA 19143-
5817. 215/724-0700.

Precision Coil Processing Co
Milnor St & Bleigh Ave,
Philadelphia PA 19136.
215/331-5200.

The CS Group
RR 3, Muncy PA 17756-
9803. 717/546-5941.

Tioga Pipe Supply Company Inc.
2450 Wheatsheaf Ln,
Philadelphia PA 19137-
1028. 215/831-0700.

WIRE SPRINGS

John Evans Sons Inc.
Spring Ave, Lansdale PA
19446. 215/368-7700.

MISCELLANEOUS FABRICATED WIRE PRODUCTS

Bridon American Corporation
101 Stevens Ln, Pittston
PA 18643-1218.
717/655-0157.

Cannondale Corporation
Airport Rd, Philipsburg
PA 16866. 814/342-
6178.

Chestnut Display Systems Inc.
6809 State Rd,
Philadelphia PA 19135-
1530. 215/335-7450.

Cornell Iron Works Inc.
Crestwood Industrial
Park, Mountain Top PA
18707. 717/474-6773.

Hanover Wire Cloth Company
500 E Middle St,
Hanover PA 17331-
2027. 717/637-3795.

Keystone Seneca Wire Cloth Co
Factory St, Hanover PA
17331. 717/637-5901.

Lift-All Co Inc.
102 S Heintzelman St,
Manheim PA 17545-
1700. 717/665-6821.

London Harness & Cable Corporation
16 E Wister St,
Philadelphia PA 19144-
5907. 215/848-8950.

Mount Joy Wire Corporation
1000 E Main St, Mount
Joy PA 17552-9332.
717/653-1461.

New York Wire Co. Weaving Division
441 E Market St, York
PA 17403-1618.
717/854-9571.

Paulsen Wire Rope Corporation
880 S 2nd St, Sunbury
PA 17801-3305.
717/286-7141.

Root Corporation
152 N Main St, Mount
Wolf PA 17347.
717/266-5626.

Sandvik Steel Co.
982 Griffin Pond Rd,
Clarks Summit PA
18411-9214. 717/587-
5191.

Williamsport Wirerope Works
100 Maynard St,
Williamsport PA 17701-
5809. 717/326-5146.

METAL FOIL AND LEAF

Circuit Foil
US Hgwy 130,
Bordentown NJ 08505.
609/298-4800.

FABRICATED METAL PRODUCTS

Banner Metals Inc.
PO Box 431, Stroudsburg
PA 18360-0431.
717/421-4110.

Diamond Manufacturing Co.
243 W 8th St, Pittston
PA 18644-1609.
717/693-0300.

Hood & Co Inc.
PO Box 485, Hamburg
PA 19526-0485.
610/562-3841.

Jersey Shore Steel Co.
PO Box 5055, Jersey
Shore PA 17740-5055.
717/398-0220.

Weinstock Conestoga
417 E Ross St, Lancaster
PA 17602-1967.
717/397-7441.

FABRICATED STRUCTURAL METAL

Deval Corporation
7341 Tulip St,
Philadelphia PA 19136-
4215. 215/332-1200.

Hub Fabricating Co.
100 Gibraltar Rd,
Reading PA 19606-3399.
610/779-2200.

Leonard Kunkin Assocs
Rt 309 & Cherry Ln,
Souderton PA 18964.
215/723-6744.

Metropolitan Steel Industries
601 Fritztown Rd,
Reading PA 19608-1511.
610/678-6411.

New Columbia Joist Company
Old Rte 15, New
Columbia PA 17856.
717/568-6761.

R-V Industries Inc.
Poplar Rd, Honey Brook
PA 19344. 610/273-2457.

SS Fisher Steel Corporation
625 Baumgardner Rd,
Lancaster PA 17603-9344. 717/464-3361.

METAL DOORS AND FRAMES

Alumo Products Co.
Regency Blvd, Mount
Carmel PA 17851.
717/339-3300.

City Aluminum Co Inc.
1909 E Hagert St,
Philadelphia PA 19125-1208. 215/425-7020.

Graham Architectural Products
1551 Mount Rose Ave,
York PA 17403-2909.
717/849-8100.

Northeast Aluminum Window Corporation
4280 Aramingo Ave,
Philadelphia PA 19124-5087. 215/535-7110.

Perkasie Industries Corporation
50 E Spruce St, Perkasie
PA 18944-1284.
215/257-6581.

Philips Products
499 W Sassafras St,
Selinsgrove PA 17870.
717/374-8163.

Thermacore Inc.
3200 Reach Rd,
Williamsport PA 17701-4154. 717/326-7325.

Weather Tite Manufacturing Corporation
645 E Erie Ave,
Philadelphia PA 19134-1208. 215/426-5350.

FABRICATED PLATE WORK

Bigbee Steel & Tank Company
99 Elizabethtown Rd,
Manheim PA 17545.
717/664-0600.

Clearfield Machine Co.
P O Box 992A, Clearfield
PA 16830-5484.
814/765-6544.

Cleaver-Brooks Co.
1500 Lehman St,
Lebanon PA 17046-3396. 717/274-7711.

Donlee Technologies
693 N Hills Rd, York PA
17402-2211. 717/755-1081.

Eastern Foundry Co.
Spring & Schaeffer Sts,
Boyertown PA 19512.
610/367-2153.

Ecolaire Corporation
1550 Lehigh Dr, Easton
PA 18042-6283.
610/250-1000.

Fuller Co.
S 10th & Mills St,
Allentown PA 18103.
610/770-7400.

Gardner Cryogenics
2136 City Line Rd,
Bethlehem PA 18017-2152. 610/264-4523.

Gruenberg Oven Co.
2121 Reach Rd,
Williamsport PA 17701-5575. 717/326-1755.

Hauck Manufacturing Company
PO Box 90, Lebanon PA
17042-0090. 717/272-3051.

Heil Co.
3249 Hempland Rd,
Lancaster PA 17601-6913. 717/397-7771.

Patterson-Kelley Co.
PO Box 458, E
Stroudsburg PA 18301-0458. 717/421-7500.

SHEET METAL WORK

A&E Manufacturing Co
2110 Hartel Ave,
Levittown PA 19057-4597. 215/943-9460.

Alumax Home Products
450 Richardson Dr,
Lancaster PA 17603-4036. 717/299-3711.

Cutler Sign Assocs
1 Oxford Valley Ofc Bldg,
Langhorne PA 19047.
215/752-5518.

Ellisco Inc.
American & Luzerne,
Philadelphia PA 19140.
215/223-3405.

**Fabral Alcan Building
Products Inc.**
3449 Hempland Rd,
Lancaster PA 17601-
1317. 717/397-2741.

Goodhart Sons Inc.
2515 Horseshoe Rd,
Lancaster PA 17601-
5939. 717/656-2404.

Edward F Grant Co
45 Lexington Ave,
Trenton NJ 08618-2320.
609/882-1164.

Herr & Sacco Inc.
Elmwood Ave, Landisville
PA 17538. 717/898-
0111.

**Kingston Metal
Specialties Co**
100 Parry St, Luzerne PA
18709-1040. 717/288-
5411.

MPC Industries
9111 River Rd,
Pennsauken NJ 08110-
3205. 609/665-1952.

Safe Walk Inc.
104 N Maple Ave, Leola
PA 17540-9799.
717/656-2326.

**Southwark Metal
Manufacturing Co.**
1600 St & Washington
Ave, Philadelphia PA
19146. 215/735-3401.

TJ Cope Inc.
305 Second Ave Rte 29,
Collegeville PA 19426-
2654. 610/489-4200.

USG Interiors
S Main St Ext, Red Lion
PA 17356. 717/244-
4071.

United Marketing Inc.
14th & Laurel Sts,
Pottsville PA 17901.
717/622-7715.

**ARCHITECTURAL AND
ORNAMENTAL METAL
WORK**

Kawneer Co Inc.
500 E 12th St,
Bloomsburg PA 17815-
8318. 717/784-8000.

Kramer Brothers Inc.
PO Box 617, Hammonton
NJ 08037-0617.
609/561-2403.

**Spring City Electrical
Manufacturing Co**
Hall & Main Drawer A,
Spring City PA 19475.
610/948-4000.

**PREFABRICATED METAL
BUILDINGS**

**Butler Manufacturing
Company**
400 N Weaber St,
Annville PA 17003-1103.
717/867-4651.

**Kaplan Building Systems
Inc.**
Rt 443 E, Pine Grove PA
17963. 717/345-4635.

**Poloron Homes Of
Pennsylvania Inc.**
74 Ridge Rd, Middleburg
PA 17842. 717/837-
1515.

**SCREW MACHINE
PRODUCTS**

Bonney Forge
Rt 522 S, Mount Union
PA 17066. 814/542-
2545.

Precision Form Inc.
148 W Airport Rd, Lititz
PA 17543-9259.
717/560-7610.

Vallorbs Jewel Company
25-99 Old Philadelphia
Pike, Bird In Hand PA
17505-9797. 717/392-
3978.

**BOLTS, NUTS, SCREWS
AND RIVETS**

**Construction Fasteners
Inc.**
Spring St & Van Reed
Rd, Reading PA 19610.
610/376-5751.

Cooper Power Systems
80 Burson St, E
Stroudsburg PA 18301-
2243. 717/476-2500.

**IRON AND STEEL
FORGINGS**

**Frog Switch &
Manufacturing Co.**
600 E High St, Carlisle
PA 17013-2608.
717/243-2454.

Gunnebo Fastening
180 S Hartman St, York
PA 17403-1853.
717/846-2200.

Lenape Forge Inc.
1280 Lenape Rd, West
Chester PA 19382-2096.
610/793-1500.

NONFERROUS FORGINGS

Phoenix Forging Co.
1000 Front St,
Catasauqua PA 18032-
2347. 610/264-2861.

AUTOMOTIVE STAMPINGS

PHC Industries Inc.
1643 Haddon Ave,
Camden NJ 08103-
3109. 609/966-0980.

CROWNS AND CLOSURES

Continental White Cap
350 Jaycee Dr, Hazleton
PA 18201-1176.
717/455-7781.

METAL STAMPINGS

Billy Penn Corporation
1831 N 5th St,
Philadelphia PA 19122-
2120. 215/426-8400.

Cook Specialty Co Inc.
North Second St, Green
Lane PA 18054.
215/234-4535.

FBF Industries Inc.
1145 Industrial Hwy,
Southampton PA 18966-
4008. 215/322-7110.

**Laubenstein
Manufacturing Co**
418 S Hoffman Blvd,
Ashland PA 17921-
1912. 717/875-2151.

**New Standard
Corporation**
Commerce Way R D 24,
York PA 17406.
717/757-9459.

**New Standard
Corporation**
125 Pinkerton Rd, Mount
Joy PA 17552-3117.
717/653-1811.

TE Dee Inc.
930 N 4th St, Allentown
PA 18102-1853.
610/432-7077.

ELECTROPLATING, PLATING AND POLISHING

Altec Industries Inc.
Second & Laird Sts,
Wilkes Barre PA 18705.
717/822-3104.

**American Nickeloid
Company**
129 Cherry St,
Walnutport PA 18088-
1608. 610/767-3841.

Apollo Metals Ltd
1001 14th Ave,
Bethlehem PA 18018-
2207. 610/867-5826.

Wade Technology Inc.
445 N 11th St,
Philadelphia PA 19123-
3722. 215/765-2453.

COATING, ENGRAVING AND ALLIED SERVICES

Armotek Industries Inc.
701 Public Rd, Palmyra
NJ 08065-1717.
609/829-6161.

Morton Intl
5 Commerce Dr, Reading
PA 19607-9700.
610/775-6600.

ENAMELED IRON AND METAL SANITARY WARE

Franke Inc.
212 Church Rd, North
Wales PA 19454-4140.
215/699-8761.

STEEL WORKS, BLAST FURNACES AND ROLLING MILLS

AIMS Company
2500 Maryland Rd,
Willow Grove PA 19090-
1216. 215/657-8821.

**Allegheny Ludlum Steel
Corporation**
900 W Valley Rd, Wayne
PA 19087-1830.
610/687-3793.

**Allegheny Ludlum Steel
Corporation**
50 S 1st Ave, Coatesville
PA 19320-3418.
610/384-4800.

**Bethlehem Steel
Corporation**
512 Township Line Rd,
Blue Bell PA 19422-
2703. 215/540-5415.

Howell Steel
Cranbury S River Rd,
Cranbury NJ 08512.
609/655-0606.

New Bishop Tube Co.
Rt 30 & Malin Rd,
Malvern PA 19355.
610/647-3450.

Pennsylvania Steel Tube
Rt 447 N, E Stroudsburg
PA 18301. 717/476-
6000.

Pittsburg Tube Co.
1121 Dodgson Rd, West
Chester PA 19382-7245.
610/399-3192.

Sandmeyer Steel Co.
1 Sandmeyer Ln,
Philadelphia PA 19116-
3598. 215/464-7100.

Tube Methods Inc.
P O Box A, Bridgeport PA
19405. 610/279-7700.

**ELECTRO-
METALLURGICAL
PRODUCTS**

**Shieldalloy Metallurgical
Corporation**
12 West Blvd, Newfield
NJ 08344-9558.
609/692-4200.

**COLD-ROLLED STEEL
SHEETS, STRIPS AND
BARS**

**Bensalem Pipe & Tube
Corporation**
1717 Woodhaven Dr,
Bensalem PA 19020-
7107. 215/639-8141.

Caine Steel Processing
22 S State St, Newtown
PA 18940-3507.

**Chapel Hill Steel Products
Inc.**
2424 State Rd, Bensalem
PA 19020-7310.
215/638-7522.

East Coast Processing
5135 Bleigh Ave,
Philadelphia PA 19136-
4202. 215/332-5030.

GM Stainless Inc.
3911 Wissahickon Ave,
Philadelphia PA 19129-
1214. 215/223-5199.

**International Trade
Service Ltd**
1801 S Pennsylvania
Ave, Morrisville PA
19067-2501. 215/736-
3500.

**Sigma Industrial Sales
Corporation**
1645 Perkiomen Ave,
Reading PA 19602-2242.
610/374-7654.

Thomson Corporation
1103 Ranck Mill Rd,
Lancaster PA 17602-
2598. 717/394-0741.

STEEL PIPES AND TUBES

**Handy & Harman Tube
Co.**
Whitehall & Twp Line Rd
R R 3, Norristown PA
19403-9803. 610/539-
3900.

Uniform Tubes Inc.
200 W 7th Ave,
Collegeville PA 19426-
2112. 610/539-0700.

**GRAY AND DUCTILE
IRON FOUNDRIES**

Dennis Raber & Assoc
5281 Nursery Rd, Dover
PA 17315-2331.
717/292-3467.

Fairmount Foundry Inc.
Front & Pine Sts,
Hamburg PA 19526.
610/562-7501.

**Griffin Pipe Products
Company**
1100 West Front St,
Florence NJ 08518-
1099. 609/499-1400.

RH Sheppard Co.
101 Philadelphia St,
Hanover PA 17331-
2038. 717/637-3751.

**The Shenango Furnace
Company**
101 Carnegie Ctr,
Princeton NJ 08540-
6231. 609/951-9400.

Wheatland Tube Co.
900 Haddon Av Ste 500,
Collingswood NJ 08108-
2114. 609/854-5400.

**MALLEABLE IRON
FOUNDRIES**

**Lancaster Malleable
Castings**
1170 Lititz Pike,
Lancaster PA 17601-
4399. 717/295-8200.

**STEEL INVESTMENT
FOUNDRIES**

Ceramet Inc.
2175 Avenue C,
Bethlehem PA 18017-
2119. 610/266-0270.

CMI-Quaker Alloy Inc.
S Cherry St, Myerstown
PA 17067. 717/866-
6511.

**Pennsylvania Precision
Castings**
633 W Lincoln Ave,
Myerstown PA 17067-
2332. 717/866-7037.

STEEL FOUNDRIES

Birdsboro Ferrocast
200 N Furnace, Birdsboro
PA 19508. 610/582-
3000.

Empire Steel Castings
1501 Frush Valley Rd,
Reading PA 19605-1927.
610/921-8101.

**Lebanon Foundry &
Machine Co**
E Lehman & 1st Sts,
Lebanon PA 17042.
717/273-1611.

**McConway & Torley
Corporation**
230 Railroad St,
Kutztown PA 19530-
1117. 610/683-7351.

**United States Pipe &
Foundry**
East Pearl St, Burlington
NJ 08016. 609/387-
6000.

PRIMARY SMELTING AND REFINIING OF NONFERROUS METALS

**Brush Wellman Inc.
Alloy Division**
Shoemakersville Rd,
Shoemakersvle PA
19555. 610/562-2211.

**Franklin Smelting &
Refining Corporation**
Castor Ave & Richmond
St, Philadelphia PA
19134. 215/634-2231.

Johnson Matthey Inc.
1401 King Rd, West
Chester PA 19380-1467.
610/648-8000.

Thermal Reduction Co.
One Pavilion Ave,
Riverside NJ 08075.
215/332-4277.

SECONDARY SMELTING AND REFINING OF NONFERROUS METALS

**Mideast Aluminum
Industries**
PO Box 98, Mountain
Top PA 18707-0098.

ROLLING, DRAWING AND EXTRUDING OF COPPER

Precision Tube Co.
Wissahickon Ave &
Church Rd, North Wales
PA 19454. 215/699-
5801.

**Reading Tube
Corporation**
PO Box 14026, Reading
PA 19612-4026.
610/926-4141.

ALUMINUM SHEET, PLATE AND FOIL

EKCO Products Inc.
PO Box 62, Clayton NJ
08312-0062. 609/881-
3600.

ALUMINUM EXTRUDED PRODUCTS

Pennex Aluminum Co.
50 Community St,
Wellsville PA 17365.
717/432-9647.

ALUMINUM ROLLING AND DRAWING

Benton Foundry Inc.
Rd 1, Benton PA 17814-
9801. 717/925-6711.

ROLLING, DRAWING AND EXTRUDING OF NONFERROUS METALS

Axel Johnson Metals
215 Welsh Pool Rd,
Exton PA 19341-1314.
610/363-0330.

NGK Metals Corporation
PO Box 13367, Reading
PA 19612-3367.
610/921-5000.

DRAWING AND INSULATING NONFERROUS WIRE

Alcan Cable
409 Reighard Ave,
Williamsport PA 17701-
4171. 717/326-3771.

Berk-Tek Inc.
R D L Box 888, New
Holland PA 17557.
717/354-6200.

**Cablec Continental
Cables Co**
2555 Kingston Rd, York
PA 17402-3780.
717/757-6600.

ALUMINUM DIE-CASTINGS

**Blue Ridge Pressure
Casting**
10th & Bridge Sts,
Lehighton PA 18235.
610/377-2510.

ALUMINUM FOUNDRIES

Doehler-Jarvis
Old Reading Pike,
Pottstown PA 19464.
610/327-5400.

Littlestown Hardware & Foundry
Charles St, Littlestown
PA 17340. 717/359-4141.

Southern Diecasters
PO Box 158, Shrewsbury
PA 17361-0158.
717/235-4804.

NONFERROUS FOUNDRIES

Allen-Stevens Corporation
Jaycee Dr Valmont Indl
Pk, Hazleton PA 18201.
717/459-1000.

Castings Co Inc.
136 Village Dr,
Boyertown PA 19512-2027. 610/369-7888.

METAL HEAT TREATING

JW Rex Co.
Eighth St & Valley Forge
Rd, Lansdale PA 19446.
215/855-1131.

PRIMARY METAL PRODUCTS

National Lamination Company
108 S Park Rd,
Vincentown NJ 08088-9752. 609/859-8110.

Reade Manufacturing Company
Ridgeway Blvd,
Lakehurst NJ 08733.
908/657-6451.

METAL CANS

American National Can Company
221 S 10th St, Lemoyne
PA 17043-1704.
717/763-7201.

American National Can Company
100 National Dr,
Fogelsville PA 18051.
610/398-2274.

Can Corporation Of America Inc.
PO Box 170, Blandon PA
19510-0170. 610/926-3044.

US Can Co.
431 Privit Rd, Horsham
PA 19044-1220.
215/674-5900.

For more information on career opportunities in the fabricated/primary metals and products industries:

Associations

AMERICAN FOUNDRYMEN'S SOCIETY
505 State Street, Des Plaines IL
60016-708/824-0181.

AMERICAN SOCIETY FOR METALS
9639 Kinsman Road, Materials Park
OH 44073-0002. 216/338-5151.

AMERICAN WELDING SOCIETY
P.O. Box 351040, 550 LeJeune Road
NW, Miami FL 33126. 305/443-9353.

Directories

DIRECTORY OF STEEL FOUNDRIES IN THE UNITED STATES, CANADA, AND MEXICO
Steel Founder's Society of America,
455 State Street, Des Plaines IL
60016. 708/299-9160.

Magazines

AMERICAN METAL MARKET
Capital Cities ABC, 825 7th Avenue,
New York NY 10019. 212/887-8580.

IRON AGE
191 South Gary, Carol Stream IL
60188. 708/462-2285.

IRON & STEEL ENGINEER
Association of Iron and Steel
Engineers, Three Gateway Center,
Suite 2350, Pittsburgh PA 15222.
412/281-6323.

MODERN METALS
625 North Michigan Avenue, Suite
2500, Chicago IL 60611. 312/654-2300.

FINANCIAL SERVICES

 *Since the 1987 stock market crash, one of the few hot financial products has been mutual funds. Jobseekers should note that while the phenomenal growth of mutual fund investing wasn't expected to continue through 1994, demographics bode well for the long-term prospects of the industry. Expect to see steady, but slower growth. Investment managers and related mutual fund service firms should reap the benefits.*

Brokerage houses posted their third straight year of record profits in 1993, and the securities industry was expected to continue at high levels in '94. According to Fortune magazine, low interest rates boosted the securities industry, but on three occasions during the Spring of 1994 the Fed raised interest rates in an attempt to ward off runaway inflation. Despite the large amount of trading, brokerage houses are continuing to shrink their staffs to keep a tight reign on costs. Uncertainty over health care reform and executive compensation have created a volatile trading environment.

ADVANTA CORPORATION
Brandywine Corporate Center, 650 Naamans Road, Claymont DE 19703. 302/791-4400. **Contact:** Human Resources. **Description:** Advanta Corporation is a consumer financial services holding company that provides financial products nationwide through its subsidiaries using direct-marketing techniques. The company mainly originates and services credit cards and mortgages. Other businesses include deposit products, equipment leasing products and credit insurance services. **Number of employees nationwide:** 1,327.

ADVANTA CORPORATION
300 Welsh Road, Building 5, Horsham PA 19044. 215/657-4000. **Contact:** Human Resources. **Description:** A consumer lending corporation.

AMERICAN EXPRESS CREDIT CORPORATION
One Rodney Square, Wilmington DE 19801. 302/594-3361. **Contact:** Angela M. Cecere, Manager/Human Resources. **Description:** A credit company dealing in commercial paper trading. **Common positions include:** Customer Service Representative. **Educational backgrounds include:** Finance; Liberal Arts. **Benefits:** 401K; Daycare Assistance; Dental Insurance; Disability Coverage; Life Insurance; Medical Insurance; Pension Plan; Tuition Assistance. **Corporate headquarters location:** This Location. **Parent company:** American Express Travel Related Services, Inc.

ASSOCIATED CREDIT BUREAU SERVICE INC.
739 Hamilton Mall, 2nd Floor, Allentown PA 18101. 215/820-6828. **Contact:** Human Resources. **Description:** A collection agency.

BERWIND CORPORATION
3000 Center Square West, 1500 Market Street, Philadelphia PA 19102. 215/563-2800. **Contact:** June Beal, Head of Human Resources. **Description:** A financial services organization, offering a wide range of consulting services.

BUTCHER & COMPANY
1528 Walnut Street, Suite 2100, Philadelphia PA 19102. 215/985-5200. **Contact:** Office Administrator. **Description:** An investment banking firm, providing a wide range of investment and financial services.

CLARK CAPITAL MANAGEMENT GROUP INC.
1735 Market Street, 34th Floor, Philadelphia PA 19103. 215/569-2224. **Contact:** Human Resources. **Description:** An investment firm.

COLLEGE CREDIT CARD CORPORATION
1500 Walnut Street, 19th Floor, Philadelphia PA 19102. 215/732-1800. **Contact:** Jay Muchnick, Director of Account Management. **Description:** Markets credit cards on-campus to college students, and designs and implements special events directed to students. **Parent company:** Campus Dimensions Inc. **Number of employees at this location:** 115.

DELAWARE MANAGEMENT CO.
1818 Market Street, 17th Floor, Philadelphia PA 19103. 215/988-1200. **Contact:** Human Resources. **Description:** A full-service financial services firm with an emphasis on mutual funds.

FIRST CLEARFIELD FUNDS INC.
1801 JFK Boulevard, Suite 1209, Philadelphia PA 19103. 215/732-2203. **Contact:** Human Resources. **Description:** A financial services firm.

FRANKLIN FIRST FINANCIAL CORPORATION
44 West Market Street, Wilkes Barre PA 18773. 717/821-7100. **Contact:** Human Resources. **Description:** A financial services firm.

HORRIGAN AMERICAN, INC.
P.O. Box 13428, Reading PA 19612-3428. 215/775-5199. **Contact:** Christine M. O'Neill, Assistant V.P./Human Resources. **Description:** Diversified financial services company. Established in 1927. **Other U.S. locations:** Chicago IL; Cincinnati OH; Reading PA. **Number of employees at this location:** 100.

JANNEY MONTGOMERY SCOTT
1801 Market Street, Philadelphia PA 19103. 215/665-6000. **Contact:** Maryanne Melchiorre, Personnel Director. **Description:** An investment firm. **Common positions include:** Accountant/Auditor; Financial Services Sales Rep.; Securities Sales Rep. **Educational backgrounds include:** Accounting. **Benefits:** Disability Coverage; Employee Discounts; Life Insurance; Medical Insurance; Profit Sharing; Savings Plan. **Corporate headquarters location:** This Location. **Operations at this facility include:** Sales. **Listed on:** American Stock Exchange; New York Stock Exchange.

OXFORD FINANCIAL SERVICES, INC.
7300 Old York Road, Philadelphia PA 19126. 215/782-7000. **Contact:** Marie Wilkins, Personnel. **Description:** A licensed finance company.

PAINEWEBBER
2 Logan Square, 24th Floor, Philadelphia PA 19103. 215/972-6800. **Contact:** Human Resources. **Description:** A securities brokerage.

PHILADELPHIA FEDERAL CREDIT UNION
BROKERAGE SERVICE
216 West Washington Square, Philadelphia PA 19106. 215/625-8700. **Contact:** Human Resources. **Description:** Offers financial services.

PHILADELPHIA STOCK EXCHANGE INC.
1900 Market Street, Philadelphia PA 19103. 215/496-5000. **Contact:** Human Resources. **Description:** A stock exchange.

PRUDENTIAL FINANCIAL SERVICES
Winchester Plaza, Suite 102, 1550 Pond Road, Allentown PA 18104. 215/391-9800. **Contact:** James C. Sharp, General Manager. **Description:** Employees market Prudential's portfolio of insurances and investment products to business owners.

PUBLIC FINANCIAL MANAGEMENT
Two Logan Square, Suite 1600, 18th & Arch Streets, Philadelphia PA 19103. 215/567-6100. **Contact:** Melinda Harris, Consultant/Recruiting Coordinator. **Description:** A financial advisory firm serving the public sector; manages $3.5 billion in public sector funds. **Common positions include:** Financial Analyst. **Educational backgrounds include:** Economics; Finance; Liberal Arts; Mathematics. **Benefits:** Dental Insurance; Disability Coverage; Employee Discounts; Life Insurance; Medical Insurance; Savings Plan; Tuition Assistance. **Special Programs:** Training Programs. **Corporate headquarters location:** This Location. **Other U.S. locations:** Los Angeles CA; San Francisco CA; Denver CO; Orlando FL; Fort Myers FL; Atlanta GA; Boston MA; Portland OR; Harrisonburg PA; Austin TX. **Parent company:** Marine Midland Bank. **Annual Revenues:** $21,000,000. **Number of employees at this location:** 135. **Projected hires for the next 12 months (This location):** 15 hires.

RITTENHOUSE TRUST COMPANY
2 Radnor Corporate Center, Suite 420, 100 Matsonford Road, Radnor PA 19087. 215/971-9300. **Contact:** Human Resources. **Description:** A financial services company.

KURT SALMON ASSOCIATES, INC.
103 Carnegie Center, Suite 205, Princeton NJ 08540. 609/452-8700. **Contact:** Ms. Marian N. Crandall, Director of Recruiting. **Description:** A financial services firm.

VANGUARD GROUP INC.
P.O. Box 2600, Valley Forge PA 19482. 215/669-6000. **Contact:** Human Resources Department. **Description:** A mutual funds company.

Note: Because addresses and telephone numbers of smaller companies change rapidly, we recommend you contact each company and verify the information below before contacting employers. Mass mailings are not recommended.

Additional medium sized employers: under 500

MANAGEMENT INVESTMENT OFFICES

Vanguard/Windsor Funds
P O Box 1100, Valley Forge PA 19482-1100. 610/669-6000.

PATENT OWNERS AND LESSORS

AAMCO Transmissions Inc.
1 Presidential Blvd, Bala Cynwyd PA 19004-1007. 610/668-2900.

Maaco Enterprises Inc.
381 Brooks Rd, Kng Of Prussa PA 19406-3169. 610/265-6606.

FEDERAL AND FEDERALLY SPONSORED CREDIT AGENCIES

Allentown General Corporation
1105 W Hamilton St, Allentown PA 18101-1043. 610/437-8135.

Eastern Mortgage
3401 Hartzdale Dr Ste 126, Camp Hill PA 17011-7238. 717/763-8924.

Keystone Farm Credit ACA
Route 222 & Scotland Rd, Quarryville PA 17566. 717/786-7007.

Oxford Finance Companies Inc.
6701 Broad St, Philadelphia PA 19126-2837. 215/276-5000.

SHORT-TERM BUSINESS CREDIT INSTITUTIONS

Citicorp Diners Club
1210 Northbrook Dr, Fstrvl Trvose PA 19053-8406. 215/355-5801.

MORTGAGE BANKERS AND LOAN CORRESPONDENTS

American General Finance Inc.
1 Oxford Ct, Langhorne PA 19047-1645. 215/757-0501.

Coml Credit Plan Consumer Disc Co
2213 Galloway Rd, Bensalem PA 19020-2917. 215/639-8580.

Franklin First Fed Savings Bank
Medical Arts Bldg, Pocono Summit PA 18346. 717/839-2582.

Maryland National Mortgage Corporation
4905 W Tilghman St, Allentown PA 18104-9130. 610/366-0110.

Meridian Mortgage Co.
555 E Lancaster Ave, Wayne PA 19087-5109. 610/293-9616.

Mortgage Access Corporation
224 N Pottstown Pike, Exton PA 19341-2212. 610/363-5800.

SECURITY BROKERS AND DEALERS

Boenning & Scattergood
1 Oxford Ct, Langhorne PA 19047-1645. 215/752-1551.

Dreyfus Service Corporation
519 Caddy Dr, Warrington PA 18976. 215/343-1300.

WH Newbold's Son & Company
1500 Walnut St, Philadelphia PA 19102-3523. 215/893-8082.

Equity Futures Inc.
3037 S Pike Ave Ste 204, Allentown PA 18103-7648. 610/791-7281.

SECURITY AND COMMODITY EXCHANGES

Options Clearing Corporation
1900 Market St, Philadelphia PA 19103-3527. 215/564-4955.

INVESTMENT ADVICE

IDS Financial Services
129 Green St, Moscow
PA 18444-9088.
717/842-8001.

**Pennsylvania Financial
Group Inc.**
1018 W 9th Ave, Kng Of
Prussa PA 19406-1225.
610/962-0400.

**SERVICES ALLIED WITH
SECURITIES AND
COMMODITIES
EXCHANGES**

BHC Financial Inc.
100 N 20th St,
Philadelphia PA 19103-
1443. 215/636-3000.

For more information on career opportunities in financial services:

Associations

FINANCIAL EXECUTIVES INSTITUTE
P.O. Box 1938, Morristown NJ
07962-1938. 201/898-4600. Fee and
membership required.

**INSTITUTE OF FINANCIAL
EDUCATION**
111 East Wacker Drive, Chicago IL
60601. 312/946-8800.

**NATIONAL ASSOCIATION OF
BUSINESS ECONOMISTS**
1801 East 9th Street, Cleveland OH
44114. 216/241-6223.

**NATIONAL ASSOCIATION OF CREDIT
MANAGEMENT**
8815 Centre Park Drive, Suite 200,
Columbia MD 21045-2158. 410/740-
5560.

**NATIONAL ASSOCIATION OF REAL
ESTATE INVESTMENT TRUSTS**
1129 20th Street NW, Suite 305,
Washington DC 20036. 202/785-
8717.

PUBLIC SECURITIES ASSOCIATION
40 Broad Street, 12th Floor, New
York NY 10004. 212/809-7000.

**SECURITIES INDUSTRY
ASSOCIATION**
120 Broadway, New York NY 10271.
212/608-1500.

**TREASURY MANAGEMENT
ASSOCIATION**
7315 Wisconsin Avenue, Suite 1250-
W, Bethesda MD 20814. 301/907-
2862.

Directories

**DIRECTORY OF AMERICAN
FINANCIAL INSTITUTIONS**
Thomson Business Publications, 6195
Crooked Creek Road, Norcross GA
30092. 404/448-1011.

**MOODY'S BANK AND FINANCE
MANUAL**
Moody's Investor Service, 99 Church
Street, New York NY 10007.
212/553-0300.

TEXAS BUSINESS DIRECTORY
American Business Directories, 5711
South 86th Circle, P.O. Box 27347,
Omaha NE 68127. 402/593-4600.

Magazines

**BARRON'S: NATIONAL BUSINESS
AND FINANCIAL WEEKLY**
Dow Jones & Co., 200 Liberty Street,
New York NY 10281. 212/416-2700.

FINANCIAL PLANNING
40 West 57th Street, 11th Floor, New
York NY 10019. 212/765-5311.

FINANCIAL WORLD
Financial World Partners, 1328
Broadway, 3rd Floor, New York NY
10001. 212/594-5030.

**FUTURES: THE MAGAZINE OF
COMMODITIES AND OPTIONS**
250 South Wacker Drive, Suite 1150,
Chicago IL 60606. 312/977-0999.

INSTITUTIONAL INVESTOR
488 Madison Avenue, 12th Floor,
New York NY 10022. 212/303-3300.

FOOD AND BEVERAGES/AGRICULTURE

While it is the nation's largest manufacturing sector, the processed food and beverage industry is experiencing sluggish growth. But improvements are expected to snowball as the effects of NAFTA and the GATT agreement take hold and boost international trade. As an example, the U.S. Commerce Department claims NAFTA provides at least three advantages to the American processed food and beverage industry sector. It is expected to: reduce mutual tariff restrictions over 15 years; abolish all Mexican import licenses; and require the mutual recognition of distinctive products, like bourbon and Tennessee whiskey -- for example, only bourbon distilled in the U.S. would be sold in Canada and Mexico.

AGRICOL CORPORATION, INC.
Plaza 1000 at Main Street, Suite 404, Voorhees NJ 08043. 609/424-9191. **Contact:** Mr. Gamil Shab, Vice President/Personnel. **Description:** A wholesale grain trading company. **Parent company:** Conagra Company.

ALLEN FAMILY FOODS, INC.
P.O. Box 63, Harbeson DE 19951. 302/684-1640. **Contact:** Barry Moore, Director of Personnel. **Description:** A processor of poultry and poultry products. **Common positions include:** Blue-Collar Worker Supervisor; Department Manager; Management Trainee; Manufacturer's/Wholesaler's Sales Rep.; Operations/Production Manager; Personnel/Labor Relations Specialist; Purchasing Agent and Manager; Quality Control Supervisor. **Educational backgrounds include:** Agricultural Science; Biology; Business Administration; Computer Science; Physics. **Benefits:** Dental Insurance; Disability Coverage; Life Insurance; Medical Insurance; Pension Plan; Savings Plan; Tuition Assistance. **Special Programs:** Training Programs. **Corporate headquarters location:** Seaford DE. **Operations at this facility include:** Manufacturing.

ALPO PET FOODS INC.
P.O. Box 25100, Lehigh Valley PA 18002-5100. 215/395-3301. **Contact:** Corporate Human Resource Manager. **Description:** Engaged in the manufacture and sales of the Alpo brand of premium canned dog and cat foods. One of the largest dogfood and catfood manufacturers and distributors in the United States.

AMERICAN HOME FOODS INC.
30 Marr Street, Milton PA 17847. 717/742-7621. **Contact:** Human Resources. **Description:** Produces canned foods.

BICKEL'S POTATO CHIP COMPANY INC.
51 North Main Street, Manheim PA 17545-0610. 717/665-2002. **Contact:** Human Resources. **Description:** Produces potato chips.

BLUE RIBBON SERVICES, INC.
7400 Oxford Avenue, Philadelphia PA 19111. **Contact:** Personnel Department. **Description:** Engaged in the food service industry, providing high-quality food and vending services. Company offers a comprehensive benefits package to full time

employees. **Common positions include:** Administrative Worker/Clerk; Cashier; Food and Beverage Service Worker; Services Sales Representative.

BORDEN INC.
PRINCE SAUCES
1550 John Tipton Boulevard, Pennsauken NJ 08110. 609/661-3253. **Contact:** Sharon Lewis, Personnel. **Description:** Manufacturers of spaghetti sauce. **Common positions include:** Accountant/Auditor; Blue-Collar Worker Supervisor; Department Manager; Financial Analyst; Food Scientist/Technologist; General Manager; Industrial Engineer; Mechanical Engineer; Operations/Production Manager; Personnel/Labor Relations Specialist; Purchasing Agent and Manager; Quality Control Supervisor. **Educational backgrounds include:** Accounting; Biology; Business Administration; Chemistry; Engineering; Finance; Liberal Arts. **Benefits:** Dental Insurance; Disability Coverage; Employee Discounts; Life Insurance; Medical Insurance; Pension Plan; Profit Sharing; Savings Plan; Tuition Assistance. **Special Programs:** Training Programs. **Corporate headquarters location:** Columbus OH. **Parent company:** Borden Inc. **Operations at this facility include:** Administration; Manufacturing. **Listed on:** New York Stock Exchange.

CAMPBELL SOUP CO.
Campbell Place, Camden NJ 08103-1799. 609/342-4800. **Contact:** Human Resources. **Description:** Headquarters location of the well-known food-processing company.

CLOFINE DAIRY PRODUCTS
1407 New Road, P.O. Box 335, Linwood NJ 08221. 609/653-1000. **Contact:** Marie Losco, Personnel. **Description:** A brokerage services company for dairy and other food products.

COLONIAL BEEF COMPANY
3333 South 3rd Street, Philadelphia PA 19148. 215/467-0900. **Contact:** Donna Bernath, Personnel Director. **Description:** A meat packing company.

CONAGRA BROILER COMPANY
255 North Rehobeth Boulevard, Milford DE 19963. 302/422-6681. **Contact:** Bob Heimbach, Assistant Division Personnel Manager. **Description:** A processor of poultry. **Common positions include:** Accountant/Auditor; Assistant Manager; Blue-Collar Worker Supervisor; Civil Engineer; Computer Programmer; Credit Manager; Customer Service Representative; Department Manager; General Manager; Instructor/Trainer; Management Trainee; Mechanical Engineer; Purchasing Agent and Manager; Quality Control Supervisor. **Educational backgrounds include:** Business Administration. **Benefits:** Dental Insurance; Disability Coverage; Employee Discounts; Life Insurance; Medical Insurance; Pension Plan; Savings Plan; Stock Option; Tuition Assistance. **Special Programs:** Internships; Training Programs. **Operations at this facility include:** Manufacturing. **Listed on:** New York Stock Exchange.

CUTLER DAIRY PRODUCTS, INC.
612 W. Sedgley Avenue, Philadelphia PA 19140. 215/229-5400. **FAX:** 215/229-5637. **Contact:** Ms. Cynthia Hart, Manager, Human Resources. **Description:** Processes and supplies eggs to the food industry on the national market level. **Common positions include:** Administrative Services Manager; Biological Scientist/Biochemist; Blue-Collar Worker Supervisor; Food Scientist/Technologist; General Manager; Heating/AC/Refrigeration Technician; Inspector/Tester/Grader; Production Manager; Truck Driver. **Educational backgrounds include:** Biology; Business Administration; Liberal Arts. **Benefits:** Dental Insurance; Life Insurance; Medical Insurance; Pension Plan;

Profit Sharing. **Corporate headquarters location:** This Location. **Other U.S. locations:** Abbeyville AL. **Operations at this facility include:** Administration; Manufacturing; Sales; Service. **Number of employees at this location:** 250. **Number of employees nationwide:** 99. **Hires/Layoffs in 1993 (This location):** 5 hires. **Hires/Layoffs in 1993 (Nationwide):** 3 hires. **Projected hires for the next 12 months (This location):** 5 hires. **Projected hires for the next 12 months (Nationwide):** 5 hires.

DEALS SEAFOOD COMPANY INC.

212 East Madison Avenue, P.O. Box 55, Magnolia NJ 08049. 609/783-8700. **Contact:** Personnel. **Description:** A seafood packing company.

DELAGRA CORPORATION

P.O. Box 126, Bridgeville DE 19933. 302/337-8206. **Contact:** Susan Larinmore, Personnel. **Description:** A food company engaged in the processing of frozen vegetables.

DIETZ AND WATSON, INC.

5701 Tacony Street, Philadelphia PA 19135. 215/831-9000. **Contact:** Personnel Department. **Description:** A sausage and prepared meats company.

DRAPER-KING COLE INC.

Chestnut Street, Milton DE 19968. 302/684-8555. **Contact:** Ron Bruerton, Personnel Director. **Description:** Processes and distributes vegetables. **Common positions include:** Accountant/Auditor; Blue-Collar Worker Supervisor; Civil Engineer; Computer Programmer; Manufacturer's/Wholesaler's Sales Rep.; Mechanical Engineer; Operations/Production Manager; Purchasing Agent and Manager; Quality Control Supervisor; Transportation/Traffic Specialist. **Educational backgrounds include:** Accounting; Business Administration; Liberal Arts; Marketing. **Benefits:** Life Insurance; Medical Insurance; Pension Plan. **Corporate headquarters location:** This Location. **Operations at this facility include:** Manufacturing; Sales.

DURKEE FRENCH FOODS

1001 Eighth Avenue, Bethlehem PA 18018. 215/867-0521. **Contact:** Lee Emery, Manager of Employee Relations. **Description:** Produces a nationally distributed line of sauce and gravy mixes, condiments, spices, extracts, and convenience foods.

EL JAY POULTRY CORPORATION

P.O. Box 778, Voorhees NJ 08043. 609/435-0900. **Contact:** Julia O'Connor, Personnel. **Description:** A poultry processing company.

FLEMING FOODS

P.O. Box 935, Oaks PA 19456. 215/935-5000. **Contact:** Al Magniarina, Assistant Manager/H.R. **Description:** One of the oldest existing cooperative grocery wholesalers in the United States, supplying dry grocery, dairy/deli, frozen food, and general merchandise to 60 member supermarkets and 175 smaller operation member retail markets. In 1983, opened a health and beauty aids/general merchandise subsidiary in Bensalem, PA (Unity Sales Co.). In 1985, the company opened Fresh Acres produce division, in Philadelphia, PA. Areas serviced include: Philadelphia metropolitan area, southern New Jersey, southeastern Pennsylvania, and northern Delaware. **Common positions include:** Accountant/Auditor; Buyer; Computer Programmer; Department Manager. **Educational backgrounds include:** Accounting; Business Administration; Finance. **Benefits:** Dental Insurance; Disability Coverage; Life Insurance; Medical Insurance; Pension Plan; Tuition Assistance; Vision Insurance. **Corporate headquarters location:** This Location. **Operations at this facility include:** Regional Headquarters.

JACK GREENBERG INC.
1717 North Delaware Avenue, Philadelphia PA 19125. 215/426-7200. **Contact:** Steve Cohn, Controller. **Description:** Distributor of frozen foods and canned goods.

HANOVER FOODS
P.O. Box 1010, Clayton DE 19938. 302/653-9281. **Contact:** Jon Andrews, Personnel Director. **Description:** A manufacturing plant that produces ingredients such as meatballs and ravioli for Campbell Soup.

HANOVER FOODS/LANCASTER DIVISION
P.O. Box 1236, Lancaster PA 17608. 717/397-6141. **Contact:** Patrick Anders, Personnel Manager. **Description:** Produces processed frozen vegetables, and manufactures ice. **Common positions include:** Management Trainee. **Benefits:** Dental Insurance; Disability Coverage; Life Insurance; Medical Insurance; Pension Plan; Savings Plan. **Special Programs:** Internships; Training Programs. **Corporate headquarters location:** Hanover PA. **Parent company:** Hanover Brands, inc. **Operations at this facility include:** Manufacturing.

HATFIELD QUALITY MEATS INC.
2700 Funks Road, P.O. Box 902, Hatfield PA 19440. 215/368-2500. **Contact:** Human Resources. **Description:** Manufactures meat products.

HERSHEY FOODS CORPORATION
100 Crystal A Drive, Hershey PA 17033. 717/534-7096. **Contact:** Gary Acker, Director/Employee Relations. **Description:** Hershey is a confectionery and chocolate manufacturer, as well as pasta maker. **Common positions include:** Accountant/Auditor; Administrator; Architectural Engineer; Attorney; Biological Scientist/Biochemist; Blue-Collar Worker Supervisor; Buyer; Chemical Engineer; Chemist; Claim Representative; Computer Programmer; Customer Service Representative; Department Manager; Draftsperson; Electrical/Electronic Engineer; Financial Analyst; Food Scientist/Technologist; General Manager; Industrial Engineer; Instructor/Trainer; Manufacturer's/ Wholesaler's Sales Rep.; Marketing Specialist; Mechanical Engineer; Operations/Production Manager; Paralegal; Personnel/Labor Relations Specialist; Public Relations Specialist; Purchasing Agent and Manager; Quality Control Supervisor; Systems Analyst; Transportation/Traffic Specialist. **Benefits:** Daycare Assistance; Dental Insurance; Disability Coverage; Employee Discounts; Life Insurance; Medical Insurance; Pension Plan; Savings Plan; Stock Option; Tuition Assistance. **Special Programs:** Internships; Training Programs. **Number of employees at this location:** 13,700. **Projected hires for the next 12 months (This location):** 50 hires.

HERSHEY PASTA GROUP
SAN GIORGIO MACARONI
749 Guilford Street, Lebanon PA 17046. 717/273-7641. **Contact:** Jo Ann Swingholm, Human Resource Coordinator. **Description:** Produces a variety of pasta products, including macaroni, spaghetti, and egg noodles. **Common positions include:** Accountant/Auditor; Blue-Collar Worker Supervisor; Computer Programmer; Customer Service Representative; Department Manager; Industrial Engineer; Personnel/Labor Relations Specialist; Quality Control Supervisor. **Educational backgrounds include:** Chemistry; Computer Science; Engineering; Finance. **Benefits:** Dental Insurance; Life Insurance; Medical Insurance; Pension Plan; Savings Plan; Tuition Assistance. **Corporate headquarters location:** Hershey PA. **Parent company:** Hershey Foods. **Operations at this facility include:** Manufacturing; Service. **Listed on:** New York Stock Exchange.

HYGRADE FOOD PRODUCTS CORPORATION

8400 Executive Avenue, Philadelphia PA 19153. 215/365-8700. **Contact:** Donna Zazada, Eastern Regional Personnel Manager. **Description:** Produces and distributes processed meats, including frankfurters, luncheon meats, and specialty meats. Facilities are located through the United States. **Common positions include:** Accountant/Auditor; Blue-Collar Worker Supervisor; Industrial Engineer; Operations/Production Manager; Personnel/Labor Relations Specialist; Production Coordinator; Safety Specialist. **Educational backgrounds include:** Business Administration; Economics; Food Science. **Benefits:** Dental Insurance; Disability Coverage; Employee Discounts; Life Insurance; Medical Insurance; Pension Plan; Profit Sharing; Savings Plan; Tuition Assistance; Vision Insurance. **Corporate headquarters location:** Cordova TN. **Parent company:** Sara Lee Corporation. **Operations at this facility include:** Manufacturing. **Listed on:** New York Stock Exchange.

J&J SNACK FOODS CORPORATION

6000 Central Highway, Pennsauken NJ 08109. 609/665-9533. **Contact:** Human Resources. **Description:** Manufactures a variety of snack foods.

KRAFT GENERAL FOODS
FOOD SERVICES DIVISION

11 East Erie Avenue, 1635 Market Street, Philadelphia PA 19124. 215/289-9000. **Contact:** Manager/Human Resources. **Description:** Processes and distributes a wide variety of frozen and cultured dairy products as a division of Kraft, Inc.

KRAFT GENERAL FOODS CORPORATION

P.O. Box 600, West North Street, Dover DE 19903. 302/734-6100. **Contact:** Personnel Director. **Description:** A branch of one of the world's largest processors and marketers of a host of familiar food and beverage products.

LEHIGH VALLEY DAIRIES INC.

880 Allentown Road, Lansdale PA 19446. 215/855-8205. **Contact:** Human Resources. **Description:** A dairy products company.

MOUNTAIRE OF DELMARVA INC.

P.O. Box 710, Selbyville DE 19975. 302/436-8241. **Contact:** Alan Slotorzynski, Personnel Director. **Description:** A leading poultry processing plant. **Corporate headquarters location:** This Location.

MRS. SMITH'S FROZEN FOODS COMPANY

P.O. Box 298, Pottstown PA 19464. 215/326-2600. **Contact:** Ron Kitlas, Human Resources Director. **Description:** Produces a broad range of nationally-recognized frozen baked products, including Mrs. Smith's brand pies and Eggo brand waffles. **Benefits:** Medical Insurance. **Parent company:** Kellogg Company.

NABISCO BISCUIT COMPANY
BAKERY AND DISTRIBUTION CENTER

P.O. Box 6119, Philadelphia PA 19115. 215/673-4800. **Contact:** Trainer Coordinator. **Description:** Philadelphia bakery of the nationally recognized producer of food products. Nabisco is an Equal Opportunity Employer MFVH. **Common positions include:** Accountant/Auditor; Blue-Collar Worker Supervisor; Department Manager; Electrical/Electronic Engineer; Food Scientist/Technologist; Industrial Manager; Operations/Production Manager; Personnel/Labor Relations Specialist; Quality Control Supervisor. **Educational backgrounds include:** Accounting; Biology; Business

Administration; Engineering; Liberal Arts. **Benefits:** Dental Insurance; Disability Coverage; Employee Discounts; Life Insurance; Medical Insurance; Pension Plan; Profit Sharing; Savings Plan; Tuition Assistance. **Special Programs:** Internships; Training Programs. **Corporate headquarters location:** East Hanover NJ. **Parent company:** RJR Nabisco. **Operations at this facility include:** Manufacturing. **Listed on:** New York Stock Exchange.

R.M. PALMER COMPANY
77 2nd Avenue, West Reading PA 19611. 215/375-2727. **Contact:** Human Resources. **Description:** Manufactures and produces quality chocolates and other confections for Halloween, Christmas, Valentine's, and Easter seasons. **Common positions include:** Accountant/Auditor; Blue-Collar Worker Supervisor; Buyer; Commercial Artist; Computer Programmer; Credit Manager; Customer Service Representative; Industrial Engineer; Operations/Production Manager; Personnel/Labor Relations Specialist; Purchasing Agent and Manager. **Educational backgrounds include:** Accounting; Business Administration; Economics; Engineering; Finance; Marketing. **Benefits:** Dental Insurance; Disability Coverage; Employee Discounts; Life Insurance; Medical Insurance; Pension Plan; Profit Sharing; Savings Plan; Tuition Assistance. **Operations at this facility include:** Administration; Manufacturing; Sales.

PEPPERIDGE FARM INC.
421 Boot Road, Downingtown PA 19335. 215/269-2500. **Contact:** Human Resources Department. **Description:** A bread and bakery products company.

PEPSI-COLA/PHILADELPHIA
11701 Roosevelt Boulevard, Philadelphia PA 19154. 215/676-6400. **Contact:** Personnel Director. **Description:** Philadelphia facility of the well-known soft drink producer and distributor.

PERDUE INC.
200 Savannah Road, Georgetown DE 19947. 302/856-0941. **Contact:** Personnel Director. **Description:** Delaware office of the nationally-known poultry products processor. **Corporate headquarters location:** Salisbury MD.

PHILADELPHIA BROKERAGE
2201 Route 38, Suite 616, Cherry Hill PA 08002. 215/467-6550. **Contact:** Human Resources. **Description:** A food brokerage company.

SNOWBALL FOODS, INC.
Sykes Lane, Williamstown NJ 08094. 609/629-4081. **Contact:** Julie Carey, Human Resource Manager. **Description:** A turkey processing plant. **Common positions include:** Accountant/Auditor; Blue-Collar Worker Supervisor; Buyer; Customer Service Representative; Food Scientist/Technologist; Management Trainee; Manufacturer's/ Wholesaler's Sales Rep.; Operations/Production Manager; Personnel/Labor Relations Specialist; Quality Control Supervisor; Transportation/Traffic Specialist. **Educational backgrounds include:** Accounting; Business Administration; Marketing. **Benefits:** 401K; Dental Insurance; Life Insurance; Medical Insurance; Tuition Assistance. **Special Programs:** Internships. **Corporate headquarters location:** This Location. **Operations at this facility include:** Administration; Manufacturing; Research and Development; Sales; Service. **Number of employees at this location:** 250.

STROH BREWERY COMPANY
LEHIGH VALLEY PLANT
P.O. Box 25013, Lehigh Valley PA 18002. 215/395-6811. **Contact:** David W. Lichtle, Industrial Relations Manager. **Description:** Brews, packages, and distributes Strohs, Schaefer, Piels and other beers. **Common positions include:** Accountant/Auditor; Administrator; Biological Scientist/Biochemist; Blue-Collar Worker Supervisor; Department Manager; Electrical/Electronic Engineer; Management Trainee; Mechanical Engineer; Operations/Production Manager; Personnel/Labor Relations Specialist; Quality Control Supervisor. **Educational backgrounds include:** Accounting; Biology; Business Administration; Engineering. **Benefits:** Dental Insurance; Disability Coverage; Employee Discounts; Life Insurance; Medical Insurance; Pension Plan; Savings Plan; Tuition Assistance; Vision Insurance. **Corporate headquarters location:** Detroit MI. **Operations at this facility include:** Manufacturing.

SUNROC CORPORATION
300 S. Pennell Road, Media PA 19037. 215/459-1100. **Contact:** Sharon Amalfitano, Personnel Director. **Description:** Manufactures a wide range of nationally-distributed water coolers and drinking fountains. **Common positions include:** Accountant/Auditor; Blue-Collar Worker Supervisor; Buyer; Computer Programmer; Credit Manager; Customer Service Representative; Draftsperson; Financial Analyst; Industrial Engineer; Personnel/Labor Relations Specialist; Purchasing Agent and Manager; Quality Control Supervisor. **Educational backgrounds include:** Accounting; Engineering; Finance; Liberal Arts. **Benefits:** Dental Insurance; Disability Coverage; Life Insurance; Medical Insurance; Profit Sharing; Tuition Assistance. **Corporate headquarters location:** This Location.

TASTY BAKING COMPANY
2801 Hunting Park Avenue, Philadelphia PA 19129. 215/221-8500. **Contact:** William Mahoney, Vice President/Human Resources. **Description:** Engaged in the manufacture and sale of a variety of small single portion cakes, pies, and cookies under the brand name Tastykake. Offers approximately 45 varieties of products. Principal markets are in the East and Northeast. **Corporate headquarters location:** This Location. **Listed on:** American Stock Exchange.

TAYLOR PACKING COMPANY INC.
P.O. Box 188, Wyalusing PA 18853. 717/746-3000. **Contact:** Human Resources. **Description:** A meat packing plant.

VENICE MAID FOODS
270 North Mill Road, Vineland NJ 08360. 609/691-2100. **Contact:** Patricia Haas, Human Resources Manager. **Description:** Venice Maid Food is one of the largest manufacturers for private brands in the country and produces over three hundred and seventy-five institutional and retail products. **Common positions include:** Accountant/Auditor; Administrative Services Manager; Chef/Cook/Kitchen Worker; Computer Operator; Customer Service Representative; Department Manager; Electrical/Electronic Engineer; Laboratory Technician; Machinist; Manufacturer's/Wholesaler's Sales Rep.; Mechanical Engineer; Operations/Production Manager; Payroll Clerk; Personnel/Labor Relations Specialist; Quality Control Supervisor; Receptionist; Secretary. **Educational backgrounds include:** Accounting; Computer Science; Engineering; Finance. **Benefits:** Dental Insurance; Disability Coverage; Employee Discounts; Life Insurance; Medical Insurance; Pension Plan; Tuition Assistance. **Corporate headquarters location:** Bala Cynwd PA. **Parent company:** Connelly Containers. **Operations at this facility include:** Administration; Manufacturing; Research and Development; Sales. **Listed on:** New York Stock Exchange. **Number of**

employees at this location: 177. **Number of employees nationwide**: 177. **Projected hires for the next 12 months (This location)**: 2 hires.

WHITMAN'S CHOCOLATE
9701 Roosevelt Boulevard, Philadelphia PA 19115. 215/464-6000. **Contact**: Edward Bowman, Personnel Director. **Description**: Produces a wide range of chocolate and other confectionery products.

Note: Because addresses and telephone numbers of smaller companies change rapidly, we recommend you contact each company and verify the information below before contacting employers. Mass mailings are not recommended.

Additional large employers: 500 +

**GROCERIES -
WHOLESALE**

Associated Wholesalers Inc.
P.O. Box 67, Rte. 422, Robesonia PA 19551. 610/693-3161.

**FROZEN FOODS -
WHOLESALE**

Keystone Foods Corporation
401 E City Ave., Bala Cynwyd PA 19004-1122. 610/667-6700.

MEAT PACKING

Moyer Packing Company
249 Allentown Rd., Souderton PA 18964-2207. 215/723-5555.

POULTRY

Empire Kosher Poultry Inc.
P.O. Box 165, River Rd., Mifflintown PA 17059. 717/436-5921.

Tyson Foods
403 S Custer Ave., New Holland PA 17557-9221. 717/354-4211.

Wampler-Longacre Turkey Inc.
Rt. 113 & Allentown Rd., Franconia PA 18924. 215/723-4335.

CANNED FOODS

Knouse Foods
800 Peach Glen-Idaville Rd., Peach Glen PA 17375-0001. 717/677-8181.

FROZEN FOODS

Seabrook Brothers & Sons Inc.
P.O. Box 5103, Seabrook NJ 08302-5103. 609/455-8080.

Progresso Foods Corp.
500 Elmer Rd., Vineland NJ 08360. 609/691-1565.

CEREAL

Kellogg Company
P.O. Box 3006, Lancaster PA 17604. 717/898-0161.

PET FOOD

Heinz Pet Products Inc.
6670 Lows St., Bloomsburg PA 17815-8613. 717/784-8200.

BAKERY PRODUCTS

Stroehmann Bakeries Inc.
P.O. Box 110, 1810 Ridge Pike, Norristown PA 19401. 610/825-1140.

Stroehmann Bakeries Inc.
255 Business Center Drive, Suite 200, Horsham PA 19044. 215/672-8010.

CANDY

H.B. Reese Candy Company
925 Reese Ave., Hershey PA 17033-2271. 717/534-4100.

M&M Mars
295 Brown St., Elizabethtown PA 17022-2127. 717/367-1500.

BOTTLED SOFT DRINKS

Philadelphia Coca Cola Bottling Company
725 East Erie Ave.,
Philadelphia PA 19134.
215/427-4500.

FOOD MANUFACTURING

Herr Foods Inc.
P.O. Box 300,
Nottingham PA 19362-9801. 610/932-9330.

Utz Quality Foods Inc.
861 Carlisle St., Hanover
PA 17331-1704.
717/637-6644.

Additional medium sized employers: under 500

BEER AND ALE WHOLESALE

Parkland Beverage Distributor
2361 Main St,
Schnecksville PA 18078-2510. 610/799-3642.

Royal Distr & Importers Inc.
2900 E State St Ext,
Trenton NJ 08619-4504.
609/587-6100.

GROCERY WHOLESALE

Bevaco Food Service
13 Rutledge Dr, Pittston
PA 18640-2264.
717/824-7826.

El-D Corporation
636 Old York Rd,
Jenkintown PA 19046-2858. 215/887-3933.

DAIRY PRODUCTS WHOLESALE

Jack & Jill Ice Cream Company
3100 Marwin Rd,
Bensalem PA 19020-6525. 215/639-2300.

CONFECTIONERY WHOLESALE

Charles Chips
Reliance Rd & Wile Av,
Souderton PA 18964.
215/723-2324.

FISH AND SEAFOOD WHOLESALE

Dockside Intl Fish Co
777 Pattison Ave,
Philadelphia PA 19148-5312. 215/271-9101.

GROCERIES AND RELATED PRODUCTS WHOLESALE

Crowley Foods Inc.
546 Foundry Rd,
Norristown PA 19403-3902. 610/272-7113.

Snyder's Of Hanover
PO Box 471, Hanover PA
17331-0471. 717/632-4477.

GRAIN AND FIELD BEANS

FM Brown Sons Inc.
188-126 W Main St,
Fleetwood PA 19522.
610/944-7654.

MEAT PACKING

Allen Clark Inc.
Irish Valley Rd, Paxinos
PA 17860. 717/648-6851.

Berks Packing Co Inc.
307 Bingaman St,
Reading PA 19602-2671.
610/376-7291.

Butler Foods Inc.
2300 E Butler St,
Philadelphia PA 19137-1012. 215/288-9920.

Robzen's Inc.
240 River St, Scranton
PA 18505-1182.
717/344-1141.

SAUSAGES AND OTHER PREPARED MEAT PRODUCTS

Casa Di Bertacchi Corporation
PO Box 327, Vineland NJ
08360-0327. 609/696-5600.

Citterio USA Corporation
PO Box A, Freeland PA
18224-0240. 717/636-3171.

Equity Group
600 Kaiser Dr, Folcroft
PA 19032-2122.
610/534-5900.

Freda Corporation
1334 S Front St,
Philadelphia PA 19147-5516. 215/336-6300.

Goodmark Foods Inc.
519 Kaiser Dr, Folcroft
PA 19032-2109.
610/586-2800.

Kunzler & Co Inc.
640-62 Manor St,
Lancaster PA 17603.
717/299-6301.

Leidy's Inc.
266 Cherry Lane,
Souderton PA 18964-
1902. 215/723-4606.

Maid Rite Steak Co
Keystone Industrial Park,
Scranton PA 18512.
717/343-4748.

Murry's Inc.
1501 Willow St, Lebanon
PA 17042-4578.
717/273-9361.

Ore-Ida Foods Inc.
700 N 5 Point Rd, West
Chester PA 19380-4206.
610/692-7575.

**William Cohen & Son
Quality Foods**
Third & Atlantic Sts,
Camden NJ 08103.
609/964-7788.

POULTRY

Agri General Inc.
370 Spicer Rd,
Gettysburg PA 17325-
7613. 717/334-9117.

College Hill Poultry Inc.
N Pine Grove St,
Fredericksbrg PA 17026.
717/865-2136.

Farmers Pride Inc.
PO Box 39, Fredericksbrg
PA 17026-0039.
717/865-6626.

Henry Colt Enterprises
Sykes Lane,
Williamstown NJ 08094.
609/629-4081.

Hi-N-Lite Farms
RR 3 Box 179A,
Tamaqua PA 18252-
9456. 717/386-5777.

Jerome Foods Inc.
1401 N Delaware Ave,
Philadelphia PA 19125-
4316. 215/427-1800.

Pennfield Farms
Rt 22, Fredericksbrg PA
17026. 717/865-2153.

RW Sauder Inc.
570 Furnace Hills Pike,
Lititz PA 17543-8902.
717/626-2074.

Round Hill Foods Inc.
South Water St, New
Oxford PA 17350.
717/624-2191.

Vineland Kosher Poultry
1100 S Mill Rd, Vineland
NJ 08360-6202.
609/692-1871.

BUTTER

Keller's Creamery Inc.
855 Maple Ave,
Harleysville PA 19438-
1031. 215/256-8871.

CHEESE

Beatrice Cheese Inc.
1002 McArthur Rd,
Whitehall PA 18052-
7002. 610/434-4822.

**DRY, CONDENSED AND
EVAPORATED DAIRY
PRODUCTS**

Dietrich's Milk Products
100 McKinley Ave,
Reading PA 19605-2117.
610/929-5736.

Holly Milk Coop
632 Park Dr, Carlisle PA
17013. 717/486-7000.

ICE CREAM

Hershey Creamery Co.
301 S Cameron St,
Harrisburg PA 17101-
2815. 717/238-8134.

MILK

**Crowley Frozen Desserts
Inc.**
1801 Hempstead Rd,
Lancaster PA 17601-
5671. 717/394-5601.

**Cumberland Farms Of
New Jersey**
RR 2, Burlington NJ
08016. 609/499-2600.

Dairy Center Inc.
485 Delaware Dr, Ft
Washington PA 19034-
2703. 215/643-1100.

Parmalat West Dairies
Bridge St & Stone Run
Rd, Spring City PA
19475. 610/948-8300.

Penn Maid Foods Inc.
2701 Red Lion Rd,
Philadelphia PA 19114-
1019. 215/934-6000.

Ready Food Products
10975 Dutton Rd,
Philadelphia PA 19154-
3288. 215/824-2800.

Rosenbergers Dairies
847 Forty Foot Rd,
Hatfield PA 19440-2870.
215/855-9074.

Rutter's Dairy Inc.
2100 N George St, York
PA 17404-1898.
717/848-9827.

Turkey Hill Dairy Inc.
Rd 2, Conestoga PA
17516-9802. 717/872-
5461.

Zausner Foods Corporation
400 S Custer Ave, New Holland PA 17557-9220. 717/354-4411.

CANNED SPECIALTIES

Breezewood Lodge
570 Potato Rd, Aspers PA 17304-9714. 717/677-9967.

Clement Pappas & Co.
W Parsonage Rd, Bridgeton NJ 08302. 609/455-1000.

DA Foodservice Inc.
29 Olney Ave, Cherry Hill NJ 08003-1615. 609/424-7788.

Spring Glen Fresh Foods Inc.
314 Spring Glen Dr, Ephrata PA 17522-9231. 717/733-2201.

CANNED FRUITS AND VEGETABLES AND JAMS

Furman Foods Inc.
R D 2, Northumberlnd PA 17857-9802. 717/473-3516.

Giorgio Foods Inc.
Blandon Rd, Temple PA 19560. 610/926-2139.

Knouse Foods Coop
421 Grant St, Chambersburg PA 17201-1631. 717/263-9177.

Knouse Foods Coop
53 E Hanover St, Biglerville PA 17307-9421. 717/677-9115.

Knouse Foods Coop
450 Gardners Station Rd, Gardners PA 17324. 717/677-7126.

Knouse Foods Coop
Cashtown-Orrtanna Rd, Orrtanna PA 17353. 717/642-8291.

Minot Food Packers
Penn & Bank Sts, Bridgeton NJ 08302. 609/451-2035.

Mott's USA
Menallen Township, Aspers PA 17304. 717/677-7121.

Ocean Spray Cranberries Inc.
104 East Park St, Bordentown NJ 08505-1424. 609/298-0905.

Sanofi Bio Inds Inc.
1741 Tomlinson Rd, Philadelphia PA 19116-3847. 215/676-3900.

Sunsweet Growers
105 S Buttonwood St, Fleetwood PA 19522. 610/944-0411.

Wilson Mushrooms Co
Rte 41 Box 489, Avondale PA 19311. 610/268-3033.

DRIED FRUITS, VEGETABLES AND SOUP MIXES

Hanover Food Corporation
Plum & Liberty Sts, Lancaster PA 17602. 717/397-6141.

PICKLED FRUITS AND VEGETABLES

Verdelli Farms Inc.
E 2nd St, Hummelstown PA 17036. 717/566-2517.

FROZEN SPECIALTIES

ASK Foods Inc.
77 N Hetrick Ave, Palmyra PA 17078-1501. 717/838-6356.

Ateeco Inc.
600 E Centre St, Shenandoah PA 17976-1825. 717/462-2745.

Bil Mar Foods Inc.
16 Union St, Medford NJ 08055-2438. 609/654-0959.

Grasso Foods Inc.
Sharptown Rd, Swedesboro NJ 08085. 609/467-2222.

Manischewitz Food Prod Corporation
214 N Delsea Dr, Vineland NJ 08360-3685. 609/692-6350.

Michele's Family Bakery
5698 Rising Sun Ave, Philadelphia PA 19120-1624. 215/725-9714.

Mrs Paul's Kitchens
5501 Tabor Ave, Philadelphia PA 19120-2197. 215/535-1151.

Van Den Bergh Foods
280 Jessup Rd, Thorofare NJ 08086. 609/848-5314.

DOG AND CAT FOOD

The Reward Co Inc.
PO Box 25100, Lehigh
Valley PA 18002-5100.

PREPARED FEEDS AND FEED INGREDIENTS

Agway Inc.
Rte 130, Bordentown NJ
08505. 609/298-4100.

Cadillac Pet Foods Inc.
9130 Griffith Morgan Ln,
Pennsauken NJ 08110.
609/662-7412.

Moyer & Son Inc.
113 E Reliance Rd,
Souderton PA 18964-
1300. 215/723-6000.

BREAD AND RELATED FOOD PRODUCTS

Amoroso's Baking Company
PO Box 1226,
Lansdowne PA 19050-
8226. 215/471-4740.

Bake Rite Rolls
2945 Samuel Dr,
Bensalem PA 19020-
7305. 215/638-2400.

Boboli
R R 1 Box 409 C-2,
Hazleton PA 18201-
9801. 717/459-6020.

Butter Krust Baking Company
249 N 11th St, Sunbury
PA 17801-2433.
717/286-5845.

Capital Bakers Division
PO Box 4469, Harrisburg
PA 17111-0469.
717/564-1891.

Chef Francisco Of Pennsylvania
250 Hansen Access Rd,
Kng Of Prussa PA
19406-2424. 610/265-
7400.

Continental Baking Co.
9801 Blue Grass Rd,
Philadelphia PA 19114-
1079. 215/969-1200.

Deer Park Baking Co.
South Egg Harbor Rd,
Hammonton NJ 08037.
609/561-2900.

Kellogg Co.
RR 2 Box 8A, Muncy PA
17756-9301. 717/546-
7383.

Maier's Bakery Inc.
2400 Northampton St,
Easton PA 18042-3823.
610/258-7131.

Maier's Sunbeam Bakery
640 Park Ave, Reading
PA 19611-1926.
610/376-7131.

Martin's Famous Pastry Shoppe
1000 Potatoe Roll Ln,
Chambersburg PA
17201-8897. 717/263-
9580.

Morabito Baking Co
757 Kohn St, Norristown
PA 19401-3739.
610/275-5419.

Philadelphia Baking Co.
Grant Ave & Roosevelt
Blvd, Philadelphia PA
19115. 215/464-4242.

Profera's Pizza Bakery
1130 Moosic St,
Scranton PA 18505-
2106. 717/342-4181.

Specialty Bakers Inc.
450 S State Rd,
Marysville PA 17053-
1012. 717/957-2131.

Stroehmann Bakeries
3375 Lycoming Creek
Rd, Williamsport PA
17701-1035. 717/494-
1191.

Stroehmann Bakeries
325 Kiwanis Blvd,
Hazleton PA 18201-
1163. 717/455-2066.

Stroehmann Bakeries
901 N Elmer Ave, Sayre
PA 18840-1835.
717/888-2289.

COOKIES AND CRACKERS

Anderson Bakery Co
2060 Old Philadelphia
Pike, Lancaster PA
17602-3413. 717/299-
2321.

DF Stauffer Biscuit Co
Belmont & 6th Ave, York
PA 17403. 717/843-
9016.

Fleetwood Snacks Inc.
18 W Poplar St,
Fleetwood PA 19522-
1505. 610/944-7623.

Quinlan Pretzel Co.
Washington & 3rd Sts,
Denver PA 17517.
215/267-7571.

FROZEN BAKERY PRODUCTS

Pet Inc.
225 W Vine St,
Chambersburg PA
17201-1164. 717/263-
4127.

Pet Inc.
Frozen Foods Division
2132 Downyflake Ln,
Allentown PA 18103-
4725. 610/797-5947.

Preferred Meal Systems
4135 Birney Ave, Moosic
PA 18507-1301.
717/457-8311.

CANE SUGAR

**Domino Sugar
Corporation**
4 & Chestnut,
Philadelphia PA 19115-
4203. 215/238-9632.

CANDY AND OTHER CONFECTIONERY PRODUCTS

American Chewing Gum
North Eagle & Lawrence
Rds, Havertown PA
19083. 610/449-1700.

Cherrydale Farms Inc.
Quakertown Rd,
Pennsburg PA 18073-
1024. 215/679-6200.

Falcon Candy Company
2300 Carpenter St,
Philadelphia PA 19146-
2502. 215/985-0774.

**Frankford Candy &
Chocolate Co Inc.**
2101 Washington Ave,
Philadelphia PA 19146-
2532. 215/735-5200.

**Gertrude Hawk
Chocolates Inc.**
9 Keystone Industrial
Park, Scranton PA
18512-1516. 717/342-
7556.

Godiva Chocolatier Inc.
650 E Neversink Rd,
Reading PA 19606-3208.
610/779-3792.

Goldenberg Candy Co.
157-165 West Wyoming
Ave, Philadelphia PA
19140. 215/455-7505.

Just Born Inc.
1300 Stefko Blvd,
Bethlehem PA 18017-
6620. 610/867-7568.

Pennsylvania Dutch Co
408 N Baltimore Ave, Mt
Holly Spgs PA 17065-
1603. 717/486-3496.

Richardson Brands Inc.
Atlantic & I Sts,
Philadelphia PA 19102.
215/634-4700.

Y&S Candies Inc.
400 Running Pump Rd,
Lancaster PA 17603-
2269. 717/299-1261.

CHOCOLATE AND COCOA PRODUCTS

Bortz Chocolate Co
PO Box 13218, Reading
PA 19612-3218.
610/376-6661.

Chester A Asher Inc.
20 E Woodlawn St,
Philadelphia PA 19144-
2238. 215/438-3774.

DE Wolfgang Candy Co
50 E 4th Ave, York PA
17404-2507. 717/843-
5536.

Wilbur Chocolate Co.
48 N Broad St, Lititz PA
17543. 717/626-1131.

SHORTENINGS, OILS AND MARGARINES

Komili Industries
20 Grayburn Dr, Marlton
NJ 08053-1922.
609/988-1310.

MALT BEVERAGES

Lion Inc.
700 N Pennsylvania Ave,
Wilkes Barre PA 18705-
2451. 717/823-8801.

WINES, BRANDY AND BRANDY SPIRITS

Charles Jacquin Et Cie
2633 Trenton Ave,
Philadelphia PA 19125-
1837. 215/425-9300.

SOFT DRINKS AND CARBONATED WATER

Regnier
Princess Rd, Trenton NJ
08648. 609/896-4500.

**Canada Dry Delaware
Valley Bottling Co.**
Whitaker Ave & Foulkrod
St, Philadelphia PA
19124. 215/533-1500.

Cloister Spring Water Co
1060 S State St, Ephrata
PA 17522-2398.
717/733-7901.

**Keystone Coca-Cola
Bottling Co.**
300 Oak St, Pittston PA
18640-3794. 717/655-
2874.

**Premium Beverage
Packers Inc.**
1090 Spring St, Reading
PA 19610-1748.
610/376-6131.

Seven-Up Bottling Co.
1103 W Ridge Pike,
Conshohocken PA
19428-1017. 610/825-
4700.

FLAVORING EXTRACTS AND SYRUPS

MacAndrews & Forbes
3rd St and Jefferson
Ave, Camden NJ 08104.
609/964-8840.

PREPARED FISH AND SEAFOOD

Deal's Seafood Co Inc.
212 E Madison Ave,
Magnolia NJ 08049-
1226. 609/783-8700.

Iceland Seafood Corporation
1250 Slate Hill Rd, Camp
Hill PA 17011-8011.
717/761-2600.

ROASTED COFFEE

Melitta USA Inc.
1401 Berlin Rd, Cherry
Hill NJ 08034-1423.
609/428-7202.

POTATO CHIPS AND SIMILAR SNACKS

Bon Ton Foods Inc.
1120 Zinns Quarry Rd,
York PA 17404-3533.
717/843-0026.

Charles Chips Inc.
3337 Marietta Ave,
Lancaster PA 17601-
1225. 717/285-5981.

El-Ge Potato Chip Co.
3553 Gillespie Dr, York
PA 17404-5838.
717/792-2611.

Frito-Lay Inc.
N Reach Rd, Williamsport
PA 17701. 717/326-
4136.

Keystone Food Products
3767 Hecktown Rd,
Easton PA 18042-2350.
610/258-0888.

Nibble With Gibble's
6647 Molly Pitcher Hwy,
Chambersburg PA
17201-9260. 717/375-
2243.

York Snacks Inc.
1000 W College Ave,
York PA 17404-3537.
717/843-0738.

PASTA

DFC Food Corporation Of Pennsylvania
595 W 11th St,
Bloomsburg PA 17815-
3616. 717/784-8906.

Nissin Foods USA Co
2901 Hempland Rd,
Lancaster PA 17601-
1386. 717/291-5901.

Paramount Macaroni
1550 John Tipton Blvd,
Pennsauken NJ 08110-
2304.

San Giorgio Macaroni
749 Guilford St, Lebanon
PA 17046-3531.
717/273-7641.

FOOD PREPARATIONS

Eastern Tea Corporation
1 Englehard Dr, Cranbury
NJ 08512-9527.

Major Smith Inc.
158 W Jackson St, New
Holland PA 17557-1641.
717/354-6560.

Pillsbury Co.
1717 Pillsbury Rd, E
Greenville PA 18041-
2298. 215/679-9571.

Sweet Street Desserts
722 Heister Ln, Reading
PA 19605-3095.
610/921-8113.

Verdelli Farms Inc.
PO Box 4920, Harrisburg
PA 17111-0920.

CIGARETTES

Casa Blanca Cigar Co.
257 E Market St, York
PA 17403-2023.
717/848-1287.

HL Neff & Co Inc.
143 W Broadway, Red
Lion PA 17356-2103.
717/244-7351.

CIGARS

House Of Windsor Inc.
S Orchard Ave,
Dallastown PA 17313.
717/244-4501.

TOBACCO STEMMING AND REDRYING

Consolidated Cigar Co.
McAdoo & Treskow Rds,
McAdoo PA 18237.
717/929-2355.

Lancaster Leaf Tobacco
198 W Liberty St,
Lancaster PA 17603-
2712. 717/394-2676.

ORNAMENTAL FLORICULTURE AND NURSERY PRODUCTS

Conard-Pyle Co.
372 Rose Hill Rd, West
Grove PA 19390-9719.
610/869-2426.

Green Leaf Enterprises
17 W Main St, Leola PA
17540-1893. 717/656-
2606.

MUSHROOMS

Giorgi Mushroom Co.
1013 Dryville Rd,
Fleetwood PA 19522.
610/944-8002.

Rain Fresh Mushroom Company
RR 3, Fleetwood PA
19522-9803. 610/944-
0554.

Sun Rise Mushroom Company
Commerce St, Temple
PA 19560. 610/921-
5565.

DAIRY FARMS

Kreider Farms
1461 Lancaster Rd,
Manheim PA 17545-
9745. 717/665-4415.

For more information on career opportunities in the food and beverage, and agriculture industries:

Associations

AMERICAN ASSOCIATION OF CEREAL CHEMISTS
3340 Pilot Knob Road, St. Paul MN
55121. 612/454-7250.

AMERICAN FROZEN FOOD INSTITUTE
1764 Old Meadow Lane, McLean VA
22102. 703/821-0770.

AMERICAN SOCIETY OF AGRICULTURAL ENGINEERS
2950 Niles Road, St. Joseph MI
49085. 616/429-0300.

AMERICAN SOCIETY OF BREWING CHEMISTS
3340 Pilot Knob Road, St. Paul MN
55121. 612/454-7250.

DAIRY AND FOOD INDUSTRIES SUPPLY ASSOCIATION
6245 Executive Boulevard, Rockville
MD 20852. 301/984-1444.

MASTER BREWERS ASSOCIATION OF THE AMERICAS
2421 North Mayfair, Suite 310,
Wauwatosa, WI 53226. 414/774-
8558.

NATIONAL AGRICULTURAL CHEMICALS ASSOCIATION
1156 15th Street NW, Suite 900,
Washington DC 20005. 202/296-
1585.

NATIONAL BEER WHOLESALERS' ASSOCIATION
1100 South Washington Street,
Alexandria VA 22314. 703/683-
4300.

NATIONAL DAIRY COUNCIL
10255 West Higgins Road, Suite 900,
Rosemont IL 60018. 708/803-2000.

NATIONAL FOOD PROCESSORS ASSOCIATION
1401 New York Avenue NW, Suite
400, Washington DC 20005.
202/639-5900.

NATIONAL SOFT DRINK ASSOCIATION
1101 16th Street NW, Washington
DC 20036. 202/463-6732.

Directories

FOOD ENGINEERING'S DIRECTORY OF U.S. FOOD PLANTS
Chilton Book Co., Chilton Way,
Radnor PA 19089. 800/695-1214.

THOMAS FOOD INDUSTRY REGISTER
Thomas Publishing Co., Five Penn
Plaza, New York NY 10001. 212/695-
0500.

Magazines

BEVERAGE WORLD
150 Great Neck Road, Great Neck NY
11021. 516/829-9210.

FOOD PROCESSING
301 East Erie Street, Chicago IL
60611. 312/644-2020.

FROZEN FOOD AGE
Maclean Hunter Media, #4 Stamford
Forum, Stamford CT 06901.
203/325-3500.

PREPARED FOODS
Gorman Publishing Co., 8750 West
Bryn Mawr, Chicago IL 60631.
312/693-3200.

GOVERNMENT

The Federal Government is the nation's largest single employer, and one of the most stable. More than 300,000 people are hired each year to work a variety of government jobs, and there is usually little change in the level of employment. The concentration of jobs is changing, however. The Department of Defense currently generates over half of all federal jobs, but both its staff and budget are being reduced due to the end of the Cold War. Other departments may suffer some job loss as a result of Vice President Al Gore's plan to "reinvent government," which was announced in September 1993, but overall, government jobs remain some of the most stable in the country. Two occupations with especially good prospects: nurses and engineers.

State: Employment opportunities in Metro Philadelphia for both state and federal government continue to decline. Over the last decade the total number of employees has dropped to 131,800. New Jersey faces a similar situation, which has forced the state to order a freeze on government hirings.

DEFENSE PERSONNEL SUPPORT CENTER
2800 South 20th Street, Philadelphia PA 19101-8419. 215/737-2000. **Contact:** Human Resources Department. **Description:** Involved in national security and international affairs.

NEW JERSEY DEPARTMENT OF LABOR
Labor and Industry Building, CN 058, Trenton NJ 08625. 609/292-2400. **Contact:** Human Resources. **Description:** A state-run job center.

PENNSYLVANIA CIVIL SERVICE COMMISSION
P.O. Box 569, Harrisburg PA 17108-0569. 717/787-1796. **Contact:** James A. Agate, Director/Employment Services. **Description:** Government administration and management at the state level. A subsidiary of the Commonwealth of Pennsylvania. **Number of employees at this location:** 60,000.

CITY OF PHILADELPHIA
1600 Arch Street, 15th Floor, Philadelphia PA 19103-1628. 215/686-2358. **Contact:** Steve Henry, Director/Employment Services. **Description:** Offices of the municipal government. Applicants must have Philadelphia residency except for engineers, librarians, registered nurses, and paramedics. Corporate headquarters location since 1701. **Common positions include:** Civil Engineer; Electrical/Electronic Engineer; Environmental Engineer; Mechanical Engineer; Sanitary Engineer. **Educational backgrounds include:** Engineering. **Benefits:** Dental Insurance; Life Insurance; Medical Insurance; Pension Plan. **Number of employees at this location:** 27,000.

STREET SANITATION DEPARTMENT
1600 Arch Street, 10th Floor, Philadelphia PA 19102. 215/686-5470. **Contact:** Human Resources Department. **Description:** City sanitation department.

U.S. GENERAL SERVICES ADMINISTRATION

The Wanamaker Building, 100 Penn Square East, Philadelphia PA 19107. 215/656-5600. **FAX:** 215/656-5594. **Contact:** Robert R. Stewart, Regional Personnel Officer. **Description:** Diversified, government-wide operation: buildings management; supply; real and personal property sales; telecommunication services; data processing; and motor vehicle operations. **Common positions include:** Civil Engineer; Computer Systems Analyst; Mechanical Engineer; Property and Real Estate Manager; Purchasing Agent and Manager; Transportation/Traffic Specialist. **Educational backgrounds include:** Business Administration; Computer Science; Engineering; Liberal Arts. **Benefits:** Life Insurance; Medical Insurance; Pension Plan; Savings Plan; Tuition Assistance. **Special Programs:** Internships; Training Programs. **Corporate headquarters location:** Washington DC. **Other U.S. locations:** San Francisco CA; Denver CO; Fort Worth DC; Atlanta GA; Auburn GA; Chicago IL; Boston MA; Kansas City MO; New York NY. **Operations at this facility include:** Regional Headquarters. **Number of employees at this location:** 2,000. **Number of employees nationwide:** 20,000.

U.S. INTERNAL REVENUE SERVICE

P.O. Box 12020, Philadelphia PA 19105. 215/597-4247. **Contact:** Dennis P. McCrossen, Chief of Labor Relations. **Description:** The mission of the IRS is to encourage and achieve the highest possible degree of voluntary compliance with tax laws and regulations. **Number of employees nationwide:** 85,000.

U.S. MARINE CORPS

4th Marine Corps District, Building 75, Philadelphia PA 19112. 215/897-6313. **Contact:** Assistant/Officer Procurement. **Description:** Procurement of male and female college undergraduates and graduates for programs leading to a commission as an officer of Marines. **Number of employees nationwide:** 200,000.

VETERANS ADMINISTRATION
INSURANCE CENTER

5000 Wissahickon Avenue, Philadelphia PA 19144. 215/438-5225. **Contact:** Human Resources Department. **Description:** A government veterans administration.

WILLOW GROVE AIR FORCE BASE

1051 Fairchild Street, Willow Grove PA 19090-5203. 215/443-1062. **Contact:** Personnel. **Description:** An air force base.

Note: Because addresses and telephone numbers of smaller companies change rapidly, we recommend you contact each company and verify the information below before contacting employers. Mass mailings are not recommended.

Additional medium sized employers: under 500

GOVERNMENT AGENCIES

Pennsylvania Department Of Public Welfare
Clarks Summit State Hospital, Clarks Summit PA 18411. 717/586-2011.

Pennsylvania Public Welfare
W Washington, Nanticoke PA 18634. 717/735-5000. SIC Code: 944001.

HEALTH CARE: SERVICE, EQUIPMENT AND PRODUCTS

Employment in the health care industry has gone up steadily during the past few years, with an average annual growth rate of eight percent -- and that doesn't include medical equipment manufacturers, who are also booming. Health care expenditures are now rising to over $800 billion a year. At press time, the Clinton Administration's health care reform plan was one of many proposals being considered by Congress. Many reforms are already underway within the industry. Best bets for jobseekers: HMOs. Also, check out nursing homes and home health care companies. Hospitals, already under tight restraints, will find things getting even tighter.

ALBERT EINSTEIN MEDICAL CENTER
5501 Old York Road, Philadelphia PA 19141. 215/456-7890. **Contact:** Human Resources Department. **Description:** A hospital.

AMCARE
650 Main Avenue, Scranton PA 18504. 717/342-2356. **Contact:** Human Resources. **Description:** A nursing care facility.

ANCORA PSYCHIATRIC HOSPITAL
202 Spring Garden Road, Ancora NJ 08037-9699. 609/561-1700. **Contact:** Human Resources Department. **Description:** An area hospital.

ARROW INTERNATIONAL INC.
3000 Bernville Road, Reading PA 19605-3505. 215/378-0131. **FAX:** 215/374-1160. **Contact:** Linda Silva, Staffing Manager. **Description:** A developer, manufacturer, and marketer of critical care and cardiovascular disposable catheters and related products which are distributed to hospital ICU/CCU, surgery, emergency, and catheter departments. **Common positions include:** Manufacturer's/Wholesaler's Sales Rep.; Mechanical Engineer. **Educational backgrounds include:** Engineering. **Corporate headquarters location:** This Location. **Other U.S. locations:** NC; NJ. **Listed on:** NASDAQ. **Number of employees nationwide:** 1,325.

ATLANTIC CITY MEDICAL CENTER
1925 Pacific Avenue, Atlantic City NJ 08401. 609/344-4081. **Contact:** Human Resources Department. **Description:** An area hospital.

B. BRAUN MEDICAL INC.
824 12th Avenue, Bethlehem PA 18018. 215/691-5400. **Contact:** Personnel Manager. **Description:** Manufactures specialized disposable plastic medical devices and syringes, and related health care products. **Parent company:** B. Braun of America.

BRYN MAWR HOSPITAL
130 S. Bryn Mawr Avenue, Bryn Mawr PA 19010. 215/526-3026. **Contact:** Human Resources Department. **Description:** A hospital.

BURDETTE TOMLIN MEMORIAL HOSPITAL
Two Stone Harbor Boulevard, Cape May Court House NJ 08210. 609/463-2170. **FAX:** 609/463-2379. **Contact:** Human Resources Department. **Description:** A 242-bed acute care community hospital. **Common positions include:** Chef/Cook/Kitchen Worker; Construction Trade Worker; Dietician/Nutritionist; EEG Technologist; EKG Technician; Electrician; Emergency Medical Technician; Medical Record Technician; Nuclear Medicine Technologist; Occupational Therapist; Physical Therapist; Radiologic Technologist; Registered Nurse; Respiratory Therapist; Social Worker; Speech-Language Pathologist; Stationary Engineer; Systems Analyst. **Benefits:** Dental Insurance; Disability Coverage; Life Insurance; Medical Insurance; Pension Plan; Tuition Assistance. **Corporate headquarters location:** This Location.

CENTRAL PARK LODGE
50 North Main Road, Broomall PA 19008. 215/356-0800. **Contact:** Human Resources. **Description:** A nursing care facility.

CENTRAL PARK LODGE/WHITEMARSH
9209 Ridge Pike, Lafayette PA 19444. 215/825-6560. **Contact:** Human Resources. **Description:** A nursing care facility.

CONTINENTAL MEDICAL SYSTEMS
600 Wilson Lane, P.O. Box 715, Mechanicsburg PA 17055. 717/790-8300. **Contact:** Human Resources. **Description:** One of the largest providers of comprehensive medical rehabilitation programs and services in the United States. Continental Medical has a significant presence in three principal sectors: inpatient rehabilitation care, outpatient rehabilitation care, and contract services. **Number of employees nationwide:** 13,500.

CROZER CHESTER MEDICAL CENTER
1 Medical Center Boulevard, Upland PA 19013. 215/447-2000. **Contact:** Human Resources Department. **Description:** An area hospital.

DELAWARE COUNTY MEMORIAL HOSPITAL
501 N. Lansdowne Avenue, Drexel Hill PA 19026. 215/284-8100. **Contact:** Human Resources Department. **Description:** An area hospital.

DOYLESTOWN HOSPITAL
595 West State Street, Doylestown PA 18901. 215/345-2200. **Contact:** Human Resources Department. **Description:** An area hospital.

EASTERN PENNSYLVANIA PSYCHIATRIC INSTITUTION
3200 Henry Avenue, Philadelphia PA 19129. 215/842-4000. **Contact:** Human Resources Department. **Description:** A state psychiatric institution.

ELWYN INSTITUTE
111 Elwyn Road, Elwyn PA 19063. 215/891-2073. **Contact:** Human Resources Department. **Description:** An area hospital.

FITZGERALD MERCY HOSPITAL
Lansdowne Avenue, Darby PA 19023. 215/237-4710. **Contact:** Human Resources Department. **Description:** An area hospital.

FOUR WOOD MANOR
1912 Marsh Road, Wilmington DE 19810. 302/529-1600. **Contact:** Personnel Director. **Description:** Operates a group of nursing homes statewide.

FOX CHASE CANCER CENTER
7701 Burholme Avenue, Philadelphia PA 19111. 215/728-2763. **Contact:** Gary J. Weyhmuller, Director of Personnel. **Description:** One of 22 comprehensive cancer centers in the United States. Facilities consist of the American Oncologic Hospital and the Institute for Cancer Research. **Corporate headquarters location:** This Location.

FRANKFORD HOSPITAL-TORRESDALE
Knights and Red Lion Roads, Philadelphia PA 19114. 215/612-4000. **Contact:** Human Resources Department. **Description:** An area hospital.

HELENE FULD MEDICAL CENTER
750 Brunswick Avenue, Trenton NJ 08638. 609/394-6000. **Contact:** Human Resources. **Description:** A medical center.

GMIS, INC.
5 Country View Road, Malvern PA 19355-1421. 215/296-3838. **Contact:** Human Resources. **Description:** A health care information company. Develops and markets automated clinical knowledge products which allow payers to access proprietary databases incorporating clinical expertise in medical claims processing. The goal is to help control health care costs. **Common positions include:** Accountant/Auditor; Computer Programmer; Dental Assistant/Dental Hygienist; Dentist; Department Manager; Employment Interviewer; Licensed Practical Nurse; Medical Record Technician; Payroll Clerk; Personnel/Labor Relations Specialist; Sales Associate; Surgical Technician; Systems Analyst. **Educational backgrounds include:** Accounting; Business Administration; Finance; Health Care; Marketing. **Benefits:** Daycare Assistance; Dental Insurance; Disability Coverage; Life Insurance; Medical Insurance; Profit Sharing. **Corporate headquarters location:** This Location. **Other U.S. locations:** Boston MA. **Operations at this facility include:** Administration; Divisional Headquarters; Research and Development; Sales; Service. **Listed on:** NASDAQ. **Annual Revenues:** $23,000,000. **Number of employees at this location:** 155. **Number of employees nationwide:** 175. **Hires/Layoffs in 1993 (This location):** 40 hires. **Hires/Layoffs in 1993 (Nationwide):** 42 hires. **Projected hires for the next 12 months (This location):** 45 hires. **Projected hires for the next 12 months (Nationwide):** 50 hires.

GERIATRIC AND MEDICAL CENTER
5601 Chestnut Street, Philadelphia PA 19139. 215/476-2250. **Contact:** Personnel Department. **Description:** A provider of skilled nursing care.

GRADUATE HOSPITAL
1800 Lombard Street, 1 Graduate Plaza, Philadelphia PA 19146. 215/893-2000. **Contact:** Human Resources Department. **Description:** An area hospital/clinic.

GRAND VIEW HOSPITAL
700 Lawn Avenue, Sellersville PA 18960. 215/453-4000. **Contact:** Human Resources Department. **Description:** An area health service.

HOLY REDEEMER HOSPITAL
1648 Huntingdon Pike, Meadowbrook PA 19046. 215/947-3000. **Contact:** Human Resources Department. **Description:** An area hospital.

HOSPITAL OF THE UNIVERSITY OF PENNSYLVANIA
3400 Spruce Street, 727 Blockley Hall, Philadelphia PA 19104. 215/662-3181. **Contact:** Staffing Development. **Description:** A 722-bed academic teaching hospital involved in patient care, education, and research. **Number of employees at this location:** 5,000.

LANKENAU HOSPITAL
100 Lancaster Avenue, Wynnewood PA 19096. 215/645-2000. **Contact:** Human Resources Department. **Description:** A hospital.

LEADER NURSING AND REHABILITATION CENTER
200 2nd Avenue, Kingston PA 18704. 717/288-9315. **Contact:** Human Resources. **Description:** A nursing home. **Other area locations:** Allentown, Carlisle, Chambersburg, Dallastown, Easton, Harrisburg, King of Prussia, Montgomeryville, Norristown, Pottsville, Reading, Sunbury, and Williamsport, PA; and West Cherry Hill, NJ.

LEHIGH VALLEY HOSPICE-POCONO
920 North 9th Street, Stroudsburg PA 18360. 717/420-0912. **Contact:** Human Resources. **Description:** A nursing home.

LOWER BUCKS HOSPITAL
501 Bath Road, Bristol PA 19007. 215/785-9251. **Contact:** Judy Mazess, RN/BSN/Employment Manager. **Description:** 250-bed community hospital in a suburban setting offering inpatient care on the following units: medical surgical, pediatrics, critical care, emergency, maternal/child intensive care and same day surgery. Extensive outpatient services and a home care department as well as physical medicine and rehabilitation are offered. On-site day care and kindergarten available for employees. **Common positions include:** Registered Nurse. **Educational backgrounds include:** Biology; Medical Technology; Nursing; Pharmacology; Physical Therapy. **Benefits:** Dental Insurance; Disability Coverage; Employee Discounts; Life Insurance; Medical Insurance; Pension Plan; Savings Plan; Tuition Assistance. **Corporate headquarters location:** This Location. **Operations at this facility include:** Service. **Number of employees at this location:** 1,100. **Projected hires for the next 12 months (This location):** 100 hires.

MAIN LINE NURSING AND REHABILITATION CENTER
283 East Lancaster Avenue, Malvern PA 19355. 215/296-4170. **Contact:** Human Resources. **Description:** A nursing home.

MEDICAL CENTER OF DELAWARE
P.O. Box 1668, Wilmington DE 19899. 302/428-6263. **Contact:** Walt Szmidt, Director of Employment. **Description:** A 1,100-bed, three-hospital system providing a full range of medical, surgical, and rehabilitation health care services. **Number of employees nationwide:** 5,000.

MEDIQ INCORPORATED
1 Mediq Plaza, Pennsauken NJ 08110-1460. 609/665-9300. **Contact:** Human Resources. **Description:** A health-care products and services firm.

MERCY CATHOLIC MEDICAL CENTER
5301 Cedar Avenue, Philadelphia PA 19143. 215/748-9000. **Contact:** Human Resources Department. **Description:** A medical center.

METHODIST HOSPITAL
2301 South Broad Street, Philadelphia PA 19148. 215/952-9000. **Contact:** Human Resources Department. **Description:** A hospital.

MONTGOMERY HOSPITAL
P.O. Box 992, Norristown PA 19404-0992. 215/270-2000. **Contact:** Human Resources Department. **Description:** A hospital.

MUHLENBERG HOSPITAL CENTER
2545 Schoenersville Road, Bethlehem PA 18017-7384. 215/861-2300. **Contact:** Jeanne Horvath, Coordinator of Employment. **Description:** A 140-bed acute care community hospital. **Number of employees at this location:** 700.

NAZARETH HOSPITAL
2601 Holme Avenue, Philadelphia PA 19152. 215/335-6260. **Contact:** Ronald J. Cori, Director of Personnel. **Description:** An acute care hospital serving the northeast Philadelphia community. **Common positions include:** Accountant/Auditor; Dietician/Nutritionist. **Educational backgrounds include:** Nursing; Physical Therapy. **Benefits:** Dental Insurance; Disability Coverage; Employee Discounts; Life Insurance; Medical Insurance; Pension Plan; Savings Plan; Tuition Assistance. **Special Programs:** Internships; Training Programs. **Number of employees nationwide:** 1,400.

NORRISTOWN STATE HOSPITAL
1001 Sterigere Street, Norristown PA 19401. 215/270-1000. **Contact:** Human Resources Department. **Description:** A hospital.

NOVACARE INC.
1016 West 9th Avenue, King of Prussia PA 19406. 215/992-7200. **Contact:** Human Resources. **Description:** The company is a provider of comprehensive medical rehabilitation services -- including speech-language pathology, occupational therapy, and physical therapy -- to patients experiencing physical disability. Services are provided 1) on a contract basis primarily to long-term health care institutions; 2) through in-patient rehabilitation hospitals and community integrated programs; and 3) through a national network of patient care centers providing orthotic and prosthetic rehabilitation services.

PENNSYLVANIA HOSPITAL
800 Spruce Street, Philadelphia PA 19107. 215/829-3000. **Contact:** Human Resources Department. **Description:** A hospital.

PHILADELPHIA GERIATRIC CENTER
5301 Old York Road, Philadelphia PA 19141. 215/456-2900. **Contact:** Human Resources Department. **Description:** A nursing home.

POTTSTOWN MEMORIAL MEDICAL CENTER
1600 East High Street, Pottstown PA 19464. 215/327-7000. **Contact:** Human Resources. **Description:** A medical center.

PRESBYTERIAN MEDICAL CENTER
51 North 39th Street, Philadelphia PA 19104. 215/662-8271. **FAX:** 215/662-8936. **Contact:** Lynn Sowden, Director of Human Resources. **Description:** A teaching hospital specializing in oncology, cardiology, and general med-surg. Job applicants may have a various health care degrees. **Common positions include:** Accountant/Auditor; Actuary; Adjuster; Administrative Services Manager; Cashier; Chemist; Chiropractor; Claim

Representative; Clerical Supervisor; Clinical Lab Technician; Computer Operator; Computer Programmer; Computer Systems Analyst; Cost Estimator; Counselor; Credit Clerk and Authorizer; Credit Manager; Dental Assistant/Dental Hygienist; Dentist; Education Administrator; EEG Technologist; EKG Technician; Employment Interviewer; Health Services Manager; Human Service Worker; Librarian; Library Technician; Licensed Practical Nurse; Line Installer/Cable Splicer; Medical Record Technician; New Accounts Clerk; Occupational Therapist; Operations Research Analyst; Optician; Order Clerk; Payroll Clerk; Personnel/Labor Relations Specialist; Physical Therapist; Physician; Physician Assistant; Podiatrist; Postal Clerk/Mail Carrier; Printing Press Operator; Psychologist; Public Relations Specialist; Purchasing Agent and Manager; Quality Control Supervisor; Radiologic Technologist; Receptionist; Recreation Worker; Registered Nurse; Respiratory Therapist; Secretary; Surgical Technician; Systems Analyst. **Educational backgrounds include:** Accounting; Biology; Business Administration; Chemistry; Communications; Computer Science; Finance; Liberal Arts. **Benefits:** Credit Union; Daycare Assistance; Dental Insurance; Disability Coverage; Life Insurance; Medical Insurance; Pension Plan; Profit Sharing; Savings Plan; Tuition Assistance. **Special Programs:** Internships; Training Programs. **Corporate headquarters location:** This Location. **Operations at this facility include:** Administration; Research and Development; Service. **Number of employees at this location:** 2,000. **Hires/Layoffs in 1993 (This location):** 500 hires. **Projected hires for the next 12 months (This location):** 400 hires.

PROCTER & GAMBLE
330 South Warminster, Hatboro PA 19040. 215/956-1000. **Contact:** Personnel. **Description:** Manufactures a variety of nationally-known health care and toiletry products. Services both the Vicks Toiletry Division and the Vicks Health Care Division of Richardson-Vicks Inc. (RVI). RVI is a developer, manufacturer, and marketer of mass-merchandised health and personal care products worldwide. RVI has a growing business in nutritional and home care products; the company also produces specialty chemicals, laboratory reagents, and diagnostic instruments for industrial, medical, and scientific use. International facilities. **Common positions include:** Chemical Engineer; Chemist; Civil Engineer; Electrical/Electronic Engineer; Industrial Engineer; Mechanical Engineer. **Educational backgrounds include:** Business Administration; Chemistry; Engineering. **Benefits:** Dental Insurance; Disability Coverage; Employee Discounts; Life Insurance; Medical Insurance; Profit Sharing; Savings Plan; Tuition Assistance. **Corporate headquarters location:** Wilton CT. **Operations at this facility include:** Manufacturing. **Listed on:** New York Stock Exchange.

REGINA COMMUNITY NURSING CENTER
230 North 65th Street, Philadelphia PA 19139. 215/472-0541. **Contact:** Human Resources. **Description:** A nursing care center.

REGINA NURSING CENTER
550 East Fornance Street, Norristown PA 19401. 215/272-5600. **Contact:** Human Resources. **Description:** A nursing care center.

REPRODUCTIVE DIAGNOSTICS INC.
1288 Valley Forge Road, Phoenixville PA 19481. 215/935-3960. **Contact:** Human Resources. **Description:** A medical laboratory.

RIVERSIDE HOSPITALS
P.O. Box 845, Wilmington DE 19899. 302/764-6120. **Contact:** Gloria Froelich, Personnel Director. **Description:** A general medical hospital. **Number of employees at this location:** 400.

SERONO DIAGNOSTICS
100 Cascade Drive, Allentown PA 18103. 215/264-2800. **Contact:** Director of Human Resources. **Description:** A manufacturer and distributor of diagnostic medical instrument systems. **Common positions include:** Accountant/Auditor; Buyer; Electrical/Electronic Engineer; Financial Analyst; Manufacturer's/Wholesaler's Sales Rep.; Marketing Specialist; Mechanical Engineer; Purchasing Agent and Manager. **Educational backgrounds include:** Accounting; Biology; Business Administration; Computer Science; Engineering; Finance; Marketing. **Benefits:** Dental Insurance; Disability Coverage; Life Insurance; Medical Insurance; Pension Plan; Savings Plan; Tuition Assistance. **Special Programs:** Internships; Training Programs. **Corporate headquarters location:** Boston MA. **Operations at this facility include:** Manufacturing; Sales.

SURGICAL LASER TECHNOLOGIES
200 Cresson Boulevard, Oak PA 19456. 215/650-0700. **Contact:** Personnel. **Description:** Manufacturers of contact surgical lasers. **Number of employees at this location:** 160.

TEMPLE UNIVERSITY HOSPITAL
3401 N. Broad Street, Philadelphia PA 19140. 215/707-2000. **Contact:** Human Resources Department. **Description:** A hospital and a physician's information bureau.

U.S. HEALTHCARE, INC.
1425 Union Meeting Road, Blue Bell PA 19422. 215/283-6816. **Contact:** HR Generalists. **Description:** Operates health maintenance organizations. **Common positions include:** Accountant/Auditor; Claim Representative; Computer Programmer; Customer Service Representative; Services Sales Representative. **Educational backgrounds include:** Accounting; Business Administration; Computer Science; Liberal Arts; Marketing. **Benefits:** Dental Insurance; Disability Coverage; Employee Discounts; Life Insurance; Medical Insurance; Pension Plan; Profit Sharing; Savings Plan; Stock Option; Tuition Assistance. **Corporate headquarters location:** This Location. **Other U.S. locations:** Shelton CT; Boston MA; Owings Mills MD; Bismark ND; Fairfield NJ; Pittsburgh PA. **Operations at this facility include:** Administration; Sales; Service. **Listed on:** NASDAQ. **Annual Revenues:** $2,190,000,000. **Number of employees nationwide:** 3,000. **Projected hires for the next 12 months (Nationwide):** 300 hires.

UNDERWOOD MEMORIAL HOSPITAL
509 N. Broad and W. Red Bank, Woodbury NJ 08096. 609/845-0100. **Contact:** Human Resources Department. **Description:** A hospital.

UNITED MEDICAL CORPORATION
56 Haddon Avenue, P.O. Box 200, Haddonfield NJ 08033. 609/354-2200. **Contact:** Human Resources. **Description:** Provides medical services and produces medical equipment.

UNIVERSAL HEALTH SERVICES, INC.
367 South Gulph Road, King of Prussia PA 19406. 215/768-3300. **Contact:** Personnel Department. **Description:** Owns and operates acute care and psychiatric hospitals. **Common positions include:** Accountant/Auditor; Computer Programmer; Marketing Specialist; Paralegal; Personnel/Labor Relations Specialist; Purchasing Agent and Manager; Systems Analyst. **Educational backgrounds include:** Accounting; Business Administration; Health Care; Nursing. **Benefits:** 401K; Dental Insurance; Disability

Coverage; Life Insurance; Medical Insurance; Tuition Assistance. **Corporate headquarters location:** This Location. **Number of employees nationwide:** 9,500.

WILSON SAFETY PRODUCTS
P.O. Box 622, Reading PA 19603. 215/376-6161. **Contact:** Rodney M. Fogelman, Director of Human Resources. **Description:** A manufacturer of personal safety protection products for head, hearing, eye, and respiratory protection. **Corporate headquarters location:** This Location.

WOODCREST PERSONAL CARE CENTER
20 Woodcrest Lane, Stevens PA 17578. 717/336-0701. **Contact:** Human Resources. **Description:** A nursing care center.

Note: Because addresses and telephone numbers of smaller companies change rapidly, we recommend you contact each company and verify the information below before contacting employers. Mass mailings are not recommended.

Additional large employers: 500+

MEDICAL INSTRUMENTS

Wampole Laboratories
Half Acre Rd., Box 1001, Cranbury NJ 08512. 609/655-6000.

DENTAL EQUIPMENT

Dentsply International
P.O. Box 872, York PA 17405-0872. 717/845-7511.

HOSPITALS AND MEDICAL CENTERS

Veterans Affairs Medical Center
1111 E End Blvd., Wilkes Barre PA 18711-0030. 717/824-3521.

West Jersey Hospital/Marlton
Rte 73 and Brick Rd., Marlton NJ 08053. 609/596-3500.

Chester County Hospital
701 E Marshall St., West Chester PA 19380-4421. 610/431-5000.

Community General Hospital
P.O. Box 1728, Reading PA 19603-1728. 610/376-2100.

Hamilton Hospital
1881 White Horse Ham Sq Rd., Trenton NJ 08690. 609/586-7900.

Roxborough Memorial Hospital
5800 Ridge Ave., Philadelphia PA 19128-1737. 215/483-9900.

Saint Mary Hospital
Langhorne Newtown Rd., Langhorne PA 19047. 215/750-2000.

Albert Einstein Medical Center
5501 Old York Rd., Philadelphia PA 19141-3098. 215/456-7010.

Childrens Hospital Of Philadelphia
34th St & Civic Center Blvd., Philadelphia PA 19104. 215/590-1000.

Community Medical Center
1822 Mulberry St., Scranton PA 18510-2398. 717/969-8000.

Cooper Hospital Univ. Medical Center
One Cooper Plaza, Camden NJ 08103-1489. 609/342-2000.

Divine Providence Hospital
1100 Grampian Blvd., Williamsport PA 17701-1995. 717/326-8181.

Jeanes Hospital
P.O. Box 57996, Philadelphia PA 19111-7996. 215/728-2000.

Medical Center Of Ocean County
2121 Edgewater Pl, Pt Pleas Bch NJ 08742-2290. 9088921100.

Memorial Hospital Salem County
310 Woodstown, Salem NJ 08079-2027. 609/935-1000.

Mercer Medical Center
P.O. Box 1658, Trenton
NJ 08607-1658.
609/394-4000.

Nesbitt Memorial Hospital
562 Wyoming Ave.,
Wilkes Barre PA 18704.
717/283-7000.

Newcomb Medical Center
65 S State St., Vineland
NJ 08360-4849.
609/691-9000.

Northeastern Hospital Of Phila
2301 E Allegheny Ave.,
Philadelphia PA 19134-4497. 215/291-3000.

Our Lady Of Lourdes Medical Center
1600 Haddon Ave.,
Camden NJ 08103-3101. 609/757-3500.

Sacred Heart Hospital
421 W Chew St.,
Allentown PA 18102-3490. 610/776-4500.

Saint Agnes Medical Center
1900 S Broad St.,
Philadelphia PA 19145-2304. 215/339-4100.

St Joseph Hospital
250 College Ave.,
Lancaster PA 17603-3378. 717/291-8211.

St Lukes Hospital
801 Ostrum St.,
Bethlehem PA 18015-1065. 610/954-4000.

Thomas Jefferson Univ. Hospital
Walnut and 11th Sts.,
Philadelphia PA 19107.
215/955-6000.

Veterans Affairs Medical Center
University & Woodland
Aves, Philadelphia PA
19104. 215/823-5800.

Episcopal Hospital
100 E Lehigh Ave.,
Philadelphia PA 19125-1098. 215/427-7000.

Memorial Hospital Burlington Cnty
175 Madison Ave.,
Mount Holly NJ 08060-2099. 609/261-7011.

Moses Taylor Hospital
700 Quincy Ave.,
Scranton PA 18510-1798. 717/963-2100.

Neumann Medical Center
1741 Frankford Ave.,
Philadelphia PA 19125-2421. 215/291-2000.

Rancocas Hospital
218-A Sunset Rd.,
Willingboro NJ 08046-1110. 609/835-2900.

South Jersey Hospital System
333 Irving Ave.,
Bridgeton NJ 08302-2123. 609/451-6600.

York Hospital
1001 S George St., York
PA 17403-3676.
717/771-2345.

Harrisburg Hospital
South Front Street,
Harrisburg PA 17101.
717/782-3131.

Easton Hospital
250 S 21st St., Easton
PA 18042-3892.
610/250-4000.

Abington Memorial Hospital
1200 York Rd., Abington
PA 19001-3720.
215/576-2001.

Allentown Osteopathic Medical Center
1736 W Hamilton St.,
Allentown PA 18104-5656. 610/770-8300.

Berwick Hospital Center
701 E 16th St., Berwick
PA 18603-2397.
717/759-5000.

Centre Community Hospital
1800 E Park Ave., State
College PA 16803-6797.
8142384351.

Cooper Hospital-Center City
1816 Spruce St.,
Philadelphia PA 19103-6603. 215/238-2000.

Deborah Heart and Lung Center
200 Trenton Rd., Browns
Mills NJ 08015-1705.
609/893-6611.

Germantown Hospital & Medical Center
1 Penn Blvd., Philadelphia
PA 19144-1498.
215/951-8000.

Allentown State Hospital
1600 Hanover Ave.,
Allentown PA 18103-2498. 610/740-3200.

Camden County Health Svc. Center
Lakeland & County
House Rds, Blackwood
NJ 08012. 609/757-3434.

Kimball Medical Center
600 River Ave.,
Lakewood NJ 08701-
5281. 9083631900.

**Reading Hospital and
Medical Center**
P.O. Box 16052, Reading
PA 19612-6052.
610/378-6000.

Shore Memorial Hospital
E New York Ave.,
Somers Point NJ 08244.
609/653-3500.

**West Jersey Hospital-
Voorhees**
101 Carnie Blvd.,
Voorhees NJ 08043-
1596. 609/772-5000.

**Wilkes-Barre General
Hospital**
N River and Auburn Sts.,
Wilkes Barre PA 18764.
717/829-8111.

Wills Eye Hospital
900 Walnut St.,
Philadelphia PA 19107-
5598. 215/928-3000.

Gettysburg Hospital
147 Gettys St.,
Gettysburg PA 17325-
2534. 717/334-2121.

**Gnaden Huetten
Memorial Hospital**
211 N 12th St.,
Lehighton PA 18235-
1195. 610/377-1300.

**Guthrie Healthcare
System**
Guthrie Square, Sayre PA
18840. 717/882-4312.

Haverford State Hospital
3500 Darby Rd.,
Haverford PA 19041-
1098. 610/525-9620.

Huntington Hospital
240 Fitzwatertown Rd.,
Willow Grove PA 19090-
2399. 215/657-4010.

**John F Kennedy
Memorial Hospital**
Langdon St and
Cheltenham Ave.,
Philadelphia PA 19124.
215/831-7000.

Metropolitan Hospital
801 Arch Street Fifth
Floor, Philadelphia PA
19107-2445. 215/238-
6700.

**Moss Rehabilitation
Hospital**
1200 W Tabor Rd.,
Philadelphia PA 19141-
3099. 215/456-9900.

Phoenixville Hospital
140 Nutt Rd.,
Phoenixville PA 19460-
3900. 610/983-1000.

Sacred Heart Hospital
1430 Dekalb St.,
Norristown PA 19401.
610/278-8200.

**West Jersey Hospital-
Camden**
1000 Atlantic Ave.,
Camden NJ 08104-
1595. 609/342-4500.

**Williamsport Hospital &
Medical Center**
777 Rural Ave.,
Williamsport PA 17701.
717/321-1000.

**PSYCHIATRIC
FACILITIES**

High Oaks Sanatorium
6617 Wissahickon Ave.,
Philadelphia PA 19119-
3798. 215/438-7200.

**REHABILITATION
HOSPITALS**

**Garden State Rehab
Hospital**
833 Route 37 W, Toms
River NJ 08755-5015.
9082440900.

Rehab Hospital of York
2791 S Queen St., York
PA 17403-9703.
717/741-5613.

**Sacred Heart Hospital &
Rehab Center**
201 Nassau Pl,
Norristown PA 19401-
3411. 610/278-6708.

Additional medium sized employers: under 500

**OFFICES AND CLINICS
OF DENTISTS**

**Eastern Dental Center
Hamilton Twp**
2103 Whitehorse Merc
Rd, Trenton NJ 08619-
2641. 609/587-0600.

The Orthodontist
2001 King Of Prusa Plz,
Kng Of Prussa PA
19406. 610/337-8080.

OFFICES AND CLINICS OF DOCTORS OF OSTEOPATHY

Community Way Medical Center
17 W Main St, Mount Joy PA 17552-1311.
717/653-4152.

OFFICES AND CLINICS OF CHIROPRACTORS

Behrman Chiropractic
120 S West End Blvd,
Quakertown PA 18951-1141. 215/538-7955.

OFFICES AND CLINICS OF HEALTH PRACTIONERS

Abington Physical Therapy Service
319 N Abington Rd,
Clarks Summit PA 18411-2309. 717/587-1575.

Back In Action
Stokes Rd & Nelson Dr,
Medford NJ 08055.
609/654-8474.

Bayada Nurses
286 Chester Ave,
Moorestown NJ 08057-3306. 609/778-4400.

Brandywine Rehabilitation Service
460 Creamery Way,
Exton PA 19341-2533.
610/363-3900.

Homestaff Of Delaware Valley
275 E Street Rd, Fstrvl
Trvose PA 19053-6157.
215/322-1552.

KQC
40 Monument Rd, Bala
Cynwyd PA 19004-1735. 610/664-2525.

Kennedy Physical Therapy
Hurffville-Cross Keys Rd,
Blackwood NJ 08012.
609/582-2842.

Keystone Works Of Burlington
3 Terri Ln, Burlington NJ
08016-4910. 609/386-8080.

Kimberly Quality Care
2550 Kingston Rd, York
PA 17402-3735.
717/755-2824.

Moorestown Visiting Nurse Assn
16 E Main St,
Moorestown NJ 08057-3325. 609/235-0462.

Newcomb Medical Center
1038E Chestnut Av,
Vineland NJ 08360.
609/794-4374.

Pro Home Health Care Agency
1 Norwegian Plz,
Pottsville PA 17901-3007. 717/628-4455.

Psychresource Associates
1100 W Chester Pike,
Havertown PA 19083-3308. 610/446-1127.

Skilled Nursing Inc.
1251 S Cedar Crest Blvd,
Allentown PA 18103-6205. 610/820-9490.

Wiley House Treatment Centers
RR 3, Saylorsburg PA
18353-9804. 610/381-3400.

19th Street Health Center
1736 W Hamilton St,
Allentown PA 18104-5656. 610/770-8741.

SKILLED NURSING CARE FACILITIES

Genesis Health Ventures
148 W State St, Kennet
Sq PA 19348-3021.
610/444-6350.

Memorial Hospital
One Hospital Dr,
Towanda PA 18848-9703. 717/265-2191.

NURSING AND PERSONAL CARE FACILITIES

Buffalo Valley Lutheran Village
211 Fairground Rd,
Lewisburg PA 17837-1207. 717/524-2221.

Cumberland County Hospice Inc.
2057 W Landis Ave,
Vineland NJ 08360-3430. 609/794-1515.

David King Care Center Atlantic City
166 S South Carolina
Ave, Atlantic City NJ
08401-7211. 609/344-2181.

Eastern Pines Convalescent Center
29 N Vermont Ave,
Atlantic City NJ 08401-5561. 609/344-8900.

Greenbriar Nurse Center Hammonton
43 White Horse Pike N,
Hammonton NJ 08037-1875. 609/567-3100.

Home Health Services/Hospice
1 Hospital Dr, Lewisburg PA 17837-9314. 717/522-2550.

Linwood Convalescent Center
New Rd & Central Av, Linwood NJ 08221. 609/927-6131.

Little Flower Manor
1201 Springfield Rd, Darby PA 19023-1115. 610/534-6000.

Lutheran Home At Moorestown
255 E Main St, Moorestown NJ 08057-2999. 609/235-5622.

Mainland Manor Nurse & Rehab Center
930 Church St, Pleasantville NJ 08232-4271. 609/646-6900.

Memorial Hospital
PO Box 15118, York PA 17405-7118. 717/843-8623.

Nursecare Health Centers
3 Station Sq, Paoli PA 19301-1321. 610/644-4051.

Oceanside Conval & Rehab Center
401 Boardwalk, Atlantic City NJ 08401-7704. 609/348-0171.

Our Lady's Residence
Glendale Av & Clematis Av, Pleasantville NJ 08232. 609/646-2450.

Paoli Memorial Hospital
255 W Lancaster Ave, Paoli PA 19301. 610/648-1000.

Saint Mary's Manor
701 Lansdale Ave, Lansdale PA 19446-2994. 215/368-0900.

Seashore Gardens
3850 Atlantic Ave, Atlantic City NJ 08401-6094. 609/345-5941.

Shore Memorial Hospital
555 Bay Ave, Somers Point NJ 08244. 609/927-9151.

GENERAL MEDICAL AND SURGICAL HOSPITALS

Allied Services Rehab Hospital
475 Morgan Hwy, Scranton PA 18508-2605. 717/348-1300.

Bucktail Medical Center
1001 Pine St, Renovo PA 17764-1620. 717/923-1000.

Caron Foundation
PO Box A, Wernersville PA 19565-0501. 610/678-2332.

Community General Osteopathic Hospital
PO Box 3000, Harrisburg PA 17105-3000. 717/652-3000.

Eastern Mercy Health System
100 Matsonford Road Suite 220, Wayne PA 19087-4527. 610/971-9770.

Farview State Hospital
PO Box 128, Waymart PA 18472-0128. 717/488-6111.

Friends Hospital
4641 Roosevelt Blvd, Philadelphia PA 19124-2399. 215/831-4600.

Geisinger Health Care System
100 N Academy Ave, Danville PA 17822. 717/271-6467.

Good Shepherd Rehab Hospital
501 St John St, Allentown PA 18103-3231. 610/776-3120.

Marian Community Hospital
100 Lincoln Ave, Carbondale PA 18407-2170. 717/282-2100.

Miners Memorial Medical Center
Seventh St, Coaldale PA 18218-1199. 717/645-2131.

Montgomery County Emergency Service
PO Box 3005, Norristown PA 19404-3005. 610/279-6100.

Mount Sinai Hospital
1429 S 5th St, Philadelphia PA 19147-5937. 215/339-3456.

Nittany Valley Rehab Hospital
550 W College Ave, Bellefonte PA 16823-7401. 814/359-3421.

Numed Psychiatric Inc.
1265 Drummers Lane Suite 107, Wayne PA 19087-1570. 610/687-5151.

Palmerton Hospital
135 Lafayette Ave, Palmerton PA 18071-1596. 610/826-3141.

Philhaven Hospital
PO Box 550, Mount
Gretna PA 17064-0550.
717/273-8871.

Pocono Medical Center
206 E Brown St, E
Stroudsburg PA 18301-
3006. 717/421-4000.

**Reading Rehabilitation
Hospital**
PO Box 250, Reading PA
19607-0250. 610/777-
7615.

Seidle Memorial Hospital
120 S Filbert St,
Mechanicsburg PA
17055-6591. 717/795-
6760.

**Shriners Hospital For
Crippled Children**
8400 Roosevelt Blvd,
Philadelphia PA 19152-
1212. 215/332-4500.

Springfield Hospital
190 W Sproul Rd,
Springfield PA 19064-
2097. 610/328-8700.

St Francis Medical Center
601 Hamilton Ave,
Trenton NJ 08629-1915.
609/599-5000.

**St Lawrence
Rehabilitation Center**
2381 Lawrenceville Rd,
Trenton NJ 08648-2024.
609/896-9500.

Taylor Hospital
E Chester Pike, Ridley
Park PA 19078.
610/595-6000.

The Devereux Foundation
PO Box 297, Malvern PA
19355-0297. 610/296-
6923.

Tyler Memorial Hospital
PO Box 273,
Tunkhannock PA 18657.
717/836-2161.

US Penitentiary Hospital
Rte 3, Lewisburg PA
17837-9803. 717/523-
1251.

Waynesboro Hospital
501 E Main St,
Waynesboro PA 17268-
2394. 717/765-4000.

**PSYCHIATRIC
HOSPITALS**

**Trenton Psychiatric
Hospital**
PO Box 7500, Trenton
NJ 08628-0500.
609/633-1500.

Tri County Respites
219 E Broad St,
Quakertown PA 18951-
1701. 215/538-2424.

SPECIALTY HOSPITALS

Clear Brook Lodge
POB 146A, Shickshinny
PA 18655. 717/864-
3116.

**Good Samaritan Regional
Medical Center**
700 E Norwegian St,
Pottsville PA 17901-
2710. 717/621-4000.

Livengrin Foundation
4833 Hulmeville Rd,
Bensalem PA 19020-
3099. 215/638-5200.

Mid-Valley Hospital
1400 Main St, Peckville
PA 18452-2098.
717/489-7546.

**Mother Bachmann
Maternity Center**
2560 Knights Rd,
Bensalem PA 19020-
3400. 215/245-4334.

**MEDICAL
LABORATORIES**

**Ashland Regional Medical
Center**
Rte 61, Ashland PA
17921. 717/875-2000.

**Omega Medical
Laboratory**
3446 Freemansburg Ave,
Bethlehem PA 18017-
5758. 610/691-2384.

**Omega Medical
Laboratory**
26 S Broad St, Nazareth
PA 18064-2156.
610/746-0972.

Omega Medical Labs
1816 W Market St,
Pottsville PA 17901-
2055. 717/622-3100.

**Quakertown Community
Hospital**
1021 Park Ave,
Quakertown PA 18951-
1551. 215/538-4500.

Riddle Memorial Hospital
Baltimore Pike Hwy 1,
Media PA 19063.
610/566-9400.

York Hospital
15505 Kenneth Rd, York
PA 17404. 717/764-
3351.

**HOME HEALTH CARE
SERVICES**

**Community Nursing
Service**
111N 6th, Vineland NJ
08360. 609/794-4261.

**Home Health Corporation
of America**
1723 W Main St,
Stroudsburg PA 18360-
1025. 717/420-0610.

Kimberly Quality Care
35 Kings Hwy E,
Haddonfield NJ 08033-
2009. 609/795-7070.

Medquist Inc.
20 Clementon Rd E,
Gibbsboro NJ 08026-
1165. 609/782-0300.

Salem Care Inc.
17 New Market St,
Salem NJ 08079-1408.
609/935-1608.

Wayne Memorial Hospital
601 Park St, Honesdale
PA 18431-1445.
717/253-8100.

**SPECIALTY OUT
PATIENT FACILITIES**

**Barnes-Kasson County
Hospital**
400 Turnpike St,
Susquehanna PA 18847-
1638. 717/853-3135.

Bloomsburg Hospital
549 Fair St, Bloomsburg
PA 17815-1463.
717/387-2100.

**Brandywine Hospital &
Trauma Center**
Rte 30 By-Pass,
Coatesville PA 19320.
610/383-8000.

Carlisle Hospital
246 Parker St, Carlisle
PA 17013-3618.
717/249-1212.

Columbia Hospital
PO Box 926, Columbia
PA 17512-0926.
717/684-2841.

**Community Hospital
Lancaster**
1100 E Orange St,
Lancaster PA 17602-
3218. 717/397-3711.

**Ephrata Community
Hospital**
PO Box 1002, Ephrata
PA 17522-1002.
717/733-0311.

Eugenia Hospital
660 Thomas Rd,
Lafayette HI PA 19444-
1199. 215/836-7700.

**Evangelical Community
Hospital**
One Hospital Dr,
Lewisburg PA 17837-
9314. 717/522-2000.

**Fulton County Medical
Center**
216 S 1st St, Mc
Connellsbg PA 17233-
1310. 717/485-3155.

Good Samaritan Hospital
Fourth and Walnut Sts,
Lebanon PA 17042.
717/270-7500.

Hanover General Hospital
300 Highland Ave,
Hanover PA 17331-
2214. 717/637-3711.

Hazleton General Hospital
700 E Broad St, Hazleton
PA 18201-6897.
717/450-4357.

**Lock Haven Hospital &
Extended Care**
24 Cree Dr, Lock Haven
PA 17745-2699.
717/893-5000.

Magee Rehab Hospital
Six Franklin Plaza,
Philadelphia PA 19102-
1177. 215/587-3000.

**The Meadows Psychiatric
Center**
RR 1, Centre Hall PA
16828-9801. 814/364-
2161.

**Medical College Hospital
Bucks County Campus**
225 Newtown Rd,
Warminster PA 18974-
5251. 215/441-6600.

**Montrose General
Hospital**
1 Grow Ave, Montrose
PA 18801-1199.
717/278-3801.

**Pottstown Memorial
Medical Center**
1600 E High St,
Pottstown PA 19464-
5008. 610/327-7000.

**Southern Chester County
Medical Center**
1015 W Baltimore Pike,
West Grove PA 19390-
9426. 610/869-1000.

**Valley Forge Medical
Center & Hospital**
1033 W Germantown
Pike, Norristown PA
19403-3998. 610/539-
8500.

**HEALTH AND ALLIED
SERVICES**

**Mercy Hospital Of
Wilkes-Barre**
POB 658, Wilkes Barre
PA 18765-0001.
717/826-3100.

**Southern Ocean County
Hospital**
Route 72 Box 1140,
Manahawkin NJ 08050-
2412. 609/597-6011.

**Vineland Development
Center Hospital**
1676 E Landis Ave,
Vineland NJ 08360-
2901. 609/696-6200.

MEDICAL, DENTAL AND HOSPITAL EQUIPMENT WHOLESALE

Wasserott's
Luzerne-Dallas Hwy,
Luzerne PA 18709.
717/344-8765.

PROFESSIONAL EQUIPMENT SUPPLIES WHOLESALE

**Cabot Medical
Corporation**
2021 Cabot Blvd W,
Langhorne PA 19047-
1875. 215/752-8300.

**Mettler Instrument
Corporation**
69 Princeton Highstown
Rd Box, Hightstown NJ
08520-1912. 609/448-
3000.

MEDICAL INSTRUMENTS

**Bear Automotive Service
Equipment Co.**
100 Werner St, Bangor
PA 18013-2852.
610/588-4400.

Krautkramer Branson
PO Box 350, Lewistown
PA 17044-0350.
717/242-0327.

Microcom Corporation
965 Thomas Dr,
Warminster PA 18974-
2878. 215/672-6300.

**Nuclear Research
Corporation**
125 Titus Ave,
Warrington PA 18976-
2424. 215/343-5900.

**Physical Acoustics
Corporation**
15 Princess Rd, Trenton
NJ 08648-2378.
609/896-2255.

Princeton Gamma-Tech
1200 State Rd, Princeton
NJ 08540-1620.
609/924-7310.

Echo Ultrasound Inc.
RR 2 Box 118, Reedsville
PA 17084-9772.
717/667-3266.

Hygeia Sciences Inc.
PO Box 1001, Cranbury
NJ 08512-0181.

I-Stat Corporation
303 College Rd E,
Princeton NJ 08540-
6605. 609/243-9300.

Interspec Inc.
110 W Butler Ave,
Ambler PA 19002-5795.
215/540-9190.

**Medical Disposables Intl
Inc.**
537 Apple St,
Conshohocken PA
19428-2903. 610/828-
2520.

North American Drager
148B Quarry Rd, Telford
PA 18969-1041.
215/723-9824.

**Nova Medical Specialties
Inc.**
449 Oakshade Rd,
Vincentown NJ 08088-
9520. 609/268-8080.

Penox Technologies
One Penox Plaza, Pittston
PA 18640. 717/655-
1421.

Pilling-Rusch Co.
420 Delaware Dr, Ft
Washington PA 19034-
2711. 215/643-2600.

**Surgical Specialties
Corporation**
50 S Museum Rd,
Reading PA 19607-2425.
610/777-1949.

Boehringer Labs Inc.
500 E Washington St,
Norristown PA 19401-
5149. 610/278-0900.

The Jerome Group Inc.
305 Harper Dr,
Moorestown NJ 08057-
3246. 609/234-8600.

DENTAL EQUIPMENT

Den-Tal-Ez Inc.
1816 Colonial Village Ln,
Lancaster PA 17601-
5891. 717/291-1161.

X-RAY APPARATUS

Air Shields
330 Jacksonville Rd,
Hatboro PA 19040-2211.
215/675-5200.

ELECTROMEDICAL AND ELECTRO-THERAPEUTIC APPARATUS

**Advanced Medical
Devices Inc.**
2733 Saunders St,
Camden NJ 08105-
1236. 609/964-8448.

American Medical Parts
3704 W Country Club
Rd, Philadelphia PA
19131-2815. 215/477-
8981.

Biomedical Sensors Ltd
293 Great Valley Pky,
Malvern PA 19355-1308.
610/296-9609.

Cardio Trace Corporation
9501 Roosevelt Blvd,
Philadelphia PA 19114-
1025. 215/673-6669.

**Cerebral Electronics
Corporation**
302 Cambridge Rd,
Cherry Hill NJ 08034-
1820. 609/667-0100.

**International Shared
Service Inc.**
1011 N Brookside Rd,
Allentown PA 18106-
9677. 610/398-7933.

Neuro Medical Systems
1327 Adams Rd Ste A,
Bensalem PA 19020-
3966. 215/638-1606.

Oakwood Technology
40 N Waterloo Rd, Devon
PA 19333-1458.
609/695-9544.

**Physio-Control
Corporation**
9600 Roosevelt Blvd,
Philadelphia PA 19115-
3932. 215/934-7853.

**Roche Medical
Electronics**
339 Kidwelly Ct, Exton
PA 19341-1495.
610/363-8899.

State Technology Inc.
510 Heron Dr, Bridgeport
NJ 08014. 609/467-
8009.

UGM Medical Systems
3401 Market St Ste 222,
Philadelphia PA 19104-
3319. 215/222-4999.

OPHTHALMIC GOODS

Balester Optical Co
388 N River St, Wilkes
Barre PA 18702.
717/824-7821.

Gentex Corporation
Main St, Carbondale PA
18407. 717/282-3550.

Pan-Optics Inc.
1700 Suckle Hwy,
Pennsauken NJ 08110.
609/665-8100.

For more information on career opportunities in the health care industry:

<u>Associations</u>

**AMERICAN ACADEMY OF FAMILY
PHYSICIANS**
8880 Ward Parkway, Kansas City MO
64114. 816/333-9700.

**AMERICAN ACADEMY OF PHYSICIAN
ASSISTANTS**
950 North Washington Street,
Alexandria VA 22314. 703/836-
2272.

**AMERICAN ASSOCIATION FOR
CLINICAL CHEMISTRY**
2101 Lovely Street NW, Suite 202,
Washington, DC 20037-1526.

**AMERICAN ASSOCIATION OF
COLLEGES OF OSTEOPATHIC
MEDICINE**
6110 Executive Boulevard, Suite 405,
Rockville MD 20852. 301/468-2037.

**AMERICAN ASSOCIATION OF
COLLEGES OF PODIATRIC MEDICINE**
1350 Piccard Drive, Suite 322,
Rockville MD 20850. 301/990-7400.

**AMERICAN ASSOCIATION OF
DENTAL SCHOOLS**
1625 Massachusetts Avenue NW,
Washington DC 20036. 202/667-
9433.

**AMERICAN ASSOCIATION OF
MEDICAL ASSISTANTS**
20 North Wacker Drive, Suite 1575,
Chicago IL 60606. 312/899-1500.

**AMERICAN ASSOCIATION OF NURSE
ANESTHETISTS**
222 South Prospect, Park Ridge IL
60068-4001. 708/692-7050.

**AMERICAN ASSOCIATION OF
RESPIRATORY CARE**
11030 Ables Lane, Dallas TX 75229-
4593. 214/243-2272.

**AMERICAN CHIROPRACTIC
ASSOCIATION**
1701 Clarendon Boulevard, Arlington
VA 22209. 703/276-8800.

AMERICAN COLLEGE OF
HEALTHCARE ADMINISTRATORS
325 South Patrick Street, Alexandria
VA 22314. 703/549-5822.

AMERICAN COLLEGE OF
HEALTHCARE EXECUTIVES
840 North Lake Shore Drive, West
1103, Chicago IL 60611. 312/943-
0544.

AMERICAN DENTAL ASSOCIATION
211 East Chicago Avenue, Chicago IL
60611. 312/440-2500.

AMERICAN DENTAL HYGIENISTS
ASSOCIATION
Division of Professional Development,
444 North Michigan Avenue, Suite
3400, Chicago IL 60611. 312/440-
8900.

AMERICAN DIETETIC ASSOCIATION
216 West Jackson Boulevard,
Chicago IL 60606. 312/899-0040.

AMERICAN HEALTH CARE
ASSOCIATION
1201 L Street NW, Washington DC
20005-4014. 202/842-4444.

AMERICAN MEDICAL ASSOCIATION
515 North State Street, Chicago IL
60610. 312/464-5000.

AMERICAN HEALTH INFORMATION
MANAGEMENT ASSOCIATION
919 North Michigan Avenue, Suite
1400, Chicago IL 60611. 312/787-
2672.

AMERICAN MEDICAL
TECHNOLOGISTS
710 Higgins Road, Park Ridge IL
60068. 708/823-5169.

AMERICAN NURSES ASSOCIATION
600 Maryland Avenue SW, Suite
100W, Washington DC 20024-2571.
202/554-4444.

AMERICAN OCCUPATIONAL
THERAPY ASSOCIATION
1383 Piccard Drive, P.O. Box 1725,
Rockville MD 20849-1725. 301/948-
9626.

AMERICAN OPTOMETRIC
ASSOCIATION
243 North Lindbergh Boulevard, St.
Louis MO 63141. 314/991-4100.

AMERICAN PHYSICAL THERAPY
ASSOCIATION
1111 North Fairfax Street, Alexandria
VA 22314. 703/684-2782. Must
send small fee in return for
information.

AMERICAN VETERINARY MEDICAL
ASSOCIATION
1931 North Meacham Road, Suite
100, Schaumburg IL 60173-4360.
708/925-8070.

NATIONAL MEDICAL ASSOCIATION
1012 Tenth Street NW, Washington
DC 20001. 202/347-1895.

NATIONAL PHARMACEUTICAL
COUNCIL
1894 Prewston White Drive, Reston
VA 22091. 202/347-1895. FAX:
703/476-0904. Fax requests to the
attention of Mary Pat.

Directories

BLUE BOOK DIGEST OF HMOs
National Association of Employers on
Health Care Alternatives, P.O. Box
220, Fort Lauderdale FL 33310.
305/361-2810.

ENCYCLOPEDIA OF MEDICAL
ORGANIZATIONS AND AGENCIES
Gale Research Inc., 835 Penobscot
Building, Detroit MI 48226. 313/961-
2242.

HEALTH ORGANIZATIONS OF THE UNITED STATES, CANADA, AND THE WORLD
Gale Research Inc., 835 Penobscot Building, Detroit MI 48226. 313/961-2242.

MEDICAL AND HEALTH INFORMATION DIRECTORY
Gale Research Inc., 835 Penobscot Building, Detroit MI 48226. 313/961-2242.

NATIONAL DIRECTORY OF HEALTH MAINTENANCE ORGANIZATIONS
Group Health Association of America, 1129 20th Street NW, Suite 600, Washington DC 20036. 202/778-3200.

Magazines

AMERICAN MEDICAL NEWS
American Medical Association, 515 North State Street, Chicago IL 60605. 312/464-5000.

CHANGING MEDICAL MARKETS
Theta Corporation, Theta Building, Middlefield CT 06455. 203/349-1054.

HEALTH CARE EXECUTIVE
American College of Health Care Executives, 840 North Lake Shore Drive, Chicago IL 60611. 312/943-0544.

MODERN HEALTHCARE
Crain Communications, 740 North Rush Street, Chicago IL 60611. 312/649-5374.

HOTELS AND RESTAURANTS

In the restaurant segment, the fastest-growing sector of the market continues to be fast-food-style establishments, although increased public concern over health has led industry leaders to develop new products and marketing strategies. McDonald's released its lower-fat "McLean Deluxe", and Kentucky Fried Chicken changed its name to "KFC" to de-emphasize the word "Fried". The take-out trend, spurred by changing demographics and eating habits, is changing the industry as a whole, not just at the fast-food end. Managerial prospects are better than average, but the industry is hampered by a shortage of entry-level workers.

The hotel industry is tied closely to other segments of the travel industry, which in turn relies on the U.S. economy as a whole. International arrivals are the fastest-growing segment of the travel industry, so hotels in major American international destinations are better positioned. Look for greater specialization within the industry, with hotels advertising as "budget", "luxury", or "corporate/meeting", for example. Hotels will also need to respond to the growing number of working couples who take shorter vacations together.

ARA HOLDING COMPANY
ARA Tower, 1101 Market Street, Philadelphia PA 19107. 215/238-3000. **Contact:** Personnel Department. **Description:** Provider of food management services to a wide range of establishments, including businesses, schools, universities, resorts, stadiums and hospitals. **Number of employees at this location:** 115,000.

BALLY'S GRAND HOTEL-CASINO
P.O. Box 1737, Atlantic City NJ 08404. 609/347-7111. **Contact:** Human Resources Department. **Description:** An area hotel and casino.

DELMAC MANAGEMENT COMPANY
18 Clover Lane, Newtown Square PA 19073. 215/356-8775. **Contact:** Personnel Department. **Description:** Operates a fast food restaurant chain.

HOTEL DU PONT
11th and Market Street, Wilmington DE 19801. 302/656-8121. **Contact:** Employment Office. **Description:** A Wilmington hotel. **Parent company:** DuPont Chemical Corporation.

NUTRITION MANAGEMENT SERVICES COMPANY
Box 725, Kimberton Road, Kimberton PA 19442. 215/935-2050. **Contact:** Personnel. **Description:** A food service management company specializing in food service programs in healthcare, retirement and acute care facilities. **Common positions include:** Dietician/Nutritionist; Food Production Worker; Food Scientist/Technologist; Food Service Manager. **Educational backgrounds include:** Food Services. **Benefits:**

Disability Coverage; Life Insurance; Medical Insurance. **Corporate headquarters location:** This Location.

OCEAN SHOWBOAT INC.
801 Boardwalk, Atlantic City NJ 08401. 609/343-4000. **Contact:** Human Resources Department. **Description:** An area hotel.

SANDS HOTEL & CASINO
Indiana Avenue & Brighton Park, Atlantic City NJ 08401. 609/441-4000. **Contact:** Human Resources Department. **Description:** A hotel and casino operation.

SERVICE AMERICA
1221 Wilson Drive, West Chester PA 19380. 215/692-9510. **Contact:** Personnel. **Description:** Engaged principally in the vending and food service business through the operations of vending machines, cafeterias, and other food and refreshment facilities, primarily for employees in industrial plants and office buildings; through the operation of vending machines at public and institutional locations; and through dining and dietary food service operations in colleges, hospitals, and nursing homes. Also operates a chain of Family Fish House restaurants; sells office furniture; provides janitorial services; and provides coin operated laundry services in apartment buildings and college dorms. **Corporate headquarters location:** Cheverly MD. **Listed on:** New York Stock Exchange.

TAJ MAHAL CASINO & HOTEL
1000 Boardwalk at Virginia Avenue, Atlantic City NJ 08401. 609/449-1000. **Contact:** Human Resources Department. **Description:** A large casino and hotel.

TROPWORLD CASINO AND ENTERTAINMENT RESORT
Morris Avenue, Atlantic City NJ 08401. **Contact:** Personnel. **Description:** Toll free number: 800/THE-TROP. A large casino and hotel. **Common positions include:** Accountant/Auditor; Administrator; Blue-Collar Worker Supervisor; Buyer; Claim Representative; Computer Programmer; Customer Service Representative; Department Manager; Financial Analyst; Hotel Manager/Assistant Manager; Marketing Specialist; Personnel/Labor Relations Specialist; Public Relations Specialist; Purchasing Agent and Manager; Services Sales Representative; Systems Analyst. **Educational backgrounds include:** Business Administration; Computer Science; Finance; Marketing. **Benefits:** Dental Insurance; Employee Discounts; Life Insurance; Medical Insurance; Pension Plan; Profit Sharing; Savings Plan; Tuition Assistance. **Corporate headquarters location:** Phoenix AZ. **Other U.S. locations:** Las Vegas NV; Laughlin NV. **Parent company:** Aztar. **Operations at this facility include:** Service. **Number of employees at this location:** 4,500.

TRUMP'S CASTLE HOTEL & CASINO
Brigantine Boulevard & Huron Avenue, Atlantic City NJ 08401. 609/441-8478. **FAX:** 609/348-4035. **Contact:** Sharon Varallo, Personnel Manager. **Description:** An area hotel and casino. **Common positions include:** Accountant/Auditor; Adjuster; Advertising Clerk; Buyer; Cashier; Claim Representative; Clerical Supervisor; Computer Operator; Computer Programmer; Computer Systems Analyst; Credit Clerk and Authorizer; Credit Manager; Customer Service Representative; Dispatcher; Electrician; Employment Interviewer; Food and Beverage Service Worker; Heating/AC/Refrigeration Technician; Hotel Manager/Assistant Manager; Hotel/Motel Clerk; Marketing Research Analyst; Marketing/Advertising/PR Manager; Payroll Clerk; Personnel/Labor Relations Specialist; Postal Clerk/Mail Carrier; Public Relations Specialist; Purchasing Agent and Manager; Receptionist; Restaurant/Food Service Manager; Retail Sales Worker;

Secretary; Services Sales Representative; Stock Clerk; Typist/Word Processor. **Educational backgrounds include:** Accounting; Business Administration; Communications; Computer Science; Finance; Marketing. **Benefits:** Dental Insurance; Life Insurance; Medical Insurance; Savings Plan; Tuition Assistance. **Special Programs:** Internships. **Corporate headquarters location:** This Location. **Number of employees at this location:** 3,700. **Projected hires for the next 12 months (This location):** 600 hires.

VALLEY FORGE CONVENTION PLAZA — *Sheraton   JoAnne Webster*
First Avenue and North Gulph Roads, King of Prussia PA 19406. 215/337-2000. **Contact:** Director of Human Resources. **Description:** National Hotel Management Company. This location includes: 2 hotels totaling almost 500 rooms as well as a convention center, 5 food and beverage outlets (including a dinner theater and nightclub) and an office building. **Common positions include:** Accountant/Auditor; Administrator; Advertising Clerk; Blue-Collar Worker Supervisor; Hotel Manager/Assistant Manager; Hotel/Motel Clerk; Personnel/Labor Relations Specialist; Public Relations Specialist; Purchasing Agent and Manager; Services Sales Representative. **Educational backgrounds include:** Accounting; Business Administration; Hotel Administration; Liberal Arts; Restaurant Management. **Benefits:** 401K; Dental Insurance; Disability Coverage; Employee Discounts; Life Insurance; Medical Insurance. **Special Programs:** Internships. **Corporate headquarters location:** Dallas TX. **Parent company:** Wyndham Hotel Co. **Operations at this facility include:** Sales; Service. **Number of employees at this location:** 550. **Projected hires for the next 12 months (This location):** 300 hires.

Note: Because addresses and telephone numbers of smaller companies change rapidly, we recommend you contact each company and verify the information below before contacting employers. Mass mailings are not recommended.

Additional large employers: 500+

MOTELS AND HOTELS

All American Plazas Inc.
P.O. Box 302, Bethel PA 19507-0302. 717/933-4146.

Resorts International Inc.
N Carolina & Boardwalk, Atlantic City NJ 08401. 609/344-6000.

Additional medium sized employers: under 500

EATING PLACES

Brock & Co Inc.
77 Great Valley Pky, Malvern PA 19355-1309. 610/647-5656.

Chefs International Inc.
62 Broadway, Pt Pleas Bch NJ 08742-2699. 908/295-0350.

Dempsey's Restaurants
Westgate Mall, Bethlehem PA 18017. 610/865-0089.

Dempsey's Restaurants
PO Box 6387, Reading PA 19610-0387.

Finley's American Restaurant
610 Middletown Blvd, Langhorne PA 19047-1854. 215/750-7003.

Hardee's Restaurant
215 S Atherton St, State College PA 16801-4002. 814/237-6101.

Italian Bistro Corporation
1008 Astoria Blvd,
Cherry Hill NJ 08003-
2327. 609/751-3300.

Kosmart Enterprises
Cal Beth Pl -A-Rm 117,
Hazleton PA 18201.
717/454-2422.

McDonald's
Laurel Mall, Hazleton PA
18201. 717/455-8315.

McDonald's
23 Carolyn Dr, Tuckerton
NJ 08087-9601.
609/296-5600.

**McDonald's Family
Restaurant**
S Brodwy, Wind Gap PA
18091. 610/863-9800.

**McDonalds Restaurant
Blackwood**
1521 Blackwood
Clementon Rd,
Blackwood NJ 08012-
4627. 609/227-9773.

Pizza Hut
5 Sterling Rd, Mount
Pocono PA 18344-1118.
717/839-7753.

Sandalwood Restaurant
4355 US Highway 1,
Princeton NJ 08540-
5705. 609/452-2044.

Taquet Restaurant
139 E Lancaster Ave,
Wayne PA 19087-3525.
610/687-5005.

Zagara's
501 Route 73 S, Marlton
NJ 08053-9617.
609/983-5700.

For more information on career opportunities in hotels and restaurants:

Associations

**AMERICAN HOTEL AND MOTEL
ASSOCIATION**
1201 New York Avenue NW, Suite
600, Washington DC 20005-3931.
202/289-3100.

**THE EDUCATIONAL FOUNDATION OF
THE NATIONAL RESTAURANT
ASSOCIATION**
250 South Wacker Drive, 14th Floor,
Chicago IL 60606. 312/715-1010.

**NATIONAL RESTAURANT
ASSOCIATION**
1200 17th Street NW, Washington
DC 20036. 202/331-5900.

Directories

**DIRECTORY OF CHAIN RESTAURANT
OPERATORS**
Business Guides, Inc., Lebhar-
Friedman, Inc., 3922 Coconut Palm
Drive, Tampa FL 33619-8321.
813/664-6700.

**DIRECTORY OF HIGH-VOLUME
INDEPENDENT RESTAURANTS**
Lebhar-Friedman, Inc., 3922 Coconut
Palm Drive, Tampa FL 33619-8321.
813/664-6700.

Magazines

**CORNELL HOTEL AND RESTAURANT
ADMINISTRATION QUARTERLY**
Cornell University School of Hotel
Administration, Statler Hall, Ithaca NY
14853. 607/255-9393.

HOTEL AND MOTEL MANAGEMENT
120 West 2nd Street, Duluth MN
55802.

INNKEEPING WORLD
Box 84108, Seattle WA 98124.
206/362-7125.

NATION'S RESTAURANT NEWS
3922 Coconut Palm Drive, Tampa, FL
33619. 212/756-5200.

INSURANCE

 *While individual life insurance and health insurance are still weak, jobseekers should look to companies that specialize in annuities, which will continue to be the industry's fastest-growing segment. Premiums of property-casualty insurers should increase by about 7- 9% in personal business, but commercial business will be tighter. Competition and mergers will increase, and life insurance companies are expected to experience further problems. The industry as a whole has been trimming back through layoffs, although the worst appears to be over.*

AIG COMPANIES
One Alico Plaza, 600 King Street, Wilmington DE 19801. 302/594-2098. **Contact:** Tom Hoffman, Vice President of Human Resources. **Description:** An international insurance organization and an underwriter of commercial and industrial insurance in the United States. **Common positions include:** Accountant/Auditor; Actuary; Administrator; Attorney; Claim Representative; Computer Programmer; Customer Service Representative; Financial Analyst; Underwriter/Assistant Underwriter. **Benefits:** Disability Coverage; Employee Discounts; Life Insurance; Medical Insurance; Savings Plan; Stock Option; Tuition Assistance. **Parent company:** American International Group, Inc. **Listed on:** London Stock Exchange; New York Stock Exchange; Tokyo Stock Exchange.

ADMIRAL INSURANCE COMPANY
1255 Caldwell Road, Cherry Hill NJ 08034. 609/429-9200. **Contact:** Personnel. **Description:** A suburban Philadelphia insurance agency.

ALLSTATE INSURANCE COMPANIES
701 Lee Road, Wayne PA 19087. 215/648-8800. **Contact:** Bill Wells, Human Resources Manager. **Description:** One of the nation's largest insurance companies. **Parent company:** Sears, Roebuck, & Company.

AMERICAN LIFE INSURANCE COMPANY
One Alico Plaza, P.O. Box 2226, Wilmington DE 19899. 302/594-2000. **Contact:** Catherine Strulson, Human Resources. **Description:** A life insurance company.

AMERICAN RE-INSURANCE COMPANY
555 College Road East, Princeton NJ 08543. 609/243-4648. **Contact:** Lisa Bronstein, Senior Employment Representative. **Description:** Primarily offers re-insurance coverage to property/casualty insurance firms. World recognized leader in the re-insurance industry. Branches throughout the U.S. and the world. **Common positions include:** Accountant/Auditor; Actuary; Administrator; Claim Representative; Department Manager; Financial Analyst; Personnel/Labor Relations Specialist; Statistician; Systems Analyst. **Educational backgrounds include:** Accounting; Business Administration; Communications; Computer Science; Finance; Marketing. **Benefits:** Dental Insurance; Disability Coverage; Life Insurance; Medical Insurance; Pension Plan; Savings Plan; Tuition Assistance. **Corporate headquarters location:** This Location. **Operations at this**

facility include: Administration; Divisional Headquarters. **Listed on:** New York Stock Exchange.

AMERICAN TRAVELLERS CORPORATION
3220 Tillman Drive, Bensalem PA 19020. 215/244-1600. **Contact:** Human Resources. **Description:** An accident and health insurance company.

BLUE CROSS & BLUE SHIELD OF DELAWARE
P.O. Box 1991, Wilmington DE 19899-1991. 302/421-3000. **Contact:** Vicki Skomsky, Human Resources Director. **Description:** The state headquarters of the national health insurance company. Includes HMO of Delaware. **Corporate headquarters location:** Chicago IL. **Other U.S. locations:** Dover DE.

CHUBB GROUP OF INSURANCE COMPANIES
1 Liberty Place, 1650 Market Street, Philadelphia PA 19103. 215/981-8163. **Contact:** Joyce Lilleston, Human Resources Manager. **Description:** Offices of the large property and casualty insurance organization. Main business is underwriting property, casualty, marine, personal, and financial services insurance worldwide. **Corporate headquarters location:** Warren NJ. **Listed on:** New York Stock Exchange. **Number of employees nationwide:** 8,500.

CIGNA COMPANIES
One Beaver Valley Road, P.O. Box 15052, Wilmington DE 19850. 302/479-6152. **FAX:** 302/479-6129. **Contact:** Gwen Thomas, Human Resources Assistant. **Description:** A division of the national insurance agency. **Common positions include:** Accountant/Auditor; Actuary; Adjuster; Attorney; Claim Representative; Clerical Supervisor; Computer Operator; Computer Systems Analyst; Department Manager; Paralegal; Personnel/Labor Relations Specialist; Secretary; Typist/Word Processor; Underwriter/Assistant Underwriter. **Educational backgrounds include:** Accounting; Business Administration; Communications; Computer Science; Insurance. **Benefits:** Daycare Assistance; Dental Insurance; Disability Coverage; Employee Discounts; Life Insurance; Medical Insurance; Pension Plan; Savings Plan; Tuition Assistance. **Special Programs:** Internships. **Corporate headquarters location:** Philadelphia PA. **Other U.S. locations:** IL; MI; NC; NY. **Operations at this facility include:** Administration; Service. **Listed on:** New York Stock Exchange. **Number of employees at this location:** 712.

CIGNA CORPORATION
STAFFING SERVICES
1601 Chestnut Street, P.O. Box 7716, Philadelphia PA 19192. **Contact:** Staffing Services Department. **Description:** A financial services firm, whose principal lines of business include property/casualty insurance, life insurance, health care insurance, and investment management services. The insurance groups offer commercial as well as individual plans. The health care group operates hospitals, manages health plans, and provides rehabilitative services. The investment group manages the portfolios of the other company groups. Number of employees worldwide: 50,000. **Common positions include:** Accountant/Auditor; Adjuster; Claim Representative; Computer Programmer; Employment Interviewer; Health Services Manager; Registered Nurse. **Educational backgrounds include:** Accounting; Computer Science. **Benefits:** Dental Insurance; Disability Coverage; Employee Discounts; Life Insurance; Medical Insurance; Pension Plan; Profit Sharing; Savings Plan; Tuition Assistance. **Corporate headquarters location:** This Location. **Operations at this facility include:** Divisional Headquarters. **Listed on:** New York Stock Exchange. **Annual Revenues:** $19,000,000,000. **Number of employees at this location:** 3,500. **Projected hires for the next 12 months (This location):** 250 hires.

COLONIAL PENN GROUP INC.
1818 Market Street, Philadelphia PA 19181. 215/988-8000. **Contact:** Human Resources Department. **Description:** An insurance company.

COLONIAL PENN PROPERTY CASUALTY CO.
P.O. Box 1998, Valley Forge PA 19482-1998. 215/650-2149. **Contact:** Human Resources. **Description:** An insurance company engaged in providing auto and homeowners insurance. **Common positions include:** Accountant/Auditor; Claim Representative; Computer Programmer; Customer Service Representative; Financial Analyst; Services Sales Representative. **Educational backgrounds include:** Accounting; Business Administration; Finance; Liberal Arts. **Benefits:** Daycare Assistance; Dental Insurance; Life Insurance; Medical Insurance; Pension Plan; Savings Plan; Tuition Assistance. **Special Programs:** Training Programs. **Corporate headquarters location:** This Location. **Parent company:** Leucadia. **Operations at this facility include:** Administration; Sales; Service. **Number of employees nationwide:** 1,260.

FIDELITY MUTUAL GROUP
250 King of Prussia Road, Radnor PA 19087. 215/964-7383. **Contact:** Beverly Morley, Assistant V.P./Employment. **Description:** A life insurance company. **Common positions include:** Accountant/Auditor; Actuary; Attorney; Computer Programmer; Customer Service Representative; Editor; Systems Analyst; Underwriter/Assistant Underwriter; Writer. **Educational backgrounds include:** Accounting; Business Administration; Computer Science; Finance; Liberal Arts; Marketing; Mathematics. **Benefits:** Dental Insurance; Disability Coverage; Employee Discounts; Life Insurance; Medical Insurance; Pension Plan; Savings Plan; Tuition Assistance. **Corporate headquarters location:** This Location. **Operations at this facility include:** Administration; Research and Development; Service.

GENERAL ACCIDENT INSURANCE
436 Walnut Street, 1 IS, Philadelphia PA 19105. 215/625-1401. **Contact:** Human Resources Department. **Description:** Sells casualty and property insurance through independent agents. **Common positions include:** Accountant/Auditor; Actuary; Administrator; Attorney; Computer Programmer; Customer Service Representative; Systems Analyst. **Educational backgrounds include:** Accounting; Business Administration; Liberal Arts; Mathematics. **Benefits:** Dental Insurance; Disability Coverage; Life Insurance; Medical Insurance; Pension Plan; Savings Plan. **Corporate headquarters location:** This Location.

HARLEYSVILLE INSURANCE COMPANIES
355 Maple Avenue, Harleysville PA 19438. 215/256-5045. **Contact:** Bruce E. McKelvy, Vice President of Human Resources. **Description:** A multiple lines property/casualty and life insurance carrier, with offices throughout the mid-Atlantic states. Products are marketed through an independent agency system. **Common positions include:** Accountant/Auditor; Actuary; Attorney; Branch Manager; Claim Representative; Commercial Artist; Computer Programmer; Customer Service Representative; Financial Analyst; Financial Services Sales Rep.; Personnel/Labor Relations Specialist; Technical Writer/Editor; Underwriter/Assistant Underwriter. **Educational backgrounds include:** Business Administration; Computer Science; Economics; Finance; Liberal Arts. **Benefits:** Dental Insurance; Disability Coverage; Employee Discounts; Life Insurance; Medical Insurance; Pension Plan; Profit Sharing; Savings Plan; Tuition Assistance. **Corporate headquarters location:** This Location. **Operations at this facility include:** Administration; Sales; Service.

INDEPENDENCE BLUE CROSS
OF GREATER PHILADELPHIA

1901 Market Street, Philadelphia PA 19103. 215/241-2400. **Contact:** Human Resources. **Description:** Independence Blue Cross has been a player in the health-care coverage industry for more than 50 years. IBC provides individual and group subscribers with health benefits that complement their lifestyles, medical and financial needs. **Common positions include:** Accountant/Auditor; Actuary; Attorney; Claim Representative; Personnel/Labor Relations Specialist; Public Relations Specialist; Services Sales Representative; Statistician; Systems Analyst; Underwriter/Assistant Underwriter. **Educational backgrounds include:** Accounting; Business Administration; Computer Science; Finance; Marketing. **Benefits:** Bonus Award/Plan; Dental Insurance; Disability Coverage; Life Insurance; Medical Insurance; Savings Plan; Tuition Assistance.

INDEPENDENCE FINANCIAL GROUP

510 Walnut Street, 17th Floor, Philadelphia PA 19106. 215/440-3636. **Contact:** Human Resources. **Description:** Carries a diversified line of financial service products including individual and group life and health insurance, individual and group pension policies, annuities, individual stocks and bonds, and professionally managed investment funds. Send resumes to: Penn Mutual Life Insurance Co., Independence Square, Philadelphia PA 19172. **Common positions include:** Branch Manager; Customer Service Representative; Department Manager; Financial Analyst; Financial Services Sales Rep.; General Manager; Insurance Agent/Broker; Management Trainee; Office Manager; Sales Manager; Systems Analyst. **Educational backgrounds include:** Accounting; Business Administration; Economics; Finance; Marketing. **Benefits:** Dental Insurance; Disability Coverage; Employee Discounts; Life Insurance; Medical Insurance; Pension Plan; Profit Sharing; Savings Plan; Tuition Assistance. **Special Programs:** Internships; Training Programs. **Corporate headquarters location:** Horsham PA. **Parent company:** Penn Mutual Life Insurance Co. **Operations at this facility include:** Sales.

INSURANCE COMPANY OF NORTH AMERICA

1601 Chestnut Street, Philadelphia PA 19192. 215/761-1000. **Contact:** Human Resources. **Description:** An insurance company.

LIBERTY MUTUAL INSURANCE COMPANY

15 Kings Grant Drive, Bala-Cynwyd PA 19004. 215/839-6600. **Contact:** Director/Hiring and Training. **Description:** Mail resumes to: 100 Berwyn Park, P.O. Box 1029, Suite 100, Berwyn, PA 19312. A full-line insurance firm offering life, medical, and business insurance, as well as investment and retirement plans. **Common positions include:** Administrator; Attorney; Claim Representative; Customer Service Representative; Insurance Agent/Broker; Sales Manager; Services Sales Representative; Underwriter/Assistant Underwriter. **Educational backgrounds include:** Business Administration; Marketing. **Corporate headquarters location:** Boston MA. **Operations at this facility include:** Divisional Headquarters.

THE PMA GROUP

PMA Building, 925 Chestnut St., 1st Floor, Philadelphia PA 19107. 215/629-5000. **Contact:** Barbara Romano, Employment. **Description:** A writer of workers' compensation insurance.

PROVIDENT MUTUAL LIFE INSURANCE CO.
OF PHILADELPHIA
1600 Market Street, Philadelphia PA 19103. 215/636-5000. **Contact:** Personnel Department. **Description:** Provides life and health insurance to individuals and groups. **Number of employees at this location:** 1,800.

PRUDENTIAL INSURANCE COMPANY
250 Gibraltar Road, Horsham PA 19044. 215/443-2000. **Contact:** Human Resources Department. **Description:** A life insurance company.

PRUDENTIAL INSURANCE COMPANY
1201 New Road, Linwood NJ 08221. 609/653-2400. **Contact:** Human Resources Department. **Description:** A life insurance company.

PRUDENTIAL INSURANCE COMPANY OF AMERICA
P.O. Box 388, Fort Washington PA 19034. 215/784-2690. **Contact:** Joan Engel, Personnel Manager. **Description:** Eastern Home Office for the largest multiline insurance company in the world with offices throughout the United States and Canada. Controls assets on $75 billion; established in 1875. **Common positions include:** Accountant/Auditor; Actuary; Administrator; Attorney; Claim Representative; Computer Programmer; Customer Service Representative; Department Manager; Facilities Engineer; Financial Analyst; General Manager; Management Trainee; Marketing Specialist; Personnel/Labor Relations Specialist; Public Relations Specialist; Purchasing Agent and Manager; Reporter; Services Sales Representative; Systems Analyst; Underwriter/Assistant Underwriter. **Educational backgrounds include:** Accounting; Business Administration; Communications; Computer Science; Economics; Finance; Liberal Arts; Marketing; Mathematics. **Benefits:** Dental Insurance; Disability Coverage; Employee Discounts; Life Insurance; Medical Insurance; Pension Plan; Savings Plan; Tuition Assistance.

RELIANCE INSURANCE CO.
4 Penn Center Plaza, Philadelphia PA 19103. 215/864-4000. **Contact:** Bruce Farbman, Vice President/Human Resources. **Description:** Provides fire and allied lines, automobile, ocean and inland marine, fidelity and surety bonds, casualty, life, accident, and health insurance. **Listed on:** Philadelphia Exchange. **Number of employees nationwide:** 3,000.

THE TRAVELERS
1000 Voorhees Drive, 4th Floor, Voorhees Township NJ 08043. 609/782-5200. **FAX:** 609/782-5900. **Contact:** Human Resources. **Description:** A large multi-line insurance and financial services company. Merged with Primerica Corporation at the end of 1993 to form The Travelers, and has over $100 billion in assets. **Common positions include:** Adjuster; Attorney; Claim Representative; Customer Service Representative; Data Entry Clerk; Employment Interviewer; Payroll Clerk; Personnel/Labor Relations Specialist; Receptionist; Registered Nurse; Secretary. **Educational backgrounds include:** Business Administration. **Benefits:** Dental Insurance; Disability Coverage; Life Insurance; Medical Insurance; Pension Plan; Savings Plan; Tuition Assistance. **Corporate headquarters location:** Hartford CT. **Parent company:** The Travelers. **Operations at this facility include:** Service. **Listed on:** New York Stock Exchange. **Number of employees at this location:** 400. **Hires/Layoffs in 1993 (This location):** 5 hires. **Projected hires for the next 12 months (This location):** 5 hires.

UNION FIDELITY LIFE INSURANCE COMPANY
Union Fidelity Office Park, Trevose PA 19049. 215/953-3000. **Contact:** Ed Anzalone, Director of Personnel. **Description:** Offers a wide range of insurance coverage. **Corporate headquarters location:** This Location.

Note: Because addresses and telephone numbers of smaller companies change rapidly, we recommend you contact each company and verify the information below before contacting employers. Mass mailings are not recommended.

Additional large employers: 500 +

INSURANCE

Penn Mutual Life Insurance Co.
Independence Sq, Philadelphia PA 19106. 215/956-8000.

Keystone Financial Inc.
P.O. Box 3660, Harrisburg PA 17105-3660. 717/233-1555.

Penn National Insurance
P.O. Box 2361, Harrisburg PA 17105-2361. 717/255-6843.

Potomac Insurance Co.
436 Walnut St., Philadelphia PA 19106-3703. 215/625-1000.

CMAC Investment Corp.
1601 Market St., Philadelphia PA 19103-2337. 215/564-6600.

Transamerica Title Insurance Company
Eight Penn Center, Philadelphia PA 19103-2125. 215/934-3400.

Additional medium sized employers: under 500

LIFE INSURANCE

American Guardian Life Assurance
PO Box 875, Blue Bell PA 19422-0875. 215/643-6400.

Corporate Health Insurance Co.
PO Box 1109, Blue Bell PA 19422-0746. 215/283-6460.

Educators Mutual Life Insurance Co
PO Box 83149, Lancaster PA 17608-3149. 717/397-2751.

Intramerica Life Insurance
1818 Market Street 24th Floor, Philadelphia PA 19181-0001. 914/577-3900.

NRG America Life Reassurance Corporation
One Penn Square West, Philadelphia PA 19107. 215/564-2603.

Providers Fidelity Life Insurance Co.
653 Skippack Pike Ste 16, Blue Bell PA 19422-1735. 215/542-7200.

Reliance Standard Life Insurance Co
2501 Parkway, Philadelphia PA 19130. 215/787-4000.

ACCIDENT AND HEALTH INSURANCE

American Travellers
3220 Tillman Dr, Bensalem PA 19020-2028. 215/244-1600.

Consumers Financial
PO Box 26, Camp Hill PA 17001-0026. 717/761-4230.

Pilgrim Life Insurance
PO Box 1679, Harrisburg PA 17105-1679.

Provident Mutual Life Insurance Co.
1600 Market St 7th Fl, Philadelphia PA 19103-7240. 215/636-5000.

HOSPITAL AND MEDICAL SERVICE PLANS

Cost Containment Associates
601 Mantua Ave, Woodbury NJ 08096-3234. 609/464-3091.

FIRE, MARINE AND CASUALTY INSURANCE

American Sentinel Insurance Co.
PO Box 1651, Harrisburg PA 17105-1651. 717/238-4559.

ARI Holdings Inc.
1000 Lenox Dr, Trenton NJ 08648-2312. 609/896-1921.

Atlantic Alliance Fid & Surety
PO Box 985, Cherry Hill NJ 08003-0985. 609/795-5575.

Boyertown Mutual Insurance Co
PO Box 478, Boyertown PA 19512-0478. 610/754-9800.

Fidelity Environmental Insurance Co
PO Box 7006, Princeton NJ 08543-7006. 609/520-1133.

First Trenton Indemnity
406 Lipponcott Drive Suite J, Marlton NJ 08053-4135. 609/983-2400.

Lackawanna Casualty Company
PO Box 450, Pittston PA 18640-0450. 717/655-5901.

Legion Insurance Company
PO Box 59239, Philadelphia PA 19102-9239. 215/851-9550.

Norguard Insurance PO Box Ah, Wilkes Barre PA 18703-0020. 717/825-9900.

Old Guard Insurance Group
PO Box 3010, Lancaster PA 17604-3010. 717/569-5361.

Pennsylvania Lumbermens Mutual Insurance Co.
The Curtis Center, Philadelphia PA 19106. 215/625-9233.

Penn-America Insurance Company
420 South York Road, Hatboro PA 19040-3990. 215/443-3600.

Pennsylvania Patriot Insurance Co.
5709 Linglestown Rd, Harrisburg PA 17112-1116. 717/540-6838.

Philadelphia Insurance Company
306 E Lancaster Ave, Wynnewood PA 19096-2104. 610/642-8400.

Physicians Insurance Company
525 Plymouth Road Suite 315, Plymouth Mtng PA 19462-1640. 610/834-6960.

Pilgrim Insurance 710 Henderson Boulevard, Folcroft PA 19032-1812. 610/534-8800.

Pioneer Mutual Insurance
6 Long Beach Lane, Glen Mills PA 19342-1740. 610/853-2660.

Spectrum General Insurance Co
PO Box 7012, Audubon PA 19407-0012. 610/630-6600.

US Insurors Company
1016 W 9th Ave Ste 201, Kng Of Prussa PA 19406-1221. 610/992-9999.

Urban Insurance Company Of Pennsylvania
3 North Delaware Avenue, Philadelphia PA 19106-1415. 215/574-0781.

SURETY INSURANCE

Atlantic Insurance Agency
4001 Chestnut St, Philadelphia PA 19104-3019. 215/382-6250.

Continental Insurance
1101 Market St, Philadelphia PA 19107-2934. 215/351-5200.

Phico Insurance Company
1 Phico Dr, Mechanicsburg PA 17055-2779. 717/766-1122.

Spear Leeds & Kellogg
1 Penn Center Plz, Philadelphia PA 19103-1821. 215/587-9458.

INSURANCE CARRIERS

National Auto Dealers Service Trenton
916 E Willow Grove Ave, Philadelphia PA 19118-1975. 215/836-5613.

For more information on career opportunities in insurance:

Associations

ALLIANCE OF AMERICAN INSURERS
1501 Woodfield Road, Suite 400
West, Schaumburg IL 60173-4980.
708/330-8500.

HEALTH INSURANCE ASSOCIATION OF AMERICA
1025 Connecticut Avenue NW, Suite 1200, Washington DC 20036-3998.
202/223-7780.

INSURANCE INFORMATION INSTITUTE
110 William Street, 24th Floor, New York NY 10038. 212/669-9200.

SOCIETY OF ACTUARIES
475 North Martingale Road, Suite 800, Schaumburg IL 60173-2226.
708/706-3500.

Directories

INSURANCE ALMANAC
Underwriter Printing and Publishing Co., 50 East Palisade Avenue, Englewood NJ 07631. 201/569-8808.

INSURANCE MARKET PLACE
Rough Notes Company, Inc., P.O. Box 564, Indianapolis IN 46206. 317/634-1541.

INSURANCE PHONE BOOK AND DIRECTORY
121 Chanlon Road, New Providence NJ 07974. 800/521-8110.

Magazines

BEST'S REVIEW
A.M. Best Co., A.M. Best Road, Oldwick NJ 08858-9988. 908/439-2200.

INSURANCE JOURNAL
9191 Towne Centre Drive, Suite 550, San Diego, CA 92122 619/455-7717.

INSURANCE TIMES
M & S Communications, 20 Park Plaza, Suite 1101, Boston MA 02116.
617/292-7117.

LEGAL SERVICES

The legal profession is undergoing a major adjustment, largely due to the rapid rise in the number of lawyers over the past two decades. In the '70s the number of lawyers doubled, and in the '80s the number rose by another 48 percent. Meanwhile, a decline in civil litigation, coupled with the recent economic downturn, has led to a "produce or perish" climate. Law schools are reporting a 10-20 percent decline in placements, and firms are laying off associates, freezing rates, and firing unproductive partners. Graduates of prestigious law schools and those who rank high in their classes will have the best opportunities.

Paralegals, or legal assistants, have a bright future. According to the U.S. Department of Labor, paralegal employment is expected to grow much faster than the average for all occupations during the next decade. As employers become aware that legal work can be done by a paralegal for less than an attorney, employment should rise sharply.

BLANK ROME COMISKY AND McCAULLEY
4 Penn Center Plaza, Philadelphia PA 19103. 215/569-5500. **Contact:** June Deitch, Personnel Director. **Description:** A Philadelphia law firm.

DEFENDER ASSOCIATION OF PHILADELPHIA
121 N. Broad Street, Philadelphia PA 19107. 215/568-3190. **Contact:** Human Resources Department. **Description:** Provides court-appointed public defenders to the Philadelphia jurisdiction of U.S. Federal Court system. **Common positions include:** Administrative Worker/Clerk; Attorney; Investigator; Paralegal; Postal Clerk/Mail Carrier; Receptionist; Secretary; Social Worker; Typist/Word Processor. **Educational backgrounds include:** Business Administration; Law/Pre-Law; Liberal Arts. **Benefits:** Dental Insurance; Disability Coverage; Life Insurance; Medical Insurance; Savings Plan. **Corporate headquarters location:** This Location. **Operations at this facility include:** Administration. **Number of employees at this location:** 500.

DRINKER BIDDLE AND REATH
1345 Chestnut Street, Philadelphia PA 19107-3496. 215/988-2790. **Contact:** Jane Sheridan, Personnel Recruiter. **Description:** A Philadelphia law firm.

DUANE MORRIS & HECKSCHER
1 Liberty Place, Philadelphia PA 19103-7396. 215/979-1000. **Contact:** Human Resources Department. **Description:** A law firm.

MORGAN LEWIS & BOCKIUS
Suite 2000, One Logan Square, Philadelphia PA 19103. 215/963-5000. **Contact:** Human Resources Department. **Description:** A law firm.

PEPPER HAMILTON & SCHEETZ
3000 Two Logan Square, 18th & Arch Streets, Philadelphia PA 19103-2799. 215/981-4000. **FAX:** 215/981-4750. **Contact:** Nadine Zlokas, Human Resources. **Description:** An international law firm. **Common positions include:** Administrator; Attorney; Computer Programmer; Financial Analyst; Personnel/Labor Relations Specialist; Purchasing Agent and Manager; Systems Analyst. **Educational backgrounds include:** Accounting; Business Administration; Computer Science; Finance; Liberal Arts. **Benefits:** Daycare Assistance; Disability Coverage; Life Insurance; Medical Insurance; Pension Plan; Savings Plan. **Special Programs:** Training Programs. **Corporate headquarters location:** This Location. **Operations at this facility include:** Administration; Regional Headquarters.

SCHNADER HARRISON SEGAL & LEWIS
1600 Market Street, Suite 3600, Philadelphia PA 19103. 215/751-2000. **Contact:** Kate Leimkuhler, Personnel Manager. **Description:** A Philadelphia law firm.

Note: Because addresses and telephone numbers of smaller companies change rapidly, we recommend you contact each company and verify the information below before contacting employers. Mass mailings are not recommended.

Additional small employers: under 100

LEGAL SERVICES

Cooper Perskie April Niedelman
1125 Atlantic Ave Suite 320, Atlantic City NJ 08401-4806. 609/344-3161.

Swartz Campbell & Detweiller
1 Veterans Sq # 106, Media PA 19063-3216. 610/566-9222.

For more information on career opportunities in legal services:

Associations

AMERICAN BAR ASSOCIATION
750 North Lake Shore Drive, Chicago IL 60611. 312/988-5000.

FEDERAL BAR ASSOCIATION
1815 H. Street NW, Suite 408, Washington DC 20006-3697. 202/638-0252.

NATIONAL ASSOCIATION OF LEGAL ASSISTANTS
1516 South Boston, Suite 200, Tulsa OK 74119-4013. 918/587-6828.

NATIONAL FEDERATION OF PARALEGAL ASSOCIATIONS
P.O. Box 33108, Kansas City MO 64114-0108. 816/941-4000.

NATIONAL PARALEGAL ASSOCIATION
P.O. Box 629, 6186 Honey Hollow Road, Doylestown PA 18901. 215/297-8333.

MANUFACTURING AND WHOLESALING: MISCELLANEOUS CONSUMER

Because the consumer products industry is so diversified, industry outlooks depend more on specific product categories. Here's a sampling.

Soaps and Detergents: One of the biggest trends in this category has been to move away from the environmentally damaging phosphates used in detergents. In fact, about 40 percent of the nation has banned phosphates altogether, instead using natural soaps made of tallow and tropical oils. Overall, employment in this area will be increasing.

Household Durables: The short-term prognosis depends on consumer confidence. Although disposable incomes have risen slightly, many consumers are replenishing savings and paying off debts instead of buying expensive new items. A recovery in housing and the aging baby-boom generation should contribute to the long-term health of this segment.

ALL-LUMINUM PRODUCTS, INC.
10981 Decatur Road, Philadelphia PA 19154. 215/632-2800. **Contact:** Mr. Ronald V. Havener, Personnel Director. **Description:** A manufacturer of casual outdoor and indoor furniture. **Common positions include:** Accountant/Auditor; Blue-Collar Worker Supervisor; Customer Service Representative; Purchasing Agent and Manager; Quality Control Supervisor. **Educational backgrounds include:** Accounting; Business Administration; Marketing. **Benefits:** Dental Insurance; Disability Coverage; Life Insurance; Medical Insurance; Profit Sharing; Savings Plan. **Corporate headquarters location:** This Location. **Operations at this facility include:** Administration; Manufacturing; Research and Development; Sales; Service.

ALLEN ORGAN COMPANY
150 Locust Street, P.O. Box 36, Macungie PA 18062. 215/966-2200. **Contact:** Harold Bloch, Personnel Manager. **Description:** A manufacturer of electronic keyboard musical instruments, principally digital computer organs and related accessories. **Corporate headquarters location:** This Location.

ALOETTE COSMETICS INCORPORATED
1301 Wright's Lane East, West Chester PA 19380. 215/692-0600. **Contact:** Human Resources. **Description:** Produces soaps and cosmetics.

BALDWIN HARDWARE CORPORATION
P.O. Box 15048, Reading PA 19612. 215/777-7811. **Contact:** Vic Carder, Vice President/Human Resources. **Description:** Manufactures builder's hardware, decorative accessories, and decorator candlesticks. **Common positions include:** Accountant/Auditor; Blue-Collar Worker Supervisor; Buyer; Chemist; Computer Programmer; Credit Manager; Customer Service Representative; Draftsperson;

Manufacturing Engineer; Product Engineer; Systems Analyst. **Educational backgrounds include:** Accounting; Business Administration; Computer Science; Engineering; Finance. **Benefits:** Dental Insurance; Disability Coverage; Employee Discounts; Life Insurance; Medical Insurance; Pension Plan; Savings Plan; Tuition Assistance. **Corporate headquarters location:** This Location. **Parent company:** MASCO. **Operations at this facility include:** Administration; Manufacturing; Research and Development; Service.

BINNEY & SMITH, INC.

1100 Church Lane, P.O. Box 431, Easton PA 18044-0431. 215/253-6271. **Contact:** Danielle Reinard, Director/Human Resources. **Description:** Produces a nationally-known line of crayons, markers, writing instruments, chalk, clay, artist kits, oils, acrylics, water colors, brushes--brand names include Crayola, Magic Marker, Liquitex, and Artista. **Common positions include:** Accountant/Auditor; Chemical Engineer; Chemist; Financial Analyst; Mechanical Engineer; Systems Analyst. **Educational backgrounds include:** Accounting; Art/Design; Business Administration; Chemistry; Communications; Computer Science; Finance; Marketing. **Benefits:** Dental Insurance; Disability Coverage; Life Insurance; Medical Insurance; Pension Plan; Savings Plan; Stock Option; Tuition Assistance. **Corporate headquarters location:** This Location. **Parent company:** Hallmark. **Operations at this facility include:** Administration; Distribution; Manufacturing; Marketing; Research and Development. **Number of employees nationwide:** 1,200.

BRITE STAR MANUFACTURING COMPANY

22 Jackson Street, Philadelphia PA 19148. 215/271-7600. **Contact:** Mr. Sandy Kinderman, Vice President. **Description:** Manufactures and imports a wide variety of Christmas decorations, trees, and other holiday items. **Common positions include:** Industrial Engineer; Purchasing Agent and Manager. **Educational backgrounds include:** Business Administration; Engineering; Finance; Marketing. **Benefits:** Disability Coverage; Life Insurance; Medical Insurance; Profit Sharing. **Corporate headquarters location:** This Location. **Operations at this facility include:** Manufacturing.

THE BUCILLA CORPORATION

One Oak Ridge Road, Hazelton PA 18201. 717/384-2525. **Contact:** Personnel Department. **Description:** A large fully-integrated needle craft company. **Common positions include:** Accountant/Auditor; Blue-Collar Worker Supervisor; Customer Service Representative; Manufacturer's/ Wholesaler's Sales Rep.; Purchasing Agent and Manager; Systems Analyst. **Educational backgrounds include:** Accounting; Art/Design; Business Administration; Computer Science; Marketing. **Benefits:** Disability Coverage; Employee Discounts; Life Insurance; Medical Insurance; Pension Plan. **Corporate headquarters location:** This Location. **Operations at this facility include:** Administration; Manufacturing; Research and Development; Sales; Service.

W. ATLEE BURPEE & CO.

300 Park Avenue, Warminster PA 18974. 215/674-4900. **Contact:** Kira Hagen-Kraiman, Director of Human Resources. **Description:** Produces gardening products. **Common positions include:** Accountant/Auditor; Blue-Collar Worker Supervisor; Buyer; Computer Programmer; Customer Service Representative; Graphic Artist; Horticulturist; Manufacturer's/Wholesaler's Sales Rep.; Marketing/Advertising/PR Manager; Operations/Production Manager; Personnel/Labor Relations Specialist; Purchasing Agent and Manager; Systems Analyst; Technical Writer/Editor. **Educational backgrounds include:** Accounting; Art/Design; Business Administration; Computer Science; Finance; Marketing. **Benefits:** 401K; Dental Insurance; Disability Coverage;

Employee Discounts; Life Insurance; Medical Insurance; Profit Sharing; Tuition Assistance. **Corporate headquarters location:** This Location.

CHURCH & DWIGHT CO., INC.
469 North Harrison Street, Princeton NJ 08543-5297. 609/683-5900. **Contact:** Human Resources. **Description:** Manufacturers of soaps, detergents, baking soda, and other products.

CONGOLEUM CORPORATION
TRENTON PLANT
3705 Quaker Bridge Road, P.O. Box 3127, Mercerville NJ 08619. 609/584-3000. **Contact:** Human Resources. **Description:** Distributes vinyl floor products to wholesalers nationwide and internationally. Parent company (Portsmouth, NH) is a diversified manufacturer/distributor, operating in the areas of home furnishings, shipbuilding, and automotive/industrial distribution.

DECORATIVE SPECIALTIES INTERNATIONAL INCORPORATED
220 Corporate Drive, Reading PA 19605. 215/926-1996. **Contact:** Joseph M. Benish, Director of Human Resources. **Description:** Produces elastic fabrics and coated papers. **Listed on:** London Stock Exchange.

DUPLEX PRODUCTS, INC.
P.O. Box 1561, York PA 17405. 717/792-2656. **Contact:** Rick Musser, Plant Manager. **Description:** Produces business forms and related products for commercial and industrial use. Maintains sales offices, manufacturing facilities, distribution centers, and warehouses throughout the United States and Puerto Rico. Product line includes continuous and unit-set business forms, office supplies, furniture, envelopes, tab cards, and other specialties. **Corporate headquarters location:** Sycamore IL. **Listed on:** American Stock Exchange.

FRANK H. FLEER CORPORATION
10th and Somerville Avenue, Philadelphia PA 19141. 215/455-2000. **Contact:** Mike Wolverton, Director of Personnel. **Description:** Produces a variety of chewing gum and trading cards.

FLEXSTEEL INDUSTRIES, INC.
LANCASTER DIVISION
P.O. Box 10908, Lancaster PA 17605. 717/392-4161. **Contact:** Lois Killian, Office Manager. **Description:** Manufactures and markets a broad line of quality upholstered furniture for the retail furniture market and the recreational vehicle field. Products include a variety of wood and upholstered chairs, rockers, sofas, sofa beds, loveseats, bucket seats, and convertible bedding units for use in office, home, vans, and recreational vehicles. The facility primarily produces upholstered living room furniture. **Common positions include:** Blue-Collar Worker Supervisor; Customer Service Representative; Purchasing Agent and Manager; Transportation/Traffic Specialist. **Educational backgrounds include:** Accounting; Business Administration; Marketing. **Benefits:** 401K; Dental Insurance; Disability Coverage; Employee Discounts; Life Insurance; Medical Insurance; Pension Plan; Tuition Assistance. **Corporate headquarters location:** Dubuque IA. **Operations at this facility include:** Divisional Headquarters; Manufacturing; Sales; Service.

FRANKLIN MINT
RR 1, Franklin Center PA 19091. 215/459-6000. **Contact:** Human Resources Department. **Description:** Manufactures jewelry/precious metals.

M. GRUMBACHER, INC.
30 Englehard Drive, Cranbury NJ 08512. 609/655-8282. **Contact:** Dennis Richardson, Director/Human Resources. **Description:** A manufacturer of artists' supplies.

KIWI BRANDS INC.
447 Old Swede Road, Douglasville PA 19518-1239. 215/385-3041. **Contact:** Philip R. Metzler, Human Resources Director. **Description:** Produces a wide range of nationally-recognized shoe care products and other household specialty chemical products.

C.F. MARTIN & CO., INC.
510 Sycamore Street, Nazareth PA 18064. 215/759-2837. **Contact:** Debbie Karlowitch, Personnel Manager. **Description:** Produces a line of world-recognized acoustic guitars, guitar strings, and is engaged in the processing of selected hardwoods.

PM COMPANY
9800 Bustleton Avenue, Philadelphia PA 19115. 215/673-4500. **Contact:** Greg Olson, Director of Personnel. **Description:** Manufactures specialized consumable products for use in office, packaging, and communications. **Common positions include:** Accountant/Auditor; Administrator; Blue-Collar Worker Supervisor; Chemical Engineer; Chemist; Computer Programmer; Credit Manager; Customer Service Representative; Department Manager; Electrical/Electronic Engineer; General Manager; Manufacturer's/Wholesaler's Sales Rep.; Marketing Specialist; Mechanical Engineer; Operations/Production Manager; Personnel/Labor Relations Specialist; Quality Control Supervisor; Systems Analyst. **Educational backgrounds include:** Accounting; Business Administration; Chemistry; Computer Science; Engineering; Finance; Marketing. **Benefits:** 401K; Daycare Assistance; Dental Insurance; Disability Coverage; Employee Discounts; Life Insurance; Medical Insurance; Pension Plan; Tuition Assistance. **Special Programs:** Internships; Training Programs. **Other U.S. locations:** CA; CO; IN; OH. **Operations at this facility include:** Administration; Manufacturing; Research and Development; Sales; Service.

PEIRCE-PHELPS, INC.
2000 North 59th Street, Philadelphia PA 19131. 215/879-7000. **Contact:** Personnel. **Description:** A distributor of a variety of electrical appliances, including washers, dryers, and air conditioners.

THE PFALZGRAFF COMPANY
140 East Market Street, York PA 17401. 717/848-5500. **Contact:** Mr. William Scott, Vice President of Corporate Human Resources. **Description:** A stoneware and dinnerware manufacturer, who also produces a line of table top accessories. **Corporate headquarters location:** This Location.

PLAYTEX FAMILY PRODUCTS CORPORATION
P.O. Box 7016, Dover DE 19903-1516. 302/674-6000. **Contact:** Human Resources Department. **Description:** Manufacturing and distribution site of the well-known national family products company. **Common positions include:** Accountant/Auditor; Administrator; Blue-Collar Worker Supervisor; Buyer; Chemist; Computer Programmer; Credit Manager; Customer Service Representative; Department Manager; Draftsperson; Electrical/Electronic Engineer; Financial Analyst; General Manager; Industrial Engineer; Mechanical Engineer; Operations/Production Manager; Personnel/Labor Relations Specialist; Purchasing Agent and Manager; Quality Control Supervisor; Systems Analyst; Transportation/Traffic Specialist. **Educational**

backgrounds include: Accounting; Business Administration; Chemistry; Computer Science; Engineering; Finance; Human Resources; Liberal Arts; Marketing. **Benefits:** Dental Insurance; Disability Coverage; Employee Discounts; Life Insurance; Medical Insurance; Pension Plan; Profit Sharing; Savings Plan; Tuition Assistance. **Special Programs:** Internships; Training Programs. **Corporate headquarters location:** Stamford CT. **Operations at this facility include:** Administration; Manufacturing; Research and Development; Service. **Number of employees nationwide:** 1,000.

THE SCORE BOARD
1951 Old Cuthbert Road, Cherry Hill NJ 08034. 609/354-9000. **Contact:** Human Resources. **Description:** The Score Board designs, markets, and distributes sports and entertainment-related products, primarily trading cards, games and memorabilia, for sale to television shopping networks, national retailers and the hobby market. **Number of employees at this location:** 228.

SIMKAR LIGHTING CO.
601 East Cayuga Street, Philadelphia PA 19120. 215/831-7700. **Contact:** Gene Christian, Vice President/Human Resources. **Description:** Manufactures fluorescent lighting fixtures. **Common positions include:** Accountant/Auditor; Customer Service Representative; Management Trainee; Manufacturer's/Wholesaler's Sales Rep.; Manufacturing Engineer. **Educational backgrounds include:** Engineering; Marketing. **Benefits:** Disability Coverage; Life Insurance; Medical Insurance; Savings Plan. **Corporate headquarters location:** This Location.

3M COMPANY
P.O. Box 119, Bristol PA 19007-0119. 215/945-2800. **Contact:** Thomas Main, Human Resources. **Description:** An international manufacturer of a vast line of consumer and industrial products, including adhesives, coatings, sealing compounds, film, magnetic recording tape, data recording tape, and many others. **Common positions include:** Buyer; Computer Programmer; Electrical/Electronic Engineer; Industrial Engineer. **Educational backgrounds include:** Business Administration; Computer Science; Engineering. **Benefits:** Dental Insurance; Disability Coverage; Employee Discounts; Life Insurance; Medical Insurance; Savings Plan; Tuition Assistance. **Corporate headquarters location:** St. Paul MN. **Listed on:** New York Stock Exchange.

VWR CORP.
1310 Goshen Parkway, West Chester PA 19380. 215/431-1700. **Contact:** Personnel Department. **Description:** Distributes laboratory equipment and supplies to high school and college science labs. **Number of employees nationwide:** 1,637.

WILTON ARMETALE
P.O. Box 600, Plumb & Square Streets, Mount Joy PA 17552. 717/653-4444. **Contact:** Kathleen Adams, Human Resource Director. **Description:** Produces Armetale (10-metal composite) giftware products.

YORKTOWNE
P.O. Box 231, 100 Redcoe Avenue, Red Lion PA 17356. 717/244-4011. **Contact:** Garth Hoffman, Vice President/Human Resources. **Description:** Produces kitchen cabinets and bathroom vanities. **Parent company:** Wickes Corporation (San Diego, CA).

Note: Because addresses and telephone numbers of smaller companies change rapidly, we recommend you contact each company and verify the information below before contacting employers. Mass mailings are not recommended.

Additional large employers: 500 +

WOODEN KITCHEN CABINETS

Aristokraft Inc.
P.O. Box 5, Keystone
St., Littlestown PA
17340. 717/359-4131.

HOUSEHOLD FURNITURE

Pennsylvania House
137 N 10th St.,
Lewisburg PA 17837-
1388. 717/523-1285.

BLINDS, SHADES, AND RELATED HARDWARE

Springs Window Fashions
P.O. Box 500,
Montgomery PA 17752.
717/547-6671.

RECORDS AND TAPES

Specialty Records Corp.
1400 E Lackawanna St.,
Olyphant PA 18447-
2151. 717/383-3291.

WEA Manufacturing Inc.
210 N Valley Ave.,
Olyphant PA 18447-
1516. 717/383-2471.

SPORTING GOODS

Prince Sports Group Inc.
1 Tennis Ct.,
Bordentown NJ 08505-
9630.

Additional medium sized employers: under 500

DURABLE GOODS WHOLESALE

JW Pepper & Son Inc.
2480 Industrial Blvd,
Paoli PA 19301-1612.
610/648-0500.

MCA Distributing Corporation
505 Wheatfield Ln,
Newtown PA 18940-
2800. 215/579-1121.

Mercuries and Associates
5000 W Tilghman St Ste
335, Allentown PA
18104-9121. 610/395-
2423.

Symbiotic & Co Inc.
637 W Dekalb Pike, Kng
Of Prussa PA 19406-
3055. 610/354-0108.

The John Wright Company
North Front St,
Wrightsville PA 17368.
717/252-3661.

TRC Electronics Inc.
961 Marcon Blvd,
Allentown PA 18103-
9521. 610/264-4995.

PRINTING AND WRITING PAPER WHOLESALE

Kurtz Bros Inc.
PO Box 392, Clearfield
PA 16830-0392.
814/765-6561.

STATIONERY AND OFFICE SUPPLIES WHOLESALE

Haverton Printing Co.
900 Sussex Blvd,
Broomall PA 19008-
4313. 610/691-5050.

WWF Paper Corporation
2 Bala Plz, Bala Cynwyd
PA 19004-1501.
610/667-9210.

INDUSTRIAL AND PERSONAL SERVICE PAPER WHOLESALE

Alling and Cory
485 Terminal Rd, Camp
Hill PA 17011-5725.
717/761-6064.

Garrett Buchanan Co.
7575 Brewster Ave,
Philadelphia PA 19153-
3206. 215/492-1776.

Inland Container
Humboldt Industrial Park,
Hazleton PA 18201.
717/384-3251.

M&C Specialties Co.
90 James Way,
Southampton PA 18966-
3816. 215/322-1600.

Springfield Paper Specialties
Limekiln Pike & Pa Tpk,
Dresher PA 19025.
215/643-2800.

PIECE GOODS AND OTHER DRY GOODS WHOLESALE

Springs Industries Inc.
Victoria Business Center,
Springfield PA 19064.
610/544-1009.

HARDWARE WHOLESALE

Safemasters
900 E 8th Ave, Kng Of
Prussa PA 19406-1324.
610/265-3200.

ELECTRICAL APPLIANCES, TELEVISIONS AND RADIOS WHOLESALE

Peirce-Phelps Inc.
2000 Block N 59th St,
Philadelphia PA 19131.
215/879-7000.

The Camera Shop Inc.
Court At King Of Prussia,
Kng Of Prussa PA
19406. 610/337-2020.

PHOTOGRAPHIC EQUIPMENT AND SUPPLIES WHOLESALE

Phillips & Jacobs Inc.
15 Twin Bride Dr,
Pennsauken NJ 08110.
609/488-7200.

OFFICE EQUIPMENT WHOLESALE

D&H Distributing Co.
2525 N 7th St,
Harrisburg PA 17110-
2511. 717/236-8001.

Executive Copy Inc.
Marlkress & Allison Rd,
Cherry Hill NJ 08003.
609/424-5898.

Paper Shop
27 Olney Ave, Cherry Hill
NJ 08003-1615.
609/424-0292.

FURNITURE WHOLESALE

Hanson Office Products
3184 Airport Rd,
Bethlehem PA 18017-
2140. 610/266-9455.

Phillips Office Products
1630 Manheim Pike,
Lancaster PA 17601-
6800. 717/560-9999.

Rishel Div Hon Industries
1201 W 3rd St,
Williamsport PA 17701-
5711. 717/326-3663.

Wallace Leisure Products
3100 & Jefferson Sts,
Philadelphia PA 19121-
3508. 215/232-9900.

HOMEFURNISHINGS WHOLESALE

Burlington House Area Rugs
One Tower Bridge,
Conshohocken PA
19428. 610/941-0440.

Durand International Inc.
Wade Blvd, Millville NJ
08332. 609/825-5620.

GTE Products Corporation
Jackson Rd, Wellsboro
PA 16901. 717/724-
8200.

PHOTOGRAPHIC EQUIPMENT

Hope Technologies
3701 Moreland Rd,
Willow Grove PA 19090-
2910. 215/657-5500.

IMR Limited
3903 Hartzdale Dr, Camp
Hill PA 17011-7829.
717/761-5412.

WATCHES, CLOCKS, AND PARTS

Gruen Marketing Corporation
150 Susquehanna Ave,
Pittston PA 18643-2668.
717/655-2111.

Harris & Mallow Division
651 New Hampshire
Ave, Lakewood NJ
08701-5452. 908/363-
9400.

SMH-US Inc.
941 Wheatland Ave,
Lancaster PA 17603-
3161. 717/394-7161.

MUSICAL INSTRUMENTS

Schulmerich Carillons
Carillon Hill, Sellersville
PA 18960. 215/257-
2771.

GAMES, TOYS AND CHILDREN'S VEHICLES

Matchbox Toys USA
6000 Midlantic Dr,
Mount Laurel NJ 08054-
1516.

Playskool
110 Pitney Rd, Lancaster
PA 17602-2616.
717/299-4301.

**SPORTING AND
ATHLETIC GOODS**

Fox Pool Corporation
3490 Board Rd, York PA
17402-9478. 717/764-8581.

Hegins Precision
RR 1 Box 13, Hegins PA
17938-9708. 717/682-3154.

**Penn Fishing Tackle
Manufacturing Co.**
3028 W Hunting Park
Ave, Philadelphia PA
19132-1121. 215/229-9415.

Prince Manufacturing
P O Box 20, Princeton NJ
08540. 609/896-2500.

**PENS AND MECHANICAL
PENCILS**

Dixon Wearever Inc.
Rte 61, Orwigsburg PA
17961. 717/366-1011.

**LEAD PENCILS,
CRAYONS AND
ARTIST'S MATERIALS**

Sargent Art Inc.
100 E Diamond Ave,
Hazleton PA 18201-5241. 717/454-3596.

MARKING DEVICES

**Graphic Controls
Corporation**
1 Carnegie Plz, Cherry
Hill NJ 08003-1020.
609/424-2200.

**CARBON PAPER AND
INKED RIBBONS**

Curtis Young Corporation
1050 Taylors Ln,
Riverton NJ 08077.
609/665-6650.

Curtis-Young Corporation
2550 Haddonfield Rd,
Pennsauken NJ 08110-1132. 609/665-6650.

Olivetti Splys Inc.
137 4th St H I A,
Middletown PA 17057-5004. 717/944-5551.

BROOMS AND BRUSHES

**Joseph Lieberman &
Sons Inc.**
1201 Jackson St,
Philadelphia PA 19148-2998. 215/336-3400.

Weiler Brush Company
One Wildwood Dr,
Cresco PA 18326.
717/595-7495.

**SIGNS AND
ADVERTISING
SPECIALTIES**

Joel Manufacturing
700 Reading Ave,
Hammonton NJ 08037.
609/567-1700.

BURIAL CASKETS

Casket Shells Inc.
First St, Archbald PA
18403. 717/876-5630.

Schuylkill Haven Casket
PO Box 179, Shuykl
Haven PA 17972-0179.
717/385-0296.

York Casket Co.
2880 Black Bridge Rd,
York PA 17402-9703.
717/854-9566.

Yorktowne Caskets
654 Lincoln St, York PA
17404-3317. 717/848-1341.

**LINOLEUM AND OTHER
HARD SURFACE FLOOR
COVERINGS**

Amitco
3131 Princeton Pike,
Trenton NJ 08648-2207.
609/896-3000.

**MANUFACTURING
INDUSTRIES**

Dimensions Inc.
641 McKnight St,
Reading PA 19601-2499.
610/372-8491.

Identicard Systems
630 E Oregon Rd,
Lancaster PA 17601.
717/569-5797.

J Kinderman & Sons
22 Jackson St,
Philadelphia PA 19148-3413. 215/271-7600.

**HOUSEHOLD AUDIO
AND VIDEO EQUIPMENT**

Lucas Hazleton Inc.
100 E Diamond Ave,
Hazleton PA 18201-5241. 717/455-7721.

**Sanyo Audio
Manufacturing USA
Corporation**
Fisher Pk, Milroy PA
17063. 717/667-2101.

RESIDENTIAL ELECTRIC LIGHTING FIXTURES

Clover Lamp Company
First Ave, Royersford PA
19468. 610/948-8600.

Del-Val Manufacturing Company
3000 Cabot Blvd W,
Langhorne PA 19047-
1800. 215/750-9400.

Greenspan Acquisitions
2401 Pennsylvania Ave
Apt 15b2, Philadelphia
PA 19130-3049.
215/289-2244.

Gross Metal Products
221-249 W Glenwood
Ave, Philadelphia PA
19140. 215/739-4411.

Philadelphia Glass Bending Co Inc.
2520 Morris St,
Philadelphia PA 19145-
1716. 215/336-3000.

Sea Gull Lighting Prdts
Wharton & 25th Sts,
Philadelphia PA 19146.
215/468-7254.

Wood River Industries
301 W Washington St,
Riverside NJ 08075-
4143. 609/764-0500.

HOUSEHOLD REFRIDERATORS AND HOME FREEZERS

Penn Refrigeration Service Co.
61-69 Woodbury St,
Wilkes Barre PA 18702.
717/825-5666.

Victory Refrigeration
Woodcraft & Burntmill
Rds, Cherry Hill NJ
08003. 609/428-4200.

ELECTRIC HOUSEWARES AND FANS

Energy Convertors Inc.
P O Box 10A, Dallas PA
18612-0010. 717/675-
5266.

Waring Products Company
1 Crystal Dr, Mc
Connellsbg PA 17233-
1208. 717/485-4871.

Wyle Laboratories
6995 Airport Highway
Ln, Merchantville NJ
08109-4384. 609/665-
6810.

HOUSEHOLD VACUUM CLEANERS

Shop Vac Corporation
2323 Reach Rd,
Williamsport PA 17701-
5582. 717/326-0502.

CUTLERY

True Temper Corporation
PO Box 8859, Camp Hill
PA 17001-8859.
717/737-1500.

LUGGAGE

York Luggage
PO Box 38, Lambertville
NJ 08530-0038.
609/397-2044.

SOAP AND OTHER DETERGENTS

Dial Corporation
1414 Radcliffe St, Bristol
PA 19007-5423.
215/788-9215.

SPECIALTY CLEANING AND POLISHING PREPARATIONS

City Cleaning Company
439 N 13th St,
Philadelphia PA 19123-
3626. 215/925-3720.

West Chemical Products
1000 Herrontown Rd,
Princeton NJ 08540-
7716. 609/921-0501.

PERFUMES, COSMETICS AND OTHER TOILET PREPARATIONS

Accupac Inc.
1501 Indl Blvd, Mainland
PA 19451. 215/256-
4151.

Conair Corporation
150 Milford Rd,
Hightstown NJ 08520-
9730. 908/287-4800.

Schoeneman Corporation
Rt 61 N, Pottsville PA
17901. 717/429-1800.

PAINTS, VARNISHES AND LACQUERS

MA Bruder & Sons Inc.
52nd St & Grays Ave,
Philadelphia PA 19143.
215/727-5104.

Penn Color Inc.
400 Old Dublin Pike,
Doylestown PA 18901-
2399. 215/345-6550.

Silberline Manufacturing Co Inc.
R D 2 Hometown,
Tamaqua PA 18252.
717/668-6050.

United Gilsonite Laboratories
1396 Jefferson Ave, Scranton PA 18509-2415. 717/344-1202.

WOOD HOUSEHOLD FURNITURE, EXCEPT UPHOLSTERED

DMI Furniture Inc.
606 York St, Gettysburg PA 17325-2011. 717/334-6231.

Donald Dean & Sons
99 Grow Ave, Montrose PA 18801-1139. 717/278-1179.

G Buehler & Co Inc.
PO Box 1068, Allentown PA 18105-1068. 610/437-4677.

Graco Metal Products
Main St, Elverson PA 19520. 610/286-0150.

SJ Bailey & Sons Inc.
PO Box 239, Clarks Summit PA 18411-0239. 717/586-1811.

SJ Bailey & Sons Inc.
445 Erie St, Honesdale PA 18431-1011. 717/253-0770.

Yerger Bros Inc.
520 Front St, Lititz PA 17543-1708. 717/626-2145.

UPHOLSTERED WOOD HOUSEHOLD FURNITURE

Comfort Designs Inc.
263 Schuyler Ave, Wilkes Barre PA 18704-3321. 717/288-6657.

Kinder Furniture & Bedding
412 Oak St, Denver PA 17517-1451. 215/267-2846.

Lambert Furniture Corporation
1301 New York Ave, Trenton NJ 08638-3311. 609/394-7000.

METAL HOUSEHOLD FURNITURE

Craftmatic Industries
2500 Interplex Dr, Fstrvl Trvose PA 19053. 215/639-1310.

Cramco Inc.
2200 E Ann St, Philadelphia PA 19134-4199. 215/427-9500.

Zenith Products Corporation
200 Commerce Dr, Aston PA 19014-3203. 610/485-4700.

HOUSEHOLD FURNITURE

Grosfillex Inc.
Old W Penn Ave, Robesonia PA 19551. 610/693-5835.

Rich Maid Kabinetry
633 W Lincoln Ave, Myerstown PA 17067-2332. 717/866-2112.

For more information on career opportunities in consumer manufacturing and wholesaling:

Associations

ASSOCIATION FOR MANUFACTURING TECHNOLOGY
7901 Westpark Drive, McLean VA 22102. 703/893-2900.

ASSOCIATION OF HOME APPLIANCE MANUFACTURERS
20 North Wacker Drive, Chicago IL 60606. 312/984-5800.

NATIONAL ASSOCIATION OF MANUFACTURERS
1331 Pennsylvania Avenue, NW, Suite 1500, Washington DC 20004. 202/637-3000.

NATIONAL HOUSEWARES MANUFACTURERS ASSOCIATION
6400 Schafer Court, Suite 650, Rosemont IL 60018. 708/292-4200.

SOAP AND DETERGENT ASSOCIATION
475 Park Avenue South, 27th Floor, New York NY 10016. 212/725-1262.

Directories

**APPLIANCE MANUFACTURER
ANNUAL DIRECTORY**
Appliance Manufacturer, 5900 Harper
Road, Suite 105, Solon OH 44139.
216/349-3060.

**HOUSEHOLD AND PERSONAL
PRODUCTS INDUSTRY BUYERS
GUIDE**
Rodman Publishing Group, 17 South
Franklin Turnpike, Ramsey NJ 07446.
201/825-2552.

**DIRECTORY OF TEXAS
MANUFACTURERS**
University of Texas at Austin, Bureau
of Business Research, Box 7459,
Austin TX 78713-7459. 512/471-
1616.

TEXAS MANUFACTURERS REGISTER
Manufacturer's News, Inc., 1633
Central Street, Evanston IL 60201.
708/864-7000.

Magazines

APPLIANCE
1110 Jorie Boulevard, Oak Brook IL
60522-9019. 708/990-3484.

COSMETICS INSIDERS REPORT
Advanstar Communications, 7500 Old
Oak Boulevard, Cleveland OH 44130.
216/243-8100.

MANUFACTURING AND WHOLESALING: MISCELLANEOUS INDUSTRIAL

In the machinery manufacturing segment, many of the biggest company names will continue to disappear due to mergers and buy outs. While hundreds of U.S. companies still make machine tools, materials-handling equipment, and compressors for American factories, the fastest-growing machinery markets are now overseas. This means that U.S. firms will have to build an overseas presence just to survive. In fact, foreign orders for a number of American-made tools remain strong.

Although mergers are often followed by layoffs, workers who survive these cuts should be better positioned for the long-term. Many manufacturers are giving workers a much greater degree of across-the-board involvement, with team-based product management allowing individual workers to gain training in a number of different job functions.

ADAGE, INC.
615 Willowbrook Lane, West Chester PA 19382. 215/430-3900. **Contact:** Human Resources. **Description:** A diversified manufacturer.

ALCO STANDARD CORPORATION
P.O. Box 834, Valley Forge PA 19482. 215/296-8000. **Contact:** Betsy Barrett, Personnel Manager. **Description:** A diversified corporation engaged in distribution and manufacturing. Company distributes paper, steel, health-science products, wine and liquor, containers, gifts and glassware, auto and truck parts; manufactures food service equipment, chemicals, rubber and plastic products, and consumer products; also engaged in investment casting and metals processing; and develops extract natural resources. **Corporate headquarters location:** This Location.

ALMO CORPORATION
9815 Roosevelt Boulevard, Philadelphia PA 19114. 215/698-4000. **Contact:** Ms. Terry Vittorelli, Personnel Director. **Description:** A manufacturer of a wide variety of industrial parts, as well as a range of consumer items.

AMERICAN BEARING AND POWER TRANSMISSION
12285 McNulty Road, Suite 101, Philadelphia PA 19154. 215/332-2900. **Contact:** Personnel Director. **Description:** A distributor of bearings and power transmission equipment.

AMERICAN METER COMPANY
300 Welsh Road, Building 1, Horsham PA 19044. 215/830-1800. **Contact:** Kelsey Brown, Director of Human Resources. **Description:** Manufacturers of vapor gas measurement products.

AMERICAN PACKAGING CORPORATION

2900 Grant Avenue, Philadelphia PA 19114. 215/698-4800. **Contact:** Mary McKeon, Director, Human Resources. **Description:** Manufactures specialty bags and laminated roll stock. **Common positions include:** Accountant/Auditor; Blue-Collar Worker Supervisor; Buyer; Chemical Engineer; Chemist; Commercial Artist; Computer Programmer; Customer Service Representative; Electrical/Electronic Engineer; General Manager; Manufacturer's/Wholesaler's Sales Rep.; Mechanical Engineer; Operations/Production Manager; Personnel/Labor Relations Specialist; Purchasing Agent and Manager; Quality Control Supervisor. **Educational backgrounds include:** Accounting; Art/Design; Business Administration; Chemistry; Computer Science; Engineering; Marketing. **Benefits:** Dental Insurance; Disability Coverage; Life Insurance; Medical Insurance; Pension Plan; Profit Sharing; Savings Plan; Tuition Assistance.

AMETEK, INC.

Station Square, Paoli PA 19301. 215/647-2121. **Contact:** Human Resources. **Description:** Designs, develops, and manufactures a broad range of industrial and scientific products and equipment. Operates in three business segments: Electro-Mechanical, Precision Instruments, and Industrial Materials. **Corporate headquarters location:** This Location. **Listed on:** New York Stock Exchange.

AQUA-CHEM, INC.
CLEAVER-BROOKS DIVISION

1500 Lehman Street, Lebanon PA 17046. 717/274-7711. **Contact:** Bruce Lovett, Director of Human Resources. **Description:** Produces industrial and commercial boilers, fire tube, and related design services. Full fabrication and manufacturing facilities including facilities for the production of burners, controls, and pressure vessels. International. **Corporate headquarters location:** Milwaukee WI.

ARMSTRONG WORLD INDUSTRIES, INC.

P.O. Box 3001, Lancaster PA 17604. 717/397-0611. **Contact:** Bing G. Spitler, Manager/Employment. **Description:** Armstrong World Industries is a manufacturer of flooring, ceiling systems, furniture, and industrial specialty products. Armstrong products are manufactured and marketed around the world. **Common positions include:** Accountant/Auditor; Chemical Engineer; Chemist; Computer Systems Analyst; Electrical/ Electronic Engineer; Industrial Engineer; Manufacturer's/Wholesaler's Sales Rep.; Mechanical Engineer. **Educational backgrounds include:** Accounting; Business Administration; Communications; Computer Science; Engineering; Liberal Arts; Marketing. **Benefits:** Dental Insurance; Disability Coverage; Employee Discounts; Life Insurance; Medical Insurance; Pension Plan; Profit Sharing; Savings Plan; Tuition Assistance. **Special Programs:** Training Programs. **Corporate headquarters location:** This Location. **Operations at this facility include:** Administration; Divisional Headquarters; Manufacturing; Research and Development; Sales; Service. **Listed on:** New York Stock Exchange. **Annual Revenues:** $2,500,000,000. **Number of employees nationwide:** 20,000. **Hires/Layoffs in 1993 (Nationwide):** 60 hires. **Projected hires for the next 12 months (Nationwide):** 60 hires.

AUTOTOTE SYSTEMS, INC.

100 Bellevue Road, P.O. Box 6009, Newark DE 19714. 302/737-4300. **Contact:** John Stevens, Director/Personnel. **Description:** Engaged in the manufacture and lease of totalisator equipment for the pari-mutuel wagering industry.

AVERY DENNISION SOABAR
7722 Dungan Road, Philadelphia PA 19111. 215/725-4700. **Contact:** Janis Von Culin, Director of Public Relations. **Description:** Manufactures marking machines used by a wide range of industrial customers, as well as tickets, tags, tapes, and related products. **Corporate headquarters location:** This Location.

BALLY ENGINEERED STRUCTURES, INC.
20 North Front Street, Bally PA 19503. 215/845-2311. **Contact:** Donna Fritzinger, Human Resources. **Description:** Manufactures walk-in coolers, freezers, and refrigerated warehouses for commercial/industrial use, along with refrigeration equipment and replacement parts for all products. Also manufactures non-refrigerated modular structures. **Common positions include:** Mechanical Engineer; Quality Control Supervisor; Systems Analyst. **Educational backgrounds include:** Accounting; Business Administration; Computer Science; Engineering. **Special Programs:** Training Programs. **Corporate headquarters location:** This Location. **Operations at this facility include:** Administration; Manufacturing.

BARRETT, HAENTJENS & COMPANY
225 North Cedar Street, Hazleton PA 18201. 717/455-7711. **Contact:** Ernest M. Stauffer, Personnel Manager. **Description:** Manufactures a wide range of centrifugal pumps. **Common positions include:** Draftsperson; Mechanical Engineer. **Educational backgrounds include:** Engineering. **Benefits:** Disability Coverage; Life Insurance; Medical Insurance; Pension Plan; Profit Sharing. **Special Programs:** Training Programs. **Corporate headquarters location:** This Location. **Operations at this facility include:** Administration; Manufacturing; Research and Development; Sales; Service.

THE BETHLEHEM CORPORATION
25th and Lennox Streets, P.O. Box 348, Easton PA 18042. 215/258-7111. **Contact:** Peggy E. Seibel, Benefits Administrator. **Description:** Engaged in the development, manufacture, and sale of equipment for environmental, energy, and continuous processing applications. Also provides subcontracting services for industrial products made to customer's specifications. Typical products include multiple-hearth furnaces, filter presses, industrial dryers, flow tubes, and transfer cars. **Common positions include:** Accountant/Auditor; Blue-Collar Worker Supervisor; Buyer; Computer Programmer; Purchasing Agent and Manager; Quality Control Supervisor. **Educational backgrounds include:** Accounting; Chemistry; Engineering. **Benefits:** Life Insurance; Medical Insurance; Pension Plan. **Operations at this facility include:** Administration; Manufacturing; Research and Development; Sales. **Listed on:** American Stock Exchange.

BRADFORD WHITE CORPORATION
Spring House Corporate Center, 323 Norristown Road, Suite 200, Ambler PA 19002-2758. 215/641-9400. **Contact:** Michael Marcellino, Personnel Manager. **Description:** Engaged in the manufacturing and marketing of water heaters. **Common positions include:** Accountant/Auditor; Administrator; Computer Programmer; Credit Manager; Customer Service Representative. **Educational backgrounds include:** Accounting; Business Administration; Engineering; Mathematics. **Benefits:** Dental Insurance; Disability Coverage; Employee Discounts; Life Insurance; Medical Insurance; Pension Plan; Savings Plan; Tuition Assistance. **Operations at this facility include:** Regional Headquarters.

BURNHAM CORPORATION
P.O. Box 3079, Lancaster PA 17604. 717/397-4701. **Contact:** K.H. Beinhauer, Personnel Manager. **Description:** Manufactures boilers, boiler/burner systems, and

related components. **Common positions include:** Accountant/Auditor; Advertising Clerk; Buyer; Computer Programmer; Department Manager; Draftsperson; General Manager; Industrial Engineer; Manufacturer's/Wholesaler's Sales Rep.; Marketing Specialist; Mechanical Engineer; Personnel/Labor Relations Specialist; Purchasing Agent and Manager; Quality Control Supervisor; Transportation/Traffic Specialist. **Educational backgrounds include:** Accounting; Business Administration; Computer Science; Economics; Engineering; Finance; Marketing; Mathematics. **Benefits:** Disability Coverage; Employee Discounts; Life Insurance; Medical Insurance; Pension Plan; Savings Plan; Tuition Assistance. **Corporate headquarters location:** This Location. **Operations at this facility include:** Administration; Divisional Headquarters; Manufacturing; Research and Development; Sales.

CSS INDUSTRIES, INC.
1845 Walnut St., Philadelphia PA 19103. 215/569-9900. **Contact:** Personnel Department. **Description:** Manufactures and distributes business forms and supplies and specialty metal containers. **Parent company:** Philadelphia Industries, Inc. **Number of employees nationwide:** 11,650.

CERTAINTEED CORPORATION
750 East Swedesword Road, Valley Forge PA 19482. 215/341-7000. **Contact:** Human Resources. **Description:** Engaged in diversified manufacturing, distribution, and sales operations in the United States. Principal products are used in residential, commercial, and industrial construction; repair and remodeling; fiberglass reinforcement applications; water and sewer systems; and other underground utility systems. Products include roofing, acoustical insulation, fiberglass thermal insulation, air handling products, glass fiber, vinyl siding, polyvinyl chloride, and asbestos-cement piping. This facility manufactures building materials, fiberglass products, and piping products. **Corporate headquarters location:** This Location.

CHARTER POWER SYSTEMS
3043 Walton Road, Plymouth Meeting PA 19462. 215/828-9000. **Contact:** Human Resources. **Description:** Produces batteries and power systems.

CONGOLEUM CORPORATION
MARCUS HOOK PLANT
Ridge Road and Yates Avenue, Marcus Hook PA 19061. 215/485-8800. **Contact:** Sonny Steele, Human Resources Manager. **Description:** One of the nation's largest manufacturers of resilient sheet vinyl flooring. **Common positions include:** Accountant/Auditor; Blue-Collar Worker Supervisor; Chemical Engineer; Chemist; Department Manager; Draftsperson; Electrical/Electronic Engineer; Industrial Engineer; Mechanical Engineer; Operations/Production Manager; Personnel/Labor Relations Specialist; Quality Control Supervisor. **Educational backgrounds include:** Accounting; Business Administration; Chemistry; Computer Science; Engineering; Finance; Liberal Arts. **Benefits:** 401K; Disability Coverage; Life Insurance; Medical Insurance; Pension Plan; Tuition Assistance. **Corporate headquarters location:** Mercerville NJ. **Operations at this facility include:** Administration; Manufacturing.

CONSARC CORPORATION
100 Indel Avenue, P.O. Box 156, Rancocas NJ 08073-0156. 609/267-8000. **Contact:** Mrs. Pat Vogel, Executive Administrator. **Description:** Consarc sells, designs and manufactures industrial melting furnaces. **Common positions include:** Buyer; Computer Programmer; Draftsperson; Electrical/Electronic Engineer; Mechanical Engineer; Operations/Production Manager. **Educational backgrounds include:** Computer Science; Engineering. **Benefits:** Disability Coverage; Life Insurance; Medical Insurance;

Profit Sharing; Tuition Assistance. **Corporate headquarters location:** This Location. **Parent company:** Inducto Therm Industries. **Operations at this facility include:** Administration.

DU PONT COMPANY
1007 Market Street, Wilmington DE 19898. 302/772-1000. **Contact:** Human Resources: Professional. **Description:** For job listings, call 302/773-6746. A corporation whose diverse activities include the manufacture of biomedical products; the manufacture of industrial and consumer products, such as photographic, data-recording, and video devices; the production of man-made fibre products, with applications in a variety of consumer and commercial industries; the production of polymer products, such as plastic resins, elastomers and films; the production of agricultural and industrial chemicals, such as herbicides and insecticides, and pigments, fluorochemicals, petroleum additives and mineral acids; the exploration for and production of crude oil and natural gas, internationally; the refining, marketing and downstream transportation of petroleum; and the mining and distribution of steam and metallurgical coals, exported mainly to overseas steel producers. **Corporate headquarters location:** This Location.

ECC INTERNATIONAL, INC.
175 Strafford Avenue, Wayne PA 19087. 215/687-2600. **Contact:** Human Resources. **Description:** Produces training simulators for the armed forces. Also manufactures Snapple beverage dispensers.

EMR PHOTOELECTRIC/SCHLUMBERGER
P.O. Box 44, Princeton NJ 08542-0044. 609/799-1000. **Contact:** Rebecca Millard, Personnel Manager. **Description:** A research, development, and manufacturing facility for Schlumberger, Ltd.; engaged in the engineering and manufacturing of critical, high-reliability transducers and transducer systems; nuclear sources and detectors for oilfield services; and sensors/transducers for high-value measurement and control. **Common positions include:** Chemical Engineer; Electrical/Electronic Engineer; Mechanical Engineer; Physicist/Astronomer. **Educational backgrounds include:** Engineering; Physics. **Benefits:** Dental Insurance; Disability Coverage; Life Insurance; Medical Insurance; Pension Plan; Profit Sharing; Savings Plan; Stock Option; Tuition Assistance. **Corporate headquarters location:** This Location. **Parent company:** Schlumberger Limited. **Operations at this facility include:** Administration; Divisional Headquarters; Manufacturing; Research and Development. **Listed on:** New York Stock Exchange. **Number of employees at this location:** 83.

EAST PENN MANUFACTURING COMPANY
Deka Road, Lyon Station PA 19536. 215/682-6361. **Contact:** Alan Hohl, Personnel Director. **Description:** Produces automotive and industrial batteries. **Common positions include:** Accountant/Auditor; Administrator; Advertising Clerk; Blue-Collar Worker Supervisor; Buyer; Chemical Engineer; Chemist; Computer Programmer; Draftsperson; Electrical/Electronic Engineer; Industrial Designer; Industrial Engineer; Marketing Specialist; Mechanical Engineer; Operations/Production Manager; Purchasing Agent and Manager; Quality Control Supervisor; Sales Associate; Transportation/Traffic Specialist. **Educational backgrounds include:** Accounting; Business Administration; Chemistry; Computer Science; Engineering; Marketing. **Benefits:** Dental Insurance; Disability Coverage; Employee Discounts; Life Insurance; Medical Insurance; Pension Plan; Profit Sharing; Savings Plan; Tuition Assistance. **Corporate headquarters location:** This Location. **Operations at this facility include:** Administration; Manufacturing; Research and Development; Sales; Service.

EFCO PEERLESS, INC.
P.O. Box 388, Boyertown PA 19512. 215/367-2153. **Contact:** Richard Smith, President. **Description:** Produces soil pipe and related fittings.

ENGINE DISTRIBUTORS
332 South 17th Street, Camden NJ 08105. 609/365-8631. **Contact:** Glen Cummins, Jr., Vice President. **Description:** Distributors for industrial engines. **Common positions include:** Branch Manager; General Manager; Manufacturer's/Wholesaler's Sales Rep.; Operations/ Production Manager.

EXIDE CORPORATION
645 Penn Street, Reading PA 19601. 215/378-0500. **Contact:** Employee Relations Manager. **Description:** Produces lead acid storage batteries for a wide variety of uses, including consumer, industrial, and automotive use. **Common positions include:** Industrial Engineer; Operations/Production Manager; Production Manager; Quality Control Supervisor. **Educational backgrounds include:** Business Administration; Communications; Engineering; Mathematics. **Benefits:** Dental Insurance; Disability Coverage; Life Insurance; Medical Insurance; Profit Sharing; Savings Plan; Tuition Assistance. **Corporate headquarters location:** Horsham PA. **Operations at this facility include:** Manufacturing.

FIBRE METAL PRODUCTS COMPANY
Route 1 & Brinton Lake Road, Concordville PA 19331. 215/459-5300. **Contact:** Sally Hamilton, Personnel Director. **Description:** Produces welding and head safety supplies.

FIFTH DIMENSION INC.
801 New York Avenue, Trenton NJ 08638-3982. 609/393-8350. **Contact:** Elaine H. Cain, Vice-President, Administration. **Description:** Manufacturer of mercury switches and relays; and glass-to-metal seals and slip rings. **Common positions include:** Administrator; Buyer; Chemical Engineer; Draftsperson; Mechanical Engineer; Operations/Production Manager; Quality Control Supervisor. **Educational backgrounds include:** Business Administration; Engineering. **Benefits:** Disability Coverage; Life Insurance; Medical Insurance; Profit Sharing; Savings Plan; Tuition Assistance. **Corporate headquarters location:** This Location. **Operations at this facility include:** Manufacturing; Research and Development. **Listed on:** NASDAQ. **Number of employees at this location:** 50.

FLEXITALLIC GASKET COMPANY
P.O. Box 286, Pennsauken NJ 08110. 609/486-4400. **Contact:** Ray Parker, Personnel. **Description:** Manufactures spiral gaskets.

GASBOY INTERNATIONAL, INC.
P.O. Box 309, Lansdale PA 19446. 215/855-4631. **Contact:** Eleanor Harding, Human Resources Manager. **Description:** Develops, manufactures, and markets petroleum dispensing pumps and computer controlled management systems and related components. Products are sold for private, commercial, industrial, and governmental use. **Common positions include:** Accountant/Auditor; Advertising Clerk; Blue-Collar Worker Supervisor; Branch Manager; Buyer; Computer Programmer; Customer Service Representative; Department Manager; Draftsperson; Electrical/Electronic Engineer; General Manager; Industrial Engineer; Management Trainee; Manufacturer's/Wholesaler's Sales Rep.; Marketing Specialist; Mechanical Engineer; Operations/Production Manager; Personnel/Labor Relations Specialist; Purchasing Agent and Manager; Quality Control Supervisor; Software Engineer; Systems Analyst; Technical Writer/Editor. **Educational backgrounds include:** Accounting; Business

Administration; Computer Science; Engineering; Liberal Arts. **Benefits:** Disability Coverage; Employee Discounts; Life Insurance; Medical Insurance; Pension Plan; Tuition Assistance. **Corporate headquarters location:** This Location. **Parent company:** Tokheim, Inc. **Operations at this facility include:** Manufacturing; Research and Development; Sales; Service.

GEORGIA-PACIFIC GYPSUM/DELAWARE
P.O. Box 310, Wilmington DE 19899. 302/658-7221. **Contact:** Robert Lindsey, Jr., Personnel. **Description:** A subsidiary operation of Georgia-Pacific Corporation, the large forest products and building products company. This plant is engaged in the manufacturing and sale of gypsum products including Wallboard and Gypcrete. **Common positions include:** Accountant/Auditor; Buyer; Computer Operator; Department Manager; Dispatcher; Electrical/Electronic Engineer; Electrician; Financial Manager; Industrial Engineer; Inspector/Tester/Grader; Mechanical Engineer; Personnel/Labor Relations Specialist. **Educational backgrounds include:** Accounting; Business Administration; Engineering; Finance; Liberal Arts; Marketing. **Benefits:** Dental Insurance; Disability Coverage; Employee Discounts; Life Insurance; Medical Insurance; Pension Plan; Savings Plan; Tuition Assistance. **Corporate headquarters location:** Atlanta GA. **Operations at this facility include:** Manufacturing; Sales. **Listed on:** New York Stock Exchange. **Number of employees at this location:** 120.

GILES & RANSOME, INC.
EARTH MOVING DIVISION
2975 Galloway Road, Bensalem PA 19020. 215/639-4300. **Contact:** Richard Smith, Manager of Personnel. **Description:** A regional distributor of Caterpillar heavy construction and industrial equipment including diesel engines and generators, construction vehicles, and material handling equipment. **Common positions include:** Accountant/Auditor; Administrator; Blue-Collar Worker Supervisor; Branch Manager; Credit Manager; Manufacturer's/Wholesaler's Sales Rep.; Mechanic; Purchasing Agent and Manager. **Educational backgrounds include:** Accounting; Business Administration; Engineering. **Benefits:** Dental Insurance; Disability Coverage; Life Insurance; Medical Insurance; Savings Plan; Tuition Assistance. **Corporate headquarters location:** This Location. **Operations at this facility include:** Administration; Regional Headquarters; Sales; Service.

HERMAN GOLDNER COMPANY
7777 Brewster Avenue, Philadelphia PA 19153. 215/365-5400. **Contact:** Michael Bannon, Sales Manager. **Description:** A distributor of plumbing parts.

W.L. GORE & ASSOCIATES, INC.
551 Paper Mill Road, P.O. Box 9206, Newark DE 19714-9206. **Contact:** Barbara Pizzala, Human Resources. **Description:** Manufactures high-technology electronic, industrial, and medical products, as well as specialty fabric products (Gore Tex R fabrics). **Common positions include:** Attorney; Chemical Engineer; Chemist; Electrical/Electronic Engineer; Mechanical Engineer; Metallurgical Engineer; Sales Engineer. **Educational backgrounds include:** Chemistry; Engineering. **Benefits:** Dental Insurance; Disability Coverage; Employee Discounts; Fitness Program; Life Insurance; Medical Insurance; Profit Sharing. **Special Programs:** Internships. **Corporate headquarters location:** This Location. **Operations at this facility include:** Manufacturing; Research and Development; Sales; Service. **Number of employees nationwide:** 5,800.

HAROWE SERVO CONTROLS, INC.
110 Westtown Road, P.O. Box 547, West Chester PA 19382. 215/692-2700.
Contact: Mary Powell, Assistant to the President. **Description:** Manufactures servo rotary controls and related systems.

HARSCO
P.O. Box 8316, Camp Hill PA 17001. 717/763-5060. **Contact:** Human Resources.
Description: Manufactures valve and pipe fittings.

IMO INDUSTRIES INC.
DELAVAL TURBINE DIVISION
P.O. Box 8788, Trenton NJ 08650-0788. 609/890-5324. **Contact:** Cheryl Pedersen, Human Resources Administrator. **Description:** Manufactures steam turbines and compressors. **Common positions include:** Accountant/Auditor; Buyer; Computer Programmer; Credit Manager; Customer Service Representative; Draftsperson; Financial Analyst; General Manager; Industrial Engineer; Mechanical Engineer; Operations/Production Manager; Personnel/Labor Relations Specialist; Purchasing Agent and Manager; Quality Control Supervisor; Systems Analyst; Technical Writer/Editor; Transportation/Traffic Specialist. **Educational backgrounds include:** Accounting; Business Administration; Engineering; Finance. **Benefits:** 401K; Dental Insurance; Disability Coverage; Life Insurance; Medical Insurance; Pension Plan; Tuition Assistance. **Operations at this facility include:** Divisional Headquarters; Manufacturing; Research and Development; Sales; Service.

INTELLIGENT ELECTRONICS, INC.
411 Eagleview Boulevard, Exton PA 19341. 215/458-5500. **Contact:** Human Resources. **Description:** Intelligent Electronics, Inc., is a leading wholesale distributor of office productivity solutions, including personal computers and related equipment. It sells primarily to small and medium-sized businesses through a network that consisted of over 1,700 franchised and affiliated customers as of January 30, 1993. **Number of employees at this location:** 2,956.

K-TRON INTERNATIONAL INCORPORATED
Routes 55 and 553, Pitman NJ 08071. 609/589-0500. **Contact:** Human Resources.
Description: Produces industrial feeders and blenders.

KBA-MOTTER CORPORATION
3900 East Market Street, P.O. Box 1562, York PA 17405. 717/755-1071. **Contact:** Janey P. Potter, Personnel Administrator. **Description:** Produces high-speed, web-fed rotogravure presses and related equipment. **Common positions include:** Accountant/Auditor; Buyer; Computer Programmer; Draftsperson; Electrical/Electronic Engineer; Machinist; Mechanical Engineer; Operations/Production Manager; Personnel/Labor Relations Specialist; Quality Control Supervisor. **Educational backgrounds include:** Accounting; Business Administration; Computer Science; Engineering; Mathematics. **Benefits:** Dental Insurance; Disability Coverage; Life Insurance; Medical Insurance; Pension Plan; Savings Plan; Tuition Assistance. **Corporate headquarters location:** This Location. **Parent company:** Koening & Bauer-Albert. **Operations at this facility include:** Administration; Divisional Headquarters; Manufacturing; Research and Development; Sales; Service. **Number of employees at this location:** 135.

DAVID B. LILLY COMPANY, INC.
P.O. Box 10527, Wilmington DE 19850-0527. 302/328-6675. **Contact:** John Judway, Controller. **Description:** A manufacturer specializing in government contract work.

MARKEL CORPORATION
School Lane, P.O. Box 752, Norristown PA 19404. 215/272-8960. **Contact:** Mr. William Hackenyos, Personnel Manager. **Description:** Produces sleevings, and wire and cable products.

MET-PRO CORPORATION
160 Cassell Road, Harleysville PA 19438. 215/723-8300. **Contact:** Human Resources. **Description:** Produces pumps and pumping equipment.

MOORE PRODUCTS COMPANY
Sumneytown Pike, Spring House PA 19477. 215/646-7400. **Contact:** Employment Manager. **Description:** Develops, manufactures, and sells industrial controls which include instruments and dimensional measuring gauges. These industrial instruments are used to measure and control temperature, pressure, flow of liquid or gas, liquid levels, and other variables found in process industries such as chemical and oil refining. **Common positions include:** Chemical Engineer; Computer Programmer; Electrical/Electronic Engineer; Industrial Engineer; Mechanical Engineer; Petroleum Engineer. **Educational backgrounds include:** Engineering. **Benefits:** Dental Insurance; Life Insurance; Medical Insurance; Pension Plan; Tuition Assistance. **Corporate headquarters location:** This Location.

PENN ENGINEERING AND MANUFACTURING
P.O. Box 1000, Danboro PA 18916. 215/766-8853. **Contact:** Human Resources. **Description:** Produces fasteners and related equipment.

PENNSYLVANIA OPTICAL
234 South Eighth Street, Reading PA 19602. 215/376-5701. **Contact:** Nancy Chiccone, Personnel Manager. **Description:** Produces a wide range of optical instruments, components, and lenses. **Parent company:** Itek Corporation.

PHILADELPHIA GEAR CORPORATION
181 South Gulph Road, King of Prussia PA 19406. 215/265-3000. **Contact:** Bruce Hamilton, Director/Industrial Relations. **Description:** Produces a wide variety of gears and gear drives for various industrial users.

SDI OPERATING PARTNERS L.P.
One Logan Square, Philadelphia PA 19103. 215/665-3650. **Contact:** Personnel Department. **Description:** Manufactures maintenance, electrical, fluid power, and glass products. **Listed on:** New York Stock Exchange. **Number of employees nationwide:** 4,000.

SCHRAMM, INC.
800 East Virginia Avenue, West Chester PA 19380. 215/696-2500. **Contact:** Personnel Manager. **Description:** Manufactures truck and crawler-mounted drilling rigs and self-propelled air compressors. Products are marketed among mining, water well and general contractors.

SELAS CORPORATION OF AMERICA
P.O. Box 200, Dresher PA 19025. 215/646-6600. **Contact:** Mr. R.W. Mason, Director of Employee Relations. **Description:** Engaged in the design, engineering, manufacture, and distribution of heat processing equipment and services to industries throughout the world. **Educational backgrounds include:** Engineering. **Benefits:** Dental Insurance; Disability Coverage; Life Insurance; Medical Insurance; Pension Plan; Savings Plan. **Corporate headquarters location:** This Location. **Operations at this facility include:** Administration; Manufacturing; Research and Development; Sales; Service. **Listed on:** American Stock Exchange. **Number of employees nationwide:** 360.

SPEAKMAN COMPANY
P.O. Box 191, Wilmington DE 19899. 302/764-7100. **Contact:** Arlene Lunbeck, Personnel Director. **Description:** A manufacturer of plumbing and heating equipment.

SPIRAX SARCO INC.
1951 Glenwood Street SW, Allentown PA 18103. 215/797-5830. **Contact:** Sam Cappello, Company Secretary. **Description:** Produces temperature and pressure regulators, steam traps, strainers, and steam humidifiers. Parent company is a diversified consumer products manufacturer. **Corporate headquarters location:** Cleveland OH. **Parent company:** White Consolidated Industries.

STOKES VACUUM
5500 Tabor Road, Philadelphia PA 19120. 215/831-5400. **Contact:** James Hughes, Director of Personnel. **Description:** A manufacturer of vacuum metalizers, vacuum pumps, vacuum freeze dryers, and other industrial equipment.

SUN DISTRIBUTORS L.P.
2600 One Logan Square, Philadelphia PA 19103. 215/665-3650. **Contact:** Personnel Department. **Description:** A wholesale distributor of diverse industrial products. **Number of employees nationwide:** 3,576.

TECHNINTROL INC.
1952 East Allegheny Avenue, Philadelphia PA 19134. 215/426-9105. **Contact:** Annamarie Meissler, Personnel Manager. **Description:** Operates in four industry segments: Electronic Products; Electrical Products; Mechanical Products; and Services. The Electronic Products segment is engaged in the production and sales of electronic scales, electronic force measuring instruments, and electronic components. Electrical Products segment is involved in the production and sales of electric transformers, and electric test stands. The Mechanical Products segment manufactures force measuring and weighing instruments, brakes, filters, and money-counting equipment. The Services segment performs installation services for customers of the company's products. **Common positions include:** Customer Service Representative. **Corporate headquarters location:** This Location. **Listed on:** American Stock Exchange.

TELEDYNE PACKAGING
4th & Townsend Streets, P.O. Box 640, Chester PA 19016. 215/494-6300. **Contact:** Mark Pass, Personnel Director. **Description:** Operates four collapsible metal tube manufacturing plants, one plastic bottle and injection-molding plant, and one impact-extrusion plant. Metal tube products include: specialty tin and aluminum tubes used by pharmaceutical manufacturers and distributors; ophthalmic ointment tubes; aluminum and lead tubes used by the cosmetics and toiletries industries; and metal tube products used for many other household and industrial products. Molding plant produces a variety of plastic bottles; impact-extrusion plant produces electrolytic

capacitor cases, alloy welding rod containers, and marking pen barrels. **Corporate headquarters location:** Los Angeles CA. **Parent company:** Teledyne, Inc.

TELEDYNE SPECIALTY EQUIPMENT

P.O. Box 15552, York PA 17405-0552. 717/848-2801. **Contact:** Plant Manager. **Description:** Manufactures an air industrial sewing machine drive motor (Variostop), which features integrated circuit control logic and a variable-speed clutch/brake system. A subsidiary of Teledyne, Inc., a high-technology multi-product corporation consisting of 130 individual companies employing 50,000 people nationwide. Operates in five industrial areas: Aviation & Electronics; Machines & Metals; Engines, Energy, and Power; Commercial and Consumer; and Insurance & Finance. **Corporate headquarters location:** Los Angeles CA. **Listed on:** New York Stock Exchange.

TELEFLEX INC.

155 South Limerick Road, Limerick PA 19468. 215/948-5100. **Contact:** Ronald Boldt, Vice President/Human Resources. **Description:** Operates in two industry segments: Technical Products and Services, and Commercial Products. The Technical Products and Services segment includes the manufacture of precision mechanical and electromechanical control equipment, and other products in the aerospace, chemical processing, and medical industries. The Commercial Products segment involves the design and manufacture of commercial controls, control systems, hydraulics, instruments, and other products with applications in the automotive, marine, and other industries.

TYLER PIPE INDUSTRIES INC.
PENN DIVISION

P.O. Box 35, Macungie PA 18062. 215/966-3491. **Contact:** Joe Rainier, Personnel Department. **Description:** Manufactures and distributes soil pipe. Company is a major national producer of both plastic and iron piping for large-volume users. **Corporate headquarters location:** Tyler TX.

VICTAULIC COMPANY OF AMERICA

P.O. Box 31, Easton PA 18044-0031. 215/252-6400. **Contact:** Corporate Recruiter. **Description:** The international marketer, manufacturer, and designer of industrial/commercial piping systems products, which include: pipe couplings, fittings, valves, piping accessories, specially designed piping products, and pre-assembled packages. **Benefits:** comprehensive benefits package. **Common positions include:** Administrator; Blue-Collar Worker Supervisor; Buyer; Computer Programmer; Credit Manager; Customer Service Representative; Department Manager; Draftsperson; General Manager; Industrial Designer; Industrial Engineer; Management Trainee; Manufacturer's/Wholesaler's Sales Rep.; Marketing Specialist; Mechanical Engineer; Metallurgical Engineer; Operations/Production Manager; Purchasing Agent and Manager; Quality Control Supervisor; Systems Analyst; Technical Writer/Editor; Transportation/Traffic Specialist. **Educational backgrounds include:** Accounting; Business Administration; Engineering; Liberal Arts; Marketing; Physics. **Operations at this facility include:** Administration; Manufacturing; Research and Development; Sales; Service.

VISHAY INTERTECHNOLOGY INC.

63 Lincoln Highway, Malvern PA 19355. 215/644-1300. **Contact:** William Spires, V.P./Industrial Relations. **Description:** Engaged in the design, manufacture, and sale of precision stress-analysis systems and services, as well as high precision resistive systems. Operates in three business segments: Measurement Group, which develops, manufactures, and markets stress analysis products; Resistive Systems Group, which

performs the same functions for the resistive products; and the Medical Systems Group, which develops, manufactures, and markets dental products. International facilities. **Corporate headquarters location:** This Location. **Listed on:** American Stock Exchange.

THE WEST COMPANY

101 Gordon Drive, P.O. Box 645, Lionville PA 19341-0645. **Contact:** Human Resources. **Description:** Designs, develops, and manufactures closures, stoppers, containers, and other packaging components and related-application machinery principally for the pharmaceutical, hospital supply, cosmetics, personal care, and beverage industries.

YORK INTERNATIONAL CORPORATION

P.O. Box 560-36BB, York PA 17405-0560. 717/771-6572. **Contact:** Jo Carol Fink, Manager of Corporate Staffing. **Description:** Manufacturers of residential, commercial, and industrial air conditioning and refrigeration equipment and systems, and food systems. Recruits internationally. **Common positions include:** Accountant/Auditor; Electrical/Electronic Engineer; Financial Analyst; Industrial Engineer; Mechanical Engineer; Purchasing Agent and Manager. **Educational backgrounds include:** Accounting; Computer Science; Engineering; Finance; Marketing. **Benefits:** Dental Insurance; Disability Coverage; Life Insurance; Medical Insurance; Pension Plan; Savings Plan; Stock Option; Tuition Assistance. **Special Programs:** Internships; Training Programs. **Corporate headquarters location:** This Location. **Operations at this facility include:** Administration; Manufacturing; Research and Development. **Listed on:** New York Stock Exchange. **Number of employees nationwide:** 11,000.

Note: Because addresses and telephone numbers of smaller companies change rapidly, we recommend you contact each company and verify the information below before contacting employers. Mass mailings are not recommended.

Additional large employers: 500 +

COMMERCIAL FURNITURE

Brodart Company
500 Arch St.,
Williamsport PA
17705. 717/326-
2461.

HEATING EQUIPMENT

Unitary Products Group
2231 E State Street
Extension, Trenton NJ
08619-3311.
609/587-3400.

TURBINES

Voith Hydro Inc.
E Berlin Rd., York PA
17404. 717/792-
7000.

FARM MACHINERY AND EQUIPMENT

Ford New Holland Inc.
36 Maple St.,
Belleville PA 17004.
717/935-2111.

Ford New Holland Inc.
500 Diller Ave., New
Holland PA 17557-
9301. 717/355-1121.

MINING MACHINERY AND EQUIPMENT

Fuller Company
2040 Avenue C,
Bethlehem PA 18017-
2188. 610/264-6011.

CRANES AND HOISTS

Acco Chain & Lifting Products
76 Acco Drive, York
PA 17402-4620.
717/741-4863.

Grove Worldwide
P.O. Box 21, Shady
Grove PA 17256-
0021. 717/597-8121.

MACHINE TOOLS

**Litton Indl.
Automation Systems**
E 6th St.,
Waynesboro PA
17268. 717/762-
2161.

DIES AND TOOLS

**Roller Bearing
Company of America
Inc.**
140 Terry Drive, Box
1237, Newtown PA
18940-1896.
215/579-4300.

PRINTING
MACHINERY AND
EQUIPMENT

**Kaumagraph
Corporation**
701 E Baltimore Pike
619, Kennet Sq PA
19348-2429.

Rockwell Intl. Corp.
200 N Park Rd.,
Reading PA 19610-
2908. 610/378-7000.

**Soabar Systems
Division**
7722 Dungan Rd.,
Philadelphia PA
19111-2733.
215/725-4700.

INDUSTRIAL
MACHINERY

Alfa-Laval Separation
955 Mearns Rd.,
Warminster PA
18974-2811.
215/443-4000.

**Kulicke & Soffa
Industries Inc.**
2101 Blair Mill Rd.,
Willow Grove PA
19090-1795.
215/784-6000.

BEARINGS

Federal-Mogul Corp.
401 W Lincoln Ave.,
Lititz PA 17543-
8701. 717/627-3623.

SKF USA Inc.
1100 1st Ave., Kng
Of Prussa PA 19406-
1312. 610/962-4300.

A/C AND HEATING
EQUIPMENT

Frick Company
345 West Main St.,
Waynesboro PA
17268-1432.
717/762-2121.

Hill Refrigeration
P.O. Box 61, Trenton
NJ 08601-0061.
609/599-9861.

Trane Company
400 Keystone
Industrial Park,
Scranton PA 18512.
717/346-7711.

MEASURING AND
CONTROLLING
DEVICES

**Brooks Instrument
Division**
407 W Vine St.,
Hatfield PA 19440-
3000. 215/362-3500.

Additional medium sized employers: under 500

PLUMBING AND
HEATING EQUIPMENT
WHOLESALE

Waxman Industries
1842 Colonial Village Ln,
Lancaster PA 17601-
6700. 717/291-5985.

York Corrugating Co.
120 S Adams St, York
PA 17404-5444.
717/845-3511.

WARM AIR HEATING
AND AIR CONDITIONING
EQUIPMENT
WHOLESALE

Fisher Brothers Inc.
7900 Rockwell Ave,
Philadelphia PA 19111-
2223. 215/728-1700.

United Refrigeration
301 N Black Horse Pike,
Mount Ephraim NJ
08059-1314. 609/933-
0333.

REFRIDGERATION
EQUIPMENT
WHOLESALE

Coca Cola Fountain
7520 Morris Court,
Fogelsville PA 18051.
610/398-7959.

FARM AND GARDEN MACHINERY WHOLESALE

Cleveland Bros Equipment Co Inc.
5300 Paxton St, Harrisburg PA 17111-2525. 717/564-2121.

INDUSTRIAL MACHNIERY WHOLESALE

Medico Industries Inc.
1500 Highway 315, Wilkes Barre PA 18711. 717/825-7711.

Modern Group Ltd
2501 Durham Rd, Bristol PA 19007-6923. 215/943-9100.

Tate Engineering Inc.
580 Turner Industrial Way, Aston PA 19014-3017. 610/485-3560.

INDUSTRIAL SUPPLIES WHOLESALE

Chestnut Group Inc.
115 Bloomingdale Ave, Wayne PA 19087-4030. 610/688-3300.

MG Industries Metal Welding Division
Fireline & Sand Quarry Rds, Palmerton PA 18071. 610/826-5700.

SKF Bearing Industries Company
525 Fame Ave, Hanover PA 17331-9539. 717/637-8981.

Xtec Office Systems
5000 Sagemore Dr, Marlton NJ 08053-4307. 609/596-7600.

SERVICE ESTABLISHMENT EQUIPMENT WHOLESALE

Fire Protection Industries
1765 Woodhaven Dr, Bensalem PA 19020-7107. 215/245-1830.

Harrisburg Paper Co.
PO Box 1337, Harrisburg PA 17105-1337. 717/561-3100.

Wilhold
Packer St, Sunbury PA 17801. 717/286-6714.

TRANSPORTATION EQUIPMENT WHOLESALE

ABB Traction Inc. A Subsidiary of ASEA
425 Phillips Blvd, Trenton NJ 08618-1430. 609/538-8095.

SCRAP AND WASTE MATERIALS WHOLESALE

Graham Recycling
505 Windsor St, York PA 17403-1054. 717/852-7744.

COMMERCIAL EQUIPMENT WHOLESALE

BLH Electronics
1 Greentree Ctr, Marlton NJ 08053-3105. 609/596-3029.

SEARCH, DETECTION, NAVIGATION AND GUIDANCE SYSTEMS

RDL Inc.
7th Ave & Freedley St, Conshohocken PA 19428. 610/825-3750.

Vega Precision Laboratories
10 Industry Dr, Lancaster PA 17603-4025.

LABORATORY APPARATUS FURNITURE

Decora Inc.
Malaga & New Brooklyn Rds, Williamstown NJ 08094. 609/728-9300.

AUTOMATIC CONTROLS ENVIRONMENTS AND APPLIANCES

Frigid Coil East
1499 E Philadelphia St, York PA 17403-1232. 717/854-3821.

PSG Industries Inc.
1225 Tunnel Rd, Perkasie PA 18944-2131. 215/257-3621.

INDUSTRIAL INSTRUMENTS FOR MEASUREMENT, DISPLAY AND CONTROL OF PROCESS VARIABLES

Bailey Controls Co.
2300 Reach Rd, Williamsport PA 17701-5578. 717/323-8501.

Heraeus Electro-Nite Company
9901 Blue Grass Rd, Philadelphia PA 19114-1013. 215/464-4200.

Red Lion Controls Co.
5 Willow Springs Cir,
York PA 17402-9428.
717/767-6511.

The Fredericks Company
2400 Philmont Ave,
Huntingdon Vy PA
19006-6232. 215/947-
2500.

**TOTALIZING FLUID
METERS AND
COUNTING DEVICES**

Porter Instrument Co.
245 Township Line Rd,
Hatfield PA 19440-1752.
215/723-4000.

**INSTRUMENTS FOR
MEASURING AND
TESTING OF
ELECTRICITY AND
ELECTRICAL SYSTEMS**

Avo Biddle Instruments
510 Township Line Rd,
Blue Bell PA 19422-
2701. 215/646-9200.

**Datcon Instrument
Company**
1811 Rohrerstown Rd,
Lancaster PA 17601-
2321. 717/569-5713.

Electron Devices
1035 Westminster Dr,
Williamsport PA 17701-
3911. 717/326-3561.

Loral Control Systems
J F Kennedy Dr, Archbald
PA 18403. 717/876-
1500.

**Rockland Scientific
Corporation**
PO Box 3135, Princeton
NJ 08543-3135.
2017677900.

Sparkomatic Corporation
PO Box 277, Milford PA
18337-0277. 717/296-
6444.

Special Devices Division
750 W Sproul Rd,
Springfield PA 19064-
4001. 610/328-4000.

Telesciences Inc.
351 New Albany Rd,
Moorestown NJ 08057-
1117. 609/235-8227.

**Tinius Olsen Testing
Machine Co**
Easton Rd, Willow Grove
PA 19090. 215/675-
7100.

**LABORATORY
ANALYTICAL
EQUIPMENT**

Kontes Glass Co.
Spruce St, Vineland NJ
08360. 609/692-8500.

Supelco Inc.
Supelco Park, Bellefonte
PA 16823. 814/359-
3441.

Wilmad Glass Co Inc.
U S Rte 40 & Oak Rd,
Buena NJ 08310.
609/697-3000.

**OPTICAL INSTRUMENTS
AND LENSES**

Plummer Precision Optics
601 Montgomery Ave,
Pennsburg PA 18073-
1597. 215/679-6272.

**CARBON AND GRAPHITE
PRODUCTS**

Carbon Products Oper
100 Stokes Ave, E
Stroudsburg PA 18301-
1222. 717/476-9017.

Pure Carbon Co.
E 2nd St, Coudersport PA
16915. 814/274-8020.

OFFICE MACHINES

Bell & Howell Co.
795 Roble Rd, Allentown
PA 18103-9111.
610/264-4510.

Brandt Inc.
1750 Woodhaven Dr,
Bensalem PA 19020-
7195. 215/638-3600.

Opex Corporation
305 Commerce Dr,
Moorestown NJ 08057-
4234. 609/727-1100.

**AUTOMATIC VENDING
MACHINES**

Amish Country Vending
147 N Ronks Rd, Ronks
PA 17572-9702.
717/399-9482.

Mars Electronics Intl
1301 Wilson Dr, West
Chester PA 19380-5954.
610/430-2500.

**Refreshment Machinery
Ind**
300 Jacksonville Rd,
Warminster PA 18974-
4894. 215/675-4200.

**AIR-CONDITIONING,
AND WARM AIR
HEATING EQUIPMENT**

Anemostat Products
888 N Keyser Ave,
Scranton PA 18504-
9723. 717/346-6586.

FES Inc.
3475 Board Rd, York PA
17402-9414. 717/767-
6411.

**Fogel Commercial
Refrigerator Co.**
5400 Eadom St,
Philadelphia PA 19137-
1303. 215/535-8300.

Glenco Star
8000 Penrose Ave,
Philadelphia PA 19153-
3810. 215/365-3000.

**Mechanical Specialties
Inc.**
Tulip & Rhawn Sts,
Philadelphia PA 19136.
215/331-5555.

**MEASURING AND
DISPENSING PUMPS**

**William M Wilson's Sons
Inc.**
Valley Forge Rd & 8th St, .
Lansdale PA 19446.
215/855-4631.

**SERVICE INDUSTRY
MACHINERY**

Capital Controls Co
3000 Advance Ln,
Colmar PA 18915-9727.
215/822-2901.

**Cochrane Environmental
Systems**
800 3rd Ave, Kng Of
Prussa PA 19406-1412.
610/265-5050.

Follett Corporation
PO Box D, Easton PA
18044-2096. 610/252-
7301.

**Garland Commercial
Industries Inc.**
185 E South St, Freeland
PA 18224-1916.
717/636-1000.

Le-Jo Enterprises Inc.
2 Lee Blvd, Malvern PA
19355-1235. 610/296-
2800.

Muskin Leisure Products
401 E Thomas St, Wilkes
Barre PA 18705-3816.
717/825-4501.

**CARBURETORS,
PISTONS AND VALVES**

Champion Parts Inc.
921 3rd Ave, Lock
Haven PA 17745-2728.
717/748-9561.

Manley Division
400 N State St, York PA
17403-1372. 717/843-
0834.

FLUID POWER PUMPS

Rexroth Corporation
2315 City Line Rd,
Bethlehem PA 18017-
2131. 610/694-8300.

**SCALES AND
BALANCES, EXCEPT
LABORATORIES**

Accu-Sort Systems
511 School House Rd,
Telford PA 18969-1148.
215/723-0981.

**INDUSTRIAL AND
COMMERICAL
MACHINERY**

Aluminum Alloys Inc.
Rt 422, Reading PA
19608. 610/678-8023.

Chalmers & Kubeck
150 Commerce Dr, Aston
PA 19014-3204.
610/494-4300.

DL Martin Machine Co
25 Harbaugh Dr,
Mercersburg PA 17236-
1796. 717/328-2141.

Delp Corporation
880 Louis Dr, Warminster
PA 18974-2819.
215/674-5850.

General Machinery Co.
1201 N 10th St, Millville
NJ 08332-2031.
609/825-7500.

Mancor Inc.
160 Olin Way, Allentown
PA 18106-9370.
610/398-2300.

OP Schuman & Sons
County Line & Titus Rd,
Warrington PA 18976.
215/343-1530.

**Pennfield Precision
Machining**
Keystone Dr, Sellersville
PA 18960. 215/257-
5191.

Zober Industries Inc.
Coventry & Magnolia
Ave, Bensalem PA
19020. 215/788-5523.

**STEAM, GAS AND
HYDRAULIC TURBINES**

**John R Hollingsworth
Company**
Nutt Road At French
Creek, Phoenixville PA
19460. 610/933-8951.

**INTERNAL COMBUSTION
ENGINES**

Johnson & Towers Inc.
Rte 38 & Briggs Rd,
Mount Laurel NJ 08054.
609/234-6990.

FARM MACHINERY AND EQUIPMENT

Ford New Holland Inc.
200 Commerce St,
Mountville PA 17554-
1697. 717/285-8201.

Philadelphia Mixers Corporation
1221 E Main St, Palmyra
PA 17078-9518.
717/838-1341.

Philadelphia Tramrail Company
2207 E Ontario St,
Philadelphia PA 19134-
2693. 215/533-5100.

True Temper Hardware Inc.
1500 S Cameron St,
Harrisburg PA 17104-
3143. 717/234-6291.

CONSTRUCTION MACHINERY AND EQUIPMENT

Darby Industries Inc.
RR 1 Box 311, Falls PA
18615-9786. 717/388-
6173.

General Engines Co
Rtes 130 & 295,
Thorofare NJ 08086.
609/845-5400.

General Machine Products Co Inc.
3111 Old Lincoln Hwy,
Fstrvl Trvose PA 19053-
4931. 215/357-5500.

Ingersoll-Rand Co.
312 Ingersoll Dr,
Shippensburg PA 17257-
9215. 717/532-9181.

LB Smith Inc.
2001 State Rd, Camp Hill
PA 17011-5946.
717/737-3431.

Linear Dynamics Inc.
79 Montgomery St,
Montgomery PA 17752-
1138. 717/547-1621.

MINING MACHINERY AND EQUIPMENT

Mineral Processing Systems Inc.
240 Arch St, York PA
17403-1410. 717/843-
8671.

Sullivan Trail Manufacturing Co.
800 Exeter Ave, Pittston
PA 18643-1745.
717/654-3355.

ELEVATORS AND MOVING STAIRWAYS

Cemcolift Inc.
PO Box 368,
Plumsteadvlle PA 18949-
0368. 215/766-0900.

Schindler Elevator Corporation
1200 Biglerville Rd,
Gettysburg PA 17325-
8012. 717/334-7651.

CONVEYORS AND CONVEYING EQUIPMENT

Fuller Co.
236 S Cherry St,
Manheim PA 17545-
2027. 717/665-2224.

SI Handling Systems
PO Box 70, Easton PA
18044-0070. 610/252-
7321.

OVERHEAD TRAVELING CRANES, HOISTS AND MONORAIL SYSTEMS

Greiner Industries Inc.
1650 Steel Way, Mount
Joy PA 17552-9515.
717/653-8111.

INDUSTRIAL TRUCKS, TRAILERS AND TRACTORS

Drexel Industries Inc.
Maple Ave, Horsham PA
19044. 215/672-2200.

Gichner Mobile Systems
401 Bridge St, Old Forge
PA 18518-2323.
717/457-7426.

Strick Corporation
9th & Oak Sts, Berwick
PA 18603. 717/752-
2708.

MACHINE TOOLS, METAL CUTTING TYPES

Garry Manufacturing Company
PO Box 3608, Harrisburg
PA 17105-3608.

Netzsch Inc.
119 Pickering Way,
Exton PA 19341-1393.
610/363-8010.

MACHINE TOOLS, METAL FORMING TYPES

Kurz-Hastings Inc.
Dutton & Darnell Rds,
Philadelphia PA 19154.
215/632-2300.

Murata Wiedemann
211 S Gulph Rd, Kng Of
Prussa PA 19406-3186.
610/265-2000.

INDUSTRIAL PATTERNS

Exact Equipment Corporation
PO Box 666, Levittown
PA 19058-0666.
215/750-9090.

Fres-Co Systems USA
10 State Rd, Telford PA
18969-1033. 215/721-4600.

Mateer-Burt Co Inc.
434 Devon Pk Dr, Wayne
PA 19087-1816.
610/293-0100.

Universal Machine Co Pottstown
525 W Vine St,
Pottstown PA 19464-6899. 610/323-1810.

SPECIAL DIES AND TOOLS

Brenner Tool & Die Inc.
921 Cedar Ave, Croydon
PA 19021-7501.
215/785-5241.

Du Pont Electronics
511 Spruce St, Clearfield
PA 16830-1942.
814/765-2431.

Kras Corporation
88 Canal Rd, Fairless Hls
PA 19030-4302.
215/736-0981.

Laneko Engineering Company
275 New Jersey Dr, Ft
Washington PA 19034-2603. 215/646-8180.

NW Controls Inc.
Shelly Rd, Harleysville PA
19438. 610/287-7871.

New Concept Manufacturing Inc.
2315 S Queen St, York
PA 17402-4938.
717/741-0840.

CUTTING TOOLS AND MACHINE TOOL ACCESSORIES

Brubaker Tool Corporation
Front & Center,
Millersburg PA 17061.
717/692-2113.

Reiff & Nestor Co.
Reiff & West Sts, Lykens
PA 17048. 717/453-7113.

ROLLING MILL MACHINERY

Positran Inc.
800 E Main St,
Norristown PA 19401-4104. 610/277-0500.

ELECTRIC AND GAS WELDING EQUIPMENT

Alloy Rods Consumables Division
801 Wilson Ave, Hanover
PA 17331. 717/637-8911.

PAPER INDUSTRIES MACHINERY

Molins Machine Company
111 Woodcrest Rd,
Cherry Hill NJ 08003-3620. 609/795-7100.

Simon LG Industries
PO Box 329, Wagontown
PA 19376-0329.
610/524-5444.

PRINTING TRADES MACHINERY

Ferag Inc.
190 Rittenhouse Cir,
Bristol PA 19007-1618.
215/788-0892.

FOOD PRODUCTS MACHINERY

Chester Jensen Co.
PO Box 908, Chester PA
19016-0908. 610/876-6276.

Multi-Flow Dispensers
1434 County Line Rd,
Huntingdon Vy PA
19006-1891. 215/322-1800.

SPECIAL INDUSTRY MACHINERY

Caddy Corporation Of America
PO Box 345, Bridgeport
NJ 08014-0345.
609/467-4222.

Chemcut Corporation
500 N Science Park Rd,
State College PA 16803-2299. 814/238-0514.

Dorr-Oliver Inc.
101 Carleton Ave,
Hazleton PA 18201-7397. 717/455-2051.

Graham Engineering Corporation
1420 6th Ave, York PA
17403-2615. 717/848-3755.

Grays Run Technologies
2401 Reach Rd #305,
Williamsport PA 17701-4193. 717/322-6310.

Jade Systems
1120 Indl Hwy,
Southampton PA 18966.
215/322-9020.

Midway Tool Engineering Co Inc.
651 Westminister Rd,
Wilkes Barre PA 18702-9601. 717/655-6844.

Quad Systems Corporation
2 Electronic Dr, Horsham
PA 19044-2250.
215/657-6202.

Royer Industries
158 Pringle St, Wilkes
Barre PA 18704-2763.
717/287-9624.

Sherman Industries
600 W Broad St, Palmyra
NJ 08065-2443.
609/829-4190.

PUMPS AND PUMPING EQUIPMENT

Blue Chip Products Inc.
1101 New Ford Mill Rd,
Morrisville PA 19067-3701. 215/736-0901.

Crane Co.
Chempump Division
175 Titus Ave,
Warrington PA 18976-2424. 215/343-6000.

Goulds Pumps Inc.
E Centre St, Ashland PA
17921. 717/875-2660.

Milton Roy Co.
Flow Central Division
201 Ivyland Rd,
Warminster PA 18974-1706. 215/441-0800.

Standard Pump
1 Pump Pl, Allentown PA
18102-5223. 610/776-6100.

BALL AND ROLLER BEARINGS

Kingsbury Inc.
10385 Drummond Rd,
Philadelphia PA 19154-3803. 215/824-4000.

National Bearings Co.
1596 Manheim Pike,
Lancaster PA 17601-3058. 717/569-0485.

Roller Bearing Co Of America
P O Box 367, Trenton NJ
08628. 609/882-7401.

AIR AND GAS COMPRESSORS

Lee Industries Inc.
W Pine St, Philipsburg PA
16866. 814/342-0460.

INDUSTRIAL AND COMMERCIAL FANS AND BLOWERS

Fuller Co.
Front & Willow Sts,
Catasauqua PA 18032.
610/266-5101.

Hefco
3651 Hempland Rd,
Lancaster PA 17601-1323. 717/285-5945.

Kooltronic Inc.
PO Box 300, Hopewell
NJ 08525-0300.
609/466-3400.

Precisionaire Industry Of Pennsylvania
Rte 895 R D 1, Auburn
PA 17922. 717/366-1466.

T-Thermal Company
Brook Rd, Conshohocken
PA 19428. 610/828-5400.

SPEED CHANGERS, INDUSTRIAL HIGH-SPEED DRIVES AND GEARS

Rexnord Corporation
2045 W Hunting Park
Ave, Philadelphia PA
19140-2813. 215/225-6000.

INDUSTRIAL PROCESS FURNACES AND OVENS

Argus International
PO Box 38, Hopewell NJ
08525-0038. 609/466-1677.

National Drying Machinery Co
2190 Hornig Rd,
Philadelphia PA 19116-4296. 215/464-6070.

Proctor & Schwartz
251 Gibraltar Rd,
Horsham PA 19044-2305. 215/443-5200.

MECHANICAL POWER TRANSMISSION EQUIPMENT

Fenner Manheim
311 W Stiegel St,
Manheim PA 17545-1747. 717/665-2421.

TB Wood's Sons Company
440 North Fifth Ave,
Chambersburg PA
17201-1778. 717/264-7161.

Warner Electric Brake & Clutch
PO Box 11, Pitman NJ 08071-0011. 609/589-0815.

GENERAL INDUSTRIAL MACHINERY AND EQUIPMENT

Central Sprinkler Corporation
451 N Cannon Ave, Lansdale PA 19446-2270. 215/362-0700.

Dougherty Brothers Co Inc.
PO Box 608, Buena NJ 08310-0608. 609/692-6100.

Hale Fire Pump Co.
700 Spring Mill Ave, Conshohocken PA 19428-1996. 610/825-6300.

Moon America Inc.
100 Greening Dr, Easton PA 18042-5770. 610/250-5656.

Vesper Corporation
11 Bala Ave, Bala Cynwyd PA 19004-3210. 2168384700.

Zeks Air Drier Corporation
Malvern Industrial Park, Malvern PA 19355. 610/647-1600.

AMMUNITION, EXCEPT SMALL ARMS

Loral Defense Systems
723 Dresher Rd, Horsham PA 19044-2205. 215/657-8811.

INDUSTRIAL VALVES

Anchor/Darling Valve Company
701 1st St, Williamsport PA 17701-5907. 717/327-4800.

France Compressor Products Division
104 Pheasant Run, Newtown PA 18940-1821. 215/968-5959.

ITT Engineered Valves
33 Centerville Rd, Lancaster PA 17603-4068. 717/291-1901.

VALVES AND PIPE FITTINGS

Anchor/Darling Valve Company
919 Conestoga Rd, Bryn Mawr PA 19010-1310. 610/527-9000.

Bonney Forge Corporation
Cedar & Meadow Sts, Allentown PA 18104. 610/435-9611.

Control Concepts Inc.
15 Terry Dr, Newtown PA 18940-1830. 215/968-4681.

Gimpel Corporation
250 Woodbourne Rd, Langhorne PA 19047-1751. 215/757-5141.

Knecht Inc.
879 Beideman Ave, Camden NJ 08105-4227. 609/966-3636.

Schrader Bellows Inc.
R D 1, Canton PA 17724-9801. 717/673-5100.

TRW Inc.
Valve Division
601 E Market St, Danville PA 17821-2099. 717/275-0170.

HEATING EQUIPMENT

Blueray Systems Inc.
Rte 61 S, Shuykl Haven PA 17972. 717/385-0780.

Monarch Manufacturing Works
2501 E Ontario St, Philadelphia PA 19134-5327. 215/739-8209.

Tampella Keeler
2600 Reach Rd, Williamsport PA 17701-4119. 717/326-3361.

HAND AND EDGE TOOLS

Gas Spring Company
92 County Line Rd, Colmar PA 18915-9606. 215/822-1982.

SAW BLADES AND HAND SAWS

Stanley Tools
1721 Stanley Dr, York PA 17404-2292. 717/767-6911.

HARDWARE

Lehigh Group
7620 Cetronia Rd, Allentown PA 18106-9299. 610/398-1233.

McKinney Products Company
820 Davis St, Scranton PA 18505-3525. 717/346-7551.

WOOD OFFICE FURNITURE

JG Furniture Systems
121 Park Ave,
Quakertown PA 18951-
1631. 215/538-5800.

OFFICE FURNITURE

Emeco Industries Inc.
805 W Elm Ave, Hanover
PA 17331-4706.
717/637-5951.

Stylex Inc.
620 Cooper St, Riverside
NJ 08075-4614.
609/461-5600.

PUBLIC BUILDING AND RELATED FURNITURE

David Edward Ltd
252 N Franklin St, Red
Lion PA 17356-1503.
717/246-2636.

WOOD OFFICE AND STORE FIXTURES, PARTITIONS AND SHELVING

Zell Brothers Inc.
PO Box 327, Red Lion PA
17356-0327. 717/244-
7661.

WOOD OFFICE AND STORE FIXTURES

American Metal Works Inc.
8701 Torresdale Ave,
Philadelphia PA 19136-
1509. 215/338-9194.

Hallmark Industries
East Ohio St, Mc Clure
PA 17841. 717/658-
8111.

Hi-Line Storage Systems Co.
Hi Line Dr & Ridge Rd,
Perkasie PA 18944.
215/257-3600.

Stanley-Vidmar Inc.
Queen City Airport Indl
Pk, Allentown PA 18103.

Trion Industries Inc.
297 Laird St, Wilkes
Barre PA 18702-6997.
717/824-1000.

DRAPERY HARDWARE AND WINDOW BLINDS

Kirsch
Reed Indl Pk, Shamokin
PA 17872. 717/672-
2591.

FURNITURE AND FIXTURES

Anton Waldmann & Assocs Inc.
S Broad St, Hughesville
PA 17737. 717/584-
2171.

For more information on career opportunities in industrial manufacturing and wholesaling:

Associations

APPLIANCE PARTS DISTRIBUTORS ASSOCIATION
228 East Baltimore Street, Detroit MI
48202. 313/875-8455.

ASSOCIATION FOR MANUFACTURING TECHNOLOGY
7901 Westpark Drive, McLean VA
22102. 703/893-2900.

NATIONAL ASSOCIATION OF MANUFACTURERS
1331 Pennsylvania Avenue, NW,
Suite 1500, Washington DC 20004.
202/637-3000.

NATIONAL SCREW MACHINE PRODUCTS ASSOCIATION
6700 West Snowville Road,
Brecksville OH 44141. 216/526-
0300.

NATIONAL TOOLING AND MACHINING ASSOCIATION
9300 Livingston Road, Fort
Washington MD 20744. 301/248-
1250.

Directories

DIRECTORY OF TEXAS MANUFACTURERS
University of Texas at Austin, Bureau
of Business Research, Box 7459,
Austin TX 78713. 512/471-1616.

TEXAS MANUFACTURERS REGISTER
Manufacturer's News, Inc., 1633
Central Street, Evanston IL 60201.
708/864-7000.

MINING/GAS/PETROLEUM/ENERGY RELATED

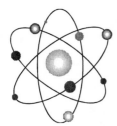

The short-term future for the petroleum industry depends upon the world economy, OPEC production, and world oil prices. U.S. crude and natural gas production is expected to remain flat, while demand for petroleum products is forecasted to rise slowly -- 1% annually, through 1997. Jobseekers, especially those with engineering backgrounds, should keep an eye out for the growing emphasis on the development of alternative fuels like methanol, and for growth in hydroelectric, geothermal, and other environmentally sound energy sources.

PENN VIRGINIA CORPORATION
200 South Broad Street, Philadelphia PA 19102. 215/545-6600. **Contact:** Cathy Stolberg, Personnel Coordinator. **Description:** An energy and resource management company engaged primarily in drilling, mining, and distributing oil, gas, and limestone. **Corporate headquarters location:** This Location. **Operations at this facility include:** Administration.

SUN COMPANY, INC.
1801 Market Street, Philadelphia PA 19103. 215/977-3782. **Contact:** Personnel Department. **Description:** Involved in: petroleum refining; distribution and retail sale of fuels, lubricants, and petrochemicals; crude oil pipelines and terminals; and marine transportation of oil. **Parent company:** Sun Company, Inc. **Number of employees nationwide:** 4,771.

WESTMORELAND COAL CO.
700 The Bellevue, 200 South Broad Street, Philadelphia PA 19102. 215/545-2500. **Contact:** C. Glenn Pierce, II, Vice President/Human Resources. **Description:** A producer of bituminous coal. **Listed on:** NASDAQ. **Number of employees nationwide:** 2,100.

Note: Because addresses and telephone numbers of smaller companies change rapidly, we recommend you contact each company and verify the information below before contacting employers. Mass mailings are not recommended.

Additional large employers: 500 +

OIL PIPELINES

Laurel Pipe Line Company
P.O. Box 368, Emmaus PA 18049-0368.
610/820-8300.

PETROLEUM REFINERIES

Amerigas Lp-Gas Products
500 N Gulph Rd., Kng Of Prussa PA 19406-2827.
610/337-7000.

BP Oil Company Inc.
Post Rd., Marcus Hook PA 19061. 610/499-7000.

Chevron USA Inc.
30th & Penrose Ave., Philadelphia PA 19145.
215/339-7000.

Additional medium sized employers: 100-499

PETROLEUM REFINING

TLJ Oil Co Inc.
166 Main St, Lakewood
NJ 08701-3305.
908/901-0020.

Witco Corporation
3300 W 4th St, Marcus
Hook PA 19061-5112.
610/494-3561.

**COAL AND LIGNITE
SURFACE MINING**

Energy Resource Group
8380 Old York Rd, Elkins
Park PA 19117-1539.
215/576-1888.

Lehigh Coal & Navigation
Rt 209, Tamaqua PA
18252-2299. 717/645-
2141.

ANTHRACITE MINING

Reading Anthracite Co.
200 Mahantongo St,
Pottsville PA 17901-
3011. 717/622-5150.

**ASPHALT FELTS AND
COATINGS**

**Atlas Minerals &
Chemicals Inc.**
Farmington Rd,
Mertztown PA 19539.
610/682-7171.

Hempt Bros Inc.
205 Creek Rd, Camp Hill
PA 17011-7418.
717/737-3411.

**Supradur Manufacturing
Corporation**
440 Katherine Rd, Wind
Gap PA 18091-1135.
610/863-4101.

**LUBRICATING OILS AND
GREASES**

Penguin Industries Inc.
Airport Industrial Mall,
Coatesville PA 19320.
610/384-6000.

Additional small employers: under 100

**CRUDE PETROLEUM
PIPELINES**

BP Oil Pipeline Co.
Cherry Tree Rd, Aston
PA 19014. 610/485-
3220.

Colonial Pipeline Co.
1060 Kirk Rd, Marcus
Hook PA 19061-1711.
610/459-8360.

**Interstate Energy
Company Inc.**
214 Shoemaker Rd,
Pottstown PA 19464-
6422. 610/323-1112.

Laurel Pipe Line Co.
3705 Trindle Rd, Camp
Hill PA 17011-4334.
717/737-8612.

Laurel Pipe Line Co.
RR 1, Mechanicsburg PA
17055-9801. 717/766-
7633.

Metropolitan Pipeline
RR 2, Montoursville PA
17754-9802. 717/433-
4731.

Mobil Pipe Line Co.
1360 Manheim Pike,
Lancaster PA 17601-
3148. 717/392-6416.

Mobile Pipe Line Co.
RR 2, New Holland PA
17557-9802. 717/354-
0898.

Sorrento Pizza
104 1 2 N Market St,
Duncannon PA 17020-
1320. 717/834-5167.

Sun Pipe Line Co.
RR 1, Saint Thomas PA
17252-9801. 717/369-
3211.

**Texas Eastern Gas
Pipeline**
RR 1, Hershey PA
17033-9801. 717/367-
4003.

**Texas Eastern Gas
Pipeline**
1462 River Rd, Marietta
PA 17547-9400.
717/426-3817.

**Texas Eastern Gas
Pipeline Co.**
1604 Industrial Dr,
Carlisle PA 17013-9614.
717/249-4218.

Texas Eastern Trans Corporation
3351 Molly Pitcher Hwy, Chambersburg PA 17201-9204. 717/264-7416.

Transcontinental Gas Pipe Line
214 Carnegie Ctr # 3, Princeton NJ 08540-6237.

Transcontinental Gas Pipe Line
60 N Bacton Hill Rd, Malvern PA 19355-1026. 610/644-7373.

BITUMINOUS COAL AND LIGNITE SURFACE MINING

Alcon Coal & Land Company Inc.
650 Blue Bell Rd, Blue Bell PA 19422-1645. 215/542-8700.

Antrim Mining Inc.
248 Main St, Blossburg PA 16912-1100. 717/638-3322.

B&B Energy
RR 1, Paxinos PA 17860-9801. 717/672-2458.

B&M Energy Resources
RR 2, Curwensville PA 16833-9802. 814/236-1650.

Chestnut Ridge Coal Company
RR 1, Frenchville PA 16836-9801. 814/263-4556.

Clyde Miles Coal & Lumber
RR 2, Newport PA 17074-9802. 814/764-3316.

Don H Richards Co.
123 Bloomingdale Ave, Wayne PA 19087-4001. 610/964-8080.

Fox Coal Co.
109 Walnut St, Tremont PA 17981-1228. 717/695-3024.

Harriman Coal Corporation
300 Grand St, Port Carbon PA 17965-1311. 717/622-4235.

Hepburnia Coal Co.
Rural Rte Rd 1, Grampian PA 16838. 814/236-0473.

L&J Energy Inc.
RR 2, Curwensville PA 16833-9802. 814/236-1091.

McDonald Land & Mining Co. Inc.
PO Box 53, Curwensville PA 16833-0053. 814/236-0110.

Pac 23 Mining Company
137 Theresa St, Shenandoah PA 17976-1437. 717/462-3716.

River Hill Coal Co. Inc.
Hoffman Dr, Karthaus PA 16845. 814/263-4506.

Underkoffler Coal Service
W Main, Lykens PA 17048. 717/453-7520.

ANTHRACITE MINING

Blaschak Coal Corporation
Rt 54, Mahanoy City PA 17948. 717/773-2113.

Kocher Coal Co.
Good Spring Rd, Valley View PA 17983. 717/682-3181.

Reading Anthracite Company
St Nichls Centrl Breaker 17948, Mahanoy City PA 17948. 717/773-3530.

OIL AND GAS FIELD SERVICES

SMC Environmental Services Group
501 Allendale Rd Box 859, Valley Forge PA 19482-0859. 610/265-2700.

PETROLEUM REFINING

Texaco Inc.
303 Fellowship Rd, Moorestown NJ 08057. 609/778-1400.

Unocal Corporation
4949 Liberty Ln, Allentown PA 18106-9524. 610/366-7336.

ASPHALT PAVING MIXTURES AND BLOCKS

AE Stone Inc.
Doughty Rd & Adams Ave, Pleasantville NJ 08232. 609/641-2781.

Eastern Industries
1010 E Market St, Bethlehem PA 18017-7018. 610/867-5008.

Eastern Industries Inc.
PO Box 177, Winfield PA 17889-0177. 717/524-2251.

Handwerk Contractors
Old Farm Rd,
Hummelstown PA
17036. 717/566-3711.

Joseph Ciccone & Sons
5290 W Coplay Rd,
Whitehall PA 18052-
2212. 610/837-1855.

South Brunswick Asphalt
2065 Route 37,
Lakehurst NJ 08733-
5646. 908/657-9700.

**Sproul Construction
Company**
101 Center St, Clarks
Summit PA 18411-1823.
717/586-7000.

**LUBRICATING OILS AND
GREASES**

Dryden Oil Co. Inc.
1020 Louis Dr,
Warminster PA 18974-
2822. 215/674-5300.

For more information on career opportunities in the mining, gas, petroleum and energy industries:

Associations

**AMERICAN ASSOCIATION OF
PETROLEUM GEOLOGISTS**
P.O. Box 979, Tulsa OK 7410-0979.
918/584-2555.

AMERICAN GEOLOGICAL INSTITUTE
4220 King Street, Alexandria VA
22302-1507. 703/379-2480.

AMERICAN NUCLEAR SOCIETY
555 North Kensington Avenue, La
Grange Park IL 60525. 708/352-
6611.

AMERICAN PETROLEUM INSTITUTE
1220 L Street NW, Suite 900,
Washington DC 20005. 202/682-
8000.

GEOLOGICAL SOCIETY OF AMERICA
3300 Penrose Place, P.O. Box 9140,
Boulder CO 80301. 303/447-2020.

**SOCIETY OF EXPLORATION
GEOPHYSICISTS**
P.O. Box 702740, Tulsa OK 74170-
2740. 918/493-3516.

Directories

**BROWN'S DIRECTORY OF NORTH
AMERICAN AND INTERNATIONAL
GAS COMPANIES**
Advanstar Communications, 7500 Old
Oak Boulevard, Cleveland OH 44130.
800/225-4569.

**NATIONAL PETROLEUM NEWS FACT
BOOK**
Hunter Publishing Co., 25 NW Point
Boulevard, Suite 800, Elk Grove
Village, IL 60007. 708/427-9512.

OIL AND GAS DIRECTORY
Geophysical Directory, Inc., P.O. Box
130508, Houston TX 77219.
713/529-8789.

Magazines

AMERICAN GAS MONTHLY
1515 Wilson Boulevard, Arlington VA
22209. 703/841-8686.

GAS INDUSTRIES
Gas Industries News, Inc., 6300 North
River Road, Suite 505, Rosemont IL
60018. 312/693-3682.

NATIONAL PETROLEUM NEWS
Hunter Publishing Co., 25 NW Point
Boulevard, Elk Grove IL 60007.
708/296-0770.

OIL AND GAS JOURNAL
PennWell Publishing Co., 1421 South
Sheridan Road, P.O. Box 1260. Tulsa
OK 74101. 918/835-3161.

PAPER AND WOOD PRODUCTS

If the economy continues to strengthen and export markets regain the momentum lost during the last few years, the industry should see revenues grow about 10 percent by the end of 1996. Technological advances should strengthen the industry both at home and abroad. Environmental concerns voiced by the public should give the paper packaging segment an advantage over plastics, as companies move to become "green."

Lumber and wood product shipments rose only slightly in 1993. Nationwide, the industry has been hit hard -- according to industry observers, more than 125 lumber and panel product mills in the Pacific Northwest, the heart of the U.S. lumber industry, have closed in the past three years due in part to poor log supplies.

AMERICAN ENVELOPE COMPANY
PHILADELPHIA DIVISION
5th and Bristol, Philadelphia PA 19140. 215/324-9200. **Contact:** Ginny Levitt, Personnel Administrator. **Description:** A division of American Envelope (Chicago), a national envelope manufacturer.

BROSIAS ELIASON COMPANY
508 South Street, New Castle DE 19720. 302/328-9481. **Contact:** Jen Englehart, Administrative Manager. **Description:** A Delaware lumber company.

CONESTOGA WOOD SPECIALTIES, INC.
245 Reading Road, P.O. Box 158, East Earl PA 17519. 717/445-6701. **Contact:** Gary Cooper, Human Resources Manager. **Description:** Produces millwork, especially panel doors, components, and moldings. **Common positions include:** Accountant/Auditor; Blue-Collar Worker Supervisor; Computer Programmer; Customer Service Representative; Department Manager; Draftsperson; Electrical/Electronic Engineer; Financial Analyst; General Manager; Industrial Engineer; Industrial Manager; Marketing Specialist; Mechanical Engineer; Operations/ Production Manager; Personnel/Labor Relations Specialist; Public Relations Specialist; Purchasing Agent and Manager; Quality Control Supervisor; Sales Associate; Systems Analyst; Transportation/Traffic Specialist. **Educational backgrounds include:** Accounting; Business Administration; Communications; Economics; Engineering; Finance; Marketing; Mathematics. **Benefits:** Dental Insurance; Disability Coverage; Employee Discounts; Life Insurance; Medical Insurance; Profit Sharing; Tuition Assistance. **Special Programs:** Training Programs. **Corporate headquarters location:** This Location. **Operations at this facility include:** Administration; Divisional Headquarters; Manufacturing; Sales; Service.

CONTAINER CORPORATION OF AMERICA
5000 Flat Rock Road, Philadelphia PA 19127. 215/984-7000. **Contact:** Carole Blessing, Personnel Manager. **Description:** A large producer of paperboard packaging. Manufacturing facilities are located throughout the United States and in foreign locations. Products include shipping containers, folding cartons, composite cans,

plastic drums, and many others. **Corporate headquarters location:** Clayton MO. **Parent company:** Jefferson/Smurfit Corporation.

CONTINENTAL PAPER BOX MANUFACTURING COMPANY
1147 North 4th Street, Philadelphia PA 19123. 215/627-4700. **Contact:** Ben Berman, President. **Description:** A manufacturer of a variety of paper packaging products.

CROWELL CORPORATION
P.O. Box 3227, Newport DE 19804. 302/998-0557. **Contact:** Joan Addleman, Vice President of Administration. **Description:** A Delaware manufacturer of paper tape.

P.H. GLATFELTER COMPANY
228 South Main Street, Spring Grove PA 17362. 717/225-4711. **FAX:** 717/225-6834. **Contact:** Kenneth N. Ross, Training and Personnel Manager. **Description:** A manufacturer of fine quality papers for the printing, book publishing, business forms, and technical specialties markets. **Common positions include:** Accountant/Auditor; Chemist; Computer Programmer; Electrical/Electronic Engineer; Manufacturer's/Wholesaler's Sales Rep.; Mechanical Engineer. **Educational backgrounds include:** Accounting; Chemistry; Computer Science; Engineering; Liberal Arts; Marketing; Mathematics. **Benefits:** Dental Insurance; Disability Coverage; Life Insurance; Medical Insurance; Pension Plan; Profit Sharing; Savings Plan; Stock Option; Tuition Assistance. **Special Programs:** Apprenticeships; Internships; Training Programs. **Corporate headquarters location:** This Location. **Operations at this facility include:** Administration; Divisional Headquarters; Manufacturing; Regional Headquarters; Research and Development; Sales; Service. **Listed on:** American Stock Exchange. **Number of employees at this location:** 1,106. **Number of employees nationwide:** 3,300. **Projected hires for the next 12 months (This location):** 10 hires. **Projected hires for the next 12 months (Nationwide):** 20 hires.

GLOBE WEIS
P.O. Box 11, Bristol PA 19007. 215/785-1531. **Contact:** Kathy Wickham, Human Resources Manager. **Description:** Produces office paper products. **Common positions include:** Accountant/Auditor; Blue-Collar Worker Supervisor; Computer Programmer; Customer Service Representative; Industrial Engineer; Operations/Production Manager; Personnel/Labor Relations Specialist. **Educational backgrounds include:** Business Administration; Computer Science; Engineering. **Benefits:** Dental Insurance; Disability Coverage; EAP; Life Insurance; Medical Insurance; Pension Plan; Savings Plan; Tuition Assistance. **Corporate headquarters location:** Baltimore MD. **Operations at this facility include:** Administration; Divisional Headquarters; Manufacturing; Sales.

G.B. GOLDMAN PAPER COMPANY
2201 East Allegheny Avenue, Philadelphia PA 19134. 215/423-8600. **Contact:** Charles Clark, Personnel. **Description:** A Philadelphia paper company.

HUNT MANUFACTURING CO. INC.
230 South Broad Street, Philadelphia PA 19102. 215/732-7700. **FAX:** 215/875-5311. **Contact:** Fran Lillo, Human Resources Assistant. **Description:** Manufactures art and office supplies and office furniture. **Common positions include:** Accountant/Auditor; Budget Analyst; Computer Operator; Computer Programmer; Computer Systems Analyst; Credit Manager; Department Manager; General Manager; Graphic Artist; Manufacturer's/Wholesaler's Sales Rep.; Marketing Research Analyst; Marketing/Advertising/PR Manager; Personnel/Labor Relations Specialist; Public Relations Specialist; Receptionist; Secretary. **Educational backgrounds include:** Accounting; Art/Design; Business Administration; Finance; Marketing. **Benefits:** Dental

Insurance; Disability Coverage; Employee Discounts; Life Insurance; Medical Insurance; Pension Plan; Profit Sharing; Savings Plan; Tuition Assistance. **Corporate headquarters location:** This Location. **Other U.S. locations:** AL; CT; KY; NC; TX; WI. **Operations at this facility include:** Administration. **Listed on:** New York Stock Exchange. **Number of employees at this location:** 1,015. Hires/Layoffs in 1993 (This location): 22 hires. Projected hires for the next 12 months (This location): 10 hires.

INTERNATIONAL PAPER COMPANY
LIQUID PACKAGING DIVISION
2100 East Byberry Road, Philadelphia PA 19116. 215/698-4100. **Contact:** Mike Siegel, Plant Manager. **Description:** One of the world's largest natural resource management companies. It produces solid wood products, including plywood, lumber, poles, and cabinets, and a variety of pulp and paper products, packaging materials, and packaging systems. In addition, the company is engaged in the development of mineral properties; health care products; formed fabrics; other products; and in the general commercial and industrial credit business. International facilities. **Corporate headquarters location:** Memphis TN. **Listed on:** New York Stock Exchange.

INTERSTATE CONTAINER CORPORATION
P.O. Box 317, Reading PA 19603. 215/376-7123. **Contact:** Carol Williamson, Personnel Administration. **Description:** Manufactures corrugated shipping containers at this location and at Lowell, MA plants. This facility also operates a paper mill which produces corrugating medium. **Common positions include:** Customer Service Representative; Department Manager; Manufacturer's/Wholesaler's Sales Rep. **Educational backgrounds include:** Business Administration; Economics; Marketing. **Benefits:** Dental Insurance; Disability Coverage; Life Insurance; Medical Insurance; Pension Plan; Savings Plan. **Corporate headquarters location:** Rosslyn VA. **Operations at this facility include:** Manufacturing.

MAIL-WELL ENVELOPE COMPANY
P.O. Box 21050, Lehigh Valley PA 18002-1050. 215/264-0535. **Contact:** Joseph Maziarz, Personnel Manager. **Description:** Produces envelopes for the direct mail market. **Common positions include:** Accountant/Auditor; Blue-Collar Worker Supervisor; Branch Manager; Credit Manager; Customer Service Representative; Department Manager; Manufacturer's/Wholesaler's Sales Rep.; Personnel/Labor Relations Specialist; Purchasing Agent and Manager. **Educational backgrounds include:** Business Administration; Finance; Graphic Design; Marketing. **Benefits:** Dental Insurance; Disability Coverage; Employee Discounts; Life Insurance; Medical Insurance; Pension Plan; Savings Plan; Tuition Assistance. **Operations at this facility include:** Administration; Manufacturing; Sales; Service. **Listed on:** New York Stock Exchange.

McARDLE-DESCO CORPORATION
P.O. Box 765, New Castle DE 19720. 302/322-5411. **Contact:** Joseph J. Pendrak, Jr., Controller/Assistant Treasurer. **Description:** Distributors for valves, gaskets, piping, and commercial plumbing supplies. **Common positions include:** Accountant/Auditor; Buyer; Computer Programmer; Credit Manager; Manufacturer's/Wholesaler's Sales Rep.; Operations/Production Manager; Purchasing Agent and Manager; Systems Manager; Warehouse Manager. **Educational backgrounds include:** Accounting; Business Administration; Computer Science; Finance; Marketing. **Benefits:** Dental Insurance; Disability Coverage; Life Insurance; Medical Insurance; Profit Sharing; Savings Plan. **Corporate headquarters location:** This Location. **Parent company:** Vail Enterprises, Inc. **Operations at this facility include:** Administration; Sales.

NVF CO. INC.

P.O. Box 68, Yorklyn DE 19736. 302/239-5281. **Contact:** Lydia Akerman, Personnel Director. **Description:** Main office with facilities in Newark and Wilmington. Produces vulcanized fiber-paper and industrial laminates.

QUAKER MAID
DIVISION OF WHITE CONSOLIDATED INDUSTRIES, INC.

State Route 61, P.O. Box H, Leesport PA 19533-9984. 215/926-3011. **Contact:** Donald Muller, Manager of Human Resources. **Description:** Manufacturer of custom wood kitchen and laminate cabinetry for all rooms. **Common positions include:** Accountant/Auditor; Buyer; Computer Programmer; Credit Manager; Customer Service Representative; Draftsperson; Industrial Engineer; Manufacturer's/ Wholesaler's Sales Rep.; Marketing Specialist; Operations/Production Manager; Personnel/Labor Relations Specialist; Purchasing Agent and Manager; Quality Control Supervisor. **Educational backgrounds include:** Accounting; Business Administration; Finance; Marketing. **Benefits:** Dental Insurance; Disability Coverage; Life Insurance; Medical Insurance; Pension Plan; Savings Plan. **Corporate headquarters location:** This Location. **Operations at this facility include:** Administration; Manufacturing; Sales.

SCOTT PAPER CO.

Front Street and Avenue of the States, Chester PA 19013. 215/874-4331. **Contact:** Human Resources Department. **Description:** A paper mill.

SIMPSON PAPER COMPANY

P.O. Box 201, Miquon PA 19452-0201. 215/828-5800. **Contact:** Personnel Manager. **Description:** Produces a wide range of paper products at mills throughout the United States. **Common positions include:** Blue-Collar Worker Supervisor; Chemical Engineer; Electrical/Electronic Engineer. **Educational backgrounds include:** Chemistry; Engineering. **Benefits:** Dental Insurance; Disability Coverage; Employee Discounts; Life Insurance; Medical Insurance; Pension Plan; Profit Sharing; Savings Plan; Tuition Assistance. **Corporate headquarters location:** San Francisco CA. **Parent company:** Seattle USA. **Operations at this facility include:** Administration; Manufacturing.

STERLING PAPER COMPANY

2155 East Castor Avenue, Philadelphia PA 19134. 215/744-5350. **Contact:** Controller. **Description:** A manufacturer of a wide variety of paper plates, cups, and other paper products.

STONE CONTAINER CORPORATION

Tulip & Decatur Streets, Philadelphia PA 19136. 215/332-0200. **Contact:** Beverly Kantner, Personnel Director. **Description:** Produces and sells paperboard packaging products in two major divisions: paperboard and corrugated containers (including this facility). Paperboard Division produces three types of paperboard, primarily for in-house sale; Corrugated Container Division is one of the 15 largest producers in the United States and sells primarily to the food and paper industries. **Corporate headquarters location:** Chicago IL. **Listed on:** New York Stock Exchange.

WILLIAM M. YOUNG LUMBER

P.O. Box 10487, Wilmington DE 19850. 302/654-4448. **Contact:** John Gormley, Personnel. **Description:** A Wilmington lumberyard.

Note: Because addresses and telephone numbers of smaller companies change rapidly, we recommend you contact each company and verify the information below before contacting employers. Mass mailings are not recommended.

Additional large employers: 500 +

HARDWOOD AND PLYWOOD

Masonite Corp. Eastern Hardboard
P.O. Box 311, Masonite Rd., Towanda PA 18848. 717/265-9121.

PAPER MILLS

Paper Corp. Of America
P.O. Box 958, Valley Forge PA 19482-0951. 610/296-8000.

COATED AND LAMINATED PAPER

Appleton Papers Inc.
2850 Appleton St., Camp Hill PA 17011-8001. 717/761-6250.

PAPER AND PAPERBOARD PRODUCTS

Berwick Industries Inc.
P.O. Box 428, Berwick PA 18603-0428. 717/752-5934.

Additional medium sized employers: under 500

PAPER MILLS

Ahlstrom Filtration Inc.
122 W Butler St, Mt Holly Spgs PA 17065-1218. 717/486-3438.

Four-M Manufacturing Company
Cardinal Dr, Mount Carmel PA 17851. 717/339-3200.

Neenah Paper Co.
75 Rittenhouse Pl, Ardmore PA 19003-2220. 610/642-1411.

Repap Technologies
2650 Eisenhower Ave, Norristown PA 19403-2314. 610/630-9630.

Stora Papyrus
170 Meredith Ave, Bryn Mawr PA 19010-1318. 610/527-8950.

Ted Lick Consulting
210 Oakleigh Ave, Harrisburg PA 17111-2245. 717/564-4205.

Webform Inc.
900 Line St, Easton PA 18042-7366. 610/258-4110.

PAPERBOARD MILLS

Gold Bond Building Products
Old Rt 15 & I-80, New Columbia PA 17856. 717/538-2531.

SETUP PAPERBOARD BOXES

Simkins Corporation
2824 N 2nd St, Philadelphia PA 19133-3515. 215/739-4033.

CORRUGATED AND SOLID FIBER BOXES

Associated Packaging
1300 Metropolitan Ave, Paulsboro NJ 08066-1823. 609/853-7000.

Beacon Container Corporation
W First & Monore Sts, Birdsboro PA 19508-2368. 610/582-2222.

Cardinal Container Corporation
Cardinal Dr, Mount Carmel PA 17851. 717/339-1611.

Connelly Containers
Righters Ferry Rd, Bala Cynwyd PA 19004. 215/839-6400.

Cor-Box Inc.
Boxwood Lane, York PA 17402. 717/757-2683.

Inland Container Corporation
136 E York St, Biglerville PA 17307-9587.
717/677-8121.

Jefferson Smurfit Corporation
100 McDonald Blvd, Aston PA 19014-3202.
610/485-8700.

McLean Packaging Corporation
3150 Salmon St, Philadelphia PA 19134-5830. 215/423-7800.

Oxford Container Co.
College Ave Ext, New Oxford PA 17350.
717/624-2122.

Oxford Innovations
5 Commerce St, Hanover PA 17331-2104.
717/632-4800.

Packaging Corporation Of America
1530 Fruitville Pike, Lancaster PA 17601-4006. 717/397-3591.

Packaging Corporation Of America
745 Cetronia Rd, Trexlertown PA 18087.
610/395-2091.

Regal Corrugated Box Co Inc.
Adams Ave & Ashland St, Philadelphia PA 19124. 215/533-6000.

Southern Container Corporation
500 Richardson Dr, Lancaster PA 17603-4096. 717/393-0436.

Specialty Industries
120 N Charles St, Red Lion PA 17356-1604.
717/246-1661.

Tim-Bar Corporation
148 Penn St, Hanover PA 17331-1952. 717/632-4727.

Union Camp Corporation
PO Box 2040, Trenton NJ 08607-2040.
609/587-2000.

Union Camp Corporation
801 Fountain Ave, Lancaster PA 17601-4532. 717/397-3741.

Visy Board Packaging
9250 Ashton Rd, Philadelphia PA 19114-3408. 215/676-5800.

Weber Display & Packaging
3500 Richmond St, Philadelphia PA 19134-6102. 215/426-3500.

Weyerhauser Company
100 E Gloucester Pike, Barrington NJ 08007-1330. 609/546-7000.

York Container Co.
138 Mt Zion Rd, York PA 17402-8985. 717/757-7611.

FIBER CANS, TUBES AND DRUMS

Natico Inc.
1600 National Hgwy, Pennsauken NJ 08110.
609/665-2900.

SANITARY FOOD CONTAINERS

Intl Paper Company Liquid Packaging Div
2100 Byberry Rd, Philadelphia PA 19116-3070. 215/698-4100.

FOLDING PAPERBOARD BOXES

Dopaco Inc.
241 Woodbine Rd, Downingtown PA 19335-3083. 610/269-1776.

Klearfold Inc.
364 Valley Rd, Warrington PA 18976-2551. 215/343-9300.

Oak Tree Packaging Corporation
Hokes Mill Rd & Lemon St, York PA 17404.
717/848-2334.

Royal-Pioneer Industries
Castor & Tulip, Philadelphia PA 19134.
215/289-8050.

Sterling Lebanon Corporation
Rts 22 & 72, Jonestown PA 17038. 717/865-5221.

PACKAGING PAPER AND PLASTICS FILM

CP Converters Inc.
15 Grumbacher Rd, York PA 17402-9417.
717/764-1193.

Paxar ASL Group
Label Ln, Troy PA 16947. 717/297-2196.

Superpac Inc.
Southampton Industrial Park, Southampton PA 18966. 215/464-3200.

COATED AND LAMINATED PAPER

Adhesive Research Inc.
Rte 216, Glen Rock PA 17327. 717/235-7979.

Amer Biltrite Tape Prod
105 Whittendale Dr, Moorestown NJ 08057-1364. 609/778-0700.

Fasson
35 Penn-Am Dr, Quakertown PA 18951-2434. 215/536-9000.

Norwood Industries
57 Markel Rd, Malvern PA 19355-1536. 610/647-3500.

PLASTICS, FOIL AND COATED PAPER BAGS

Atlantic Cheinco Corporation
William St, Burlington NJ 08016. 609/386-2800.

Trinity Packaging Corporation
13 Indl Pk Rd, Lewistown PA 17044. 717/242-2355.

Union Camp Corporation
Humboldt Indl Pk R R 1, Hazleton PA 18201-9801. 717/384-4674.

DIE-CUT PAPER AND PAPERBOARD

American Packaging Corporation
Grant & Ashton, Philadelphia PA 19114. 215/698-4800.

Autokraft Box Corporation
PO Box 128, Red Lion PA 17356-0128. 717/244-4041.

National Fiberstok Corporation
2801 Grant Ave, Philadelphia PA 19114-1098. 215/464-8700.

Sharp Corporation
Carland Rd & Ridge Pike, Conshohocken PA 19428. 610/279-3550.

ENVELOPES

Allen Envelope Corporation
1001 Cassatt Rd, Berwyn PA 19312-1151. 610/296-0500.

Tri-State Envelope Corporation
20th & Market Sts, Ashland PA 17921. 717/875-0433.

STATIONERY, TABLETS AND RELATED PRODUCTS

Atapco Office Prdts Group
7 Wood Ave, Bristol PA 19007-4816. 215/785-1531.

CONVERTED PAPER AND PAPERBOARD PRODUCTS

Beistle Co.
PO Box 10, Shippensburg PA 17257-0010. 717/532-2131.

Papel-Freelance Inc.
2530 U S Hwy 130, Cranbury NJ 08512. 609/395-0022.

Paper Magic Group
401 Adams Ave, Scranton PA 18510-2025. 717/961-3863.

Paper Manufacturers
9800 Bustleton Ave, Philadelphia PA 19115-2197. 215/673-4500.

Roosevelt Paper Co.
7601 State Rd, Philadelphia PA 19136-3496. 215/331-5000.

Stenco Paper Products
1101 Kings Hwy N, Cherry Hill NJ 08034-1913. 609/482-0050.

Unique Industries Inc.
2400 Weccacoe Ave, Philadelphia PA 19148-4298. 215/336-4300.

Woodstream Corporation
69 N Locust St, Lititz PA 17543-1714. 717/626-2125.

York Wall Coverings
750 Linden Ave, York PA 17404-3373. 717/846-4456.

RECONSTITUTED WOOD PRODUCTS

Conwed Bonded Fiber Company
Coopertown Rd, Riverside NJ 08075. 609/461-3400.

Denlinger Inc.
Rt 30, Paradise PA 17562. 717/768-8244.

Homasote Co.
PO Box 7240, Trenton
NJ 08628-0240.
609/883-3300.

WOOD PRODUCTS

Ginsey Industries
281 Benigno Blvd,
Bellmawr NJ 08031-
2585. 609/933-1300.

HARDWOOD DIMENSION AND FLOORING MILLS

Catawissa Lumber &
Specialty Co Inc.
PO Box 176, Catawissa
PA 17820-0176.
717/356-2349.

Catawissa Lumber &
Specialty Co Inc.
Rt 487, Paxinos PA
17860. 717/644-1928.

Walter H Weaber & Sons
Inc.
R D 4, Lebanon PA
17042-9804. 717/867-
2212.

MILLWORK

Allensville Planing Mill
Main St, Allensville PA
17002. 717/483-6386.

Gunton Building Products
2550 General Armistead
Ave, Norristown PA
19403-5214. 610/631-
9500.

Middle Atlantic Millwork
PO Box 529, Woodbury
Hgts NJ 08097-0529.
609/848-8000.

Mohawk Flush Doors
Rte 11, Northumberlnd
PA 17857. 717/473-
3557.

Morgan Products Ltd
299 Mulberry Dr,
Mechanicsburg PA
17055-3139. 717/697-
0346.

Wenco Inc. Of
Pennsylvania
W Main St, Ringtown PA
17967. 717/889-3173.

Young Door Co Inc.
215 Packer St, Sunbury
PA 17801-1227.
717/286-5691.

WOOD KITCHEN CABINETS

Adelphi Kitchens Inc.
Penn Ave & Freeman St,
Robesonia PA 19551.
610/693-3101.

Heritage Custom
Kitchens Inc.
215 Diller Ave, New
Holland PA 17557-1611.
717/354-4011.

Kountry Kraft Kitchens
Inc.
PO Box 570,
Newmanstown PA
17073-0570. 610/589-
4575.

Quality Custom Kitchens
Inc.
125 Peters Rd, New
Holland PA 17557-9205.
717/656-2721.

HARDWOOD VENEER AND PLYWOOD

Columbia Forest Products
Constitution Ave, New
Freedom PA 17349.
717/235-3802.

Keystone Veneers Inc.
240 N Reach Rd,
Williamsport PA 17701-
9101. 717/322-4400.

STRUCTURAL WOOD MEMBERS

Berks Products
Corporation
726 Spring St, Reading
PA 19604-2208.
610/374-5131.

For more information on career opportunities in the paper and wood products industries:

Associations

AMERICAN FOREST AND PAPER
ASSOCIATION
1111 19th Street NW, Suite 700,
Washington DC 20036. 202/463-
2700.

AMERICAN FOREST AND PAPER
ASSOCIATION
260 Madison Avenue, New York NY
10016. 212/340-0600.

AMERICAN FOREST AND PAPER ASSOCIATION
1250 Connecticut Avenue NW, Washington DC 20036. 202/463-2700.

FOREST PRODUCTS RESEARCH SOCIETY
2801 Marshall Court, Madison WI 53705. 608/231-1361.

NATIONAL PAPER TRADE ASSOCIATION
111 Great Neck Road, Great Neck NY 11021. 516/829-3070.

PAPERBOARD PACKAGING COUNCIL
888 17th Street NW, Suite 900, Washington DC 20006. 202/289-4100.

TECHNICAL ASSOCIATION OF THE PULP AND PAPER INDUSTRY
P.O. Box 105113, Atlanta GA 30348. 404/446-1400.

Directories

DIRECTORY OF THE FOREST PRODUCTS INDUSTRY
Miller Freeman Publications, Inc., 600 Harrison Street, San Francisco CA 94107. 415/905-2200.

LOCKWOOD-POST'S DIRECTORY OF THE PAPER AND ALLIED TRADES
Miller Freeman Publications, Inc., 600 Harrison Street, San Francisco CA 94107. 415/905-2200.

POST'S PULP AND PAPER DIRECTORY
Miller Freeman Publications, Inc., 600 Harrison Street, San Francisco CA 94107. 415/905-2200.

Magazines

PAPERBOARD PACKAGING
Advanstar Communications, 131 West First Street, Duluth MN 55802. 218/723-9200.

PULP AND PAPER WEEK
Miller Freeman Publications, Inc., 600 Harrison Street, San Francisco CA 94107. 415/905-2200.

WOOD TECHNOLOGIES
Miller Freeman Publications, Inc., 600 Harrison Street, San Francisco CA 94107. 415/905-2200.

PERSONAL SERVICES

There are a variety of services which fall under this industry. Here's a sampling:

Animal Caretakers: Non-farm caretakers include people who feed, water, groom, bathe and exercise animals. They are usually employed by kennels, veterinary facilities and stables. Employment should grow faster than the national average through the year 2005. In addition to an expansion of the population and economy, the growing pet population will also contribute to the growth of this field.

Barbers and Cosmetologists: Overall employment in this field is expected to do quite well through the next decade. Population growth, rising incomes and a growing demand for these services will spur further expansion. Most of the employment growth will be for cosmetologists, as the trend to personalized, full-service, unisex salons continues.

KEYSTONE AUTO CLUB OF AMERICA
AAA
2040 Market Street, Philadelphia PA 19103. 215/864-5000. **Contact:** Judith Compagno, Staffing and Employment. **Description:** Philadelphia office of the well-known automotive services company.

NUTRI/SYSTEM INC.
410 Horsham Road, Horsham PA 19044. 215/442-5300. **Contact:** Manager/Human Resources. **Description:** A chain of weight loss centers providing professionally supervised services through a network of 1700 company-owned and franchised centers in the U.S., Canada, England, and Australia. Privately held. **Common positions include:** Accountant/Auditor; Attorney; Computer Programmer; Customer Service Representative; Dietician/Nutritionist; Food Scientist/Technologist; Marketing Specialist; Systems Analyst; Technical Writer/Editor. **Educational backgrounds include:** Accounting; Computer Science; Marketing. **Benefits:** 401K; Dental Insurance; Disability Coverage; Life Insurance; Medical Insurance; Pension Plan; Profit Sharing. **Special Programs:** Internships; Training Programs. **Corporate headquarters location:** This Location. **Operations at this facility include:** Administration; Research and Development. **Number of employees at this location:** 4,000.

Note: Because addresses and telephone numbers of smaller companies change rapidly, we recommend you contact each company and verify the information below before contacting employers. Mass mailings are not recommended.

Additional medium sized employers: under 500

TRUCK RENTAL AND LEASING

Rollins Truck Rental & Leasing
180 Greenfield Rd,
Lancaster PA 17601-5832. 717/299-5224.

Ryder Truck Rental & Leasing
RR 3, Denver PA 17517-9803. 717/336-3861.

Altra Auto Rental
2555 Nazareth Rd,
Easton PA 18042-2712.
610/250-1974.

PASSENGER CAR RENTAL

Enterprise Rent-A-Car
2110 Route 70 E, Cherry Hill NJ 08003-1203.
609/751-7272.

Enterprise Rent-A-Car
970 Loucks Rd, York PA 17404-2273. 717/854-4151.

Express Car & Trunk Rental
1750 The Fairway,
Jenkintown PA 19046.
215/885-1400.

Half-A-Car
550 Heath Rd, Merion Sta PA 19066-1423.
610/664-8221.

Lehigh Valley Ford Rental
333 State Ave, Emmaus PA 18049-3023.
610/965-6202.

UTILITY TRAILER AND RECREATIONAL VEHICLE LEASING

Strick Lease Inc.
111 Carolina Way,
Carlisle PA 17013-8813.
717/258-5665.

FUNERAL SERVICE AND CREMATORIES

Spencer T Videon Inc. & Assocs
Garrett Rd & Shadeland Av, Drexel Hill PA 19026. 610/259-2200.

MISCELLANEOUS PERSONAL SERVICES

Capitol Rent A Tux
Park City Center,
Lancaster PA 17601.
717/392-3290.

Food Abuse Center-Introspect
2321 N Broad St, Colmar PA 18915-9702.
215/997-3600.

Invisions Inc.
100 Canal Pointe Blvd,
Princeton NJ 08540-7063. 609/452-1331.

Jenny Craig Weight Loss Centre
910 E Woodland Ave,
Springfield PA 19064.
610/328-0929.

Jenny Craig Weight Loss Centers
4395 W Swamp Rd,
Doylestown PA 18901-1039. 215/348-7331.

Smalls Formal Wear
Willow Grove Prk Mall,
Willow Grove PA 19090.
215/659-3068.

Weight Watchers
25 Gateway Dr # 113,
Mechanicsburg PA 17055-2908. 717/763-1290.

LAWN AND GARDEN SERVICE

Brickman Industries
375 S Flowers Mill Rd,
Langhorne PA 19047-2939. 215/757-9400.

Buck & Doe Turf Farm
Cannery Rd, Coatesville PA 19320. 610/486-6073.

S&S Landscape Designs
41 Fairview Ave, Mount Pocono PA 18344-1646.
717/839-9154.

Waterloo Gardens Inc.
200 N Whitford Rd,
Exton PA 19341-2099.
610/363-0800.

ORNAMENTAL SHRUB AND TREE SERVICE

Quaker City Tree Inc.
501 New Jersey Av,
Glassboro NJ 08028.
609/863-8800.

POWER LAUNDRIES

Angelica Health Care
58 & Lindbergh Blvd,
Philadelphia PA 19143.
215/724-7800.

Millville Laund & Dry Cleaners
26 W McNeal St, Millville NJ 08332-3799.
609/825-0360.

GARMENT PRESSING

Apex Cleaners & Laundries
507 Baltimore Pike, Springfield PA 19064-3811. 610/565-8539.

Fairway Cleaners
Twining Rd & Limeklin Pke, Dresher PA 19025.
215/646-1338.

Parkway One Hour Cleaners
929 S High St, West Chester PA 19382-5466.
610/692-4366.

PRINTING AND PUBLISHING

Cuts in print advertising have hurt the printing industry in recent years, but as the U.S. economy improves and more money is spent on advertising, things will improve for printers. They will still face tight profit margins because of rising supply costs -- the price of paper is expected to remain soft, with paper mill capacity outstripping demand; and the costs of other materials, like film, chemicals, and plates, are expected to gradually rise in response to an improving economy. But despite these pressures, increased sales should mean that after years of layoffs, printers will begin hiring again. Job opportunities for bindery workers and printing press operators will experience a growth rate similar to all other professions, while openings for prepress workers will be slightly below that average.

Newspaper and magazine publishers have also been suffering from shrinking advertising dollars, but they expected 1994 to be a good year, as the overall economy improved and clients increased their advertising budgets. For the long-term, look for newspaper companies to target specific readers in order to attract advertisers.

An improving economy will also help book publishers, who were hit hard by the recession of the early 1990s. As the economic recovery continues and disposable income increases, sales of adult trade books will climb. The expanding 5-14 year-old age group should also prompt a rise in sales of juvenile books. Employment in the book publishing industry was expected to jump to 77,000 in 1994, a gain of roughly 1,000 nationwide. Those jobs were expected in editorial, marketing and administrative positions.

BIOSIS, INC.
2100 Arch Street, Philadelphia PA 19103. 215/587-4800. **Contact:** Personnel. **Description:** A not-for-profit educational institution that provides bibliographic retrieval products and services in the life sciences. Abstracts scientific literature. **Common positions include:** Computer Programmer; Marketing Specialist; Public Relations Specialist; Systems Analyst; Technical Writer/Editor. **Educational backgrounds include:** Biology; Chemistry; Computer Science; Marketing. **Benefits:** Dental Insurance; Disability Coverage; Flextime Plan; Life Insurance; Medical Insurance; Pension Plan; Savings Plan; Tuition Assistance. **Special Programs:** Training Programs. **Corporate headquarters location:** This Location.

BRACELAND BROS. INC.
7625 Suffolk Avenue, Philadelphia PA 19153. 215/492-0200. **Contact:** Kelly Monteforte, Personnel Director. **Description:** A Philadelphia printing company.

BUCKS COUNTY COURIER TIMES, INC.

8400 Route 13, Levittown PA 19057. 215/949-4000. **Contact:** Personnel Department. **Description:** Publishes a daily newspaper (Bucks County Courier Times), with a circulation of more than 65,000.

CHILTON COMPANY

201 King of Prussia Road, Radnor PA 19089. 215/964-4000. **Contact:** Marilyn McLaughlin, Employment Manager. **Description:** A large magazine and book publisher, also engaged in providing commercial printing services. Magazines include industrial and trade, tennis, and travel magazines. The Book Division produces Chilton auto manuals, educational materials, and non-fiction books. The Printing Division prints magazines and catalogs for other publishers, and is engaged in offset printing services. **Corporate headquarters location:** This Location.

CLAKINS NEWSPAPERS INC.

P.O. Box 858, Doylestown PA 18901. 215/345-3000. **Contact:** Human Resources. **Description:** A newspaper publisher.

COURIER-POST NEWSPAPER

P.O. Box 5073, Cherry Hill NJ 08034. 609/663-6000. **Contact:** Human Resources. **Description:** A newspaper.

DELMAR NEWS AGENCY, INC.

P.O. Box 7169, Newark DE 19714. **Contact:** Human Resources. **Description:** A distributor of periodicals.

DOW JONES & COMPANY, INC.

P.O. Box 300, Princeton NJ 08543-0300. 609/520-4000. **Contact:** Personnel. **Description:** New Jersey office of the financial news service and publishing company. Publications include The Wall Street Journal.

THE DUNMOREAN

P.O. Box 164, Dunmore PA 18512. 717/941-0105. **Contact:** Human Resources. **Description:** A newspaper publisher.

THE EXPRESS TIMES

30 North Fourth Street, P.O. Box 391, Easton PA 18044-0391. 215/258-7171. **Contact:** Human Resources. **Description:** A newspaper publisher.

FAULKNER TECHNICAL REPORTS, INC.
d.b.a. FAULKNER INFORMATION SERVICES

7905 Browning Road, 114 Cooper Center, Pennsauken NJ 08109-4319. 609/662-2070. **Contact:** Betsey Thomas, Operations - Personnel Administrator. **Description:** Faulkner Information Services is an independent publishing and research company that has specialized in providing technical information and insight to end users and communication and IS professionals for nearly three decades. **Educational backgrounds include:** Accounting; Liberal Arts; Marketing. **Benefits:** 401K; Dental Insurance; Disability Coverage; Life Insurance; Medical Insurance; Tuition Assistance. **Number of employees at this location:** 68.

FRY COMMUNICATIONS INC.

800 West Church Road, Mechanicsburg PA 17055. 717/766-0211. **Contact:** Human Resources. **Description:** A newspaper publisher.

INDEPENDENT NEWSPAPER COMPANY
P.O. Box 7001, Dover DE 19903. 302/674-4750. **Contact:** Personnel Department. **Description:** Publishers of the Delaware State News, a daily Delaware newspaper. In addition, company publishes a variety of weekly papers in Delaware, Florida, Arizona, and Maryland.

INSTITUTE FOR SCIENTIFIC INFORMATION
3501 Market Street, Philadelphia PA 19104. 215/386-0100. **Contact:** Marianne Creelman, Employment Manager. **Description:** Produces more than 50 products, including indexes and data bases that provide essential information from journals, books, and other significant materials published in the sciences, social sciences, and the arts and humanities. **Common positions include:** Accountant/Auditor; Computer Programmer; Customer Service Representative; Data Entry Clerk; Database Management Specialist; Indexer; Manufacturer's/Wholesaler's Sales Rep.; Marketing Specialist; Operations/Production Manager; Proofreader; Purchasing Agent and Manager; Quality Control Supervisor; Systems Analyst; Technical Writer/Editor; Translator; Typist/Word Processor. **Educational backgrounds include:** Accounting; Biology; Chemistry; Communications; Computer Science; Finance; Liberal Arts; Library Science; Marketing; Mathematics; Word Processing. **Corporate headquarters location:** Philadelphia PA.

LANCASTER NEWSPAPERS, INC.
P.O. Box 1328, Lancaster PA 17608. 717/291-8681. **Contact:** Susan Glouner, Personnel Coordinator. **Description:** Publishes the morning Intelligencer Journal, the evening Lancaster New Era, and the Sunday News, with a combined daily circulation of over 100,000. **Common positions include:** Accountant/Auditor; Administrator; Advertising Clerk; Blue-Collar Worker Supervisor; Buyer; Commercial Artist; Computer Programmer; Credit Manager; Customer Service Representative; Department Manager; Editor; Financial Analyst; General Manager; Management Trainee; Mechanical Engineer; Operations/Production Manager; Quality Control Supervisor; Reporter; Services Sales Representative; Systems Analyst; Technical Writer/Editor. **Educational backgrounds include:** Accounting; Art/Design; Business Administration; Communications; Computer Science; Finance; Journalism; Liberal Arts; Marketing. **Benefits:** Dental Insurance; Disability Coverage; Employee Discounts; Life Insurance; Medical Insurance; Pension Plan.

MACK PRINTING COMPANY
1991 Northampton Street, Easton PA 18042-3189. 215/258-9111. **Contact:** Michael Tirrell, Corporate Industrial Relations Manager. **Description:** Provides a wide range of printing and publications services, including publication and catalog printing, photo composition, and binding.

THE MAPLE PRESS COMPANY
Willow Springs Lane, P.O. Box 2695, York PA 17405. 717/764-5911. **Contact:** Shirley Baker, Personnel Manager. **Description:** Principally engaged in the book manufacturing business, producing hardcover and paperback books upon order from publishers. Book manufacturing services include photo composition, printing, and binding. **Corporate headquarters location:** This Location.

MARS GRAPHIC SERVICES INCORPORATED
1 Deadline Drive, Westville NJ 08093. 609/456-8666. **Contact:** Human Resources. **Description:** A printer and lithographer.

McMILLAN PUBLISHING COMPANY
100 Front Street, Box 500, Riverside NJ 08075. 609/461-6500. **Contact:** Human Resources Department. **Description:** A book publishing company.

MONTGOMERY NEWSPAPERS COMPANY
P.O. Box 1628, Fort Washington PA 19034. 215/646-5100. **Contact:** Dolly Gilman, Business Manager. **Description:** Publishes a daily newspaper in Hatboro/Warminster ('Today's Spirit') and weekly newspapers in Ambler, Glenside, Huntingdon, Valley Jenkintown, King of Prussia, Springfield, and Willow Grove. **Corporate headquarters location:** This Location.

MORNING CALL
P.O. Box 1260, Allentown PA 18105. 215/820-6500. **Contact:** Human Resources. **Description:** A newspaper publisher.

NATIONAL NEWS BUREAU INC.
P.O. Box 43039, Philadelphia PA 19219. 215/546-8088. **Contact:** Human Resources. **Description:** A news publishing service.

NATIONAL PUBLISHING COMPANY
24th and Locust Street, Philadelphia PA 19103. 215/732-1863. **Contact:** Charles Keenan, Personnel Director. **Description:** Publishers of the King James version of the Bible; also involved in binding a variety of books for other publishers.

THE NEWS-JOURNAL CO.
950 West Basin Road, New Castle DE 19720. 302/324-2500. **Contact:** Joan Driver, Personnel Director. **Description:** Publishes a daily newspaper as part of the Gannett Newspapers Group (Arlington, VA). Weekday circulation exceeds 64,000; more than 145,000 on Sunday. **Common positions include:** Accountant/Auditor; Administrator; Advertising Clerk; Blue-Collar Worker Supervisor; Commercial Artist; Computer Programmer; Credit Manager; Customer Service Representative; Department Manager; Editor; Marketing Specialist; Operations/Production Manager; Personnel/Labor Relations Specialist; Public Relations Specialist; Purchasing Agent and Manager; Reporter; Services Sales Representative; Systems Analyst; Technical Writer/Editor. **Educational backgrounds include:** Accounting; Art/Design; Business Administration; Communications; Computer Science; Journalism; Marketing. **Benefits:** 401K; Dental Insurance; Disability Coverage; Employee Discounts; Life Insurance; Medical Insurance; Pension Plan; Profit Sharing. **Special Programs:** Internships; Training Programs. **Number of employees at this location:** 620. **Projected hires for the next 12 months (This location):** 45 hires.

NEWS AMERICA PUBLICATIONS, INC./TV GUIDE
100 Matsonford Road, #4 Radnor Corporate Center, Radnor PA 19088. 215/293-8500. **Contact:** Human Resources Department. **Description:** Publishers of TV Guide magazine. **Common positions include:** Accountant/Auditor; Computer Programmer; Financial Analyst; Operations/Production Manager. **Educational backgrounds include:** Accounting; Business Administration; Communications; Computer Science. **Benefits:** Dental Insurance; Employee Discounts; Life Insurance; Medical Insurance; Pension Plan; Profit Sharing; Savings Plan; Tuition Assistance. **Special Programs:** Internships. **Corporate headquarters location:** This Location. **Operations at this facility include:** Administration; Sales; Service. **Number of employees at this location:** 1,300.

NORTH AMERICAN PUBLISHING COMPANY
401 North Broad Street, Philadelphia PA 19108. 215/238-5300. **Contact:** Director of Human Resources. **Description:** A publisher of trade and business magazines. **Common positions include:** Advertising Clerk; Customer Service Representative; Editor; Secretary; Services Sales Representative; Writer. **Educational backgrounds include:** Journalism; Liberal Arts; Marketing. **Benefits:** Medical Insurance; Profit Sharing; Savings Plan; Tuition Assistance. **Corporate headquarters location:** This Location.

PACKARD PRESS
1 Penn Center at Suburban Station, 1617 JFK Boulevard, 19th Floor, Philadelphia PA 19103. 215/563-9000. **Contact:** Mr. Thomas McShane, Personnel. **Description:** A publisher and printer of a wide range of books and magazines concerning the securities, legal, and general finance industries.

PARIS BUSINESS FORMS INCORPORATED
122 Kissel Road, Burlington NJ 08016. 609/387-7300. **Contact:** Human Resources. **Description:** Produces business forms.

PATRIOT NEWS
P.O. Box 2265, Harrisburg PA 17105. 717/255-8100. **Contact:** Personnel. **Description:** A newspaper publisher.

PERFECT PHOTO, INC.
5729 North Broad Street, Philadelphia PA 19141. 215/224-9080. **Contact:** Personnel Manager. **Description:** Provides a wide range of photo and photofinishing services.

PHILADELPHIA BUSINESS JOURNAL
400 Market Street, Suite 300, Philadelphia PA 19106. 215/238-1450. **Contact:** Personnel. **Description:** A weekly business journal.

PHILADELPHIA DAILY NEWS
P.O. Box 7788, Philadelphia PA 19101. 215/854-5984. **FAX:** 215/854-5910. **Contact:** Human Resources. **Description:** A large daily newspaper established in 1925.

PHILADELPHIA INQUIRER
400 North Broad Street, Philadelphia PA 19130. 215/854-2000. **Contact:** Christine Bonanducci, Employee Relations Manager. **Description:** Publishes one of America's largest daily newspapers, with a weekday circulation of more than 700,000. Sunday circulation is more than 1,000,000. **Common positions include:** Accountant/Auditor; Administrator; Advertising Clerk; Blue-Collar Worker Supervisor; Buyer; Computer Programmer; Customer Service Representative; Department Manager; Editor; Financial Analyst; General Manager; Management Trainee; Marketing Specialist; Mechanical Engineer; Operations/ Production Manager; Personnel/Labor Relations Specialist; Purchasing Agent and Manager; Reporter; Systems Analyst. **Parent company:** Knight-Ridder Newspaper Group.

THE PRESS
1000 West Washington Avenue, Pleasantville NJ 08232. 609/272-1100. **Contact:** Human Resources. **Description:** A newspaper publisher.

QUEBECOR PRINTING INC.
P.O. Box 465, Atglen PA 19310. 215/593-5173. **Contact:** Human Resources Department. **Description:** A lithographic commercial printer.

REAL NEWS
P.O. Box 50386, Philadelphia PA 19132. 215/634-7170. **Contact:** Human Resources. **Description:** A newspaper publisher.

RODALE PRESS INC.
33 East Minor Street, Emmaus PA 18098. 215/967-5171. **Contact:** John Volanski, Personnel Director. **Description:** Publishes a wide variety of general-interest trade books.

RUNNING PRESS
125 South 22nd Street, Philadelphia PA 19103. 215/567-5080. **FAX:** 215/568-2919. **Contact:** Human Resources. **Description:** A book publishing company. Publishes non-fiction, children's books, art books, and literature.

SBF COMMUNICATION GRAPHICS
3747 Ridge Avenue, Philadelphia PA 19132. 215/226-1705. **Contact:** John Frock, President. **Description:** A printer of business forms.

W.B. SAUNDERS COMPANY
The Curtis Center, Independence Square, Suite 300, Philadelphia PA 19106. 215/238-7870. **Contact:** Director of Personnel. **Description:** A division of Harcourt Brace & Company. Parent company in business since 1888. Publishes text books, clinical reference books, and periodicals for the medical, nursing and health related professions. Most positions are in editing, production, marketing, advertising, design/illustration, proofreading, sales and clerical. **Common positions include:** Advertising Clerk; Customer Service Representative; Department Manager; Editor; Marketing Specialist; Services Sales Representative; Technical Writer/Editor. **Educational backgrounds include:** Art/Design; Business Administration; English; Marketing; Science. **Benefits:** 401K; Dental Insurance; Disability Coverage; Education Assistance; Employee Discounts; Life Insurance; Meal Discounts; Medical Insurance; Pension Plan; Savings Plan; Scholarship Program; Stock Option; Tuition Assistance. **Corporate headquarters location:** Chestnut Hill MA. **Other U.S. locations:** San Diego CA; Orlando FL; Fort Worth TX; Austin TX. **Parent company:** Harcourt General. **Operations at this facility include:** Administration; Manufacturing; Sales; Service. **Listed on:** New York Stock Exchange. **Number of employees at this location:** 400. **Number of employees nationwide:** 5,000.

SCANFORMS INCORPORATED
Keystone Park, 181 Rittenhouse Circle, Bristol PA 19007. 215/785-0101. **Contact:** Human Resources. **Description:** Produces forms for direct-mail advertising.

E.W. SCRIPPS CO.
1403 Foulk Road, Wilmington DE 19803. 302/478-4141. **Contact:** Human Resources. **Description:** The E.W. Scripps Co. is a diversified media company. The company operates three principal business segments: publishing, broadcasting, and cable television.

SHOPPER'S GUIDE INC.
P.O. Box 5600, Pennsauken NJ 08110. 609/663-8100. **Contact:** Human Resources. **Description:** A publisher.

SMITH-EDWARDS-DUNLAP COMPANY
2867 East Allegheny Avenue, Philadelphia PA 19134. 215/425-8800. **Contact:** Tom Dougherty, Personnel. **Description:** A commercial printer.

UNITED STATES BANKNOTE COMPANY
680 Blair Mill Road, Horsham PA 19044. 215/657-3480. **Contact:** Barbara Butler, Assistant Personnel Manager. **Description:** A financial specialty printing firm, engaged primarily in the engraving and printing of securities, documents, and currency.

YORK TAPE & LABEL CORPORATION
P.O. Box 1309, York PA 17405. 717/846-4840. **Contact:** Deidra McMeans, Personnel Manager. **Description:** Printers and converters of pressure-sensitive labels sold to Fortune 1000 companies and used for primary production decoration. **Common positions include:** Accountant/Auditor; Blue-Collar Worker Supervisor; Buyer; Commercial Artist; Credit Manager; Customer Service Representative; Industrial Engineer; Manufacturer's/Wholesaler's Sales Rep.; Mechanical Engineer; Personnel/Labor Relations Specialist; Printing Press Operator. **Educational backgrounds include:** Accounting; Business Administration; Engineering. **Benefits:** Dental Insurance; Disability Coverage; Employee Discounts; Life Insurance; Medical Insurance; Pension Plan; Savings Plan; Spending Account; Tuition Assistance. **Special Programs:** Training Programs. **Corporate headquarters location:** This Location. **Parent company:** Uarco, Inc.

Note: Because addresses and telephone numbers of smaller companies change rapidly, we recommend you contact each company and verify the information below before contacting employers. Mass mailings are not recommended.

Additional large employers: 500 +

NEWSPAPERS PUBLISHING OR PRINTING

Journal Register Company
50 W State St., Trenton NJ 08608-1298. 609/396-2200.

South Jersey Publishing Company
1000 W Washington Ave., Pleasantville NJ 08232-3861. 609/272-7000.

The Times
500 Perry St., Trenton NJ 08618-3932. 609/396-3232.

BOOK PUBLISHING

McGraw-Hill Inc.
Princeton Rd., Hightstown NJ 08520. 609/426-5000.

BOOK PRINTING

Arcata Graphics/Fairfield
100 N Miller St., Fairfield PA 17320. 717/642-5871.

Brown Printing Company
R R 2 Rt 29 N, E Greenville PA 18041-9802. 215/679-4451.

Haddon Craftsmen Inc.
1001 Wyoming Ave., Scranton PA 18509-2909. 717/348-9211.

COMMERCIAL PRINTING

Jostens Printing & Publishing
401 S Science Park Rd., State College PA 16803-2217. 8142375771.

Deluxe Check Printers
Indl. Blvd. 4, Paoli PA 19301. 610/647-7660.

Lehigh Press Inc.
51 Haddonfield Rd., Cherry Hill NJ 08002-1453. 609/665-5200.

Panel Prints Inc.
1001 Moosic Rd., Old Forge PA 18518-2036. 717/457-8334.

GREETING CARDS

Paper Magic Group Inc.
101 Indl. Park Rd.,
Elysburg PA 17824.
717/644-0842.

TYPESETTING

Intl. Computaprint Corp.
475 Virginia Drive, Ft
Washington PA 19034-
2792. 215/641-6000.

Additional medium sized employers: under 500

BOOKS, PERIODICALS AND NEWSPAPERS WHOLESALE

Brauninger News
121 New York Ave,
Trenton NJ 08638-5299.
609/396-1100.

NEWSPAPER PUBLISHING

Acme Newspapers Inc.
311 East Lancaster Ave,
Ardmore PA 19003-
1403. 610/642-4300.

Burlington Times Inc.
Rte 130, Willingboro NJ
08046. 609/871-8000.

Calkins Newspapers
333 N Broad St,
Doylestown PA 18901-
3407. 215/345-3000.

Central States Publishing
500 Mildred Ave, Clifton
Hgts PA 19018-2914.
610/622-8800.

Centre Daily Times
3400 E College Ave,
State College PA 16801-
7528. 814/238-5000.

Citizens' Voice Inc.
75 N Washington St,
Wilkes Barre PA 18701-
3109. 717/821-2000.

Daily Pennsylvanian
4015 Walnut St,
Philadelphia PA 19104-
6198. 215/898-6581.

Hazleton Standard-Speaker Inc.
21 N Wyoming St,
Hazleton PA 18201-
6068. 717/455-3636.

JH Zerbey Newspapers
111 Mahantongo St,
Pottsville PA 17901-
3008. 717/622-3456.

Norristown Herald Inc.
410 Markley St,
Norristown PA 19401-
4617. 610/272-2500.

Pocono Record
511 Lenox St,
Stroudsburg PA 18360-
1599. 717/421-3000.

Press-Enterprise Inc.
3185 Lackawanna Ave,
Bloomsburg PA 17815-
3398. 717/784-2121.

Princeton University Press
3175 Princeton Pike,
Trenton NJ 08648-2308.
609/896-2111.

Progressive Publishing Company
206 E Locust St,
Clearfield PA 16830-
2423. 814/765-6593.

Public Opinion
77 N 3rd St,
Chambersburg PA
17201-1803. 717/264-
6161.

Scrantonian Tribune
338 N Washington Ave,
Scranton PA 18503-
1502. 717/344-7222.

Suburban Publications
134 N Wayne Ave,
Wayne PA 19087-3315.
610/688-3000.

Sun-Gazette Co.
252 W 4th St,
Williamsport PA 17701-
6102. 717/326-1551.

The Express-Times
PO Box 391, Easton PA
18044-0391. 610/258-
7171.

The Gloucester County Times
309 S Broad St,
Woodbury NJ 08096-
2406. 609/845-3300.

The Patriot-News Co.
812 Market St,
Harrisburg PA 17101-
2808. 717/255-8100.

The Princeton Packet
300 Witherspoon St,
Princeton NJ 08542-
3477. 609/924-3244.

The Reporter
307 Derstine Ave,
Lansdale PA 19446-
3532. 215/855-8440.

The Times Leader
15 N Main St, Wilkes
Barre PA 18711-0201.
717/829-7100.

The Trentonian
PO Box 231, Trenton NJ
08602-0231. 609/989-
7800.

**Times & News Publishing
Co.**
18 Carlisle St,
Gettysburg PA 17325-
1800. 717/334-1131.

Times News
Iron & 1st Sts, Lehighton
PA 18235. 610/377-
2051.

York Newspaper Co.
1891 Loucks Rd, York
PA 17404-9708.
717/767-6397.

PERIODICAL PUBLISHING

Cowles Magazines
PO Box 8200, Harrisburg
PA 17105-8200.
717/657-9555.

Monroe Printing Co.
34 N Crystal St, E
Stroudsburg PA 18301-
2129. 717/421-9033.

**Princeton University
Press**
41 William St, Princeton
NJ 08540-5237.
609/258-4900.

Springhouse Corporation
1111 Bethlehem Pike,
Spring House PA 19477-
1114. 215/646-8700.

BOOK PUBLISHING

Excerpta Medica
105 Raider Blvd, Belle
Mead NJ 08502-1510.
609/896-9450.

Farm Journal Inc.
230 W Washington Sq,
Philadelphia PA 19106-
3522. 215/829-4700.

Herff Jones Yearbooks
525 Boyds School Rd,
Gettysburg PA 17325-
8015. 717/334-9123.

Houghton Mifflin Co.
101 Campus Dr,
Princeton NJ 08540-
6400. 609/452-0200.

**Intelligencer Printing
Company**
330 Eden Rd, Lancaster
PA 17601-4218.
717/291-3100.

JB Lippincott Co.
227 E Washington Sq,
Philadelphia PA 19106-
3719. 215/238-4200.

**National Business
Services Inc.**
1120 Wheeler Way,
Langhorne PA 19047-
1711. 215/752-4200.

Nevins Publishing
172 Orchard Rd, Skillman
NJ 08558-2502.
908/874-5939.

Peterson's Guides Inc.
PO Box 2123, Princeton
NJ 08543-2123.
609/243-9111.

Tab Books
Monterey & Pinola Aves,
Blue Ridge Sm PA
17214. 717/794-2191.

BOOK PRINTING

Bloomsburg Craftsmen
4411 Old Berwick Rd,
Bloomsburg PA 17815-
3599. 717/784-7394.

**Kutztown Publishing
Company Inc.**
PO Box 346, Kutztown
PA 19530-0346.
610/683-7341.

**North American Directory
Corporation**
Rt 924 S, Hazleton PA
18201. 717/459-5700.

**Offset Paperback
Manufacturers Inc.**
Rte 309, Dallas PA
18612-1295. 717/675-
5261.

Suburban Publishers
Stevens Lane, Pittston
PA 18643. 717/655-
6881.

**MISCELLANEOUS
PUBLISHING**

**American Soc Testing &
Materials**
1916 Race St,
Philadelphia PA 19103-
1108. 215/299-5400.

Daily Local News
Bradford Av & Strausberg
Rd, West Chester PA
19382. 610/696-1775.

**Daily Racing Form
Company**
10 Lake Dr, Hightstown
NJ 08520-5321.
609/448-9100.

**Datapro Information
Services**
600 Delran Pkwy,
Riverside NJ 08075-
1255. 609/764-0100.

Reuben H Donnelley Corporation
211 Wyoming Ave,
Scranton PA 18503-
1427. 717/348-3355.

COMMERCIAL PRINTING, LITHOGRAPH

BSC Litho
3000 Canby St,
Harrisburg PA 17103-
2167. 717/238-8378.

Baum Printing House
9985 Gantry Rd,
Philadelphia PA 19115-
1001. 215/671-9500.

Consolidated Drake Press
5050 Parkside Ave,
Philadelphia PA 19131-
4794. 215/879-1400.

Decorating Resources
430 Andbro Dr, Pitman
NJ 08071-1251.
609/589-3800.

FW Dodge Co.
1234 Market St 5th Fl,
Philadelphia PA 19107-
3721. 215/496-4900.

Grafika Commercial Printing Inc.
710 Johnston St,
Reading PA 19608.
610/678-8630.

ICS Corporation
2225 Richmond St,
Philadelphia PA 19125-
4324. 215/427-1540.

International Litho Corporation
11631 Caroline Rd,
Philadelphia PA 19154-
2178. 215/677-9000.

Interprint
2100 Frost Rd, Bristol PA
19007-1517. 215/785-
0700.

Lebanon Valley Offset
E Main St, Annville PA
17003. 717/867-4601.

Lehigh Press Lithographers
7001 North Park Dr,
Merchantville NJ 08109-
4399. 609/665-5200.

Magna Graphic South
121 Rose Twig Lane,
Chalfont PA 18914.
215/997-2002.

Moore Response Marketing Service
4 Neshmnyinterplex,
Fstrvl Trvose PA 19053.
215/244-0300.

Payne Printery Co Inc.
Center Hill Rd, Dallas PA
18612. 717/675-1147.

Pearl-Pressman-Liberty
5th & Poplar Sts,
Philadelphia PA 19123.
215/925-4900.

Pomco Graphics Inc.
4411 Whitaker Ave,
Philadelphia PA 19120-
4698. 215/455-9500.

Regency Thermographers Inc.
725 Clayton Ave,
Waynesboro PA 17268-
2000. 717/762-7161.

Regency-Thermographers Inc.
64 N Conahan Dr,
Hazleton PA 18201-
7355. 717/455-8811.

Robins-Le Cocq Corporation
261 Old York Rd,
Jenkintown PA 19046-
3254. 215/887-5700.

Sheridan Press
450 Fame Ave, Hanover
PA 17331-9581.
717/632-3535.

SLC Graphics Inc.
50 Rock St, Pittston PA
18640. 717/655-9681.

Standard Register Co.
121 Mt Zion Rd, York PA
17402-8985. 717/755-
1051.

Sullivan Graphics Inc.
215 N Zarfoss Dr, York
PA 17404-5837.
717/792-4623.

The Paper Magic Group
1 Eureka Dr, Troy PA
16947-1422. 717/297-
2135.

Today's Sunbeam
PO Box 20, Salem NJ
08079-0020. 609/935-
1500.

Winchell Co.
1315 Cherry St,
Philadelphia PA 19107-
2083. 215/568-1770.

COMMERCIAL PRINTING, GRAVURE

Phototype Color Graphics
7890 Airport Hwy,
Merchantville NJ 08109-
4304. 609/663-4100.

COMMERCIAL PRINTING

Allen Lane & Scott Inc.
2867 E Allegheny Ave,
Philadelphia PA 19134-
5903. 215/561-2300.

American Bank Note Company
680 Blair Mill Rd,
Horsham PA 19044-
2271. 215/657-3480.

Celebrations Wedding
681 Main St, Lumberton
NJ 08048-1102.
609/261-5200.

Eureka Security Printing Co Inc.
101 Church St, Jessup
PA 18434-1048.
717/489-7538.

Globe Ticket & Label Company
300 Constance Dr,
Warminster PA 18974-
2815. 215/443-7960.

Malcom Printing
1770 E Market St Ste
203, York PA 17402-
2874. 717/757-5111.

Metal Lithographic
6 Litho Rd, Trenton NJ
08648-3304. 609/883-
4300.

National Designers Inc.
PO Box 518, Thorofare
NJ 08086-0518.
609/663-5042.

National Label Company
2025 Joshua Rd,
Lafayette HI PA 19444-
2431. 610/825-3250.

Norton Performance Plastics
150 N Delaware Ave,
Atlantic City NJ 08401-
5260. 609/348-5898.

Patton Industries
390 New Albany Rd,
Moorestown NJ 08057-
1116. 609/778-8500.

Tursack Printing Inc.
Rte 23 At 100 R D 2,
Pottstown PA 19464.
610/469-0260.

USA Direct Inc.
4075 N George St Ext,
Manchester PA 17345-
9639. 717/266-5601.

Yorkship Business Supplies Inc.
22 Springdale Rd, Cherry
Hill NJ 08003-1617.
609/424-9510.

MANIFOLD BUSINESS FORMS

Data Papers Inc.
R D 2, Muncy PA 17756-
9802. 717/546-2201.

Forms Inc.
Easton Rd and Pa Tpke,
Willow Grove PA 19090.
215/659-4000.

Moore Business Forms & Systems
100 American Dr,
Quakertown PA 18951-
2433. 215/536-8200.

Moore Business Forms & Systems
Indl Pk, Lewisburg PA
17837. 717/524-2224.

Moore Business Forms & Systems
110 4th St, Honesdale
PA 18431-1891.
717/253-2400.

NCR Corporation Business Forms Division
1160 E Main St, Mount
Joy PA 17552-9337.
717/653-1801.

Rapidforms Inc.
301 Grove Rd, Thorofare
NJ 08086-9400.
609/933-0480.

Reynolds & Reynolds Company
Hood & Commerce Sts,
Chambersburg PA
17201. 717/263-1326.

Safeguard Business Systems Inc.
1180 Church Rd,
Lansdale PA 19446-
3969. 215/361-2300.

Safeguard Business Systems Inc.
217 Church Rd, North
Wales PA 19454-4137.
215/699-3544.

Willamette Inds Inc.
1050 Wheeler Way,
Langhorne PA 19047-
1708. 215/752-1521.

GREETING CARDS

Rousana Cards
145 Lehigh Ave,
Lakewood NJ 08701-
4527. 908/905-6700.

BLANKBOOKS AND LOOSELEAF BINDERS

Buchan Industries Inc.
Penn & Jefferson Sts,
Clifton Hgts PA 19018.
610/622-3500.

JIK Limited
361 W Gordon St,
Allentown PA 18102-
3029.

BOOKBINDING AND RELATED WORK

General Bindery Co.
Third & Hunting Park Aves, Philadelphia PA 19140. 215/457-2515.

Oxford Bookbinding Company
3101 Red Lion Rd, Philadelphia PA 19114-1122. 215/632-0400.

TYPESETTING

Bell Atlantic Directory
2500 Monroe Blvd, Norristown PA 19403-2418. 610/650-5000.

Bi-Comp Inc.
210-234 E York St, York PA 17403. 717/848-1147.

Comcom
834 N 12th St, Allentown PA 18102-1319. 610/437-9656.

Tapsco Inc.
309 Colonial Dr, Akron PA 17501-1210. 717/859-2006.

Volt Information Sciences
1 Sentry Pkwy 1000, Blue Bell PA 19422. 610/825-7720.

Waldman Graphics Inc.
9100 Pennsauken Hwy, Pennsauken NJ 08110-1206. 609/662-9111.

York Graphic Service Inc.
3600 W Market St, York PA 17404-5813. 717/792-3551.

PLATEMAKING

Herff Jones Inc.
1509 Maple St, Scranton PA 18505-2707. 717/346-2095.

For more information on career opportunities in printing and publishing:

Associations

AMERICAN INSTITUTE OF GRAPHIC ARTS
919 3rd Avenue, 22nd Floor, New York NY 10003-3004. 212/807-1990.

NEWSPAPER ASSOCIATION OF AMERICA
Newspaper Center, 11600 Sunrise Valley Drive, Reston VA 22091. 703/648-1000.

AMERICAN SOCIETY OF NEWSPAPER EDITORS
P.O. Box 4090, Reston VA 22090-1700. 703/648-1144.

ASSOCIATION OF GRAPHIC ARTS
330 7th Avenue, 9th Floor, New York NY 10001-5010. 212/279-2100.

BINDING INDUSTRIES OF AMERICA
70 East Lake Street, Suite 300, Chicago IL 60601. 312/372-7606.

THE DOW JONES NEWSPAPER FUND
P.O. Box 300, Princeton NJ 08543-0300. 609/520-4000.

GRAPHIC ARTISTS GUILD
11 West 20th Street, 8th Floor, New York NY 10011. 212/463-7730.

INTERNATIONAL GRAPHIC ARTS EDUCATION ASSOCIATION
4615 Forbes Avenue, Pittsburgh PA 15213. 412/682-5170.

MAGAZINE PUBLISHERS ASSOCIATION
575 Lexington Avenue, Suite 540, New York NY 10022. 212/752-0055.

NATIONAL ASSOCIATION OF PRINTERS AND LITHOGRAPHERS
780 Pallisade Avenue, Teaneck NJ 07666. 201/342-0700.

NATIONAL NEWSPAPER ASSOCIATION
1525 Wilson Boulevard, Arlington VA 22209. 703/907-7900.

NATIONAL PRESS CLUB
529 14th St. NW, 13th Floor, Washington DC 20045. 202/662-7500.

THE NEWSPAPER GUILD
Research and Information Department,
8611 2nd Avenue, Silver Spring MD
20910. 301/585-2990.

PRINTING INDUSTRIES OF AMERICA
100 Dangerfield Road, Arlington VA
22314. 703/519-8100.

**TECHNICAL ASSOCIATION OF THE
GRAPHIC ARTS**
Box 9887, Rochester NY 14623.
716/475-7470.

WRITERS GUILD OF AMERICA WEST
8955 Beverly Boulevard, West
Hollywood CA 90048. 310/550-
1000.

Directories

**EDITOR & PUBLISHER
INTERNATIONAL YEARBOOK**
Editor & Publisher Co. Inc., 11 West
19th Street, New York NY 10011.
212/675-4380.

GRAPHIC ARTS BLUE BOOK
A.F. Lewis & Co., 79 Madison
Avenue, New York NY 10016.
212/679-0770.

**JOURNALISM CAREER AND
SCHOLARSHIP GUIDE**
The Dow Jones Newspaper Fund,
P.O. Box 300, Princeton NJ 08543-
0300. 609/520-4000.

Magazines

AIGA JOURNAL
American Institute of Graphic Arts,
1059 Third Avenue, New York NY
10021. 212/752-0813.

EDITOR AND PUBLISHER
Editor & Publisher Co. Inc., 11 West
19th Street, New York NY 10011.
212/807-1990.

GRAPHIC ARTS MONTHLY
249 West 49th Street, New York NY
10011. 212/463-6836.

GRAPHIS
141 Lexington Avenue, New York NY
10016. 212/532-9387.

PRINT
104 Fifth Avenue, 19th Floor New
York NY 10011. 212/463-0600.

Special Book and Magazine Programs

**THE NEW YORK UNIVERSITY
SUMMER PUBLISHING PROGRAM**
48 Cooper Square, Room 108, New
York NY 10003. 212/998-7219.

**THE RADCLIFFE PUBLISHING
COURSE**
77 Brattle Street, Cambridge MA
02138. 617/495-8678.

**RICE UNIVERSITY PUBLISHING
PROGRAM**
Office of Continuing Studies, P.O. Box
1892, Houston TX 77251-1892.
713/520-6022.

**UNIVERSITY OF DENVER PUBLISHING
INSTITUTE**
2075 South University Boulevard, #D-
114, Denver CO 80208. 303/871-
4868.

REAL ESTATE

Solid opportunities for job seekers will appear for those looking to enter the real estate game. Residential and commercial land sales will help keep up employment opportunities for real estate agents, brokers and appraisers. The number of job openings in these occupations are expected to mimic the number of openings for most other careers nationwide. Most of these openings, however, will be replacement positions, as agents retire or leave the field, rather than new positions being created.

Property and real estate managers will have even greater luck finding employment, as more openings appear for these positions than other occupations. The people with the most qualified backgrounds for these positions will be those with college degrees in business administration and other related fields.

A.D. MORTGAGE CORPORATION
1608 Walnut Street, Suite 1303, Philadelphia PA 19103. 215/546-1600. **Contact:** Human Resources. **Description:** Offers mortgage services.

ACADEMY MORTGAGE SERVICES, INC.
1111 Street Road, Suite 312, Southampton, PA 18966. 215/364-5750. **Contact:** Human Resources. **Description:** A real estate loan company.

AETNA FEDERAL SAVINGS DIVISION
1722 South Broad Street, Philadelphia, PA 19145. 215/463-1800. **Contact:** Human Resources. **Description:** A real estate loan company.

AMERDEL CORPORATION
826 North Lewis Road, Royersford PA 19468. 215/495-7101. **Contact:** Human Resources. **Description:** A land developer.

BINSWANGER
1635 Market Street, Philadelphia PA 19103. 215/448-6000. **Contact:** Cheryl Fortunato, Director of Human Resources. **Description:** One of Philadelphia's largest real estate services firms. **Corporate headquarters location:** This Location.

COMMONWEALTH LAND TITLE INSURANCE CO.
8 Penn Center, 5th Floor, Philadelphia PA 19103. 215/241-6169. **FAX:** 215/241-1450. **Contact:** Steve Eisen, Employment Manager. **Description:** Provides title insurance, relocation assistance, and residential appraisal services. **Common positions include:** Accountant/Auditor; Attorney; Budget Analyst; Clerical Supervisor; Computer Operator; Computer Programmer; Department Manager; Draftsperson; Employment Interviewer; Paralegal; Payroll Clerk; Secretary; Systems Analyst; Typist/Word Processor. **Educational backgrounds include:** Accounting; Computer Science; Finance;

Real Estate. **Benefits:** Dental Insurance; Disability Coverage; Employee Discounts; Life Insurance; Medical Insurance; Pension Plan; Savings Plan; Tuition Assistance. **Corporate headquarters location:** This Location. **Parent company:** Reliance Group Holdings Inc. **Annual Revenues:** $900,000,000. **Number of employees at this location:** 200. **Number of employees nationwide:** 4,800. **Projected hires for the next 12 months (This location):** 50 hires. **Projected hires for the next 12 months (Nationwide):** 1,000 hires.

COMMERCIAL CREDIT PLAN
CONSUMER DISCOUNT COMPANY
P.O. Box 52220, Philadelphia, PA 19115. 215/677-3102. **Contact:** Human Resources. **Description:** A real estate loan company.

COMMONWEALTH FEDERAL SAVINGS BANK
70 Valley Stream, Valley Forge, PA 19482. 215/677-2500. **Contact:** Human Resources. **Description:** A real estate loan institution.

CORESTATES FIRST BANK
341 West Cheltenham Avenue, Philadelphia, PA 19126. 215/635-5686. **Contact:** Human Resources. **Description:** A real estate loan institution.

CRUSADER SAVINGS BANK
6526 Castor Avenue, Philadelphia, PA 19149. 215/744-0640. **Contact:** Human Resources. **Description:** A real estate loan institution.

FIRST NATIONAL BANK OF CANTON
5 West Main Street, Canton, PA 17724. 717673-5127. **Contact:** Human Resources. **Description:** A real estate loan institution.

1429 WALNUT STREET ASSOCIATES
1429 Walnut Street, Philadelphia PA 19102. 215/563-5111. **Contact:** Human Resources. **Description:** A non-residential building operator.

GE CAPITAL INC.
P.O. Box 5260, Cherry Hill NJ 08034. 609/661-6100. **Contact:** Human Resources Department. **Description:** A real estate loans company.

GMAC MORTGAGE CORPORATION
8360 Old York Road, Elkins Park PA 19117. 215/881-3343. **Contact:** Sharon Blumberg, Staffing Supervisor. **Description:** Provides a wide range of mortgage banking and related financial services. **Common positions include:** Accountant/Auditor; Computer Programmer; Customer Service Representative; Systems Analyst. **Educational backgrounds include:** Business Administration; Communications; Finance; Marketing. **Benefits:** Dental Insurance; Disability Coverage; Employee Discounts; Life Insurance; Medical Insurance; Savings Plan. **Corporate headquarters location:** This Location. **Operations at this facility include:** Administration.

GILPIN, VAN TRUMP, & MONTGOMERY
1400 North Dupont Street, P.O. Box 8715, Wilmington DE 19899. 302/656-5400. **Contact:** Kathy Edwards, Personnel Manager. **Description:** A Delaware real estate services firm, specializing in residential and commercial real estate, relocation services, property management, and mortgage banking.

MERIDIAN SAVINGS BANK
7578 Haverford Avenue, Philadelphia, PA 19151. 215/878-1100. **Contact:** Human Resources. **Description:** A real estate loans institution.

MERIDIAN SAVINGS BANK
65 Woodland Avenue, Philadelphia PA 19142. 215/720-1980. **Contact:** Human Resources. **Description:** A real estate loan company.

EDWARD H. MEYER & SON REALTORS
1531 Orthodox Street, Philadelphia PA 19124. 215/535-5289. **Contact:** Human Resources. **Description:** A real estate agency.

NORTHWEST FINANCIAL CONSUMER DISTRICT COMPANY
2201 Cottman Avenue, Philadelphia PA 19149. **Contact:** Human Resources. **Description:** A real estate loan company.

PNC BANK
11830 Bustleton Avenue, Philadelphia PA 19116. 215/676-0300. **Contact:** Human Resources. **Description:** A real estate loan company.

RS FINANCIAL CORPORATION
2000 Market Street, Philadelphia, PA 19138. 215/567-3850. **Contact:** Human Resources. **Description:** A real estate loan company.

READING COMPANY
1 Penn Square West, 30 South 15th Street, Suite 1300, Philadelphia PA 19102-4813. 215/569-3344. **Contact:** Personnel. **Description:** A real estate firm.

TRANSNATIONAL MORTGAGE CORPORATION
1210 Tasker Street, Philadelphia PA 19148. 215/465-8662. **Contact:** Human Resources. **Description:** A real estate loan company.

VARTAN ENTERPRISES, INC.
3601 Vartan Way, Harrisburg PA 17110. 717/657-0100. **Contact:** Human Resources. **Description:** A real estate agency.

Note: Because addresses and telephone numbers of smaller companies change rapidly, we recommend you contact each company and verify the information below before contacting employers. Mass mailings are not recommended.

Additional medium sized employers: under 500

OPERATORS OF APARTMENT BUILDINGS

Amity Gardens Apartments
20 Cedar House # A, Douglassville PA 19518-1424.
610/385-3071.

Browns Woods
Lawrence Dr, Browns Mills NJ 08015.
609/893-5665.

Carriage Hill Apartments
2098 Butler Pike, Conshohocken PA 19428-1203.
610/825-4947.

Clover Hill Gardens
Garden, Mount Holly
NJ 08060. 609/267-
1647.

**Eastampton Garden
Apartments**
Bentley Rd, Mount
Holly NJ 08060.
609/267-4071.

Glendora Court
230 E Evesham Rd,
Glendora NJ 08029-
1320. 609/939-0054.

Goshen Manor
101 North Five Points
Rd, West Chester PA
19380. 610/436-
5768.

Greenway Apartments
State Hwy No 73 W,
West Berlin NJ
08091. 609/767-
7080.

**Hidden Village
Apartments**
1943 Pinehurst Rd,
Bethlehem PA 18018-
1528. 610/866-0600.

**Lancaster Court
Apartments**
1127 Wabank Rd,
Lancaster PA 17603-
6888. 717/392-0242.

**Manor House
Apartments**
1415 Spencer Ave,
Lancaster PA 17603-
6520. 717/393-0465.

Market House
39 S Poplar St,
Elizabethtown PA
17022-2159.
717/367-8007.

Plymouth Gardens

1300 Fayette St,
Conshohocken PA
19428-1320.
610/825-1770.

**Springetts Manor
Apartments**
50 Eisenhower Dr,
York PA 17402-2699.
717/757-1565.

The Leasing Center
226 Highland Ave,
State College PA
16801-4934.
814/237-7191.

Timberfalls At Blakely
Route 6, Olyphant PA
18447. 717/489-
3288.

**United Stinson Ltd
Partnership**
15th St & Arbor Dr,
Chester PA 19013.
610/874-1421.

**Valley View
Apartments**
600 W Schuylkill Rd,
Pottstown PA 19464-
7433. 610/326-4223.

**OPERATORS OF
RESIDENTAL MOBILE
HOME SITES**

Eastwood Village
Greenfield Rd,
Lancaster PA 17601.
717/397-8745.

Tricia Meadows
27 Patricia Ln, Mount
Laurel NJ 08054-
4405. 609/866-1331.

**REAL ESTATE
AGENTS AND
MANAGERS**

**Balcor Management
Group**

110 Marter Ave,
Moorestown NJ
08057-3124.
609/273-9301.

**Brenneman Appraisal
Service Inc.**
18 S George St, York
PA 17401-1425.
717/854-5757.

**Brode & Brooks
Realtors**
Route 63, Green Lane
PA 18054. 215/234-
4508.

Burgdorff Realtors
4 Bridge St, Stockton
NJ 08559-2101.
908/782-5628.

Chase Hampton Inc.
2277 Golden Rod Ct,
Jamison PA 18929-
1738. 215/343-5252.

**Chelbourne Plaza
Condominiums**
46 Township Line Rd,
Elkins Park PA 19117-
2252. 215/663-8088.

**Dusco Property
Management Inc.**
146 Park City Center,
Lancaster PA 17601-
2706. 717/393-1583.

**English Manner
Apartments**
243 W Tulpehocken
St, Philadelphia PA
19144-3235.
215/843-9424.

Executive Terrace
455 S Gulph Rd, Kng
Of Prussa PA 19406-
3114. 610/337-1937.

Fox & Lazo Inc.
Realtors
438 E Baltimore Pike,
Media PA 19063-
3840. 610/566-2500.

Fox & Lazo Inc.
Realtors
9 S Main St,
Morrisville PA 19067-
1510. 215/493-1891.

Fox & Lazo Inc.
Realtors
560 E Lancaster Ave,
Wayne PA 19087-
5049. 610/687-5200.

Fox and Lazo Inc.
Realtors
725 Skippack Pike,
Blue Bell PA 19422-
1741. 215/643-3537.

Glen Hollow
Apartments
1100 Newportville
Rd, Croydon PA
19021-5055.
215/788-3384.

John T Henderson
Real Estate
1 S Main St,
Morrisville PA 19067-
1528. 215/493-0300.

Kravco Co.
234 Goddard Blvd,
Kng Of Prussa PA
19406. 610/768-
6300.

Loralean Corporation
650 Skippack Pike,
Blue Bell PA 19422-
1710. 215/542-9235.

New Market Realty
3 Pennsylvania Ave,
Malvern PA 19355-
2417. 610/647-2222.

Patten Corporation
Valley View Estates,
Albrightsvlle PA
18210. 717/722-
9970.

Plato Professional
Development Center
7660 Imperial Way #
A101, Allentown PA
18195-1016.
610/481-0461.

Richard A Weidel
Corporation Realtors
Summit Square Shopg
Center, Newtown PA
18940. 215/968-
0140.

Richard A Weidel
Corporation Realtors
The Grist Mill,
Morrisville PA 19067.
215/493-1954.

Sample Associates
3620 Stephen Crane
Ln, Bethlehem PA
18017-1550.
610/865-3303.

Simpson Real Estate
Corporation
PO Box 451, Clarks
Summit PA 18411-
0451. 717/586-3411.

Thornbury Hunt
34 Fox Brook Ln,
Thornton PA 19373-
1129. 610/399-0700.

Weichert Co Realtors
3010 William Penn
Hwy, Easton PA
18042-5214.
610/252-6666.

Weichert Realtors
111 N Wayne Ave,
Wayne PA 19087-
3577. 610/687-4400.

9600 Condominium
Association
9600 Atlantic Ave,
Margate City NJ
08402-2224.
609/822-9600.

LAND SUBDIVIDERS
AND DEVELOPERS

Bucks County
Industrial
Development
Corporation
2 E Court St,
Doylestown PA
18901-4300.
215/348-9031.

FPA Corporation
2507 Philmont Ave,
Huntingdon Vy PA
19006-6236.
215/947-8900.

Seitzinger Bros
Developer & Lessors
459 Claude A Lord
Blvd, Pottsville PA
17901. 717/628-
4304.

Thornbury Hunt
Thornton Rd & Bonnie
Ln, Thornton PA
19373. 610/558-
3500.

For more information on career opportunities in real estate:

Associations

INSTITUTE OF REAL ESTATE MANAGEMENT
430 North Michigan Avenue, Chicago IL 60611. 312/661-1930.

INTERNATIONAL ASSOCIATION OF CORPORATE REAL ESTATE EXECUTIVES
440 Columbia Drive, Suite 100, P.O. Box 1408, West Palm Beach FL 33409. 407/683-8111.

Magazines

JOURNAL OF PROPERTY MANAGEMENT
Institute of Real Estate Management, 430 North Michigan Avenue, Chicago IL 60610. 312/661-1930.

NATIONAL REAL ESTATE INVESTOR
6151 Powers Ferry Road, Atlanta GA 30339. 404/955-2500.

REAL ESTATE FORUM
12 West 37th Street, New York NY 10018. 212/563-6460.

REAL ESTATE NEWS
3525 West Peterson, Suite 100, Chicago IL 60659. 312/465-5151.

RETAIL

Over the past few years, much of the retail industry has been struggling against low consumer confidence, but with many prices now coming down, analysts believe that sales of some big-ticket items, like computers, will rise. The housing rebound is also spurring sales of appliances, home electronics equipment and furniture. Meanwhile, discount department stores keep booming. This trend holds true for both merchandise and apparel stores, as well as for other broad product areas like health and beauty aides. Unfortunately for professionals, most new jobs will be entry-level, where there is currently a major labor shortage.

ANGELO BROTHERS COMPANY
12401 McNulty Road, Philadelphia PA 19154. 215/671-2000. **FAX:** 215/464-4115. **Contact:** Cathy Lane, Personnel Director. **Description:** A Philadelphia company engaged in the sale of light bulbs, lighting fixtures, replacement glassware, wall plates, lighting hardware and other categories. **Common positions include:** Accountant/Auditor; Adjuster; Administrative Services Manager; Advertising Clerk; Assistant Manager; Buyer; Clerical Supervisor; Commercial Artist; Computer Operator; Computer Programmer; Computer Systems Analyst; Credit Clerk and Authorizer; Credit Manager; Customer Service Representative; Employee Benefits Administrator; Food and Beverage Service Worker; Industrial Manager; Manufacturer's/Wholesaler's Sales Rep.; Marketing/ Advertising/PR Manager; Order Clerk; Receptionist; Secretary; Services Sales Representative; Stock Clerk; Truck Driver; Typist/Word Processor; Wholesale and Retail Buyer. **Educational backgrounds include:** Accounting; Art/Design; Computer Science; Economics; Finance; Liberal Arts; Marketing. **Benefits:** Dental Insurance; Employee Discounts; Life Insurance; Medical Insurance; Profit Sharing; Savings Plan; Tuition Assistance. **Corporate headquarters location:** This Location. **Other U.S. locations:** Santa Fe Springs CA; Jacksonville FL; Chicago IL; Bensalem PA. **Operations at this facility include:** Distribution; Divisional Headquarters; Regional Headquarters; Sales; Service. **Number of employees at this location:** 425. **Number of employees nationwide:** 125. **Hires/Layoffs in 1993 (This location):** 30 hires. **Hires/Layoffs in 1993 (Nationwide):** 17 hires. **Projected hires for the next 12 months (This location):** 5 hires. **Projected hires for the next 12 months (Nationwide):** 0.

A. H. ANGERSTEIN, INC.
315 New Road, Wilmington DE 19805. 302/996-3500. **Contact:** Marge Mesler, Personnel Director. **Description:** A Wilmington company engaged in the sale of building materials, glass fixtures, and kitchen and bathroom appliances.

AVON PRODUCTS INC.
2100 Ogletown Road, Newark DE 19712. 302/453-7700. **Contact:** Susan Calvetti, Human Resources Manager. **Description:** The main east coast office engaged in the sales and distribution of cosmetics. **Corporate headquarters location:** New York NY.

BON-TON

2801 East Market Street, York PA 17402. 717/757-7660. **Contact:** Ted Johnson, Junior V.P./Personnel. **Description:** A full-line department store. **Common positions include:** Branch Manager; Buyer; Department Manager; Management Trainee. **Educational backgrounds include:** Business Administration; Marketing. **Benefits:** Dental Insurance; Disability Coverage; Employee Discounts; Life Insurance; Medical Insurance; Pension Plan; Profit Sharing; Savings Plan. **Corporate headquarters location:** New York NY. **Parent company:** Allied Stores, Inc. **Listed on:** New York Stock Exchange.

BURLINGTON COAT FACTORY

1830 Route 130 North, Burlington NJ 08016. 609/387-7800. **Contact:** Sarah R. Orleck, Executive Director of Human Resources. **Description:** A progressive, off-price apparel discounter. The all-name-brand apparel lines include: coats, sportswear, childswear, menswear, juvenile furniture, linens, shoes, and accessories. **Listed on:** New York Stock Exchange.

BUTEN/THE PAINT AND PAPER PEOPLE

5000 Ridge Avenue, Philadelphia PA 19128. 215/483-7500. **Contact:** Michael B. Steinberg, Vice President/Operations. **Description:** Retailer/wholesaler of paints, wallcoverings, window treatments, and related items. **Common positions include:** Branch Manager; Management Trainee. **Educational backgrounds include:** Business Administration; Marketing. **Benefits:** Disability Coverage; Employee Discounts; Life Insurance; Medical Insurance; Pension Plan. **Special Programs:** Training Programs. **Corporate headquarters location:** This Location. **Operations at this facility include:** Administration; Regional Headquarters; Sales.

CONSOLIDATED STORES CORPORATION

1105 North Market Street, Suite 1300, P.O. Box 8985, Wilmington DE 19899. 302/478-4896. **Contact:** Human Resources. **Description:** Operates a chain of retail stores that sell close-out merchandise. Sells similar merchandise on a wholesale basis. In 1991-92, Consolidated Stores introduced a new venture under the name All For One, which now totals 170 stores. **Number of employees nationwide:** 13,880.

DEB SHOPS, INC.

9401 Blue Grass Road, Philadelphia PA 19114. 215/676-6000. **Contact:** Pamela A. Dunlap, Administrative Assistant. **Description:** Deb Shops, Inc. is a growing chain of specialty apparel stores offering moderately-priced, fashionable, coordinated sportswear, dresses, coats, and accessories. Operates over 350 stores in 34 states. Deb Shops seeks career-oriented individuals for store management positions. **Common positions include:** Assistant Manager; Store Manager. **Educational backgrounds include:** Art/Design; Business Administration; Communications; Fashion; Liberal Arts; Marketing; Merchandising. **Benefits:** Employee Discounts; Life Insurance; Medical Insurance; Savings Plan.

DELAWARE CADILLAC

1606 Pennsylvania Avenue, Wilmington DE 19806. 302/656-3100. **Contact:** Andy Chatham, General Manager. **Description:** A Wilmington automotive dealership.

DELAWARE OLDS, INC.

P.O. Box 906, Wilmington DE 19899. 302/764-6200. **Contact:** Chandler Luke, General Manager. **Description:** An area dealer of new and used automobiles.

S.P. DUNHAM & COMPANY INC.
2495 U.S. Highway 1, Lawrenceville NJ 08648-4097. 609/989-7777. **Contact:** Store Manager. **Description:** A department store.

EDMUND SCIENTIFIC COMPANY
101 East Gloucester Pike, Barrington NJ 08007. 609/573-6279. **Contact:** Virginia Lamelas, Personnel Director. **Description:** A mail order house.

HAPPY HARRYS INC.
315 Ruthar Drive, Newark DE 19711. 302/366-0335. **Contact:** Dennis Gossert, Director of Personnel. **Description:** A Delaware valley area drug store chain.

HIT OR MISS, INC.
1221 Chestnut Street, Philadelphia PA 19107. 215/972-7030. **Contact:** Mel Rappleyea, Human Resource Director. **Description:** A chain of women's fashion stores; over 500 stores in 32 states. A division of TJX, Inc., which includes Chadwicks of Boston, Winners of Canada, Homegoods, and T.J. Maxx. **Common positions include:** Assistant Manager; Buyer; General Manager; Management Trainee. **Educational backgrounds include:** Art/Design; Business Administration; Fashion; Retail Management. **Benefits:** Dental Insurance; Disability Coverage; Employee Discounts; Life Insurance; Medical Insurance; Stock Option. **Special Programs:** Internships; Training Programs. **Corporate headquarters location:** Stoughton MA. **Operations at this facility include:** Sales; Service. **Listed on:** New York Stock Exchange. **Number of employees nationwide:** 5,000. **Projected hires for the next 12 months (This location):** 3 hires.

JCPENNEY COMPANY
5000 Dover Mall, Dover DE 19901. 302/674-4200. **Contact:** Patricia Collins, Personnel Assistant. **Description:** A national company which operates a chain of department stores and thrift drug stores, and which also provides banking services. Area locations in Wilmington (302/998-1131) and Newark (302/366-7680).

JCPENNEY COMPANY
905 Wheeler Way, Box County Business Park, Langhorne PA 19047. 215/752-5300. **Contact:** Lin Andruschkevich, District Personnel Manager. **Description:** One of the nation's largest retail merchandise sales and service corporations, with department stores and catalog centers located in many major United States cities and several foreign locations. **Common positions include:** Management Trainee. **Benefits:** Dental Insurance; Disability Coverage; Employee Discounts; Life Insurance; Medical Insurance; Pension Plan; Profit Sharing; Savings Plan. **Corporate headquarters location:** Dallas TX. **Listed on:** New York Stock Exchange.

KIRKWOOD DODGE INC.
4800 Kirkwood Highway, Wilmington DE 19808. 302/999-0541. **Contact:** Personnel. **Description:** A Wilmington area automotive dealership.

LERNER NEW YORK
1200 Market Street, Philadelphia PA 19107. 215/627-3360. **Contact:** Jennifer Mack, District Manager. **Description:** A national women's and children's moderately-priced specialty apparel store chain. Lerners is a division of Limited, Inc., with over 2,300 stores nationwide operating under such names as Limited Express, Victoria Secret, Lane Bryant, and Size Unlimited. Also operates mail order catalog business. **Common positions include:** Assistant Manager; Customer Service Representative; Department Manager; General Manager; Management Trainee; Operations/Production Manager.

Educational backgrounds include: Business Administration; Liberal Arts; Marketing. **Benefits:** Dental Insurance; Disability Coverage; Employee Discounts; Life Insurance; Medical Insurance; Pension Plan; Savings Plan. **Corporate headquarters location:** New York NY. **Operations at this facility include:** Sales; Service. **Listed on:** New York Stock Exchange.

T.H. MANDY
1 Ellisburg Circle, Cherry Hill NJ 08034. 609/429-1912. **Contact:** Manager. **Description:** A women's specialty retailer. **Common positions include:** Management Trainee; Sales Associate; Store Manager.

MARTIN OLDSMOBILE INC.
298 East Cleveland Avenue, Newark DE 19711. 302/738-5200. **Contact:** Doug Buchanan, Controller. **Description:** A Delaware automobile dealership.

McCRORY STORES
2955 E. Market St., York PA 17402. 717/757-8269. **Contact:** Douglas Reeder, Human Resources Manager. **Description:** A national retail variety chain with 1,100 units in 38 states; food service operations. **Corporate headquarters location:** This Location. **Number of employees nationwide:** 28,000.

MERCANTILE STORES COMPANY, INC.
1100 North Market Street, Wilmington DE 19801. 302/575-1816. **Contact:** Human Resources. **Description:** Operates department stores in the South and Midwest.

O.A. NEWTON & SON COMPANY
P.O. Box 397, Bridgeville DE 19933. 302/337-8211. **Contact:** Bill Farlow, President. **Description:** A company involved in the sale of a wide variety of home appliance products.

THE PEP BOYS--MANNY, MOE & JACK
3111 West Allegheny Avenue, Philadelphia PA 19132. 215/227-9000. **FAX:** 215/227-7513. **Contact:** Jim McKnight, Human Resources Manager. **Description:** Primarily engaged in the retail sale of a wide range of automotive parts and accessories, and the installation of automobile components and merchandise. The Pep Boys have over 400 stores in 24 states. **Common positions include:** Accountant/Auditor; Administrative Services Manager; Assistant Manager; Automotive Mechanic/Body Repairer; Branch Manager; Buyer; Cashier; Claim Representative; Computer Operator; Computer Programmer; Construction Contractor and Manager; Credit Manager; Customer Service Representative; Department Manager; Economist/Market Research Analyst; Financial Manager; Graphic Artist; Marketing Research Analyst; Payroll Clerk; Personnel/Labor Relations Specialist; Printing Press Operator; Receptionist; Retail Sales Worker; Secretary; Wholesale and Retail Buyer. **Educational backgrounds include:** Accounting; Art/Design; Business Administration; Communications; Computer Science; Finance; Liberal Arts; Marketing; Mathematics. **Benefits:** Dental Insurance; Disability Coverage; Employee Discounts; Life Insurance; Medical Insurance; Savings Plan; Tuition Assistance. **Special Programs:** Training Programs. **Corporate headquarters location:** This Location. **Operations at this facility include:** Administration. **Listed on:** New York Stock Exchange. **Annual Revenues:** $1,200,000,000. **Number of employees at this location:** 600. **Number of employees nationwide:** 15,000. **Hires/Layoffs in 1993 (This location):** 100 hires. **Hires/Layoffs in 1993 (Nationwide):** 11,000 hires. **Projected hires for the next 12 months (This location):** 125 hires.

RITE AID CORPORATION

P.O. Box 3165, Harrisburg PA 17105. 717/761-2633. **Contact:** Doug Stone, Director of Pharmacy Personnel. **Description:** A retail pharmaceutical company. Note: employee and projected hire numbers below are for pharmacists only. **Common positions include:** Pharmacist. **Educational backgrounds include:** Pharmacology. **Benefits:** Dental Insurance; Disability Coverage; Employee Discounts; Life Insurance; Medical Insurance; Pension Plan; Profit Sharing; Savings Plan. **Special Programs:** Internships; Training Programs. **Corporate headquarters location:** This Location. **Other U.S. locations:** AL; CT; DC; DE; FL; GA; IN; KY; MA; MD; ME; MI; NC; NH; NJ; NY; OH; PA; RI; SC; TN; VA; VT; WV. **Listed on:** New York Stock Exchange. **Number of employees nationwide:** 5,100. **Projected hires for the next 12 months (Nationwide):** 750 hires.

SEARS, ROEBUCK & COMPANY

4640 Roosevelt Boulevard, Philadelphia PA 19124. 215/697-8888. **Contact:** Personnel Department. **Description:** Applicants must appear in person. One of the world's largest retailers with subsidiaries also engaged in the insurance and real estate businesses. Merchandise consists of merchandising, credit, and international units for which financial statements are presented; merchandising distributes broad lines of merchandise and services through more than 850 retail stores and more than 2,775 sales offices and other facilities. Credit provides credit services to merchandising customers; other business segments include Allstate Insurance, engaged primarily in the property/liability and life insurance lines, as well as providing financial services, primarily in the United States and Canada. Real estate operations are handled through subsidiary Coldwell Banker, which invests in, develops, and operates real estate and performs related financial services, including savings and loan, mortgage banking, and mortgage guaranty insurance activities. facilities. **Corporate headquarters location:** Chicago IL. **Listed on:** New York Stock Exchange. **Number of employees nationwide:** 39,000.

SILO, INC.

6900 Lindbergh Boulevard, Philadelphia PA 19142. 215/492-7726. **Contact:** Nancy Nessler, Employment Recruiter. **Description:** A retailer of appliances and electronics. **Common positions include:** Accountant/Auditor; Advertising Clerk; Blue-Collar Worker Supervisor; Buyer; Management Trainee; Operations/Production Manager; Services Sales Representative. **Educational backgrounds include:** Accounting; Art/Design; Business Administration; Liberal Arts; Marketing. **Benefits:** Disability Coverage; Employee Discounts; Life Insurance; Medical Insurance; Pension Plan; Profit Sharing; Tuition Assistance. **Corporate headquarters location:** Brighton MI. **Parent company:** Fretter, Inc. **Operations at this facility include:** Administration; Regional Headquarters; Service. **Number of employees nationwide:** 3,700. **Projected hires for the next 12 months (This location):** 50 hires.

THE SOUTHLAND CORPORATION

2711 Easton Road, Willow Grove PA 19090. 215/672-5711. **Contact:** Treasa Gallaway-Davis, Human Resources Manager. **Description:** Southland is the world's largest convenience retailer, with approximately 7,000 7-Eleven and other convenience units in the U.S. and Canada. In addition, area licensees and affiliates operate almost 5,300 7-Eleven stores in the United States and 19 foreign countries. Southland, which owns a 50 percent interest in Citgo Petroleum Corporation is among the nation's largest independent gasoline retailers. **Common positions include:** Management Trainee; Marketing Specialist; Merchandiser. **Educational backgrounds include:** Accounting; Business Administration; Communications; Marketing. **Benefits:** Disability Coverage; Life Insurance; Medical Insurance; Pension Plan; Profit Sharing.

SPENCER GIFTS INC.
6826 Black Horse Pike, Pleasantville NJ 08232. 609/645-3300. **Contact:** Terri Coyle, Personnel Manager. **Description:** A retailer of novelty and joke items. **Common positions include:** Accountant/Auditor; Assistant Manager; Buyer; Management Trainee. **Educational backgrounds include:** Accounting; Business Administration; Liberal Arts; Marketing. **Operations at this facility include:** Administration; Sales; Service. **Number of employees nationwide:** 4,000. **Projected hires for the next 12 months (This location):** 2 hires.

STRAWBRIDGE & CLOTHIER
100 Christiana Mall, Newark DE 19702-3202. 302/366-7399. **Contact:** Personnel. **Description:** A retail store. **Corporate headquarters location:** Philadelphia PA.

STRAWBRIDGE & CLOTHIER
4747 Concord Pike, Wilmington DE 19803. 302/478-1860. **Contact:** Susan McClure, Personnel Director. **Description:** Operates a chain of retail stores. **Corporate headquarters location:** Philadelphia PA.

STRAWBRIDGE AND CLOTHIER
801 Market Street, Philadelphia PA 19107. 215/629-7888. **Contact:** Anne Hayden, Manager of Employment. **Description:** Operates a full-line of department stores, with branches in Delaware, Pennsylvania, and New Jersey. Buyers training program begins in September (150 hours). **Common positions include:** Accountant/Auditor; Department Manager; Management Trainee. **Educational backgrounds include:** Business Administration; Economics; Fashion; Liberal Arts; Marketing; Merchandising; Retail Management. **Benefits:** 401K; Dental Insurance; Disability Coverage; Education Assistance; Employee Discounts; Life Insurance; Medical Insurance; Pension Plan; Prescription Drugs; Savings Plan; Tuition Assistance. **Special Programs:** Internships; Training Programs. **Corporate headquarters location:** This Location. **Operations at this facility include:** Regional Headquarters. **Number of employees nationwide:** 12,000.

SUPER RITE FOODS, INC.
P.O. Box 2261, Harrisburg PA 17105. 717/232-6821. **Contact:** Personnel. **Description:** Super Rite Corporation is a full-service grocery wholesaler and retailer, serving customers in Pennsylvania, New Jersey, Maryland, Delaware, Virginia, and West Virginia. As one of the largest grocery wholesalers in the Middle Atlantic region, the company supplies more than 13,000 regional brand and 1,000 private label grocery division currently operates supermarkets under the name Basics in the Metropolitan Baltimore and Washington areas.

JOHN WANAMAKER
1300 Market Street, Philadelphia PA 19107. 215/422-1863. **Contact:** Mary Morrison, Management Placement Coordinator. **Description:** One of Philadelphia's oldest and most respected full-line department stores. **Common positions include:** Credit Manager; Customer Service Representative; Department Manager; Management Trainee; Personnel/Labor Relations Specialist. **Educational backgrounds include:** Art/Design; Business Administration; Liberal Arts; Marketing. **Benefits:** Dental Insurance; Disability Coverage; Employee Discounts; Life Insurance; Medical Insurance; Pension Plan; Savings Plan; Tuition Assistance. **Corporate headquarters location:** Washington DC. **Parent company:** Woodward and Lathrop. **Operations at this facility include:** Divisional Headquarters; Sales.

WAWA INC.
260 Baltimore Pike, Wawa PA 19063. 215/358-8000. **Contact:** Personnel. **Description:** Management offices for a convenience store chain.

WINNER FORD NEWARK
303 East Cleveland Avenue, Newark DE 19711. 302/764-5900. **Contact:** Jack Cooper, Manager. **Description:** An automotive dealership.

ZALLIE SUPERMARKETS
1230 Blackwood-Clementon Road, Clementon NJ 08021. 609/627-6501. **Contact:** Personnel Department. **Description:** Corporate offices for a chain of six Shop-Rite supermarkets.

Note: Because addresses and telephone numbers of smaller companies change rapidly, we recommend you contact each company and verify the information below before contacting employers. Mass mailings are not recommended.

Additional large employers: 500 +

DEPARTMENT STORES

Hess's Department Stores Inc.
9th & Hamilton Mall,
Allentown PA 18101.
610/821-4377.

GENERAL MERCHANDISE STORES

Reynolds Bros Inc.
1000 Airport Rd.,
Lakewood NJ 08701-5960. 9083675600.

GROCERY STORES

Giant Food Stores Inc.
1149 Harrisburg Pike,
Carlisle PA 17013-1618.
717/249-4000.

Laneco Inc.
3747 Hecktown Rd.,
Easton PA 18042-2399.
610/253-7155.

Uni-Marts Inc.
477 E Beaver Ave., State College PA 16801-5690.
8142346000.

Weis Markets Inc.
1000 S 2nd St., Sunbury PA 17801-3318.
717/286-4571.

MEN'S CLOTHING STORES

Today's Man Inc.
835 Lancer Drive,
Moorestown NJ 08057-4225. 609/235-5656.

WOMEN'S CLOTHING STORES

Conston Corporation
P.O. Box 358,
Hightstown NJ 08520-0358.

SHOE STORES

C&J Clark Retail Inc.
440 Madison St.,
Hanover PA 17331-4700. 717/632-2444.

Additional medium sized employers: under 500

DRUG STORES AND PROPRIETARY STORES

Clover Stores
2201 Cheltenham Av,
Cheltenham PA 19012.
215/885-2753.

Eckerd Drugs
200 Tuckerton Rd,
Medford NJ 08055-8806. 609/983-9393.

GPS Pharmacy Services
764 Sans Souci Pky,
Wilkes Barre PA 18702-1331. 717/821-0842.

King's Pharmacy
Rts 662 & 73, Oley PA
19547. 610/987-9877.

LF Widmann Inc.
PO Box 149, Lock Haven
PA 17745-0149.
717/769-6483.

Pathmark
Aramingo Av & Venango,
Philadelphia PA 19134.
215/533-4140.

Phar-Mor
3849 Union Deposit Rd,
Harrisburg PA 17109-
5920. 717/561-9707.

Phar-Mor
Fairgrounds Square Mall,
Reading PA 19605.
610/929-4942.

**Prescription Delivery
Systems**
49 S York Rd, Hatboro
PA 19040-3231.
215/674-1565.

Rea & Derick Inc.
1848 Lycoming Creek
Rd, Williamsport PA
17701-1500. 717/323-
1338.

Shelly's Pharmacy
2313 E Venango St,
Philadelphia PA 19134-
4622. 215/289-0691.

Thrift Drug
Larchmont Commons,
Mount Laurel NJ 08054.
609/778-7748.

Thrift Drug
Kendig Square, Willow
Street PA 17584.
717/464-1720.

Thrift Drug
1425 Main St, Olyphant
PA 18447-1350.
717/383-9811.

Thrift Drug
Bridge At Fox Croft Sq,
Jenkintown PA 19046.
215/572-1290.

Weis Market Pharmacy
2160 White St, York PA
17404-4900. 717/845-
1318.

Weis Market Pharmacy
Five Point Plaza,
Montgomeryvle PA
18936. 215/361-0488.

**USED MERCHANDISE
STORES**

**Goodwill Industries Mid
Eastern Pennsylvania**
Route 222 & Meridian
Drive, Trexlertown PA
18087. 610/391-8822.

Wearguard
1455 Franklin Mills Cir,
Philadelphia PA 19154-
3141. 215/281-9223.

**SPORTING GOODS AND
BICYCLE SHOPS**

Bowling Palace
Rt 30, Downingtown PA
19335. 610/269-9999.

Boy Scouts Of America
Plymouth Meeting Mall,
Plymouth Mtng PA
19462. 610/828-4102.

Champ's Sports
Deptford Mall, Woodbury
NJ 08096. 609/845-
9449.

**Cross-Country Ski
Outfitters**
State Hwy No 29,
Lambertville NJ 08530.
609/397-3366.

**Gold Medal Sporting
Goods Inc.**
237 Route 73 S, Marlton
NJ 08053-4122.
609/985-1800.

Playdrome Toms River
Conifer & State Hwy No
37, Toms River NJ
08753. 908/349-5345.

Sports Page
Montgomery Mall, North
Wales PA 19454.
215/361-8220.

The Sports Authority
113 E Swedesford Rd,
Exton PA 19341-2333.
610/594-9368.

BOOK STORES

Beaver College Bookstore
Easton & Church Rd,
Glenside PA 19038.
215/884-9407.

**Book-Of-The-Month Club
Inc.**
1225 S Market St,
Mechanicsburg PA
17055-4728. 717/697-
0311.

Encore Books
10 Schalks Crossing Rd,
Plainsboro NJ 08536-
1612. 609/275-0270.

Farley's Bookshop
Princeton Forrestal
Village, Princeton NJ
08540. 609/520-1244.

Reading Center II
72 S Clinton Ave,
Trenton NJ 08609-1238.
609/695-3804.

STATIONERY STORES

Phillips Office Products
100 N Hanover St,
Carlisle PA 17013-2421.
717/249-8117.

Standard Forms Inc.
8 S Maple Ave, Marlton
NJ 08053-2002.
609/988-8800.

Wagner's Office Products Inc.
212 N George St, York
PA 17401-1108.
717/846-7777.

JEWELRY STORES

Barclay Jewelers
Quaker Bridge Mall,
Trenton NJ 08648.
609/275-8200.

Belden Jewelers
2300 E Lincoln Hwy,
Langhorne PA 19047-
1805. 215/752-5024.

Gemstone Jewerly Inc.
Coventry Mall, Pottstown
PA 19464. 610/323-
1913.

Kay Jewelers
Montgomery Mall,
Montgomeryvle PA
18936. 215/362-1778.

Littman Jewelers
King Of Prussia Mall,
King Of Prussia PA
19406. 610/265-4595.

Piercing Pagoda
2801 Whiteford Rd, York
PA 17402-8976.
717/840-1712.

Piercing Pagoda
Lycoming Mall, Muncy
PA 17756. 717/546-
2555.

Piercing Pagoda
Park City Shopping
Center, Lancaster PA
17601. 717/397-8849.

Plumb Gold
Court King Of Prussia,
Kng Of Prussa PA
19406. 610/265-7552.

Topkapi Boutiques
127 Park City Center,
Lancaster PA 17601-
2705. 717/295-9280.

HOBBY, TOY AND GAME SHOPS

AC Moore Co.
2633 MacArthur Rd,
Whitehall PA 18052-
3818. 610/264-4003.

Kay-Bee Toys
2495 US Highway 1,
Trenton NJ 08648-4099.
609/883-1466.

Pets Crafts & Things
3765 Nicholas St, Easton
PA 18042-5115.
610/252-1004.

Pets Crafts & Things
Rt 115, Easton PA
18042. 610/253-6962.

Playland Toy Store
Lycoming Mall, Muncy
PA 17756. 717/546-
7444.

Rag Shop Fabrics & Crafts
Crispin Square, Marlton
NJ 08053. 609/985-
1537.

Western Publishing Co.
Jonaires Ln, Stroudsburg
PA 18360. 717/476-
7510.

GIFT AND NOVELTY SHOPS

Creative Hands
Montgomery Shopping
Cntr, Rocky Hill NJ
08553. 609/924-3355.

Dollar Discount Stores
Barclay Square Shopping
Center, Upper Darby PA
19082. 610/623-6536.

San Francisco Music Box Co.
310 Echelon Towers,
Voorhees NJ 08043-
2323. 609/770-8215.

Spain's Gifts & Cards
Venango & Aramingo,
Philadelphia PA 19134.
215/744-7004.

Thrift Drug
2127 Route 130,
Willingboro NJ 08046-
1441. 609/877-1281.

Thrift Drug
Rancocas Plaza,
Willingboro NJ 08046.
609/877-6860.

LUGGAGE AND LEATHER GOODS

Leather Loft
Rockvale Sq, Lancaster
PA 17602. 717/397-
6580.

SEWING AND NEEDLEWORK STORES

Dannemann Fabrics
601 E Lancaster Ave,
Reading PA 19607-1366.
610/777-1331.

Jo-Ann Fabrics
Mifflin County Commons,
Lewistown PA 17044.
717/242-2350.

Rag Shop Fabrics & Crafts
State Hwy No 37 &
Washington, Toms River
NJ 08753. 908/929-
2787.

CATALOG AND MAIL-ORDER HOUSES

National Media Corporation
1700 Walnut St,
Philadelphia PA 19103-
6013. 215/482-9800.

DIRECT SELLING ESTABLISHING

Proficient Food Company
2910 Old Tree Dr,
Lancaster PA 17603-
4082. 717/293-0081.

LIQUIFIED PETROLEUM PRODUCTS

Pennsylvania & Southern Gas Co.
102 Desmond St, Sayre
PA 18840-2002.
717/888-6600.

TOBACCO STORES

DES Tobacco Corporation
Benjamin Fox Pavillion,
Jenkintown PA 19046.
215/885-3250.

Tinder Box International Ltd
3 Bala Plz, Bala Cynwyd
PA 19004-3481.
610/668-4220.

NEWS DEALERS AND NEWSSTANDS

Encore Books
The Village At Newtown,
Newtown PA 18940.
215/579-2140.

OPTICAL GOODS STORES

Eyeland Optical
2364 MacArthur Rd,
Whitehall PA 18052-
4524. 610/432-3937.

Lens Crafters
129 Hamilton Mall,
Pleasantville NJ 08232.
609/484-8400.

Lenscrafters
Berkshire Mall, Reading
PA 19610. 610/374-
3323.

Nuvision Optical
Hamilton Mall,
Pleasantville NJ 08232.
609/484-0004.

Wall & Ochs Outlet
2060 Cottman Ave,
Philadelphia PA 19149-
1120. 215/722-8505.

York County Energy Partners
2146 White St, York PA
17404-4900. 717/843-
3889.

MISCELLANEOUS RETAIL STORES

ATI Communications
14 Union Hill Rd,
Conshohocken PA
19428-2719. 610/825-
8200.

Ben Franklin Arts Crafts
4880 Carlisle Pike,
Mechanicsburg PA
17055-3026. 717/975-
0490.

Coon Industries Inc.
278 Union St, Luzerne
PA 18709-1412.
717/287-9601.

Delcrest Medical Products
1710 Dekalb Pike, Blue
Bell PA 19422-3352.
610/275-2277.

Lifeline
701 E Marshall St, West
Chester PA 19380-4412.
610/431-5011.

Packaging Corporation Of America
38 Cabot Blvd E,
Langhorne PA 19047-
1802. 215/949-2080.

Pencor Services Inc.
463 Delaware Ave,
Palmerton PA 18071-
1908. 610/826-2552.

Prestige Fragrance & Cosmetics
Hill Av & Park Rd,
Reading PA 19610.
610/373-8081.

Prints Plus
Hamilton Mall,
Pleasantville NJ 08232.
609/383-6022.

Red Rose Systems Inc.
4139 Oregon Pike,
Ephrata PA 17522-9550.
717/738-8310.

SAIC
1645 E Main St,
Waynesboro PA 17268-
1874. 717/765-4334.

Saxco Intl Inc.
200 Gibraltar Rd,
Horsham PA 19044-
2318. 215/443-8100.

**Sugerman's Hearing Aid
Center**
Scrn-Carbndl Hwy,
Archbald PA 18403.
717/876-4821.

**Sunglass Hut Of Park
City**
501 Park City Center,
Lancaster PA 17601-
2713. 717/394-5768.

The Camera Shop Inc.
King Of Prussia Plaza,
Kng Of Prussa PA
19406. 610/265-6556.

Thomas Somerville Co.
780 Eden Rd, Lancaster
PA 17601-4271.
717/569-7321.

Thrift Drug
The Market Sq Of
Chestnut Hill,
Philadelphia PA 19144.
215/242-8022.

UARCO Business Forms
355 N 21st St Ste 102,
Camp Hill PA 17011-
3707. 717/761-3489.

**Weis Market Colonial
Bakery**
Route 309, Dallas PA
18612-1295. 717/675-
3115.

**LUMBER AND OTHER
BUILDING MATERIALS
DEALERS**

HM Stauffer & Sons
33 Glenola Dr, Leola PA
17540-1902. 717/656-
2811.

JC Snavely & Sons
150 Main St, Landisville
PA 17538-1244.
717/898-2241.

**Lowe's Of Chambersburg
Inc.**
1320 Lincoln Way E,
Chambersburg PA
17201-3037. 717/264-
1941.

**Vineland Tran Mix
Concrete Co.**
366 Shell Rd, Penns
Grove NJ 08069-2750.
609/299-1090.

**PAINT, GLASS AND
WALLPAPER STORES**

Finnaren & Haley Inc.
901 Washington St,
Conshohocken PA
19428-2379. 215/878-
6200.

MAB Paints
3559 W Chester Pike,
Newtown Sq PA 19073-
3701. 610/353-0440.

HARDWARE STORES

L&H Plumbing & Heating
621 Blackhorse Pike,
Williamstown NJ 08094.
609/629-5005.

**RETAIL NURSERIES,
LAWN AND GARDEN
SUPPLY STORES**

Agway Inc-Farm & Home
633 Mercer St,
Hightstown NJ 08520-
2917. 609/448-1470.

Frank's Nursery & Crafts
2730 Dekalb Pike,
Norristown PA 19401-
1821. 610/277-5866.

Gardenville Supply
6805 Easton Rd,
Pipersville PA 18947-
9717. 215/766-8871.

Holly Millville Orchards
Cumberland Rd, Millville
NJ 08332. 609/825-
4959.

LW Myers Nurseries
758 Union St, Lancaster
PA 17603-5538.
717/393-2440.

Princeton Nurseries
Lake Rd, Kingston NJ
08528. 609/924-1776.

DEPARTMENT STORES

**Abe Feinberg & Sons
Company**
864 Main St, Darby PA
19023-2109. 215/727-
0300.

Accessory Place
900 Market St,
Philadelphia PA 19107-
4228. 215/238-0725.

Adolfo
830 Oley St, Reading PA
19604-2546. 610/378-
1694.

Aeropostale
2000 Route 38, Cherry
Hill NJ 08002-2170.
609/486-4414.

Aileen Factory Outlet
Manufactures Outlet
Mall, Morgantown PA
19543-9301. 610/286-
6959.

American Asian Discount
1601 S 7th St,
Philadelphia PA 19148-
1212. 215/551-3550.

American Tourister Factory Outlet
Vf Outlet Complex,
Reading PA 19610.
610/374-1120.

Ames Department Store
Route 61, Shamokin PA
17872. 717/648-4651.

Ames Department Store
666 E Main St, Lansdale
PA 19446-2964.
215/855-5188.

Ames Department Store
500 Valley Rd, Hamburg
PA 19526-9203.
610/562-8684.

Ames Department Store
5370 Allentown Pike,
Temple PA 19560-1200.
610/921-9291.

Ames Department Store
County Line Plaza,
Souderton PA 18964.
215/721-4990.

Ames Department Store
Boyrtwn Plz Shopg Ctr,
Boyertown PA 19512.
610/367-6975.

Annie's Attic
9309 Krewstown Rd #
A, Philadelphia PA
19115-3734. 215/464-
0624.

Archie Jacobson Outlet
12123 Knights Rd,
Philadelphia PA 19154-
3104. 215/281-7890.

B&B Distribution Center
254 Drum Point Rd, Brick
NJ 08723-6312.
908/920-3300.

Baby's Outlet
828 Penn Ave, Reading
PA 19610-3016.
610/372-8781.

Bachman Company The Retail Store
Vf Outlet, Reading PA
19610. 610/373-3906.

Bag & Baggage Outlet
Manufactures Outlet
Mall, Morgantown PA
19543-9301. 610/286-
6988.

Bagazio
2950 Advance Ln,
Colmar PA 18915-9787.
215/822-9024.

Ben Franklin Variety & Craft Stores
324 N Lewis Rd,
Royersford PA 19468-
1509. 610/948-8486.

Bernard Chaus Retail Outlet
801 Hill Ave, Reading PA
19610-3026. 610/376-
8843.

Best Products Co Inc.
4152 Quakerbridge Rd,
Trenton NJ 08648-4703.
609/799-2901.

Best Products Co Inc.
31 Lawrence Rd,
Broomall PA 19008-
3918. 610/353-5300.

Best Products Co Inc.
Rt 1 Sproul Rd,
Springfield PA 19064.
610/544-9910.

Best Value
5691 Rising Sun Ave,
Philadelphia PA 19120-
1625. 215/745-7425.

BJ's Wholesale Club
2054 Red Lion Rd,
Philadelphia PA 19115-
1603. 215/676-2400.

Bloomingdale's
2400 W Moreland Rd,
Willow Grove PA 19090-
4001. 215/657-8100.

Bloomingdale's
660 W Dekalb Pike, Kng
Of Prussa PA 19406-
2958. 610/337-6300.

Boston Trader's Connection
601 N Park Rd, Reading
PA 19610-2910.
610/374-1780.

Bradlees
US Hwy No 38 &
Cuthbert Blvd, Cherry Hill
NJ 08002. 609/665-
1073.

Bradlees
State Hwy No 42,
Blackwood NJ 08012.
609/228-7060.

Bradlees
222 S White Horse Pike,
Stratford NJ 08084-
1541. 609/346-9300.

Bradlees
Blackhorse Pike Shop
Ctr, Audubon NJ 08106.
609/547-3434.

Bradlees
Five Points Plaza,
Montgomeryvle PA
18936. 215/361-0900.

Bradlees
50 N MacDade Blvd,
Glenolden PA 19036-
1223. 610/534-4900.

Bradlees
Village Mall, Horsham PA
19044. 215/675-1772.

Bradlees
Germantown Pike,
Norristown PA 19401.
610/275-4600.

Bradlees
Coventry Mall, Pottstown
PA 19464. 610/327-
3200.

Bradless
Springfield Rd & Wst
Chstr Pke, Broomall PA
19008. 610/359-1166.

Brights
1241 Blakeslee
Boulevard Dr E,
Lehighton PA 18235-
2497. 717/386-5811.

Budget Express Inc.
1901 E Westmoreland
St, Philadelphia PA
19134-2521. 215/427-
9230.

Bugle Boy Factory Outlet
916 Windsor St, Reading
PA 19604-2317.
610/372-3611.

Caldor
Washington Plaza,
Blackwood NJ 08012.
609/228-9000.

Caldor At Suburban Plaza
1700 Nottingham Way,
Trenton NJ 08619-3567.
609/586-5600.

Caldor
11000 Roosevelt Blvd,
Philadelphia PA 19116-
3961. 215/673-2900.

Cambridge Dry Goods
Vanity Fair Complex,
Reading PA 19610. ´
610/376-4236.

Capacity Factory Outlet
Manufactures Outlet
Mall, Morgantown PA
19543-9301. 610/286-
7388.

Cape Isle Knitters
122 Village Blvd,
Princeton NJ 08540-
5761. 609/520-9833.

Cape Isle Knitters
Vf Factory Outlet,
Reading PA 19610.
610/376-7050.

Carole Hochman Lingerie
807 N 9th St, Reading
PA 19604-2450.
610/372-7588.

**Carters Child Wear
Factory Outlet**
843 N 9th St, Reading
PA 19610-1717.
610/372-9822.

Cedar Beauty Supply
613 Cedar Ave,
Lansdowne PA 19050-
4002. 610/622-4338.

Chai's Discount Store
4925 N Broad St,
Philadelphia PA 19141-
2215. 215/329-0555.

**Champion Hanes Active
Wear**
801 Hill Ave, Reading PA
19610-3026. 610/376-
5249.

Charles Bargain Store
5510 Chester Ave,
Philadelphia PA 19143-
5328. 215/724-7004.

Clover Stores
2005 Marlton Pike E,
Cherry Hill NJ 08003-
1201. 609/424-1800.

Clover Stores
Cuthbert Rd & MacArthur
Blvd, Collingswood NJ
08108. 609/858-8900.

Clover Stores
Baltimore Pk &
Middletown Rd, Media
PA 19063. 610/565-
4844.

Clover Stores
250 W Chester Pike,
Havertown PA 19083-
4628. 610/789-6300.

Clover Stores
Rising Sun & Adams Av,
Philadelphia PA 19120.
215/722-8808.

Clover Stores
8500 Ridge Av,
Philadelphia PA 19128.
215/483-9700.

Clover Stores
8800 Frankford Ave,
Philadelphia PA 19136-
1313. 215/333-1400.

Clover Stores
2001 Cottman Ave,
Philadelphia PA 19149-
1118. 215/722-8400.

Clover Stores
Island Av & Lindbergh
Blvd, Philadelphia PA
19153. 215/492-0603.

Clover Stores
Rts 63 & 463, Lansdale
PA 19446. 215/855-
5858.

Corning Factory Store
831 Oley St, Reading PA
19604. 610/373-5650.

Corning Revere Factory Store
12 Market Hall, Princeton NJ 08540-5734.
609/987-2330.

Cos-Medic World
401 Germantown Pike, Lafayette HI PA 19444-1803. 610/825-5775.

DE Jones Inc.
4536 Frankford Ave, Philadelphia PA 19124-3602. 215/535-9601.

David Thomas Factory Store
10175 Northeast Ave, Philadelphia PA 19116-3713. 215/677-7390.

Delmont Discount
4102 Lancaster Ave, Philadelphia PA 19104-1727. 215/387-1233.

Delta Hosiery Outlets
503 Penn St, Reading PA 19601-3410. 610/373-2973.

Discount Stores Inc.
55 E Germantown Pike, Norristown PA 19401-1545. 610/277-7765.

Dollar Bill's
32 Snyder Ave, Philadelphia PA 19148-2711. 215/339-1996.

Dollar Depot
4836 Frankford Ave, Philadelphia PA 19124-2606. 215/288-3707.

Dollar Depot
3067 Kensington Ave, Philadelphia PA 19134-2415. 215/426-1135.

Dollar Discount Stores
200 MacDade Blvd, Lansdowne PA 19050-3835. 610/259-2020.

Dollar Land Inc.
2050 Richmond St # A, Philadelphia PA 19125-4323. 215/365-1200.

Doug's Outlet II
5630 Woodbine Ave, Philadelphia PA 19131-1322. 215/763-8873.

Dress Barn
Manufactures Outlet Mall, Morgantown PA 19543-9301. 610/286-0719.

Eagle's Eye Company Outlet
8 & Hill Av, Reading PA 19610. 610/378-5711.

Easy Spirit & Co.
801 Hill Ave, Reading PA 19610-3026. 610/374-7044.

Elkay Factory Outlet
44 W Chelten Ave, Philadelphia PA 19144-2702. 215/849-3890.

Everything 99 Cents Store Inc.
1175 Berkshire Blvd, Reading PA 19610-1244. 610/376-0608.

F&G Consignment Shop
4216 Princeton Ave, Philadelphia PA 19135-1719. 215/333-7406.

FW Woolworth Co.
119 E State St, Trenton NJ 08608-1709.
609/393-4223.

FW Woolworth Co.
Quaker Bridge Mall, Trenton NJ 08648.
609/799-8600.

FW Woolworth Co.
1841 Bethlehem Pike, Flourtown PA 19031-1109. 215/233-4226.

FW Woolworth Co.
1330 Chestnut St, Philadelphia PA 19107-4589. 215/735-7578.

FW Woolworth Co.
Huntingdon Pke, Philadelphia PA 19111. 215/379-3613.

FW Woolworth Co.
1 Olney Sq, Philadelphia PA 19120. 215/224-4556.

FW Woolworth Co.
7310 Frankford Ave, Philadelphia PA 19136-3827. 215/624-6422.

FW Woolworth Co.
52 & Market St, Philadelphia PA 19139. 215/476-2936.

FW Woolworth Co.
5611 Germantown Ave, Philadelphia PA 19144-2241. 215/438-3833.

FW Woolworth Co.
164 W Chelten Ave, Philadelphia PA 19144-3302. 215/848-8483.

FW Woolworth Co.
2013 S Broad St, Philadelphia PA 19148-5505. 215/467-4414.

FW Woolworth Co.
King Of Prussia Plaza,
Kng Of Prussa PA
19406. 610/265-0256.

Family Dollar Stores
115 S Black Horse Pike,
Bellmawr NJ 08031-
2310. 609/931-6635.

Family Dollar Stores
36 Berlin Rd, Clementon
NJ 08021-4546.
609/435-3012.

Family Dollar Stores
8445C Frankford Ave,
Philadelphia PA 19136-
2420. 215/332-8780.

Family Dollar Stores
1929 W 9th St, Chester
PA 19013-2719.
610/494-9088.

Family Dollar Stores
3764 L St, Philadelphia
PA 19124-5530.
215/743-0315.

Family Dollar Stores
7161 Ogontz Ave,
Philadelphia PA 19138-
2015. 215/424-6156.

Farah Factory Store
807 N 9th St, Reading
PA 19604-2450.
610/374-1166.

Fashion Flair
Manufactures Outlet
Mall, Morgantown PA
19543-9301. 610/286-
0880.

Filenes Basement
Franklin Mills Mall,
Philadelphia PA 19154.
215/281-0616.

**Flemington Fashion
Outlet**
Manufactures Outlet
Mall, Morgantown PA
19543-9301. 610/286-
6990.

**Flemington Fashion
Outlet**
800 Heister Ln, Reading
PA 19605-3035.
610/929-4460.

Grimm's Variety
1916 Welsh Rd,
Philadelphia PA 19115-
4655. 215/464-1889.

**Hamilton Watch & Clock
Shoppe**
Reading Outlet Ctr,
Reading PA 19604.
610/372-7560.

**Hartstrings Child Wear
Outlet**
830 Oley St, Reading PA
19604-2546. 610/376-
8808.

Health Fair
1416 Chestnut St,
Philadelphia PA 19102-
2505. 215/972-0499.

Health Fair
1720 Chestnut St,
Philadelphia PA 19103-
5120. 215/972-0566.

Health Fair
942 Market St,
Philadelphia PA 19107-
4220. 215/925-7380.

Health Fair
1619 Grant Ave,
Philadelphia PA 19115-
3167. 215/464-5752.

Health Fair
5522-24 N 5 St,
Philadelphia PA 19120.
215/924-5110.

Health Fair
4642 Frankford Ave,
Philadelphia PA 19124-
5828. 215/744-2986.

Health Fair
3175 Kensington Ave,
Philadelphia PA 19134-
2426. 215/739-3223.

Health Fair
7257 Frankford Ave,
Philadelphia PA 19135-
1010. 215/332-0950.

Health Fair
The Gallery, Philadelphia
PA 19107. 215/627-
1989.

Izod Factory Store
801 Hill Ave, Reading PA
19610-3026. 610/378-
0455.

J Crew
810 Windsor St, Reading
PA 19604-2315.
610/378-9106.

JM Fields Inc.
Germantown Pke,
Norristown PA 19401.
610/275-0654.

Jaeger Outlet
801 N 9th St, Reading
PA 19610-1717.
610/375-3316.

Jamesway
Minck & Walker Av,
West Berlin NJ 08091.
609/768-5800.

Jamesway Department Store
Hilltown Plaza Shopping Center, Souderton PA 18964. 215/723-8968.

Jamesway Department Store
290 Main St, Harleysville PA 19438-2416. 215/256-8558.

Jamesway Department Store
Rt 100 & State, Pottstown PA 19464. 610/970-0534.

Jessica McClintock Outlet
921 Douglass St, Reading PA 19604-2454. 610/478-0810.

Joan & David
807 N 9th St, Reading PA 19604-2450. 610/372-2830.

John Henry & Friends For Men
801 N 9th St, Reading PA 19604-2400. 610/376-0581.

John Wanamaker
901 Old York Rd, Jenkintown PA 19046-1427. 215/887-8300.

John Wanamaker
Berkshire Mall, Reading PA 19610. 610/374-4311.

Just A Buck
1048 South St, Philadelphia PA 19147-1935. 215/627-1760.

K-Mart Discount Store
US Hwy No 1 & Province Line Rd, Trenton NJ 08648. 609/452-2777.

K-Mart Discount Store
7101 Roosevelt Blvd, Philadelphia PA 19149-1431. 215/333-4500.

K-Mart Discount Store
8801 Torresdale Ave, Philadelphia PA 19136-1510. 215/333-8940.

K-Mart Discount Store
424 W Oregon Ave, Philadelphia PA 19148-4605. 215/755-3960.

K-Mart Discount Store
3975 Columbia Ave, Mountville PA 17554-1805. 717/285-2220.

K-Mart Discount Store
328 S White Horse Pike, Berlin NJ 08009-1936. 609/768-0090.

K-Mart Discount Store
1445 Brace Rd, Cherry Hill NJ 08034-3524. 609/428-1827.

K-Mart Discount Store
7500 S Crescent Blvd, Merchantville NJ 08109-4104. 609/665-8505.

K-Mart Discount Store
133 York Rd, Hatboro PA 19040. 215/674-5610.

Kid Kot'N
632 W Germantown Pike, Plymouth Mtng PA 19462-1003. 610/834-7599.

Kids Creations
807 N 9th St, Reading PA 19604-2450. 610/374-5534.

Lane Department Store
Kings Mall, Kutztown PA 19530. 610/683-6080.

Leather Loft
832 Oley St, Reading PA 19604-2500. 610/375-9799.

Leggs Hanes Bail Factory Outlet
810 Moss St, Reading PA 19604-2425. 610/376-3155.

Leggs Hanes Bali Factory Outlet
Manufactures Outlet Mall, Morgantown PA 19543-9301. 610/286-0625.

Leslie Fay Factory Outlets
830 Oley St, Reading PA 19604-2546. 610/372-9733.

Leslie Lady
126 Village Blvd, Princeton NJ 08540-5761. 609/734-0855.

Linens & Much More
801 N 9th St, Reading PA 19604-2400. 610/375-6901.

Linens & Much More
730 N 8th St, Reading PA 19604-2455. 610/375-8660.

Little Red Shoe House
Manufactures Outlet Mall, Morgantown PA 19543-9301. 610/286-0043.

Liz Claiborne Outlet Center
830 Oley St, Reading PA 19604-2546. 610/372-9655.

London Fog Factory Store
801 Hill Ave, Reading PA 19610-3026. 610/371-0772.

Lord & Taylor
Quaker Bridge Mall, Trenton NJ 08648. 609/799-9500.

Macy's
State Hwy No 38, Cherry Hill NJ 08002. 609/665-5000.

Macy's
1250 Baltimore Pike, Springfield PA 19064-2798. 610/328-1234.

Macy's
The Court At King Of Prussia, Kng Of Prussa PA 19406. 610/337-9350.

Macy's
Montgomery Mall, North Wales PA 19454. 215/362-9100.

Marshalls Discount Store
1356 Franklin Mills Cir, Philadelphia PA 19154-3141. 215/281-3757.

Marshalls Department Store
801 Bethlehem Pike, North Wales PA 19454-1421. 215/362-7433.

Marshalls Department Store
9173-75 Roosevelt Blvd, Philadelphia PA 19114. 215/676-3025.

Marshalls Department Store
Ridge & Butlr Pke, Conshohocken PA 19428. 610/828-7081.

McCrory's Store
N Olden Av Ex & Princeton Av, Trenton NJ 08609. 609/396-5865.

McCrory's Store
U S Hwy No 1, Trenton NJ 08648. 609/883-7521.

McCrory's Store
51 Scotch Rd, Trenton NJ 08628-2512. 609/883-0330.

Mikasa Factory Outlet
Hill Ave & Park Rd, Reading PA 19606. 610/376-2928.

Mondo Collection Factory Outlet
951 N 6th St, Reading PA 19601-1800. 610/373-6788.

Moon Discount Store
2864 N Mascher St, Philadelphia PA 19133-3525. 215/739-0514.

Napier Company Factory Store
951 N 6th St, Reading PA 19601-1800. 610/478-7365.

National Merchandise Liquid Inc.
7360 Wissinoming St, Philadelphia PA 19136-4218. 215/331-7166.

Nautica Of Reading
843 N 9th St, Reading PA 19604-2453. 610/478-9980.

New Health Aid Center
4658 Frankford Ave, Philadelphia PA 19124-5828. 215/537-0891.

Nolan's Department Store
33 E Franklin St, Topton PA 19562-1203. 610/682-2447.

Oneida Factory Store
Vanity Fair Indutrial Park, Reading PA 19610. 610/375-3778.

Ports Of The World
300 E Godfrey Ave, Philadelphia PA 19120-1634. 215/745-4700.

Ports Of The World
Logan Square Shopping Center, Norristown PA 19401. 610/277-3550.

Price Wise Family Health Center
1834 E Passyunk Ave, Philadelphia PA 19148-2140. 215/468-1777.

Prince Gardner Inc.
Manufactures Outlet Mall, Morgantown PA 19543-9301. 610/286-7999.

Quality Plus Discount
27 W State St, Media PA 19063-3348. 610/566-9445.

Polo Ralph Lauren Factory Store
845 N 9th St, Reading PA 19604-2416. 610/373-5900.

Reading Bag Company
Vf Factory Outlet, Reading PA 19610. 610/372-4544.

Reading China & Glass Co.
RR 9 Box 9382, Reading PA 19605-9650. 610/378-0413.

Reading Station Outlet Center
951 N 6th St, Reading PA 19601-1800.
610/478-7000.

Ross Dress For Less
105 Mercer St, Princeton NJ 08540-6809.
609/520-8878.

Ross Stores
Red Lion and Norcom Rd, Philadelphia PA 19154-2398. 215/676-5869.

Ross Stores
2333 W Main St, Lansdale PA 19446-1346. 215/361-8159.

Ross Stores
751 Horsham Rd, Lansdale PA 19446-6489. 215/362-5585.

Ross Stores
400 S State Rd, Springfield PA 19064-1243. 610/544-1517.

Saks Fifth Ave Clearinghouse
1618 Franklin Mills Cir, Philadelphia PA 19154-3142. 215/632-5600.

Sam's Club
1000 Franklin Mills Cir, Philadelphia PA 19154-3190. 215/632-2299.

Santerian Department Store
Line & Penn Lansdale, Lansdale PA 19446.
215/855-0700.

Scent Cellar
801 N 9th St, Reading PA 19604-2400.
610/373-5124.

Ship & Shore Lady Factory Outlet
902 Windsor St, Reading PA 19604-2317.
610/372-9500.

Ship N Shore
801 N 9th St, Reading PA 19604-2400.
610/376-6099.

Simpson Variety
1247 S 2nd St, Philadelphia PA 19147-5420. 215/467-0788.

Specials
12123 Knights Rd, Philadelphia PA 19154-3104. 215/632-3636.

Spiegel Ultimate Outlet
1990 Franklin Mills Cir, Philadelphia PA 19154-3142. 215/632-6680.

Sports Warehouse
Manufactures Outlet Mall, Morgantown PA 19543-9301. 610/286-7320.

Strawbridge & Clothier
Ardmore & Montgomery Avs, Ardmore PA 19003.
610/645-1399.

Strawbridge & Clothier
2600 E Moreland Rd, Willow Grove PA 19090-4001. 215/830-0200.

Strawbridge & Clothier
640 W Dekalb Pike, Kng Of Prussa PA 19406-2900. 610/337-8400.

Strawbridge & Clothier
Germantown Pke & Hickory, Plymouth Mtng PA 19462. 610/825-1700.

TJ Maxx
US Hwy No 1, Trenton NJ 08648. 609/452-7092.

TJ Maxx
1495 Old York Rd, Abington PA 19001-1923. 215/884-3840.

TJ Maxx
City Line Shpg Ctr, Philadelphia PA 19151.
215/879-2602.

TJ Maxx
1634 Franklin Mills Cir, Philadelphia PA 19154-3142. 215/281-0929.

TJ Maxx
3130 Dekalb Pike, Norristown PA 19401-1527. 610/275-7331.

TJ Maxx
949 Church Rd, Cherry Hill NJ 08002-1301.
609/667-0730.

The Casual Shop
3612 Lancaster Ave, Philadelphia PA 19104-2604. 215/222-3351.

The Gap
8600 Germantown Ave, Philadelphia PA 19118-2841. 215/247-7463.

Timberland Factory Outlet
Reading Outlet Center, Reading PA 19604.
610/375-8489.

Totes Factory Outlet
815 N 9th St, Reading PA 19604-2416.
610/373-5543.

Totes Factory Outlet
Vanity Fair Complex,
Reading PA 19610.
610/376-2050.

Toy Liquidators
Rockvale Sq Factory
Outlet Mal, Lancaster PA
17602. 717/397-9386.

Unishops Inc.
24 & McKean,
Philadelphia PA 19148.
215/463-9632.

Urban Outfitters Inc.
1801 Walnut St,
Philadelphia PA 19103-
4903. 215/569-3131.

Urban Outfitters Inc.
404 Locust St,
Philadelphia PA 19106-
3710. 215/387-0373.

Valu-Plus Inc.
4628 Frankford Ave,
Philadelphia PA 19124-
5804. 215/535-8222.

Valu-Plus Inc.
1501 Unity St,
Philadelphia PA 19124-
3998. 215/744-4707.

Valu-Plus Inc.
2330 N Front St,
Philadelphia PA 19133-
3716. 215/739-1784.

Valu-Plus Inc.
6339 Woodland Ave,
Philadelphia PA 19142-
2036. 215/724-2386.

Valu-Plus Inc.
5619 Germantown Ave,
Philadelphia PA 19144-
2241. 215/844-2233.

Value City
721 W Sproul Rd,
Springfield PA 19064-
1215. 610/690-2400.

**Van Heusen Factory
Outlet**
126 Village Blvd,
Princeton NJ 08540-
5761. 609/520-0767.

**Van Heusen Factory
Outlet**
825 Oley St, Reading PA
19604-2547. 610/372-
4518.

**Van Heusen Factory
Outlet**
Exit 22 Penna Turnpike,
Morgantown ,PA 19543.
610/286-6995.

**Van Heusen Factory
Outlet**
Vanity Fair Outlet,
Reading PA 19610.
610/378-5550.

Wal-Mart Discount Cities
5900 Perkiomen Ave,
Reading PA 19606-3635.
610/582-0505.

Watt & Shand Inc.
Two E King St, Lancaster
PA 17603-3824.
717/397-5221.

**West Point Pepperell Mill
Store**
951 N 6th St, Reading
PA 19601-1800.
610/375-1305.

Windsor Shirt Company
801 Hill Ave, Reading PA
19610-3026. 610/378-
0100.

Woolworth
6900 Torresdale Ave,
Philadelphia PA 19135-
1994. 215/624-2135.

Yi's Korner
4535 Frankford Ave,
Philadelphia PA 19124-
3638. 215/743-0318.

Young Generations
951 N 6th St, Reading
PA 19601-1800.
610/373-8990.

99 Cent Store
901 Brunswick Ave,
Trenton NJ 08638-3946.
609/989-1688.

VARIETY STORES

FW Woolworth Co.
601 2000 Rt 38, Cherry
Hill NJ 08002. 609/663-
1892.

Kelly's Korner
2501 Kensington Ave,
Philadelphia PA 19125-
1399. 215/291-9800.

GROCERY STORES

CR's Friendly Mini Market
Moselem Springs,
Fleetwood PA 19522.
610/944-0281.

Davisville Center Inc.
800 E Street Rd,
Warminster PA 18974-
3317. 215/355-4070.

**Dutchway Farm Market
Inc.**
701 E Lincoln Ave,
Myerstown PA 17067-
2295. 717/866-5758.

Genuardi Super Markets
Easton & Old Dublin Pike,
Doylestown PA 18901.
215/345-1830.

Giant Markets Inc.
501 S Washington Ave,
Scranton PA 18505-
3803. 717/343-2401.

Insalaco's Market
Country Club Shopping
Center, Dallas PA 18612.
717/675-6100.

Martin's Country Market
1717 W Main St, Ephrata
PA 17522-1129.
717/738-3754.

Shop Rite Exec Office
954 Route 166, Toms
River NJ 08753-6562.
908/341-0700.

Shop Rite Of Marlton
State Hwy No 70 &
State Hwy No, Marlton
NJ 08053. 609/983-
7370.

Turkey Hill Minit Market
2501 N Reading Rd,
Denver PA 17517-9330.
215/484-2646.

Zippy Food Bag
804 E 5th St, Berwick
PA 18603-3923.
717/752-3661.

FRUIT AND VEGETABLE MARKETS

Produce Junction Inc.
126 Bridge St, Mont
Clare PA 19453-5014.
610/935-8727.

CANDY, NUT AND CONFECTIONERY STORES

Garrahy's Fudge Kitchen
1140 Chambersburg Rd,
Gettysburg PA 17325-
3396. 717/334-9141.

RETAIL BAKERIES

Buns Galore
1024 E Lancaster Ave,
Bryn Mawr PA 19010-
1449. 610/527-9272.

Italian Peoples Bakery
Mercerville Shopping
Center, Trenton NJ
08619. 609/586-1868.

MISCELLANEOUS FOOD STORES

Bucks County Nut & Coffee Co
168 Eagleview Blvd,
Exton PA 19341-3012.
610/363-6910.

Cafe Pilon Espresso Coffee
825 Route 38, Mount
Holly NJ 08060-2981.
609/261-0009.

Diamond Station
1160 S State St, Ephrata
PA 17522-2618.
717/733-9787.

Penn Dutch Pullet Farm
RR 2, Duncannon PA
17020-9802. 717/834-
4805.

MOTOR VEHICLE DEALERS

Bennett Infiniti Inc.
4800 W Tilghman St,
Allentown PA 18104-
9365. 610/398-9100.

Faulkner Toyota Inc.
Street & Mechanicsville
Rd, Bensalem PA 19020.
215/244-9300.

Frederick Toyota
1507 Quentin Rd,
Lebanon PA 17042-
7431. 717/274-1461.

Griffith Honda Of York
2108 S Queen St, York
PA 17403-4809.
717/848-2600.

Haldeman Lincoln Mercury Inc.
2443 Lehigh St,
Allentown PA 18103-
4704. 610/791-4900.

Keenan Motors
856 N Easton Rd,
Doylestown PA 18901-
1007. 215/348-0800.

Kelly Car & Truck Center
1986 State Rd,
Lancaster PA 17601-
1808. 717/898-4000.

Ladd-Hanford Mazda
2247 Cumberland St,
Lebanon PA 17042-
2521. 717/270-2908.

Scott Chevrolet Inc.
3333 Lehigh St, Emmaus
PA 18049. 610/967-
4151.

USED CAR DEALERS

Apsche Motors II
7103 Rt 13, Levittown
PA 19057. 215/946-
1530.

Conicelli Used Cars
1201 W Ridge Pike,
Conshohocken PA
19428-1019. 610/834-
0620.

Continental Pre-Owned
3315 Walnut St,
Harrisburg PA 17109-
3563. 717/541-9410.

Fairless Motors Inc.
501 Lincoln Hwy,
Fairless Hls PA 19030-
1401. 215/736-3033.

AUTO AND HOME SUPPLY STORES

A&A Auto Stores
360 N 9th St,
Stroudsburg PA 18360-
1804. 717/424-0776.

Avellinos Tire & Auto Service Co
4309 County Line Rd,
Chalfont PA 18914-
1823. 215/822-3000.

Bastian Tire Sls Bloomsburg
232 W Main St,
Bloomsburg PA 17815-
1607. 717/784-5920.

Firestone Tire & Service Centers
220 W Lincoln Hwy,
Exton PA 19341-2623.
610/363-0650.

Firestone
3117 Bridge Ave, Pt
Pleas Bch NJ 08742-
3456. 908/295-2424.

McCarthy Tire Service Company
340 Kidder St, Wilkes
Barre PA 18702-5606.
717/822-3151.

STS Car Service Center
7720 Main St, Fogelsville
PA 18051-1630.
610/391-0300.

MEN'S AND BOYS' CLOTHING STORES

Quality Discount Apparel
810 Moss St, Reading
PA 19604-2425.
610/376-2177.

Smalls Formal Wear
69th & Market Sts,
Upper Darby PA 19082.
610/734-0230.

Triple A Trouser Manufacturing Co.
Penn Av & Larch St,
Scranton PA 18509.
717/342-9194.

WOMEN'S CLOTHING STORES

Annie Sez
933 Montgomery Ave,
Narberth PA 19072-
1501. 610/664-9482.

Cooper Sportswear
801 N 9th St, Reading
PA 19604-2400.
610/375-3470.

Country Road Australia
700 N 8th St, Reading
PA 19604-2522.
610/375-8208.

David Thomas Factory Store
401 Race St, Philadelphia
PA 19106-1820.
215/922-4659.

Doneckers Inc.
409 N State St, Ephrata
PA 17522-2100.
717/733-2231.

Express
1067 W Baltimore Pike,
Media PA 19063-5121.
610/565-6128.

Jonathan Logan Inc.
801 Hill Ave, Reading PA
19610-3026. 610/372-
3819.

Junior Colony Inc.
1871 S 5th St,
Allentown PA 18103-
4991. 610/791-3131.

Mandee Shop
New Britain Village Sq,
Chalfont PA 18914.
215/997-9097.

Maurices Inc.
Lebanon Plaza Shopping
Center, Lebanon PA
17042. 717/272-9987.

Merry Go Round
Stroud Mall, Stroudsburg
PA 18360. 717/420-
0227.

Rainbow Shops
2051 W Oregon Ave,
Philadelphia PA 19145-
4224. 215/755-8558.

Rave
Granite Run Mall, Media
PA 19063. 610/566-
6692.

Robert Scott & David Brooks
951 N 6th St, Reading
PA 19601-1800.
610/478-9883.

Saks Fifth Avenue
2 Bala Cynwyd Plaza,
Bala Cynwyd PA 19004.
610/667-1550.

The Avenue
100 Black Horse Pike,
Pleasantville NJ 08232.
609/484-9720.

WOMEN'S ACCESSORY AND SPECIALTY STORES

VF Factory Outlet
801 Hill Ave, Reading PA 19610-3026. 610/378-0408.

CHILDREN'S WEAR STORES

House Of Bargains Inc.
70 Portland Rd, Conshohocken PA 19428-2717. 610/834-1600.

SHOE STORES

Banister Shoe Store
2980B Whiteford Rd, York PA 17402-8978. 717/757-7119.

Dolcis Shoe Store
1228 Plymouth Meeting Mall, Plymouth Mtng PA 19462-1327. 610/825-0734.

Florsheim Thayer McNeil
2 Neshaminy Mall, Bensalem PA 19020. 215/357-1693.

Foot Locker
Shore Mall, Pleasantville NJ 08232. 609/646-1762.

Irving Shoes Inc.
York Galleria Mall, York PA 17402. 717/840-1167.

Irving Stride Rite
Park City Center, Lancaster PA 17601. 717/299-2994.

Lady Footlocker
160 N Gulph Rd, Kng Of Prussa PA 19406-2924. 610/265-6018.

Littonian Shoe Co.
31 Keystone St, Littlestown PA 17340-1662. 717/359-5194.

Nine West
1201 Hooper Ave, Toms River NJ 08753-3330. 908/286-7751.

Parade Of Shoes
Village West Shopping Center, Allentown PA 18104. 610/435-8171.

Payless Shoe Source
Burlington Center, Burlington NJ 08016. 609/386-8309.

Payless Shoe Source
Park City Mall, Lancaster PA 17601. 717/293-9817.

Payless Shoe Source
Manoa Shopping Center, Havertown PA 19083. 610/789-9240.

Picway Shoes
1238 Greensprings Dr, York PA 17402-8825. 717/757-4212.

Picway Shoes
Valley Forge Mall, Phoenixville PA 19460. 610/935-1393.

Shoe-Town
1800 Clements Bridge Rd, Woodbury NJ 08096-2021. 609/853-8198.

Stride Rite East End
East End Center, Wilkes Barre PA 18702. 717/825-9697.

The Shoe Works
Wyoming Valley Mall, Wilkes Barre PA 18702. 717/823-9313.

MISCELLANEOUS APPAREL AND ACCESSORY STORES

A&H Sportswear Co.
50 Sycamore St, Nazareth PA 18064-1037. 610/746-0922.

Astor Swimwear Outlet Stores
1722 N 10th St, Reading PA 19604-1503. 610/929-3322.

Banana Republic
315 Goddard Blvd, Kng Of Prussa PA 19406. 610/768-9007.

Carroll Reed Outlet
1001 Washington St, Conshohocken PA 19428-2381.

Gold Medal Sporting Goods Inc.
1011 Cedar Ave, Bensalem PA 19020-6302. 215/785-1234.

Hats In The Belfry
525 S 3rd St, Philadelphia PA 19147-2307. 215/922-6770.

Life Uniform
Moorestown Mall, Moorestown NJ 08057. 609/235-2965.

The Sweatshirt Co.
34 S Willowdale Dr,
Lancaster PA 17602-
1476. 717/293-9360.

Touchdown Sportswear
Plymouth Meeting Mall,
Plymouth Mtng PA
19462. 610/834-8675.

**Wilson Suede & Leather
Co Inc.**
Hamilton Mall,
Pleasantville NJ 08232.
609/646-6012.

Work 'N Gear Stores
1692H Clements Bridge
Rd, Woodbury NJ
08096-3010. 609/848-
7676.

Z&H Uniforms
2188 Plymouth Meeting
Mall, Plymouth Mtng PA
19462-1328. 610/825-
7238.

FURNITURE STORES

Bombay Co.
2300 E Lincoln Hwy,
Langhorne PA 19047-
1805. 215/752-5762.

Jetronic Industries Inc.
4200 Mitchell St,
Philadelphia PA 19128-
3538. 215/482-7660.

Just Cabinets
6295 Allentown Blvd,
Harrisburg PA 17112.
717/541-9232.

**Mr Sandman Discount
Sleep Center**
3500 Cottman Ave,
Philadelphia PA 19149-
1606. 215/624-7335.

Naked Furniture
Route 6 Scranton
Carbondale Hw, Olyphant
PA 18447. 717/383-
9633.

**Nationwide Discount
Sleep Centers**
State Hwy No 38, Mount
Holly NJ 08060.
609/265-7771.

**Nationwide Discount
Sleep Centers**
3721 W Chester Pike,
Newtown Sq PA 19073-
2303. 610/359-1720.

**Nationwide Discount
Sleep Centers**
9356 Old Bustleton Ave,
Philadelphia PA 19115-
4611. 215/676-1296.

**Nationwide Discount
Sleep Centers**
2440 E Venango St,
Philadelphia PA 19134-
4618. 215/831-8100.

**FLOOR COVERING
STORES**

Rickel Floor Store
120 N MacDade Blvd,
Darby PA 19023-1609.
610/461-9460.

**MISCELLANEOUS
HOMEFURNISHINGS
STORES**

Albert E Price Inc.
Interstate Business Park,
Bellmawr NJ 08031.
609/933-1111.

Bell Electric
650 Wyoming Ave,
Scranton PA 18509-
3016. 717/343-2461.

Happy Viking Ltd
Rt 309, Hatfield PA
19440. 215/362-1900.

Lechters Housewares
Baltimore Pike & Rte
320, Springfield PA
19064. 610/328-2815.

**Remington Factory
Service Center**
King Of Prussia Plaza,
Kng Of Prussa PA
19406. 610/265-3731.

**RADIO, TELEVISION AND
CONSUMER
ELECTRONICS STORES**

Bookland Video
Dairyland Shopping
Center, Red Lion PA
17356. 717/244-1435.

**Radio Shack
A Division Tandy
Corporation**
Kendig Sq, Willow Street
PA 17584. 717/464-
3641.

**Strouds Jewelers &
Distributors**
Chipperfield Dr & Rt 611,
Stroudsburg PA 18360.
717/424-2111.

Unclaimed Freight Co.
2260 Industrial Dr,
Bethlehem PA 18017-
2138. 610/861-1250.

**COMPUTER AND
COMPUTER SOFTWARE
STORES**

EMC Corporation
488 Norristown Rd, Blue
Bell PA 19422-2352.
610/834-7740.

Essex Corporation
6 State Rd Ste 108,
Mechanicsburg PA
17055-7933. 717/766-
2699.

Execu-Flow Systems
2250 Hickory Rd,
Plymouth Mtng PA
19462-1047. 610/941-
6667.

Reohr Group Inc.
1150 1st Ave Ste 1035,
Kng Of Prussa PA
19406-1316. 610/768-
7150.

**United Systems
Technology Inc.**
1035 Broadway,
Westville NJ 08093-
1439. 609/742-0060.

Wolf Computer Systems
2 Neshaminy Interplex,
Fstrvl Trvose PA 19053.
215/244-9653.

**RECORD AND
PRERECORDED TAPE
STORES**

Listening Booth
Viewmont Mall, Scranton
PA 18508. 717/342-
8343.

Schwartz Brothers Inc.
822 Montgomery Ave
Ste 204, Narberth PA
19072-1937.

Square Circle
Hamilton Mall, Mays
Landing NJ 08330.
609/484-1990.

**Wall To Wall Sound
Video**
Baltimore Pike & Rte
320, Springfield PA
19064. 610/328-3430.

**MUSICAL INSTRUMENT
STORES**

Guitarmakers Connection
10 W North St, Nazareth
PA 18064-1424.
610/759-2064.

Keyboard World
Nittany Mall, State
College PA 16801.
814/238-2956.

For more information on career opportunities in retail:

<u>Associations</u>

**INTERNATIONAL ASSOCIATION OF
CHAIN STORES**
3800 Moor Place, Alexandria VA
22305. 703/549-4525.

**INTERNATIONAL COUNCIL OF
SHOPPING CENTERS**
665 Fifth Avenue, New York NY
10022. 212/421-8181.

**NATIONAL AUTOMOTIVE DEALERS
ASSOCIATION**
8400 Westpark Drive, McLean VA
22102. 703/821-7000.

**NATIONAL INDEPENDENT
AUTOMOTIVE DEALERS
ASSOCIATION**
2521 Brown Boulevard, Suite 100,
Arlington TX 76006. 817/640-3838.

NATIONAL RETAIL FEDERATION
325 7th Street NW, Suite 1000,
Washington DC 20004. 202/783-
7971.

<u>Directories</u>

**AUTOMOTIVE NEWS MARKET DATA
BOOK**
Automotive News, Crain
Communication, 1400 Woodbridge
Avenue, Detroit MI 48207-3187.
313/446-6000.

STONE, CLAY, GLASS AND CONCRETE PRODUCTS

Production of stone, clay, glass, concrete and related materials is expected to increase as residential, commercial and public works construction spur demand. By looking at the future of these types of projects, the growth rate of the stone and materials industry will be slow. Construction is expected to have a significant increase in 1995, even though infrastructure construction is dependent on ever shrinking governmental budgets. Even so, shipments of most of these materials are only expected to increase by 1 or 2 percent.

ANCHOR GLASS CONTAINER CORPORATION
83 Griffith, Salem NJ 08079. 609/935-4000. **Contact:** Bernie Bettwy, Personnel Manager. **Description:** Manufacturers of a variety of container products.

THE J.E. BAKER COMPANY
232 East Market Street, P.O. Box 1189, York PA 17405. 717/848-1501. **Contact:** Human Resources. **Description:** Produces refractory products, including dolomite and agriculture limestone. **Common positions include:** Accountant/Auditor; Administrator; Blue-Collar Worker Supervisor; Buyer; Ceramics Engineer; Chemist; Computer Programmer; Customer Service Representative; Department Manager; Draftsperson; Electrical/Electronic Engineer; Financial Analyst; Geologist/Geophysicist; Manufacturer's/Wholesaler's Sales Rep.; Mechanical Engineer; Personnel/Labor Relations Specialist; Purchasing Agent and Manager; Systems Analyst. **Educational backgrounds include:** Accounting; Business Administration; Chemistry; Computer Science; Engineering; Finance; Geology; Marketing. **Benefits:** 401K; Dental Insurance; Disability Coverage; Employee Discounts; Life Insurance; Medical Insurance; Profit Sharing; Savings Plan; Tuition Assistance. **Corporate headquarters location:** This Location. **Operations at this facility include:** Administration; Manufacturing; Research and Development; Sales; Service.

ESSROC MATERIALS INC.
P.O. Box 32, Nazareth PA 18064. 215/837-6725. **Contact:** Human Resources. **Description:** A cement manufacturing company.

HIGH CONCRETE STRUCTURES
125 Denver Road, Denver PA 17517. 717/336-9300. **Contact:** Joyce Griffith, Personnel. **Description:** Manufacturers of precast concrete for use by the construction industry.

LEONE INDUSTRIES
P.O. Box 400, 443 Southeast Avenue, Bridgeton NJ 08302. 609/455-2000. **Contact:** Personnel. **Description:** Manufactures flint for clear glass containers. **Common positions include:** Accountant/Auditor; Buyer; Customer Service Representative; Draftsperson; Electrical/Electronic Engineer; General Manager; Industrial Engineer; Management Trainee; Mechanical Engineer; Operations/Production Manager;

Purchasing Agent and Manager; Quality Control Supervisor. **Educational backgrounds include:** Accounting; Business Administration; Engineering; Finance; Marketing. **Benefits:** Dental Insurance; Life Insurance; Medical Insurance; Pension Plan; Tuition Assistance. **Corporate headquarters location:** This Location. **Operations at this facility include:** Manufacturing.

Note: Because addresses and telephone numbers of smaller companies change rapidly, we recommend you contact each company and verify the information below before contacting employers. Mass mailings are not recommended.

Additional large employers: 500+

ASPHALT

Harsco Corp.
P.O. Box 8888, Camp Hill PA 17001-8888.
717/763-7064.

GLASS AND GLASS PRODUCTS

PPG Industries/Glass Division
635 Park Drive, Carlisle PA 17013. 717/486-3366.

Owens-Illinois Inc.
Crystal Ave., Vineland NJ 08360. 609/692-3600.

Schott Glass Technologies Inc.
400 York Ave., Pittston PA 18642-2036.
717/457-7485.

PQ Corporation
P.O. Box 840, Valley Forge PA 19482-0840.
610/293-7200.

TILE

American Olean Tile Company
1000 N Cannon Ave., Lansdale PA 19446-1872. 215/855-1111.

POTTERY PRODUCTS

Susquehanna Pfaltzgraff Company
140 E Market St., York PA 17401-1219.
717/848-5500.

BRICK AND CONCRETE PRODUCTS

Glen-Gery Corp.
1166 Spring St Box 7001, Reading PA 19610-1723. 610/374-4011.

TREATED MINERALS AND EARTHS

Murata Erie North America
1900 W College Ave., State College PA 16801-2723. 8142371431.

MINERAL WOOL

Owens-Corning Fiberglass
P.O. Box 8, Barrington NJ 08007-0008.
609/547-9200.

Additional medium sized employers: under 500

POTTERY PRODUCTS

Boehm Edward Marshall
PO Box 5051, Trenton NJ 08638-0051.
609/392-2207.

CONCRETE BLOCK AND BRICK

EP Henry Corporation
201 Park Ave, Woodbury NJ 08096-3523.
609/845-6200.

Ralph Clayton & Sons
515 Lakewood-New Egypt Rd, Lakewood NJ 08701. 908/363-1995.

York Building Products Company Inc.
1020 N Hartley St, York PA 17404-2849.
717/848-2831.

CONCRETE PRODUCTS

Atlantic Concrete Products Inc.
8900 Old Rte 13, Bristol PA 19007. 215/945-5600.

Atlas Building Systems Inc.
PO Box 245, Marlton NJ 08053-0245. 609/767-0884.

Bogert Precast Inc.
163 Catawissa Ave, Williamsport PA 17701-4170. 717/322-6130.

Glenn O Hawbaker Inc.
325 W Aaron Dr, State College PA 16803-3045. 814/237-1444.

Nitterhouse Concrete Prod Inc.
PO Box N, Chambersburg PA 17201-0813. 717/264-6154.

Roman Mosaic & Tile Company
1105 Saunders Ct, West Chester PA 19380-4295. 610/692-3100.

Rotondo Penn Cast
514 Township Line Rd, Telford PA 18969-1186. 215/257-8081.

Schuylkill Products Inc.
Gordon Nagle Trail, Cressona PA 17929. 717/385-2352.

Terre Hill Concrete Products Inc.
Rte 897, Terre Hill PA 17581. 215/445-6736.

READY MIX CONCRETE

Pennsylvania Supply
1001 Paxton St, Harrisburg PA 17104-1645. 717/233-4511.

Trap Rock Industries
PO Box 419, Kingston NJ 08528-0419. 609/924-0300.

Valley Transit Mix Co.
169 Quarry Rd, Chambersburg PA 17201-8496. 717/263-9186.

LIME

Bellefonte Lime Co Inc.
N Thomas St, Bellefonte PA 16823. 814/355-4761.

Centre Lime & Stone Company Inc.
Airport Rd & Rt 64, Bellefonte PA 16823. 814/359-2773.

Corson Lime Co.
500 Stenton Ave, Plymouth Mtng PA 19462-1231. 610/828-4300.

Martin Limestone Inc.
PO Box 550, Blue Ball PA 17506-0550. 717/354-1300.

Wimpey Minerals Pennsylvania Inc.
Rt 422, Annville PA 17003. 717/867-4441.

GYPSUM PRODUCTS

Byers Choice Ltd
94 County Line Rd, Colmar PA 18915-9606. 215/822-6700.

Genstar Flintkote Building
1101 S Front St, Camden NJ 08103-3200. 609/966-7600.

National Gypsum Co.
1818 River Rd, Burlington NJ 08016-2132. 609/499-3300.

CUT STONE AND STONE PRODUCTS

Anthony Dally & Sons
PO Box 27, Pen Argyl PA 18072-0027. 610/863-4172.

Rynone Manufacturing Corporation
N Thomas Ave, Sayre PA 18840. 717/888-5272.

Wildon Industries Inc.
Rte 512, Mount Bethel PA 18343. 610/588-1212.

MINERALS AND EARTHS

ISP Minerals Inc.
16001 Charmian Rd, Blue Ridge Sm PA 17214. 717/794-2184.

Lycoming Silica Sand Company
R D 1, Montoursville PA 17754-9801. 717/368-2481.

MINERAL WOOD

Manville/Schuller
Atlantic Ave C-N 130, Berlin NJ 08009. 609/767-5000.

Pacor Inc.
1900 N 6th St, Philadelphia PA 19122-2104. 215/978-7100.

FLAT GLASS

AFG Industries
2600 River Rd, Riverton
NJ 08077-1600.
609/829-0400.

GLASS CONTAINERS

Lake Glass
481 Linden Grove Rd,
Ephrata PA 17522-8539.
717/445-9483.

**PRESSED AND BLOWN
GLASS**

**Lurex Manufacturing Co
Inc.**
PO Box 22, Vineland NJ
08360-0022. 609/692-
5600.

Wilbur Scientific
North Rd, Middlebry Ctr
PA 16935. 717/376-
5221.

**GLASS PRODUCTS,
MADE FROM
PURCHASED GLASS**

Bellco Glass Inc.
340 Edrudo Rd, Vineland
NJ 08360-3457.
609/691-1075.

Falconer-Lewistown
1 Belle Ave, Lewistown
PA 17044-2435.
717/242-2571.

JE Berkowitz LP
Delsea Dr & Harvard Ave,
Westville NJ 08093.
609/456-7800.

HYDRAULIC CEMENT

Lafarge Corporation
5160 Main St, Whitehall
PA 18052-1827.
610/262-7831.

Lone Star Industries
401 W Prospect St,
Nazareth PA 18064-
2727. 610/759-4210.

**BRICK AND
STRUCTURAL CLAY TILE**

Certech Inc.
550 Stewart Rd, Wilkes
Barre PA 18706-1455.
717/823-7400.

**CERAMIC WALL AND
FLOOR TILE**

Dal-Tile Corporation
211 N 4th St, Gettysburg
PA 17325-1604.
717/334-1181.

Dal-Tile Corporation
2938 York Rd,
Gettysburg PA 17325-
8229. 717/334-9151.

Wenczel Tile Co.
PO Box 5408, Trenton
NJ 08638-0408.
609/599-4503.

**CRUSHED AND BROKEN
LIMESTONE**

Eastern Industries Inc.
Rd 3 Box 150, Center
Valley PA 18034-9803.
610/866-0932.

**CRUSHED AND BROKEN
STONE**

Keystone Cement Co.
7311 Airport Rd, Bath PA
18014-8808. 610/837-
1881.

**CONSTRUCTION SAND
AND GRAVEL**

The Morie Company
1201 N High St, Millville
NJ 08332-2530.
609/327-4500.

INDUSTRIAL SAND

US Silica Co.
RR 1 Box 1885,
Mapleton Dep PA 17052-
9700. 814/542-2561.

**For more information on career opportunities in stone, clay, glass and concrete
products:**

Associations

NATIONAL GLASS ASSOCIATION
8200 Greensboro Drive, McLean VA
22102. 703/442-4890

Magazines

GLASS MAGAZINE
National Glass Association, 8200
Greensboro Drive, McLean VA 22102.
703/442-4890

THE NORTH AMERICAN CEMENT REVIEW
Douglas M. Queen, Inc., 2143 Old Spring Road, Williamstown MA 01267. 413/458-8364.

ROCK PRODUCTS
MacLean Hunter Publishing Co., Chicago IL 60606. 312/726-2805.

TRANSPORTATION

 *All four major transportation segments -- airlines, railroad, trucking and water transport -- expect modest growth as the nation's economy slowly recovers.* *According to analysts, airline traffic should continue to grow both domestically and abroad, but carriers will still have to balance costs and fares. Regional carriers will continue to outpace larger airlines. According to the U.S. Labor Department, the hiring picture of airlines will improve over the long-term.*

On the railroads, the use of both freight and passenger trains will climb. On the road, truckers will see an increase in opportunities, but a jump in operating costs will squeeze profit margins. Job opportunities should be good for truck drivers and mechanics, as the number of trucking and warehouse jobs are projected to grow by 25 percent over the next several years. According to the U.S. Commerce Department, increased trade and stronger freight rates should help the performance of U.S. flag liner companies operating in the Asian markets. Domestic use of water transportation should also increase, especially between Alaska and the lower 48 states.

A.C.T.S. INC.
P.O. Box 28741, BWI Airport MD 21240. 717/854-8554. **Contact:** Human Resources. **Description:** An air transportation company.

AERO SERVICES INTERNATIONAL INC.
660 Newtown-Yardley Road, Newtown PA 18940. 215/860-5600. **Contact:** Human Resources. **Description:** An air transportation service.

AL EL ISRAEL AIRLINES
1515 Market Street, Philadelphia PA 19102. 215/563-8011. **Contact:** Human Resources. **Description:** An air transportation company.

AMTRAK
30th Street Station, 3rd Floor South Tower, Philadelphia PA 19104. 215/349-1108. **Contact:** Hattie McCoy, Senior Human Resources Representative. **Description:** Manages and operates an interstate passenger rail service with connections throughout the United States, and major routes serving the Northwest. This office is responsible for Amtrak hiring in Philadelphia and Wilmington, DE. **Benefits:** Dental Insurance; Disability Coverage; Employee Discounts; Life Insurance; Medical Insurance; Pension Plan; Savings Plan; Tuition Assistance. **Special Programs:** Internships; Training Programs.

ASSOCIATED AIR FREIGHT
Turnpike Industrial Drive, Middletown PA 17057. 215/758-8270. **Contact:** Human Resources. **Description:** An air transportation company.

BROOKS ARMORED CAR SERVICE
P.O. Box 1223, Governor Prince Boulevard, Wilmington DE 19899-1223. 302/762-5444. **Contact:** Ed Strauser, Personnel. **Description:** A local provider of armored vehicles, serving banks and other clients in need of security-intensive transportation services.

BUCKEYE PIPE LINE CO.
3900 Hamilton Boulevard, P.O. Box 368, Emmaus PA 18049. 215/820-8300. **FAX:** 215/820-3823. **Contact:** Suzanne E. Peacock, Manager/Employee Relations. **Description:** Provides common-carrier liquid pipeline transportation services (refined petroleum products). **Common positions include:** Accountant/Auditor; Attorney; Chemical Engineer; Civil Engineer; Computer Programmer; Draftsperson; Electrical/Electronic Engineer; Financial Analyst; Instructor/Trainer; Mechanical Engineer; Systems Analyst; Technical Writer/Editor. **Special Programs:** Internships; Training Programs. **Operations at this facility include:** Administration. **Listed on:** New York Stock Exchange. **Annual Revenues:** $163,000,000. **Number of employees at this location:** 620. **Projected hires for the next 12 months (This location):** 25 hires.

THE BUDD COMPANY
2450 Hunting Park Avenue, Philadelphia PA 19129-1397. 215/221-7100. **Contact:** Personnel Manager. **Description:** A diversified transportation manufacturing firm with three primary operating segments: Automotive Products Group, which manufactures products such as auto body parts, frames, wheels, brakes, etc; the Industrial Products Group, which manufactures such items as railway cars, truck trailers, iron castings, plastic auto parts, and specialized fibers and nylon for industrial products; and the International Group, with facilities in West Germany, France, Argentina, and Mexico. A manufacturing plant in Philadelphia produces auto body components. **Corporate headquarters location:** Troy MI.

CONSOLIDATED RAIL CORPORATION/CONRAIL
P.O. Box 41417, Philadelphia PA 19101-1417. 215/209-5099. **Contact:** Human Resources. **Description:** A railroad company.

CONTINENTAL AIRLINES CARGO FACILITY
Philadelphia Intl. Airport, Philadelphia PA 19153. 215/492-4301. **Contact:** Human Resources. **Description:** Provides air transportation services.

DUTCHLAND AVIATION
P.O. Box 174, Smoketown PA 17576. 717/293-9824. **Contact:** Human Resources. **Description:** An air transportation company.

HORTMAN AVIATION INC.
11301 Norcom Road, Philadelphia PA 19154. 215/969-5066. **Contact:** Human Resources. **Description:** Provides aviation services.

INCHCAPE
700 Lafayette Building, 437 Chestnut Street, Philadelphia PA 19106. 215/923-9300. **Contact:** Personnel Department. **Description:** Engaged in providing maritime transportation as an agent. **Common positions include:** Customer Service Representative; Department Manager; Transportation/Traffic Specialist. **Educational backgrounds include:** Business Administration; Liberal Arts. **Benefits:** Dental Insurance; Disability Coverage; Life Insurance; Medical Insurance; Pension Plan; Savings Plan. **Operations at this facility include:** Administration; Sales; Service.

KEREK AIR FREIGHT
2811 Turnpike Industrial Park, Middletown PA 17057. 717/939-8125. **Contact:** Human Resources. **Description:** An air transportation company. **Other U.S. Locations:** Lancaster, PA; Folcroft, PA.

LYNDEN AIR FREIGHT
P.O. Box 1384, Sharon Hill PA 19079. 215/532-6323. **Contact:** Human Resources. **Description:** An air transportation company.

MATLACK, INC.
P.O. Box 8789, Wilmington DE 19899. 302/426-2700. **Contact:** Human Resources. **Description:** A trucking company.

NEW PENN MOTOR EXPRESS INC.
P.O. Box 630, Lebanon PA 17042. 717/274-2521. **Contact:** Human Resources. **Description:** A trucking company.

P.T.L. TRANSPORTATION SERVICES
555 North Lane, Conshohocken PA 19428. 215/832-1800. **Contact:** Jane Gunkle, Human Resources. **Description:** A trucking company.

PILOT AIR FREIGHT
Ambassador One Building, Diplomat Drive, Lester PA 19113. 215/521-6200. **Contact:** Human Resources. **Description:** An air transportation company.

PILOT AIR FREIGHT
744 Roble Road, Allentown PA 18103. 215/264-8777. **Contact:** Human Resources. **Description:** An air transportation company.

PILOT AIR FREIGHT CORPORATION
P.O. Box 97, Lima PA 19037. 215/891-8100. **Contact:** Human Resources. **Description:** An air transportation company.

RLC CORPORATION
P.O. Box 1791, Wilmington DE 19899. 302/426-2700. **Contact:** Vickie Dobrowski, Personnel Manager. **Description:** Company leases and rents trucks.

SERVICE BY AIR INC.
407 Elmwood Avenue, Elmwood Court One, Sharon Hill PA 19079. 215/534-7142. **Contact:** Human Resources. **Description:** An air transportation company.

SOUTHEASTERN PENNSYLVANIA TRANSPORATION AUTHORITY (SEPTA)
841 Chestnut Street, 6th Floor, Philadelphia PA 19107. 215/580-7325. **Contact:** Sylvia P. Chandler, Director of Personnel. **Description:** Operates complete public transportation facilities for the city of Philadelphia and surrounding areas.

U.S. NAVAL SHIP SYSTEMS NAVAL WARFARE SYSTEM
Building 47, Code 3210, Naval Base, Philadelphia PA 19112-5083. 215/897-7414. **Contact:** Personnel Staffing Specialist. **Description:** In-service engineering for hull, mechanical, and electrical ship systems. **Number of employees nationwide:** 1,800.

UNION PACIFIC
Eighth and Eaton Avenue, Bethlehem PA 18018. 215/861-3200. **Contact:** Personnel Department. **Description:** A diversified conglomerate including railroad, holding companies, oil and petroleum, real estate, and other operations.

VIKING YACHT COMPANY
Route 9 & Garden State Pkwy., New Gretna NJ 08224. 609/296-6000. **Contact:** Human Resources. **Description:** Manufactures yachts.

Note: Because addresses and telephone numbers of smaller companies change rapidly, we recommend you contact each company and verify the information below before contacting employers. Mass mailings are not recommended.

Additional large employers: 500 +

RAILROADS

Missouri Pacific RR
Eighth & Eaton Avenues, Bethlehem PA 18018. 4022715000.

NON-LOCAL TRUCKING

United Transport/Marlton
2 Eves Drive, Marlton NJ 08053-3193. 609/424-3777.

PACKING AND CRATING SERVICES

Princeton Packaging Inc.
20 Jaycee Drive, Hazleton PA 18201-1142. 717/455-7741.

Additional medium sized employers: under 500

RAILROADS, LINE HAULING OPERATORS

Monongahela Ry
Six Penn Center Plaza, Philadelphia PA 19103-2919. 215/977-5099.

LOCAL AND SUBURBAN TRANSIT

Levy School Bus Co.
114 N Broad St, Allentown PA 18104-5346. 610/434-5110.

TRUCKING

Al Hamilton Contracting
RR 1 Box 87, Woodland PA 16881-9705. 814/857-7677.

Allentown Cement Company
PO Box 199, Blandon PA 19510-0199. 610/926-1024.

C&C Carriage Mushroom
PO Box 388, Avondale PA 19311-0388. 610/268-3773.

Capitol Bus Co.
1061 S Cameron St, Harrisburg PA 17104-2530. 717/233-7673.

Central Enterprises Inc.
1111 Ellsworth St, Philadelphia PA 19147-4605. 215/551-8383.

Chester Carriers Inc.
PO Box 231, Easton PA 18044-0231. 610/253-4271.

Farm and Home Oil
420 State St, Telford PA 18969-1024. 215/257-0131.

IMI Express Inc.
1515 Market St 17th Fl, Philadelphia PA 19102-1921. 215/448-4000.

Jonas P Donmoyer Inc.
PO Box 74, Ono PA 17077-0074. 717/865-2148.

Maximizer Transportation
225 Lincoln Hwy, Fairless Hls PA 19030-1103. 215/949-3600.

Ohio Oil Gathering Corp.
100 Matsonford Rd Ste 400, Wayne PA 19087-4527. 610/293-0410.

Pennsylvania Truck Lines
555 N Lane,
Conshohocken PA
19428. 610/832-1800.

Tioga Transport Inc.
5 East Ave, Wellsboro PA
16901-1613. 717/724-
4808.

Trenwyth Industries
PO Box 438, Emigsville
PA 17318-0438.

Trimac
2950 State Rd, Bensalem
PA 19020-7318.
215/244-8170.

**Ward Trucking
Corporation**
1115 Slate Hill Rd, Camp
Hill PA 17011-7824.
717/761-1334.

**Kuhn Transportation
Company Inc.**
1670 York Rd,
Gettysburg PA 17325-
8264. 717/337-3131.

Lebarnold Inc.
4410 Industrial Park Rd,
Camp Hill PA 17011-
5739. 717/761-3004.

NRM Trucking Co.
PO Box 3050, Malvern
PA 19355-0750.
610/644-6700.

PE Kramme Inc.
Main St, Monroeville NJ
08343. 609/358-8151.

**Valley Farms Equipment
Co Inc.**
1860 E 3rd St,
Williamsport PA 17701-
3992. 717/234-6000.

Louderback Trans Co.
260 Hansen Access Rd,
Kng Of Prussa PA
19406-2424. 610/265-
5500.

**REFRIDGERATED
WAREHOUSING**

**United States Cold
Storage Inc.**
100 Dobbs Ln, Cherry
Hill NJ 08034-1435.
609/354-8181.

**GENERAL
WAREHOUSING**

Donecker's Self Storage
115 W Chestnut St,
Ephrata PA 17522-2027.
717/738-9516.

Xtra Space Self Storage
947 Bethlehem Pike,
Montgomeryvle PA
18936-9607. 215/661-
9199.

SPECIAL WAREHOUSING

Laurelwood Self Storage
611 Blackwood
Clementon Rd,
Clementon NJ 08021-
5903. 609/627-5888.

**DEEP SEA DOMESTIC
TRANSPORT OF
FREIGHT**

Maritrans Partners LP
1 Logan Sq, Philadelphia
PA 19103-6932.
215/864-1200.

**MARINE CARGO
HANDLING**

**South Jersey Port
Corporation**
2500 Broadway, Camden
NJ 08104-2409.
609/541-8500.

**AIRPORTS, FLYING
FIELDS AND SERVICES**

Stambaugh Air Service
427 2nd St, Highspire PA
17034-1560. 717/939-
1300.

TRAVEL AGENCIES

**AAA East Pennsylvania
Travel Agency**
95 S Hanover St,
Pottstown PA 19464-
5950. 610/323-6300.

AAA Travel Agency
3433 Trindle Rd, Camp
Hill PA 17011-4459.
717/761-8347.

**Bon-Ton World Wide
Travel**
Berkshire Mall, Reading
PA 19610. 610/371-
0100.

Liberty Travel
Lycoming Mall, Muncy
PA 17756. 717/326-
2671.

Liberty Travel
457 W Germantown
Pike, Plymouth Mtng PA
19462-1301. 610/825-
4950.

Liberty Travel
3050 State Hill Rd # 5,
Reading PA 19610-1436.
610/921-8161.

Rosenbluth Travel
Princeton-Hightstown Rd,
Cranbury NJ 08512.
609/443-0520.

**ARRANGEMENT OF
TRANSPORTATION OF
FREIGHT**

Danzas Corporation
777 Henderson Blvd,
Folcroft PA 19032.
610/237-0556.

**BOAT BUILDING AND
REPAIR**

**Silverton Marine
Corporation**
301 Riverside Dr, Millville
NJ 08332-6717.
609/825-4117.

Trojan Yacht
167 Greenfield Rd,
Lancaster PA 17601-
5814. 717/397-2471.

RAILROAD EQUIPMENT

ACF Industries Inc.
2nd & Arch Sts, Milton
PA 17847. 717/742-
7601.

**Keystone Railway
Equipment Co**
Simpson Ferry Rd, Camp
Hill PA 17011. 717/761-
3690.

**Morrison-Knudsen
Corporation**
Crestwood Dr Crestwood
Indl Pk, Mountain Top PA
18707. 717/474-0850.

Trinity Industries Inc.
48 Magnolia Ct,
Doylestown PA 18901-
2650. 215/340-1990.

**MOTORCYCLES,
BICYCLES AND PARTS**

**Electric Mobility
Corporation**
591 Mantua Blvd N,
Sewell NJ 08080-1000.
609/468-0270.

For more information on career opportunities in transportation:

Associations

AMERICAN BUREAU OF SHIPPING
2 World Trade Center, 106th Floor,
New York NY 10048. 212/557-9520.

AMERICAN MARITIME ASSOCIATION
485 Madison Avenue, 15th Floor,
New York NY 10022. 212/319-9217.

**AMERICAN SOCIETY OF TRAVEL
AGENTS**
1101 King Street, Alexandria VA
22314. 703/739-2782. For
information, send a SASE with $.75
postage to the attention of Fulfillment
Department.

AMERICAN TRUCKING ASSOCIATION
2200 Mill Road, Alexandria VA
22314-4677. 703/838-1700.

**ASSOCIATION OF AMERICAN
RAILROADS**
50 F Street NW, Washington DC
20001. 202/639-2100.

**INSTITUTE OF TRANSPORTATION
ENGINEERS**
525 School Street SW, Suite 410,
Washington DC 20024. 202/554-
8050.

MARINE TECHNOLOGY SOCIETY
1828 L Street NW, Suite 906,
Washington DC 20036. 202/775-
5966.

**NATIONAL MARINE
MANUFACTURERS ASSOCIATION**
401 North Michigan Avenue, Suite
1150, Chicago IL 60611. 312/836-
4747. Subscription to job listing
publication available for a fee.

**NATIONAL MOTOR FREIGHT TRAFFIC
ASSOCIATION**
2200 Mill Road, Alexandria VA
22314. 703/838-1810.

NATIONAL TANK TRUCK CARRIERS
2200 Mill Road, Alexandria VA
22314. 703/838-1700.

Directories

**MOODY'S TRANSPORTATION
MANUAL**
Moody's Investors Service, Inc., 99
Church Street, New York NY 10007.
212/553-0300.

NATIONAL TANK TRUCK CARRIER DIRECTORY
2200 Mill Road, Alexandria VA 22314. 703/838-1700.

OFFICIAL MOTOR FREIGHT GUIDE
1700 West Courtland Street, Chicago IL 60622. 312/278-2454.

Magazines

AMERICAN SHIPPER
P.O. Box 4728, Jacksonville FL 32201. 904/355-2601.

TRAFFIC WORLD MAGAZINE
741 National Press Building, Washington DC 20045. 202/383-6140.

FLEET OWNER
707 Westchester Avenue, White Plains NY 10604-3102. 914/949-8500.

HEAVY DUTY TRUCKING
Newport Communications, P.O. Box W, Newport Beach CA 92658. 714/261-1636.

MARINE DIGEST AND TRANSPORTATION NEWS
P.O. Box 3905, Seattle WA 98124. 206/682-3607.

SHIPPING DIGEST
51 Madison Avenue, New York NY 10010. 212/689-4411.

TRANSPORT TOPICS
2200 Mill Road, Alexandria VA 22314. 703/838-1772.

UTILITIES: ELECTRIC, GAS AND SANITATION

The major forces shaping the U.S. utilities industry are decreased regulation and competition from newly emerging alternative energy sources. Job prospects for those entering the utilities industry vary by sector; the best sector right now is electric, and at the bottom is the stagnant nuclear industry.

AMERICAN WATER SYSTEM
1025 Laurel Oak Road, Voorhees NJ 08043. 609/346-8200. **Contact:** Jack Markel, Director, Personnel Administration. **Description:** Acquires, manages, and services water companies across the country.

ATLANTIC ELECTRIC
P.O. Box 1500-MLC, Pleasantville NJ 08232. 609/645-3500. **Contact:** Bob Pavlovski, Senior Employment Representative. **Description:** An electric utility company. Company jobline: 609/625-5848. **Common positions include:** Accountant/Auditor; Civil Engineer; Electrical/Electronic Engineer; Mechanical Engineer; Personnel/Labor Relations Specialist; Systems Analyst. **Educational backgrounds include:** Accounting; Computer Science; Engineering. **Benefits:** Dental Insurance; Disability Coverage; Life Insurance; Medical Insurance; Pension Plan; Prescription Drugs; Savings Plan; Tuition Assistance; Vision Plan. **Parent company:** Atlantic Energy. **Operations at this facility include:** Administration. **Listed on:** New York Stock Exchange.

C&D CHARTER POWER SYSTEMS INC.
3043 Walton Road, Plymouth Meeting PA 19462. 215/828-9000. **Contact:** Gerry Barr, Human Resources. **Description:** A manufacturer and supplier of products and services to the standby power and motive power markets.

COLUMBIA GAS SYSTEMS SERVICE, INC.
P.O. Box 420, 20 Montchanin Road, Wilmington DE 19807-0020. 302/429-5000. **Contact:** Ms. Lois G. Hubbs, Manager, Placement. **Description:** A gas company.

DELAWARE ELECTRIC CO-OP
P.O. Box 600, Greenwood DE 19950. 302/398-9090. **Contact:** Fay Shockley, Personnel Director. **Description:** A Delaware electric company.

DELMARVA POWER & LIGHT COMPANY
800 King Street, P.O. Box 231, Wilmington DE 19899. 302/429-3164. **Contact:** Peggy Symes, Coordinator of Management Employment. **Description:** An electric and gas utility. **Common positions include:** Accountant/Auditor; Attorney; Blue-Collar Worker Supervisor; Buyer; Chemist; Civil Engineer; Computer Programmer; Customer Service Representative; Department Manager; Draftsperson; Economist/Market Research Analyst; Electrical/Electronic Engineer; Financial Analyst; General Manager; Marketing Specialist; Mechanical Engineer; Operations/Production Manager; Personnel/Labor Relations Specialist; Public Relations Specialist; Systems Analyst; Transportation/Traffic Specialist. **Educational backgrounds include:** Accounting;

Communications; Economics; Engineering; Finance. **Benefits:** Dental Insurance; Disability Coverage; Employee Discounts; Life Insurance; Medical Insurance; Pension Plan; Savings Plan; Tuition Assistance. **Corporate headquarters location:** This Location. **Operations at this facility include:** Administration.

EASTERN SHORE NATURAL GAS
P.O. Box 615, Dover DE 19903. 302/734-6720. **Contact:** Rich Felton, Personnel Director. **Description:** A Delaware distributor of natural gas.

PENNSYLVANIA POWER & LIGHT CO.
Two North Ninth St., Allentown PA 18101. 215/774-5273. **Contact:** Janice L. Williams, Manager/Placement. **Description:** An electric utility company providing light and power. **Number of employees nationwide:** 8,000.

PHILADELPHIA ELECTRIC COMPANY
2301 Market Street, P.O. Box 8699, Philadelphia PA 19101. **Contact:** Human Resources Department. **Description:** A public utility which provides electric, gas, and steam service to customers through southeast Pennsylvania. Total area served covers more than 2,000 square miles, with a service population of 3.6 million. **Educational backgrounds include:** Engineering; Physics. **Corporate headquarters location:** This Location.

PHILADELPHIA GAS WORKS
800 West Montgomery Avenue, Philadelphia PA 19122. 215/978-3000. **Contact:** Kenneth E. Buggelin, Industrial Relations Manager. **Description:** Provides natural gas utility services throughout the Philadelphia area. **Common positions include:** Civil Engineer.

PHILADELPHIA SUBURBAN
762 Lancaster Avenue, Bryn Mawr PA 19010. 215/527-8000. **Contact:** Human Resources. **Description:** A water utilities.

PUBLIC SERVICE ELECTRIC & GAS
P.O. Box 236, Hancocks Bridge NJ 08038. 609/935-6000. **Contact:** Human Resources Department. **Description:** An electric and gas utility company.

ROLLINS ENVIRONMENTAL SERVICES
P.O. Box 2349, Wilmington DE 19899. 302/426-2700. **Contact:** Human Resources. **Description:** A refuse systems and waste management company.

UGI CORP.
P.O. Box 858, North Church Street, Valley Forge PA 19482. 215/337-1000. **Contact:** Personnel Department. **Description:** A gas and electric utility involved in gas production and distribution in Pennsylvania. **Number of employees nationwide:** 5,229.

Note: Because addresses and telephone numbers of smaller companies change rapidly, we recommend you contact each company and verify the information below before contacting employers. Mass mailings are not recommended.

Additional large employers: 500+

NATURAL GAS DISTRIBUTION

South Jersey Gas Company
One South Jersey Plaza Rte. 54, Hammonton NJ 08037-9160. 609/561-9000.

ELECTRIC SERVICES

Metropolitan Edison Co.
P.O. Box 16001, Reading PA 19640-0002. 610/929-3601.

Philadelphia Electric Power Company
2301 Market St., Philadelphia PA 19103-1380. 215/841-4000.

GAS AND/OR WATER SUPPLY

Pennsylvania Gas & Water Company
39 Public Sq., Wilkes Barre PA 18711-0600. 717/829-8600.

Pennsylvania-American Water Company
800 W Hershey Park Drive, Hershey PA 17033-2400. 717/533-5000.

REFUSE SYSTEMS

BCM Engineers Inc.
1 Plymouth Meeting Mall, Plymouth Mtng PA 19462-1326. 610/825-3800.

Additional medium sized employers: 100-499

ELECTRIC SERVICES

Archbald Co-Generation
170 Power Blvd, Archbald PA 18403-2046. 717/876-5600.

Lakewood Project Management Inc.
150 Airport Rd, Lakewood NJ 08701-6910. 908/370-7070.

Metropolitan Edison Company
2121 Sullivan Trl, Easton PA 18042-9310. 610/258-0463.

Metropolitan-Edison Company
501 Parkway Blvd, York PA 17404-2699. 717/848-7100.

Pennsylvania Electric Company
820 S 4th St, Clearfield PA 16830-2008. 814/765-1685.

Safe Harbor Water Power Corporation
PO Box 97, Conestoga PA 17516-0097. 717/872-5441.

Tri County Rural Electric Cooperative
RR 3, Coudersport PA 16915-9803. 814/274-8740.

WATER SUPPLY

Holly Mount Water Co.
84 Mill St, Mount Holly NJ 08060-1899. 609/267-0540.

New Jersey American Water Co
515 Grove St, Haddon Hgts NJ 08035-1756. 609/547-1700.

REFUSE SYSTEMS

Eastern Environmental Service Inc.
PO Box 368, Drums PA 18222-0368. 717/788-6075.

York Waste Disposal Company
1110 E Princess St, York PA 17403-2543. 717/845-1557.

Additional small employers: under 100

ELECTRIC SERVICES

Adams Electric Cooperative Inc.
1380 Biglerville Rd, Gettysburg PA 17325-8018. 717/334-2171.

Adams Electric Cooperative Inc.
204 W King St, Shippensburg PA 17257-1126. 717/532-2214.

Adams Electric Cooperative Inc.
153 N Stratton St, Gettysburg PA 17325-1822. 717/334-9211.

Citizen's Electric Company
1775 Industrial Blvd, Lewisburg PA 17837-1276. 717/524-2231.

Claverack Rural Electric Coop Inc.
RR 2 Box 17, Wysox PA 18854-9781. 717/265-2167.

Sullivan County Rural Electric
PO Box 65, Forksville PA 18616-0065. 717/924-3381.

Tri Country Rural Electric Cooperative
PO Box 526, Mansfield PA 16933-0526. 717/662-2175.

West Penn Power Co.
N Grant, Waynesboro PA 17268. 717/762-2171.

NATURAL GAS DISTRIBUTION

Entrade Corporation
1930 Route 70 E, Cherry Hill NJ 08003-2146. 609/751-4640.

Equitable Gas Co Governmental Affairs
423 Walnut St, Harrisburg PA 17101-1906. 717/233-7043.

Gas-Oil Products Inc.
1507 Parkway Ave, Trenton NJ 08628-2799. 609/882-6696.

Pennsylvania Energy Marketing Co.
30 N Franklin St, Wilkes Barre PA 18701-1301. 717/825-2900.

Pennsylvania Gas & Water Co.
135 Jefferson Ave, Scranton PA 18503-1701. 717/348-3811.

Philadelphia Gas Works
212 W Chelten Ave, Philadelphia PA 19144-3803. 215/236-0500.

Southern Jersey Gas Company
2 Heather Croft, Pleasantville NJ 08232-4601. 609/641-9292.

South Jersey Gas Company
965 Asbury Ave, Ocean City NJ 08226-3535. 609/398-0444.

South Jersey Gas Company
111 N Franklin Ave, Pleasantville NJ 08232-2507. 609/645-2690.

Suburban Propane
1124 White Horse Pike S, Hammonton NJ 08037-1024. 609/561-0820.

REFUSE SYSTEMS

Day Products Inc.
540 Pedricktown Rd, Bridgeport NJ 08014. 609/467-5522.

Ecoflo
4402 Congress Ct, North Wales PA 19454-3735. 215/368-8122.

H&H Disposal Service
205 E Grand Ave, Tower City PA 17980-1123. 717/647-9391.

For more information on career opportunities in the utilities industry:

Associations

AMERICAN PUBLIC GAS ASSOCIATION
P.O. Box 11094D, Vienna VA 22183. 703/352-3890.

AMERICAN PUBLIC POWER ASSOCIATION
2301 M Street NW, Washington DC 20037. 202/467-2970.

AMERICAN RURAL ELECTRIC COOPERATIVE ASSOCIATION
1800 Massachusetts Avenue NW, Washington DC 20036. 202/797-5441.

AMERICAN WATER WORKS ASSOCIATION
6666 West Quincy Avenue, Denver CO 80235. 303/794-7711.

Directories

MOODY'S PUBLIC UTILITY MANUAL
Moody's Investors Service, Inc., 99 Church Street, New York NY 10007. 212/553-0300.

Magazines

PUBLIC POWER
2301 M Street NW, Washington DC 20037. 202/467-2900.

EMPLOYMENT SERVICES OF GREATER PHILADELPHIA

EMPLOYMENT AGENCIES AND TEMPORARY SERVICES OF PHILADELPHIA

NOTE: While every effort is made to keep the addresses and phone numbers of employment agencies up-to-date, many of these organizations are small and move frequently. Please notify the publisher if you find any discrepancies.

ADIA PERSONNEL SERVICES
1760 Market Street, 6th Floor, Philadelphia PA 19103. 215/567-2390. An employment agency. Offers temporary and permanent placement.

ADVANCE PERSONNEL, INC.
P.O. Box 8383, Reading, PA 19603. **Contact:** Sam Lamanna, Sr. 215/374-4089. Employment agency; temporary help agency. Founded 1980. Established firm with clients in the Philadelphia suburbs and in southern New Jersey. Non-specialized. **Positions commonly filled:** Administrative Assistant; Bookkeeper; Claims Representative; Clerk; Customer Service Rep; Data Entry Clerk; Executive Secretary; Legal Secretary; Medical Secretary; Receptionist; Secretary; Stenographer; Typist; Word Processor. Company pays fee. **Placements per year:** 201-500.

ALEXANDER PERSONNEL ASSOCIATES
One Oxford Valley, Suite 702, Langhorne PA 19047. 215/757-4935. **Contact:** Joyce Beck, Manager. Appointment required. Founded 1984. **Specializes in:** Accounting; Engineering; General Management; Industrial; Insurance; Manufacturing; Secretarial; Technical and Scientific. **Positions commonly filled:** Accountant; Administrative Assistant; Bookkeeper; Chemical Engineer; Clerk; Credit Manager; Customer Service Representative; Data Entry Clerk; Executive Secretary; Electrical Engineer; Industrial Designer; Industrial Engineer; Manufacturing Engineer; Mechanical Engineer; Metallurgical Engineer; Operations and Production Specialist; Quality Control Supervisor; Receptionist; Sales Representative; Secretary; Technical Writer/Editor; Word Processing Specialist; Word Processor; Typist. Company pays fee.

AMATO & ASSOCIATES
1313 Medford Road, Suite 100, Wynnewood PA 19096-2418. **Contact:** Bobbi Amato, President. 610/642-9696. **FAX:** 610/642-9797. Appointment required. Founded 1980. **Specializes in:** Insurance. **Positions commonly filled:** Claims Representative; Insurance Broker; Underwriter. Company pays fee. **Placements per year:** 1-49.

AMERICAN TEMPORARY SERVICE
255 East Street Road, Box 285, Feasterville PA 19053. 215/364-3838. **Contact:** Carolyn Anderson, Operations Manager. Temporary help service. Appointment preferred. Non-specialized.

ATOMIC PERSONNEL, INC.
P.O. Box 11244, Philadelphia, PA 19117-0244. 215/885-4223. **FAX:** 215/885-4225. **Contact:** Arthur L. Krasnowm, President. Employment agency and executive search firm. Appointment required. Founded 1959. **Positions commonly filled include:** Biochemist, Biologist, Biomedical Engineer, Ceramics Engineer, Chemical Engineer, Chemist, Civil Engineer, Electrical Engineer, Industrial Engineer, Manufacturing Engineer, Mechanical Engineer, Metallurgical Engineer, Quality Control Supervisor, Sales Representative, Safety Engineer, Control Engineer. **Specializes int the areas of:** Construction, Engineering, Health/Medical, Industrial, Manufacturing, Sales and Marketing, Technical and Scientific, Fossil and Nuclear Power, Cogeneration, Environmental. Company pays fee.

AVAILABILITY/AVAIL-A-SEARCH
2938 Columbia Avenue, Suite 1502, Lancaster PA 17603. 717/291-1871. **Contact:** Anthony J. Spinelli, President. Employment agency. Founded 1974. **Specializes in:** Accounting and Finance; Clerical; Engineering; Legal; MIS/EDP; Manufacturing; Minorities; Sales and Marketing; Technical and Scientific; Veterans; Women.

BECKER TEMPORARY SERVICES, INC.
One Bala Plaza, Suite LL36, Bala Cynwyd PA 19004. 215/667-3023. **Contact:** Dan Becker, Manager. Temporary help service. Appointment requested. Founded 1967. Non specialized.

BORIS ASSOCIATES
375 Warner Road, Wayne PA 19087. 215/687-8165. **Contact:** Ted Boris. An employment agency.

BRENTWOOD SEARCH CONSULTANTS
327 Shawmut Avenue, Suite D, Philadelphia PA 19128-0381. 215/487-7199. An employment agency.

CAPITAL AREA TEMPORARY SERVICES
P.O. Box 32, Lemoyne PA 17043. **Contact:** Paul V. Gaughan, President. 717/761-0133. Temporary help service. Appointment requested. Founded 1971. Member NATS; ITSA. **Specializes in:** Clerical; Manufacturing. **Positions commonly filled:** Bookkeeper; Clerk; Demonstrator; Factory Worker; General Laborer; Legal Secretary; Light Industrial Worker; Office Worker; Receptionist; Secretary; Stenographer; Typist; Word Processing Specialist.

CAREERS U. S.A.
1825 JFK Boulevard, Philadelphia PA 19103. 215/561-3800. A temporary and permanent employment agency.

CORE STAFF
P.O. Box 15444, Philadelphia PA 19149-5444. **Contact:** J. Kiefer, Secretary/Treasurer. 215/864-0113. Temporary help service. Appointment requested. Founded 1978. Non specialized. Company pays fee. **Placements per year:** 1,001 +.

DENTAL POWER OF DELAWARE VALLEY, INC.
1528 Walnut Street, Suite 1802, Philadelphia PA 19102. An employment service specializing in staffing dental offices.

DOUGHERTY & ASSOCIATES, INC.
1730 Walton Road, Suite 304, Blue Bell PA 19422. 215/825-2131. **Contact:** George J. Dougherty. An employment agency.

DUNHILL PERSONNEL SYSTEMS OF PHILADELPHIA
801 W. Street Road, Feasterville PA 19053. 215/357-6590. **Contact:** Dave Bontempo, President. Employment agency. **Specializes in:** Accounting and Finance; Office Services; Sales and Marketing.

EAGLE STAFFERS & PLACERS, INC.
610 East Baltimore Pike, P.O. Box 743, Ardmore PA 19063. 215/891-1904. A personnel placement and temporary employment service.

EDEN AND ASSOCIATES, INC.
794 N. Valley Rd., Paoli PA 19301. 215/889-9993. **Contact:** Brooks Eden, President. Employment agency and consulting firm. Appointment required. Founded 1981. Grown from one employee to 12. Specializes in the Food Industry; Supermarket Chains; and Food Wholesalers. Deal on exclusive basis. Company pays fee. **Placements per year:** 201-500.

EMPLOYMENT CORPORATION OF AMERICA
2250 Hickory Road, Plymouth Meeting PA 19103. 215/941-0800. An employment agency.

EVERETT KELLY ASSOCIATES, INC.
1601 Market Street, Suite 325, Philadelphia PA 19103. 215/981-0800. An employment agency.

EXPRESS PERSONNEL SERVICE
260 South Broad Street, Suite 1810, Philadelphia PA 19102. 215/893-1200. An employment agency.

F-O-R-T-U-N-E PERSONNEL CONSULTANTS OF ABINGTON , INC.
Baederwood Office Plaza, P.O. Box 282, Abington PA 19001. 215/886-9020. An employment agency.

F-O-R-T-U-N-E PERSONNEL CONSULTANTS OF PHILADELPHIA, INC.
1528 Walnut Street, Suite 1625, Philadelphia PA 19102. 215/546-9490. An employment agency.

JERRY GOLDBERG AND ASSOCIATES, INC.
1404 East Market Street, York PA 17403. **Contact:** Jerry Goldberg, President. 717/843-0041. Employment agency. Appointment preferred. Founded 1962. Working with all types of industries, with products ranging from small precision parts to very large equipment. **Specializes in:** Accounting and Finance; Banking; Computer Hardware and Software; Engineering; Manufacturing; MIS/EDP; Personnel and Human Resources; Technical and Scientific; Technical Sales and Marketing. **Positions commonly filled:** Aerospace Engineer; Accountant; Biomedical Engineer; Buyer; CAD/CAM; CAE/CIM; Ceramics Engineer; Chemical Engineer; Chemist; Computer Programmer; Credit Manager; Draftsperson; EDP Specialist; Electrical Engineer; Facilities Engineer/Manager; Financial Analyst; Food Technologist; General Manager; Industrial Designer; Industrial and Manufacturing Engineer; MIS Specialist; Mechanical Engineer; Metallurgical Engineer; Operations/Production Specialist; Personnel and Labor Relations Specialist; Physicist; Plant and Manufacturing Manager; Purchasing Agent; Quality Control Supervisor; Systems Analyst; Technical Sales Representative; Technical Writer/Editor; Technician. Company pays fee.

ROBERT HALF OF PHILADELPHIA, INC.
2000 Market Street, 18th Floor, Philadelphia PA 19103. An employment agency.

HEALTH AND SCIENCE CENTER
P.O. Box 213, Lima PA 19037. 215/891-0714. **Contact:** J. Timothy McGrath, Executive Director. Employment agency. Appointment requested. Founded 1970. **Specializes in:** Health and Medical; Technical and Scientific.

HORIZON TEMPORARY SERVICES INC.
P.O. Box 37, Media PA 19063. 215/565-1036. **Contact:** Jay G. Godwin, Manager. Temporary help service. Appointment requested. Founded 1977. Non specialized.

HOSKINS HAINS ASSOCIATES
3835 Walnut Street, Harrisburg PA 17109. **Contact:** Patricia Hoskins, Owner. 717/657-8444. Employment agency. Appointment requested. Founded 1980. **Specializes in:** Accounting and Finance; Banking; Clerical; Computer Hardware and Software; Engineering; Manufacturing; MIS/EDP; Minorities; Personnel and Human Resources; Resume Services; Sales and Marketing; Technical and Scientific; Women. **Positions commonly filled:**

Accountant; Administrative Assistant; Bank Officer/Manager; Computer Operator; Computer Programmer; Credit Manager; Data Entry Clerk; Draftsperson; EDP Specialist; Electrical Engineer; Financial Analyst; Industrial Engineer; MIS Specialist; Mechanical Engineer; Metallurgical Engineer; Personnel and Labor Relations Specialist; Purchasing Agent; Quality Control Supervisor; Receptionist; Sales Representative; Secretary; Statistician; Systems Analyst; Technical Writer/Editor; Typist; Word Processing Specialist. Company pays fee; individual pays fee.

INNOVATIVE STAFFING, INC.
100 Old York Road, Suite 221, Jenkintown PA 19046. 215/854-1800. An employment agency.

INTERIM PERSONNEL, INC.
1617 JFK Boulevard, Suite 240, Philadelphia PA 19103. 215/561-3322. **Contact:** Linda Totten, Area Manager. 215/337-3725. A full-service permanent and temporary employment agency. Appointment requested. Founded 1983. **Specializes in:** Clerical; Office Automation. **Positions commonly filled:** Administrative Assistant; Bookkeeper; Clerk; Computer Operator; Data Entry Clerk; Legal Secretary; Medical Secretary; Office Worker; Receptionist; Secretary; Stenographer; Typist; Word Processing Specialist. Company pays fee. **Placements per year:** 201-500.

JEWISH EMPLOYMENT AND VOCATIONAL SERVICE
1845 Walnut Street, 7th Floor, Philadelphia PA 19103. 215/854-1800. An employment agency.

KATHY KARR PERSONNEL, INC.
2512 West Main Street, Norristown PA 19403. 215/630-0760. **Contact:** Kathy Karr, President. Employment agency; temporary help service. Appointment requested. **Specializes in:** Clerical.

KELLY SERVICES, INC.
1055 Westlakes Drive, Berwin PA 19312. 215/251-9813. **Contact:** Nicholas F. Regaldi, Regional Vice President. Temporary help service. No appointment required. Founded 1946. **Specializes in:** Clerical.

KEY PERSONNEL SERVICE
845 Wyoming, Street, Allentown PA 18103. **Contact:** Walter Moyer, Manager. 215/435-6355. Employment agency; temporary help service. No appointment required. Founded 1983. Non specialized. **Positions commonly filled:** Aerospace Engineer; Buyer; Ceramics Engineer; Chemical Engineer; Chemist; Civil Engineer; Computer Programmer; Credit Manager; Draftsperson; EDP Specialist; Electrical Engineer; Financial Analyst; General Manager; Industrial Engineer; MIS Specialist; Marketing Specialist; Mechanical Engineer; Metallurgical Engineer; Operations/Production Specialist; Personnel and Labor Relations Specialist; Purchasing Agent; Quality Control Supervisor; Technical Writer/Editor. Company pays fee.

LONDON PERSONNEL SERVICES
7024 Terminal Square, Upper Bay PA 19082. 215/734-3223. An employment agency.

MANLINE PERSONNEL SERVICE, INC.
P.O. Drawer 448, Bala Cynwyd PA 19004. 215/667-1820. **Contact:** Mr. W.T. Newmaster, Manager. Employment agency. Appointment requested. Founded 1967. **Specializes in:** Engineering; Technical and Scientific.

MANPOWER TEMPORARY SERVICES
709 North Easton Road, Willow Grove PA 19090. 215/657-0500. **Contact:** Jean Costello, Branch Manager. Temporary help service. Appointment preferred. **Specializes in:** Clerical.

MICHAEL J. McCOLLIGAN AND ASSOCIATES
7341 West Chester Pike, Upper Darby PA 19082. 215/352-8110. **Contact:** Mike McColligan, Senior Technical and Management Recruiter. Employment agency. Appointment requested. Founded 1976. **Specializes in:** Biomedical Engineering; Computer Hardware and Software; Defense Electronics; Engineering; Health and Medical; MIS/EDP; Technical and Scientific.

EDP/TEMPS OF PENNSYLVANIA
401 City Line Avenue, Suite 215, Bala Cynwyd PA 19004. 215/667-2990. Temporary help service. No appointment required. Founded 1976. Branch offices located in: California; Connecticut; Illinois; Maryland; Massachusetts; Michigan; New York; Ohio; Virginia. **Specializes in:** Accounting and Finance; Banking; Computer Hardware and Software; Engineering; Insurance; Manufacturing; MIS/EDP; Nonprofit; Personnel and Human Resources; Printing and Publishing; Technical and Scientific.

MINORITY PERSONNEL SERVICES
5424 North 5th Street, Philadelphia PA 19120. 215/457-2672. An employment agency.

THE MORRIS GROUP
1024 East Lancaster Avenue, Philadelphia PA 19010. 215/520-0100. An employment agency.

NORCON ASSOCIATES, INC.
P.O. Box 405, Newtown Square PA 19073-0405. 215/359-1707. An employment agency. **Specializes in:** Technical.

OLSTEN TEMPORARY SERVICES OF ALLENTOWN
1227 Liberty Street, Suite 103A, Allentown PA 18102. 215/435-0553. **Contact:** Owner/Manager. Temporary help service. No appointment required. Founded 1981. **Specializes in:** Accounting and Finance; Advertising; Banking; Clerical; Computer Hardware and Software; Construction; Insurance; Legal; Manufacturing; Personnel and Human Resources; Sales and Marketing.

OLSTEN TEMPORARY SERVICES OF PHILADELPHIA
1617 J.F.K. Boulevard, Suite 420, Philadelphia PA 19103. 215/568-7795. **Contact:** Placement. Temporary help service. Appointment requested. Non specialized.

OLSTEN SERVICES
4720 Carlisle Pike, Mechanicsburg PA 17005. **Contact:** Rosemary Kaufman, Branch Manager. 717/731-6100. Temporary help agency. No appointment required. Founded 1950. Olsten Services is a national supplier of temporary help with over 430 offices nationwide. **Specializes in:** Accounting; Advertising; Computer Hardware and Software; Construction; Food Industry; Industrial and Interior Design; Insurance; Legal; Manufacturing; Nonprofit; Printing and Publishing; Sales and Marketing; Secretarial and Clerical; Technical and Scientific. **Positions commonly filled:** Accountant; Administrative Assistant; Bookkeeper; Claims Representative; Computer Programmer; Customer Service Representative; Data Entry Clerk; Draftsperson; EDP Specialist; Executive Secretary; Factory Worker; Financial Analyst; General Laborer; Industrial Designer; Insurance Agent/Broker; Legal Secretary; Light Industrial Worker; Mechanical Engineer; Medical Secretary; Purchasing Agent; Receptionist; Records Manager; Sales Representative; Secretary; Statistician; Stenographer; Systems Analyst; Technical Writer/Editor; Technician; Typist; Word Processor. **Placements per year:** 1,000+.

PRN CONSULTANTS
Durham Road, Langhorne PA 19047. 215/750-6161. An employment agency. **Specializes in:** Nursing.

PAL
1239 Vine Street, Philadelphia PA 19107. An employment agency. **Specializes in:** Blue Collar.

PERSONNEL RESOURCES ORGANIZATION
121 South Broad Street, Suite 1030, Philadelphia PA 19107. 215/735-7500.

PERSONNEL SYSTEMS
2030 Tilghman Street, Suite 201A, Allentown PA 18104. 215/825-9114. **Contact:** Elaine Glose, President, President. Employment agency; temporary help agency. Appointment required. Founded 1985. **Specializes in:** Secretarial and Clerical.

PHILADELPHIA SEARCH GROUP, INC.
One Cherry Hill, Suite 510, Cherry Hill NJ 08002. 609/667-2300. An employment agency.

POWERS PERSONNEL
1530 Chestnut Street, Suite 310, Philadelphia PA 19102. 215/563-5520. **Contact:** Jean Powers, President. Employment agency; temporary help agency. Appointment required. Founded 1975. **Specializes in:** Legal; Secretarial and Clerical.

PRATT PERSONNEL
The Atlantic Financial Building, 1547 Pratt Street, Suite 300, Philadelphia PA 19124. 215/537-1212. **Contact:** Joseph P. Egan, C.P.C., President. Employment agency. Appointment requested. Founded 1959. Member, National Association of Personnel Consultants and Pennsylvania Association of Personnel Consultants. **Specializes in:** Clerical; Engineering; Manufacturing.

PROFESSIONAL RECRUITERS, INC.
GSB Building, Suite 103, Bala Cynwyd PA 19004. 215/667-9355. An employment agency.

PROTOCOL
400 Market Street, 4th Floor, Philadelphia PA 19106. 215/592-7111. Temporary help service. Appointment requested. Founded 1961. Branch offices located in: Arizona; California; Connecticut; District of Columbia; Florida; Georgia; Illinois; Indiana; Kansas; Louisiana; Maryland; Massachusetts; Michigan; Minnesota; Missouri; Nevada; New Jersey; New Mexico; New York; Ohio; Oklahoma; Oregon; Rhode Island; Tennessee; Texas; Virginia; Washington. Non specialized. **Positions commonly filled:** Accountant; Administrative Assistant; Bookkeeper; Clerk; Companion; Computer Operator; Computer Programmer; Customer Service Representative; Data Entry Clerk; Demonstrator; Draftsperson; Driver; EDP Specialist; Factory Worker; General Laborer; Health Aide; Legal Secretary; Light Industrial Worker; Medical Secretary; Nurse; Office Worker; Public Relations Worker; Receptionist; Sales Representative; Secretary; Stenographer; Technician; Typist; Word Processing Specialist. Company pays fee. **Placements per year:** 1,001+.

QUEST SYSTEMS, INC.
1150 First Avenue, King of Prussia PA 19406. 215/265-8100. **Contact:** Charles Lagana, Manager. No appointment required. Founded 1968. **Specializes in:** Computer Hardware and Software. **Positions commonly filled:** Computer Programmer; EDP Specialist; MIS Specialist; Software Engineer; Systems Analyst; Technical Recruiter. Company pays fee. **Placements per year:** 1,000+.

RSVP SERVICES
P.O. Box 8369, Cherry Hill NJ 08002. An employment agency. **Specializes in:** Electronics and computers.

THE RICHARDS GROUP
2 Penn Center Plaza, Suite 710, Philadelphia PA 19102. 215/751-0805. An employment agency.

ROMAC & ASSOCIATES
Delaware Valley, 1700 Market Street, Suite 2702, Philadelphia PA 19103. 215/568-6810. An employment agency. Temporary and permanent placement.

TOM SAWCHAK ACTION OF PENNSYLVANIA
206 Grant Street, Olyphant PA 18447. **Contact:** Tom Sawchak, Owner. 717/383-0271. Employment agency. No appointment required. Founded 1975. **Specializes in:** Clerical; Engineering; Insurance; Manufacturing; Sales and Marketing. **Positions commonly filled:** Bookkeeper; Civil Engineer; Claim Representative; Computer Operator; Computer Programmer; Construction Worker; Credit Manager; Customer Service Representative; Driver; Electrical Engineer; Factory Worker; General Manager; Hotel Manager/Assistant Manager; Industrial Engineer; Insurance Agent/Broker; Legal Secretary; Mechanical Engineer; Nurse; Office Worker; Purchasing Agent; Quality Control Supervisor; Receptionist; Secretary; Systems Analyst; Typist; Underwriter. Company pays fee; individual pays fee. **Placements per year:** 50.

SELECT PERSONNEL, INC.
Neshaminy Plaza 2, 3070 Bristol Pike, Salem PA 19020. 215/741-4700; **FAX:** 215/752-4582. **Contact:** Marjorie Stilwell, President. Appointment preferred. Founded 1989. **Specializes in:** Computer Hardware and Software; Engineering; Finance; Hybrids; Industrial; Manufacturing; Personnel/Human Resources; Sales and Marketing; Technical and Scientific; Semiconductors; Women. **Positions commonly filled:** Accountant; Aerospace Engineer; Architect; Biochemist; Biologist; Bookkeeper; Buyer; Ceramics Engineer; Chemical Engineer; Chemist; Civil Engineer; Computer Programmer; Customer Service Representative; Electrical Engineer; Industrial Engineer; Manufacturing Engineer; Marketing Specialist; Mechanical Engineer; Metallurgical Engineer; MIS Specialist; Operations and Production Specialist; Purchasing Agent; Quality Control Supervisor; Sales Representative; Software Engineer; Systems Analyst; Technical Illustrator; Technical Writer/Editor; Technician. Company pays fee. No fee to applicant. **Placements per year:** 100-199.

A. L. SINGMASTER PERSONNEL SERVICES
P.O. Box 708, Devon PA 19333. **Contact:** Alan Singmaster, Owner. 215/687-4970. Employment agency. No appointment required. Founded 1980. Firm specializes in Heavy Industry, particularly Metals/Materials. Past experience in personnel management (14 years). **Specializes in:** Manufacturing; Technical and Scientific. **Positions commonly filled:** Biochemist/Chemist; Ceramics Engineer; Chemical Engineer; Electrical Engineer; General Manager; Industrial Engineer; Mechanical Engineer;

Metallurgical Engineer; Personnel Director; Sales Representative. Company pays fee. **Placements per year:** 0-50.

SNELLING PERSONNEL SERVICES
12 S. 12th Street, Suite 3201, Philadelphia PA 19107. 215/922-4700. **Contact:** Richard Cheek, Owner. Employment agency. Appointment required. Founded 1976. Specializes in the placement of Sales, Marketing and Management personnel in the Temporary Help industry.

SNELLING PERSONNEL SERVICES
200 Butler Avenue, Lancaster PA 17601. **Contact:** Richard Conley, Manager. 717/394-7180. Temporary help service. No appointment required. Founded 1978. A division of Robscot, Inc. **Specializes in:** Clerical; Construction; Janitorial Labor; Manufacturing. **Positions commonly filled:** Accountant; Bookkeeper; Clerk; Computer Programmer; Data Entry Clerk; Demonstrator; Factory Worker; General Laborer; Legal Secretary; Light Industrial Worker; Maintenance Janitor; Office Worker; Receptionist; Secretary; Skilled Laborer; Typist.

SOURCE EDP
150 South Warner Road, Suite 238, King of Prussia PA 19406. 215/341-1960. Employment agency. Appointment requested. Founded 1962. **Specializes in:** Computer Hardware and Software; MIS/EDP; Technical and Scientific.

KEN SPINRAD, INC.
P.O. Box 4095, Reading PA 19606. 215/779-0944. **Contact:** Ken Spinrad, President. Employment agency. No appointment required. **Specializes in:** Apparel; Fashion; Textile Industry.

STAFF BUILDERS, INC. HEALTH CARE SERVICES
One Bala Plaza, Suite 127, Bala Cynwyd, PA 19004-1411. 215/783-0306. Temporary help service. Appointment requested. Founded 1961. Branch offices located in: Arizona; California; Connecticut; District of Columbia; Florida; Georgia; Illinois; Indiana; Kansas; Louisiana; Maryland; Massachusetts; Michigan; Minnesota; Missouri; Nevada; New Jersey; New Mexico; New York; Ohio; Oklahoma; Oregon; Rhode Island; Tennessee; Texas; Virginia; Washington. Non specialized. **Positions commonly filled:** Accountant; Administrative Assistant; Bookkeeper; Clerk; Companion; Computer Operator; Computer Programmer; Customer Service Representative; Data Entry Clerk; Demonstrator; Draftsperson; Driver; EDP Specialist; Factory Worker; General Laborer; Health Aide; Legal Secretary; Light Industrial Worker; Medical Secretary; Nurse; Office Worker; Public Relations Worker; Receptionist; Sales Representative; Secretary; Stenographer; Technician; Typist; Word Processing Specialist. Company pays fee. **Placements per year:** 1,001 + .

STAFF BUILDERS, INC. OF PHILADELPHIA
Castor Avenue, Philadelphia PA 19149. 215/677-7600. Temporary help service. Appointment requested. Founded 1961. Branch offices located in: Arizona; California; Connecticut; District of Columbia; Florida; Georgia; Illinois; Indiana; Kansas; Louisiana; Maryland; Massachusetts; Michigan; Minnesota; Missouri; Nevada; New Jersey; New Mexico; New York; Ohio; Oklahoma; Oregon; Rhode Island; Tennessee; Texas; Virginia; Washington. Non specialized.

STROHL SYSTEMS
500 North Gulf Road, Suite 500, King of Prussia, PA 19406. 215/825-6220. **Contact:** Myles L. Strohl, President. Employment agency; temporary help service. No appointment required. Founded 1968. **Specializes in:** MIS/EDP.

TAC/TEMPS INC. OF PENNSYLVANIA
200 North Warner Road, Suite 313, King of Prussia PA 19406. 215/768-0300. Temporary help service. No appointment required. Branch offices located in: California; Connecticut; District of Columbia; Maryland; Massachusetts; New Hampshire; New York; Rhode Island; Virginia. **Specializes in:** Accounting and Finance; Advertising; Banking; Clerical; Education; Health and Medical; Insurance; Legal; Manufacturing; Nonprofit; Personnel and Human Resources; Printing and Publishing; Sales and Marketing; Transportation.

TAC/TEMPS INC. OF PENNSYLVANIA
1617 JFK Boulevard, Suite 326, Philadelphia PA 19103. 215/568-4466. Temporary help service. No appointment required. Branch offices located in: California; Connecticut; District of Columbia; Maryland; Massachusetts; New Hampshire; New York; Rhode Island; Virginia. **Specializes in:** Accounting and Finance; Advertising; Banking; Clerical; Education; Health and Medical; Insurance; Legal; Manufacturing; Nonprofit; Personnel and Human Resources; Printing and Publishing; Sales and Marketing; Transportation.

TECH/AID OF PENNSYLVANIA
630 West Germantown Pike, Suite 361, Plymouth Meeting PA 19462. 215/834-7340. Temporary help service. No appointment required. Founded 1969. Tech/Aid is a division of Technical Aid Corporation and has branch offices located in: Arizona; California; Connecticut; Illinois; Maryland; Massachusetts; New Hampshire; Rhode Island; Texas; Virginia. **Specializes in:** Architecture; Cable Television; Computer Hardware and Software; Construction; Engineering; Manufacturing; Technical and Scientific.

TEMP FORCE OF PENNSYLVANIA
827 Cumberland Street, Lebanon PA 17042. **Contact:** Phyllis Showers, Owner. 717/273-8813. Temporary help service. No appointment required. Founded 1965. Branch offices located in: Alabama; Arkansas; California; Colorado; Connecticut; Florida; Illinois; Indiana; Kansas; Maryland; Massachusetts; Michigan; Mississippi; Nevada; New Jersey; New Mexico; New York; Ohio; Oklahoma; Tennessee; Utah; Vermont; Virginia. Non-

specialized. **Positions commonly filled:** Accountant; Bookkeeper; Clerk; Computer Operator; Computer Programmer; Customer Service Representative; Data Entry Clerk; Demonstrator; Driver; Factory Worker; General Laborer; Legal Secretary; Light Industrial Worker; Medical Secretary; Office Worker; Purchasing Agent; Receptionist; Secretary; Statistician; Stenographer; Typist; Word Processing Specialist.

TENCO SERVICES, INC.
15 Park Avenue, P.O. Box 369, Ambler PA 19002. 215/643-6930. **Contact:** Gerald Johns, Executive Officer. Temporary help service. No appointment required. Founded 1953. **Specializes in:** Clerical; Engineering; Technical and Scientific.

TODAY'S STAFFING SERVICES, INC.
5601 Chesnut Street, Philadelphia PA 19139. 215/748-8844. An employment agency.

UNITED TECHNICAL ASSOCIATES, INC. OF PENNSYLVANIA
100 North Wilkes-Barre, Suite 110, Wilkes Barre PA 18702. **Contact:** Alice Skiro, Manager. 717/824-6420. Temporary help service. No appointment required. Founded 1974. **Specializes in:** Clerical; Computer Hardware and Software; Construction; Engineering; Food Industry; Manufacturing; MIS/EDP; Technical and Scientific. **Positions commonly filled:** Accountant; Administrative Assistant; Aerospace Engineer; Biochemist; Biologist; Biomedical Engineer; Bookkeeper; Ceramics Engineer; Chemical Engineer; Chemist; Civil Engineer; Clerk; Computer Operator; Computer Programmer; Data Entry Clerk; Draftsperson; EDP Specialist; Electrical Engineer; Factory Worker; General Laborer; Industrial Designer; Industrial Engineer; Legal Secretary; Light Industrial Worker; Mechanical Engineer; Medical Secretary; Metallurgical Engineer; Mining Engineer; Office Worker; Petroleum Engineer; Physicist; Quality Control Supervisor; Receptionist; Secretary; Statistician; Stenographer; Systems Analyst; Technical Writer/Editor; Technician; Typist; Word Processing Specialist. **Placements per year:** 501-1,000.

UNITED TECHNICAL ASSOCIATES, INC. OF PENNSYLVANIA
1259 South Cedarcrest Boulevard, Suite 225, Allentown PA 18103. 215/434-6446. **Contact:** John F. Pavlick, Manager. Temporary help service. No appointment required. Founded 1974. **Specializes in:** Clerical; Computer Hardware and Software; Construction; Engineering; Food Industry; Manufacturing; MIS/EDP; Technical and Scientific.

UNITED TECHNICAL ASSOCIATES, INC. OF PENNSYLVANIA
3917 Jonestown Road, Harrisburg PA 17109. **Contact:** Craig Miller, Manager. 717/657-3106. Temporary help service. No appointment required. Founded 1974. **Specializes in:** Clerical; Computer Hardware and Software; Construction; Engineering; Food Industry; Manufacturing; MIS/EDP; Technical and Scientific. **Positions commonly filled:** Accountant; Administrative Assistant; Aerospace Engineer; Biochemist; Biologist; Biomedical Engineer; Bookkeeper; Ceramics Engineer; Chemical Engineer;

Chemist; Civil Engineer; Clerk; Computer Operator; Computer Programmer; Data Entry Clerk; Draftsperson; EDP Specialist; Electrical Engineer; Factory Worker; General Laborer; Industrial Designer; Industrial Engineer; Legal Secretary; Light Industrial Worker; Mechanical Engineer; Medical Secretary; Metallurgical Engineer; Mining Engineer; Office Worker; Petroleum Engineer; Physicist; Quality Control Supervisor; Receptionist; Secretary; Statistician; Stenographer; Systems Analyst; Technical Writer/Editor; Technician; Typist; Word Processing Specialist. **Placements per year:** 501-1,000.

UNITED TECHNICAL ASSOCIATES, INC. OF READING
50 Stevens Street, Reading, PA 19609. 215/678-5882. **Contact:** Margaret Hildebrand, Manager. Temporary help service. No appointment required. Founded 1975. 80% Drafting and Designing; Tooling and Machine. **Specializes in:** Technical.

VISITING NURSE ASSOCIATION OF YORK COUNTY
218 E. Market Street, York PA 17403. **Contact:** Patricia Heilind, Personnel Manager. 717/846-9900. Employment agency. Appointment required. Founded 1908. Health Care to the community, private duty, Medicare certified, Home Health and Hospital Care. **Positions commonly filled:** Administrative Assistant; Bookkeeper; Claims Representative; Data Entry Clerk; Dietician/Nutritionist; Executive Secretary; Home Health Aide; Marketing Specialist; Medical Secretary; Nurse; Personnel Director; Public Relations Worker; Receptionist; Secretary; Therapist; Typist. Individual pays fee. **Placements per year:** 0-50.

VOGUE PERSONNEL, INC.
One Penn Center, 1617 JFK Boulevard, Philadelphia PA 19103. **Contact:** Ronald Madison, Manager. 215/564-0720. Employment agency. Appointment requested. Founded 1969. **Specializes in:** Women. **Positions commonly filled:** Administrative Assistant; Bookkeeper; Customer Service Representative; Legal Secretary; Medical Secretary; Model; Receptionist; Sales Representative; Secretary; Stenographer; Typist; Word Processing Specialist. Company pays fee. **Placements per year:** 201-500.

YORKTOWNE PERSONNEL
P. O. Box 2343, York PA 17405. 717/843-0079; **FAX:** 717/843-5792. **Contact:** Roger M. Geiger, Owner. Appointment required. Founded 1981. **Specializes in:** Accounting; Affirmative Action; Engineering; Finance; Food Industry; General Management; Industrial; Manufacturing; Personnel/Human Resources; Technical and Scientific. **Positions commonly filled:** Accountant; Buyer; Chemical Engineer; Electrical Engineer; Industrial Designer; Industrial Engineer; Manufacturing Engineer; Mechanical Engineer; Metallurgical Engineer; Operations and Production Specialist; Purchasing Agent; Quality Control Supervisor; Software Engineer. **Placements per year:** 50-99.

EMPLOYMENT AGENCIES AND TEMPORARY SERVICES OF DELAWARE

CALDWELL TEMPORARY SERVICES
405 Newark Shopping Center, Newark DE 19711. **Contact:** Office Manager/Technical Representative. 302/731-1111. Temporary help service. Appointment requested. Founded 1969. **Specializes in:** Clerical; Labor; Light Industrial; Technical and Scientific. **Positions commonly filled:** Accountant; Administrative Assistant; Agricultural Engineer; Architect; Biochemist; Biologist; Biomedical Engineer; Bookkeeper; Chemical Engineer; Chemist; Clerk; Computer Operator; Computer Programmer; Construction Worker; Data Entry Clerk; Demonstrator; Draftsperson; Driver; EDP Specialist; Electrical Engineer; Factory Worker; General Laborer; Industrial Engineer; Legal Secretary; Light Industrial Worker; Mechanical Engineer; Medical Secretary; Office Worker; Receptionist; Secretary; Stenographer; Systems Analyst; Technician; Typist; Word Processing Specialist.

CALDWELL TEMPORARY SERVICES
905 Shipley Street, Wilmington DE 19801. Employment agency; temporary help agency. Founded 1968. **Specializes in:** Accounting; Banking and Finance; Insurance; Legal; Sales and Marketing; Secretarial. **Positions commonly filled:** Accountant; Administrative Assistant; Biomedical Engineer; Bookkeeper; Clerk; Computer Programmer; Credit Manager; Customer Service Representative; Data Entry Clerk; Draftsperson; Executive Secretary; Financial Analyst; Industrial Engineer; Legal Secretary; Light Industrial Worker; Medical Secretary; Receptionist; Sales Representative; Secretary; Statistician; Stenographer; Systems Analyst; Technician; Typist; Work Processor; etc. Company pays fee. **Placements per year:** 51-100.

CASEY EMPLOYMENT SERVICES, INC.
820 West Street, Wilmington DE 19801. **Contact:** Daniel G. Kasal, President. 302/658-6461. Employment agency; temporary help agency. Appointment required. Founded 1953. **Specializes in:** Accounting; Engineering; Industrial and Interior Design; Sales and Marketing; Secretarial; Technical and Scientific. **Positions commonly filled:** Accountant; Administrative Assistant; Biochemist/Chemist; Biologist; Biomedical Engineer; Bookkeeper; Civil Engineer; Claims Representative; Clerk; Computer Programmer; Credit Manager; Customer Service Representative; Data Entry Clerk; Industrial Designer; Draftsperson; Driver; EDP Specialist; Electrical Engineer; Executive Secretary; Factory Worker; Financial Analyst; General Laborer; General Manager; Industrial Engineer; Insurance Agent/Broker; Legal Secretary; Light Industrial Worker; Management Consultant; Marketing Specialist; Mechanical Engineer; Medical Secretary; Metallurgical Engineer; Personnel Director; Public Relations Worker; Purchasing Agent; Receptionist; Sales Representative; Secretary; Statistician; Stenographer; Technical

Writer/Editor; Technician; Typist; Underwriter; Word Processor. Company pays fee. **Placements per year:** 201-500.

FIDELITY PERSONNEL
4010 Concord Pike, Wilmington DE 19803. **Contact:** Donald Giangiacomo, Manager. 302/478-6996. Employment agency. Appointment requested. Founded 1969. **Specializes in:** Accounting and Finance; Banking; Clerical; Computer Hardware and Software; Engineering; Insurance; Legal; MIS/EDP; Technical and Scientific. **Positions commonly filled:** Accountant; Actuary; Administrative Assistant; Bank Officer/Manager; Bookkeeper; Buyer; Claim Representative; Clerk; Computer Operator; Computer Programmer; Credit Manager; Customer Service Representative; Data Entry Clerk; Draftsperson; EDP Specialist; Economist; Financial Analyst; General Manager; Legal Secretary; MIS Specialist; Marketing Specialist; Medical Secretary; Office Worker; Personnel and Labor Relations Specialist; Purchasing Agent; Quality Control Supervisor; Receptionist; Sales Representative; Secretary; Statistician; Stenographer; Systems Analyst; Technical Writer/Editor; Technician; Typist; Underwriter; Word Processing Specialist. Company pays fee; individual pays fee. **Placements per year:** 201-500.

NORRELL SERVICES
301 North Walnut Street, Suite 106, Wilmington DE 19801. 302/656-8340. **Contact:** Karen Russo, Branch Manager. Temporary help service. No appointment required. Founded 1977. Non-specialized.

SNELLING PERSONNEL SERVICES
3617-A Silverside Road, Wilmington DE 19810. **Contact:** King G. Morton, Co-Owner/General Manager. 302/478-6060. Employment agency. Appointment requested. Founded 1963. **Specializes in:** Accounting and Finance; Banking; Clerical; Computer Hardware and Software; Engineering; Fashion; Food Industry; Personnel and Human Resources; Sales and Marketing; Technical and Scientific; Transportation. **Positions commonly filled:** Accountant; Administrative Assistant; Bank Officer/Manager; Biomedical Engineer; Bookkeeper; Buyer; Ceramics Engineer; Civil Engineer; Claim Representative; Clerk; Computer Operator; Computer Programmer; Credit Manager; Customer Service Representative; Data Entry Clerk; EDP Specialist; Electrical Engineer; Financial Analyst; Food Technologist; General Manager; Hotel Manager/Assistant Manager; Industrial Engineer; Insurance Agent/Broker; Legal Secretary; Marketing Specialist; Mechanical Engineer; Metallurgical Engineer; Petroleum Engineer; Medical Secretary; Office Worker; Personnel and Labor Relations Specialist; Purchasing Agent; Receptionist; Reporter/Editor; Sales Representative; Secretary; Stenographer; Systems Analyst; Typist; Word Processing Specialist. Company pays fee; individual pays fee. **Placements per year:** 101-200.

SUSSEX EMPLOYMENT SERVICES
204C North Race, Georgetown DE 19947. **Contact:** Joyce Westen, Manager. 302/856-7308. Employment agency; temporary help service. Appointment requested. Founded 1982. **Specializes in:** Clerical. **Positions commonly filled:** Accountant; Administrative Assistant; Bookkeeper; Clerk; Computer Operator; Computer Programmer; Construction Worker; Customer Service Representative; Data Entry Clerk; Draftsperson; EDP Specialist; Factory Worker; General Laborer; Legal Secretary; Light Industrial Worker; Medical Secretary; Office Worker; Receptionist; Secretary; Stenographer; Typist; Word Processing Specialist. Company pays fee; individual pays fee. **Placements per year:** 101-200.

WILMINGTON SENIOR CENTER-EMPLOYMENT SERVICES
1909 North Market Street, Wilmington DE 19802. **Contact:** Barbara Washam, Community Relations. 302/651-3440. Employment agency; temporary help service. No appointment required. Founded 1974. **Specializes in:** Elderly (service to all persons 55 years or older). **Positions commonly filled:** Accountant; Bookkeeper; Clerk; Companion; Driver; Gardener; Home Repair Worker; Office Worker; Receptionist; Sales Representative; Secretary; Typist. **Placements per year:** 201-500.

EMPLOYMENT AGENCIES AND TEMPORARY SERVICES OF NEW JERSEY

ALTERNATIVE
Forrestal Center, 211 College Road East, Princeton NJ 08540. 609/452-0020. Temporary help service. Appointment requested. Founded 1961. Branch offices located in: Arizona; California; Connecticut; District of Columbia; Florida; Georgia; Illinois; Indiana; Kansas; Louisiana; Maryland; Massachusetts; Michigan; Minnesota; Missouri; Nevada; New Jersey; New Mexico; New York; Ohio; Oklahoma; Oregon; Pennsylvania; Rhode Island; Tennessee; Texas; Virginia; Washington. Non-specialized.

BLAKE & ASSOCIATES
P.O. Box 1425, Pleasantville NJ 08232-1425. 609/645-3330; **FAX:** 609/383-0320. **Contact:** Ed Blake, Manager. Appointment required. Founded 1979. **Specializes in:** Accounting; Administration, MIS/EDP; Architecture/Construction/Real Estate; Banking; Computer Hardware and Software; Engineering; Finance; Food Industry; General Management; Health/Medical; Industrial; Insurance; Legal; Manufacturing; Retail; Sales and Marketing; Secretarial; Technical and Scientific; Transportation. **Positions commonly filled:** Accountant; Administrative Assistant; Aerospace Engineer; Architect; Biochemist; Biologist; Biomedical Engineer; Bookkeeper; Chemical Engineer; Chemist; Civil Engineer; Claims Representative; Computer Operator; Computer Programmer; Credit Manager; Customer Service

Representative; Data Entry Clerk; Draftsperson; EDP Specialist; Executive Secretary; Electrical Engineer; Hotel Manager; Industrial Designer; Industrial Engineer; Legal Secretary; Manufacturing Engineer; Mechanical Engineer; Medical Secretary; Metallurgical Engineer; MIS Specialist; Purchasing Agent; Quality Control Supervisor; Receptionist; Sales Representative; Secretary; Software Engineer; Systems Analyst; Technician; Word Processing Specialist; Typist; Word Processor. **Placements per year: 50-99.**

CAREERS FIRST, INC.
305 U. S. Route 130, Cinnaminson NJ 08077-3398. 609/786-0004. **Contact:** Gail Duncan, President. Employment agency. Appointment required. Founded 1970. Small technical agency recruiting and placing computer personnel primarily in New Jersey, Delaware and Pennsylvania. **Specializes in:** Computer Hardware and Software; MIS/EDP; Technical and Scientific.

CHURCHILL & HARRIMAN, INC.
601 Ewing Street, Suite B7, Princeton NJ 08540. 609/921-3551; **FAX:** 609/921-1061. **Contact:** Mr. Ken Peterson, President. Appointment required. Founded 1986. **Specializes in:** Administration, MIS/EDP; Affirmative Action. **Positions commonly filled:** Computer Programmer; EDP Specialist; MIS Specialist; Software Engineer; Systems Analyst. Company does not pay fee. **Placements per year: 1-49.**

DUNHILL OF CHERRY HILL
1040 Kings Highway North, Suite 400, Cherry Hill NJ 08034. 609/667-9180. **Contact:** Bill Emerson, Owner. Employment agency; temporary help service. Founded 1972. Non-specialized.

IMPACT PERSONNEL, INC.
3371 Route 1, Lawrenceville NJ 08648. 609/987-8888; **FAX:** 609/987-9020. **Contact:** Guy James, President. No appointment required. Founded 1985. **Specializes in:** Accounting; Advertising; Administration, MIS/EDP; Banking; Computer Hardware and Software; Engineering; Fashion; Finance; Food Industry; General Management; Health/Medical; Industrial; Insurance; Legal; Manufacturing; Printing/Publishing; Retail; Sales and Marketing; Secretarial; Technical and Scientific. **Positions commonly filled:** Accountant; Administrative Assistant; Bookkeeper; Chemical Engineer; Claims Representative; Clerk; Commercial Artist; Computer Operator; Computer Programmer; Customer Service Representative· Data Entry Clerk; Driver; Executive Secretary; Electrical Engineer; Factory Worker; General Laborer; Hotel Manager; Industrial Designer; Industrial Engineer: Legal Secretary; Light Industrial Worker; Mechanical Engineer; Medical Secretary; Quality Control Supervisor; Receptionist; Sales Representative; Secretary; Software Engineer; Technical Recruiter; Technician; Word Processing Specialist; Typist; Word Processor. Company pays fee. **Placements per year: 500-999.**

PERSONNEL ONE
20 Nassau Street, Princeton NJ 08542. 609/799-4636. **Contact:** Kathleen Sereni, Branch Manager. Employment agency; temporary help agency. No

appointment required. Founded 1979. Parent company is Science Management Corporation. **Specializes in:** Secretarial and Clerical.

RSVP
P.O. Box 8369, Cherry Hill NJ 08002. 609/667-4488. **Contact:** Howard Levin, Director. Employment agency. Appointment required. Founded 1966. Member of National Personnel Associates (world's largest employment network), NAPC, MAAPC. **Specializes in:** Computer Hardware and Software; Electrical Engineering; MIS/EDP.

RECRUITMENT ALTERNATIVES, INC.
York House East, Box 554, Moorestown NJ 08057. 609/273-1066. **Contact:** Thomas J. Jaskel, Senior Vice President. Appointment required. Founded 1986. **Specializes in:** Personnel/Human Resources. **Positions commonly filled:** Human Resource Generalist; Human Resource Specialist; Technical Recruiter. Company pays fee. **Placements per year:** 1-49.

SCIENTIFIC SEARCH, INC.
Plaza Office Center, Suite 309, 560 Fellowship Road, Mt. Laurel NJ 08054. 609/866-0200; **FAX:** 609/722-5307. **Contact:** Robert I. Greenberg, President. Appointment required. Founded 1983. **Specializes in:** Computer Hardware and Software; Health/Medical; Sales and Marketing; Technical and Scientific. **Positions commonly filled:** Computer Programmer; Customer Service Representative; EDP Specialist; MIS Specialist; Nurse; Sales Representative. Company pays fee. **Placements per year:** 50-99.

SELECTIVE PERSONNEL
214 Highway 18, East Brunswick NJ 08816. 609/497-2900. Employment agency; temporary help service. **Specializes in:** Accounting and Finance; Banking; Clerical; Computer Hardware and Software; Engineering; Health and Medical; Insurance; Legal; Manufacturing; MIS/EDP; Personnel and Human Resources; Sales and Marketing; Technical and Scientific.

SNELLING PERSONNEL SERVICES
5425 Route 70, Pennsauken NJ 08109. 609/662-5424. **Contact:** Chris Deegler, Owner/Manager. Employment agency. No appointment required. Snelling Personnel Services has over 500 offices throughout the United States. **Specializes in:** Accounting and Finance; Banking; Clerical; Food Industry; Health and Medical; Personnel and Human Resources; Sales and Marketing.

SUPPORTIVE CARE OF NEW JERSEY
383 North Kings Highway, Cherry Hill NJ 08034. 609/482-6630. **FAX:** 609/482-6632. **Contact:** Ann E. Matthews, Manager. Temporary help service. Appointment requested. Founded 1984. **Specializes in:** Health and Medical.

EXECUTIVE SEARCH FIRMS OF PHILADELPHIA

ACCOUNTANTS ON CALL
1600 Market Street, Suite 1418, Philadelphia PA 19103. 215/568-5600. **Contact:** Mark S. Libes, President. Executive search firm. Appointment requested; unsolicited resumes accepted. **Specializes in:** Accounting; Banking; Finance.

J. ALLEN ENTERPRISES
33 West Lancaster Avenue, Ardmore PA 19003. 215/642-8347; **FAX:** 215/642-8347. **Contact:** Joel M. Allen, Owner. Appointment required. **Specializes in:** Accounting; Advertising; Administration, MIS/EDP; Computer Hardware and Software; Engineering; Food Industry; General Management; Health/Medical; Industrial; Insurance; Legal; Manufacturing; Non-Profit; Personnel/Human Resources; Printing/Publishing; Retail; Sales and Marketing; Secretarial; Technical and Scientific; Transportation. **Positions commonly filled:** Accountant; Administrative Assistant; Aerospace Engineer; Architect; Biochemist; Biologist; Biomedical Engineer; Bookkeeper; Buyer; Ceramics Engineer; Chemical Engineer; Chemist; Civil Engineer; Claims Representative; Clerk; Commercial Artist; Computer Operator; Computer Programmer; Construction Worker; Credit Manager; Customer Service Representative; Data Entry Clerk; Draftsperson; Driver; EDP Specialist; Executive Secretary; Electrical Engineer; Factory Worker; General Laborer; Hotel Manager; Industrial Designer; Industrial Engineer; Legal Secretary; Light Industrial Worker; Manufacturing Engineer; Marketing Specialist; Mechanical Engineer; Medical Secretary; Mechanical Engineer; Medical Secretary; Metallurgical Engineer; MIS Specialist; Operations and Production Specialist; Public Relations Worker; Purchasing Agent; Quality Control Supervisor; Receptionist; Reporter/Editor; Sales Representative; Secretary; Software Engineer; Systems Analyst; Technical Illustrator; Technical Recruiter; Technical Writer/Editor; Technician; Word Processing Specialist; Word Processor; Typist. Company pays fee. **Placements per year:** 50-99.

AMATO & ASSOCIATES
1313 Medford Road, Suite 100, Wynnewood PA 19096-2418. 610/642-9797. **FAX:** 610/642-9696. **Contact:** Bobbi Amato, President. Appointment required. Founded 1980. **Specializes in:** Insurance. **Positions commonly filled:** Account Executives, Claims, CSR's, Loss Control, Managers, Marketing Reps., Producers, Risk Managers, Underwriters. Types of firms: Agents, Brokers, Excess, Personal Lines, Primary Carriers, Property/Casualty, Reinsurance, Umbrella, Wholesalers, Workers Comp. Company pays fee.

ANDRE GROUP, INC.
500 N. Gulph Road, Suite 210, King of Prussia PA 19406. **Contact:** Richard Andre, President. 215/337-0600. Executive search firm. Appointment requested; unsolicited resumes accepted. Founded 1969. **Specializes in:** Personnel and Human Resources. **Searches conducted per year:** 150-200.

BARR ASSOCIATES
93 South West End Boulevard, Suite 105B, Quakertown PA 18951. 215/538-9411; **FAX:** 215/538-9466. **Contact:** Sharon Barr, Owner. No appointment required. Founded 1987. **Specializes in:** Engineering; Sales and Marketing. **Positions commonly filled:** Chemical Engineer; Electrical Engineer; Mechanical Engineer; Quality Control Supervisor. Company pays fee. **Placements per year:** 1-49.

CMIS
24 Hagerty Boulevard, Suite 9, West Chester PA 19382. 215/430-0013; **FAX:** 215/430-6878. **Contact:** Peter DiNicola, President. Appointment required. **Specializes in:** Administration, MIS/EDP; Computer Hardware and Software; General Management; Sales and Marketing. **Positions commonly filled:** Computer Programmer; MIS Specialist; Sales Representative; Systems Analyst. Company pays fee. **Placements per year:** 1-49.

CLIFFORD ASSOCIATES, INC.
306 Corporate Drive East, Langhorne PA 19047. 215/968-1980; **FAX:** 215/968-6680. **Contact:** Cliff Milles, Owner. Appointment required. Founded 1985. **Specializes in:** Computer Hardware and Software. **Positions commonly filled:** Programmer/Analyst. Company pays fee. **Placements per year:** 1-49.

COURTRIGHT & ASSOCIATES
P. O. Box 503, Clarks Summit PA 18411. 717/586-0735. **Contact:** Robert Courtright, President. Appointment required. Founded 1989. **Specializes in:** Biotechnology/Biopharmaceutical. Company pays fee. **Placements per year:** 1-49.

DIVERSIFIED SEARCH, INC.
One Commerce Square, 2005 Market Street, Suite 3300, Philadelphia PA 19103. 215/732-6666. An executive search and consulting service.

DOW-TECH ASSOCIATES
P.O. Box 323, Thorndale PA 19372. 610/383-5051; **FAX:** 610/383-5052. **Contact:** Karen Paulson, Senior Corporate Recruiter. Placement in New York, New Jersey, and Washington D.C. as well as Pennsylvania. Appointment required. **Specializes in of the areas of:** Computer Hardware and Software; Engineering; Sales and Marketing. **Positions commonly filled:** Computer Programmer; Electrical Engineer; Mechanical Engineer; Sales Representative; Software Engineer; Technician. Company pays fee. **Placements per year:** 50-99.

DUNHILL OF LANCASTER, INC.

1801 Lititz Pike, Lancaster PA 17601. **Contact:** President. 717/569-4802. Professional/technical search firm. Founded 1969. **Specializes in:** Accounting and Finance; Data Processing; Sales and Marketing; Technical and Engineering. **Positions commonly filled:** Accounting Manager; Data Processing VP, Manager, Supervisor; Financial Controller; Mechanical, Plant, Industrial, Manufacturing, Quality Control Manager and Supervisor.

EDEN & ASSOCIATES, INC.

160 Valley Forge Plaza, King of Prussia PA 19406. 215/265-3535; **FAX:** 215/265-5083. **Contact:** Brooks D. Eden, President. Appointment required. Founded 1981. **Specializes in:** Food & Drug Retailers and Distributors; Food & Beverage Manufacturers; Specialty & Mass Merchandising Retailers. Concentrating in disciplines including retail operations, distribution, manufacturing, finance, data processing, sales and marketing, merchandising, procurement, real estate development, engineering, human resources and general management. Deal on exclusive basis. Company pays fee.

HOWARD FISCHER ASSOCIATES, INC.

1530 Chestnut Street, Suite 800, Philadelphia PA 19102. An executive search firm.

HEALTH & SCIENCE CENTER

P.O. Box 213, Lima PA 19037. 215/891-0714. **Contact:** J. Timothy McGrath, Executive Director. Executive search firm. Founded 1970. **Specializes in:** Health and Medical; Technical and Scientific. **Searches conducted per year:** 51-100.

J.J. & H., JACOBSON ASSOCIATES

5 Neshaniny Interplex, Suite 113, Trevors, 19053.. 215/639-5890. **FAX:** 215/922-2368. Executive search firm. No appointment necessary. Founded in 1971. **Specializes in:** Insurance. **Positions commonly filled:** Accountant, Administrative Assistant, Claims Representative, EDP Specialist, Legal Secretary, Marketing Specialist, MIS Specialist, Operations and Production Specialist, Sales Representative, Systems Analyst, Attorney, Senior Level Executive. Company pays fee. **Placements per year:** 100-199.

LAMONTE OWENS, INC.

805 East Willow Grove Avenue, Suite 1A, P.O. Box 27742, Philadelphia PA 19118. 215/248-0500; **FAX:** 215/233-3737 and 215/248-9880. **Contact:** Lamonte Owens, President. Executive search firm. Appointment requested; unsolicited resumes accepted. Founded 1970. Specialist in Minority and Female Recruiting. 25% contingency; 75% retainer and search. **Searches conducted per year:** 25.

LAWRENCE PERSONNEL
Suite 110, 1000 Valley Forge Circle, King of Prussia PA 19406-1111. 610/783-5400; **FAX:** 610/783-6008. **Contact:** Larry Goldberg, General Manager. Executive Search Firm -- Contingency Recruiter. Appointment required. Founded 1957. **Specializes in:** Engineering; Industrial; Manufacturing; Technical and Scientific; Telecommunications. **Positions commonly filled:** Biomedical Engineer; Electrical Engineer; Industrial Engineer; Manufacturing Engineer; Telecommunications Engineer. Company pays fee. **Placements per year:** 1-49.

MANAGEMENT RECRUITERS OF BUCKS COUNTY
One Greenwood Square, Suite 235, Bensalem PA 19020. 215/245-1551. **Contact:** Ted Mashack, Manager. Executive search firm. Appointment required; no phone calls; unsolicited resumes accepted. Founded 1965. World's largest contingency search firm. Five hundred offices nationwide, doing business under the names of "Management Recruiters", "Sales Consultants", "CompuSearch" and "OfficeMates5". Specializes in mid-management/professional positions, $25,000-75,000 per annum. **Specializes in:** Accounting; Administration, MIS/EDP; Advertising; Affirmative Action; Architecture; Banking and Finance; Communications; Computer Hardware and Software; Construction; Electrical; Engineering; Food Industry; General Management; Health and Medical; Human Resources; Industrial and Interior Design; Insurance; Legal; Manufacturing; Operations Management; Printing and Publishing; Procurement; Real Estate; Retailing; Sales and Marketing; Technical and Scientific; Textiles; Transportation. Contingency.

MANAGEMENT RECRUITERS OF DELAWARE COUNTY
90 South Newtown Street, Suite 9 Newtown Square PA 19073. 215/356-8360. **Contact:** M. A. (Sandy) Bishop, Manager. Executive search firm. Appointment required; no phone calls; unsolicited resumes accepted. Founded 1965. World's largest contingency search firm. Five hundred offices nationwide, doing business under the names of "Management Recruiters", "Sales Consultants", "CompuSearch" and "OfficeMates5". Specializes in mid-management/professional positions, $25,000-75,000 per annum. **Specializes in:** Accounting; Administration, MIS/EDP; Advertising; Affirmative Action; Architecture; Banking and Finance; Communications; Computer Hardware and Software; Construction; Electrical; Engineering; Food Industry; General Management; Health and Medical; Human Resources; Industrial and Interior Design; Insurance; Legal; Manufacturing; Operations Management; Printing and Publishing; Procurement; Real Estate; Retailing; Sales and Marketing; Technical and Scientific; Textiles; Transportation. Contingency.

MANAGEMENT RECRUITERS OF KING OF PRUSSIA
P.O. Box 1803, Southeastern PA 19399-1803. 215/964-1200. **Contact:** John Zerkle, Manager. Executive search firm. Appointment required; no phone calls; unsolicited resumes accepted. Founded 1965. World's largest contingency search firm. Five hundred offices nationwide, doing business under the names of "Management Recruiters", "Sales Consultants", "CompuSearch" and "OfficeMates5". Specializes in mid-

management/professional positions, $25,000-75,000 per annum. **Specializes in:** Accounting; Administration, MIS/EDP; Advertising; Affirmative Action; Architecture; Banking and Finance; Communications; Computer Hardware and Software; Construction; Electrical; Engineering; Food Industry; General Management; Health and Medical; Human Resources; Industrial and Interior Design; Insurance; Legal; Manufacturing; Operations Management; Printing and Publishing; Procurement; Real Estate; Retailing; Sales and Marketing; Technical and Scientific; Textiles; Transportation. Contingency.

MANAGEMENT RECRUITERS OF LEHIGH VALLEY
1414 Millard Street, Bethlehem PA 18018. **Contact:** Fred Meyer, Manager. 215/974-9770. Executive search firm. Appointment required; no phone calls; unsolicited resumes accepted. Founded 1965. World's largest contingency search firm. Five hundred offices nationwide, doing business under the names of "Management Recruiters", "Sales Consultants", "CompuSearch" and "OfficeMates5". Specializes in mid-management/professional positions, $25,000-75,000 per annum. **Specializes in:** Accounting; Administration, MIS/EDP; Advertising; Affirmative Action; Architecture; Banking and Finance; Communications; Computer Hardware and Software; Construction; Electrical; Engineering; Food Industry; General Management; Health and Medical; Human Resources; Industrial and Interior Design; Insurance; Legal; Manufacturing; Operations Management; Printing and Publishing; Procurement; Real Estate; Retailing; Sales and Marketing; Technical and Scientific; Textiles; Transportation. Contingency.

MANAGEMENT RECRUITERS OF WILLOW GROVE
2500 Office Center, Suite 612, Willow Grove PA 19090. 215/657-6250. **Contact:** Rowland Norris, General Manager. Executive search firm. Appointment required; no phone calls; unsolicited resumes accepted. Founded 1965. World's largest contingency search firm. Five hundred offices nationwide, doing business under the names of "Management Recruiters", "Sales Consultants", "CompuSearch" and "OfficeMates5". Specializes in mid-management/professional positions, $25,000-75,000 per annum. **Specializes in:** Accounting; Administration, MIS/EDP; Advertising; Affirmative Action; Architecture; Banking and Finance; Communications; Computer Hardware and Software; Construction; Electrical; Engineering; Food Industry; General Management; Health and Medical; Human Resources; Industrial and Interior Design; Insurance; Legal; Manufacturing; Operations Management; Printing and Publishing; Procurement; Real Estate; Retailing; Sales and Marketing; Technical and Scientific; Textiles; Transportation. Contingency.

MANAGEMENT RECRUITERS
& COMPU-SEARCH MANAYUNK/CHESTNUT HILL
4419 Main Street, Philadelphia PA 19127-1324. 215/482-6881; **FAX:** 215/482-7518. **Contact:** Scott Quitel, President. Appointment required. Founded 1991. **Specializes in:** Administration, MIS/EDP; Computer Hardware and Software; Health/Medical; Legal; Sales and Marketing; Technical and Scientific. **Positions commonly filled:** Attorney; Biochemist; Biologist; Biomedical Engineer; Computer Operator; Computer Programmer; Electrical

Engineer; MIS Specialist; Nurse; Software Engineer; Systems Analyst; Technical Writer/Editor. Company pays fee. **Placements per year:** 50-99.

MANAGEMENT RECRUITERS OF PHILADELPHIA
Robert Morris Building, 100 North 17th Street, Philadelphia PA 19103. 215/665-9430. **Contact:** Tom Lucas, Manager. Executive search firm. Appointment required; no phone calls; unsolicited resumes accepted. Founded 1965. World's largest contingency search firm. Five hundred offices nationwide, doing business under the names of "Management Recruiters", "Sales Consultants", "CompuSearch" and "OfficeMates5". Specializes in mid-management/professional positions, $25,000-75,000 per annum. **Specializes in:** Accounting; Administration, MIS/EDP; Advertising; Affirmative Action; Architecture; Banking and Finance; Communications; Computer Hardware and Software; Construction; Electrical; Engineering; Food Industry; General Management; Health and Medical; Human Resources; Industrial and Interior Design; Insurance; Legal; Manufacturing; Operations Management; Printing and Publishing; Procurement; Real Estate; Retailing; Sales and Marketing; Technical and Scientific; Textiles; Transportation. Contingency.

GEORGE R. MARTIN EXECUTIVE SEARCH
P.O. Box 673, Doylestown, PA 18901. **Contact:** George R. Martin, Owner/Manager. 215/348-8146. Executive search firm. Appointment requested; no phone calls; unsolicited resumes accepted. Founded 1973. **Specializes in:** Affirmative Action; Computer Hardware and Software; Engineering; Insurance; Manufacturing; Personnel and Human Resources; Sales and Marketing; Technical and Scientific; Women. Non-contingency. **Searches conducted per year:** 26-50.

OFFICEMATES5 OF KING OF PRUSSIA
P.O. Box 1803, Southeastern PA 19399-1803. 215/964-1200. **Contact:** John Zerkle, Manager. Executive search firm. Appointment required; no phone calls; unsolicited resumes accepted. Founded 1965. World's largest contingency search firm. Five hundred offices nationwide, doing business under the names of "Management Recruiters", "Sales Consultants", "CompuSearch" and "OfficeMates5". Specializes in mid-management/professional positions, $25,000-75,000 per annum. **Specializes in:** Accounting; Administration, MIS/EDP; Advertising; Affirmative Action; Architecture; Banking and Finance; Communications; Computer Hardware and Software; Construction; Electrical; Engineering; Food Industry; General Management; Health and Medical; Human Resources; Industrial and Interior Design; Insurance; Legal; Manufacturing; Operations Management; Printing and Publishing; Procurement; Real Estate; Retailing; Sales and Marketing; Technical and Scientific; Textiles; Transportation. Contingency.

PRO EM PERSONNEL SERVICE, INC.
120 S. York Road, Suite #8, Hatboro PA 19040. 215/674-4040. **Contact:** Norman V. Pomplas, President. Executive search firm. No appointment required. Founded 1970. Technical recruiting specialist to the Chemical

Process industry. Personnel search and employment specialist on a nationwide basis.

QUESTOR CONSULTANTS, INC.

2515 North Broad Street, Colmar PA 18915. 215/997-9262; **FAX:** 215/997-9226. **Contact:** Sal Bevivino, President. No appointment required. Founded 1984. **Specializes in:** Insurance. **Positions commonly filled:** Claims Representative. Company pays fee. **Placements per year:** 1-49.

THE RICHARDS GROUP

2 Penn Center, Suite 710, Philadelphia PA 19102. 215/751-0805; **FAX:** 215/854-0791. **Contact:** Larry Winitsky, President. Appointment required. Founded 1991. **Specializes in:** General Management; Health/Medical; Personnel/Human Resources; Retail; Sales and Marketing; Secretarial. **Positions commonly filled:** Administrative Assistant; Buyer; Commercial Artist; Computer Operator; Computer Programmer; Data Entry Clerk; EDP Specialist; Executive Secretary; Legal Secretary; Marketing Specialist; Nurse; Receptionist; Sales Representative; Secretary; Software Engineer; Systems Analyst; Typist; Word Processing Specialist; Word Processor. Company pays fee. **Placements per year:** 100-199.

S-H-S INTERNATIONAL

101 East Lancaster Avenue, Wayne PA 19087. 215/687-6104. **Contact:** Paul Reitman, General Manager. Executive search firm. Appointment required; unsolicited resumes accepted. Founded 1969. **Specializes in:** Accounting; Administration, MIS/EDP; Banking and Finance; Chemicals and Pharmaceuticals; Computer Hardware and Software; Construction; Construction Building Material; Electrical Engineering; Health and Medical; Human Resources; Industrial and Interior Design; Insurance; Legal; Manufacturing; Sales and Marketing; Technical and Scientific; Textiles; Women. Out placement. Contingency. **Searches conducted per year:** 501+.

SALES CONSULTANTS OF PHILADELPHIA

301 Oxford Valley Road, Suite 204, Yardley PA 19067. 215/321-4100. **Contact:** Manager. Executive search firm. Appointment required; no phone calls; unsolicited resumes accepted. Founded 1965. World's largest contingency search firm. Five hundred offices nationwide, doing business under the names of "Management Recruiters", "Sales Consultants", "CompuSearch" and "OfficeMates5". Specializes in mid-management/professional positions, $25,000-75,000 per annum. **Specializes in:** Accounting; Administration, MIS/EDP; Advertising; Affirmative Action; Architecture; Banking and Finance; Communications; Computer Hardware and Software; Construction; Electrical; Engineering; Food Industry; General Management; Health and Medical; Human Resources; Industrial and Interior Design; Insurance; Legal; Manufacturing; Operations Management; Printing and Publishing; Procurement; Real Estate; Retailing; Sales and Marketing; Technical and Scientific; Textiles; Transportation. Contingency.

SALES CONSULTANTS OF PHILADELPHIA/WEST
2500 Office Center, Willow Grove PA 19090. 215/657-6250. **Contact:** Rowland Norris, Manager. Executive search firm. Appointment required; no phone calls; unsolicited resumes accepted. Founded 1965. World's largest contingency search firm. Five hundred offices nationwide, doing business under the names of "Management Recruiters", "Sales Consultants", "CompuSearch" and "OfficeMates5". Specializes in mid-management/professional positions, $25,000-75,000 per annum. **Specializes in:** Accounting; Administration, MIS/EDP; Advertising; Affirmative Action; Architecture; Banking and Finance; Communications; Computer Hardware and Software; Construction; Electrical; Engineering; Food Industry; General Management; Health and Medical; Human Resources; Industrial and Interior Design; Insurance; Legal; Manufacturing; Operations Management; Printing and Publishing; Procurement; Real Estate; Retailing; Sales and Marketing; Technical and Scientific; Textiles; Transportation. Contingency.

SCHNEIDER, HILL, & SPANGLER, INC.
Rose Tree Corporate Center, P.O. Box 70, Media PA 19063-0070. 215/566-9550; **FAX:** 215/566-9555. **Contact:** Steven A. Schneider, Senior Managing Partner. Executive Search Firm. Appointment required. Founded 1956. **Specializes in the areas of:** Accounting; Finance; General Management; Health/Medical; Manufacturing; Non-Profit; Personnel/Human Resources. **Positions commonly filled include:** Senior Operating Management; Outside Directors. Company pays fee. **Placements per year:** 50-99.

SELECT SEARCH INCORPORATED
1411 Walnut Street, Suite 200, Philadelphia PA 19102. 215/564-6550. 215/564-6121. **Contact:** Susan Alder, President/Carol Baker, Vice President. Appointment required. Founded 1991. Non-specialized. **Positions commonly filled:** Accountant; Administrative Assistant; Bookkeeper; Buyer; Claims Representative; Computer Operator; Computer Programmer; Credit Manager; Customer Service Representative; EDP Specialist; Executive Secretary; Hotel Manager; Legal Secretary; Marketing Specialist; Medical Secretary; MIS Specialist; Nurse; Optician; Purchasing Agent; Quality Control Supervisor; Receptionist; Restaurant Manager; Sales Representative; Secretary; Software Engineer; Systems Analyst; Travel Agent/Manager; Word Processing Specialist; Word Processor; Typist. Company pays fee. **Placements per year:** 1-49.

SELECTIVE MANAGEMENT SERVICES, INC.
319 South Sixteenth Street, Philadelphia PA 19102. 215/545-7111. **Contact:** Alan M. Schwartz, President. Executive search firm. Appointment requested; unsolicited resumes accepted. Founded 1972. **Specializes in:** Computer Hardware and Software; Insurance; Packaging; Printing and Publishing. Contingency. **Searches conducted per year:** 26-50.

SPENCER STUART
One Commerce Square, 2005 Market Street, Suite 2350, Philadelphia PA 19103. 215/563-0010. An executive search firm.

SYSTEMS PERSONNEL, INC.
115 West State Street, Media PA 19063. 215/565-8880; **FAX:** 215/565-1482. **Contact:** Jerry Reynolds/Jim Doherty, Partners. Appointment required. Founded 1974. **Specializes in:** Computer Hardware and Software. **Positions commonly filled:** Computer Programmer; EDP Specialist; MIS Manager; MIS Specialist; Software Engineer; Systems Analyst. Company pays fee. **Placements per year:** 100-199.

YORKTOWNE PERSONNEL
103 East Market Street, York PA 17401. 717/843-0079; **FAX:** 717/843-5792. **Contact:** Roger Geiger, Owner. Appointment required. Founded 1981. **Specializes in:** Accounting; Affirmative Action; Engineering; Finance; Food Industry; General Management; Industrial; Manufacturing; Personnel/Human Resources; Technical and Scientific. **Positions commonly filled:** Accountant; Buyer; Chemical Engineer; Electrical Engineer; Industrial Designer; Industrial Engineer; Manufacturing Engineer; Mechanical Engineer; Metallurgical Engineer; Operations and Production Specialist; Purchasing Agent; Quality Control Supervisor; Software Engineer. **Placements per year:** 50-99.

EXECUTIVE SEARCH FIRMS OF DELAWARE AND NEW JERSEY

BLAKE & ASSOCIATE
P.O. Box 1425, Pleasantville NJ 08232-1425. 609/645-3330; **FAX:** 609/383-0320. **Contact:** Ed Blake, Manager. Appointment required. Founded 1979. **Specializes in:** Accounting; Administration, MIS/EDP; Architecture/Construction/Real Estate; Banking; Computer Hardware and Software; Engineering; Finance; Food Industry; General Management; Health/Medical; Industrial; Insurance; Legal; Manufacturing; Retail; Sales and Marketing; Secretarial; Technical and Scientific; Transportation. **Positions commonly filled:** Accountant; Administrative Assistant; Aerospace Engineer; Architect; Biochemist; Biologist; Biomedical Engineer; Bookkeeper; Chemical Engineer; Chemist; Civil Engineer; Claims Representative; Computer Operator; Computer Programmer; Data Entry Clerk; Draftsperson; EDP Specialist; Executive Secretary; Electrical Engineer; Hotel Manager; Industrial Designer; Industrial Engineer; Legal Secretary; Manufacturing Engineer; Mechanical Engineer; Medical Secretary; Metallurgical Engineer; MIS Specialist; . **Placements per year:** 50-99.

CHURCHILL & HARRIMAN, INC.
601 Ewing Street, Suite B7, Princeton NJ 08540. 609/921-3551; **FAX:** 609/921-1061. **Contact:** Mr. Ken Peterson, President. Appointment required. Founded 1986. **Specializes in:** Administration, MIS/EDP; Affirmative Action. **Positions commonly filled:** Computer Programmer; EDP Specialist; MIS

Specialist; Software Engineer; Systems Analyst. Company does not pay fee. **Placements per year:** 1-49.

HEALTH CARE RECRUITERS OF PHILADELPHIA

Three Evens Drive, Suite 303, Marlton NJ 08053. 609/596-7179; **FAX:** 609/596-6895. **Contact:** Frank Rosamilca, President. Appointment required. Founded 1985. **Specializes in:** Health/Medical; Technical and Scientific. **Positions commonly filled:** Biochemist; Biologist; Biomedical Engineer; MIS Specialist; Marketing Manager; Nurse; Quality Control Supervisor; Sales Manager; Software Engineer; Technical Recruiter. Company pays fee. **Placements per year:** 50-99.

HUFF ASSOCIATES

500 Bay Avenue, N., Suite B, Ocean City NJ 08226. 609/399-2867. **Contact:** W.Z. Huff, President. All Ph.D.'s. **Specializes in:** Health/Medical; Manufacturing; Technical and Scientific. **Positions commonly filled:** Biomedical Engineer; Ceramics Engineer; Chemical Engineer; Chemist; Civil Engineer; Electrical Engineer; Hotel Manager; Manufacturing Engineer; Mechanical Engineer; Nurse; Operations and Production Specialist; Physicians. Company pays fee. **Placements per year:** 1-49.

IMPACT PERSONNEL, INC.

3371 Route 1, Lawrenceville NJ 08648. 609/987-8888; **FAX:** 609/987-9020. **Contact:** Guy James, President. No appointment required. Founded 1985. **Specializes in:** Accounting; Advertising; Administration, MIS/EDP; Banking; Computer Hardware and Software; Engineering; Fashion; Finance; Food Industry; General Management; Health/Medical; Industrial; Insurance; Legal; Manufacturing; Printing/Publishing; Retail; Sales and Marketing. **Positions commonly filled:** Accountant; Administrative Assistant; Bookkeeper; Chemical Engineer; Claims Representative; Clerk; Commercial Artist; Computer Operator; Computer Programmer; Customer Service Representative; Electrical Engineer; Factory Worker; General Laborer; Hotel Manager; Industrial Designer; Industrial Engineer; Legal Secretary; Light Industrial Worker; Mechanical Engineer; Medical Secretary.

ANN FITTON LEES AND COMPANY

116 Magnolia Lane, Princeton NJ 08540. 609/921-6518; **FAX:** 609/921-7187. **Contact:** Ann Lees, President. Appointment required. Founded 1991. **Specializes in:** Health/Medical; Technical and Scientific. **Positions commonly filled:** Biochemist; Biologist; Biomedical Engineer; Chemical Engineer; Chemist; Nurse; Operations and Production Specialist; Quality Control Supervisor. Company pays fee. **Placements per year:** 1-49.

MANAGEMENT RECRUITERS

P.O. Box 639, Claymont DE 19703. **Contact:** Penny Via, Owner. 302/475-4320. Executive search firm. Appointment required; no phone calls; unsolicited resumes accepted. Founded 1965. World's largest contingency search firm. Five hundred offices nationwide, doing business under the names "Management Recruiters", "Sales Consultants", "CompuSearch" and

"OfficeMates5". Specializes in mid-management/professional positions, $25,000-75,000 per annum. **Specializes in:** Accounting; Administration, MIS/EDP; Advertising; Affirmative Action; Architecture; Banking and Finance; Chemicals and Pharmaceuticals; Communications; Computer Hardware and Software; Construction; Electrical; Engineering; Food Industry; General Management; Health and Medical. Contingency.

MANAGEMENT RECRUITERS OF MEDFORD
520 Stokes Road, Building A, Medford NJ 08055. 609/654-9109; **FAX:** 609/654-9166. **Contact:** Norman Talbot, President. Appointment required; no phone calls. Founded 1989. **Specializes in:** Engineering; General Management; Industrial. **Positions commonly filled:** Aerospace Engineer; Biochemist; Biomedical Engineer; Chemical Engineer; Chemist; Civil Engineer; Draftsperson; Electrical Engineer; Industrial Engineer; Industrial Hygienist; Manufacturing Engineer; Mechanical Engineer; Metallurgical Engineer; Quality Control Supervisor; Safety Engineer; Software Engineer; Systems Analyst. All positions are fee paid by the employer. **Placements per year:** 50-99.

ROBERT MICHAELS ASSOCIATES, INC.
33 Boothby Drive, Mt. Laurel NJ 08054. 609/778-8118. **Contact:** Robert M. Slivinski. Appointment required. Founded 1987. **Specializes in:** Accounting; Advertising; Administration, MIS/EDP; Engineering; Finance; Food Industry; General Management; Legal; Manufacturing; Personnel/Human Resources; Retail; Sales and Marketing; Secretarial; Transportation. **Positions commonly filled:** Accountant; Administrative Assistant; Biochemist; Bookkeeper; Buyer; Chemist; Civil Engineer; Commercial Artist; Computer Operator; Computer Programmer; Credit Manager; Customer Service Representative; Draftsperson; Executive Secretary; Electrical Engineer; Industrial Engineer; Purchasing Agent; Quality Control Supervisor. Company pays fee.

PRINCETON PLANNING CONSULTANTS
P.O. Box 341, Princeton NJ 08540. 609/452-0909; **FAX:** 212/752-1285. **Contact:** Barbara Cohen, President. Appointment required. Founded 1990. **Specializes in:** Legal--Attorneys only. Company pays fee. **Placements per year:** 1-49.

RECRUITMENT ALTERNATIVES, INC.
York House East, Box 554, Moorestown NJ 08057. 609/273-1066. **Contact:** Thomas J. Jaskel, Senior Vice President. Appointment required. Founded 1986. **Specializes in:** Personnel/Human Resources. **Positions commonly filled:** Human Resource Generalist; Human Resource Specialist; Technical Recruiter. Company pays fee. **Placements per year:** 1-49.

ROBERT SCOTT ASSOCIATES
P.O. Box 486, Rancocas NJ 08073-0486. 609/835-2224; **FAX:** 609/835-1933. **Contact:** Bob Scott, President. Appointment required. Founded 1979. **Specializes in:** Engineering; Manufacturing; Technical and Scientific; Pulp and Paper; Film and Conversion Products; Chemicals. **Positions commonly filled:** Biochemist; Biologist; Biomedical Engineer; Ceramics Engineer; Chemical

Engineer; Chemist; Civil Engineer; Electrical Engineer; Industrial Engineer; Manufacturing Engineer; Mechanical Engineer; Metallurgical Engineer. Company pays fee.

SNELLING PERSONNEL SERVICES
3617-A Silverside Road, Wilmington DE 19810. **Contact:** King Morton, Co-Owner. 302/478-6060. Executive search firm. Appointment requested; unsolicited resumes accepted. Founded 1965. **Specializes in:** Accounting; Administration, MIS/EDP; Construction; Engineering; Fashion; Finance; Food Industry; General Management; Insurance; Legal. **Number of searches per year:** 101-200.

WORLCO COMPUTER RESOURCES, INC.
901 Route 38, Cherry Hill NJ 08002. 609/665-4700; **FAX:** 609/665-8142. **Contact:** Frank Parisi, Managing Partner. No appointment required. Founded 1982. **Specializes in:** Administration, MIS/EDP; Computer Hardware and Software; Sales and Marketing. **Positions commonly filled:** Computer Operator; Computer Programmer; EDP Specialist; Marketing Specialist; MIS Specialist; Sales Representative. **Placements per year:** 100-199.

INDEX TO PRIMARY EMPLOYERS

NOTE: *Below is an alphabetical index of Philadelphia's primary employer listings included in this book. Those employers in each industry that fall under the headings "Additional large employers" or "Small to medium sized employers" are not indexed here.*

AVAILABLE AT YOUR LOCAL BOOKSTORE

Knock 'em Dead
The Ultimate Job Seeker's Handbook
The all-new 1994 edition of Martin Yate's classic now covers the entire job search. The new edition features a special section on what to do when a layoff is imminent. *Knock 'em Dead* also includes the best overall advice on mounting a successful job search campaign and Yate's famous great answers to tough interview questions. When it comes to proven tactics that give readers the competitive advantage, Martin Yate is the authority to turn to. 6x9", 304 pages, $8.95.

Resumes That Knock 'em Dead
Martin Yate reviews the marks of a great resume: what type of resume is right for each applicant, what always goes in, what always stays out, and why. Every single resume in *Resumes That Knock 'em Dead* was actually used by a job hunter to successfully obtain a job. No other book provides the hard facts for producing an exemplary resume. 8-1/2x11", 216 pages, $7.95.

Cover Letters That Knock 'em Dead
The final word on not just how to write a "correct" cover letter, but how to write a cover letter that offers a powerful competitive advantage in today's tough job market. *Cover Letters That Knock 'em Dead* gives the essential information on composing a cover letter that wins attention, interest, and job offers. 8-1/2x11", 204 pages, $7.95.

ALSO OF INTEREST...

The JobBank Series
There are now 20 *JobBank* books, each providing extensive, up-to-date employment information on hundreds of the largest employers in each job market. Recommended as an excellent place to begin your job search by *The New York Times, The Los Angeles Times, The Boston Globe, The Chicago Tribune,* and many other publications, *JobBank* books have been used by hundreds of thousands of people to find jobs.

Books available: *The Atlanta JobBank--The Boston JobBank--The Carolina JobBank--The Chicago JobBank--The Dallas-Ft. Worth JobBank--The Denver JobBank--The Detroit JobBank--The Florida JobBank--The Houston JobBank--The Los Angeles JobBank--The Minneapolis JobBank--The New York JobBank--The Ohio JobBank--The Philadelphia JobBank--The Phoenix JobBank--The St. Louis JobBank--The San Francisco JobBank--The Seattle JobBank--The Tennessee JobBank--The Washington DC JobBank.* Each book is 6x9", over 300 pages, paperback, $15.95.

If you cannot find a book at your local bookstore, you may order it directly from the publisher. Please send payment including $4.50 for shipping and handling (for the entire order) to: Bob Adams, Inc., 260 Center Street, Holbrook, MA 02343. Credit card holders may call 1-800/USA-JOBS (in Massachusetts, 617/767-8100). Please check first at your local bookstore.